YUCATÁN
PENINSULA
HANDBOOK

YUCATÁN
PENINSULA
HANDBOOK
SIXTH EDITION

CHICKI MALLAN

MOON
TRAVEL
HANDBOOKS

YUCATÁN HANDBOOK
SIXTH EDITION

Published by
Moon Publications, Inc.
P.O. Box 3040
Chico, California 95927-3040, USA

Printed by
Colorcraft Ltd.

ISBN: 1-56691-122-2
ISSN: 1098-6707

Editors: Don Root, Karen Gaynor Bleske
Map Editors: Don Root, Diane Wurzel
Production & Design: Carey Wilson, Rob Warner
Cartography: Chris Folks, Mike Morgenfeld, Bob Race
Index: Gregor Krause

Front cover photo: Oz Mallan

All photos by Oz Mallan unless otherwise noted.

Distributed in the United States and Canada by Publishers Group West

Printed in China

Please send all comments,
corrections, additions,
amendments, and critiques to:

**YUCATÁN HANDBOOK
MOON TRAVEL HANDBOOKS
P.O. BOX 3040
CHICO, CA 95927-3040, USA
e-mail: travel@moon.com
www.moon.com**

Printing History
1st edition—1986
6th edition—October 1998

To the newest generations—the "grands":
Stephanie, Kellianne, Misty, Jena, Jasmine,
Kara, Courtney, Becky, Peter, Chelsea, Brittany,
Tyler, Bryant, Serra, Aaron, Alexander, Michael,
Stanley, Rosie, Trevor, Caleb, and Cortney.

CONTENTS

ABBREVIATIONS

a/c—air-conditioning
C—Celsius
d—double occupancy
km—kilometer

pp—per person
s—single occupancy
s/n—*sin numero* (without a
street number)

t—triple occupancy
tel.—telephone

ACCOMMODATIONS PRICE KEY

Shoestring: under US$15
Budget: US$15-35

Inexpensive: US$35-55
Moderate: US$55-80

Expensive: US$80-120
Premium: US$120+

KEEPING CURRENT

We strive to keep our book as up to date as possible and would appreciate your help. Prices go up and down and it's virtually impossible to keep up with them; the prices and price categories in this book are not guaranteed and are intended as a guide only. But if you find a hot new resort or attraction, or if we have neglected to include an important bit of information, please let us know. Our mapmakers take extraordinary care to be accurate, but if you find an error, let us know that as well.

We're especially interested in hearing from female travelers, RVers, outdoor enthusiasts, expatriates, and local residents. And we'd also welcome comments from the Mexican tourist industry, including hotel owners and individuals who specialize in accommodating visitors to their country. Address your letters to:

> ***Yucatán Peninsula Handbook***
> Moon Travel Handbooks
> P.O. Box 3040
> Chico, CA 95927-3040, USA

ACKNOWLEDGMENTS

I wish there were a way to say thanks to the entire population of the Yucatán Peninsula for their help in bringing this sixth edition of Yucatán Peninsula Handbook together. In every state there were those who offered help—from providing use of a cool office-safe for storing exposed film, to providing directions to new and exciting places. Countless perfect strangers were perfectly willing to interrupt their workday to show us the way, either on foot or in an old clunker or a fine new "bug." The people on the Peninsula are grand. Thanks to all. And how can we forget our readers—you're the best!

MAPS

MAP SYMBOLS

– – – –	INTERNATIONAL BOUNDARY	o	TOWNS	– – – –	FERRY
– · – · –	STATE BOUNDARY	O	CITIES		GAS STATION
——	FOUR LANE ROAD		WATER	●	HOTELS, ACCOMMODATIONS
——	PAVED ROAD	✕ ✕	AIRPORT		
– – – –	UNPAVED ROAD				SNORKELING
(18)	FEDERAL HIGHWAY		ARCHAEOLOGICAL SITE		BRIDGE
▲6km▲	DISTANCES BETWEEN SELECTED POINTS			– · – · –	TRAIL
■	POINTS OF INTEREST		SWIMMING		AQUATIC SPORTS
			CHURCH		

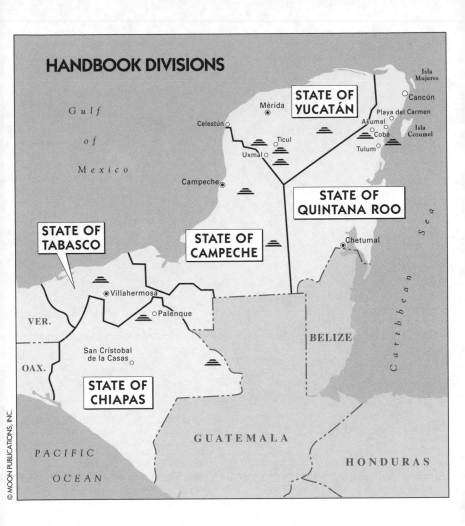

HANDBOOK DIVISIONS

STATE OF
YUCATÁN

STATE OF
QUINTANA ROO

STATE OF
CAMPECHE

STATE OF
TABASCO

STATE OF
CHIAPAS

Gulf

of

Mexico

Mérida

Isla
Mujeres

Cancún

Playa del Carmen

Celestún

Akumal

Isla
Cozumel

Ticul

Cobá

Uxmal

Tulum

Campeche

Chetumal

Caribbean Sea

Villahermosa

Palenque

VER.

BELIZE

OAX.

San Crístobal
de la Casas

GUATEMALA

PACIFIC

OCEAN

HONDURAS

© MOON PUBLICATIONS, INC.

KATHY ESCOVEDO SANDERS

INTRODUCTION

An ancient Maya homeland flanked by the Gulf of Mexico and the dazzling Caribbean Sea, the Yucatán Peninsula is a truly magical place. Its sparkling white beaches ring a rugged interior where dense jungles conceal a fairyland of trees, ferns, and blossoms. Rising out of these jungles and above the beaches, the grand stone ruins of the Maya have been uncovered, renovated, and made tourist-friendly. These ancient relics harbor clues to the rise and fall of the great Maya civilization and provide insights into the lifestyle of today's Maya; scattered around these archaeological zones and across the Peninsula lie villages where descendants of the Yucatán's early inhabitants create beautiful textiles and ceramics and carry on centuries-old traditions.

The Mexican government is aware of the assets they have in the Maya world, and anyone who spends much time in this living museum will run into special people devoted to the preservation of all of these gifts.

LAND AND CLIMATE

The Yucatán Peninsula occupies an area of approximately 113,000 square km, with a shoreline of over 1,600 km. It comprises the Mexican states of Yucatán on the north coast, Campeche on the west along the Gulf of Mexico, and Quintana Roo on the east along the Caribbean coast. To the south are the countries of Belize and Guatemala; to the southwest the Mexican states of Tabasco and Chiapas (which are also covered in this Handbook).

Geologically, this flat shelf of limestone and coral composition is like a stone sponge; rain is absorbed into the ground and delivered to natural stone-lined sinks and underground rivers. The abundant limestone provided the early Maya with sturdy material to create the mammoth structures that survived hundreds of years to become one of the region's chief attractions. The soft rock was readily cut with handhewn implements but created a problem in the Maya's search for

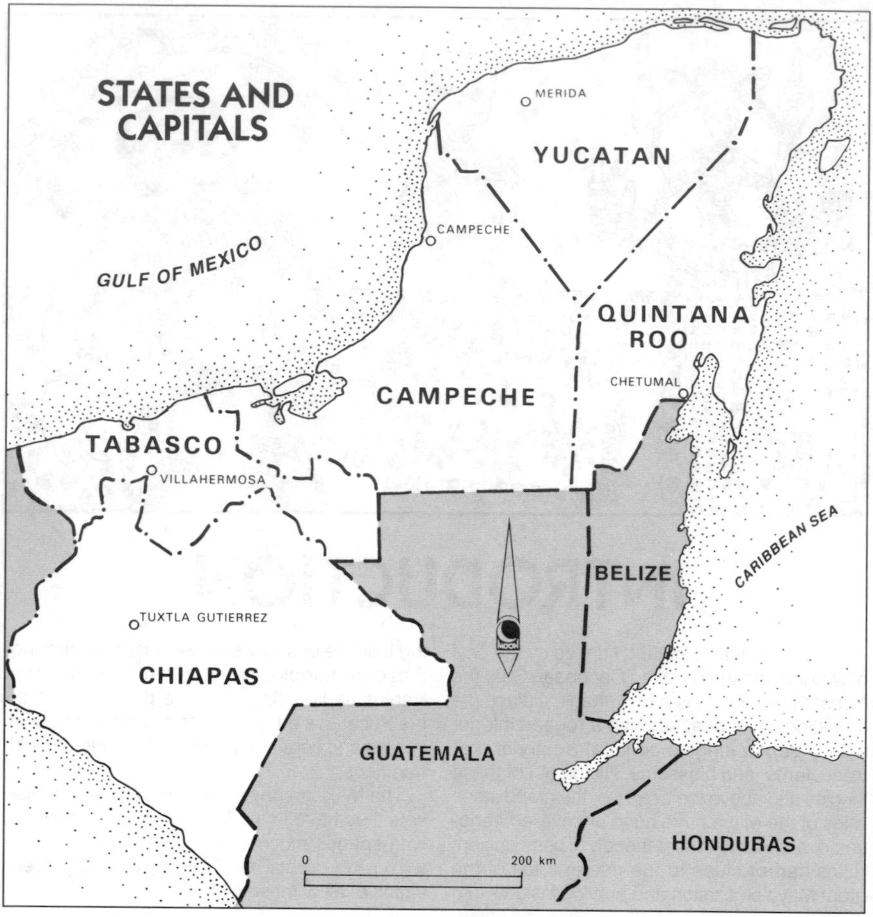

STATES AND CAPITALS

MERIDA

YUCATAN

GULF OF MEXICO

CAMPECHE

QUINTANA ROO

CAMPECHE

CHETUMAL

TABASCO

VILLAHERMOSA

BELIZE

CARIBBEAN SEA

TUXTLA GUTIERREZ

CHIAPAS

GUATEMALA

HONDURAS

0   200 km

water; thanks to the predominantly porous rock, there are few surface rivers and lakes in Quintana Roo. Only in the extreme south does a sizeable river exist—the Río Hondo cuts a natural boundary between Belize and Quintana Roo, at the city of Chetumal. Four shallow lakes at Cobá are scattered between ancient ruins.

Cenotes

The early inhabitants found their water mostly in cenotes (natural wells). Limestone and coral create eerie shorelines, caves, and, fortunately, waterholes. When flying over the Peninsula you can see circular ground patterns caused by the hidden movement of underground rivers and lakes. The water level rises and falls with the cycle of rain and drought. The constant ebb and flow erodes the underside of these limestone containers, creating steep-walled caverns; the surface crust eventually wears so thin that it caves in, exposing the water below. Around these water sources Maya villages grew. Some of the wells are shallow, seven meters below the jungle floor; some are treacherously deep, with the surface of the water as much as 90 meters below. In times of drought, the Maya fetched water by carving stairs into slick limestone walls or by hanging long ladders into abysmal hollows that lead to underground lakes.

John Stephens's book, *Incidents of Travel in The Yucatán,* covers his 1841 expedition with Frederick Catherwood. Catherwood's realistic art reproduces accurately how the Indians in the northern part of the Peninsula survived from year to year with little or no rainfall by burrowing deep into the earth to retrieve water. The two American explorers observed long lines of naked Indian men carrying calabash containers of the precious liquid from deep holes.

The Peninsula Coast

The west and north coasts are composed of many lagoons, sandbars, and mangrove swamps. The east coast is edged with coral reefs and several islands—Cozumel, Isla Mujeres, and Contoy. The fifth-largest reef in the world, the Belize Reef, extends from the tip of Isla Mujeres 250 km south to the Bay of Honduras. Many varieties of coral—including rare black coral found at great depths—grow in the hills and valleys of the often-deep reef that protects the east coast of the Peninsula. Diving for coral is prohibited in many places along the reef, and where permitted it makes for a dangerous, but lucrative, occupation. Since tourists are willing to buy it, the local divers continue to retrieve it from the crags and crevices of underwater canyons. In addition to attracting profit-seekers, the coral ridges of the reef draw thousands of sport divers from all over the world each year.

Climate

The weather in the Yucatán falls into a wet season May-October and a dry season November-April. Though most travelers prefer the milder conditions of the dry season, you can enjoy the area any time of year. Travelers to the Yucatán Peninsula in the dry season can expect hot days, occasional brief storms called *nortes,* and plenty of tourists. Travel in the wet season can be more difficult, with regular rains and hot, muggy air. May and June are infamous in the Yucatán for heat and humidity both on the sweaty side of 90 (° F/%).

Hurricane season runs July-November with most activity occurring from mid-August to mid-September. Though tropical storms are common this time of year and sometimes disrupt travel plans, full-fledged hurricanes, like Hurricane Gilbert, are relatively rare. However, don't make the mistake of thinking you can tough out one of these monsters! Leave the area quickly if a hurricane is headed your way.

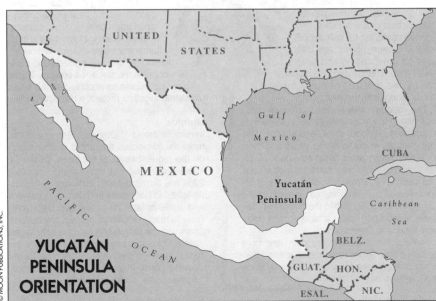

YUCATÁN
PENINSULA
ORIENTATION

FLORA AND FAUNA

Quintana Roo's forests are home to mangroves, bamboo, and swamp cypresses. Ferns, vines, and flowers creep from tree to tree and create a dense growth. On topmost limbs, orchids and air ferns reach for the sun. The southern part of the Yucatán Peninsula, with its classic tropical rainforest, hosts tall mahoganies, *campeche, zapote,* and *kapok,* also covered with wild jungle vines.

Many exotic animals found nowhere else in Mexico inhabit the state's flatlands and thick jungles. With patience it's possible to observe animals not normally seen in the wild. If you're serious about this venture, bring a small folding stool (unless you prefer to sit in a tree), a pair of binoculars, a camera, and plenty of bug repellent.

FLORA

Palms

A wide variety of palm trees and their relatives grows on the Peninsula—tall, short, fruited, and even oil-producing varieties. Though similar, various palms have distinct characteristics.

Royal palms are tall with smooth trunks. Queen palms are often used for landscaping and bear a sweet fruit. Thatch palms are called *chit* by the Indians, who use the fronds extensively for roof thatch.

The coconut palm serves the Yucatecan well; one of the most useful trees in the world, it produces oil, food, drink, and shelter. The tree matures in six to seven years and then for five to seven years bears coconuts, which are valued by locals as a nutritious food source and cash crop. Presently, this source of income has all but disappeared on much of the Quintana Roo coast due to the "yellowing" disease, a condition that's attacked palm trees from Florida to Central America.

Henequen is a cousin to the palm tree; from its fiber come twine, rope, matting, and other products. New uses are sought constantly since this plant is locally abundant.

From Fruit to Flowers

Quintana Roo grows delicious sweet and sour oranges, limes, and grapefruit. Avocado is abundant, and the papaya tree is practically a weed. The mamey tree grows tall (15-20 meters) and full, providing not only welcome shade but also an avocado-shaped fruit, brown on the outside with a vivid, salmon-pink flesh that makes a sweet snack (the flavor similar to a sweet yam's). Another unusual fruit tree is the guaya, a member of the litchi nut family. This rangy evergreen thrives on sea air and is common along the coast and throughout the Yucatán Peninsula. Its small, green, leathery pods grow in clumps like grapes and contain a sweet, yellowish, jellylike flesh—tasty! The calabash tree, a friend to the Indian for many years, provides gourds used for containers.

The tall ceiba is a very special tree to those close to the Maya religion. Considered the tree of life, even today locals leave it undisturbed, even if it sprouts in the middle of a fertile milpa (cornfield).

When visiting in the summer, you can't miss the beautiful *framboyanes* (royal poinciana). As its name implies, when in bloom it is the most flamboyant tree around, with wide-spreading branches covered in clusters of brilliant orange-red flowers. These trees line sidewalks and plazas and when clustered together present a dazzling show.

Orchids

In remote areas of Quintana Roo one of the more exotic blooms, the orchid, is often found on the highest limbs of tall trees. Of the 71 species reported on the Yucatán Peninsula, 20% are terrestrial and 80% are epiphytic, attached to host trees and deriving moisture and nutrients from the air and rain. Both types grow in many sizes and shapes: tiny buttons spanning the length of a long branch, large-petaled blossoms with ruffled edges, or intense, tiger-striped miniatures. The lovely flowers come in a wide variety of colors, some subtle, some brilliant.

BOB RACE

Nature's Hothouse

In spring, flowering trees are a beautiful sight—and sound: hundreds of singing birds gather in the treetops throughout the mating season. While wandering through jungle landscapes, you'll see, thriving in the wild, a gamut of plants that we so carefully nurture and coax to survive on windowsills at home. Here in its natural environment, the croton exhibits wild colors, the pothos grows 30-cm leaves, and the philodendron splits every leaf in gargantuan glory.

White and red ginger are among the more exotic herbs that grow on the Peninsula. Plumeria (in the South Pacific called frangipani) has a wonderful fragrance and appears in many colors. Hibiscus and bougainvillea bloom in an array of bright hues. A walk through the jungle will introduce you to many delicate strangers in the world of tropical flowers. But you'll find old friends too, such as the common morning glory creeping and climbing for miles over bushes and trees. Viny coils thicken daily. Keeping jungle growth away from the roads, utility poles, and wires is a constant job for local authorities, because warm, humid air and ample rainfall encourage a lush green wonderland.

CORAL REEFS

The spectacular coral reefs that grace the Yucatán's east coast are made up of millions of tiny carnivorous organisms called polyps. Coral grows in innumerable shapes: delicate lace, trees with reaching branches, pleated mushrooms, stovepipes, petaled flowers, fans, domes, heads of cabbage, and stalks of broccoli. The

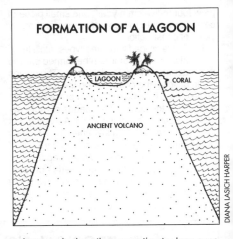

FORMATION OF A LAGOON

LAGOON — CORAL — ANCIENT VOLCANO

DIANA LASICH HARPER

polyps can be less than a centimeter long or as big as 15 cm in diameter. Related to the jellyfish and sea anemone, polyps need sunlight and clear saltwater no colder than 20° C to survive. Coral polyps have cylinder-shaped bodies. One end is attached to a hard surface (the bottom of the ocean, the rim of a submerged volcano, or the reef itself) and the other, the mouth, is circled with tiny tentacles that capture its minute prey with a deadly sting.

Coral reefs are formed when polyps attach themselves to each other. Stony coral, for example, makes the connection with a flat sheet of tissue between the middle of both bodies. They develop their limestone skeletons by extracting calcium out of the seawater and depositing calcium carbonate around the lower half of the body. They reproduce from buds or eggs. Occasionally small buds appear on the adult polyp; when mature, they separate from the adult and add to the growth of existing colonies. Eggs, on the other hand, grow into tiny forms that swim away and settle on the ocean floor. When developed, the egg begins a new colony.

As these small creatures continue to reproduce and die, their sturdy skeletons accumulate. Over eons, broken bits of coral, animal waste, and granules of soil all contribute to the strong foundation for a reef, which slowly rises toward the surface. To grow, a reef must have a base no more than 25 meters below the water's surface, and in a healthy environment it can

THE WORLD'S LONGEST REEFS

Great Barrier Reef, Australia: 1,600 km
S.W. Barrier Reef, New Caledonia:
  600 km
N.E. Barrier Reef, New Caledonia:
  540 km
Great Sea Reef, Fiji Islands: 260 km
Belizean Reef: 250 km
S. Louisiade Archipelago Reef, PNG:
  200 km

grow four to five cm a year. One small piece of coral represents millions of polyps and many years of construction.

Reefs are divided into three types: atoll, fringing, and barrier. An atoll can be formed around the crater of a submerged volcano. The polyps begin building their colonies on the round edge of the crater, forming a circular coral island with a lagoon in the center. Thousands of atolls occupy tropical waters of the world. A fringing reef is coral living on a shallow shelf that extends outward from shore into the sea. A barrier reef runs parallel to the coast. Water separates it from the land, and it can be a series of reefs with channels of water in between. This is the case with some of the largest barrier reefs in the Pacific and Indian oceans.

The Yucatán Peninsula's Belize Reef (the most common of several names) extends from the tip of Isla Mujeres to Sapodilla Caye in the Gulf of Honduras. This reef is 280 km long, fifth longest in the world. The beauty of the reef attracts divers and snorkelers from distant parts of the world to investigate its unspoiled marinelife.

Conservation

The Mexican government has strict laws governing the reef, to which most divers are more than willing to comply in order to preserve this natural treasure and its inhabitants. It takes hundreds of years to form large colonies, so please don't break off pieces of coral for souvenirs. After a very short time out of water the polyps lose their color and you have only a piece of

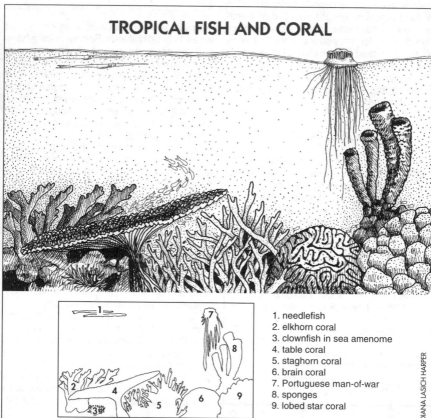

TROPICAL FISH AND CORAL

1. needlefish
2. elkhorn coral
3. clownfish in sea amenome
4. table coral
5. staghorn coral
6. brain coral
7. Portuguese man-of-war
8. sponges
9. lobed star coral

DIANA LASICH HARPER

CARIBBEAN FISH

blue chromis	barred cardinal
toadfish	trumpetfish
porkfish	sand tilefish
trunkfish	triggerfish
queen angelfish	sergeant major
grouper	big eye
stoplight parrot fish	bluestriped grunt
French grunt	butterfly indigo hamlet
spotted drum	barracuda
angelfish	hogfish

chalky white coral—just like the pieces you see while beachcombing. Stiff fines await those who remove anything from the reef, and spearfishing along the reef is strictly prohibited.

FISH

The fish and other sealife of the Yucatán coast are world-famous among divers and snorkelers. The barrier reef that runs the length of the Peninsula from Isla Mujeres to Belize is home to myriad fish species, including parrot fish, candy bass, moray eels, spotted scorpionfish, turquoise angelfish, fairy basslets, flame fish, and gargantuan manta rays. Several species of shark thrive in the waters off Quintana Roo, though they're not considered a major threat to swimmers and divers.

Sport fish including sailfish, marlin, and bluefin tuna inhabit the outer Caribbean waters. Check with a hotel or tourist office to arrange a fishing trip. Hard-fighting bonefish and pompano can be found in the area's lagoons.

In the shark caves off Isla Mujeres, sharks "sleep" on the cave floor due to low water salinity. Though some divers boast of petting the sluggish predators, most choose not to disturb them.

The clear waters of the cenotes, or giant wells, of the Yucatán are home to several species of blind fish, which live out their existence in darkness.

The Meaning of Color

Most people interested in a reef already know they're in for a brilliant display of colored fish. In the fish world, color isn't only for exterior dec-

oration. Fish change hues for a number of reasons, including anger, protection, and sexual attraction. This is still a little-known science. For example, because of the many colors grouper appear in, marine biologists are uncertain how many species (or moods) there are. A male damselfish clearly imparts his aggression—and his desire for love—by turning vivid blue. Some fish have as many as 12 different recognizable color patterns, and they can change within seconds.

These color changes, along with other body signals, combine to make communication simple between species. Scientists have discovered that a layer of color-bearing cells lies just beneath a fish's transparent scales. These cells contain orange, yellow, black, or red pigments: some fish combine their colors to make yellow or green. A crystalline tissue adds white, silver, or iridescence. Color changes when the pigmented cells are revealed, combined, or masked.

Fish communicate in many other surprising ways, including electrical impulses and flashing bioluminescence (cold light). If fish communication intrigues you, read Robert Burgess's book, *Secret Languages of the Sea* (Dodd, Mead and Company).

REPTILES

Although reptiles thrive in Yucatán's warm, sunny environment, humans are their worst enemy. In the past some species were greatly reduced in number because they were hunted for their unusual skin. Though this activity is against the laws of most countries today, a few black marketeers still take their toll on the species.

Iguanas

This group of American lizards—family Iguanidae—includes various large plant-eaters seen frequently in Quintana Roo. The iguana grows to one meter long and has a blunt head and long flat tail. Bands of black and gray circle its body, and a serrated column reaches down the middle of its back almost to the tail. The young iguana is bright emerald green.

The lizard's forelimbs hold the front half of its body up off the ground while its two back limbs are kept relaxed and splayed alongside its hindquarters. However, when the iguana is frightened, its

iguana

OZ MALLAN

hind legs do everything they're supposed to, and the iguana crashes quickly (though clumsily) into the brush searching for its burrow and safety. This reptile is not aggressive, but if cornered it will bite and use its tail in self-defense.

The iguana mostly enjoys basking in the bright sunshine along the Caribbean. Though they are herbivores, the young also eat insects and larvae. Certain varieties in some areas of the Peninsula are almost hunted out—for example, the spiny-tailed iguana in the central valley of Chiapas. In isolated parts of Quintana Roo it is not unusual to see locals along dirt paths carrying sturdy specimens by the tail to put in the cookpot.

From centuries past, recorded references attest to the iguana's medicinal value, which partly explains the active trade of live iguana in the marketplaces of some parts of the Peninsula. Iguana stew is believed to cure or relieve various human ailments such as impotence. Another reason for their popularity at the market is their delicate white flesh, which tastes a lot like a very firm chicken but is much more expensive.

Other Lizards

You'll see a great variety of other lizards as well, from the skinny two-inch miniature gecko to the chameleonlike black anole that changes colors to match its environment, either when danger is imminent or as subterfuge to fool the insects that it preys on. At mating time, the male anole's bright-red throat-fan is puffed out to make sure that all female lizards will see it.

Some lizards are brightly striped in various shades of green and yellow; others are earth colors that blend with the gray and beige limestone that dots the landscape. Skinny as wisps of thread running on hind legs, or chunky and waddling with armorlike skin, the range is endless and fascinating!

Coral Snakes

In North and South America are several species of true coral snakes, which are close relatives of cobras. Many false coral snakes with similar coloring are around, though harmless. The coral snakes found from the southern part of the Yucatán Peninsula to Panama grow much larger (1-1.5 meters) than the ones in the southern United States. The body is slender, with no pronounced distinction between head and neck.

The two North American coral snakes have prominent rings around their bodies in the same sequence of black, yellow or white, and red. Nocturnal, coral snakes spend the day under rocks or logs. They don't look for trouble and seldom strike, but will bite if stepped on; their short fangs, however, can be stopped by shoes or clothing. Even though the Mexicans call this the "20-minute snake," meaning if you are bitten and don't get antivenin within 20 minutes, you die, it's actually more like a 24-hour period. According to Mexico's Instituto Nacional de Higiene, an average of 135 snake-bite deaths per year (mostly children) are reported for the country, the number declining as more villages receive antivenin.

Chances of the average tourist being bitten by a coral (or any other) snake are slim. However, if you plan on extensive jungle exploration, check with your doctor before you leave home. Antivenin is available in Mexico, and it's wise to be prepared for an allergic reaction to the antivenin by bringing antihistimine and Adrenalin. The most important thing to remember if bitten: *don't panic and don't run.* Physical exertion and panic cause the venom to travel through your body much faster. Lie down and stay calm; have someone carry you to a doctor.

Tropical Rattlesnakes

The tropical rattlesnake, called *cascabel* in Mexico and Mesoamerica, is the deadliest and most treacherous species of rattler. It differs slightly from other species by having vividly contrasting neck bands. Contrary to popular myth, this serpent doesn't always rattle a warning of its impending strike. It grows 2-2.5 meters long and is found mainly in higher, drier areas of the tropics.

Caymans

The cayman is part of the crocodilian order. Its habits and appearance are similar to those of crocodiles; the main difference is its underskin. The cayman's skin is reinforced with bony plates on the belly, making it useless for the leather market. (Alligators and crocodiles, with smooth belly skin and sides, have been hunted almost to extinction in some parts of the world.)

Of the five species of cayman, several frequent the brackish inlet waters near the estuaries on the north edge of the Yucatán Peninsula along the Río Lagartos (loosely translated to mean "River of Lizards"). They are broad-snouted and often look as though they sport a pair of spectacles. A large cayman can be 2.5 meters long and very dark gray-green with eyelids that look swollen and wrinkled. Some species have eyelids that look like a pair of blunt horns. They are quicker than alligators and have longer, sharper teeth. Their disposition is vicious and treacherous; don't be fooled by the old myth that on land they're cumbersome and slow. When cornered they move swiftly and are known for their viciousness toward people. The best advice you can heed is to give the cayman a wide berth when you spot one.

Sea Turtles

At one time many species of giant turtles inhabited the coastal regions of Quintana Roo, laying their eggs in the warm Caribbean sands. Though many hatchlings didn't survive birds, crabs, and sharks, thousands of turtles managed to return each year to their birthplace. The Sea Turtle Rescue Organization claims that in 1947, during one day, over 40,000 nesting Kemp's ridley sea turtles were counted. In 1984 fewer than 500 Kemp's ridleys nested during the entire season.

In spite of concentrated efforts by the Mexican government, the number of turtles is still decreasing. They were a valuable source of food for the Maya Indians for centuries. But only in recent years has the wholesale theft of turtle eggs, coupled with the senseless slaughter of the hawksbill for its beautiful shell, begun to deplete these species. Refrigeration and freezer holds enable large fishing boats to capture thousands of turtles at one time and smuggle meat by the ton into various countries, to be canned as soup or frozen for the unwary consumer; processors often claim the turtle meat in their product is from the legal freshwater variety.

Another problem is the belief that turtle eggs cure impotence. Despite huge fines for anyone possessing turtle eggs, every summer nesting grounds along the Yucatán Peninsula are raided. There is no hunting season for these threatened creatures, and the meat is illegal on menus throughout the state, though some restaurants ignore the law and verbally offer turtle meat. The eggs are kept much more secretively.

Ecological organizations are trying hard to save the dwindling turtle population. Turtle eggs are kept in captivity; when the hatchlings break through their shells, they are brought to a beach and allowed to rush toward the sea, hopefully imprinting a sense of belonging there so that they will later return to the spot. After a while at the beach, the hatchlings are scooped up and placed in tanks to grow larger before being released into the open sea. All of these efforts are in the experimental stage; the results will not be known for years. The government is enforcing tough penalties for people who take turtle eggs or capture, kill, sell, or imprison animals on the endangered list.

Pronatura is a grassroots Yucatecan organization valiantly working against the tide, trying to save sea turtles from extinction. They also maintain a deer reproduction center, engage in coastal and reef management planning, study toucan habitat and jaguar populations, and manage general conservation funds. For more information or to make a donation, write Pronatura, Calle 1d #254a, entre 36 y 38, Col. Campestre, Mérida, Yucatán 97120, Mexico; tel./fax (99) 44-2290. Specify your interest. Donations made out to "Friends of Pronatura" are U.S. tax deductible.

MAMMALS

Nine-banded Armadillos

This strange creature looks like a miniature prehistoric monster. The size of a small dog, its most unusual feature is the tough coat of plate armor that encases it. Even the tail has its own armor! Flexibility comes from nine bands (or external "joints") that circle the midsection. Living on a diet of insects, the armadillo's extremely keen sense of smell can locate grubs 15 cm underground. Its front paws are sharp, enabling it to dig easily into the earth and build underground burrows. After digging the hole, the animal carries down as much as a bushel of grass to make its nest. Here it bears and rears its young and sleeps during the day. Unlike some armadillos that roll up into a tight ball when threatened, this species will race for the burrow, stiffly arch its back, and wedge in so that it cannot be pulled out. The tip of the Yucatán Peninsula is a favored habitat due to its scant rainfall and warm temperatures; too much rain floods the burrow and can drown young armadillos.

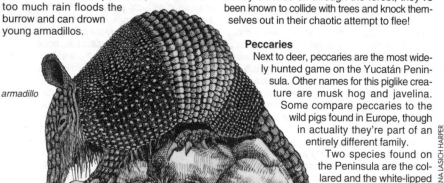

armadillo

DIANA LASICH HARPER

Giant Anteaters

This extraordinary cousin of the armadillo measures two meters from the tip of its tubular snout to the end of its bushy tail. Its body is colored shades of brown-gray; the hindquarters become darker in tone, while a contrasting wedge-shaped pattern of black outlined with white decorates the throat and shoulders. This creature walks on the knuckles of its paws, keeping the foreclaws razor sharp. Its claws allow it to rip open the leathery mud walls of termite or white ant nests, the contents of which are a main food source. After opening the nest, the anteater begins flicking its tongue. Ants don't have a chance; the long, viscous tongue quickly transfers them to a toothless, elongated mouth.

While particularly dangerous to ants, its longs claws are capable of injuring humans, making the anteater a deadly beast when threatened.

Tapirs

South American tapirs are found from the southern part of Mexico to southern Brazil. A stout-bodied animal, it has short legs and tail, small eyes, and rounded ears. The nose and upper lip extend into a short but very mobile proboscis. Totally herbivorous, tapirs usually live near streams or rivers in the forest. They bathe daily and also use the water as an escape when hunted either by humans or by their prime predator, the jaguar. Shy and unaggressive, these nocturnal animals have a definite home range, wearing a path between the jungle and their feeding area. If attacked, the tapir lowers its head and blindly crashes off through the forest; they've been known to collide with trees and knock themselves out in their chaotic attempt to flee!

Peccaries

Next to deer, peccaries are the most widely hunted game on the Yucatán Peninsula. Other names for this piglike creature are musk hog and javelina. Some compare peccaries to the wild pigs found in Europe, though in actuality they're part of an entirely different family.

Two species found on the Peninsula are the collared and the white-lipped peccaries. The feisty col-

MANATEE BREEDING PROGRAM

The state of Florida, under the auspices of the Miami Seaquarium and Dr. Jesse White, has begun a captive breeding program hoping to learn more about the habits of the manatee and to try to increase the declining numbers. Several manatees have been born in captivity; they along with others that have recuperated from injury or illness will be or have been released into Florida's Crystal River, where boat traffic is restricted. They are tagged and closely observed.

Florida maintains a 24-hour hotline where people report manatees in need of help for any reason. Rescues can include removing an adult male from a cramped storm drain or rushing to the seaquarium newborns that somehow managed to get separated from their mothers and have washed ashore. These newborns are readily accepted by surrogate-mother manatees and are offered nourishment (by way of a thumb-sized teat under the front flipper) and lots of TLC. Medical aid is given to mammals that have been slashed by boat propellers as a result of cruising boats. The manatee has a playful curiosity and investigates anything found in its underwater environment, many times sustaining grave damage.

a close-up of the truncated snout and prehensile lips of the manatee, which surprisingly is a distant relative of the elephant

OZ MALLAN

lared peccary stands 50 cm at the shoulder and can be one meter long, weighing as much as 30 kilograms. It is black and white with a narrow, semicircular collar of white hair on the shoulders. In Spanish *javelina* means "spear," descriptive of the two spearlike tusks that protrude from its mouth. This more familiar peccary is found in the desert, woodlands, and rainforests, and travels in groups of 5-15. Also with tusks, the white-lipped peccary is reddish brown to black and has an area of white around its mouth. This larger animal, which can grow to 105 cm long, is found deep in tropical rainforests and lives in herds of 100-plus.

Cats

Seven species of cats are found in North America, four tropically distributed. The jaguar is heavy-chested with sturdy, muscled forelegs. It has small, rounded ears and its tail is relatively short. Color ranges from tan on top and white on the underside to pure black. The male can weigh 65-115 kilograms, females 45-85 kilograms.

Largest of the cats on the Peninsula, the jaguar is about the same size as a leopard. Other cats found in Quintana Roo are the ocelot and puma. In tropical forests of the past the large cats were the only predators capable of controlling the populations of hoofed game such as deer, peccaries, and tapirs. If hunting is poor and times are tough, the jaguar *(el tigre)* will go into rivers and scoop up fish with its large paws. The river is also one of the jaguar's favorite spots for hunting the large tapir when it comes to drink.

Manatees

Probably the most unusual mammal, the manatee is an elephantine creature of immense proportions with gentle manners and the curiosity of a kitten. Though today seldom seen, this enormous animal, often referred to as the sea cow, at one time roamed the shallow inlets, bays, and estuaries of the Caribbean in large numbers. The manatee is said to be the basis for seamen's myths of mermaids. In South America this particular mammal is revered by certain Indian tribes. The manatee image is frequently seen in the art of the ancient Maya, who hunted it for its flesh. In modern times, the population has been reduced by the encroachment of large numbers of people in the manatees' habitats along the riverways and shorelines. Ever-growing numbers of motorboats inflict often-deadly gashes on the nosy creatures.

At birth the manatee weighs 30-35 kilograms; it can grow up to four meters long and weigh over a ton. Gray with a pinkish cast and shaped like an Idaho potato, it has a spatulate tail, two forelimbs with toenails, pebbled coarse skin, tiny sunken eyes, numerous fine-bristled hairs scattered sparsely over its body, and a permanent Mona Lisa smile. The head of the mammal seems small for its gargantuan body, and its preproboscidean lineage includes dugongs (in Australia), hyrax, and elephants. The manatee's truncated snout and prehensile lips help push food into its mouth. The only aquatic mammal that exists on vegetation, the manatee grazes on bottom-growing grasses and other aquatic plantlife. It ingests as much as 225 kilograms per day, cleaning rivers of oxygen-choking growth. It is unique among mammals in that it constantly grows new teeth—to replace worn ones, which fall out regularly. Posing no threat to any other living thing, it has been hunted for its oil, skin, and flesh, which is said to be tasty.

The mammal thrives in shallow, warm water; in Quintana Roo the manatee has been reported in shallow bays between Playa del Carmen and Punta Allen, but very infrequently anymore. One recent spring evening, in a small bay in Belize near the Chetumal border, a curious manatee spent about an hour lazily swimming the cove, lifting its truncated snout, and often its entire head, out of the water about every four minutes. The few people (this author included) standing on a small dock in the bay were thrilled to be seeing the shy animal.

In neighboring Guatemala, the government is sponsoring a manatee reserve in Lago de Izabal. In the U.S. the mammal is found mostly in the inshore and estuarine areas of Florida. It is protected under the Federal U.S. Marine Mammal Protection Act of 1972, the Endangered Species Act of 1973, and the Florida Manatee Sanctuary Act of 1978. It is estimated that its total population numbers about 2,000.

BIRDS

Since a major part of the Yucatán Peninsula is still undeveloped and covered with trees and brush, it isn't surprising to find exotic, rarely seen birds all across the landscape. The Mexican government is beginning to realize the great value in this (almost) undiscovered treasure trove of nature and is making initial efforts to protect nesting grounds. The birds of the Yucatán, which attract scientists and laypeople alike, have until recent years been free from pesticides, smog, and human beings' encroachment. If you're a serious birdwatcher, you probably know all about Quintana Roo. Undoubtedly, however, change is coming as more people intrude into the rangeland of the birds, exploring these still undeveloped tracts on the Yucatán Peninsula. Hopefully, stringent regulations will take hold before many of these lovely birds are chased away or destroyed.

Cobá, with its marshy-rimmed lakes, nearby cornfields, and relatively tall, humid forest, is worth a couple of days to the ornithologist. One of the more impressive birds to look for is the keel-billed toucan, often seen perched high on a bare limb in the early hours of the morning. Others include chachalacas (held in reverence by the Maya), screeching parrots, and occasionally the ocellated turkey. For an excellent bird book that deals with the Yucatán Peninsula, check out *100 Common Birds of the Yucatán Peninsula*, written by Barbara MacKinnon. A well-known birdwatcher, Barbara has lived in the Cancún area for many years and is donating all the profits of her book to the Sian Ka'an Reserve. Available for US$30 through Amigos de Sian Ka'an, Apdo. Postal 770, Cancún, Quintana Roo 77500, Mexico.

Sooty Terns

In Cancún, on a coral island just offshore from the Camino Real Hotel, a breeding colony of sooty terns has been discovered. The sooty tern is one of several seabirds that lack waterproof feathers. It is the only one that will not venture to land on a passing ship or drifting debris. Feeding on tiny fish and squid that swim near the ocean surface, the bird hovers close to the water, snatching unsuspecting prey.

The sooty tern nests from April till September. The Camino Real Hotel is being urged to warn guests to stay away from the rocky island. Humans are the sooty tern's only predator. If frightened, the parent birds panic, leaving the eggs exposed to the hot tropical sun or knocking the young into the sea where they drown immediately.

Flamingos

The far north end of the Peninsula at Río Lagartos plays host to thousands of long-necked, long-legged flamingos during the nesting season (June-August). They begin arriving around the end of May, when the rains begin. This homecoming is a breathtaking sight: a profusion of pink/salmon colors clustered together on the white sand, or sailing across a blue sky, long, curved necks straight in flight, the flapping movement exposing contrasting black and pink on the undersides of their wings. The estimated flamingo population on the Yucatán Peninsula is 30,000. This wildlife refuge, called **El Cuyo**, protects the largest colony of nesting American flamingos in the world.

Many of these flamingos winter in Celestún, a small fishing village on the northwest coast a few km north of the Campeche-Yucatán state border. Celestún lies between the Gulf of Mexico and a long tidal estuary known as La Cienega. Since the disruption of Hurricane Gilbert, a flock of flamingos has found a new feeding ground near Chicxulub. If you're visiting Mérida and want to see flamingos during the winter season, it's a closer drive to Celestún or Chicxulub (about one hour) than to Río Lagartos (about three hours). don't forget your camera and color film!

Estuary Havens

Estuaries play host to hundreds of bird species. A boat ride into one of them will give you an opportunity to see a variety of ducks; this is a wintering spot for many North American flocks. Among others, you'll see the blue-winged teal, northern shoveler, and lesser scaup. You'll also see a variety of wading birds feeding in the shallow waters, including numerous types of heron, snowy egret, and, in the summer, white ibis. Seven species of birds are endemic to the Yucatán Peninsula: ocellated turkey, Yucatán whippoorwill, Yucatán flycatcher, orange oriole, black catbird, yellow-lored parrot, and the quetzal.

Quetzals

Though the ancient Maya made abundant use of the dazzling quetzal feathers for ceremonial costumes and headdresses, they hunted other fowl in much larger quantities for food; nonetheless, the quetzal is the only known bird from the pre-Cortesian era that is almost extinct. These birds live only in the very high cloud forests where they thrive on the constant moisture. Today they are still found (rarely) in the cloud forest of Chiapas and in Guatemala, where the government has established a quetzal sanctuary not too far from the city of Cobán. The beautifully designed reserve is open to hikers, with several km of good trails leading up into the cloud forest. For the birder this could be a worthwhile detour to search out the gorgeous quetzal. The tourist office in Cobán, INGUAT, hands out an informative leaflet with a map and description of the quetzal sanctuary.

INSECTS AND ARACHNIDS

Those pesky air-breathing invertebrates are unavoidable in any tropical locale. Some are annoying (mosquitoes and gnats), some are dangerous (black widows, bird spiders, and scorpions), and others can cause pain when they bite (red ants), but many are beautiful (butterflies and moths), and *all* are fascinating studies in evolved socialization and specialization. Note:

DIFFERENTIATING MOTHS AND BUTTERFLIES

1. Butterflies fly during the day; moths fly at dusk or at night.

2. Butterflies rest with their wings folded straight up over their bodies; most moths rest with their wings spread flat.

3. All butterflies have bare knobs at the end of both antennae (feelers); moths' antennae are either plumy or hairlike and end in a point.

4. Butterflies have slender bodies; moths are plump. Both insects are of the order Lepidoptera. So, lepidopterists, you are in butterfly heaven in the jungle areas of the Yucatán Peninsula.

Cockroaches also live in the jungle, so don't be surprised if you run into one.

Butterflies and Moths

The Yucatán has an abundance of beautiful moths and butterflies. Of the 90,000 types of butterflies in the world, a large percentage is seen in Quintana Roo. You'll see, among others, the magnificent blue morpho, orange-barred sulphur, copperhead, cloudless sulphur, malachite, admiral, calico, ruddy dagger-wing, tropical buckeye, and emperor. The famous monarch is also a visitor during its annual migration from the Florida Peninsula. It usually makes a stopover on Quintana Roo's east coast, including Cancún and Cozumel, on its way south to the Central American mountains and Mexican highlands where it spends the winter. Trying to photograph a live butterfly is a testy business. Just when you have it in your crosshairs, the comely critter flutters off to another spot!

SIAN KA'AN

With the growing number of visitors to Quintana Roo and the continual development of its natural wonders, there's a real danger of decimating the wildlife and destroying the ancient culture of its people. In 1981, authorities and scientists collaborated on a plan to stem that threat. The plan, which takes into account land titles, logging, hunting, agriculture, cattle ranching, and tourist development—and which local people feel comfortable with—culminated in the October 1986 establishment of the **Reserva de la Biosfera Sian Ka'an,** part of UNESCO's World Network of Biosphere Reserves.

Ongoing environmental efforts address several important issues, among them deforestation, which is becoming commonplace in Quintana Roo as the growing population clears more land for farms and ranches. Even in traditional fishing villages, growth is affecting the environment. In Punta Allen, to supplement their income fishermen were turning to the ancient method of slash-and-burn agriculture that for centuries had worked fine for the small groups of people inhabiting the Quintana Roo region. But with the continued systematic destruction of the forest to create new growing fields, the entire rainforest

WHAT IS A BIOSPHERE RESERVE?

The biosphere is the thin mantle of the earth in which we live. It consists of parts of the lithosphere, hydrosphere, and atmosphere. The biosphere maintains our life and that of all organisms. We need to protect it and keep it liveable.

The program *Man and Biosphere* was created by UNESCO in 1971, and it deals with the interaction of man with his environment. The program contains various projects, among which the concept of biosphere reserve has gained popularity and has become very important worldwide.

The idea of a biosphere reserve is new in conservation. It promotes the protection of different natural ecosystems of the world, and at the same time allows the presence of human activities through the rational use and development of natural resources on an ecological basis.

A biosphere reserve has a nucleus which is for conservation and limited scientific investigation only. A buffer zone would surround this nucleus in which people may live and use the resources on a regulated, ecological basis. Conservation in a biosphere reserve is the challenge of good use rather than prohibiting use. This concept sets it apart from the national parks in which people are only observers. Biosphere reserves are especially appropriate in Mexico where conservation and economic development are equally important.

—from the bulletin of the
Amigos de Sian Ka'an

along the Caribbean could be destroyed in just a few years.

The people need an alternative means to support their families. Many of the people are fishermen. Many more are being trained as guides and learning about the flora and fauna of their reserve, and they're learning English along the way.

Among other problems receiving attention is the plight of the palm tree. The palm is an important part of the cultural and practical lifestyle of the indigenous people of Quintana Roo. The Maya have for years used two particular types of palm, *Thrinax radiata* and *Coccothrinax readdi,* as thatch for the roofs of their houses, and in the past 10 years fishermen have been cutting *Thrinax* to construct lobster traps. This palm is growing increasingly rare in the reserve today. Amigos de Sian Ka'an, with the World Wildlife Fund, is studying the palms' growth patterns and rates, anticipating a management plan that will encourage future growth. Other projects on the table include limiting commercial fishing, relocating an entire fishing village to an area that will better support the families, halting tourist development where it would endanger the ecology, and studying the lobster industry and its future. A number of other worthwhile projects are waiting in line. Like most ambitious endeavors, these take a lot of money. If you're inter- ested in helping out, join the booster club. Your donation will help a worthy cause, and you'll get a newsletter with fascinating facts about the area and its people as well as updates on current projects. For more detailed information write to: Amigos de Sian Ka'an, Apdo. Postal 770, Cancún, Quintana Roo 77500, Mexico.

Ecology Publications
For birders or any visitor intrigued with wildlife and interested in helping the ecological preservation of the Yucatán Peninsula, a fairly new book, *100 Common Birds Of The Yucatán Peninsula* by Barbara MacKinnon, is available through the Amigos de Sian Ka'an.

HISTORY OF THE YUCATÁN

ANCIENTS

Earliest Humans
People and animals from Asia crossed the Bering land bridge into North America in the Pleistocene Epoch about 50,000 years ago, when sea levels were much lower. The epic human trek south continued until only 3,000 years ago, when anthropologists say people first reached Tierra del Fuego, at the tip of South America.

As early as 10,000 B.C., Ice Age humans hunted woolly mammoth and other large animals roaming the cool, moist landscape of Central Mexico. Between 7000 and 2000 B.C., society evolved from hunters and gatherers to farmers. After about 6000 B.C., corn, squash, and beans were independently cultivated in widely separated areas of Mexico. The remains of clay figurines from the Preclassic period, presumed to be fertility symbols, marked the rise of religion in Mesoamerica, beginning around 2000 B.C.

Around 1000 B.C. the Olmec Indian culture, believed to be the region's earliest, began to spread throughout Mesoamerica. Large-scale ceremonial centers grew along Gulf coast lands, and much of Mesoamerica was influenced by these Indians' religion of worship- ping jaguarlike gods. Also at this time, the New World's first calendar and a beginning system of writing were developed.

Classic Period
The Classic period, beginning about A.D. 300, is now hailed by many as the peak of cultural development among the Maya Indians and other cultures throughout Mexico. Until A.D. 900, phenomenal progress was made in the development of artistic, architectural, and astronomical skills. Impressive buildings were constructed during this period, and codices (folded bark books) were written and filled with hieroglyphic symbols that detailed complicated mathematical calculations of days, months, and years. Only the priests and the privileged held this knowledge, and continued

---

HISTORICAL PERIOD CLASSIFICATIONS

PERIOD	BEGINNING DATE
ARCHAIC	2000 B.C.
EARLY PRECLASSIC	800 B.C.
MIDDLE PRECLASSIC	300 B.C.
LATE PRECLASSIC	A.D. 250
EARLY CLASSIC	A.D. 600
LATE CLASSIC	A.D. 900
EARLY POST-CLASSIC	A.D. 1200
LATE POST-CLASSIC	A.D. 1530

to learn and develop it until, for an unknown reason, the growth halted suddenly.

Post-Classic

After A.D. 900, the Toltec influence took hold, marking the end of the most artistic era and the birth of a new militaristic society built around a blend of ceremonialism, civic and social organization, and conquest.

THE COLONIAL ERA

Hernán Cortés

Following Columbus's arrival in the New World, other adventurers traveling the same seas soon found the Yucatán Peninsula. In 1519, 34-year-old Hernán Cortés sailed from Cuba against the wishes of the Spanish governor. With 11 ships, 120 sailors, and 550 soldiers he set out to search for slaves, a lucrative business with or without the government's blessing. His search began on the Yucatán coast and would eventually encompass most of Mexico. However, he hadn't counted on the ferocious resistance and cunning of the Maya Indians. The fighting was destined to continue for many years—a time of bloodshed and death for many of his men. (This

Hernán Cortés

"war" didn't really end on the Peninsula until the Chan Santa Cruz Indians finally signed a peace treaty with the Mexican federal government in 1935, over 400 years later.) By the time Cortés died in 1547 (while exiled in Spain), the Spanish military and Franciscan friars were well entrenched in the Yucatán Peninsula.

Diego de Landa

The Franciscan priests were shocked by Mayan religious customs such as body mutilation and human sacrifice, which they believed to be influences of the devil. The Franciscans believed it their holy duty to eliminate the Maya religion and convert the Indians.

Diego de Landa arrived in Mexico in 1549 as a 25-year-old friar and was instrumental in the destruction of many thousands of Maya idols. He oversaw the burning of 27 codices filled with characters and symbols that he could not understand, but which he believed contained only superstitions and the devil's lies. Since then, only three codices have been found and studied, and only parts of them have been completely deciphered. While Landa was directly responsible for destroying the history of these ancient people, his reputation is partly redeemed by his writing the most complete and detailed account of Maya life in his book *Relaciones de las Cosas de Yucatán.* Landa's book describes daily living in great detail, including the growth and preparation of food, the structure of society, the priesthood, and the sciences. Although he was aware of the sophisticated "count of ages," he didn't understand it. Fortunately, he left a one-line formula which, used as a mathematical and chronological key by later researchers, opened up the science of Maya calculations and their great knowledge of astronomy.

Landa was called back to Spain in 1563 after colonial civil and religious leaders accused him of "despotic mismanagement." He spent a year in prison, and while his fate was being decided, he wrote the book as a defense against the charges. During his absence, his replacement, Bishop Toral, acted with great compassion toward the Indians. Landa was ultimately cleared and was allowed to return to the New World in 1573, where he became a bishop and resumed his previous methods of proselytizing. He lived in the Yucatán until his death in 1579.

THE *ENCOMIENDA*

Only through the extraordinary efforts and the cunning of Cortés and the men he led was the New World conquered. These adventurers provided and paid for their own equipment, ships, and arms. Neither Cortés nor his soldiers received pay checks on the first of each month. Many went into debt in order to proceed with their explorations, having faith that the booty of war would be worth the deaths of comrades and the wounds they all suffered.

Down to the last man they expected grand treasures in gold. In many cases what they received in the end was a trifle of what they expected, and it wasn't gold. Only the leaders and the original conquistadors actually received a reward, in the form of immense tracts of land.

Almost immediately after Cortés conquered the Indians in Mexico, he realized that it would be easy to use the Spanish *encomienda* (guardianship) system as used after the reconquest of Moorish lands in Spain. The lands were divided up among the conquistadors, and the Indians on the land were in essence given as well. This plan gave the Spaniards the power to collect tribute (as the Indian ruler Moctezuma had done before them). The Indians performed the labor that it took to give the Spanish *encomendero* power and money. In return, the *encomendero* was to convert his Indians to Christianity, to look after them as a father, and to keep the peace in the village. History tells a different story.

Franciscan Power

Bishop Toral was cut from a different cloth. A humanitarian, he was appalled by the unjust treatment of Indians. Though Toral, after Landa's imprisonment, tried to impose sweeping changes, was unable to make inroads into the power held by the Franciscans in the Yucatán. Defeated, he retired to Mexico. However, shortly before his death in 1571, his reforms were implemented with the "Royal Cedula," which prohibited friars from shaving the heads of Indians against their will, flogging them, or keeping prison cells in monasteries. It also called for the immediate release of all Indian prisoners.

Catholicism

Over the years, the majority of Indians were baptized into the Catholic faith. Most priests did their best to educate the people, teach them to read and write, and protect them from the growing number of Spanish settlers who used them as slaves. The Indians, then and now, practice Catholicism in their own manner, combining their ancient beliefs, handed down through centuries, with Christian doctrine. These mystic yet Christian ceremonies are performed in baptism, courtship, marriage, illness, farming, house-building, and fiestas.

Further Subjugation

While all of Mexico dealt with the problems of economic colonialism, the Yucatán Peninsula had an additional one: harassment by vicious pirates who made life on the Gulf coast unstable. Around 1600, when silver production began to wane, Spain's economic power faltered. In the following years, haciendas (self-supporting estates or small feudal systems) began to thrive, overrunning communal villages jointly owned by the Maya. But later, between 1700 and 1810 as Mexico endured the backlash of several government upheavals in Europe, Spanish settlers on the Peninsula began exploiting the native Maya in earnest. The passive Indians were ground down, their lands taken away, and their numbers greatly reduced by the white man's epidemics and mistreatment.

Caste War

The Spaniards grabbed the Maya land and planted it with tobacco and sugarcane year after year until the soil had worn out. Added to the other abuses, it was inevitable that the Indians' rage would eventually explode in a furious attack. This bloody uprising in the 1840s was called the Caste War. Though the Maya were farmers, not soldiers, this savage war saw them taking revenge on every white man, woman, and child by means of rape and murder. European survivors made their way to the last Spanish strongholds of Mérida and Campeche. The governments of the two cities appealed for help to Spain, France, and the United States. No one answered the call, and it was soon apparent that the remaining two cities would be wiped out. But fate would not have it that way; just as the governor of Mérida was about to begin evacuating the city, the Maya picked up their primitive weapons and walked away.

Attuned to the signals of the land, the Maya knew that the appearance of the flying ant was the first sign of rain and signaled the time to plant corn. When, on the brink of destroying the enemy, the winged ant made an unusually early appearance, the Indians turned their backs on certain victory and returned to their villages to plant corn.

This was just the breather the Spanish settlers needed. Help came from Cuba and Mexico City, as well as 1,000 U.S. mercenary troops. Vengeance was merciless. Most Maya were killed indiscriminately. Some were taken prisoner and sold to Cuba as slaves; others left their villages and hid in the jungles, in some cases for decades. Between 1846 and 1850, the population of the Yucatán Peninsula was reduced from 500,000 to 300,000. Quintana Roo along the Caribbean coast was considered a dangerous no-man's-land for almost another hundred years.

Growing Maya Power

Many Maya Indians escaped slaughter during the Caste War by fleeing to the isolated territory known today as Quintana Roo. The Maya revived the "Talking Cross," a pre-Cortesian oracle representing gods of the four cardinal directions. This was a religious/political marriage. Three determined survivors of the Caste War—a priest, a master spy, and a ventriloquist—all wise leaders, knew their people's desperate need for divine leadership. As a result of the words from the "talking cross," shattered Indians came together in large numbers and began to organize. The community guarded the cross's location, and advice from it continued to strengthen the Maya.

They called themselves Chan Santa Cruz (meaning "People of the Holy Cross"). As their confidence developed, so did the growth and power of their communities. Living in dense forests very close to the border with British Honduras (now Belize), they found they had something their neighbors wanted: timber. The Chan Santa Cruz Maya began selling timber to the British and were given arms in return. These weapons gave the Maya even more power. From

1855 to 1857 internal strife weakened the relations between Campeche and Mérida. While the Spaniards were dealing with the problem on the Gulf coast, the Maya took advantage of the vulnerability of Fort Bacalar and in 1857 took it over, gaining control of the entire Caribbean coast from Cabo Catouche in the far north to the border of British Honduras in the south. In three years they destroyed all of the Spanish settlements while slaughtering or capturing thousands of whites.

The Indians of the coastal community of Chan Santa Cruz, also known as Cruzobs, for years had murdered their captives. But starting in 1858 they took lessons from the colonials and began to keep whites for slave labor in the fields and forest; women were put to work doing household chores and some became concubines. For the next 40 years, the Chan Santa Cruz Indians kept the east coast of the Yucatán for themselves; a shaky truce with the Mexican government endured. The Indians were financially independent, self-governing, and, with no roads in, totally isolated from technological advancements beginning to take place in other parts of the Peninsula. They were not at war as long as everyone left them alone.

The Last Stand

Only when Pres. Porfirio Díaz took power in 1877 did the Mexican federal government began to think seriously about the Yucatán Peninsula. Over the years, Quintana Roo's isolation and the strength of the Maya in their treacherous jungle had foiled repeated efforts by Mexican soldiers to capture the Indians. The army's expeditions were infrequent, but it rankled Díaz that a handful of Indians had been able to keep the Mexican federal army at bay for so long. An assault in 1901, under the command of Gral. Ignacio Bravo, broke the government's losing streak. The general captured a village, laid railroad tracks, and built a walled fort. Supplies arriving by rail kept the fort stocked, but the Indian army held the fort under siege for an entire year. When reinforcements arrived from the capital, the upstarts were finally put down. Thus began another cycle of brutal Mexican occupation until 1915. The scattered Indians didn't give up. They persisted with guerilla raids from the rainforest until the Mexicans, finally defeated once again, pulled out and returned Quintana Roo to the Maya.

From 1917 till 1920, hundreds of thousands of Indians died from influenza and smallpox epidemics introduced by the Spanish. An Indian leader, General May, took stock of his troops and saw clearly that the old soldiers were fading. They had put up a long tough battle to hold onto their land and culture. The year 1920 marked the end of their independent reign in Quintana Roo's jungle. Foreign gummakers initiated the chicle boom, bringing *chicleros* to work the trees. It was then that General May demanded (and received) a negotiated settlement. In 1935 the Chan Santa Cruz Indians signed a peace treaty with the Mexican Federals.

MODERN TIMES

Meanwhile, in the northern part of the Peninsula, international demand for the henequen plant brought prosperity to Mérida, capital of the state of Yucatán. Twine and rope made from the sword-shaped leaves of this variety of agave plant were in demand all over the world. Soon after the henequen boom began in 1875, Mérida had become the jewel of the Peninsula. Spanish haciendas staffed by Indian slaves cultivated the easily grown plant, and for miles the outlying areas were planted with the henequen, which required little rainfall and thrived in the Peninsula's thin, rocky soil. Beautiful mansions were built by entrepreneurs who led the gracious life,

THE WALLS OF MEXICO

Some might say a wall is a wall is a wall. Not in Mexico. A wall may be the remnant of a 1,000-year-old structure built by Indians and incorporated into a 500-year-old Spanish structure. Walls are truthful. No matter that some past contractor may have painted over them, in most cases the paint won't adhere to the ancient stone for long—they proudly show their antiquity. Some of the finest walls are found in patios of churches—they deserve a little extra time of careful study. Surprisingly, a long look finds remnants of ancient frescoes, bits of color and often a carved design worn down with age. Each is different, each a mystery, each a discovery.

sending their children to school in Europe, cruising with their wives to New Orleans in search of new luxuries and entertainment. Port towns were developed on the Gulf coast, and a two-km-long wharf named Progreso was built to accommodate the large ships that came for sisal (hemp from the henequen plant).

The only thing that didn't change was the lifestyle of the *peones*. The Indian peasants' life was still devoid of human rights. They labored long, hard hours, living in constant debt to the company store, where their meager peso wage was spent before it was received. The Indians were caught up in a cycle of bondage that endured for many years in Mérida. One story holds than it was during this time that the lovely *huipil* (Indian dress) was mandated to be worn by all Indians and mestizos (those of mixed blood) on the Peninsula. There would then be no problem distinguishing Indians from pure-blooded Spaniards.

Hacienda Wealth

The outside world was becoming aware of the Peninsula, its newly found economic activity, and its rich *patrones.* In 1908, an American journalist, John Kenneth Turner, stirred things up when he documented the difficult lives of the Indian plantation workers, and the accompanying opulence enjoyed by the owners. From this time forward, reform was inevitable. In 1915, wealthy hacienda owners were compelled to pay an enormous tax to Pres. Venustiano Carranza. This tax was forcibly extracted under the watchful eye of General Alvarado and 7,000 armed soldiers, who needed the money to put down revolutionaries Emiliano Zapata and Pancho Villa in the northern regions of Mexico. Millions of pesos changed hands.

The next thorn in the side of the hacienda owners was upstart Felipe Carrillo Puerto, the first socialist governor of Mérida. Under his tutelage the Indians set up a labor union, educational center, and political club that amounted to leagues of resistance. These leagues gave the *peones* the first secular hope ever held out to them. Through them, workers wielded a power that wealthy Yucatecans were forced to acknowledge. Carrillo pushed on, making agrarian reforms at every turn. He decreed that abandoned haciendas were up for appropriation by the government. He was so successful that his

Hacienda Yaxcopoil dates from the turn of the century.

opponents began to worry seriously about the power he was amassing. With the number of his followers growing, conservatives saw only one way to stop him. In 1923, Felipe Carrillo Puerto was assassinated.

The Revolution

The fight against wealthy landowners and the power elite did not die with Carrillo. In the south, Emiliano Zapata was demanding land reform; shortly thereafter, the revolution put an end to the elitist control of wealth in the country. The constitution of 1917 had made some inroads. It was instrumental in dividing up the large haciendas, giving the country back to the people (*some* of the people), and making sweeping political changes. The education of all children was mandated and many new schools were built. Power of the church was curtailed and church land redistributed.

In this war of ideals, however, Indian villages were broken up along with the large haciendas, and turmoil continued. Again it was the rich against the poor; a whole new class of rich had been created, those who had the new power. In 1936, Pres. Lázaro Cárdenas declared Quintana Roo a territory of the Mexican government. It wasn't until later years that some of the Indians received favorable treatment, when President Cárdenas gave half the usable land in Quintana Roo to the poor. In 1974, with the promise of tourism, the territory was admitted to the Federation of States of Mexico.

Mexican Unity

Between 1934 and 1940, the Mexican government nationalized most foreign companies, which were taking more out of the country than they were putting in. Mexico suffered through a series of economic setbacks but gained unity and national self-confidence. Like a child learning to walk, the country took many falls. But progress continued; the people of the country saw more jobs, fairer wages, and more products on the market. The progress lasted until the 1970s, when inflation began to rise. By 1976 it was totally out of hand. Mexico was pricing itself out of the market, both for tourists and capital investors. Eventually, a change in the monetary policy let the peso float, finding its own value against the dollar. The policy brought back tourists and investors.

The condition of the peso is a boon for visitors, but a burden for the people. The belief is that enough tourism will create more jobs so that the economic condition will ultimately remedy itself. Smart Mexican businesspeople began developing the natural beauty of the Caribbean coast, and indeed visitors are coming from all over the world.

GOVERNMENT AND ECONOMY

GOVERNMENT

Theoretically, Mexico enjoys a constitutional democracy modeled after that of the United States. A president, a two-house congress, and a judiciary branch see to the business of running the country. Theoretically, Mexico's elections are free. Realistically, for 66 years the country has been controlled by one party, the PRI (Partido Revolución Institutional, or Institutional Revolution Party). Political dissent—represented primarily by PAN (Partido Acción Nacional) and PMS (Partido Mexicano Socialista)—has never had much voice. The president, who can serve only a single six-year term, handpicks the next PRI candidate who historically has been guaranteed the office through use of the state-controlled media and dubious election procedures.

In addition to Mexico's 32 states, the country has the *Distrito Federal,* or Federal District in Mexico City, which encompasses the government center. The states are allowed a small measure of autonomy, but the reach of the federal government is long. City mayors, called *presidentes municipales,* appoint federal *delegatos* to represent the national government at the municipal level.

Fraud and corruption have been ugly mainstays of Mexican government from its beginning. In the 1988 presidential election, PRI candidate Carlos Salinas Gortari officially garnered 51% of the vote, a figure many critics believe was invented by the PRI after polls closed. (A suspicious "breakdown" in the election computer delayed the results for several days.)

But Salinas's term will likely be remembered as a time of historic reforms, such as expanding the number of Senate seats to allow more for the opposition, limiting campaign spending, and changing the rules of the body that oversees Mexican elections.

The only certainty in Mexico's tumultuous political arena is that, after decades of a government static in its ways, things are changing fast. The U.S. Congress's passage of NAFTA in 1993 sealed a free-trade deal between Mexico, the U.S., and Canada that will likely change Mexico's economic landscape forever—the political ramifications of which are still unclear. The March 1994 election-year shooting of PRI presidential candidate Luis Donaldo Colosio in Tijuana was Mexico's first major political assassination since 1928. Soon after, Colosio's campaign manager, technocrat Ernesto Zedillo, was nominated to fill the candidacy. Mexico's political future is anyone's guess.

ECONOMY

Mexico's chief industries are tourism, oil, and mining. Mexican oil is produced by Pemex, the national corporation, and most is shipped at OPEC prices to the U.S. (its number-one customer), Canada, Israel, France, and Japan. Rich in natural gas, the country sends the U.S. 10% of its total output. Two-thirds of Mexico's export revenue comes from fossil fuels.

The Yucatán

The leading industry on the Yucatán Peninsula is the oil business. Along the Gulf coast from Campeche south into the state of Tabasco, the oil industry is booming. Yucatán cities are beginning to show signs of good financial health.

Yucatecan fisheries are abundant along the Gulf coast. At one time fishing was not much more than a ma-and-pa business here, but today fleets of large purse seiners with their adjacent processing plants can be seen on the Gulf of Mexico just south of the city of Campeche and on Isla del Carmen. With the renewed interest in preserving fishing grounds for the future, the industry could continue to thrive for many years.

Tourism is developing into the number-one contributor to the economy. Going with a good thing, the government has set up a national trust to finance a program of developing beautiful areas of the country to attract visitors. Cancún is the most successful thus far.

Cancún

Until the tourism boom of the 1970s, Quintana Roo's economy amounted to very little. For a few years the chicle boom brought a flurry of activity up and down the state. At that time chicle, used to make chewing gum, was shipped from the harbor of Isla Cozumel. Native and hardwood trees have always been in demand; coconuts and fishing were the only other natural resources that added to the economy—but neither on a large scale. With the development of an offshore sandbar—Cancún—into a multimillion-dollar resort, tourism is now its number-one money-maker. Cancún is one of Mexico's most modern and popular resorts. Construction is continuing south along the coast. Other naturally attractive sites are earmarked for future development, and the corridor south of Cancún is already showing signs of growth with several new resorts, a marina, an 18-hole golf course, and talk of another international airport. New roads give access to previously unknown beaches and often-unseen Maya structures. Extra attention is going to archaeological zones ignored for hundreds of years, and to building restrooms, ticket offices, and fences to keep out vandals.

Agriculture

The land in the northernmost part of the Yucatán was described by Diego de Landa, an early Spanish priest, as "a country with the least earth ever seen, since all of it is one living rock." Surprisingly, the thin layer of soil is enough to support agriculture. This monotonous landscape is dotted with a multitude of sword-shaped plants called henequen. At the turn of the century, Spanish settlers on the Peninsula made vast fortunes growing and selling henequen, which was used for rope-making. However, it was the Maya who showed the Spanish its many valuable uses, especially for building their houses. Without nails or tools, houses were tied together with handmade henequen twine. Wherever *palapa*-style structures are built today by the Indians, the same nail-free method is used.

With careful nurturing of the soil, the early Indians managed to support a large population of people on the land. Though rainfall is spotty and unreliable, the land is surprisingly fertile and

each year produces corn and other vegetables on small farms. The northern tip of the Peninsula can be dry and arid. On the northwest edge where trade winds bring more rain, the land is slightly greener. As you travel south, the desert gradually becomes green until you find yourself in a jungle plain fringed by the turquoise Caribbean and the Río Hondo.

Along the coast of Quintana Roo, remnants of large coconut plantations, now broken up into small tracts and humble ranchitos, are being developed by farmers with modest government assistance. At one time it was commonplace to see copra lining the roadside, drying in the sun. The number of coconut trees afflicted with "yellowing disease" in the Yucatán has greatly decreased the output of copra in the state. The disease and Hurricane Gilbert combined to turn what was once a mixture of thick, lush coconut trees and rich, verdant jungle into what looks like a war zone, with dead limbs and topless coconut trees. Fortunately the jungle rejuvenates quickly, and within a few more years nature will cover the dead with new growth. As for the coconut trees, new strains are being planted that are resistant to this dreadful disease.

Different parts of the Peninsula produce different crops. In most areas juicy oranges grow, which you can find for sale everywhere; in the marketplace and at roadside stands, vendors often remove the green peel, leaving the sweet fruit ready to eat. The earliest chocolate drink was developed by the Indians in Mexico and presented to the Spanish. Today chocolate manufactured in Mexico is shipped all over the world. Bananas of many kinds, from finger-size to 15-inch red plantains, are grown in thick groves close to the Gulf coast. Tabasco bananas are recognized worldwide as among the finest.

Many of the crops now produced by American farmers were introduced by the Maya and Aztecs, including corn, sweet potatoes, tomatoes, peppers, squash, pumpkin, and avocados. Many other products favored by Americans are native to the Yucatán Peninsula: papaya, cotton, tobacco, rubber, vanilla, and turkey.

PEOPLE

Today, 75-80% of the entire population of Mexico is estimated to be mestizo (mixed blood, mostly Indian and Spanish), with 10-15% pure Indian. For comparison, as recently as 1870, pure-blooded Indians made up over 50% of the population. While no statistics are available, it's believed most of the country's pure Indians live on the Peninsula (including the state of Chiapas).

Language
The farther you go from a city, the less Spanish and more Mayan, or a dialect of Mayan, you'll hear. The government estimates that of the 10 million Mexican Indians in the country, about 25% speak only an Indian dialect. Of the original 125 native languages, 70 are still spoken, 20 of which are classified as Maya languages, including Tzeltal, Tzotzil, Chol, and Yucatec Mayan. Mexican education was made compulsory in 1917, though like most laws this one didn't reach the Yucatán Peninsula till quite recently. Despite efforts to integrate the Indian into Mexican society, many remain content with the status quo. Schools throughout the Peninsula use Spanish-language books, even though many children speak only a Maya dialect. In some of the smaller, more rural, schools (such as in Akumal), bilingual teachers are recruited to help children make the transition.

Higher Education
Though education is free, many rural parents need their children to help with work on the *ranchito*. That and the cost of books still prevent many Yucatecan children from getting a higher education. For years, Peninsula students wanting an education had to travel to the university at Mérida. Now though the number of students going on to college grows with each generation, and universities are slowly being built, the state of Quintana Roo still does not have a university. College is available in Campeche and Tabasco, and another one has been built in Mérida.

Housing and Family
The major difference in today's rural housing is the growth of the *ranchito,* typically one hut on a family farm that raises corn, sometimes a few pigs and turkeys, and maybe even a few head of cattle. While far from posh, the Indians' homes have become slightly more comfortable than their ancestors', commonly furnished with a table and chairs, a lamp, and maybe a metal bathtub.

Abundance of wood explains the difference in rural housing between the north and south ends of the Quintana Roo Caribbean coastline. In the north, where wood is less abundant, structures are commonly made with walls of stucco or slender saplings set close together. Small houses

teacher and students

OZ MALLAN

in the south are built mostly of milled board, with either thatch or tin roofs. Many huts have electric lighting and TV antennae and some even have refrigerators.

Until recently families usually had many children. A man validated his masculinity and gained respect by having a large family. The labor around the family plot was doled out to children as they came along.

The Maya

Maya men and women average 1.62 meters (five feet six inches) and 1.5 meters (four feet eleven inches) tall respectively. Muscular bodied, they have straight black hair, round heads, broad faces with pronounced cheekbones, aquiline noses, almond-shaped dark eyes, and eyelids with the epicanthic or Mongolian fold.

Bishop Diego de Landa writes in his *Rela-* *ciones* that when the Spanish arrived, the Maya still practiced the ancient method of flattening a newborn's head with a wooden press. By pressing the infant's forehead, the fronto-nasal portion of the face was pushed forward, as can be seen in carvings and other human depictions from the pre-Cortesian period. This was considered a beautiful trait by the Maya. They also dangled a bead in front of a baby's eyes to encourage cross-eyedness, another Maya beauty mark. Dental mutilation was practiced by filing the teeth to give them different shapes or by inlaying carvings with pyrite, jade, or turquoise. Tattooing and scarification were accomplished by lightly cutting a design into the skin and purposely infecting it, creating a scar of beauty. Adult noblemen often wore a phony nosepiece to give the illusion of an even longer nose sweeping back into the long, flat forehead.

ANCIENT CULTURE OF THE YUCATÁN PENINSULA

EARLY MAYA

The origins of the Maya world lie in the Pacific coastal plains of Chiapas and Guatemala. From here, Maya culture slowly moved north and west to encompass all of Guatemala, the Yucatán Peninsula, most of the states of Chiapas and Tabasco, and the western parts of Honduras and El Salvador. The earliest traces of human presence found in this area are obsidian spear points and stone tools dating back to 9000 B.C. The Loltún caves in the Yucatán contain a cache of extinct mammal bones, including mammoth and early horse, which were probably dragged there by a roving band of hunters. As the region dried out and large game disappeared over the next millennia, tools of a more settled way of life appeared, like grinding stones for preparing seeds and plant fibers. The first sedentary villages began to appear after 2000 B.C. With them came the hallmarks of a more developed culture: primitive agriculture and ceramics.

Proto-Maya

Archaeologists believe that the earliest people we can call Maya, or proto-Maya, lived on the Pacific coast of Chiapas and Guatemala. These tribes lived in villages that may have held over 1,000 inhabitants and made beautiful painted and incised ceramic jars for food storage. After 1000 B.C. this way of life spread north to the highlands site of Kaminaljuyú (now part of Guatemala City) and, over the next millennium, to the rest of the Maya world. Meanwhile, in what are now the Mexican states of Veracruz and Tabasco to the northwest, another culture, the Olmecs, was developing what is now considered Mesoamerica's first civilization. Its influence was felt throughout Mexico and Central America. Archaeologists believe that before the Olmecs disappeared around 300 B.C. they contributed two crucial cultural advances to the Maya: the long-count calendar and the hieroglyphic writing system, though some researchers think the latter may have actually originated in the Zapotec culture of Oaxaca.

Izapa and Petén

During the Late Preclassic era (after 300 B.C.), that same Pacific coastal plain saw the rise of a Maya culture at a place called Izapa near Tapachula, Chiapas. The Izapans worshipped gods that are obviously precursors of the Classic

Maya pantheon and commemorated religious and historical events in bas-relief carvings that emphasized costume and finery. All that was missing were long-count dates and hieroglyphs. Those appeared as the Izapan style spread north into the Guatemalan highlands. This was the heyday of Kaminaljuyú, which grew to enormous size, with over 120 temple-mounds and numerous stelae. The earliest calendar inscription that researchers are able to read comes from a monument found at El Baúl to the southwest of Kaminaljuyú; it has been translated as A.D. 36. The Izapan style's northernmost reach was Yucatán's Loltún caves, where an Izapan warrior-relief is carved out of the rock at the cave entrance.

In the Petén jungle region just north of the highlands, the dominant culture was the Chicanel, whose hallmarks are elaborate temple-pyramids lined with enormous stucco god-masks (as in Kohunlich). The recently excavated Petén sites of Nakbé and El Mirador are the most spectacular Chicanel cities yet found. El Mirador contains a 70-meter-tall temple-pyramid complex that may be the most massive structure in Mesoamerica. Despite the obvious prosperity of this region, there is almost no evidence of long-count dates or writing systems in either the Petén jungle or the Yucatán Peninsula just to the north.

The great efflorescense of the southern Maya world stops at the end of the Late Preclassic (A.D. 250). Kaminaljuyú and other cities were abandoned, and researchers believe that the area was invaded by Teotihuacano warriors extending the reach of their Valley of Mexico-based empire. On the Yucatán Peninsula, there is evidence of Teotihuacano occupation at the Río Bec site of Becán and at Acanceh near Mérida. You can see Teotihuacano-style costumes and gods in carvings at the great Petén city of Tikal and at Copán in Honduras. By A.D. 600, the Teotihuacano empire had collapsed, and the stage was set for the Classic Maya era.

CLASSIC AND POST-CLASSIC MAYA

Maya Heartland

The heartland of the Classic Maya (A.D. 600-800) runs from Copán in Western Honduras through the Petén region to Tikal, and ends at Palenque in Chiapas. The development of these city-states, which also included Yaxchilán and Bonampak, almost always followed the same pattern. Early in this era, a new and vigorous breed of rulers founded across the region a series of dynasties bent on deifying themselves and their ancestors. All the arts and sciences of the Maya world, from architecture to astronomy, were focused on this goal. The long-count calendar and the hieroglyphic writing system were the most crucial tools in this effort, as the rulers needed to recount the stories of their dynasty and of their own glorious careers. During the Classic era, painting, sculpture, and carving reached their climax; objects like Lord Pacal's sarcophagus lid from Palenque are now recognized as among the finest pieces of world art.

Royal monuments stood at the center of large and bustling cities. Cobá and Dzibilchaltún each probably hosted 50,000 inhabitants, and there was vigorous intercity trade. In the northern area, the largest Classic-era cities, including the Río Bec sites and Cobá, are more obscure to travlelers due to their relatively poor state of preservation. Each Classic city-state reached its apogee at a different time—the southern cities generally peaked first—but by A.D. 800 nearly all of them had collapsed and were left in a state of near-abandonment.

The Classic Maya decline is one of the great enigmas of Mesoamerican archaeology. There are a myriad of theories—disease, invasion, etc.—but many researchers now believe the collapse was caused by starvation brought on by overpopulation and destruction of the environment. With the abandonment of the cities, the Classic Maya's cultural advances disappeared as well. The last long-count date was recorded in 909, and many religious customs and beliefs were never seen again.

Northern Yucatán

However, Maya culture was far from dead; the new heartland was the northern end of the Yucatán Peninsula. Much archaeological work remains to be done in this area, and there are a number of controversies now raging as to who settled it where and when. For a brief period between A.D. 800 and 925, it was the Puuc region's turn to prosper. The art of architecture reached its climax in city-states like Uxmal, where the Nunnery Quadrangle and the Governor's Palace are considered among the finest Maya buildings. After the Puuc region was abandoned, almost certainly due to a foreign invasion, the center of Maya power moved east to Chichén Itzá. The debate rages as to who built (or rebuilt) Chichén, but the possibilities have narrowed to two tribes: Putún Maya warrior-traders or Toltecs escaping political strife in their Central Mexican homeland. Everyone agrees that there is Mexican influence at Chichén; the question is, was it carried by the Putún or by an invading Toltec army?

During the Early post-Classic era (A.D. 925-1200), Chichén was the great power of northern Yucatán. Competing city-states either bowed before its warriors or, like the Puuc cities and Cobá, were destroyed. After Chichén's fall in 1224—probably due to an invasion—a heretofore lowly tribe calling themselves the Itzá became the Late Post-Classic (1200-1530) masters of Yucatecan power politics. The Itzá's ruling Cocom lineage was finally toppled in the mid-15th century.

Northern Yucatán dissolved into an unruly group of jealous city-states ready to go to war with each other at a moment's notice. By the time of the Spanish conquest, culture was once again being imported from outside the Maya world. Putún Maya seafaring traders brought new styles of art and religious beliefs back from their trips to Central Mexico. Their influence may be seen in the Mixtec-style frescoes at Tulum on the Quintana Roo coast.

Mayapán

Kukulcán II of Chichén Itzá founded Mayapán between A.D. 1263 and 1283. After his death and the abandonment of Chichén, an aggressive Itzá lineage named the Cocom seized power and used Mayapán as a base to subjugate northern Yucatán. They succeeded through wars using Tabascan mercenaries and intermarrying with other powerful lineages. Foreign lineage heads were forced to live in Mayapán where they could easily be controlled. At its height, the city covered 6.5 square km within a defensive wall that contained over 15,000 inhabitants. Architecturally, Mayapán leaves much to be desired; the city plan was haphazard, and its greatest monument was a sloppy, smaller copy of Chichén's Pyramid of Kukulcán.

The Cocom ruled for 250 years until A.D. 1441-1461, when an upstart Uxmal-based lineage named the Xiu rebelled and slaughtered the Cocom. Mayapán was abandoned and Yucatán's city-states weakened themselves in a series of bloody intramural wars that left them hopelessly divided when it came time to face the conquistadors.

RELIGION AND SOCIETY

The Earth

The Maya saw the world as a layered flat square. At the four corners (each representing a cardinal direction) stood four bearded gods called Becabs who held up the skies. In the underworld, four gods called Pahuatuns steadied the earth. The layered skies and underworld were divided by a determined number of steps up and down. Each god and direction was associated with a color: black for west, white for north, yellow for south, and most important, red for east. In the center of the earth stood the Tree of Life, "La Ceiba." Its powerful roots reached the underworld, and its lofty foliage swept the heavens, connecting the two. The ceiba tree was associated with the color blue-green *(yax)* along with all important things—water, jade, and new corn.

The Indians were terrified of the underworld and what it represented: odious rivers of rotting flesh and blood and evil gods such as Jaguar, god of the night, whose spotty hide was symbolized by the starry sky. Only the priests could communicate with and control the gods. For this reason, the populace was content to pay tribute to and care for all the needs of the priests.

Ceremonies

Ceremony appears to have been a vital part of the daily lives of the Maya. Important rituals took place on specific dates of their accurate calendar; everyone took part. These activities were performed in the plazas, on the platforms, and around the broad grounds of the temple-cities. Sweat baths apparently were incorporated into the religion. Some rituals were secret and only priests took part within the inner sanctums of the temple. Other ceremonies included fasts, abstinences, purification, dancing, prayers, and simple sacrifices of food, animals, or possessions (jewelry, beads, and ceramics) amid clouds of smoky incense.

The later Maya took part in self-mutilation. Carvings found at several sites depict an Indian pulling a string of thorns through a hole in his tongue or penis. The most brutal ceremonies involved human sacrifice. Sacrificial victims were thrown into a sacred well; if they didn't drown within a certain length of time (often overnight), they were rescued and then expected to relate the conversation of the spirits who lived in the bottom of the well. Other methods of sacrifice were spearing, beheading, or removing the heart of the victim with a knife and offering it still beating to the spirits.

Although old myths and stories say young female virgins were most often sacrificed in the sacred cenotes, anthropological dredging and diving in the muddy water in various Peninsula ruins has turned up evidence suggesting most of the victims were young children, both male and female.

Time

The priests of the Classic period represented time as a parade of gods who were really numbers moving through Maya eternity in careful mathematical order. They were shown carrying heavy loads with tumplines around their heads. The combination of the gods and their burdens reflected the exact number of days gone by since the beginning of the Maya calendar count. Each god has particular characteristics; number nine, an attractive young man with the spots of a serpent on his chin, sits leaning forward, jade necklace dangling on one knee, right hand reaching up to adjust his tumpline. His load is the screech owl of the *baktun* (the 144,000-day period). Together, the two represent nine times 144,000, or 1,296,000 days—the number of days elapsed since the beginning of the Maya day count and the day the glyph was carved, maybe 1,275 years ago. Archaeologists call this a long-count date. Simpler methods also were used, including combinations of dots and bars (ones and fives, respectively, with special signs for zero). Most Mayanists agree that the date of the beginning of the long count was 10 August 3114 B.C.

Status

If the Maya's sophisticated calendar sounds complicated, so will the complex, stratified society that made up the Maya civilization. Their society of many classes was headed by the elite,

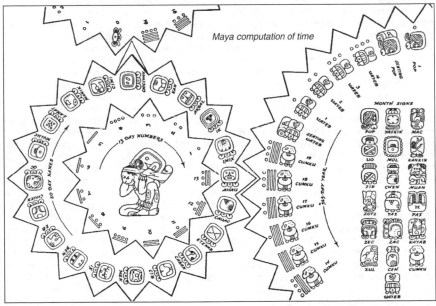

Maya computation of time

who controlled matters of warfare, religion, government, and commerce. Also in this group were architects who designed the magnificent temples and pyramids. Skilled masons belonged to a class that included servants of royalty. Priests directed the people in the many rites and festivals demanded by a pantheon of gods.

Farmers were instrumental in maintaining the social order. They battled a hostile environment, constantly fighting the jungle and frequent droughts. Creativity enabled them to win out most of the time. They slashed fields from rainforest, constructed raised plots in swampy depressions, and built irrigation canals. In some areas farmers terraced the land to conserve soil and water. The results of working by hand and using stone and wood tools were sufficient to feed a growing population. All aspects of Maya life were permeated by the society's religion.

Housing

Thanks to remaining stone carvings, we know that the ancient Maya lived in houses almost identical to the *palapa* huts that many Yucatán residents still live in today. These huts were built with tall, thin sapling trees placed close together to form the walls, then topped with a *palapa* roof. This type of house provided air circulation through the walls, and the thick *palapa* roof allowed the rain to run off easily, keeping the inside snug and dry. In the early years there were no real doors, and furnishings were sparce. Then as now, families slept in hammocks, the coolest way to sleep. For the rare times when it turned cold, tiny fires were built on the floor below the hammocks to keep the family warm. Most of the cooking was done either outdoors or in another hut. Often a small group of people—extended family—built their huts together on one plot and lived an almost communal lifestyle. If one member of the group brought home a deer, everyone shared in this trophy. Though changing, this is still commonplace throughout the rural areas of the Peninsula.

Maya "Basketball"

Ball courts were prevalent in the ceremonial centers located throughout the Yucatán Peninsula. Though today's Maya are peaceful, at one time bloody games were part of the ancient culture, as may be seen from the remaining artwork (for example the panel in Chichén Itzá's Temple of the Bearded Man). The carvings graphically show that the losing (or as a few far-out researchers have suggested, the winning) team was awarded a bloody death. The players were heavily padded with cotton padding stuffed with salt, and the object of the game was to hit a hard rubber ball into a cement ring attached to a wall eight meters off the ground. Legend says the game went on for hours and the winners (or losers) were awarded clothes and jewelry from the spectators.

THE ARTS

Pottery

The Maya were outstanding potters. Some of the earliest Maya pottery, found at Izapan, dates to 36 B.C. Evidence of artistic advancement is apparent in the variety of new forms, techniques, and artistic motifs that developed during the Classic period. Growth has been traced from simple monochrome ceramics of early periods to bichrome and later to rich polychrome. Polychrome drawings on pottery work have been found with recognizable color still visible. Three-legged plates with a basal edge and small conical supports, as well as covered and uncovered vessels, were prevalent. A jar with a screw-on lid was found recently in Río Azul, a Maya site in an isolated corner of Guatemala.

Figurines, especially those found in graves on the island of Jaina, were faithful reproductions of the people and their times. Many decorated pottery vessels used for everyday purposes tell us something about these people who enjoyed beauty even in mundane objects. Decorative motifs ranged from simple geometric designs to highly stylized natural figures to simple true-to-life reproductions. We have learned much from Maya artists' realistic representations of body alterations, garments, and adornments typical of their time. All social classes are represented: common men and women, nobility, priests, musicians, craftspeople, merchants, warriors, ball players, even animals. Many of these clay figurines were used as flutes, whistles, ocarinas, rattles, or incense holders. Noteworthy is the quantity of female figurines that represent the fertility goddess Ix Chel.

Sculpture

The Maya used their great talent for sculpture almost exclusively to decorate temples and sanctuaries. They employed a number of techniques, which varied depending on the area and the natural resources available. They excelled in freestanding stone carving, such as the stelae and altars. In areas such as Palenque, where stone wasn't as available, stucco art is outstanding. The Indians added rubber to the plaster-and-water mixture, creating an extremely durable surface that would polish to a fine luster. In Palenque you'll see marvelous examples of stucco bas-reliefs adorning pyramids, pillars, stairways, walls, friezes, masks, and heads. Sculpting was done not only in stone but also in precious materials such as gold and silver. Some of the Maya's finest work was done in jade, a substance they held in great reverence.

Painting

Paints were of mineral and vegetable origin in hues of red, yellow, brown, blue, green, black, and white. Mural painting was highly refined by the Maya. Murals found in several ancient sites depict everyday life, ceremonies, and battle scenes in brilliant colors. Bright color was also applied to the carved stone structures, pyramids, and stelae. Today all color has disappeared from the outside of these buildings along with most of the finishing plaster that was used as a smooth coating over large building stones. When Cortés's men first viewed the coast of Tulum, it must have been quite a sight to behold: brilliantly colored buildings in the midst of lush green jungle overlooking a clear turquoise sea.

SCIENCE

Maya inscriptions relate to calculations of time, mathematics, and the gods. Astronomy was also a highly developed science. The Maya shared their calendar system and concept of zero with other Mesoamerican groups, but they went on to perfect and develop their sophisticated calendar, more exact to a ten-thousandth of a day than the Gregorian calendar in use today.

Hieroglyphics

The hieroglyphics the Maya used in scientific calculations and descriptions are seen everywhere on the Yucatán Peninsula, in carved temple panels, on pyramid steps, and in stelae commonly installed in front of the great structures, carrying pertinent data about the buildings and people of that era. The most important examples of the system are the three codices that survived the coming of the conquistadors. In the codices, symbols were put carefully on pounded fig bark with brushes and various dyes developed from plants and trees. As with all fine Maya art, it was the upper class and priests who learned, developed, and became highly skilled in hieroglyphics. Science and artwork ceased suddenly with the end of the Classic period, around A.D. 900.

EARLY AGRICULTURE

Enriching the Soil

Scientists believe Maya priests studied celestial movements. A prime function performed in

serpent head from Chichén Itzá

OZ MALLAN

the elaborate temples, which were built to strict astronomical guidelines, may have been charting the changing seasons and deciding when to begin the planting cycle. Farmers used the slash-and-burn method of agriculture, and still do today. Before the rains began in the spring, Indians cut the trees on a section of land, leaving stumps about a half meter above ground. Downed trees were spread evenly across the landscape in order to burn uniformly; residual ash was left to nourish the soil. At the proper time, holes were made with a pointed stick, and precious maize kernels were dropped into the earth, one by one. At each corner (the cardinal points) of the cornfield, offerings of *pozole* (maize stew) were left to encourage the gods to give forth great rains. With abundant moisture, crops were bountiful and rich enough to provide food even into the following year.

The Maya knew the value of allowing the land to lay fallow after two seasons of growth, and each family's milpa (cornfield) was moved from place to place around the villages scattered through the jungle. Often, squash and tomatoes were planted in the shade of towering corn stalks to make double use of the land. Today, you see windmills across the countryside (many stamped "Chicago, Inc."); with the coming of electricity to the outlying areas, pumps are being used to bring water from underground rivers and lakes to irrigate crops. Outside of irrigation methods, the Maya follow the same ancient pattern of farming their ancestors did.

Maize

Corn was the heart of Maya nutrition, eaten at each meal. From it the Indians made tortillas, stew, and beverages—some of them alcoholic. Corn cultivation was such a vital part of Maya life that it is represented in drawings and carvings along with other social and religious symbols. In their combination of beans and corn, the Maya enjoyed all the protein they needed. They did not raise livestock until Spanish times.

Corn tortillas are still a main staple of the Mexican people. Native women in small towns can be seen early in the morning carrying bowls of corn kernels on their heads to the tortilla shop for grinding into tortilla dough. This was done by hand for centuries—and still is in isolated places. With the advent of electricity on the Peninsula, it's become much quicker to pay a peso or two to grind dough automatically. Others pay a few more pesos (price is controlled by the government) and buy their tortillas by the kilo hot off the griddle.

CORN: A MAYA MAINSTAY

Corn was much more than food to the ancient Maya. The crop was apparently intertwined in Maya legend with the notion of the beginning of life. It's depicted in many of the remaining ancient Maya carvings and drawings; a fresco at the ruins of Tulum, for example, shows human feet as corn.

The crop was so significant to the Maya that everything else would stop when the signs implied it was time to plant the fields. In ancient times, it was Maya priests who calculated—by means of astronomical observation—the perfect time to fire the fields before the rains. While some Maya farmers still refer to the calendar keeper of their village for the proper planting date, today most base their planting date on observation of natural phenomena, such as the swarming of flying ants or the rhythm and frequency of croaking frogs—a Maya version of a Farmer's Almanac.

Corn is not the critical staple it was before the days of stores and supermarkets, but many poor villages still rely for their survival on what the people raise in their small *milpas*, or cornfields. The *milpas* are planted in the centuries-old method. The process begins with a plea to the Chacs—the Maya rain gods. Performed at the end of each April, the ceremony arouses the Chacs from their seasonal sleep. Bowls of corn porridge are left at the four corners of a family's *milpa* for the age-old deities, who are still treated with great respect. To anger the Chacs could bring a drought and without the yearly rains the corn crop fails. With the Chacs satisfied, the farmers then cut trees and grasses and leave them in the field to dry before setting them aflame. The fire is allowed to burn until all is reduced to ash. A stick is used to poke holes in the ash-covered earth, and seeds are then dropped into the holes one by one.

THE ANTHROPOLOGICAL MUSEUM OF MEXICO

Many flights to the Yucatán Peninsula from the U.S. make a stop in Mexico City for a change of planes. If you have a chance to layover there for a day or two on your way to Mayaland, a highly informative adjunct to your trip would be a visit to the Anthropological Museum of Mexico in Chapultepec Park.

The Anthropological Museum complex was built in 1963-64 after a beautiful design by Pedro Ramírez Vásquez. In the Salon of the Maya you'll see some of the finest treasures found on the Yucatán Peninsula. The terra-cotta figures from the Island of Jaina are remarkable images of people, portraying various lifestyles. Reproductions of the colored frescoes found in Bonampak are outstanding, as are the delicate carvings from Chichén Itzá.

The museum shop stocks a great selection of catalogs, brochures, and informative books (in several languages) on many subjects including the Indian cultures of ancient Mexico. Some of the finer reproductions of Maya art are available here at reasonable prices. (Unfortunately, the store doesn't ship to the States, so you must either lug your purchases around with you on the rest of your trip or take the time to wrap and ship them yourself.)

After visiting the museum and seeing the artifacts, you will have gained a greater understanding of the people who created the mysterious structures you visit on the Yucatán Peninsula.

ENTER THE SPANIARDS

When the conquistadors arrived in 1517, the Maya of northern Yucatán were too divided to put up a successful long-term resistance. Nevertheless, they fought fiercely, and Francisco de Montejo was not able to establish his capital, Mérida, until 1542. Sporadic revolts by Yucatecan Maya have continued over the centuries, with the last ending only in the early 1900s. In the late 19th century, the Chiapan Maya fought several pitched battles with the Mexican army. The Guatemalan Maya city-states were conquered by the brutal Pedro de Alvarado, ending almost all resistance by 1541. However, one tribe managed to evade the conquistadors and settled deep in the jungle on an island in the middle of Lake Petén. Their traditional Maya city-state, called Tayasol, thrived until 1697, when a Spanish army finally penetrated that remote zone.

KATHY ESCOVEDO SANDERS

ON THE ROAD
RECREATION AND ENTERTAINMENT

BULLFIGHTING

The bullfight is not for everyone. Many foreigners feel it's inhumane treatment of a helpless animal. The bullfight is a bloodsport; if you can't tolerate this sort of thing, you'd probably be happier not attending. Bullfighting is big business in Mexico, Spain, Portugal, and South America. The *corrida de toros* (running of the bulls) is made up of a troupe of (now) well-paid men all playing an important part in the drama. On Sundays and holidays, 50,000 people fill the country's largest arena in Mexico City for each performance. The afternoon starts off promptly at 4 p.m. with music and a colorful parade of solemn pomp with matadors, picadors on horseback, and banderilleros, plus drag mules and many ring attendants. The matadors ceremoniously circle the crowded arena to the roar of the crowd. The afternoon has begun!

Traditional customs of the ring have not changed in centuries. The matador is the star of the event. This ceremony is a test of a man and his courage. He's in the arena for one purpose, to kill the bull—but bravely and with artful moves. First the preliminary *quites* and then a series of graceful veronicas heighten the excitement, brushing the treacherous horns with each move. The matador wills the animal to come closer with each movement of the muleta. An outstanding bullfighter performs his ballet as close to the bull's horns as possible, to the crowd's wild cheers. He must elude the huge beast with only a subtle turn of his body. To add to the excitement, he does much of this on his knees. At the hour of truth, the judge gives the matador permission to dedicate the bull to a special person in the crowd. He throws his *montera* (hat) to the honored person and prepares for his final, deadly maneuvers.

At just the right moment, he slips the *estoque* (sword) into the bull's neck. A perfect blow will sever the aorta, killing the huge animal instantly. If the matador displays extraordinary grace, skill, and bravery, the judge awards him the ears and the tail, and the crowd their uncontrollable respect.

Bullfighting has long been one of the most popular events in Mexico. Aficionados of this Spanish artform thrill to the excitement of the crowd, the stirring music, the grace and courage of a noble matador, and the bravery of a good bull. A student of Mexican culture will want to take part in the corrida, to learn more about this powerful art.

Art is the key word. A bullfight is not a fight, it is an artistic scene of pageantry and ceremony, handed down from the Middle Ages, that was once celebrated all over Europe.

Records of the first primitive bullfight come to us from the island of Crete, 2,000 years before the time of Christ. At the same time in Spain, savage wild bulls roamed the Iberian Peninsula. When faced with killing one of these vicious animals, young men, not to be outdone by the Cretans, would "dance" as close as possible to the brute to show their bravery before finally killing the animal with an ax.

The Romans began importing Spanish wild bulls for Colosseum spectacles and the Arabs in Spain encouraged *tauromaquia* (bullfighting). In 1090, El Cid (Rodrigo Díaz de Vivar), the hero of Valencia and subject of romantic legend, is believed to have fought in the first organized bull festival. He lanced and killed a wild bull from the back of his horse. In that era, only noblemen were allowed to use a lance, and the corrida soon became the sport of kings. Even Julius Caesar is said to have gotten in the ring with a wild bull. Bullfighting quickly became popular and stood out as the daring event for the rich. In Spain, bullfights were held in that country's ancient Roman colosseums. A feast day celebration wasn't complete without a *corrida de toros*. Predictably, the number of noblemen killed while participating in this wild event began to grow and the bullfight soon became the subject of controversy.

In the 16th century, Pope Pius V issued a papal ban threatening to excommunicate anyone killed while bullfighting. This didn't dull the enthusiasm of the Spanish; the pope withdrew the ban, and the fights continued. Queen Isabella and then King Philip ordered the bullfights halted, and the fights ceased.

Since the lance was forbidden, commoners intrigued with the event began fighting bulls on foot, using a cape to hide the sword *(estoque)* and confuse the bull. This was the beginning of the corrida as we know it today.

The corrida has changed little in the past 200 years. The beautiful clothes originally designed by the famous artist Goya are still used. Richly embroidered silk capes draped over the arena railing add a festive touch. Even in the smallest Yucatán village corrida, the costume design persists. Though made of simple cotton, rather than rich satin and gold-trimmed silk, delicately embroidered with typical designs of the Yucatán, the torero's garb is striking.

Gone are the wild bulls; the animals, all of Spanish ancestry, are bred on large Mexican ranches just for the bullring. Only the finest, those showing superior strength, cunning, and bravery, are sent to the ring. *El toro* is trained for one shining day in the arena.

The season begins in December and lasts three months. The rest of the year the *novilleros* (neophyte matadors) are seen in plazas across the country. They must prove themselves in the arena before they are acknowledged as respected and highly paid matadors. Bullfighting is as dangerous now as when the pope tried to have it banned in the 16th century. Almost half of the most renowned matadors in the past 250 years have died in the ring.

Bullfights usually take place on Sunday afternoons; the best seats on the shady side of the arena *(la sombra)* cost more. Ask at your hotel or local travel agency for ticket information. But remember, the corrida is not for everyone.

SNORKELING AND SCUBA DIVING

Not everyone who travels to the Yucatán Peninsula is a diver or even a snorkeler—at first! One peek through the "looking glass"—a diving mask—changes that. The Caribbean is one of the most notoriously seductive bodies of water in the world. Turquoise blue and crystal clear with perfect tepid temperature, Yucatán coastal waters, protected by offshore reefs, are ideal for a languid float during hot, humid days.

Snorkeling
You'll find that the sea is where you'll want to spend a good part of your trip. So even if you

snorkeling in Xelha Lagoon

these amazing little animals create exotic displays of shape and form, dense or delicate depending on species, depth, light, and current. Most need light to survive; in deeper, low-light areas, some species of coral take the form of a large plate, thereby performing the duties of a solar collector. The sponge is another curious underwater creature and it comes in all sizes, shapes, and colors, from common brown to vivid red.

Choosing a Dive Company

Diving lessons are offered at nearly all the dive shops on the Peninsula. Before you make a commitment, ask about the instructor and check his accident record, then talk to the harbormaster, or if you're in a small village, ask at the local cantina. Most of these divers (many are American) are conscientious, but a few are not, and the locals know whom to trust.

Bringing your own equipment to Mexico might save you a little money, depending on the length of your trip and means of transportation. But if you plan on staying just a couple of weeks and want to join a group on board a dive boat by the day, it's generally not much more to rent a tank, which will save you the hassle of carrying your own.

Choose your boat carefully. Look it over first. Some aren't much more than fishing boats, with little to make the diver comfortable. Ask questions; most of the divemasters speak English. Does it have a platform for getting in and out of the water? How many tanks of air may be used per trip? How many dives? Exactly where are you going? How fast does the boat go and how long will it take to get there? Remember, some of the best dive spots might be farther out at sea. A more modern boat, while more expensive, might get you extra diving time.

Detailed information is available for divers and snorkelers who wish to know about the dive sites you plan to visit. Once you're on the Yucatán Peninsula, you'll find pamphlets and books available in dive shops on reefs, depths, and especially currents. Wherever diving is good, you'll almost always find a dive shop. There are a few high-adventure dives where diving with an experienced guide is recommended (see "Scuba Diving" in the "Isla de Cozumel" section).

never considered underwater sports in the past, you'll probably be eager to learn. First-timers should have little trouble learning to snorkel. Once you master breathing through a tube, it's simply a matter of relaxing and floating. Time disappears once you are introduced, through a four-inch diameter glass window, to a world of fish in rainbow colors of garish yellow, electric blue, crimson, and a hundred shades of purple. The longer you look, the more you'll discover: underwater caverns, tall pillars of coral, giant tubular sponges, shy fish hiding on the sandy bottom, and delicate wisps of fine grass.

Scuba Diving

For the diver, there's even more adventure. Reefs, caves, and rugged coastline harbor the unknown. Ships wrecked hundreds of years ago hide secrets as yet undiscovered. Swimming among the curious and brazen fish puts you into another world. This is raw excitement!

Expect to see an astounding variety of fish, crustaceans, and corals. Even close to shore,

Underwater Hazards and First Aid

A word here about some of the less inviting members of marine society. Anemones and sea urchins are everywhere. Some can be dangerous if touched or stepped on. The long-spined, black sea urchin can inflict great pain and its poison can cause an uncomfortable infection. Don't think that you're safe in a wetsuit and booties or even if wearing gloves. The spines easily slip through the rubber. In certain areas, such as around the island of Cozumel, the urchin is encountered at all depths and is very abundant close to shore where you'll probably be wading in and out; keep your eyes open. If diving at night, use your flashlight. If you should run into one of the spines, remove it quickly and carefully, disinfect the wound, and apply antibiotic cream. If you have difficulty removing the spine, or if it breaks, see a doctor—pronto!

Cuts from coral, even if just a scratch, will often cause an infection. Antibiotic cream or powder will usually take care of it. If you get a deep cut, or if minute bits of coral are left in the wound, a serious and long-lasting infection can ensue. See a doctor.

EMERGENCY ASSISTANCE FOR DIVERS

Check with your divemaster about emergency procedures before your boat goes out to sea. Also check with your medical insurance company; generally they will pay for emergency recompression and air-evacuation services.

Cozumel Recompression Chamber:
(987) 2-2387

Divers Alert Network (DAN):
(919) 684-8111 or 684-4326 (24 hours); non-emergency, (919) 684-2949; members call (800) 446-2671

Aeromedical Group:
tel. (619) 278-3822

Life Flight:
tel. (800) 392-4357 from Mexico; (713) 704-3590 in Houston, TX; (800) 231-4357 elsewhere in the U.S.

Wise divers watch out for the color red, as many submarine hazards bear that hue. If you scrape against red coral, or "fire coral," you'll feel a burning sensation that lasts anywhere from a few minutes to five days. On some, it causes an allergic reaction and will raise large red welts. Cortisone cream will reduce inflammation and discomfort.

Fire worms (also known as bristle worms), if touched, will deposit tiny, cactuslike bristles in the skin. They can cause the same reaction as fire coral. *Carefully* scraping the skin with the edge of a sharp knife (as you would to remove a bee stinger) might remove the bristles. Any leftover bristles will ultimately work their way out, but you can be very uncomfortable in the meantime. Cortisone cream helps relieve this inflammation, too.

Several species of sponges have fine, sharp spicules (hard, minute, pointed calcareous or siliceous bodies that support the tissue) that you should not touch with a bare hand. The attractive red fire sponge can cause great pain; a mild solution of vinegar or ammonia (or urine if there's nothing else) will help. The burning lasts a couple of days, and cortisone cream soothes. But don't be fooled by dull-colored sponges. Many have the same sharp spicules, and touching them with a bare hand is risky at best.

Some divers feel the need to touch the fish they swim with. A few beginners want an underwater picture taken of them feeding the fish— bad news! When you offer fish a tasty morsel from your hand, you could start an underwater riot. Fish are always hungry and always ready for a free meal. Some of those denizens of the deep may not be so big, but in the frenzy to be first in line, their very efficient teeth have been known to miss the target. Another way to save your hands from unexpected danger is to keep them out of cracks and crevices, where moray eels live. A moray will usually leave you alone if you do likewise, but their many needle-sharp teeth can cause a painful wound that's apt to get infected.

A few seagoing critters resent being stepped on, and they can retaliate with a dangerous wound. The scorpion fish, hardly recognizable with its natural camouflage, lies hidden most of the time on a reef shelf or the bottom of the sea. If you should step on or touch it you can expect a painful, dangerous sting. If this happens, see a doctor immediately.

Another sinister fellow is the ray. There are several varieties in the Caribbean, including the yellow and southern stingrays. If you leave them alone they're generally peaceful, but if you step on them they will zap you with a tail that carries a poisonous sting, which can cause anaphylactic shock. Symptoms include respiratory difficulties, fainting, and severe itching. Go quickly to the doctor and tell him what caused the sting. Jellyfish can inflict a miserable sting. Avoid particularly the long streamers of the Portuguese man-of-war, though some of the smaller jellyfish are just as hazardous.

Whatever you do, don't let these what-ifs discourage you from an underwater adventure. Thousands of people dive in the Caribbean every day of the year and only a small number of accidents occur.

Note: Please don't touch the coral; doing so is a death sentence to the polyps!

OTHER OUTDOOR ACTIVITIES

Water-skiing, Parasailing, Windsurfing
With so many fine beaches, bays, and coves along the Caribbean, all water sports are available. Because so many beaches are protected by the reef that runs parallel to Quintanta Roo's east coast, calm **swimming beaches** are easy to find. Also, many hotels have pools. Water-skiing is good on Nichupté Bay in Cancún, and parasailing is popular there also. Windsurfing lessons and rental boards are available at most resort areas: Cozumel, Cancún, Akumal, and Playa del Carmen.

Fishing
A fishing license is required for all anglers 16 years or older. Good for three days, one month, or a year, licenses are available for a small fee at most fresh- and saltwater fishing areas. Ask in the small cafes at the more isolated beaches. Check with the closest Mexican consulate about where you can get a permit for your sportfishing craft; you can also get current information there on fishing seasons and regulations which vary from area to area. Fishing gear may be brought into Mexico without customs tax; however, the customs officials at the border crossing from Brownsville, Texas, into Mexico are notorious

for expecting to have their palms greased before allowing the RVer or boater to cross the border. If you find yourself in this position, start with dollar bills (bring lots of them with you); several people need to be soothed before you can cross. If you choose not to pay the bribe, they can keep you hanging around for hours, even days, before they will allow you to cross. Sadly, it's a no-win situation. For more fishing information write to: General de Pesca, Av. Alvaro Obregón 269, Mexico 7, D.F.

Spearfishing is allowed in some areas along the Yucatán coast, but not on the reef. The spear must be totally unmechanical and used free-hand or with a rubber band only (no spear guns). If you plan on spearfishing, a Mexican fishing license is required. You can obtain one from sportfishing operations and bait and tackle shops in Cancún and Cozumel. If you're visiting a remote fishing lodge, ask if they supply licenses. For further information write to Oficina de Pesca, 2550 Fifth Ave., Suite 101, San Diego, CA 92103-6622; tel. (619) 233-6956.

Birdwatching and Flora Fancying
Birdwatching is wonderful throughout the Yucatán. From north to south the variety of birds is broad and changes with the geography and the weather. Bring binoculars and wear boots and lightweight trousers if you plan on watching in jungle areas.

Studying tropical flora is also a popular activity. For this you most certainly will be in the backcountry—don't forget bug repellent, and be prepared for an occasional rain shower, even in the dry season. For most orchids and bromeliads, look up in the trees, but remember, the Yucatán also has ground orchids. And please, don't take anything away with you except pictures.

Photography
There's a world of beauty to photograph here, what with the sea, the people, and the natural landscape of the Peninsula. If you plan on **video-taping,** check with your local Mexican tourist office for information on what you can bring into the country. Most archaeological zones prohibit tripods. For the photographer who wants to film *everything,* small planes are available for charter in the larger cities and resorts. In Cancún, for instance, you can take pictures from a plane that

tours for about 15 minutes over Cancún and the surrounding coast. Per-person price is US$30-40. (For further information see "Photography" under "Services and Information," below.)

Golf and Tennis

Tourist-oriented Quintana Roo is the best bet for golf and tennis aficionados. Golf courses are few, but you can plan on playing in Cancún, Playacar, and Puerto Aventuras. Tennis courts are scattered about Quintana Roo; the large hotels at Cancún, Akumal, Cozumel, and Puerto Aventuras have them. Bring your own racket.

FIESTAS

Mexico knows how to give a party! Everyone who visits the Yucatán should take advantage of any holidays falling during the visit. Workers are given a day off on legal holidays. See the special topic "Holidays and Fiestas" for dates of the biggest fiestas.

As well as the public festivities listed, a birthday, baptism, saint's day, wedding, departure, return, good crop, and many more reasons than we'd ever think of are good excuses to celebrate with a fiesta. One of the simplest but most charming celebrations is Mother's Day in Playa del Carmen, Mérida, and many other colonial cities. Children both young and old serenade mothers (often with a live band) with beautiful music outside their windows on the evening of the holiday. If invited to a fiesta, join in and have fun.

Village Festivities

Half the fun of any fiesta is watching preparations, which generally take all day and involve everyone. Fireworks displays are set up by *especialistas* who wrap and tie bamboo poles together with packets of paper-wrapped explosives. At some point this often-tall *castillo* (structure holding the fireworks) will be tilted up and set off with a spray of light and sound followed by appreciative cheers of delight.

Village fiestas are a wonderful time of dancing, music, noise, colorful costumes, good food, and usually lots of drinking. A public fiesta is generally held in the central plaza surrounded by temporary stalls where you can get Mexican fast food: tamales (both sweet and meat), *buñuelos* (sweet

---

PAPELES PICADOS

Anyone who has traveled in Mexico knows the locals love to throw a party. It can be religious, or for a birthday, wedding, feast day, or other holiday. The Mexicans entertain all the senses! Fiesas feature great music, tasty food, and brightly colored decorations, often including *papeles picados*—row upon row of rectangles of paper hung from above, dancing to the slightest breeze.

Literally translated as "pricked papers," the *papeles picados* are pricked or stamped with a certain design that is apropos to the occasion. You'll see them strung across the streets above the traffic, or hung on wires in front of a church or inside the home, looking like lace paper doilies or table placemats.

If there is a drawback to this tradition, it's that the pieces of paper are left blowing in the wind until the next holiday. Soon all that's left are torn bits of colored paper and the memories of the fine fiesta they commemorated.

---

rolls), tacos, *refrescos* (soft drinks), *churros* (fried dough dusted with sugar), *carne asada* (barbecued meat), and plenty of beer chilling in any convenient ice-filled container.

Beware "The Egg"

You'll find innocent-looking little old ladies selling eggshells filled with confetti, ready to be smashed on an unsuspecting head. So be prepared if you're the only gringo around! The more you respond good-naturedly, the more you will continue to be the target—and what the heck, whether the headache is from too much beer or too many eggs doesn't matter. (Besides, it might be time for you to plunk out a few pesos for your own bombs!)

A Marriage of Cultures

Many festivals in Mexico honor religious feast days. You'll see a unique combination of religious fervor and ancient beliefs mixed with plain old good times. In the church plaza, dances passed down from family to family since before Cortés introduced Christianity to the New World continue for hours. Dancers dress in symbolic costumes of bright colors, feathers, and bells,

HOLIDAYS AND FIESTAS

Jan. 1: **New Year's Day.** Legal holiday.

Jan. 6: **Día de los Reyes Magos.** Day of the Three Kings. On this day Christmas gifts are exchanged.

Feb. 2: **Candelaria.** Candlemas. Many villages celebrate with candlelight processions.

Feb. 5: **Flag Day.** Legal holiday.

Feb./March: **Carnaval.** The week before Ash Wednesday, the beginning of Lent. Some of the best planned festivals of the year are held this week. In Mérida, Isla Mujeres, Cozumel, Campeche: Easter parades with colorful floats, costume balls, and sporting events. Chetumal: a parade with floats, music, and folk dances from all over Mesoamerica.

March 21: **Birthday of Benito Juárez** (1806). Legal holiday.

Vernal Equinox. Chichén Itzá: A phenomenon of light and shadow displays the pattern of a serpent slithering down the steps of the Pyramid of Kukulcán.

May 1: **Labor Day.** Legal holiday.

May 3: **Day of the Holy Cross.** Dance of the Pig's Head performed during fiestas at Celestún, Felipe Carrillo Puerto, and Hopelchén.

May 5: **Battle of Puebla,** also known as **Cinco de Mayo.** In remembrance of the 1862 defeat of the French. Legal holiday.

May 12-18: **Chankah Veracruz** (near Felipe Carrillo Puerto). Honors the Virgin of the Immaculate Conception. Maya music, bullfights, and religious procession.

May 15: **San Isidro Labrador.** Festivals held at Panaba (near Valladolid) and Calkini (southwest of Mérida).

May 20-30: **Becal.** Jipi Fiesta in honor of the plant *jipijapa,* used in making Panama hats, the big moneymaker for most of the population.

June 29: **Day Of San Pedro.** All towns with the name of San Pedro. Fiestas held in Sanah-cat and Cacalchen (near Mérida), Tekom, and Panaba (near Valladolid).

Early July: **Ticul** (near Uxmal). Weeklong fiesta celebrating the establishment of Ticul. Music, athletic events, dancing, and fireworks.

Sept. 15: **Independence Day.** Legal holiday.

Sept. 27-Oct. 14: **El Señor de las Ampollas** in Mérida. Religious holiday. Big fiesta with fireworks, religious services, music, and dancing.

Oct. 4: **Feast Day of San Francisco de Asisi.** Usually a weeklong fiesta precedes this day in Uman, Hocaba, Conkal, and Telchac Pueblo (each near Mérida).

Oct. 12: **Columbus Day.** Legal holiday.

Oct. 18-28: **Izamal.** Fiesta honoring El Cristo de Sitilpech. A procession carries an image of Christ from Sitilpech to the church in Izamal. Religious services, fireworks, music, and dancing. Biggest celebration on the 25th.

Oct. 31: **Eve of All Souls' Day.** Celebrated all through the Yucatán. Flowers and candles placed on graves, the beginning of an eight-day observance.

Nov. 1-2: **All Souls' Day and Day of the Dead.** Graveside and church ceremonies. A partylike atmosphere in all the cemeteries. Food and drink vendors do a lively business, as well as candy makers with their sugar skulls and skeletons. A symbolic family meal is eaten at the gravesite.

Nov. 8: **Conclusion of El Día de Muerte.** Day of the Dead.

Nov. 20: **Día de la Revolución.** Revolution Day of 1910. Legal holiday.

Dec. 8: **Feast of the Immaculate Conception.** Fiestas at Izamal, Celestún (including a boat procession), and Champotón (boat procession carrying a statue of Mary, water-skiing show, other aquatic events, dancing, fair).

Dec. 12: **Our Lady of Guadalupe.**

Dec. 25: **Christmas.** Legal holiday.

reminding local onlookers about their Maya past. Inside the church is a constant stream of the candle-carrying devout, some traveling long distances on their knees to the church, repaying a promise made to a deity months before in thanks for a personal favor, a healing, or a job found.

Some villages offer a corrida (bullfight) as part of the festivities. Even a small town will have a simple bullring; in the Yucatán these rings are frequently built of bamboo. In Maya fashion, no nails are used—only henequen twine to hold together a two-tiered bullring! The country corrida has a special charm. If celebrating a religious holiday, a procession carrying the image of the honored deity might lead off the proceedings. The bull has it good here; there are no bloodletting ceremonies and the animal is allowed to live. Only a tight rope around its middle provokes sufficient anger for the fight. Local young men perform in the arena with as much heart and grace as professionals in Mexico City. And though the clothes are not satin and velvet, they are simple cotton heavily embroidered with beautiful flowers and designs. The crowd shows its admiration with shouts, cheers, and of course *música!*—even if the band is composed only of a drum and a trumpet. In the end, someone unties the bull—*very carefully!* Good fun for everyone, even those who don't understand the art of the corrida.

Religious Feast Days

Christmas and Easter are wonderful holidays. The *posada* (procession) of Christmas begins nine days before the holiday, when families and friends take part in processions that portray Mary and Joseph and their search for lodging before the birth of Christ. The streets are alive with people, bright lights, and colorful nativity scenes. Families provide swinging piñatas (pottery covered with papier-mâché in the shape of a popular animal or perky character and filled with candy and small surprises); children and adults alike enjoy watching the blindfolded small fry swing away with a heavy board or baseball bat while an adult moves and sways the piñata with a rope, making the fun last, giving everyone a chance. Eventually, someone gets lucky and smashes the piñata with a hard blow (it takes strength to break it), and kids skitter around the floor retrieving the loot. Piñatas are common, not only for Christmas and Easter but also for birthdays and other special occasions in the Mexican home.

The Fiesta and Visitors—Practicalities

A few practical things to remember about fiesta times. Cities will probably be crowded. If you know in advance that you'll be in town, make hotel and car reservations as soon as possible. Easter and Christmas at any of the beach hotels will be crowded, and you may need to make reservations as far as six months in advance. Some of the best fiestas are in more isolated parts of the Yucatán and neighboring states. Respect the privacy of people; the Indians have definite feelings and religious beliefs about having their pictures taken, so ask first and abide by their wishes.

ACCOMMODATIONS AND FOOD

The Yucatán Peninsula offers a wide variety of accommodations. There's a myriad of hotels to choose from in cities, villages, beach resorts, and offshore islands, in all price ranges. If you like the idea of light housekeeping and preparing your own food, condos are available in many locales. If your lifestyle is suited to outdoor living, beach camping is wonderful along the Caribbean, and the number of small bungalows for tourists is growing rapidly.

CAMPING

If you are traveling in your own vehicle, you must obtain a vehicle permit when entering the country. Camping with a vehicle allows you to become a "luxury camper," bringing all the equip-

Some beach huts offer little more than sapling walls, thatch roof, and hammock hooks; this one goes further with hanging beds and mosquito netting.

ment you'll need (and more!). A van or small camper truck will fit on almost any road you'll run into. With an RV you can "street camp" in the city. Parking lots of large hotels (check with the manager) or side streets near downtown activities are generally safe and offer easy access to entertainment.

Vehicle Supplies

A few reminders and some common-sense planning make a difference when traveling and camping with a vehicle. Near the Caribbean coast are many swampy areas, so check for marshy ground before pulling off the road. When beach camping, park above the high-tide line. Remember that gas stations are not as frequently found on the Peninsula as in most parts of Mexico. If you plan on traveling for any length of time, especially in out-of-the-way places, carry extra gas, and fill up whenever the opportunity arises. Along with your food supply, always carry enough water for both the car and passengers. Be practical and come prepared with a few necessities (see our checklist).

Sleeping Outdoors

Sleeping under a jeweled sky in a warm clime can be either a wonderful or an excruciating experience. (Two factors that will make or break it are the heat and the mosquito population in the immediate vicinity.) Some campers sleep in tents to get away from biting critters, which helps but is no guarantee; also, heat hangs heavily inside a closed tent. Sleeping bags cushion the ground but tend to be much too warm. If you have a bag that zips across the bottom, it's cooling to let your feet hang out (well marinated in bug repellent or wearing a pair of socks—a dark color the mosquitoes might not notice). An air mattress or foam pad softens the ground (bring along a patch kit). Mexican campers often just roll up in a lightweight blanket, covering all skin, head to toe, to defy possible bug attacks.

For a very small fee, many rural resorts provide *palapa* hammock-huts that usually include water (for washing only); these places are great if you want to meet other backpackers. Though they are fast giving way to bungalow construction, a few hammock-huts are still found along the Caribbean coast and in Palenque, Chiapas.

HOTELS

Price Categories
Accommodations prices in this book are listed by price category. Although prices change frequently, the categories will give you a good idea of what to expect.

The price categories used in this book are as follows:

Shoestring: Under US$15
Budget: US$15-35
Inexpensive: US$35-55
Moderate: US$55-80
Expensive: US$80-120
Premium: US$120 and over

The ranges are based on high season (Dec. 15-April 15) rates, and don't include the 12% room tax. We *cannot* guarantee the prices of hotels; changes are too frequent. Use our range as a guide.

Reservations
Traveling during the peak season (15 Dec.-15 April) requires a little planning if you wish to stay at the popular hotels. (The smartest budget traveler will visit Cozumel during any season but high season.) Make reservations in advance. Many hotels can be contacted through an 800 number, travel agency, or auto club. A few of the well-known American chains are represented in the larger resorts (Cancún, Playa del Carmen, Mérida, Villahermosa), and their international desks can make reservations for you. Many now have fax numbers, much quicker than regular mail. If you're traveling May-June or Sept.-Oct., rooms are generally available.

Budget
Travelers looking to spend nights cheaply can find a *few* overnight accommodations in Cancún (the downtown area); more in Cozumel, Isla Mujeres, Playa del Carmen, Mérida, Villahermosa, Campeche, Tuxtla Gutiérrez, San Cristóbal de las Casas, and along the Caribbean and Gulf of Mexico coasts. During the

peak season in Cancún it takes a little (sometimes a lot of) nosing around (starting out early in the day helps).

For the adventurer in small rural villages, ask at the local cantina, cafe, or city hall for hotel or boardinghouse-type accommodation. These hotels are *usually* clean, and more than likely you'll share a toilet and (maybe) a shower. Sometimes you'll share the room itself, a large area with enough hammock hooks scattered around the walls to handle several travelers. The informed budget traveler carries his or her hammock (buy it on the Yucatán Peninsula if you don't already have one—they're the best made) when wandering around the Caribbean. When staying in the cheaper hotels in out-of-the-way places, come prepared with toilet paper, towel, soap, and bug repellent, and expect to buy bottled drinking water. Most of the villages have a small cantina that serves a *comida corrida* (set lunch), or ask your host; credit cards are *not* the norm. However, the price will be right and the family that runs it will offer a cultural experience you won't forget.

Youth hostels, though few and far between, are good bargains on the Peninsula, especially in Cancún.

Moderate

In most cities on the Peninsula it's not difficult to find moderate hotels; even in downtown Cancún and a few scattered locations within the hotel zone, moderate hotels are available. They aren't nearly as glitzy, probably don't have telephones or multiple restaurants and bars, maybe not even a swimming pool, and they are not on the beach. However, the better ones provide transportation or are close to a bus stop. Prices can be one-third the cost of those in the hotel zone.

Luxury

Some of the familiar hotel names found on the Peninsula are the Presidente, Camino Real, Hyatt, and Sheraton. They offer endless luxuries, including lovely bathrooms—some with hair dryers, marble fixtures, separate showers, and thick, fluffy towels—in-room safes, cable television, mini-bars, a/c, good beds, suites, junior suites, balconies, terraces, gorgeous ocean views, green garden areas, pools (one is a kilometer long) with swim-up bars, nightclubs and fabulous restaurants, entertainment, travel agents, car rentals, gift shops, and delicatessens; almost all accept credit cards. Refunds are handled on an individual basis.

Condominiums

Cancún has hundreds of condos lining the beach and many under construction. Isla Mujeres, Cozumel, Playa del Carmen, and Akumal have a few condominiums, and others are sprouting up along the southern coastal beaches as well. If you're vacationing with family or a group, condo living can be a real money-saver while still providing the fine services of a luxury hotel. Fully equipped kitchens make cooking a snap. In many cases the price includes daily maid service. Some condos (like the Condumel on Isla Cozumel) welcome you with a refrigerator stocked with food basics; you pay only for the foods and beverages that you use each day. Details are given in the appropriate travel sections.

Time Shares

Time-share mania is putting down roots. One of the biggest complaints from travelers to Cancún, Puerto Aventuras, and Cozumel in the last couple of years concerns the salespeople who pester visitors to buy condos and time-share accommodations. Their come-on is an offer for a free breakfast and often a free day's rental of a motorbike, or some other freebies. After the breakfast or lunch, they give a sales presentation, a tour of the facilities, and then each guest gets a hard pitch from a very experienced salesperson. These people have learned American sales methods down to the nitty-gritty. If you succumb to the offer of free breakfast and aren't interested in buying, better practice saying *"No."*

FOOD

Taste as many different dishes as possible! You'll be introduced to spices that add a new dimension to your diet. Naturally, you won't be wild about everything—it takes a while to become

OZ MALLAN

accustomed to squid served in its own black ink, for instance! A hamburger might not taste like one from your favorite fast-food place back home. It should also not come as a shock to find that your favorite downhome Tex-Mex enchiladas and tacos are nothing like those you order in Mexican restaurants.

Seafood

You won't travel far before realizing that one of Yucatán's specialties is fresh fish. All along the Caribbean and Gulf coasts are opportunities to indulge in piscine delicacies: lobster, shrimp, red snapper, seabass, halibut, barracuda, and lots more. Even the tiniest cafe will prepare sweet fresh fish à la Veracruz, using ripe tomatoes, green peppers, and onions. Or if you prefer, ask for the fish *con ajo,* sautéed in garlic and butter—scrumptious! Most menus offer an opportunity to order *al gusto* (cooked to your pleasure).

Try the unusual conch *(kahnk),* which has been a staple in the diet of the Maya along the Caribbean coast for centuries. It's often used in ceviche. Some consider this dish raw; actually, the conch or fish is marinated in a lime dressing with onions, peppers, and a host of spices—very tasty! Often conch is pounded, dipped in egg and cracker crumbs, and sautéed quickly (like abalone steak in California), with a squirt of fresh lime. (If it's cooked too long it becomes tough and rubbery.)

If you happen to be on a boat trip during which the crew prepares a meal of fresh fish on the beach, more than likely you'll be served *tik n' chik* cooked over an open fire. The whole fish (catch of the day) is placed on a wire rack and seasoned with onions, peppers, and *achiote,* a fragrant red spice grown on the Peninsula since the time of the early Maya. Bishop Diego de Landa identified *achiote* in his *Relaciones,* written in the 1500s.

Wild Game

The Yucatecans are hunters, and if you explore the countryside very much, you'll commonly see men and boys on bicycles, motorscooters, or horses with rifles slung over their shoulders and full game bags tied behind them. Game found in the jungle varies. *Pato* (wild duck) is served during certain times of the year and is prepared in several ways that must be tried.

TORTILLAS

The staple of the Mexican diet, tortillas are still made by hand in many homes, but a large percentage of people now buy them ready-made for a reasonable price, saving hours of work on the *metate* (grinder) and the *tomal* (griddle). In any public market, the tortilla shop is always the busiest place. Folks line up to purchase two, four, or six kilograms of tortillas every day. One traveler tells of spending 20 minutes in fascinated concentration observing the whole operation: 50-pound plastic sacks of shucked corn kernels stacked in a corner of the stall, the machinery that grinds it, the pale yellow dough, the unsophisticated conveyor belt that carries the dough across the live-flame cooking surface, the patrons who patiently line up for the fresh results, and the baker who hands the traveler several tortillas hot off the fire along with a friendly smile that says thanks for being interested.

tortilla-makers at work

MEXICAN WINE

It would seem the most natural thing in the world for Mexico to produce good wines, considering the Spanish conquistadors came from a land with a long history of growing rich flavorful grapes and were experts in the field of fermentation. Pre-Hispanics didn't have wine as the Spanish knew it, but did make fermented beverages from such things as corn. It was not long before vine cuttings were brought to the New World and colonists were tending vineyards. By 1524 wine was so successful that Mexican wines were soon competing with Spanish wines. Pressure from vintners at home forced King Felipe II to outlaw its production in Mexico. However, over the years church use continued and no doubt many gallons of the forbidden drink found their way to private cellars. But for all practical purposes and development, the industry was stopped before it had the opportunity to make itself known around the world.

Not until 1939 under Pres. Lázaro Cárdenas did Mexican winemaking begin to make a name for itself. Experts from around the world are beginning to recognize the industry in general and several of the wines are considered world-class. Over 125,000 acres of vineyards are under cultivation in the states of Baja California Norte, Aguascalientes, Querétaro, and Zacatecas; the vineyards of Baja produce almost 80% of the country's wines. Some of the well-known wineries from this area are **Domecq, L.A. Cetto,** and **Santo Tomas.**

The wineries **Cavas de San Juan** and **Casa Martell,** are found in Querétaro, some 2,000 miles south of Baja. This was due to the suggestion of a University of California professor of enology who came to the conclusion that the area's 6,100-foot elevation compensated for its location outside the celebrated "wine belt." Zacatecas is the location of the relatively new and promising **Unión Vinícola Zacateca,** while **La Esplendida** and **Valle Redondo** are from Aguascalientes.

According to Walter Stender of ACA Imports, some Mexican wines are now being imported to the United States. Note: Mexican wines don't age well and you need not be impressed by dates. In other words, the whites are ready for the table when released to market; the reds need age no more than 18 months.

If you want champagne, remember to ask for *vino espumoso* or "bubbly wine." A label that reads *methode champenoise* means that the French system for producing sparkling wine was used. Mexico signed an agreement with the French government not to label its domesticly produced sparkling wines "champagne."

Of course there are many imported wines from all over the world available in the fine restaurants of Cancún—many from California—but while in Mexico be adventurous and try the Mexican wine. A personal favorite is L.A. Cetto's white.

Restaurants

Most small cafes that cater to Mexican families are open all day and late into the night. The Mexican custom is to eat the heavier meal of the day 1-4 pm. In most of these family cafes a generous *comida corrida* (set lunch) is served at this time. If you're hungry and want an economical (but filling) meal, that's what to ask for; though you don't know exactly what's coming, you get a tableful of delights. Always expect a large stack of tortillas and five or six small bowls filled with the familiar and the unfamiliar: it could be black beans, a cold plate of tomatoes and the delicious Yucatán avocado, or *pollo pibil* (chicken in banana leaves). Cafes in the larger hotels that cater to tourists don't serve this set meal. Late in the evening, a light supper is served 9-11 p.m. Hotels with foreign tourists offer dinner earlier to cater to British, Canadian, and American tastes. Some restaurants add a service charge onto the bill. If so, the check will say *incluido propina*. It's still gracious to leave a few coins for the waiter. If the tip isn't added to the bill, leaving 10-15% is customary. Remember, in Mexico it's considered an insult if a waiter submits a bill before it's requested; when you're ready to pay, say, *"La cuenta, por favor"* ("The bill, please").

Strolling musicians are common in Mexican cafes. If you enjoy the music, 10 pesos is a considerate gift. In certain cities, cafes that cater to Mexicans will commonly serve free snacks in the afternoon with a beer or cocktail. The Café Prosperidad (Calle 56 #456A) in downtown Mérida is very generous with its *antojitos* (snacks). The place is always packed with locals ordering the *comida corrida,* complete with live entertainment and waitresses wearing a long version of the *huipil.* Here you'll get the real essence of the city, and you may be the only gringo present. Remember, we didn't say the cafe is spotless!

Yucatán has its own version of junk food. You'll find hole-in-the-wall stands selling *tortas* (sandwiches), tacos, tamales, or *licuados* (fruit drinks), as well as corner vendors selling mangos on a stick, slices of pineapple, peeled oranges, candies of all kinds (including tall pink fluffs of cotton candy), and barbecued meat. The public markets have foods of every description, usually very cheap. In other words, there's a huge variety to choose from, so have fun.

A ploy used by many seasoned adventurers when they're tired of eating cold food from their backpacks: In a village where there isn't a cafe of any kind, go to the local cantina (or grocery store, church, or city hall) and ask if there's a woman in town who (for a fee) would be willing to include you at her dinner table. Almost always you'll find someone, usually at a fair price (determine price when you make your deal). With any luck you'll find a woman renowned not only for her *tortillas por manos* but also for the tastiest *poc chuc* this side of Ticul. You gain a lot more than food in this arrangement; the culture swap is priceless.

Food Safety

When preparing your own food in the backcountry, a few possible sources of bacteria are fresh fruit and vegetables, especially those with thin skins that don't get peeled, like lettuce or tomatoes. When washing these foods in local water (and they should definitely be washed thoroughly before consuming), add either bleach or iodine (8-10 drops per quart) to the water. Soaking vegetables together in a container or plastic bag for about 20 minutes is easy; carrying along Ziploc bags is essential. If at the beach and short of water, substitute seawater (for everything but drinking). Remember not to rinse the bleached food with contaminated water, just pat dry, and if they have a distasteful lingering flavor, a squirt of lime juice tastes great and is very healthy. Nature has packaged some foods hygienically; a banana has its own protective seal so is considered safe (luckily, since they're so abundant on the Peninsula). Foods that are cooked and eaten immediately are also considered safe.

TRANSPORTATION

For centuries, getting to the Yucatán Peninsula required a major sea voyage to one of the few ports on the Gulf of Mexico, followed by harrowing and uncertain land treks limited to mule trains and narrow paths through the tangled jungle. Today the Peninsula is accessible from anywhere in the solar system! Arrive via modern airports, a network of new (good) highways, a reasonably frequent train system (very limited), or an excellent bus service that reaches large cities as well as an incredible number of small villages in remote areas.

BY CAR

Renting a car in Mexico is usually a simple matter but can cost much more than in the U.S.— and is always subject to Murphy's Law. If you know exactly when you want the car and where, it's helpful to make reservations in the U.S. in advance. If you wait until you get to Mexico, you pay the going rate, which can add up to about $60 per day for a small car; most offices give little or no weekly discount. This is not to say that you can't take part in the favorite Mexican pastime: bargaining.

Car Rental

If it's just before closing time, and if someone has cancelled a reservation, and if it's off-season on the Peninsula, it's possible to get a car for a good rate. However, that's a lot of ifs to count on when you want and need a car as soon as you arrive. Also, it's often difficult to get a car without reservations; you may have to wait around for one to be returned.

Hertz, Avis, and Budget franchise representatives can be found in many parts of Mexico. American corporate offices will honor a contract price made in the U.S. before your arrival in Mexico. Avis is currently the cheapest of the big

DRIVING DISTANCES
IN KM

RIO LAGARTOS
PROGRESO   33   48   TIZIMIN   CANCUN
63   MERIDA   52   159   68
CELESTUN   160   PLAYA
DEL CARMEN
VALLADOLID   37
YUCATAN   AKUMAL
194   26
233   TULUM
FELIPE   98
CARRILLO
CAMPECHE   PUERTO

GULF OF MEXICO   QUINTANA
ROO

CAMPECHE   134
213   151   154   CHETUMAL
CIUDAD   ESCARCEGA   110
DEL CARMEN   XPUJIL
FRONTERA   93   159
(99 mi)
75   206
TABASCO
VILLAHERMOSA   BELIZE CITY
115   CARIBBEAN
278   27   PALENQUE   BELIZE   SEA
207   GUATEMALA
CHIAPAS
83
TUXTLA   SAN CRISTOBAL
GUTIERREZ   DE LAS CASAS

0   100 km

© MOON PUBLICATIONS, INC.

three (Avis, Hertz, and Budget all list 800 numbers in the Yellow Pages; ask for the international desk). Make your arrangements before you leave home. Always ask for the best deal, usually a weekly arrangement. Even if you only plan to use the car for four or five days, use your calculator; it might still be a better deal, especially with unlimited mileage thrown in. If you belong to AAA or other auto clubs, the car rental agency might give you a 10-20% discount (be sure you bring your membership card), but not in conjunction with another special deal.

Another advantage to making advance reservations is the verification receipt. Hang onto it; when you arrive at the airport and show your verification receipt (be sure you get it back), a car will almost always be waiting for you. Once in a

while you'll even get an upgrade for the same fee if your reserved car is not available. On the other side of the coin, be sure that you go over the car carefully before you take it far. Drive it around the block and check the following:

• Make sure there's a spare tire and working jack.

• All doors lock and unlock, including trunk.

• The seats move forward, have no sprung backs, etc.

• All windows lock, unlock, roll up and down properly.

• The proper legal papers are in the car, with address and phone numbers of associate car rental agencies in cities you plan to visit (in case of an unexpected car problem).

- Horn, emergency brake, and foot brakes work properly.

- Clutch, gearshift, all gears (including reverse) work properly.

- Get directions to the nearest gas station; the gas tank may be empty. If it's full it's wise to return it full, since you'll be charged top dollar per liter of gas. Ask to have any damage, even a small dent, missing doorknob, etc., noted on your contract, if it hasn't been already.

- Note the hour you picked up the car and try to return it before that time: a few minutes over will cost you another full day's rental fee.

When you pick up your rental car, the company makes an imprint of your credit card on a blank bill, one copy of which is attached to the papers you give the agent when you return the car. Keep in mind that the car agency has a limit on how much you can charge on one credit card at one time. If you go over the limit, be prepared to pay the balance in cash or with another credit card. If you pick up a car in one city and return it to another, there's a hefty drop-off fee (per km). Most agents will figure out in advance exactly how much it will be so that there aren't any surprises when you return the car.

In 99 cases out of 100, all will go smoothly. However, if you run into a problem or are overcharged, don't panic—charge everything and save all your paperwork; when you return home, make copies of everything and call the company; chances are very good that you'll get a refund.

Insurance

Rental car insurance runs about US$6 per day and covers only 80% of the damages. However, it's dangerous to skip insurance; in most cases in Mexico, when there's an accident the police take action first and ask questions later. With an insurance policy, most of the problems are eased over. Rental agencies also offer medical insurance for US$4 per day. Your private medical insurance should cover this (check). Also, ask your credit-card provider exactly what insurance they provide when you rent a car.

Documents

An international driver's license is not required to drive or rent a car in Mexico. However, if you feel safer with it, get one from an auto club. At AAA in California you will need two passport pictures and US$10, along with a current driver's license from your home state. The international license is another good form of identification if you should have an accident or other driving problems.

When you cross the border from the U.S. into Mexico, your car insurance is no longer valid. You can buy insurance from AAA or an auto club before you leave home. Numerous insurance agencies at most border cities sell Mexican insurance: Sanborn's is one of the largest. Ask Sanborn's for their excellent free road maps of the areas you plan to visit. For more information write: Sanborn's Mexican Insurance Service, P.O. Box 1210, McAllen, TX 78501; tel. (512) 682-3401.

In the last 15 years highway construction has been priority work on the Peninsula. A growing number of well-engineered roads—many of them expensive toll roads—provide access to cities and towns. However, before taking your car into the country, consider the manufacturer and the condition of the car. Will parts be available in the event of a breakdown? Volkswagen, Renault, Ford, General Motors, and Chrysler have Mexican branches and parts should be available. If you drive an expensive foreign sports car or a large luxury model, you might be better off making other arrangements. Repairs might be unavailable and you could be stranded in an unlikely place for days waiting for a part. It's always wise to make sure you and the mechanic understand the cost of repairs before he begins—just like at home! **Note:** Selling your car in Mexico is illegal.

Driving Tips

In Mexico, it's recommended that you don't drive outside the cities at night unless it's a necessity. The highways have no streetlights—it's hard to see a black cow on a black road in the black night. Also, pedestrians have no other place to walk; shoulders are nonexistent on the roads. Public phones are few and far between, and gas stations close when the sun goes down. If you should have a problem while driving during daylight hours on a *main* road, stay with your car. The Green Angels, a government-sponsored tow truck service, cruise the roads several times a day on the lookout for drivers in trouble. They carry gas and small parts and are prepared to fix tires. Each car is equipped with a CB radio and the driver is trained to give first aid, or will call a doctor. If you foolishly travel an isolated road after dark and break down, your best bet is to lock yourself in and stick it out for the night; go for help in the morning. The Mexican people are friendly, especially when they see someone in trouble; sometimes you have more help than you want.

Toll Roads vs. Free Roads

Toll roads are springing up all over Mexico. The fees are high and generally the highways are in great shape. In almost all cases, you can still use the old roads to get to your destination (which is what the budget minded locals use). On the free roads expect *topes* traffic bumps all along the highways. In some cases there's a sign to warn you, in others it will be a big surprise, and the underside of the car can be damaged. These roads can be very slow. Look for the signs that say *libre* (free); the toll road is the *cuota*. If you can't find the old road, ask a local.

BY PLANE

Two of the three international airports on the Yucatán Peninsula are in Quintana Roo. The newest and most modern is at Cancún; jets arrive daily, with connections from most countries in the world. It's also possible to fly internationally to the small island of Cozumel. Elsewhere in Quintana Roo are several small landing strips for private planes and small commuter airlines. More airports are in the planning stage in QR. The third international airport on the Peninsula is in Mérida.

BY TRAIN

For many years Mexico has had a fairly efficient railway service, but recent reports say the service is slipping. Traveling by train used to be relaxing and the scenery outstanding. You still can make

---

AIRLINES SERVING THE YUCATÁN PENINSULA

American: tel. (800) 433-7300; flies from Dallas/Fort Worth to Cancún.

Aeromexico: tel. (800) 237-6639; flies from Los Angeles and Houston to Cancún and Mérida.

Continental: tel. (800) 231-0856; flies from Houston to Cancún and Cozumel; connecting flights (via Houston) from Los Angeles, San Francisco, and Denver.

Mexicana: tel. (800) 531-7921; flies from Newark, Los Angeles, San Francisco, San Jose, Denver, San Antonio, and Chicago to Cancún and Cozumel.

---

an entire trip from the U.S. to Mérida by rail (then take a 45-minute flight to Cancún). From several stateside cities along the border, buses or trains drop off passengers at Mexican train connections. For information on other departure points along the border plus schedules, prices, etc., deal directly with the railway companies; schedules and prices change frequently. Some travel agents have train information. Government tourist offices can give you schedules and prices for a specific trip, but some of these sources may not be accurate. Note: We have heard reports of robberies on some of the train routes in the Yucatán Peninsula.

BY BUS

Bus service on the Peninsula is efficient. Fares will fit the most meager budget, scheduling is frequent, and even the smallest village is accessible from most Yucatán cities. From the U.S. it's smart to make reservations with Greyhound or Trailways to your final destination on the Peninsula. The bus driver will take you to the border and then help you make the transfer (including your luggage) to a Mexican bus line. This service saves you a lot of time and confusion when in a strange bus station. When making return reservations, book them for cross-border travel, even if only to the first town on the U.S. side;

again you will have an easier time crossing the border and making the connection. When NAFTA matures, transport across the border to Mexican destinations may become less complicated.

Class Choice

You have a choice of Plus, super-deluxe, deluxe, first-, second-, and third-class buses. Third-class passengers can bring their animals (and often do); second- and third-class buses are usually older models, with no toilets or a/c. Third-class bus tickets are cheap (as little as a Mexican taco at Taco Bell in the U.S.). First-class and above buses have assigned seats. Any bus with the word Plus attached is one of the really upscale buses that have airline seats, cold drinks, TVs, are faster (usually no stops), and quite comfortable. The price is much higher, but still not prohibitive. Deluxe are comfortable, have fewer seats, and are often triple the price, but are still very moderate compared to U.S. prices. Make reservations in advance. Your ticket will read *asiento* (seat) with a number. Some first-class buses sell food and drinks onboard. If you're traveling a long distance, buy at least first class; the difference in comfort is worth the small added expense. Second- and third-class buses stop for anyone who flags them, and at every small village along the way. First class operates almost exclusively between terminals. This cuts a lot of time off a long journey.

Luggage

If it fits in the overhead rack, almost anything can be carried on. Usual allowance is 25 kilograms, but unless you're ridiculously overloaded, no one ever objects to what you bring aboard. If a driver should refuse your load, you can usually come to an amicable (monetary) agreement. Larger luggage is carried in the cargo hold under the bus where breakables have a short lifespan. Purses and cameras are best kept between your feet on the floor, rather than in the overhead rack—just in case. Luggage should always be labeled, inside and out, with your name, address, and telephone number.

Seat Comfort

If you can, choose the shady side of the bus during the day: going south sit on the left side, and going north sit on the right. At night sit on the right, which eliminates the glare of oncoming headlights. The middle of the bus is the best place to be. Steer clear of seats near the bathroom, usually the last few rows. They can be smelly and the aisle traffic and constant door activity can keep you awake. Bring a book and just relax.

BY CRUISE SHIP

One of the fastest-growing industries in tourism is ocean cruising. What was once reserved for the idle rich is becoming commonplace for the ordinary vacationer. Cruising is no longer a means of getting from point A across an ocean to point B; cruise ships are for fun! And the more luxurious the better—though for obvious financial reasons some ships cater to fun-seekers rather than luxury-seekers. Daily prices can start as low as US$150 pp, on up to US$700 pp.

More and more cruise ships are being built yearly, and some of the new ships can carry as many as 5,000 people. Mexico (especially in the Caribbean) is getting its share! Each year a few more glamorous ships anchor offshore at Cozumel and Playa del Carmen, and if rumors are to be believed, soon we'll see them at Calica (next to Xcaret) and Majahual (on the Xcalak Peninsula).

Special-interest groups are finding a ship the perfect gathering place. For groups ranging from Smithsonian Associates' naturalists and archaeologists to theater guilds, appropriate speakers and plans are coordinated with the ship's personnel.

The Money Factor

Shop carefully if price is the most important factor; prices are competitive. A variety of ships offer mass market Las Vegas-type cruises aimed at younger passengers interested in short three- to five-day trips. Upscale luxury boats reminiscent of first-class on the "Queens"—Mary and Elizabeth—cruise for two weeks or longer and will cost the most. These are the ones with large cabins, restaurants where one orders from a complete menu, and passengers who are pampered outrageously, with a price tag to match. For the adventurer, small, casual ships capable of traveling narrow river passages into often vir-

cruising to Cozumel

OZ MALLAN

gin territory where nature and people have not been exposed to the diluting effects of tourism—for a while at least—run a gamut of prices from moderate to exorbitant.

Ways to Cut Costs

Go standby. Once you put your name on the list, you'll have no choice of cabin location or size, and airfare is usually not included. Passengers are notified two weeks prior to departure. **Last-minute travel clubs** and **discount agencies** include cruises available at the last minute in their inventories. These clubs charge a yearly membership fee, around US$50; for that, the member receives a newsletter with phone numbers, a list of trips, and other pertinent information that provides access to upcoming values. Those who are willing to pack up at a moment's notice (two weeks) can save 10-50%.

By the same token, some cruise lines will give a substantial discount to folks who book and buy passage six months to a year in advance. **Cunard, Princess, Holland America,** and **Royal Cruise Line** are all willing to give a 10-50% discount. Often, ships offer specials for various reasons; study the travel sections of newspapers and get to know your travel agent. Let him or her know what you would like, and ask him or her to call you if and when the price is right.

Sharing a quad room generally gives you a good discount. If you don't have any roomies to bring along, some lines will sell you a same-sex quad for a set price.

Ask for **senior citizen discounts;** though not many lines give them, there are a few.

To Quintana Roo

Several passenger ships make stops at Quintana Roo's islands and ports. Many sail out of Miami, stopping at Key West before continuing to the Caribbean and Mexico's Playa del Carmen and Isla Cozumel. Many lines will drop you off either at Cancún, Cozumel, or Playa del Carmen. Check with Princess Lines, Chandris, and Carnival Cruises; your travel agent can give you the names of others that stop along the Yucatán coast. New cruise ships are continually adding the Mexican Caribbean to their ports of call.

Cruise passengers have the opportunity to make shore excursions from the Caribbean coast ports to Chichén Itzá, Tulum, Cobá, and Xelha, or they can just lie around the white beach, enjoy the turquoise sea, or shop at the many *tiendas* for typical souvenirs.

Some cruise ships to the Quintana Roo coast specialize in diving and might carry a dive doctor, a small decompression chamber for treating the bends, and air compressors for filling tanks. Divers can either bring their own equipment or rent on board. Certification courses in scuba diving are offered as well as a multitude of watersports equipment and events. Dress is casual on these ships and fine entertainment can be had on board at the disco, pool, bars, or cinema. Fitness centers, shops, and film-processing make ship life convenient and pleasant.

GROUP TRAVEL

Travel agents offer many choices of escorted tours. You pay a little extra, but all arrangements and reservations are made for you to tour by plane, train, ship, or RV caravan. Special-interest tours with a guest expert are another possibility. For instance, archaeology buffs can usually find a group through a university that includes a knowledgeable professor to guide them through chosen Maya ruins. Evenings are spent together reviewing the day's investigation and discussing the next day's itinerary.

Archaeology laypeople will find many opportunities, including trips offered through Earthwatch, P.O. Box 403, Watertown, MA 02172; volunteers can work on a dig under the supervision of professionals. Destinations change regularly. *Transitions Abroad,* 18 Hulst Rd., Box 344, Amherst, MA 01004, is a magazine that offers information about study and teaching opportunities around the world. Travel agencies, student publications, and professional organizations can give you more information. Or call **Yucatán Reservations Central,** tel. (800) 952-4550.

NOTES FOR THE PHYSICALLY CHALLENGED

Mexico hasn't caught up with many parts of the world that have made life a little easier for the physically challenged. Sidewalks are narrow, and often hazardous due to myriad holes and cracks. Streets in the older cities are often cobblestone. Curbs are exceptionally steep, sometimes requiring more than one pushing person to maneuver. And the majority of the small resorts along the Quintana Roo coast are sand resorts—even some of the dining rooms are sand-floored. Fortunately, Cancún and Cozumel both have paved streets, but Isla Mujeres still has sand streets and it's hard to roll a wheelchair.

Toilets are not designed for anyone but the physically agile. Few hotels offer ramps for wheelchairs, and many—the old colonial buildings, especially—don't have elevators. The more upscale the hotel, the more preparation for the challenged. Always ask in advance, there is seldom more than one handicapped room. Caveat Emptor!

WHAT TO TAKE

Whatever time of year you travel to Mexico's Caribbean coast, you can expect warm weather, which means you can pack less in your suitcase. Most airlines allow you to check two suitcases, and you can bring another carry-on bag that fits either under your seat or in the overhead rack; this is great if you're planning a one-destination trip to a self-contained resort hotel and want a change of clothes each day. But if you plan on moving around a lot, keep it light.

Experienced travelers pack a small collapsible pocketbook into their compartmented carry-on, which then gives them only one thing to carry while en route. And be sure to include a few overnight necessities in your carry-on in the event your luggage doesn't arrive when you do. Valuables and medications are safest in your carry-on stowed under the seat in front of you rather than in the overhead rack, whether you're on a plane, train, or bus.

Clothing

How you dress depends on where you are. In today's Mexico, *almost* any clothing is acceptable, but look to see what the people of the area are wearing and follow their dress codes. A swimsuit is a must, and if you're not staying at one of the larger hotels, bring a beach towel. Beach attire is best worn at the beach; it isn't appropriate in urban areas, especially churches. A few beaches may be designated "nude" or "clothing optional," although nude sunbathing in Mexico is almost always inappropriate and unsafe—and *always* illegal.

If traveling during November, December, or January, bring along a light jacket since it can cool off in the evening. The rest of the year you'll probably carry the jacket in your suitcase. For women, a wraparound skirt is a useful item that can quickly cover up shorts when traveling through villages and cities (many small-village residents

KEEPING THE INSECTS AWAY

Of the many insect repellents around, some are better than others. Read the labels and ask questions. Some formulas were designed to spray the outdoors, some a room, others your clothes—none of these are for the skin. Some repellents are harmful to plants and animals, some can dissolve watch crystals, and others can damage plastic eyeglass lenses. This can be a particular problem if labels are written in a foreign language that you cannot read. It's best to bring your repellent from home.

Many of the most efficient repellents contain diethyl-toluamide (DEET). Test it out before you leave home; the more concentrated solutions can cause an allergic reaction in some people, and for children a milder mix is recommended. Avoid use on skin with sores and abrasions.

When using repellents, remember:
- If redness and itching begin, wash off with soap and water.
- Apply repellent by pouring into the palms of your hands, then rubbing together and applying evenly to the skin. If you're sweating, reapply every two hours. Use caution if perspiration mixed with repellent runs down your forehead and into your eyes—an absorbent headband helps.
- If you swim, reapply after coming out of the water.
- It's helpful to dip your socks, spray them heavily, or (as suggested by the World Health Organization) dip strips of cotton cloth, two or three inches wide, and wrap around your lower legs. One strip is effective for several weeks. Mosquitoes hover close to the ground in many areas.
- Apply liberally around the edges of your sleeves, pants cuffs, or shorts cuffs.

Sleeping in an a/c room with tight-fitting windows is one good way to avoid nighttime buzzing attacks; in other situations use a mosquito net over the bed. It helps if the netting has been dipped in repellent, and make sure it's large enough to tuck well under the mattress. A rectangular shape is more efficient than the usual conical, giving you more room to sit up so you'll avoid contact with the critters that might bite through the net.

An Alternative

Long Road Travel Supplies, 111 Avenida Dr., Berkeley, CA 94708, USA, tel. (800) 359-6040 or (510) 540-4763, fax (510) 540-0652, has come up with the **Indoor Travel Tent.** This lightweight, portable, net housing is made of ultrafine mesh netting and fits right on top of the bed. A nylon floor and lightweight poles provide you with a roomy rectangular shape and free-standing protection from both flying and crawling insects that can make sleeping impossible. It's convenient with a zipper door, folding flap for extra foot room, and inside pocket for keeping valuables close at hand. Packed in its own carrying bag, it weighs just 2.3 pounds (for single bed) and costs US$79; the double weighs 2.8 pounds and costs US$99. Ask about the budget-priced Indoor Tent II, with a drawstring door; single size is US$49 and weighs 1.25 pounds.

gawk at women wearing shorts; whatever you do, don't enter a church wearing them). The wraparound skirt also makes a good shawl for coolish evenings. Cotton underwear stays cool in the tropics, but nylon is less bulky and dries overnight, cutting down on the number needed. Be sure that you bring broken-in, comfortable walking shoes; blisters can wreck a vacation.

Necessities

If you wear glasses and are planning an extended trip in Mexico, it's a good idea to bring an extra pair or carry the lens prescription. The same goes for medications (make sure the prescription is written in general terms), though many Mexican pharmacies sell prescription drugs over the counter.

Avid readers in any language besides Spanish should bring a supply of books; English-language reading materials are for sale in limited quantities, mostly in big hotel gift shops and only a few bookstores. Both small and large hotels have book-trading shelves. Ask at the desk to see their collection. Most travelers are delighted to trade books.

A Note on Toilets

Many of Mexico's public toilets consist of a hole in the floor. Whether you're in that situation or trekking the jungle, a couple of items make it easier. For women, **Le Funelle** is a scooplike paper funnel with a wide mouth and easy-to-hold handle that enables women to stand up to urinate in comfort and safety. Made of biodegradeable paper, it can be tossed down the toilet when finished. Each Le Funnelle is packaged with a couple of tissues in an envelope about the size of a playing card—comes with instructions. A pack of four is US$2.85, pack of 20 is US$8.99.

This and some other really clever toilet articles and traveling items can be seen in a great little catalog called **Magellan's, Essentials For The Traveler.** Take a look at the anti-bacterial wipes (pre-moistened towelettes with germ killers). A box of 20 costs US$4.85. A disinfectant spray also serves as a good room deodorizer. To receive your own catalog, call (800) 962-4943.

The smaller the town, the more difficulty you'll have in finding a toilet. You can always go into a restaurant, buy a cold drink, and use the facilities. If there are no restaurants in the village, you must either stop at the local *tienda* or cantina and ask, *"¿Dónde está el baño?"* ("Where is the bathroom?"), or take a walk into the countryside. There was a time not too many years ago when you could not find facilities at any of the archaeological sites; however, in all of the mid- to large-size sites today, you will find a restroom.

Note! When you see a wastebasket in the stall with toilet paper in it, do not flush paper down the toilet; instead drop the used paper into the wastebasket. Often, the toilet will overflow if you put paper in it.

Backpackers

If you plan on hitchhiking or using public transportation, don't use a large external-frame pack; it won't fit in most small cars or public lockers. Smaller packs with zippered compartments that will accommodate mini-padlocks are most practical. A strong bike cable and lock secures the pack to a YH bed or a bus or train rack. None of the above will deter the real criminal, but might make it difficult enough to discourage anyone else.

Experienced backpackers travel light with a pack, an additional canvas bag, a small water-purifier and mosquito-proof tent, a hammock, and mosquito netting.

Campers

For the purist who vows to cook every meal, here's a list for a handy carried kitchen:

- single-burner stove, two fuel cylinders (fuel not allowed on commercial airlines)
- one large, sharp, machete-type knife; one small, sturdy, sharp knife
- pair of pliers—good hot pot grabber
- plastic pot scrubber
- can opener (with bottle hook)
- hot pad, two if there's room
- two pots that nest, one Silverstone skillet
- wire holder to barbecue fish or meat over open fire
- small sharpening stone
- soap and laundry detergent
- plate, cup, fork, and spoon, plastic or metal
- two large metal cooking spoons
- one long-handled wooden spoon
- one egg spatula
- three fast-drying dish towels (not terry-cloth)
- plastic Ziploc bags, large trash bags
- paper towels or napkins
- two or three plastic containers with tight-fitting lids, nested
- coffee drinkers who don't like instant will want a coffee pot
- several short candles and matches
- flashlight (batteries are usually easy to find)

DOCUMENTS

U.S. and Canadian citizens can obtain a free tourist card with proof of citizenship (birth certificate, passport, voter's registration, or notarized affidavit) good for 180 days. It can be obtained at any Mexican consulate or tourist office, at all border entry points, or from airport ticket offices for those traveling by plane. Hang onto your tourist card for the entire trip. You won't need it after you go through customs until it's time to leave the country. Then you must give it back. If you're visiting Mexico for 72 hours or less, you don't need a tourist card. Ask at the Mexican consulate about extensions for longer periods. If you're a naturalized citizen, carry your naturalization papers or passport. Citizens of the U.S. or Canada are not required to obtain certificates of vaccination to enter Mexico; other nationals should check with a local Mexican consulate. Those under 18 without a parent or legal guardian must present a notarized letter from the parents or guardian granting permission to travel alone in Mexico. If a single parent is traveling with a minor, he or she should carry a notarized letter from the other parent granting permission. This is important going in both directions.

Passport

If you have a passport, bring it along even though it's not required (tuck your tourist card inside); it's the simplest ID when cashing traveler's checks, registering at hotels, and going through immigration. If you're visiting an area that has a current health problem and you have a health card with current information, keep that with the passport also. Keep all documents in a waterproof plastic case and in a safe place. Contact the **Centers For Disease Control** for the most recent information about isolated areas that might be on the list for immunization. If traveling to such places, you'll need proof of vaccination to get back into the U.S., and perhaps other countries as well.

Driving Procedures

If you're driving, the tourist card serves as a vehicle permit when completed and validated at the border point of entry. Vehicle title or registration and driver's license are required. If you should happen to reach a remote border crossing at night, you may find it unstaffed. Do not cross the border with your car until you have obtained the proper papers; if you do, it will cause problems when you exit the country. Mexican vehicle insurance is available at most border towns 24 hours a day.

Pets

If you're traveling with a pet, a veterinarian's certificate verifying good health and a rabies inoculation within the last six months is required. This certificate will be validated by any Mexican consulate for a small fee.

Purchases

When departing by land, air, or sea, you must declare at the point of reentry into your own country all items acquired in Mexico. To facilitate this procedure, it is wise to register any foreign-made possessions with customs officials before entering Mexico and to retain the receipts for purchases made while there. Limitations on the value of imported, duty-free goods vary from country to country and should be checked before traveling. U.S. citizens are allowed to carry through customs US$600 worth of purchases pp duty free and up to US$1,000 for 10% tax. However, about 2,700 items are exempt from this limit, most of which are handcrafted or manufactured in Mexico. Consular offices or embassies in Mexico City can supply additional information on exempt items. Plants and certain foods are not allowed into the U.S. and Mexico. Authentic archaeological finds, colonial art, and other original artifacts cannot be exported from Mexico. And, of course, trying to bring marijuana or any other narcotic into or out of Mexico or the U.S. is foolhardy. Jail is one place in Mexico a visitor would prefer to avoid.

HEALTH AND SAFETY

TURISTA

Some travelers to Mexico worry about getting sick the moment they cross the border. But with a few simple precautions, it's not a foregone conclusion that you'll come down with something in Mexico. The most common illness to strike visitors is turista, Montezuma's Revenge, the trots, travelers illness, or in plain Latin—diarrhea. No fun, it can cause uncomfortable cramping, fever, dehydration, and the need to stay close to a toilet for the duration. It's caused, among other things, by various strains of bacteria in food or water.

Statistics show that most tourists get sick on the third day of their visit. Interested doctors note that this traveler's illness is common in every country. They say that in addition to bacteria, a change in diet is equally to blame and suggest that the visitor slip slowly into the eating habits of Mexico. In other words, don't blast your tummy with the *habanera* or *jalapeño* pepper right off the bat. Work into the fried food, drinks, local specialties, and new spices gradually; take your time changing over to foods that you may never eat while at home, including the large quantities of wonderful tropical fruits that you'll want to eat every morning. Turista can also be blamed on alcohol mixed with longer-than-usual periods of time in the tropical sun.

The Water

Water is probably the worst culprit. Carry bottled water at all times. Many parts of the Yucatán Peninsula (such as Cancún and the newer developments along the Caribbean coast) have modern sewage systems, but the small villages and more isolated areas still have little or none—all waste is redeposited in the earth and can contaminate the natural water supply. While in these places you should take special precautions.

In the backcountry, if necessary, boil it, or purify it with chemicals, whether the source is the tap or a crystal-clear cenote. That goes for brushing your teeth as well. If you have nothing else, a bottle of beer will make a safe (though maybe not

sane) mouth rinse. If using ice, ask where it was made and if it's pure. Think about the water you're swimming in; some small local pools might be better avoided.

The easiest way to purify the water is with purification tablets; Hidroclonozone and Halazone are two, but many brands are available at drugstores in all countries—in Mexico ask at the *farmacia*. Another common method is to carry a small plastic bottle of liquid bleach (use 8-10 drops per quart of water) or iodine (called *yodo*, five to seven drops per quart). Whichever you use, let the water stand for 20 minutes to improve the flavor. If you're not prepared with any of the above, boiling the water for 20-30 minutes will purify it. Even though it takes a heck of a lot of fuel that you'll probably be carrying on your back, don't get lazy in this department. You can get very sick drinking contaminated water and you can't tell by looking at it—unless you travel with a microscope!

When camping on the beach where fresh water is scarce, use seawater to wash dishes and even yourself. If you have access to a sporting goods or marine store, ask for Sea Saver soap. Otherwise, use Castille soap. It only takes a small squirt of the soap to do a good job. (A rub of soap on the backsides of pots and pans before setting them over an open fire makes for easy cleaning after cooking.)

In the larger cities, purified water is generally provided in bottles in each room, or if the hotel is large enough it maintains its own purification plant on the premises. In Cozumel, for example, the Sol Caribe Hotel has a modern purification plant behind glass walls for all to see, and they're proud to show it off and explain how it works. If the tap water is pure, a sign over the spigot will specify this. If you're not sure about the water, ask the desk clerk; he'll let you know the status—they prefer healthy guests who will return.

Other Sources of Bacteria

Handling money can be a source of germs. Wash your hands frequently, don't put your fingers in your mouth, and carry individual foil packets of disinfectant cleansers, like Wash Up (handy and refreshing in the tropic heat) or liquid disinfectants that just rub dry. Hepatitis is another bug that can be contracted easily if you're around it.

When in backcountry cafes, remember that fruits and vegetables, especially those with thin, edible skins (like tomatoes), are a possible source of bacteria. If you like to eat food purchased from street vendors (and some should not be missed), use common sense. If you see the food being cooked (killing all the grubby little bacteria) before your eyes, have at it. If it's hanging there already cooked and nibbled on by small flying creatures, pass it by. It may have been there all day, and what was once a nice sterile morsel could easily have gone bad in the heat or been contaminated by flies. When buying food at the marketplace to cook yourself, use the hints given in "Food."

Treatment

Remember, it's not just the visiting gringo who gets sick because of bacteria. Many Mexicans die each year from the same germs, and the Mexican government is working hard to remedy their sanitation problems. Tremendous improvements have taken place that ultimately will be accomplished all over Mexico, but it's a slow process. In the meantime, many careful visitors come and go each year with nary a touch of turista.

If after all your precautions you still come down with traveler's illness, many medications are available for relief. Most can be bought over the counter in Mexico, but in the U.S. you'll need a prescription from your doctor. Lomotil and Imodium A-D are common and certainly turn off the faucet after a few hours of dosing; however, each has the side effect of becoming a plug. It does not cure the problem, only the symptoms; if you quit taking it too soon your symptoms reappear and you're back to square one. In its favor, Lomotil probably works faster than any of the other drugs, and if you're about to embark on a 12-hour bus ride across the Yucatán Peninsula you might consider Lomotil a lifesaver. A few other over-the-counter remedies are Kaopectate in the U.S., Imodium and Donamycin in Mexico. Be sure to read and follow the directions. If you're concerned, check with your doctor before leaving home. Also ask him or her

about some new formulas called Septra and Bactrim. While traveling, we count on a combination of Imodium (which stops the symptoms fairly quickly) and Septra or Bactrim, which supposedly kills the bug. Don't forget the common Pepto-Bismol. Some swear by it; be aware that it can turn the tongue a dark brownish color—nothing to be alarmed about. Septra and Bactrim must be bought in the U.S. with a prescription under a different name; check with your doctor.

For those who prefer natural remedies, lime juice and garlic are both considered good when taken as preventatives. They need to be taken in large quantities. Douse everything with the readily available lime juice (it's delicious on salads and fresh fruit and in drinks). You'll have to figure out your own ways of using garlic (some believers carry garlic capsules, available in most U.S. health-food stores). Mexicans imbibe fresh coconut juice (don't eat the oily flesh, it makes your problem worse!). Plain boiled white rice and chamomile tea *(té de manzanillo)* also soothe the stomach. While letting the ailment run its course, stay away from spicy and oily foods and fresh fruits. Don't be surprised if you have chills, nausea, vomiting, stomach cramps, and a fever. This could go on for about three days. If the problem persists, see a doctor.

SUNBURN

Sunburn can spoil a vacation quicker than anything else, so approach the sun cautiously. Expose yourself for short periods the first few days; wear a hat and sunglasses. Use a good sunscreen, and apply it to all exposed areas of the body (don't forget feet, hands, nose, backs of your knees, and forehead—especially if you have a receding hairline). Remember that after each time you go into the water for a swim, sunscreen lotion must be reapplied. Even after a few days of desensitizing your skin, when spending a day snorkeling wear a T-shirt in the water to protect your exposed back, and thoroughly douse the back of your neck with sunscreen lotion. The higher the number on sunscreen bottles, the more protection. Some users are allergic, so try a small patch test before leaving home. If you have a reaction, investigate the new "natural" sunblocks using mica. Ask at your pharmacy.

ÖZ MALLAN

pool games at the Hyatt Regency, Cancún

If, despite precautions, you still get a painful sunburn, do not return to the sun. Cover up with clothes if it's impossible to find protective deep shade (like in the depths of a dark, thick forest). Keep in mind that even in partial shade (such as under a beach umbrella), the reflection of the sun off the sand or water will burn your skin. Reburning the skin can result in painful blisters that easily become infected. Soothing suntan lotions, coconut oil, vinegar, cool tea, and preparations like Solarcaine will help relieve the pain. Drink plenty of liquids (especially water) and take tepid showers. A few days out of the sun is the best medicine.

HEALING

Most small cities on the Yucatán Peninsula have a resident doctor. He or she may or may not speak English, but will usually make a house call. When staying in a hotel, get a doctor quickly by asking the hotel manager; in the larger resorts, an English-speaking doctor is on call 24 hours a day. If you need to ask someone to get you a doctor, say, *"¡Necesito doctor, por favor!"* Emergency clinics are found in all but the smallest villages, and a taxi driver can be your quickest way to get there when you're a stranger in town. In small rural villages, if you have a serious problem and no doctor is around, you can usually find a *curandero*. These healers deal with the old natural methods (and maybe just a few chants thrown in for good measure), and can be helpful in a desperate situation away from modern technology.

Self Help
The smart traveler carries a first-aid kit of some kind. If backpacking, carry at least the following:

> adhesive tape
> alcohol
> antibiotic ointment
> aspirin
> baking soda
> Band-Aids
> cornstarch
> gauze
> hydrogen peroxide
> insect repellent
> iodine
> Lomotil
> pain pills
> sewing needle
> sunscreen
> water purification tablets

Many of these products are available in Mexico, but certain items, like aspirin and Band-Aids, are sold individually in small shops and are much cheaper in your hometown. Even if not out in the wilderness, you should carry at least a few Band-Aids, aspirin, and an antibiotic ointment or powder or both. Travelers should be aware that in the tropics, with its heavy humidity, a simple scrape can become infected more easily than in a dry climate. So keep cuts and scratches as clean and dry as possible.

Another great addition to your first-aid kit is David Werner's book, *Where There Is No Doctor*. Also published in Spanish, it can be ordered from the Hesperian Foundation, P.O. Box 1692, Palo Alto, CA 94302. David Werner drew on his experience living in Mexico's backcountry when creating this informative book.

Shots

Check on your tetanus shot before you leave home, especially if you're backpacking in isolated regions. A gamma globulin shot may also be necessary; ask your physician.

SIMPLE FIRST-AID GUIDE

Acute Allergic Reaction: This, the most serious complication of insect bites, can be fatal. Common symptoms are hives, rash, pallor, nausea, tightness in chest or throat, and trouble in speaking or breathing. Be alert for symptoms. If they appear, get prompt medical help. Start CPR if needed and continue until medical help is available.

Animal Bites: Bites, especially on face and neck, need immediate medical attention. If possible, catch and hold the animal for observation, taking care not to be bitten. Wash the wound with soap and water (hold under running water for two to three minutes unless the bleeding is heavy). Do not use iodine or other antiseptics. Bandage. This also applies to bites by human beings. In the case of human bites the danger of infection is high.

Bee Stings: Apply cold compresses quickly. If possible, remove the stinger by gentle scraping with a clean fingernail and continue cold applications till the pain is gone. Be alert for symptoms of acute allergic reaction or infection requiring medical aid.

Bleeding: For severe bleeding apply direct pressure to the wound with a bandage or the heel of the hand. Do not remove cloths when blood-soaked, just add others on top and continue pressure till bleeding stops. Elevate the bleeding part above heart level. If bleeding continues, apply a pressure bandage to arterial

points. Do not put on a tourniquet unless advised by a physician. Do not use iodine or other disinfectants. Get medical aid.

Blister On Heel: It is better not to open a blister if you can rest the foot. If you can't, wash the foot with soap and water. Make a small hole at the base of the blister with a needle sterilized in 70% alcohol or in a match flame. Drain the fluid and cover with a strip bandage or moleskin. If a blister breaks on its own, wash with soap and water, bandage, and be alert for signs of infection (redness, festering) that call for medical attention.

Burns: For minor burns (redness, swelling, pain), apply cold water or immerse the burned part in cold water immediately. Use burn medication if necessary. For deeper burns (blisters develop), immerse in cold water (not ice water) or apply cold compresses for one to two hours. Blot dry and protect with a sterile bandage. Do not use antiseptic, ointment, or home remedies. Consult a doctor. For deep burns (skin layers destroyed, skin may be charred), cover with sterile cloth; be alert for breathing difficulties and treat for shock if necessary. Do not remove clothing stuck to the burn. Do not apply ice. Do not use burn remedies. Get medical help quickly.

Cuts: For small cuts, wash with clean water and soap. Hold the wound under running water. Bandage. Use hydrogen peroxide or another antiseptic. For large wounds, see "Bleeding." If a finger or toe has been cut off, treat the severed end to control bleeding. Put the severed part in clean cloth for the doctor (it may be possible to reattach it by surgery). Treat for shock if necessary. Get medical help at once.

Diving Accident: There may be injury to the cervical spine (such as a broken neck). Call for medical help. (See "Drowning.")

Drowning: Clear the airway and start CPR even before trying to get water out of the lungs. Continue CPR till medical help arrives. In case of vomiting, turn the victim's head to one side to prevent inhalation of vomitus.

Food Poisoning: Symptoms appear a varying number of hours after eating and are generally like those of the flu—headache, diarrhea, vomiting, abdominal cramps, fever, a general sick feeling. See a doctor. A rare form, botulism, has a high fatality rate. Symptoms are double vision, inability to swallow, difficulty in speaking, respiratory paralysis. Get to an emergency facility at once.

Fractures: Until medical help arrives, do not move the victim unless absolutely necessary. Suspected victims of back, neck, or hip injuries should not be moved. Suspected breaks of arms or legs should be splinted to avoid further damage before the victim is moved, if moving is necessary.

Heat Exhaustion: Symptoms are cool moist skin, profuse sweating, headache, fatigue, and drowsiness with essentially normal body temperature. Remove the victim to cool surroundings, raise feet and legs, loosen clothing, and apply cool cloths. Give sips of salt water—one teaspoon of salt to a glass of water—for rehydration. If the victim vomits, stop fluids and take the victim to an emergency facility as soon as possible.

Heatstroke: Rush the victim to a hospital. Heatstroke can be fatal. The victim may be unconscious or severely confused. The skin feels hot and is red and dry, with no perspiration. Body temperature is high. Pulse is rapid. Remove the victim to a cool area, sponge with cool water or rubbing alcohol; use fans or a/c and wrap the victim in wet sheets, but do not overchill. Massage arms and legs to increase circulation. Do not give large amounts of liquids. Do not give liquids if the victim is unconscious.

Insect Bites: Be alert for an acute allergic reaction that requires quick medical aid. Otherwise, apply cold compresses and soothing lotions. If the bites are scratched and infection starts (fever, swelling, redness), see a doctor.

Jellyfish Stings: Symptom is acute pain and may include feeling of paralysis. Immerse the affected area in ice water from for 5-10 minutes or apply aromatic spirits of ammonia to remove venom from the skin. Be alert for symptoms of acute allergic reaction and/or shock. If this happens, get the victim to a hospital as soon as possible.

Motion Sickness: Get a prescription from your doctor if boat travel is anticipated and this illness is a problem. Many over-the-counter remedies are sold in the U.S.; Bonine and Dramamine are two. If you prefer not to take chemicals or if you get drowsy, the new Sea Band is a cloth band that you place around the pressure point of the wrist. For more information write: Sea Band, 1645 Palm Beach Lake Blvd., Suite 220, W. Palm Beach, FL 33401 USA. Also available by prescription from your doctor is medication administered in adhesive patches behind the ear.

Muscle Cramps: Usually a result of unaccustomed exertion; "working" the muscle or kneading it with the hand relieves cramp. If in water, head for shore (you can swim even with a muscle cramp), or knead the muscle with your hand. Call for help if needed. Do not panic.

Mushroom Poisoning: Even a small ingestion may be serious. Induce vomiting immediately if there is any question of mushroom poisoning. Symptoms—vomiting, diarrhea, difficult breathing— may begin in one to two hours or up to 24 hours. Convulsions and delirium may develop. Go to a doctor or emergency facility at once.

Nosebleed: Press the bleeding nostril closed, or pinch the nostrils together, or pack them with sterile cotton or gauze. Apply a cold cloth or ice to the nose and face. The victim should sit up, leaning forward, or lie down with head and shoulders raised. If bleeding does not stop in 10 minutes, get medical help.

Obstructed Airway: Find out if the victim can talk by asking, "Can you talk?" If he or she can talk, encourage the victim to cough the obstruction out. If he or she can't speak, a trained person must apply the Heimlich maneuver. If you are alone and choking, try to forcefully cough the object out. Or press your fist into your upper abdomen with a quick upward thrust, or lean forward and quickly press your upper abdomen over any firm object with a rounded edge (back of chair, edge of sink, porch railing). Keep trying till the object comes out.

Plant Poisoning: Many plants are poisonous if eaten or chewed. If the leaves of the diffenbachia (common in the Yucatán jungle) are chewed, one of the first symptoms is swelling of the throat. Induce vomiting immediately. Take the victim to an emergency facility for treatment.

Poison Ivy, Oak, or Sumac: After contact, wash the affected area with an alkali-base laundry soap, lathering well. Have a poison-ivy remedy available in case itching and blisters develop.

Puncture Wounds: Usually caused by stepping on a tack or a nail, these often do not bleed, so try to squeeze out some blood. Wash thoroughly with soap and water and apply a sterile bandage. Check with a doctor about tetanus. If pain, heat, throbbing, or redness develops, get medical attention at once.

Rabies: Bites from bats, raccoons, rats, or other wild animals are the most common threat of rabies today. Try to capture the animal, avoiding getting bitten, so it can be observed; do not kill the animal unless necessary and try not to injure the head so the brain can be examined. If the animal can't be found, see a doctor, who may decide to use antirabies immunization. In any case, flush the bite with water and apply a dry dressing; keep the victim quiet and see a doctor as soon as possible.

Scrapes: Sponge with soap and water; dry. Apply antibiotic ointment or powder and cover with a nonstick dressing (or tape on a piece of cellophane). When healing starts, stop the ointment and use an antiseptic powder to help a scab form. Ask a doctor about tetanus.

Shock: Can be a side effect in any kind of injury. Get immediate medical help. Symptoms may be pallor, clammy skin, shallow breathing, fast pulse, weakness, or thirst. Loosen clothing, cover the victim with blanket but do not apply other heat, and place the victim on his or her back with the feet raised. If necessary, start CPR. Do not give water or other fluids.

Snakebite or Lizard Bite: If the reptile is not poisonous, tooth marks usually appear in an even row (an exception, the poisonous gila monster, shows even tooth marks). Wash the bite with soap and water and apply a sterile bandage. See a doctor. If the snake is poisonous, puncture marks (one to six) can usually be seen. Kill the snake for identification if possible, taking care not to be bitten. Keep the victim quiet, immobilize the bitten arm or leg, keeping it on a lower level than the heart. If possible, phone ahead to be sure antivenin is available and get medical treatment as soon as possible. Do not give alcohol in any form. If treatment must be delayed and a snakebite kit is available, use as directed.

Spider Bites: The black widow bite may produce only a light reaction at the place of the bite, but severe pain, a general sick feeling, sweating, abdominal cramps, and breathing and speaking difficulty may develop. The more dangerous brown recluse spider's venom produces a severe reaction at the bite, generally in two to eight hours, plus chills, fever, joint pain, nausea, and vomiting. Apply a cold compress to the bite in either case. Get medical aid quickly.

Sprain: Treat as a fracture till the injured part has been X-rayed. Raise the sprained ankle or other joint and apply cold compresses or immerse in cold water. If the swelling is pronounced, try not to use the injured part till it has been X-rayed. Get prompt medical help.

Sunburn: For skin that is moderately red and slightly swollen, apply wet dressings of gauze dipped in a solution of one tablespoon baking soda and one tablespoon cornstarch to two quarts of cool water. Or take a cool bath with a cup of baking soda to a tub of water. Sunburn remedies are helpful in relieving pain. See a doctor if the burn is severe.

Sunstroke: This is a severe emergency. See "Heatstroke." The skin is hot and dry; body temperature is high. The victim may be delirious or unconscious. Get medical help immediately.

Ticks: Cover ticks with mineral oil or kerosene to exclude air from them, and they will usually drop off or can be lifted off with tweezers in 30 minutes. To avoid infection, take care to remove the whole tick. Wash the area with soap and water. Check with a doctor or health department to see if deadly ticks are in the area.

Wasp Sting: Apply cold compresses to the sting and watch for acute allergic reaction. If such symptoms develop, get the victim to a medical facility immediately.

HAZARDS

Security

It's smart to keep passports, traveler's checks, money, and important papers on your person or in a safe deposit box at all times. (It's always a good idea to keep a separate list of document numbers in your luggage and leave a copy with a friend back home. This expedites replacement in case of loss.) The do-it-yourselfer can sew inside pockets into clothes; buy extra-long pants that can be turned up and sewn three-fourths of the way around, the last section closed with a piece of Velcro. Separate shoulder-holster pockets, money belts, and pockets around the neck inside clothing—all made of cotton—are available commercially. If you're going to be backpacking and sloshing in jungle streams, etc., put everything in Ziploc plastic bags before placing them in pockets. Waterproof plastic tubes will hold a limited number of items around your neck while you swim.

Before You Leave Home

Probably the best way to save money is to make sure you don't lose anything along the way. Be practical; leave expensive jewelry at home. Take five minutes to go through your wallet before leaving and remove all credit cards you won't be using and put a good part of your money in traveler's checks. Make two copies of your passport-picture page and any credit cards you carry. Leave one copy of each with someone at home you can reach in case of emergency. After you get your visitor's card, also make a copy of that for your wallet if possible. Keep these copies where you'll have them in the event your wallet and cards are stolen—in another piece of luggage. If your cards should get pinched, the copies will expedite replacement wherever you are in the world. Keep the original visitor's card with your passport in a hotel safe when sightseeing or swimming.

The Hotel Safe

Even the smallest hotels have safe-deposit boxes or some other security system for their guests. Many of the more upscale hotels have in-room safes now, which is very convenient. Use it for your airline tickets and passports as well as other valuables. Don't leave anything valuable lying around your room. Why create a tempting situation? Most hotel employees are honest (honestly); working in a hotel is a good job, and for the most part that's far more important to the employee than stealing. However (you knew a *however* was coming didn't you?), you might be the unlucky person to draw the unscrupulous thief/maid/bell boy.

A hotel robbery is less common than, say, a setup on the street (a jostle, attention diverted by one person while the other grabs your purse or cuts the strap of a carry bag). Take precautions, act sensibly, be aware of what is going on around you at all times; don't flash large wads of cash, and don't give your room number to strangers. If you're invited to go anywhere with a stranger, suggest meeting him/her there; let someone know where you are going, even if it's the desk clerk.

Pickpockets

Don't forget pickpockets! They love fairs and all celebrations where there are lots of people; it's really easy to jostle people in crowds (that includes buses), so make sure you've got your money where a quick hand can't get to it, like a money belt, or a holster worn over your shoulder under your clothing. Many types are available; check out the trendy travel stores and catalogs. It's a good idea to put everything in a plastic bag before you stash it in your belt/holster; sweat makes ink run.

Legal Help

If after all precautions you still have a problem, contact the 24-hour national hotline of the office of **La Procuradoría de Protección al Turista** (Attorney General for the Protection of Tourists.) Each state has an office. The following number is located in Mexico City; tell the English-speaking operator you have an emergency and she will direct your call; tel. (5) 250-0293, 250-0151, or 250-0589.

In the event you should be arrested, contact the nearest American Consul's office. If nothing else, they will visit you and advise you of your rights. Whatever you do, don't get caught with illegal substances; there's little that anyone can do given the current U.S. pressures to stop drug trafficking.

Insurance

Most homeowner's policies cover loss of property while on vacation; check it out before you leave home. *Do* make a police report if you're robbed. It's a long bureaucratic chore, but sometimes your property is recovered as a result. It also helps to have the report in hand when you deal with your insurance back home.

Lastly (yes, this is a repeat), always a make a copy of the front pages of your passport with pictures and all the vital information, numbers, etc., in the event of losing your passport. Then, when you go to your American consul or ambassador, this will expedite getting the passport replaced.

Women Travelers

A solo female traveler is considered very approachable by scammers and con artists. The "May I Join You?" scam is typical in tourist areas. A seemingly harmless man may ask if he can join you; he orders a drink (or more), and you foot the bill. If you really would like some company, make sure to specify *"Cuentos separados por favor"* ("Separate checks please") to your waiter.

Hitchhiking

Neither men nor women are advised to hitch-hike. When walking at night, find other travelers or trustworthy companions. Let your hotel staff know your plans; they can often provide you with a reliable list of taxi drivers, etc., and look out for your well-being.

SERVICES AND INFORMATION

PHOTOGRAPHY

Bring a camera to the Yucatán Peninsula! Nature and the Maya combine to provide unforgettable panoramas, well worth taking home with you on film to savor again at your leisure. Many people bring simple cameras such as Instamatics or disc types, which are easy to carry and are uncomplicated. For boat trips and snorkeling the new disposable waterproof cameras are great. Others prefer 35-mm cameras, which offer higher-quality pictures, are easier than ever to use, and are available in any price range. They can come equipped with built-in light meter, automatic exposure, self-focus, and self-advance—with little more to do than aim and click.

Film

Two reasons to bring film with you: it's cheaper and more readily available in the United States. Two reasons *not* to bring lots of film: space may be a problem and heat can affect film quality, both before and after exposure. If you're traveling for more than two weeks in a car or bus a good part of the time, carry film in an insulated case. You can buy a soft-sided insulated bag in most camera shops or order one out of a professional photography magazine. For the average vacation, if your film is kept in your room, there should be no problem. Many varieties of Kodak film are found in camera shops and hotel gift shops on the Yucatán Peninsula. In the smaller towns along the Caribbean coast you may not be able to find slide film.

X-ray Protection

If you carry film with you when traveling by plane, take precautions. Each time film is passed through the security X-ray machine, a little damage is done. It's cumulative, and perhaps one time won't make much difference, but most photographers won't take the chance. Request hand inspection. With today's tight security at airports, some guards insist on passing your film and camera through the X-ray machine. If your film is packed in your checked luggage, it's wise to keep it in protective lead-lined bags, available at camera shops in two sizes; the larger size holds up to 22 rolls of 35-mm film, the smaller holds eight rolls. If you use fast film, ASA 400 or higher, buy the double lead-lined bag designed to protect more sensitive film. Carry an extra lead-lined bag for your film-loaded camera if you want to drop it into a piece of carry-on luggage. (These bags also protect medications from X-ray damage.)

If you decide to request hand examination (rarely if ever refused at a Mexican airport), make it simple for the security guard. Have the film out of boxes and canisters placed together in one clear plastic bag that you can hand him for quick examination both coming and going. He'll also want to look at the camera; load it with film *after* crossing the border.

Film Processing

For processing film, the traveler has several options. Most people take their film home and have it processed at a familiar lab. Again, if the trip is lengthy and you are shooting lots of photos, it's impractical to carry used rolls around for more than a couple of weeks. Larger cities have one-hour photo labs, but they only handle color prints; color slides must be processed at a lab in Mexico City, which usually takes a week or two. If you'll be passing through the same city on another leg of your trip, the lab is a good cool place to store your slides while you travel. Just tell the lab technician when you think you'll be picking them up. Kodak mailers are another option but most photographers won't let their film out of sight until they reach their own favorite lab.

Camera Protection

Take a few precautions with your camera while traveling. At the beach remember that a combination of wind and sand can really gum up the works and scratch the lens. On 35-mm cameras keep a clear skylight filter on the lens instead of a lens cap so the camera can hang around your neck or in a fanny pack always at the ready for that spectacular shot that comes when least expected. If something is going to get scratched, better a $15 filter than a $300 lens.

It also helps to carry as little equipment as possible. If you want more than candids and you carry a 35-mm camera, basic equipment can be simple. Padded camera cases are good and come in all sizes. A canvas bag is lighter and less conspicuous than a heavy photo bag, but doesn't have the extra protection the padding provides. At the nearest army/military surplus store you can find small military bags and webbed belts with eyelet holes from which to hang canteen pouches and clip holders for extra equipment. It helps to have your hands free while climbing pyramids or on long hikes.

Safety Tips

Keep your camera dry; carrying a couple of big Ziploc bags affords instant protection. Don't *store* cameras in plastic bags for any length of time because the moisture that builds up in the bag can damage a camera as much as leaving it in the rain.

It's always wise to keep cameras out of sight in a car or when camping out. Put your name and address on the camera. Chances are if it gets left behind or stolen it won't matter whether your name is there or not, and don't expect to see it again; however, miracles do happen. (You *can* put a rider on most homeowner's insurance policies for a nominal sum that will cover the cost if a camera is lost or stolen.) It's a nuisance to carry cameras every second when traveling for a long period. During an evening out, you can leave your cameras and equipment (out of sight) in the hotel room—unless it makes you crazy all evening worrying about it! Some hotel safes are large enough to accommodate your equipment.

Cameras can be a help or a hindrance when you're trying to get to know the people. In the backcountry, you'll run into folks who are frightened of being photographed—put your camera away until the right moment. The main thing to remember is to ask permission first and then if someone doesn't want his/her picture taken, accept their refusal with a gracious smile and move on.

Camera Fees

There is an additional charge of US$8-10 to use a video camera at most archaeological sites. There is talk of a similar charge for still cameras as well, though we had no problems using a camera, without tripod, on our last visit. To be sure, check with the tourist office in Mérida before you visit the ruins.

*street snacks,
Quintana Roo*

OZ MALLAN

MONEY

New Pesos

After the collapse of the stock market in 1994, the peso plunged in value. Mexicans in all walks of life are suffering as U.S. residents would if without warning the US$1 was suddenly worth US50 cents. Their buying power was stifled, and every individual and business with debt was pushed deeper into the hole. Things have leveled off somewhat; however, when the peso drops, the dollar becomes more valuable in Mexico. So, sadly, what is a hardship on Mexicans becomes a boon to the traveler. Don't expect bargains in upscale hotels. Their prices are geared to the foreign traveler, and those prices have risen to make up some of the difference. It's in the smaller towns and businesses that you'll notice "cheap." The exchange rate can go up or down in today's volatile financial climate in Mexico; most of the prices are quoted in US$, since that seems to be fairly stable. Some of the prices are quoted in pesos. And when you tip, remember that these service people make a minuscule salary, so do tip as you would in the United States.

Cashing personal checks in Mexico is not easy; however, it is possible to withdraw money against your credit card in some banks and instant teller machines. Wearing a money belt is always a good idea while traveling—in any country.

Exchange

Usually your best rate of exchange is at the bank, but small shops frequently give a good rate if you're making a purchase. Hotels notoriously give the poorest exchange. Check to see what kind of fee, if any, is charged. You can learn the current exchange rate daily in all banks and most hotels. Try not to run out of money over the weekend because the new rate often is not posted until noon on Monday; you will get the previous Friday's rate of exchange even if the weekend newspaper may be announcing an overwhelming difference in your favor.

Note: According to many foreign travelers in Mexico, it's easier to exchange U.S. dollars for pesos than many other currencies (perhaps with the exception of Canadian dollars). So, foreign travelers might want to come prepared with either U.S. dollars or American traveler's checks. Also, try to spend all your coinage before leaving the country, since most banks or money changers will not buy peso coins with U.S. dollars.

Always go with pesos in hand to the small rural areas of Mexico. And even more convenient, take them in small denominations. In most cases it's a real hassle to cash dollars or traveler's checks.

The Cost of Traveling?

If we had a crystal ball, we could provide an answer to this question. But, like supply and demand, costs constantly change. A conservative estimate for *real* budget travelers is around **US$30-35** pp, per day. Moderate spenders who want more leeway can expect to spend **US$35-85** pp, per day; and luxury seekers can expect to

---

TIPPING

Tipping is of course up to the individual, but for a guideline on the Yucatán Peninsula the following seems to be average:

Porters: About US$1 per bag. If you're staying at a hotel with no elevator and three flights of stairs and you have lots of luggage, you may wish to be more generous.

Hotel Maids: If staying more than one night, US$1-2 per day left at the end of your stay.

Waiters/Waitresses: If not already included on the bill, 10-15% is average.

Tour Guides: Tour guides should receive about US$5 for a half-day trip and US$10-20 day for longer trips, if they do a good job of course! Also customary is US$5 for the driver.

Informal Site Guides: When visiting a ruin, cave, or lighthouse you will usually be shown the way by a young boy—US$0.50 is customary.

Gas station Attendants: Usually tipped about US$0.50 for pumping gas, cleaning the windshield, checking the oil and water, and providing other standard services.

Tipping **taxi drivers** is not customary.

Note: For the most part, American coins are useless in Mexico since moneychangers, whether banks or stores, will not accept them.

start their daily spending with US$100. Of course, when it comes to luxury, the sky's the limit in resort areas such as Cancún. Everyone must add more if renting a car, and deduct a little if you're traveling by twos. A lot depends on how you get around; taxis are a lot more expensive than buses, and trekkers get the best bargain of all. So what it means is, that it is impossible for me to predict!

Credit Cards

Major credit cards are accepted at all of the larger hotels, upscale restaurants in big cities, travel agencies, and many shops throughout Mexico. But don't take it for granted; ask. The smaller businesses do not accept them. In some cases you will be asked to pay a fee on top of the charged amount. In Mexico, universally, gas stations *do not* accept credit cards.

Hours for Banks and Businesses

Banks are open Mon.-Fri. 9 a.m.-1:30 p.m. Business offices are open from between 8 and 9 a.m. to 6 p.m., closing for an hour or more in the early afternoon. Government offices are usually open until 3 p.m. Stores in cities are generally open 10 a.m.-7 p.m., closing for a time between 1 and 4 p.m. Government offices, banks, and stores are closed on national holidays.

Moneda

The "$" sign in Mexico means pesos. Shops that accept dollars will often price items with the abbreviation "Dlls." If you see a price that says "m.n.," that indicates pesos, *moneda national*. Most large airports have money exchange counters, but the hours generally depend on the flight schedules.

Traveler's Checks

Traveler's checks are the easiest way to carry money. However, certain moneychangers will pay more for cash and some banks charge a fee, so always ask before making a transaction. If you're in a really small town, don't expect the shops or vendors to cash a traveler's check; gas stations deal *only* in pesos—so far. Be prepared. If you need to change money after bank hours, look for a sign that says Casa de Cambio.

The favored credit cards in Mexico are Bancomer (Visa) and Carnet (MasterCard)—way down the list is American Express; in fact most businesses refuse Amex as well as Diners Club. Look for ATMs in the more modern banks. Before leaving home, ask your bank teller if your particular card is authorized for use in Mexico, and, if so, at which branches.

Admission Fees

Admissions to the archaeological sites have taken large leaps in the past few years. INAH (Instituto Nacional de Antropología e Historia) is the arm of the government that directs the museums and archaeological sites of the country. The increase in fees certainly goes hand in hand with the improvements made on the sites. All the larger sites now have or will soon have modern visitor centers with restrooms, gift shops, snack shops, museums, and auditoriums. Most of the smaller sites will eventually have restrooms. INAH also sets the fees. There are still one or two sites in *way* out-of-the-way places that have not added restrooms or visitor's amenities and don't charge at all. Admission to all sites and museums is free on Sunday.

Remember that your video camera might cost more than you do to get into the archaeological grounds, about US$10.

Admission fees do not include the services of a guide; having an English-speaking guide is really worthwhile, but be sure to establish your fee (for your entire group), how long the guide will be with you, and where he will take you, before saying yes! A good starting point for negotiations for up to six people is US$25-30. If he was *really* good, a tip is fair. By yourself, expect to pay at least US$10 in the larger sites (much cheaper by the dozen) for a half day.

As at the sites, admission to state and national parks is free on Sunday. Fees range US$0.75-5.

Taxes

Note: 12% IVA tax is added to room rates, restaurant and bar tabs, and gift purchases. When checking in or making reservations at a hotel, ask if tax has already been added. And once again, don't forget that when you leave the country or travel from Mexican city to Mexican city, you must pay an **airport departure tax.** National departures, **US$6;** international departures, **US$12.**

Watching Your Pesos

No matter where you travel in the world, it's wise to guard your money. A money belt worn under the clothes is probably the most unobtrusive. They come in a variety of styles, from a shoulder holster to a flat pocket worn around the neck, or even an honest-to-goodness leather belt with a fine flat zipper opening on the inside, where you can insert a few folded bills for an emergency. Using hotel safe facilities is also very practical. In most cases visitors encounter no problems, but take precautions—it only takes one pickpocket to ruin a good vacation.

Bargaining

This is one way a visitor really gets to know the people. Although the influx of many outsiders who don't appreciate the delicate art of bargaining has deteriorated this traditional verbal exchange, it's still a way of life among Mexicans, and it can still build a bridge between the gringo and the Yucatecan. Some Americans accustomed to shopping with plastic money either find bargaining distasteful or go overboard and insult the merchant by offering far too little. It would not be insulting to begin the bargaining at 50% below the asking price; expect to earn about a 20% discount (and new respect) after a lively, often jovial, repartee between buyer and seller. Bargaining is only done in the public markets, and some of the artisans' markets.

COMMUNICATIONS AND MEDIA

Mailing and Shipping

Mailing and shipping from Mexico is easy within certain limitations. Packages of less than US$25

in value can be sent to the United States. The package must be marked "Unsolicited Gift—Under $25" and addressed to someone other than the traveler. Only one package per day may be sent to the same addressee. Major stores will handle shipping arrangements on larger items and duty must be paid; this is in addition to the US$400 carried in person across the border.

Almost every town of any size in the Yucatán has a post office. If you can't find it by looking, ask—it may be located in someone's front parlor. Airmail postage is recommended for the best delivery. Post offices will hold travelers' mail for one week if it is marked a/c Lista de Correos ("care of General Delivery"). Hotels will extend the same service for mail marked "tourist mail, hold for arrival."

Telephone

One of the newest additions to the Yucatán Peninsula as well as other parts of Mexico is a scattering of Direct Dial USA telephone booths. Shiny new touch-tone phones bring you in direct contact with an American operator who will either charge the call to your telephone credit card or make it collect. Look for phones labeled **Ladatel**. Many of these phones use telephone cards available at small markets and pharmacies. The cards are sold in 10, 20, 30, and 50 peso amounts; when you use the card a digital screen shows how much money your call is costing and deducts it from the value of the card. It comes in very handy when calling ahead to confirm hotel rooms or making other arrangements, and it's certainly better than carrying peso coins. The card is quick and efficient and eliminates the language barrier as well as the often-long waits.

However, until the phones are installed in the small towns, expect the same old rules. Hotels (if they have phones) add enormous service charges to direct calls—always ask what it will be first. Calling collect is cheaper, and going to a *larga distancia* office is the most economical. Remember that although the Ladatel phones are really convenient, they are costly if you talk for any length of time, collect or not. Many think the "user-friendly" quality is worth the price.

Note: Fax machines are becoming very common, but can also be expensive. In some smaller towns, one fax services the entire town, so messages can be delayed because the sender

---

YUCATÁN PENINSULA POSTAL CODES

Cancún	77500
Campeche	24000
Chetumal	77000
Cozumel	77600
Isla Mujeres	77400
Playa del Carmen	77710
Mérida	97000
San Cristóbal	29200

YUCATÁN PENINSULA TELEPHONE AREA CODES

Campeche	981
Cancún	98
Chetumal	983
Chiapa de Corzo	968
Chichén Itzá	985
Cozumel	987
Felipe Carillo Puerto	983
Isla Mujeres	987
Izama	995
Mérida	99
Palenque	934
Piste	985
Playa del Carmen	987
Puerto Celestun	991
San Cristóbal	967
Ticul	997
Tuxtla	961
Uxmal	99
Valladolid	985
Villahermosa	93

must compete with everyone else and encounters a constant busy signal.

Radio and Television

AM and FM radio stations, in Spanish, are scattered throughout the Peninsula. Television is becoming more common as well. In the major cities, hotel rooms have TV entertainment. The large resort hotels in Cancún, Cozumel, and Mérida and surroundings have one or more cable stations from the U.S., on which you can expect to see all the major baseball and football games, news, and latest movies, sometime CNN.

STANDARDS AND MEASUREMENTS

Time

The states of the Yucatán Peninsula are in the U.S. Central Standard Time Zone. From April to October, all states except Quintana Roo switch to daylight saving time (or Central Daylight Time).

Electricity

Electric current has been standardized throughout Mexico, using the same 60-cycle, 110-volt AC current common in the United States. Small travel appliances can be used everywhere; if you have a problem, it will be because there's no electricity at all. In some areas electricity is supplied by small generators and is usually turned off at 10 p.m. Those hotels usually will offer you gas lanterns for use after the lights go out. Some areas use solar and wind generators for electric lights only, if the sun is behind clouds for a couple of days, or the wind dies, lights can be really dim.

Measurements

Mexico uses the metric system of weights and measures. Distances are measured in km, weights are measured in grams and kilograms, gasoline is sold by the liter, and temperatures are given on the Celsius scale. A chart at the back of this book will help visitors accustomed to the Anglo-American system of measurement make the appropriate conversions.

OTHER VISITOR SERVICES

Studying In Mexico

In addition to fulfilling the requirements for a tourist card, students wishing to study in Mexico must present documents to a Mexican consulate demonstrating that they have been ac-

USEFUL TELEPHONE NUMBERS

Assistance

Emergencies	06
Directory Assistance (within Mexico)	01
Long-distance Operator	02
International operator (English)	09

Long-Distance Dialing
Mexico long-distance: 91 (92 for person-to-person) + area code + number
International long-distance: 98 (99 for person-to-person) + area code + number
U.S. long-distance: 95 (96 for person-to-person) + area code + number

Long-Distance via U.S. Services:

AT&T	001-95-800-462-4240
MCI	001-95-800-674-7000
Sprint	001-95-800-877-8000

cepted at an educational institution and that they are financially solvent. A number of courses and workshops lasting two to eight weeks are offered throughout Mexico in addition to full-time study programs. Many adults as well as younger folks take part in language programs in which the student lives with a Spanish-speaking family for a period of two to four weeks and attends language classes daily. This total immersion into the language, even for a short time, is quite successful and popular as a cultural experience.

Write to the National Registration Center for Study Abroad (NRCSA), 823 N. Second St., Milwaukee, WI 53203 USA. Request their "Directory of Educational Programs," which describes programs in a number of cities in Mexico.

Churches and Clubs

Mexico is predominantly a Catholic country. However, you'll find a few churches of other denominations in the larger cities; evangelical churches are becoming common. Local telephone books and hotel clerks have these listings. Many international organizations like the Lions, Rotary, Shriners, and foreign social groups have branches on the Yucatán Peninsula which welcome visitors.

U.S. Embassies and Consulates

If an American citizen finds him- or herself with a problem of any kind, the nearest consul will provide advice or help. Travel advisories with up-to-the-minute information about traveling in remote areas of Mexico are available.

DIANA LASICH HARPER

KATHY ESCOVEDO SANDERS

QUINTANA ROO

INTRODUCTION

The Land and Sea

The state of Quintana Roo (kin-taw-nuh-ROW) is on the Yucatán Peninsula's east coast and bordered by the Mexican states of Yucatán to the northwest and Campeche to the west, and the countries of Belize and Guatemala to the south. Quintana Roo occupies 50,350 square km and has a population of over 600,000. Mostly flat, this long, isolated state is covered with tropical forest and boasts the most beautiful white-sand beaches on the Peninsula. Several islands lie offshore, and the magnificent 250-km-long Belize Reef—whose abundant undersea life makes for world-class diving—runs parallel to the Caribbean coast from the tip of Isla Mujeres to the Bay of Honduras. Chetumal, capital of the state, borders Belize.

History

The east coast of Quintana Roo is lined with Maya ruins, ranging from tiny "watchtowers" in Cancún to the relative grandeur of Tulum. Al-

though there is evidence of earlier occupation, particularly in Tancah, Xcaret, and Xelha, and although some structures may even post-date the Spanish Conquest, most of the Maya structures were built during the Late Post-Classic period (A.D. 1200-1530). This was the heyday of the Putún Maya traders, who frequented the Gulf and Caribbean coasts of Mesoamerica in large, seagoing canoes (Columbus encountered one off the coast of Honduras on his final voyage). Most of the Late Post-Classic buildings along Quintana Roo's coast were probably built either by the Putún or at their urging to serve as ports, way stations, and lighthouses for their trade.

Mexico ignored this stretched-out coastal region longer than the rest of the Peninsula because of its dense jungle and notorious Chan Santa Cruz Indians. The only real Spanish settlement, Bacalar, on the southern end of the state, was destroyed once by pirates and again by rioting Maya during the Caste War. When defeated by the Spanish, many Maya took refuge in this coastal territory, easily keeping would-be intruders at bay until the beginning of the 20th century.

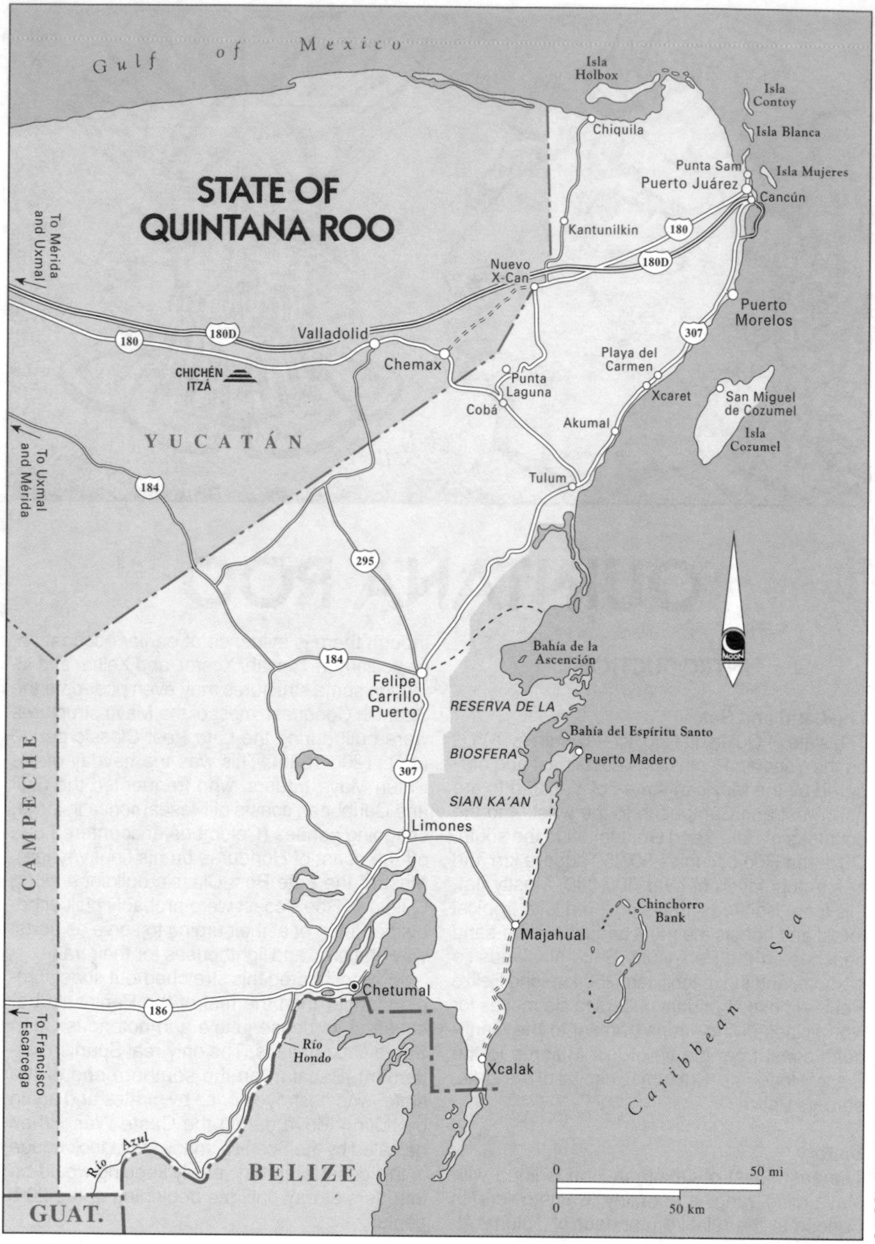

STATE OF QUINTANA ROO

Gulf of Mexico

Isla Holbox
Chiquila
Isla Contoy
Isla Blanca
Punta Sam
Puerto Juárez
Isla Mujeres
Cancún
Kantunilkin
180
Nuevo X-Can
180D
Puerto Morelos
307

To Mérida and Uxmal

180
180D
Valladolid
Chemax
CHICHÉN ITZÁ

Playa del Carmen
Punta Laguna
Cobá
Xcaret
San Miguel de Cozumel
Akumal
Isla Cozumel

YUCATÁN

To Uxmal and Mérida

184
295
Tulum

184

Felipe Carrillo Puerto

Bahía de la Ascención

RESERVA DE LA

307
BIOSFERA
Bahía del Espíritu Santo
Puerto Madero

SIAN KA'AN

Limones

CAMPECHE

Chinchorro Bank

Majahual

Caribbean Sea

To Francisco Escárcega

186
Chetumal
Río Hondo
Xcalak

Río Azul
BELIZE

GUAT.

0   50 mi
0   50 km

© MOON PUBLICATIONS, INC.

ARCHAEOLOGICAL ZONES OF QUINTANA ROO

Tulum	Xelha
Cobá	Kohunlich

For many years, the east coast of the Yucatán Peninsula remained a desolate no-man's land; it had no name because few people ever spoke about it. But when it became a territory, it needed a name. As is often the custom in Mexico, the territory was named for an army general, undoubtedly a sterling soldier who deserved the honor. But sadly the man had not fought a battle in, nor had he ever traveled to, the territory of this Caribbean paradise. His name was Andrés Quintana Roo.

Quintana Roo was held as a territory of the Republic for 73 years, then admitted as Mexico's 30th state in 1974. Highways weren't built here until the 1970s, when Mexico finally realized that

Quintana Roo possessed all the elements necessary to make it one of the world's most beautiful resort areas.

Economy

Native hardwood trees on the southern end of the peninsula have always been in demand, coconuts and fishing have long contributed to the economy, and for a few years in the early 1900s, the chicle boom brought a flurry of activity centered around the harbor of Isla Cozumel. But none of these industries amounted to much, and life in Quintana Roo was slow and gentle until 1968—the year road construction began to and from the sand dune now known as Cancún. Now the face of Quintana Roo has changed. Tourism is the state's number-one attraction, and Cancún is a multimillion-dollar resort with 24,000 rooms luring tourists to sea and sand. Building and construction continue expanding south down the Peninsula, bringing new roads to previously unknown beaches and unseen Maya structures.

CANCÚN

In 1967 a data-crunching computer selected a small, swampy finger of land in an isolated part of the Mexican Caribbean as Mexico's most promising tourist town—Cancún resort was born. Lying on an island connected by bridges with the mainland, the city was designed from the ground up. The resort sprang into being with new infrastructure, modern electrical plants, purified tap water, paved tree-lined avenues, and buildings resembling Maya temples. When the first hotel opened its doors in 1972, visitors began coming and haven't stopped since.

For some, the name Cancún conjures immediate images of sugar-fine sand, a palette-blue sea, and flashing dollar signs. Absolutely! The beaches *are* stunning and the water *is* enticing, but it can be costly to enjoy Cancún—especially if you just "drop in" at one of the fabulous resorts in the hotel zone. However, with careful shopping for package deals from your travel agent or in the travel pages of your local newspaper, you'll find something to fit your pocketbook.

Curiously, even high prices haven't slowed down the visitors. Today not only Americans

and Canadians come to Cancún; the hotels are filled with visitors from all over the globe, and one of the many cruise ships calling on Cancún travels back and forth from Italy.

SIGHTS

Archaeological Zones

Cancún's archaeological zones are minor compared to the big sites spread throughout the Yucatán Peninsula. But structures uncovered on this narrow strip of land have contributed important information to our knowledge about the people who lived here hundreds of years ago. Remnants of two sites, **Ruinas del Rey** on the south end of the island (at the Caesar Park Cancún Resort), and **Yamil Lu'um** next to the Sheraton Hotel, are both worth a look.

To view Ruinas del Rey, head for the golf course on the lagoon side of the resort. The remains of the Post-Classic structure consist of a few platforms, two plazas, and a small pyramid. It is said that when the ruins were originally ex-

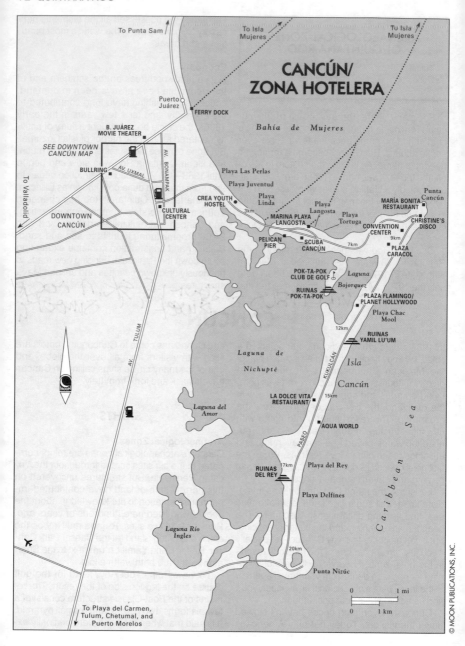

To Punta Sam

To Isla
Mujeres

Tu Isla
Mujeres

CANCÚN/
ZONA HOTELERA

Puerto
Juárez

FERRY DOCK

Bahía de Mujeres

B. JUÁREZ
MOVIE THEATER

*SEE DOWNTOWN
CANCÚN MAP*

BULLRING

AV. UXMAL

AV. BONAMPAK

AV.

CULTURAL
CENTER

DOWNTOWN
CANCÚN

To Valladolid

Playa Las Perlas

Playa Juventud

CREA YOUTH
HOSTEL

Playa
Linda

3km

Playa
Langosta

Playa
Tortuga

MARÍA BONITA
RESTAURANT

Punta
Cancún

MARINA PLAYA
LANGOSTA

CONVENTION
CENTER

CHRISTINE'S
DISCO

PELICAN
PIER

SCUBA
CANCÚN

7km

9km

PLAZA
CARACOL

POK-TA-POK
CLUB DE GOLF

*Laguna
Bojorquez*

RUINAS
POK-TA-POK

PLAZA FLAMINGO/
PLANET HOLLYWOOD

Playa Chac
Mool

12km

RUINAS
YAMIL LU'UM

AV. TULUM

*Laguna de
Nichupté*

*Isla
Cancún*

KUKULCAN

LA DOLCE VITA
RESTAURANT

15km

*Laguna del
Amor*

AQUA WORLD

C a r i b b e a n   S e a

PASEO

RUINAS
DEL REY

17km

Playa del Rey

Playa Delfines

*Laguna Río
Ingles*

20km

Punta Nizúc

0   1 mi

0   1 km

To Playa del Carmen,
Tulum, Chetumal, and
Puerto Morelos

© MOON PUBLICATIONS, INC.

enjoying the sun and the sea, Cancún

cavated, a skeleton believed to be a king was un-covered, hence the "del Rey" ("of the King").

Yamil Lu'um is on the highest point of mostly flat Cancún. The two small temples (15 meters high) were probably used as watchtowers and lighthouses along this navigational route. Between 400 and 700 years old, they were first noted in 1841 by two intrepid American explorers, John L. Stephens and Frederick Catherwood.

Laguna de Nichupté

This large lagoon, ringed by Paseo Kukulcán, is fed by a combination of freshwater from underground springs and saltwater that enters from two openings to the sea. In certain areas where the water is still and swampy, mangroves provide hiding places for the cayman, little brother of large crocodilians found on other parts of the Peninsula. Birdlife is plentiful, with a treasure trove of over 200 cataloged species including herons, egrets, ospreys, parrots, and parakeets; the sooty tern returns here to nest each year.

The best way to see the lagoon and its wildlife is by boat. You can arrange a boat and guide at your hotel or at any travel agent in town.

Along the north end of the large lagoon the marinas bustle with activity, and the trim greens of the Pok Ta Pok golf course extend out over the water. Nichupté is a favorite for water-skiing, sailing (Sunfish and Hobie Cat rentals), riding Wave Runners, and sailboarding.

BEACHES

All of Cancún is scenic. But the most scenic beaches are on the seaward side of the island, a 21-km stretch along Paseo Kukulcán. Walking along the coast is rated a five-star activity, and it's free (all beaches in Mexico are public). The panorama is capricious—the color of the sea changes subtly throughout the day from pale aqua at dawn to deep turquoise at noon to cerulean blue under the blazing afternoon sun to pink-splashed purple during the elegant sunset.

Hotel Beaches

The hotel-zone hotels all have beaches; some provide their guests with a variety of facilities, including *palapa* sun shelters, volleyball courts, aerobics classes, bars, restaurants, showers, restrooms, towels, and lifeguards. Note, however, that everyone is free to use the 18-meter (60-foot) strip of sand along the sea on any part of Cancún; signs indicating this are prominently posted everywhere by SECTUR, the Ministry of Tourism.

Public Beaches

Don't expect lifeguards or showers on these beaches; some have snack stands and good parking areas. **Playa Linda** is close to the city (10 minutes by bus) on Paseo Kukulcán near the Nichupté bridge. Two km past Playa Linda on Paseo Kukulcán is **Playa Tortuga,** where the water is clear, calm, and deep and a *palapa*-covered snack bar serves beachgoers.

Playa Chac Mool is beyond the Convention Center, around Punta Cancún and then south. This stunning beach displays the vibrant colors that make the Caribbean famous. You can walk out to sea 14 meters in shallow water before it begins to drop off. Check the tide conditions on the sign just south of the beach cafe—the water at times gets rough. **Playa Delfines** at the south end of the hotel zone is a favorite of locals, since this stretch of sand is free of hotels thus far. Sunset-watching from the low rise over the beach here is particularly fine.

Swimming

The calmest and most protected ocean beaches face Bahía de Mujeres on the north end of the island; the stretch of beach from the youth hostel to Playa Linda usually provides calm water. The lagoon is also usually calm, but not as clear as the sea.

The water on the ocean side of Cancún can be hazardous. Many beaches do *not* have lifeguards. None of the Cancún beaches are suitable for surfing, but from Punta Cancún to Punta Nizúc the surf can be as high as three feet, and at certain times you'll encounter an undertow. Pay particular attention to warning flags (green is okay, yellow is dangerous, and red is STAY OUT). If you don't see a water-condition sign, ask at the concession stand; when in doubt, don't swim. Each year a few people drown off the beaches of Cancún because of a lack of respect for the power of this beautiful sea.

Getting to the Beach

Cancún is one big beach, or more accurately, a series of breathtaking beaches laid end to end. It's simple to reach any beach by bus; the bus route begins in downtown Cancún and makes a circuit the length of Paseo Kukulcán and back. The buses are modern, comfortable, and inexpensive. Remember that the locals use these buses to get to and from work, so expect them to be crowded during the commute hours. Fare is about US$0.40 anywhere, and buses run 24 hours a day. Bus stops are numerous and marked with blue signs that read "Parada." Most drivers will also stop for a waving arm almost anywhere (if there's room).

WATER SPORTS

Snorkeling

Cancún's sandy sea floor doesn't hold the cool caves and rocky crevices that attract abundant sea life; expert snorkelers will want to head for one of the several nearby reefs. In the immediate vicinity the most popular are Chital, Cuevones, and Manchones Reefs (see "Scuba Diving," below), which are composed of a variety of uniquely shaped and textured coral and are home to large populations of reef fish, including blue chromis and barracuda. Dive boats make scuba trips to these reefs and will usually take snorkelers along (room permitting).

For beginners (including children), Cancún is a great place to learn to snorkel. Though not as full of sea life as the reefs, the many areas of calm water around the hotel zone are by no means barren; you'll see plenty of sun-loving fish such as tanned beauties and burnt-back beach nappers. Guests at the Camino Real Cancún have access to a calm, artificial lagoon ideal for viewing tropical fish and sea turtles from small to large. Intermediates can head to Punta Nizúc, where coral outcroppings attract large numbers of fish. Parque Nacional El Garrafón, across from Cancún on Isla Mujeres, is another good spot for beginners and intermediates; tour boats go there daily from Cancún and carry snorkeling equipment. Snorkeling equipment is also available for rent at all the marinas and some of the hotels.

Scuba Diving

For the experienced scuba diver, Cancún would be a distant second choice to Cozumel, but as dive spots go, none of the Caribbean is dull.

At **Punta Nizúc** (next to Club Med), divers and snorkelers can explore the starting point of the Belize Barrier Reef, which runs parallel to the Quintana Roo coast some 250 km (150 miles) south to the Gulf of Honduras. It's the world's fifth-longest reef. Unfortunately, all the boat activity around Punta Nizúc has had a heavy impact and most of the coral here is dead. Tropical fish still swarm to the area, however.

One of the most popular local reefs, despite its shallow depths, is **Chital,** a short distance north of the Hotel Presidente. The reef is made up of two sections, both about 20 meters wide. Expect a one-knot current and clear visibility up to 33 meters.

At **Cuevones Reef,** about three km north of Punta Cancún, the body of the reef is comprised of elkhorn, rock, and brain corals. Several small caves *(cuevones)* at a depth of about 10 me-

boats will give you a good fast ride if the wind is up. Negotiate for the fee—sometimes you can get a good daily rate, better than the hourly rate posted.

In a brisk breeze, sailboards (aka Windsurfers) provide exhilarating rides—skimming across the waves at mind-blowing speeds. Lessons are available at most of the marinas or at the International Windsurfer Sailing School at Playa Tortuga, tel. (98) 84-2023. Usually six hours of lessons will give you a good start. Sailboards are available for rent at many of the hotels and marinas.

Parasailing

Parasailing is popular at the busy beaches. The rider, strapped into a colorful parachute and safety vest, is pulled high over the sand and surf by a speedboat; after about 10 minutes of "flying" he or she is gently deposited back on land with the help of two catchers. Once in a while the rider is inadvertently dropped in the bay—usually to the guffaws of the beach crowd. Most hotels post signs stating they are not responsible for parasailing accidents and injuries that occur by their beaches. Accidents do happen; watch a few passengers take the trip before you go up, and check the harnesses for wear and tear.

Marina Aqua Ray, on the lagoon by Lorenzillo's restaurant, tel. (98) 83-3007, has the newest angle on parasailing with its Skyrider Parasail, a two-seater attached to the parachute, giving the riders an enhanced sense of comfort and safety.

Other Water Sports

Water-skiing is popular in Cancún; most skiers prefer Laguna Nichupté, although some can often be seen on calm days in Bahía de Mujeres north of the island. Equipment and instruction information are available from the marinas.

You'll see a lot of **personal watercraft**—Jet Skis and Wave Runners—on the lagoon. These speedy water-cycles really move! **Kayaking** is becoming popular in the Caribbean, and many hotels now offer kayaks to their guests free of charge.

At the Marinas

Marina Aqua Ray, Paseo Kukulcán Km 10.5 (on the lagoon at Lorenzillo's restaurant), tel. (98) 83-3007 or 83-1773, U.S. tel. (800) 833-5402, is one of the largest operations in Can-

OZ MALLAN

Cancún parasailing

ters attract large schools of reef fish, groupers, amberjack, and the ever-lurking predatory barracudas. Visibility to 45 meters.

Manchones Reef is a shallow reef closer to Isla Mujeres (three km south) than to Cancún (eight km northeast). Its 10-meter depth, 60-meter visibility, lack of current, and abundant sea life make it an ideal dive site for beginners.

Cancún has a good selection of dive shops that provide equipment rentals and instruction; check with the marinas for recommendations. Before a diver can rent equipment, it's necessary to show a certified diver's card. Resort courses (for one dive accompanied by the divemaster) and certification classes are offered. For information, call **Mundo Marina** (PADI), tel. (98) 83-0554; **Neptune** (NAUI), tel. (98) 83-0722; **Aqua Tours,** tel. (98) 83-0400, fax (98) 83-0403; or **Scuba Cancún,** (NAUI and PADI), tel. (98) 83-1011.

Sailing and Windsurfing

Hobie Cat and Sunfish rentals are available at a few hotels and most of the marinas. These small

cún, with a good safety record and a responsible attitude toward Cancún's fragile ecology. They rent Wave Runners, Jet Skis, water skis, kayaks, and snorkeling and diving gear, and operate several different tours to the lagoons and reefs. Their **Aqua Ray Jungle Tour** is a 2.5-hour boat trip through the lagoons, with a stop for snorkeling near Punta Nizúc. The **Reef Express** is a 30-minute boat shuttle to Marina Aqua Ray's floating water-sports center just off Punta Nizúc, where you can hang out on an anchored dock (with refreshments and sun deck), snorkel in the surrounding shallow reefs, or catch a ride on the **SubSea Explorer,** which has below-deck windows for viewing undersea life. The marina also offers parasailing, sportfishing, diving, and sightseeing tours.

Aqua Tours marina, Paseo Kukulcán Km 6.25 (by Fat Tuesday's), tel. (98) 83-0400 or 83-1860, fax (98) 83-0403, offers scuba diving, snorkeling, jungle tours, sportfishing, water-skiing, Isla Mujeres cruises, a floating casino cruise, and a lobster dinner cruise. **Royal Yacht Club,** Paseo Kukulcán Km 16.5 (by the Captain's Cove restaurant and Royal Mayan hotel), tel. (98) 85-0391 or 85-2930, offers a variety of water sports and tours plus canoe rentals, and has showers and lockers at the rental area.

Pelican Pier, Paseo Kukulcán Km 5.5, tel. (98) 83-0315, offers sportfishing trips as well as spectacular flights over Cancún in an ultralight plane. They also have a Cessna used for air-taxi service. **Mundo Marina,** Paseo Kukulcán Km 5.5, tel. (98) 83-0554, offers snorkeling, diving, sportfishing, and cruises. **Marina Playa Langosta,** Paseo Kukulcán at Playa Langosta, tel. (98) 83-2802, arranges sportfishing trips and cruises.

FISHING

Anglers come to Cancún for some of the world's finest sportfishing. Charters are available and easily arranged with a day or two advance reservation; call the marinas or check with your hotel. Sportfishing trips including gear for up to six passengers run about US$320 per trip for four hours, US$520 for eight hours. On full-day trips you can cap off the afternoon with a fish barbecue on the beach (ask the captain in advance). One of the most exciting game fishes, the sail-

fish, runs from March to mid-July. Bonito and dorado run from May to early July, wahoo and kingfish from May to September. Barracuda, red snapper, bluefin, grouper, and mackerel are plentiful all year.

Another trip currently popular among anglers is a flyfishing excursion south of Cancún for permit, bonefish, and tarpon (all catch and release). Ask at your hotel.

LAND-BASED SPORTS

Golf and Tennis

The **Pok Ta Pok Club de Golf,** Paseo Kukulcán Km 7.5, tel. (98) 83-1277 or 82-1230, fax (98) 83-3358, has tennis courts and a well-kept 18-hole golf course designed by Robert Trent Jones. The golf club is a great sports center, with a pro shop, swimming pool, marina, restaurant, bar, and even its own small restored Maya ruin near the 12th hole, discovered when the course was built. Temporary club membership allows you to play golf or tennis at the club; arrangements can be made through your hotel. Greens fees are about US$50, with an additional US$30 for golf cart rental.

Another fine golf course is at **Caesar Park Cancún Resort,** right at the water's edge. This par-72 course surrounds small Maya ruins in a beautifully landscaped environment. More golf courses are found along the Caribbean coast going south.

Many of the hotels on the island have tennis courts, some with night lighting, open to non-guests for a fee.

Horseback Riding

Rancho Loma Bonita, south of Cancún near Puerto Morelos, tel. (98) 84-0907, provides horses for rides along the sea or into the jungle in a wide variety of locations. Transportation to and from the ranch, drinks, lunch, and a guide are included in the rates. Make arrangements through your hotel tour desk or call the ranch directly.

Spectator Sports

Bullfighting has long been a popular pageant for Latin countries. Cancún's bullring is on Av. Bonampak at Sayil, tel. (98) 84-5465 or 84-8372. Bullfights are held every Wednesday at 3:30 p.m. and are preceded by a Mexican fiesta with folkloric dance performances at 2:30 p.m. Tickets are available through tour desks or at the bullring.

Jai-alai is Cancún's newest spectator sport and is played in the enormous purple **Gambling Palace,** on Paseo Kukulcán by Playa Linda, which opened in 1993. Jai-alai games are played nightly 6 p.m.-midnight; dinner is served on the upper level of the viewing area, and betting on the players is encouraged. Also in the palace is the Super Book, tel. (98) 83-9000, where viewers bet on major sporting events and horse races broadcast over satellite television from the United States. Super Book is open daily 1 p.m.-midnight.

TOURS AND DAY-TRIPS

Boat Tours to Isla Mujeres

A variety of boat tours go from Cancún to nearby Isla Mujeres. You can ride in a glass-bottom boat and slowly drift above flamboyant undersea gardens, take a musical cruise that lets you dance your way over to the small island, or enjoy cruises based on any number of other themes and activities. These tours often include snorkeling, and the necessary equipment is furnished (though there may be an added rental charge).

The **Aqua-Quin** is a motorized trimaran going twice daily for snorkeling at Playa Garrafón; it includes a buffet lunch, open bar, music, and fun. Reservations required. The **Crucero Tropical Cruiser Morning Express** includes a continental breakfast, snorkeling at Garrafón, time for shopping, lunch at the Pirate's Village on the island, and an open bar. The boat is a/c and departs from the Playa Langosta dock at 10:30 a.m., returning at 4:30 p.m. Fare is US$45 pp; tel. (98) 83-3268.

The **B/M Carnaval Cancún,** a large triple decker, serves an onboard buffet lunch with an open bar, stops for snorkeling, and allows time for shopping in downtown Isla Mujeres. Called the **Caribbean Funday** tour, the boat leaves the Fat Tuesday pier daily. Fare is US$50, plus US$5 to rent snorkel gear; tel. (98) 84-3760. The same ship is used for the evening Caribbean Carnaval cruise to Isla Mujeres, which includes a buffet dinner, open bar, and Caribbean floor show for US$60 pp.

Atlantis is an imitation submarine that takes visitors to the edges of Manchones Reef to view the fish and coral, and to the nearby wreck of the SS *Elizabeth.* It's an adventure second only to being in scuba gear and swimming the reef. The boat then proceeds to Isla Mujeres beach where you can go swimming or just relax in the restaurant and bar. *Atlantis* departs from Cancún's Playa Linda hourly. For more information call (98) 83-3021.

Dolphin Express offers another good daytrip to Isla Mujeres. This all-inclusive trip takes you to Pirate Village to see and swim with the dolphins; continental breakfast on board and lunch at the village are included. The trip fare is about US$30; to swim with the dolphins is another US$65 (rumors have it the price is going up). Departure time from Playa Langosta Pier is 10 a.m., return 4:30 p.m. For reservations, call (98) 83-3283 or 83-1488.

For information on getting to Isla Mujeres on your own, see "Getting There" in the Isla Mujeres section.

Aqua World

This water park in the hotel zone on Paseo Kukulcán opposite the Melia Cancún Hotel, tel. (98) 85-2288, offers all the water toys you could ask for, plus jungle tours, diving trips, and deepsea fishing trips. It's also the departure point for the **Cancún Queen** paddleboat dinner/party cruise.

Xcaret

One of the most popular day-trips from Cancún goes to **Xcaret,** a manmade water park a half-hour drive south of Cancún. Wildly decorated a/c buses depart between 9 and 10 a.m. from the Xcaret terminal on Paseo Kukulcán across from Plaza Caracol, next to the Fiesta Americana Coral Beach Hotel, returning in late afternoon. The tour costs US$30, including transportation and park entrance; meals and dolphin activities within the park are not included. Tours including the ruins of Tulum with a stop at Xcaret are also available. Call (98) 83-0654 or 83-0743 for information.

Taxi Tours

One way to make sure you see the sights you want to see around Cancún without having to follow a group itinerary is to hire an English-speaking taxi driver for an hour or a day. Rates start at US$10 per hour if you stay within the Cancún limits, and get higher the farther you travel. For information, contact the taxi drivers' union, tel. (98) 83-1840 or 83-1844.

Isla Holbox

One of the best side trips from Cancún for nature lovers is to diminutive Isla Holbox off the north coast of the Yucatán Peninsula. A natural preserve and bird refuge, Holbox is mostly mangrove swamp and marks the division between the Gulf of Mexico and the Caribbean Sea. Only a few hundred people live on the island, supporting themselves by fishing and hammock weaving. There's a hammock loom in front of nearly every house; this is a great place to see how they're made. The islanders are not accustomed to tourists, and your presence will likely be greeted with curious stares and friendly advances.

To get to Holbox you'll need a rental car and a sense of adventure. Drive west out of Cancún toward Mérida on the old road (not the *autopista*). Near the town of Vicente Guerrero you'll see a road on the right heading north to Kantunilkin. If you miss that, there's another side road heading north near Nuevo X-Can. Your ultimate destination is Chiquila—ask for directions often. The paved road heads north to Kantunilkin past small ranches and pueblos; after about 65 miles you will reach the tiny settlement of Chiquila on the north coast. A fishing community with few residents and even fewer guests, Chiquila is the departure point for the car ferry to Isla Holbox, which runs only a few days a week, and then only if the demand is high enough. A few *palapa* restaurants on the beach here serve cold drinks and superb lunches of fresh fish and lobster. As an alternative to the unpredictable ferry, you can hire a captain and boat from among the Chiquila fishermen; a typical tour of the island will take about four hours. There are no hotels in Chiquila or on Holbox, but camping is permitted, or you may be able to arrange to stay in a local home. We've had reports that you can also hire a boat in Punta Sam or on Isla Mujeres for a tour around Isla Holbox.

Tikal

The Guatemalan airline **Aviateca** operates a one-day tour that takes you by air from Cancún to the spectacular Maya ruins of Tikal, in the Guatemalan highlands. The plane departs Cancún at 6 a.m. and lands at Flores, about a 20-minute drive from the ruins. You get five hours to explore Tikal, which many consider to be the most spectacular of the Maya sites. Wildlife is abundant; spider monkeys swing from the treetops along heavily wooded paths, and parrots fly overhead. Vendors sell Guatemalan crafts and folk art in the ruins parking lot for prices far lower than those at Cancún shops, where Guatemalan crafts have overshadowed those from Mexico. The plane returns to Cancún at 6 p.m. For information, contact your hotel tour desk or Aviateca at Plaza Mexico, Av. Tulum 200, tel. (98) 84-3938 or 87-1386.

Other airlines flying from Cancún to Flores include **Mexicana** airlines (which also offers Tikal tours), tel. (98) 84-2000, and Aerocaribe, with flights on Tuesday, Thursday, Saturday, and Sunday for about US$69 one-way.

Other Nearby Destinations

Flights are available from Cancún to **Cuba,** which is still off-limits to American citizens. The U.S. State Dept. will not help Americans who go there and get into trouble, but many folks take the chance. Flight information is easy to get at any of the many travel agencies scattered about Cancún.

From Cancún you can fly to **Belize City** on Aerocaribe. Planes leave Tuesday, Thursday, Saturday, and Sunday; fare is about US$79 one-way. This is a new service and anything can happen. I've heard that the flight is canceled if there aren't enough passengers; you'd be wise to check with your travel agent. From Belize City it's easy to rent a car or hop a bus to the Maya sites, or find a boat to take you to the many beautiful offshore cays.

Aviateca, Plaza Mexico, Av. Tulum 200, tel. (98) 84-3938 or 87-1386, also offers extended tours of Guatemala and flights to **Guatemala City.**

ACCOMMODATIONS

At last count, Cancún held 122 hotels and more than 24,000 rooms. Budget hotels are few. At the other end of the spectrum, the luxury accommodations of Cancún's hotel zone are the most modern hostelries on Mexico's Caribbean coast.

USEFUL HOTEL ZONE TELEPHONE NUMBERS

MORE HOTELS

Cancún Playa Oasis	(98) 85-1111
Caribbean Princess Resort . . .	(98) 83-2579
Caribbean Village	(98) 85-0112
Continental Villas Plaza	(98) 83-0102
Holiday Inn Express Cancún . .	(98) 83-2200
Jack Tar Village Resort	(98) 85-1366
Marriott Casa Magna Cancún. .	(98) 85-2000
Melia Cancún	(98) 85-1114
Oasis Cancún	(98) 85-0867
Omni Cancún Hotel & Villas. . .	(98) 85-0714
Piramides Cancún Beach Resort	(98) 85-1333
Royal Sands Presidential Retreat	(98) 83-4939
Sierra Radisson Plaza.	(98) 83-2444
Sun Palace.	(98) 85-1555
Yalmakan Cancún	(98) 85-2222

GOLF COURSES

Caesar Park	(98) 81-8000
Melia Cancún	(98) 85-1114
Pok-ta-Pok	(98) 83-0871

Shuttle Boats to Isla Mujeres and Cozumel:
(98) 83-3448 or 83-3583. Boats leave from
Playa Tortugas Terminal (next to Fat Tuesday)
several times each day. Roundtrip fare to
Cozumel US$26, to Isla Mujeres, US$13.

Rates are lowest in late spring and fall; some hotels raise their rates in August when Mexicans and Europeans typically take long vacations. Rates rise 20-50% around Thanksgiving and again at Christmas, with some hotels actually doubling their rates for the week between Christmas and New Year's Day. Package deals provide the best prices year-round. As one hotel representative told us, "Nobody books a room at rack rates in Cancún anymore." Packages vary and may include reduced airfare, reduced rates for stays of three or more nights, reduced car rental rates, and perks such as welcome cocktails, free meals, and free use of sports/fitness facilities. Have your travel agent check all these op-

tions, and keep an eye out for package deals advertised in newspapers and magazines. You can get amazing bargains when occupancy is low, even in the high season. Keep in mind that most prices you'll be quoted do not include the 12% room tax.

Zona Hotelera
Almost every hotel in the hotel zone falls into our Premium price category. Most offer one or more swimming pools; good beaches and beach activities; an assortment of restaurants, bars, and nightlife; gardens; travel, tour, and car-rental agencies; and laundry and room service.

Shoestring: The best bargain in Cancún is the CREA Youth Hostel, tel. (98) 83-1337, on Paseo Kukulcán next to Club Verano Beat. The hostel has a beach (not always in the best condition), swimming pool, bar, inexpensive dining room, and 650 bunk beds in women's and men's dorms.

Expensive: The several low-rise buildings of **Days Inn El Pueblito,** tel. (98) 85-0797, fax (98) 85-0731, U.S. tel. (800) 325-2525, are staggered down a slight hill above the sea. Swimming pools flow between the buildings; the largest sports a swim-up bar. Kids hang out at the water slide, while quiet-seeking grownups will find plenty of lounging room away from all the commotion. El Pueblito is a good choice for families, since the rooms are comfortable rather than fancy, and the grounds and beach offer plenty of play space.

The **Carrousel,** tel. (98) 83-2312, fax (98) 83-2312, U.S. tel. (800) 333-1212, is simple but comfy and on the beach. The **Aristos,** tel. (98) 83-0011, fax (98) 83-0078, U.S. tel. (800) 527-4786, is popular with families and Mexican tourists. Closer to the major malls, discos, and restaurants are **Calinda Viva,** on a nice beach near Plaza Caracol, tel. (98) 83-0800, fax (98) 83-2087, U.S. tel. (800) 221-2222; and **Miramar Mission,** tel. (98) 83-1755, fax (98) 83-1136, which is popular with tour groups.

Premium: One of the all-time favorites is the durable **Camino Real Cancún,** tel. (98) 83-0100, fax (98) 83-2965, U.S. tel. (800) 722-6466. You have plenty of space at this place, which is spread out on lovely grounds on the tip of the island. The rooms have beautiful views with private balconies and cable TV. Other amenities include beaches, a pool, and a small artificial "la-

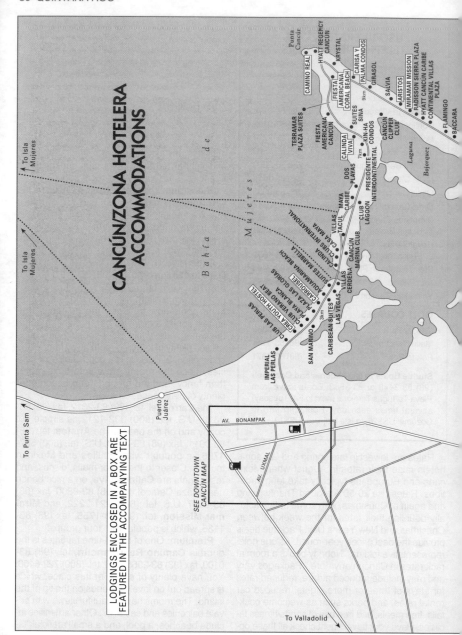

CANCÚN/ZONA HOTELERA ACCOMMODATIONS

To Punta Sam

To Isla Mujeres

To Isla Mujeres

Bahía   de   Mujeres

Puerto Juárez

Punta Cancún

HYATT REGENCY CANCUN
CAMINO REAL
CRYSTAL
CARISA Y PALMA CONDOS
GIRASOL
FIESTA AMERICANA CORAL BEACH
SALVIA
MIRAMAR MISSION
RADISSON SIERRA PLAZA
HYATT CANCUN CARIBE
CONTINENTAL VILLAS PLAZA
FLAMINGO
BACCARA
ARISTOS
TERRAMAR PLAZA SUITES
FIESTA AMERICANA CANCUN
SUITES SINA
KIN-HA
CANCUN CLIPPER CLUB
CONDOS
CALINDA VIVA
DOS PLAYAS
PRESIDENTE INTERCONTINENTAL
VILLAS TACUL
MAYA CARIBE
CASA MAYA
CANCUN MARINA CLUB
CLUB LAGOON
CALINDA CLUBS INTERNATIONAL
VILLAS CERDENA
SUITES MARBELLA
DURAMHINA BEACH
CARHOUSE
PLAYA LAS GLORIAS
PLAZA LAS BLANCA
CREA YOUTH HOSTEL
LAS VEGAS
CARIBBEAN SUITES
SAN MARINO
CLUB LAS PERLAS
IMPERIAL LAS PERLAS

9km

7km

Laguna

Bojorquez

3km

SEE DOWNTOWN CANCUN MAP

AV. BONAMPAK

AV. UXMAL

To Valladolid

LODGINGS ENCLOSED IN A BOX ARE
FEATURED IN THE ACCOMPANYING TEXT

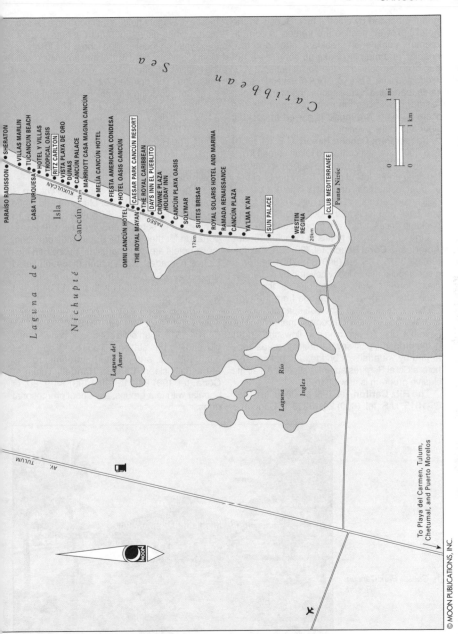

© MOON PUBLICATIONS, INC.

goon" inhabited by colorful fish. Guests in the hotel's "Tower" section are treated to complimentary continental breakfast, afternoon tea, snacks, and morning wake-up service—a hot cup of coffee served by the Tower butler at your requested time. Take your pick of several restaurants, bars, and coffee shops; the Maria Bonita restaurant, across the road, is superb. In the main building, live music is played at cocktail hour and in the evening.

Caesar Park Cancún Resort, U.S. tel. (800) 228-3000, is a self-contained resort spread luxuriously on 250 acres near the lagoon. It features lounging areas, lots of grass, many pools, several great restaurants, and an 18-hole golf course built around an ancient Maya ruin; a shuttle takes you back and forth to the golf club. Ask about package prices, which are good value here.

One of the largest hotels in Cancún, **Fiesta Americana Coral Beach,** tel. (98) 83-2900, fax (98) 83-3076, U.S. tel. (800) 343-7821, features a spectacular atrium lobby covered by a stained-glass dome. A string quartet plays in the lobby each afternoon—a nice change from the typical happy-hour scene. The 602 spacious suites all have ocean-view balconies; master suites have hot tubs. A swimming pool flows the length of the property, past several sunning areas separated by waterfalls, a bridge, and palms. The hotel's Coral Reef restaurant is superb. An all-inclusive program is now offered.

The **Ritz Carlton,** tel. (98) 85-0808, fax (98) 85-1015, U.S. tel. (800) 241-3333, is Cancún's most extravagant hotel, a fact you'll note as soon as the white-gloved doorman ushers you into the crystal-chandelier-filled lobby. The lushly opulent rooms are filled with luxury amenities, while the health club offers steam rooms, saunas, and massage. The private Club Lounge overlooks an atrium, providing a soothing yet formal setting for afternoon tea, and the Club Grill has become a favorite hideaway for locals; the food is excellent and the desserts are as extravagant as the decor. The Ritz is the ultimate for those seeking unparalleled service and elegance.

Downtown

The biggest drawback to staying downtown is the absence of beach. But blue sea and white sand are easily accessible; buses run every 15 minutes, and some hotels provide free transportation for their guests. Sometimes crowded, these hotels are good bargains. Yucatecan ambience pervades. Each accommodation listed below has a swimming pool, bar, one or more restaurants, and rooms with private bath, hot water, and phone.

Budget: Hotel Cotty, Uxmal 44 (between Tulum and Yaxchilán), tel. (98) 84-0550, tel./fax (98) 84-1319, is an oldie but goodie conveniently close to the bus station. All 38 rooms now offer a/c, cable TV, and private bathrooms; rooms are usually clean. **Cancún Handall,** Tulum at Cobá, tel. (98) 84-1122, fax (98) 84-9280, is popular with tour groups; ask about promotional rates.

Caesar Park Cancún Resort

OZ MALLAN

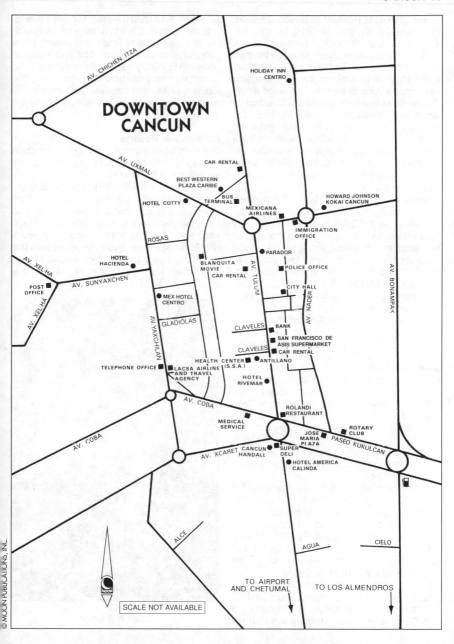

DOWNTOWN CANCUN

AV. CHICHEN ITZA

AV. UXMAL

HOLIDAY INN CENTRO

CAR RENTAL

BEST WESTERN PLAZA CARIBE

HOTEL COTTY

BUS TERMINAL

MEXICANA AIRLINES

HOWARD JOHNSON KOKAI CANCUN

IMMIGRATION OFFICE

ROSAS

PARADOR

HOTEL HACIENDA

POLICE OFFICE

AV. XEL-HA

BLANQUITA MOVIE

AV. SUNYAXCHEN

CAR RENTAL

CITY HALL

POST OFFICE

AV. XELHA

MEX HOTEL CENTRO

AV. TULUM

AV. NADER

AV. BONAMPAK

GLADIOLAS

AV. YAXCHILAN

CLAVELES

BANK

SAN FRANCISCO DE ASIS SUPERMARKET

CLAVELES

CAR RENTAL

TELEPHONE OFFICE

HEALTH CENTER (S.S.A.)

ANTILLANO

LACSA AIRLINE AND TRAVEL AGENCY

HOTEL RIVEMAR

AV. COBA

ROLANDI RESTAURANT

MEDICAL SERVICE

AV. COBA

ROTARY CLUB

JOSE MARIA PLAZA

PASEO KUKULCAN

AV. XCARET

CANCUN HANDALL

SUPER DELI

HOTEL AMERICA CALINDA

ALCE

AGUA

CIELO

TO AIRPORT AND CHETUMAL

TO LOS ALMENDROS

SCALE NOT AVAILABLE

© MOON PUBLICATIONS, INC.

Inexpensive: Howard Johnson Cancún, Av. Uxmal 26, tel. (98) 84-3218, fax (98) 84-4335, is on a quiet block of Uxmal near Av. Nader. The four-story hotel has 48 standard rooms, 12 suites with kitchens, a/c, a lobby bar, swimming pool, jacuzzi, small roof garden, and free transportation to the beach. A small dining room in the lobby serves continental breakfast for about US$3. **Antillano,** Claveles at Tulum, tel. (98) 84-1532, fax (98) 84-1878, sits right in the middle of the action. Its quieter rooms face the inner courtyard. Rooms at **Hotel Rivemar,** Av. Tulum 49, tel. (98) 84-1999, have private baths, tile floors, and a/c. The hotel is clean and in a great location.

Moderate: Hotel Hacienda, Av. Sunyaxchen 39, tel. (98) 84-3672, U.S. tel. (800) 458-6888, U.S. fax (714) 494-5088, is a pleasant, low-key hotel with 40 a/c rooms, a swimming pool, pool bar, beach transportation, a cafe, parking, and a travel agency on the premises. **Mex Hotel Centro,** Av. Yaxchilán 31, tel. (98) 84-3478 or 84-3888, fax (98) 84-1309, U.S. tel. (800) 221-6509, has been around a long time and gets better every year. It's conveniently located in the middle of the city, with scores of cafes and shops within walking distance. Rooms are smallish, but have a/c and TV. Other amenities include a pool, restaurant, coffee shop, and a free shuttle that takes guests to the beach (beach towels are provided). Terra-cotta pottery, tile floors, and colorful textiles give the hotel a pleasant Mexican flavor.

Hotel America Calinda, Av. Tulum at Calle Brisa, tel. (98) 87-7500, fax (98) 84-1953, U.S. tel. (800) 262-2656, is a large commercial-type hotel with clean rooms, a pool, a/c, and a coffee shop. It's within walking distance of good food and interesting shops, and a free shuttle takes guests to the beach.

Also getting high marks is the **Parador,** Av. Tulum 26, tel. (98) 84-1310 or 84-1043, fax (98) 84-9712, in the center of downtown next to Pop, a favorite budget cafe. Each of the 66 rooms has a private bath and a/c. Purified drinking water is available in the hall, and a pool and grassy area make sun worshippers happy. The fine little **Best Western Plaza Caribe,** Av. Tulum 13, tel. (98) 84-1377, has been around a long time and has comfortable rooms and a pool.

The most expensive downtown hotel (and one of the nicest) is the **Holiday Inn Centro,** Av. Nader 1, tel. (98) 87-4455, fax (98) 84-7945, U.S. tel. (800) HOLIDAY. It offers all the amenities of the beachside hotels and provides free transportation to the sand. The pretty peach-and-white four-story building sits at the end of Av. Nader, far from just about everything. The 100 rooms face an inner courtyard and large swimming pool; banquet and meeting facilities are available.

All-Inclusive Resorts

The all-inclusives that are springing up include meals and activities in their rates and can be economical in the long run.

Club Med, tel. (98) 85-2300, fax (98) 85-2290, U.S. tel. (800) 258-2633, is quite a distance from downtown Cancún, but taxis are always lined up at the gate; fare to town runs about US$8 each way. All Club Med guests must pay a US$30 initiation fee; if you stay more than five nights you must pay an additional US$50 membership fee. Room rates start at $142 pp for a standard room, $156 pp for an ocean view.

Cancún coastline

Other all-inclusives include **Sun Palace,** in the hotel zone at Paseo Kukulcán Km 20, tel. (98) 85-1555, fax (98) 85-2040, U.S. tel. (800) 346-8225, 150 suites, US$504 d; and **Beach Palace,** also in the hotel zone, tel. (98) 83-1177, fax (98) 85-0439, U.S. tel. (800) 346-8225, US$444 d.

Condominiums

Cancún is sprouting condos everywhere you look. While they may make you wonder when the building will end, condos do provide some of the best bargains in town for families or small groups. For as low as US$150 a night, a family of five can stay in lovely surroundings near the beach with a pool, cooking facilities, often two bathrooms, and daily maid service included in the price.

Rates can soar much higher or at certain times of the year can even be less. Travel agents can help you find a condo to suit. For the daring, good buys come if you just arrive on the scene without reservations, go from condo to condo, and negotiate the price of one that isn't reserved. However, you run the risk of not finding what you want, especially during the winter months.

Popular choices include **Carisa y Palma** condos, in the heart of the hotel zone near the Convention Center, tel. (98) 83-0211, fax (98) 83-0932, and the units available from **Vacation Clubs International,** tel. (98) 83-0855, fax (98) 83-0206. Call for prices.

FOOD

It would take a year to sample each of the more than 400 fine restaurants in Cancún. Most budget cafes with both American and Mexican cuisine are found downtown near Av. Tulum and Av. Yaxchilán. The epicurean explorer can find Argentine, Swiss, French, Chinese, Italian, Mexican, Arabic, Polynesian, Texan, Yucatecan, continental, and vegetarian cuisine. This is gourmet headquarters for the state of Quintana Roo—all you have to do is look! Most restaurants accept credit cards.

A curious food fact: Mexico is one of the world's leading coffee producers, but most restaurants in Mexico serve instant coffee. Cancún is the exception; almost all of its cafes serve good brewed coffee, and a few even offer brewed decaf (try the delicious decaf at La Dolce Vita). On some Cancún menus you can find a traditional favorite, *café de olla* (coffee cooked, sweetened with raw sugar and cinnamon, and served in a small earthen mug).

Mexican

Just across from the the Camino Real, the **Maria Bonita** restaurant, tel. (98) 83-1730, is a dazzler offering great Mexican food in a colorful, music-filled setting reminiscent of a Mexican village. Reservations suggested.

El Café, in front of a commercial building on Av. Nader, tel. (98) 84-1584, has a vast breakfast menu, including platters of fresh papaya, pineapple, and bananas; baskets of homemade pastries and breads; fresh orange-papaya juice; and bargain-priced *molletes* (rolls split and covered with beans and melted cheese). The *chilaquiles* are the best we've had in Cancún, and *pozole* is prepared daily. A blossoming *framboyán* tree shades the outdoor patio beside the sidewalk. It's a casual place and obviously a big hit with local office workers and *políticos.*

Perico's, at Av. Yaxchilán 71 downtown, tel. (98) 84-3152, continues to draw crowds. The decor alone is worth a visit; the bar seats are saddles, and a fanciful mural depicting Mexican heroes and Hollywood movie stars covers the wall. The emphasis is on fun, with amiable waiters dressed as bandits liberally pouring tequila. The food is dependably good; look for generous portions of barbecued ribs and chicken and huge Mexican combination plates. Make sure to tour the whole restaurant, including restrooms.

Also downtown, **La Habichuela,** Margaritas 25, tel. (98) 84-3158, is another longtime favorite offering gourmet Mexican cuisine in a romantic, candlelit setting. Lush plants fill the bilevel courtyard and dining room, and carvings of Maya gods and rulers sit in niches and on platforms in the dining areas. Try the shrimp in a sauce of *huitlacoche* (a black, mushroomlike fungus grown in corn), or go all out with the *cocobichuela* (shrimp and lobster in curry sauce) served in a coconut shell. Open for lunch and dinner; reservations suggested.

Los Almendros, Av. Bonampak at Av. Sayil downtown, tel. (98) 84-0807, is one of the few places in Cancún serving authentic Yucatecan dishes such as *cochinita pibil* and *poc-chuc.* **Flamingos,** near Punta Sam, and **Mandingo's,** right next to the Puerto Juárez ferry pier, serves the freshest fish *tikin xic*-style or grilled with garlic and oil. These two huge *palapa* restaurants are favored by locals who settle in for afternoon-long lunches of seafood cocktails and ceviche, huge platters of fish, and plenty of ice-cold beer.

For a full night of fine dining, dancing, and entertainment visit **El Mexicano,** La Mansión-Costa Blanca mall in the hotel zone, tel. (98) 83-2220. Caribbean and Mexican shows accompany gourmet Mexican dishes, many flambéed tableside. The setting is elegant, and though tour groups tend to congregate here, even solo diners receive impeccable service.

Iguana Wana, in Plaza Caracol, tel. (98) 83-0829, has something for everyone on its enormous menu, with such unusual finds as conch fritters, vegetarian fajitas, fried bananas, and chicken with *chipotle* sauce; frozen yogurt, and a dazzling pastry tray as well.

Italian

The longtime favorite for Italian-food lovers is **La Dolce Vita,** tel. (98) 85-0150, now in the Hotel Zone next to the lagoon, across from the Marriott Hotel. From *zuppa* to antipasto to *tutta* pasta to *pesce e frutta del mare* to the hazelnuts in your dessert, the food is scrumptious. If you like fish, try *boquinete Dolce Vita,* which consists of white snapper stuffed with shrimp and mushrooms, then baked in golden puff pastry (shaped like a fish, of course)—*delizioso!* The decaf coffee is fresh brewed and rich. A meal with wine averages about US$30-40 pp. Casual atmosphere. Open for lunch and dinner; reservations necessary.

Restaurant Rolandi, Av. Cobá 12, tel. (98) 84-4047, might be more familiar to old-timers as Pizzeria Rolandi. No matter the name, the pizzas are still great, with thin, crisp crusts covered with an eclectic selection of toppings. Pastas, calzones, and a great garlicky antipasto round out the menu; save room for the coconut ice cream topped with Kahlúa. Casual atmosphere. Open for lunch and dinner.

Other Italian selections include: **Cenacolo,** Plaza Kukulcán, tel. (98) 85-3603, offering outdoor seating; **Savios,** Plaza Caracol, tel. (98) 83-2085, an elegant bistro serving northern Italian cuisine; **Augustus Caesar,** in La Mansión-Costa Blanca, tel. (98) 83-3384, an enduring favorite since 1980 and open for lunch and dinner (reservations advised); and **Cilantro,** at the Hyatt Regency, tel. (98) 83-0966, upscale and quiet, featuring a Mexican and Italian menu with a weekly salad-and-pasta buffet (reservations suggested).

American

It's impossible to ignore the proliferation of U.S.-based restaurants and fast-food chains throughout Cancún, among them McDonald's, Burger King, Wendy's, Subway, and Kentucky Fried Chicken.

T.G.I. Friday's, tel. (98) 83-3542, was one of the first franchises in Cancún (even the locals have come to love their burgers) and enjoys an enviable location across the street from the Convention Center. **Planet Hollywood,** Plaza Flamingo, tel. (98) 85-0723, serves California cuisine in a raucous setting with music videos, movies on four screens, and a boutique selling Planet Hollywood paraphernalia. Open 11 a.m.-2 a.m.

The Seafood Market, at the Hyatt Regency, tel. (98) 83-0966, displays shrimp, lobster, and fresh fish on ice—diners select their dinner. Reservations suggested. At **Pop,** Av. Tulum 26 (next to city hall), tel. (98) 84-1991, you can enjoy a straightforward, no-nonsense, American-style breakfast, lunch, or dinner. Open daily 8 a.m.-11 p.m.

CAFE DE OLLA

Served at the Sheraton Towers Breakfast Buffet

Recipe:
1 small earthen pot
3 tbsp. dark roasted coarse ground coffee
1 cinnamon stick
3 cloves
dark brown sugar to taste
1 liter of water

Bring water to boiling in pot, add coffee, cinnamon, and sugar. Bring to boil again, strain, and serve. Optional: Add tequila to taste. Especially good brewed over an open fire!

Other Ethnic

Blue Bayou, at the Hyatt Cancún Caribe Villas and Resort, tel. (98) 83-0044, offers a Cajun menu, great blackened fish, and butter-tender beef fillet; reservations recommended. **Gypsy's,** opposite the Continental Villas Plaza Hotel on the lagoon, tel. (98) 83-2015, brings a little bit of Spain to Mexico with paella and a flamenco show twice nightly; the inexpensive breakfast buffet is a big hit as well. Open 8 a.m.-midnight. Authentic Japanese food is served at **Yamamoto,** downtown at Av. Uxmal 31, tel. (98) 87-3366; open 1:30-11 p.m.

Vegetarian

100% Natural, downtown at Av. Sunyaxchen 6, tel. (98) 84-3617, serves good vegetarian dishes, crispy salads with a good selection of veggies, great healthy shakes—you can really be creative here! Open daily 8 a.m.-midnight. A second location at Plaza Terramar in the hotel zone, tel. (98) 83-1180, is open 24 hours.

Groceries

The *mercado municipal* is six blocks north of the bus station on Av. Tulum. At the *mercado* look for La Chiquita del Caribe, which serves superb seafood (try the garlic shrimp!) at affordable prices. **Javier Rojo Gómez,** behind the post office on Sunyaxchen, is a smaller version of the *mercado municipal.* Old favorite **San Francisco de Asis Super Market** on Tulum now has a new location in the hotel zone. These are modern, well-stocked markets designed for one-stop shopping. **Comercial Mexicana,** Av. Uxmal at the traffic circle, is an enormous grocery and department store. **Super Deli** is the current favorite for imported cheeses, cookies, crackers, even frozen Sara Lee pastries and Haagen Dazs ice cream, and has a good bakery and deli section. Both locations—one downtown on Av. Uxmal, the other at Plaza Nautilus in the hotel zone—are open 24 hours and have cafes serving great sandwiches and full meals. The **Super Gourmet Deli** in Plaza Kukulcán has a similar selection, but the prices are outrageously high.

Bakeries

Indulge yourself in fine Mexican and French pastries and crusty *bolillos* at **La Francesca Panadería** on Av. Uxmal at Av. Nader. A small-er bakery is **Los Globos,** on Tulipanes just west of Av. Tulum. **Super Deli** (on Av. Tulum and in Plaza Nautilus), offers a great selection of breakfast pastries and breads. At **Ciao,** Av. Cobá 30, cappuccino and espresso are served with sublime pastries, cakes, and pies. The prices are high, but so is the quality, and there's nothing like a strong cup of coffee and a sticky pecan roll to lift flagging spirits.

ENTERTAINMENT

Cancún has a marvelous choice of nighttime entertainment. It's easy to dance the night away at a number of inviting places. Most of the hotels on the island have discos in motion until the early morning hours. Some cantinas offer live bands ranging from jazz to popular marimba to reggae, and several hotels offer Mexican "fiestas" weekly, including *típico* dinners, traditional dances, and colorful costumes.

Traditional Dance

The casual **Mexican Fiesta** at the Hyatt Regency, tel. (98) 83-0966, has been running nightly for years, packing in guests for a lavish buffet and folkloric dance performances. **Ballet Folklórico de México** performs nightly at 7 p.m. during a Mexican buffet at the Continental Villas Plaza Hotel, tel. (98) 85-1444.

Discos

Cancún has some of Mexico's most upscale, modern discos. Many don't even open until 10 p.m. and don't get wild till after midnight. Dress codes are enforced; most of the fancier discos do not allow tank tops, sandals, or other casual wear. Men can usually get by with a nice T-shirt or polo shirt and dressy shorts (some discos don't allow shorts) or long pants. Women tend to wear sundresses. Expect cover charges of US$5 or more and high drink prices.

Christine's Disco, next to Hotel Krystal, tel. (98) 83-1133, is dressy and features a superb sound and light show. The high-tech **La Boom,** Paseo Kukulcán Km 3.5, tel. (98) 83-1372, has fog and wind machines and a sound system that reflects the disco's name. **Dady'O,** Paseo Kukulcán Km 9.5, tel. (98) 83-3333, is known for its bikini contests and boisterous young crowd. The

OZ MALLAN

Fiesta Night at the Hyatt Regency Hotel

superextravagant **Up & Down,** in front of the Oasis Cancún, tel. (98) 85-2909, offers a restaurant with mellow music upstairs and a full-scale disco downstairs.

Latin Music
Azúcar, next to the Camino Real, tel. (98) 83-0100, is a classy club with a tropical garden decor and live salsa bands. **Batacha,** by the Miramar Mission Hotel, tel. (98) 83-1755, is more casual and attracts couples of all ages who love the Latin beat. **Cat's Reggae Bar,** downtown on Av. Yaxchilán (no phone), is the best spot for Caribbean music.

Other Bars and Nightclubs
Rock 'n' roll oldies get dancers on the floor at **Hard Rock Cafe,** tel. (98) 83-1266, and **Planet Hollywood,** tel. (98) 85-0723, both on Paseo Kukulcán.

Classy spots for music and conversation are: the **Lobby Bar** and **Reflejos,** both at the Hyatt Regency, tel. (98) 83-0966; **Tropical Oasis**

Piano Bar, at the Hotel and Villas Tropical Oasis; the **Oasis Bar** at the Hyatt Cancún Caribe Villas and Resort, tel. (98) 83-0044, offering live jazz and dancing; and the **Club Grill** at the Ritz Carlton Hotel, tel. (98) 85-0808, an elegant restaurant with a cozy lounge where well-dressed couples dance to romantic music.

For zany fun with wild and comedic waiters as well as exceptionally good food, head to either **Carlos'n Charlie's** or **Señor Frog's,** both on Paseo Kukulcán. Similar in ambience and decor, but with a more authentically Mexican flair, is **Perico's** on Av. Yaxchilán downtown.

For a serene, romantic spot to begin or end an evening, watch Cancún's sensational sunset or glittering stars in **La Palapa,** at Hotel Club Lagoon Caribe on Paseo Kukulcán; the mellow *palapa* bar sits over the lagoon at the end of its own pier. La Palapa serves snacks and exotic drinks and offers live music and dancing 9 p.m.-1:30 a.m.

Dinner Cruises
The **Columbus Lobster Dinner Cruise** leaves the Royal Mayan Marina dock (hotel zone) daily at 4 p.m. and 7:30 p.m. The *Columbus,* tel. (98) 83-3268 or 83-3271, is a 62-foot motor-sailing vessel that cruises for three hours at sunset or under the starry sky while guests enjoy an open bar and dine on delicious broiled lobster or steak. Dress is casual, reservations necessary. On the **Pirate's Night Adventure,** tel. (98) 83-3268 or 83-3283, diners cruise on the *Crucero Tropical Cruiser* to Treasure Island (actually a beach on Isla Mujeres facing Cancún). Once onshore, passengers enjoy a buffet dinner and free drinks while watching a floor show with lively games and lots of audience participation. Departs nightly (except Sunday) from the Playa Langosta Pier at 6 p.m., returning at 11 p.m.

The *Cancún Queen* is the only paddleboat on the lagoon (so far). Its dinner cruise offers gourmet steak and lobster, as well as an open bar, live music, dancing, and games. Board on Paseo Kukulcán, opposite the Melia Cancún Hotel; tel. (98) 85-2288. Reservations suggested.

Centro Convenciones Cancún
Cancún's smashing Convention Center, at Paseo Kukulcán Km 9, offers 108,000 square feet of convention space with the latest high-

tech audiovisual equipment. It's in the heart of the Cancún hotel zone, five minutes' walking distance from 4,000 upscale hotel rooms and 15 km (nine miles) from the international airport. For more information contact PS Enterprises, U.S. tel. (800) 538-0424 or (202) 797-1222.

Cinema

The majority of films shown in Cancún are American-made, in English with Spanish subtitles. Expect the bill to change every three or four days. **Cines Cancún,** Av. Xcaret 112, tel. (98) 84-1646, and **Cine Royal,** Av. Tulum, present Mexican films.

SHOPPING

Cancún's malls are sleek and spectacular; no bargaining here (at least in most businesses). In downtown Cancún you'll find small streetside shopping marts, often fronted by touts urging you in. You won't find vendors on the beach—it's illegal, and the law is enforced. Almost all businesses in Cancún accept credit cards.

Shopping Centers

La Mansión-Costa Blanca is a small, exclusive mall featuring unique boutiques, several of the city's top restaurants, a money exchange, and a bank. The shops at **El Parian** are constructed around a small garden off to one side of the Convention Center.

Plaza Caracol, one of Cancún's biggest and most contemporary shopping centers, is conveniently located in the hub of the hotel zone, fully a/c, and elaborately finished with marble floors and lots of windows. The two-story mall holds over 200 shops and boutiques.

Even more good shopping is found at: **Plaza la Fiesta,** a huge one-floor department store featuring Mexican crafts; **Plaza Lagunas,** at the center of the hotel zone; **Plaza Nautilus,** a modern, two-story plaza; **Terramar,** opposite the Fiesta Americana Hotel; **Kukulcán Plaza,** a two-story, a/c plaza near Casa Turquesa that also holds a bowling alley and movie theaters; **Plaza México** on Av. Tulum, an a/c mall specializing in Mexican crafts; **Plaza Safa,** a lovely arcade that fronts Av. Tulum; and **Tropical Plaza,** next door to Plaza México.

Crafts Markets

In the hotel zone, next to the Convention Center, **Coral Negro** is a collection of approximately 50 stalls selling handicrafts from all parts of Mexico. **Ki Huic,** downtown on Av. Tulum, is Cancún's main crafts market, with over 100 vendors and just about every kind of craft and souvenir you can imagine. **Plaza Garibaldi,** also downtown at the intersection of Av. Tulum and Uxmal, contains several stalls of serapes, tablecloths, traditional clothing, onyx, and other handcrafted items.

SERVICES AND INFORMATION

Medical Information

Most hotels in Cancún can provide the name of a doctor who speaks English. For simple first aid downtown, stop at **Cruz Roja,** Av. Labná 2, tel. (98) 84-1616. If the problem is more serious, head to **Total Assist Hospital,** Claveles 5 (at Av. Tulum), tel. (98) 84-1092 or 84-8116. This small, walk-in 24-hour emergency hospital is geared more to tourists than to locals; an English-speaking doctor is usually on call. For other questions call the American Consulate, tel. (98) 84-2411.

TO GET MARRIED IN CANCÚN

Call (98) 4-1311, ext. 129, to make an appointment with Señor Pedro Solis Rodríguez, official of the Civil Registry. When they go to the Civil Registry Office at the city hall, located downtown on Av. Tulum, bride and groom should have:

√ Tourist cards

√ Birth certificates

√ Blood tests

√ Passports or driver's licenses

√ Final divorce decrees if applicable

√ The names, addresses, ages, nationalities, and tourist card numbers of four witnesses

√ Fee to pay the cashier at the city hall, about US$35.

√ Filled-out application given to you by the judge.

Very important: these things must be done at *least* two days before the wedding.

Pharmacies are tourist-oriented and at most of them a little English is spoken. Hotel delivery service is usually available. The pharmacy at Caracol Plaza in the hotel zone, tel. (98) 83-1894 or 83-2827, is open daily 9 a.m.-10 p.m.

Post Office and Telegrams

The post office is on Av. Sunyaxchen (west of Av. Tulum) at Av. Xel-Ha, tel. (98) 84-1418; open Mon.-Fri. 8 a.m.-7 p.m., Saturday 9 a.m.-noon. Call the telegraph office at (98) 84-1529.

Consulate Representatives

The **U.S. Consular Office,** Av. Nader 40, tel. (98) 84-2411 or 84-6399, keeps hours Mon.-Fri. 9 a.m.-2 p.m. and 3-6 p.m. The **Canadian Consulate** is at Plaza México #312, second floor, and open Mon.-Fri. 11 a.m.-2 p.m.; for emergencies outside business hours call the Canadian Embassy in Mexico City at (915) 724-7900. The **French Consulate** is at Instituto Internacional de Idiomas, Av. Xel-Ha 113, tel. (98) 84-6078; open Mon.-Fri. 8-11 a.m. and 5-7 p.m. The consular representative of **Spain** is in the Oasis Building on Paseo Kukulcán, tel. (98) 83-2466; open Mon.-Fri. 10 a.m.-1 p.m. The **Italian Consulate** is in La Mansión-Costa Blanca Mall, tel. (98) 83-2184; open 9 a.m.-2 p.m.

Tourist Information

The **state tourist office** is on Av. Tulum at the Plaza Municipal Benito Juárez, next to the Multibanco Comermex, tel. (98) 84-8073; open Mon.-Sat. 9 a.m.-5 p.m. *Cancún Tips* is a helpful, free tourist information booklet available in hotels and shops; the publishers also operate tourist information offices in Plaza Caracol, Plaza Kukulcán, the Convention Center, and at Playa Langosta Pier. The chamber of commerce, tel. (98) 84-4315, is also a good source of information. Booths with tourist information signs abound

along Av. Tulum and Paseo Kukulcán; be warned—most are operated by time-share companies offering free tours and meals in exchange for your presence at a timeshare presentation.

Legal Matters

In recent years, the college crowd began descending upon Cancún during Easter break (shades of Florida). The city fathers didn't like this unleashed orgy of pleasure. Now, young people are handed a document that spells out the rules. The legal age for drinking alcohol is 18. When a person 16 years old or older is tossed into jail they are treated like the adult prisoners. Purchase, possession, and consumption of drugs is illegal. Public nudity is also illegal, although you will find nude sunbathers on some of the out-of-the-way beaches along the coast to the south and on Isla Mujeres.

Immigration

Remember that you must turn in your Mexican visitor's card when you leave the country. The card is normally good for 30 days. If you need an extension (*before* your card expires), go to the main immigration office at Av. Nader 1 downtown, tel. (98) 84-1749, fax (98) 84-0918; open Mon.-Fri. 8:30 a.m.-noon. You will be asked to leave your card and pick it up the following day. A second immigration office at the airport, tel. (98) 84-2992, can also answer questions and provide assistance.

Tours and Travel Agencies

With the advent of the tour guide's union, tours around the area are supposed to be the same price at all agencies; however, we are hearing that's not always the case. So, try bargaining the price. All the larger hotels in Cancún have travel agencies available to help you with your travel needs locally and internationally. Many more are scattered about the city. Most offices close 1-3 p.m., then reopen till 7 p.m. or 8 p.m. **Turismo Aviomar,** Av. Yaxchilán downtown, tel. (98) 84-8831, fax (98) 84-5385, offers many tours of the city and surrounding area in modern a/c buses. The agency can make reservations for party boats to Isla Mujeres and arrange most of your vacation plans. The **American Express** office is downtown at Av. Tulum 208 (at Calle Agua), tel. (98) 84-1999. A few other good firms

---

CANCÚN EMERGENCY NUMBERS

Police.	(98) 84-1913
Fire	(98) 84-1202
Red Cross	(98) 84-1616
Air-Vac Medical Life Service (Houston, Texas)	(713) 961-4050

are **Intermar Caribe,** Av. Bonampak at Calle Cereza, tel. (98) 84-4266, fax (98) 84-1652; **PTT Travel,** Av. Cobá 12-20, tel. (98) 84-8831; and **Viaje Bojórquez,** Calle Alcatraces 12, tel. (98) 87-1156, fax (98) 84-1652.

Mayaland Tours, downtown at the Hotel America on Av. Tulum, tel. (98) 87-5411 or 87-2450, offers many day-trips and packages that begin in Cancún and continue on to Chichén Itzá, Uxmal, Palenque, Mérida, and more. Some of the packages include hotels and autos—a real bargain. Their modern a/c double-decker buses have friendly, knowledgeable guides and onboard attendants. Most travel agencies and tour desks in town have information and can make reservations for Mayaland Tours. **Yucatán Central Reservations,** U.S. tel. (800) 555-8842, specializes in all parts of the Yucatán Peninsula and can create custom trips—including making hotel and airline reservations—for visitors.

GETTING THERE AND AROUND

By Air

Cancún's international airport is 20 km (12 miles) south of Cancún. Along with everything else around this young city, the airport continues to grow and add to its facilities each season. It now has two runways, but no storage lockers; most hotels are willing to check your tagged luggage for you.

Airlines serving Cancún include: **Mexicana,** Av. Cobá 39, tel. (98) 87-4444, airport tel. (98) 86-0120; **Aeromexico,** Av. Cobá 80, tel. (98) 84-3571, airport tel. (98) 86-0018; **Continental,** airport tel. (98) 86-0040; **Lacsa,** Av. Bonampak at Av. Cobá, tel. (98) 87-3101, airport tel. (98) 86-0014; **Taesa,** Av. Yaxchilán, tel. (98) 87-4314, airport tel. (98) 86-0206; and **Aviacsa,** Av. Cobá, tel. (98) 87-4214 or 87-4211. **Aerocaribe** and **Aerocozumel,** Av. Tulum 29, tel. (98) 84-2000, airport tel. (98) 86-0083, offer daily flights to and from Isla Cozumel. **Aviateca,** airport tel. (98) 86-0155, flies to Guatemala. Several airlines run charter flights to Cancún from major U.S. gateways at reduced fares. Ask your travel agent to check out this option.

Car rentals, taxis, and *colectivos* are available at the airport. The *colectivo* vans are cheaper than taxis and they *will* be filled to capacity. Buy your ticket near the baggage pickup for US$10 pp. It's always a good idea to watch each person remove his or her luggage on the way to your hotel, just to avoid a mix-up. When you depart from Cancún, you will have to take a taxi since the *colectivos* only run one-way. Depending on the number of people in the cab, it will cost US$10-15 from downtown, about US$20 from the hotel zone. Be sure you set aside US$12 for departure tax to be paid at the airport.

By Bus

Buses operate daily between Cancún, Mérida, and Chetumal, linking smaller villages en route. The bus terminal is downtown on Av. Tulum. Call or go to the terminal for complete schedules—they change frequently. You will find the first- (**ADO**) and second-class (**Autotransportes del Caribe**) bus stations next door to each other, across from the Hotel Plaza Caribe at the intersection of Avenidas Tulum and Uxmal and at Av. Pino, a small side street off Uxmal. These buses run frequently and fares are cheap. Try to buy your ticket well ahead of your departure since the traffic is heavy.

Playa Express on Av. Pino, offers a/c minibus and regular bus service between Cancún, Playa del Carmen, Tulum, Felipe Carillo Puerto, and Chetumal. The minibuses do not have large luggage compartments. Right across the street, **Interplaya** operates minibuses between Cancún and Playa del Carmen (with stops at all the beach areas) every half-hour 5 a.m.-10 p.m. **InterCaribe** runs first-class, nonstop buses to Mérida and Chetumal.

Caribe Express, on Av. Pino, around the corner from ADO, tel. (98) 87-4174, runs between Cancún, Chetumal, Campeche, and Mérida. These first-class luxury buses are the 747s of the road, featuring a/c, earphones, TV, music, bathrooms, and an attendant who will serve you drinks and cookies.

Expresso de Oriente, on Av. Uxmal, tel. (98) 84-5542 or 84-4804, offers deluxe service between Cancún and Mérida; 11 buses daily run nonstop, others stop in Playa del Carmen, Tulum, and Valladolid. Reservations must be confirmed two hours before departure or they will be canceled.

By Car

Car rentals are available at Cancún airport and many hotels. Most companies rent jeeps, sedans, and Volkswagen bugs, and accept credit cards. You may find that you get the best rates by reserving your car in advance through U.S.-based agencies, though some of the small local agencies offer great deals when business is down.

The 320-km, four-hour drive from Mérida to Cancún is on a good highway (Hwy. 180) through henequen-dotted countryside, past historic villages and archaeological ruins. The new toll highway cuts 30-60 minutes off the drive, though the straight, high-speed, eight-lane road is somewhat monotonous. The tolls from Cancún to Mérida run about US$17 each way. New roads are going in along the Cancún-Tulum corridor (now known as the Maya Riviera); when asked if these would be free roads, we've gotten different answers. Right now the free Hwy. 307 from Cancún to Chetumal (343 km) is a four-hour drive along a well-maintained two-lane highway (two more lanes have been under construction for years). The road runs parallel to the Caribbean coast.

DRIVING DISTANCES FROM CANCÚN

Airport	20 km
Akuma	104 km
Aventuras (playa)	107 km
Bacalar	320 km
Chemuyil	109 km
Chetumal	382 km
Chichén Itzá	192 km
Club Med	25 km
Cobá	167 km
Kohunlich	449 km
Mérida	312 km
Pamul	92 km
Playa del Carmen	65 km
Puerto Juárez	2 km
Puerto Morelos	32 km
Punta Sam	7 km
Tulum	130 km
Valladolid	152 km
Xcaret	72 km
Xelha	123 km

ISLA MUJERES

Finger-shaped Isla Mujeres lies 13 km (eight miles) east of Cancún across Bahía Mujeres. The island is small—just eight km (five miles) long and 400 meters at its widest point—but many visitors return year after year to spend a few hedonistic days relaxing or diving on the island's outlying reefs.

Though the overflow of tourists from Cancún and Cozumel is noticeable, the island is relatively quiet, especially in the off-season (June and September are great!). The easygoing populace still smiles at backpackers, and travelers can easily find suitable lodging in all price ranges, though in the budget category it's getting harder.

Isla Mujeres holds a large naval base, so you'll see many ships in its harbor. Note that the Mexican navy doesn't like people photographing the base, ships, or on-duty sailors, so if you're struck with the urge to photograph everything, ask someone in charge first. Before tourism, fishing was the island's prime industry, with turtle, lobster, and shark the local specialties. Today the turtle is protected; with a few specific exceptions, it is illegal to hunt them or take their eggs. Stiff fines face those who break this law.

The weather here is about the same as on the entire coast. Hurricanes are not common, but Isla Mujeres is nevertheless prepared; 25 hurricane shelters dot the flat island, and all the hotels know just what to do should a hurricane blow ashore.

History

One legend tells us that the name Isla Mujeres ("Island of Women") comes from the buccaneers who stowed their female captives here while conducting their nefarious business on the high seas. Another more prosaic (and probably correct) version refers to the large number of female-shaped clay idols found on the island when the Spaniards arrived. Archaeologists presume the island was a stopover for the Maya Indians on their pilgrimages to Cozumel to worship Ix Chel, female goddess of fertility and an important deity to Maya women.

SIGHTS

Orientation

The "city" of Isla Mujeres, at the north end of the island, is 10 blocks long and five blocks wide. On Av. Hidalgo, the main street, you'll find the central plaza, city hall, police station, cinema, *farmacia,* and a large supermarket. Most streets are really only walkways, with no vehicles allowed (although they frequently squeeze by anyway). The ferry dock is three blocks from the plaza; if you're traveling light, you can walk to most of the hotels when you get off the ferry. Otherwise, taxis queue up along Av. Rueda Medina close to the ferry dock.

Parque Nacional El Garrafón

At this national park five km (three miles) south of town, the snorkeling has been heralded for years. It's a great spot for beginners, thanks to a close-in coral reef, little swell, and water only a meter deep for about five meters offshore (after which the bottom drops off abruptly to six meters). Brazen Bermuda grubs gaze at you eye-to-eye through your mask, practically begging to have their picture taken. Swim past the reef and you'll see beautiful angelfish that seem to enjoy hanging around a coral-encrusted anchor and a couple of antiquated ship's cannons. This is a good place to introduce children to the undersea world (though beware, the water here can get surgy).

The coral here, both in and out of the water, is beautiful, but should be avoided for both its sake and yours. It can be razor sharp, so never touch or walk on it. And don't wear suntan lotion into the water; it contains chemicals toxic to these fragile creatures. (Alternatively, ask your pharmacist for an ecological lotion that will not harm the fish and coral.)

Nonsnorkeling visitors to the park can relax in beach chairs on the sand or under *palapa* sun shelters—that is, until the tourist boats from Cancún arrive. So many day-trippers come from Cancún that the beach gets terribly crowded and loses its tranquillity between around 10 a.m. and 2 p.m.; even the fish seem to flee the tourist

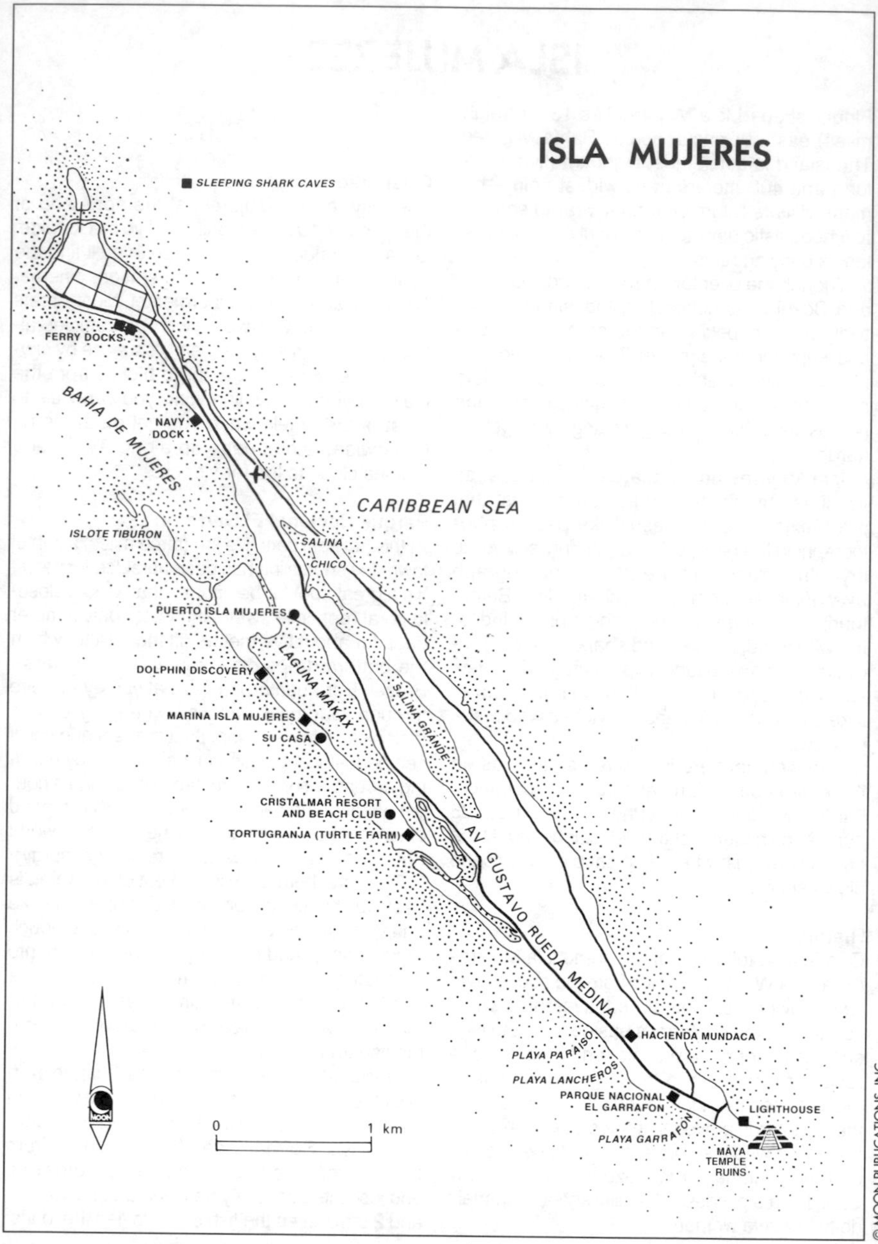

ISLA MUJERES

SLEEPING SHARK CAVES

FERRY DOCKS

BAHIA DE MUJERES

NAVY DOCK

CARIBBEAN SEA

ISLOTE TIBURON

SALINA CHICO

PUERTO ISLA MUJERES

LAGUNA MAKAX

DOLPHIN DISCOVERY

MARINA ISLA MUJERES

SU CASA

SALINA GRANDE

CRISTALMAR RESORT AND BEACH CLUB

TORTUGRANJA (TURTLE FARM)

AV. GUSTAVO RUEDA MEDINA

HACIENDA MUNDACA

PLAYA PARAISO

PLAYA LANCHEROS

PARQUE NACIONAL EL GARRAFON

LIGHTHOUSE

PLAYA GARRAFON

MAYA TEMPLE RUINS

0   1 km

© MOON PUBLICATIONS, INC.

hordes then, heading off to go hang out someplace else. So come early. The park is officially open 8 a.m.-5 p.m., but someone is usually there before 8 a.m. to let early-birds in; admission is US$2 pp.

Built into the steep cliff that backs the beach are a dive shop (snorkel, mask, and fins rent for about US$6 per day), seafood cafe, lockers, showers, and changing rooms. Taxi fare from town to Garrafón is about US$4 for up to four passengers.

Tortugranja Turtle Farm
A low-key, no-frills environment to protect sea turtles, this farm is on Carreterra Sac Bajo, on the

beach south of the Cristalmar Resort and Beach Club. One section of sand is fenced off as the hatchery, where the turtles dig their nests and lay their eggs. Eggs are collected from beach nests and put into incubation pens. After they hatch, they are placed in three large pools, to grow in a protected environment until they are at least a year old. An experimental holding area in the sea is roped and netted off to keep adult turtles close by and within easy reach of the hatchery beach. This guarantees they will come to *this* shore to lay their eggs under the watchful eye of marine biologists. Once the laying season is over, they are released back to the open sea. Staff at the farm give information (in Spanish)

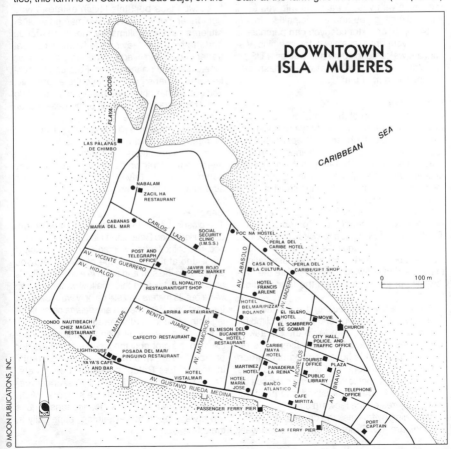

DOWNTOWN
ISLA MUJERES

and might let you hold some of the smaller turtles. On the grounds you'll find restrooms, a gift shop (proceeds from T-shirt sales help take care of the turtles), and great ice cream bars. Admission is US$1.50.

Swim with Dolphins

Relatively new on Isla is **Dolphin Discovery,** whose main attraction is a big saltwater pen holding six dolphins you can swim with for a fee. First you'll watch an instructive video explaining what not to do, where you can touch the dolphins and where you can't. Then you join these marvelous animals in the water. It really is a frolic, dolphins jumping over you, pulling you and swimming with you. A trainer is with you at all times, directing you and the dolphins. Cost is US$110; for an extra cost you can purchase a video of your entire swim with the dolphins. Visitors are welcome to come and watch for US$3. A restaurant on the premises offers a tasty buffet lunch 11 a.m.-1 p.m.

Maya Ruins

At the southern tip of the island on a cliff overlooking the sea, an ancient Maya temple once used as a coastal observation post has been reconstructed. To get there, continue south from Parque Nacional El Garrafón on the main road until you see the lighthouse road going off to the right. Park your vehicle in the small clearing near the lighthouse and follow the dirt path to the ruins. These ruins were first seen and described by Francisco Hernández de Córdoba in 1517. The temple was devoted to worship of Ix Chel, goddess of fertility, and was also used for making the sophisticated astronomical observations that were part of Maya daily life—note the narrow slits in the walls facing the four cardinal points.

Ask the caretaker if you can go up in the lighthouse; it's 10 meters high and worth the climb for the vista. Yes, it is polite to tip the caretaker. Sometimes you have to call for him, since he might be behind his house hoeing his garden of tomatoes, peppers, and watermelons. This is a magnificent spot to see both the open sea on the windward side of the island and peaceful Bahía Mujeres on the leeward side.

If traveling by taxi, ask the driver to wait while you look around. Or let him go—you can walk back to Playa Garrafón and catch a taxi to town (till 5 p.m.). The walk all the way back to town is long and sweaty—figure about two hours.

Hacienda Mundaca

A touching local legend from the mid-1800s tells of a swashbuckling, slave-trading pirate, Fermín Mundaca de Marechaja, who fell in love with a young woman on Isla Mujeres. Her name was Prisca Gómez (aka *Trigueña* or "Brunette"), and depending on which version of the story you hear she was either a visitor from Spain or a native of the island. After 10 years of plying the seas and buying and selling slaves, Mundaca retired to the island to court Gómez, unsuccessfully. Mundaca built this lavish estate to woo her further, but to no avail. She married another Mujeres man and ultimately moved to Mérida and the high life, leaving the heartsick slave-trader behind. He lived out the remainder of his lonely life here on the island. Fate can be fickle—and perhaps just. But if you're a romantic, you'll feel a haunting melancholy while strolling in the once-gracious gardens of this deserted, almost destroyed estate.

The government is slowly restoring Hacienda Mundaca and making it into a park. It's still not much more than trails through the bush. To get there from downtown, follow the main highway south approximately 4.5 km (2.7 miles) to a signed turnoff to the left.

Beaches

The closest beach to downtown is **Playa Norte,** also called Coco Beach and Nautibeach (perhaps because of the topless women?), on the lee side of the island at the north edge of town. Here you can relax in the sun and swim in a blue sea that's as calm as a lake. In this shallow water you can wade out 35 meters and still be only waist deep. At the west end of the beach are *palapa* cafes serving both soft and hard beverages.

If you see a rugged-looking, sun-tanned muscle man, it's probably the local beach character named Tarzan, who runs the equipment rental in front of Las Palapas Chimbo beach cafe. Tarzan rents sailboards, water skis, and three-wheeled "bikes" that float. He's also a PADI-trained diver and offers scuba lessons. Prices are always open to bargaining, especially in the off-season.

At the south end of the island, toward Playa Garrafón on the main road out of town, are **Playa Paraíso** and **Playa Lancheros,** both quiet beaches where people formerly swam and rode the backs of giant sea turtles. Today the turtles are protected by law from such indignities, but you can still enjoy the sun, sand, and sea here; an open *palapa* restaurant specializes in seafood.

Isla Contoy

If you've ever dreamed of visiting Gilligan's Island, a trip to Contoy is a must. A national bird sanctuary, Contoy is 24 km (14 miles) north of Isla Mujeres and is home to herons, brown pelicans, frigates, and cormorants to name a few. The island's only structures are a three-story viewing tower, remnants of old informational displays explaining the island's ecology, and old bunkhouses once used by biologists. The rest of the island is lush tropical jungle, surrounded by crystal-clear water. Recently reopened to the public, Contoy was closed for a while as biologists worried its popularity was ruining the ecology.

Day-trips leave from Mujeres. Check with the Tourist Office at Av. Hidalgo 6 or with the Boatman's Cooperative next to the ferry pier, tel. (987) 7-0036. Many of the boats are slow and have wooden seats, so if comfort is a necessity double check which boat you'll be on. Even if you are on a slow boat, this is forgotten as the verdant island with hundreds of birds soaring in the wind comes into view. Exploration of the small island is left to you with plenty of time to enjoy swimming or snorkeling in the warm shallow waters. Fresh fruit is served on arrival. A delicious lunch of fresh barbecued fish (caught on the way), Spanish rice, bread, soft drinks and beer is served on the beach. Our crew drank as much beer as we did and were very jovial. (Obviously, all captains are different.)

WATER SPORTS

Snorkeling and Scuba Diving

The snorkeler on Isla Mujeres has many choice locations to choose from. **Parque Nacional El Garrafón** is a good introduction to the feast for the eyes. Another good option is the east end of **Playa Norte,** where visibility can be up to 33 meters (109 feet) near the wooden pier; occasional-

dive boat, Isla Mujeres

ly the sea gets choppy here, clouding the water. The windward side of the island is never good for snorkeling as the sea is seldom calm; don't snorkel or even swim on the windward side on a rough day and risk being hurled against the sharp rocks. An open wound caused by coral laceration often becomes infected in this humid climate.

The dive shops on the island sponsor excursions to nearby reefs. A lot of press has been devoted to Isla Mujeres's **Sleeping Shark Caves.** Ask at the dive shop for detailed information. Although some divemasters will take you in among the sluggish though dangerous fish, others feel that it isn't a smart dive. Bill Horn, experienced diver and owner of Aqua Safari Dive Shop on Isla Cozumel, warns that there's always danger when you put yourself into a small area with a wild creature. In a cave, even if a large fish isn't trying to attack, the swish of a powerful tail could easily send you crashing against the wall. Reasons given for the sharks' somnambulant state vary with the teller: salinity of the water or low carbon dioxide. Divers must dive to depths of 150 feet or more to see the sharks, which may or may not be around. Local divemasters say that divers have a 30% chance of spotting the sharks. Between Cancún and Isla Mujeres, experienced divers will find excitement diving **Chital, Cuevones, La Bandera,** and **Manchones Reefs.**

Scuba diving and snorkeling trips or rental equipment can be arranged at **Carnavalito Dive Shop,** tel. (987) 7-0118, **Mexico Divers,** tel. (987) 7-0131, and **La Bahía Dive Shop,** tel. (987) 7-0340. All three are on Av. Rueda Medina in the vicinity of the ferry docks. These shops are qualified, reliable, and give excellent service. Remember, always check out the divemaster's certification and consider what kind of a divemaster it is who doesn't ask to see yours.

Fishing

Deep-sea fishing trips can be arranged through any of the marinas. Spring is the best time to catch the big ones: dorado, marlin, and sailfish. The rest of the year you can bring in good strings of grouper, barracuda, tuna, and red snapper. **Mexico Divers,** on Av. Rueda Medina next to the boat dock, tel. (987) 7-0131, offers a day-long deep-sea fishing trip that includes bait, tackle, and lunch. The **Boatmen's Cooperative,** on the waterfront just north of the ferry pier, tel. (987) 7-0036, and the **Club de Yates,** on Av. Rueda Medina next to the Pemex station, tel. (987) 7-0211 or 7-0086, also offer deep-sea fishing trips and boat rentals.

Dock Facilities

The marinas in Isla Mujeres are getting more sophisticated, with many services available. **Pemex Marina** in the bay offers electricity, water, diesel, and gasoline. You'll find a mechanic at the navy-base dock, tel. (987) 7-0196. **Laguna Makax** offers only docking facilities. In boating emergencies, call the Coast Guard ("Neptuno") on VHF channel 16.

ACCOMMODATIONS

You'll find a surprising number of hotels on this miniscule island. Besides the few luxury-class establishments, most are simple, family-run inns. Many are downtown near the oceanfront.

Yucatecan boatmen keep a sharp watch for the reef between Isla Mujeres and Isla Contoy. Hundreds of ships in the past 400 years have been wrecked on the reef, which parallels the Caribbean coast for about 250 kilometers.

Shoestring

The youth hostel, **Poc Na,** Av. Matamoros 91, tel. (987) 7-0090, fax (987) 7-0059, offers clean, dormitory-style rooms with fans, communal baths and toilets, and either mattresses or hammocks. The cafeteria is simple with few choices, but its food is adequate and inexpensive. Rates start at US$5 for mattress and sheet, US$2.50 for a hammock, and US$1 for a towel, with a US$7 deposit required for all rentals.

Budget

Low-priced hotels are no longer as easy to find here as they once were. Look at budget places carefully before paying your money—what can be clean and friendly one season can go downhill the next. And at any lodgings in this category, hot water can be an elusive, unreliable item.

Marcianito, Av. Abasolo 10, tel. (987) 7-0111,

is a clean little family run hotel, right downtown. This is the ultimate in simplicity, and maybe one of the only true budget hotels left.

On the oceanfront, the **Hotel Vistalmar,** Av. Rueda Medina s/n, between Abasolo and Matamoros, tel. (987) 7-0209, fax (987) 7-0096, is really spartan, but offers a friendly ambience and good location. Each of the clean rooms has a ceiling fan and a private bathroom with hot water. At the end of the day, guests gather at the tables and chairs out on the big common balconies—a good place to meet fellow travelers. A small restaurant overlooks the sea and serves simple but tasty meals.

For another peso saver, take a look at the simple, multistoried **Caribe Maya,** Av. Madero 9, tel. (987) 7-0190. Old but clean, the 20 rooms each have a private bath and thrift-store furnishings; some have a/c, the rest have fans. Air circulation is better on the upper floors.

Another old-timer with a repeat clientele is the **Hotel Martínez,** Av. Madero 14, tel. (987) 7-0154. The 14 rooms are dependably clean, and all have fans and bathrooms. Don't be shocked to find closed doors after 10 p.m.; a few loud knocks will rouse one of the family members and you will be let in.

Hotel El Isleño, Calle Vicente Guerrero at Madero, tel. (987) 7-0302, shouldn't be your first choice for low-priced accommodations, since cleanliness is not its hallmark. But if the other places mentioned here are full, check here; shared bath. **Hotel María José,** on Av. Madero at Av. Rueda Medina, tel. (987) 7-0130, is another good choice, with street-facing balconies in some rooms.

Moderate

Marina Isla Mujeres, tel./fax (987) 7-0594, is a private little resort on the waterfront with efficiency suites, each including kitchenette, living room, bathroom, bedroom, a/c and fan. Rates include complimentary breakfast. Pleasant, though out of town.

Su Casa, south of town on Laguna Mekax, U.S. tel. (800) 552-4550, is a delightfully low-key, eight-room resort right on its own beach. It's rustic, private, peaceful, and exudes a happy ambience. Each fan-cooled room has a bedroom, sitting area, and small kitchen.

Facing the windward side of the island, **Hotel Perla del Caribe,** Av. Madero 2, tel. (987) 2-

0444, fax (987) 7-0011, U.S. tel. (800) 258-6454, offers pleasant rooms with private bathrooms and a/c or fan. Rooms have terraces and balconies, so be sure to ask for one facing the sea. Other amenities include a snack bar and pool. The hotel's (rough-water) beach is good for sunbathing and walking; swim only when the sea is calm. The concrete *malecón* walkway along the backside of the island is conveniently close to La Perla. Credit cards are okay. Prices drop considerably during the low season.

El Mesón del Bucanero, Av. Hidalgo 11, tel. (987) 7-0210, fax (987) 7-0126, is a small hotel above the Bucanero restaurant. The rooms are pleasant and clean, with private bathrooms and hot water, though their location above the busy restaurant can be noisy.

According to one reader, the **Hotel Gomar,** Av. Rueda Medina 150, tel. (987) 7-0142, is "better than average." The hotel is conveniently located across from the ferry in a long, narrow, four-story building. It's simple, colorfully decorated, and clean, with comfortable beds, private bathrooms, fans, and a friendly staff.

At **Hotel Francis Arlene,** on Av. Guerrero near the Casa de la Cultura, tel./fax (987) 7-0310, the owners keep a close eye on the condition of the immaculately clean rooms, which have a/c or fan, tiled baths, and good mattresses. Some rooms have refrigerators, toasters, and coffee makers, and some have stoves.

Moderate/Expensive

Posada del Mar, Av. Rueda Medina 15A, tel. (987) 7-0212, fax (987) 7-0266, is an older complex (though newly decorated) with your choice of bungalows or hotel rooms. This is a happy place with many return customers each year—always a good sign. You can go swimming in the bay (right across the street) or in the hotel's own lovely pool, which is fed by a stone, colonial-style aqueduct. A low-key *palapa* bar, where swings substitute for barstools and hammocks hang in the shade, sits next to the pool; ask bartenders Romie or Miguel for a Maya Sacrifice, a drink that lights up the *palapa* with flame and fun! The restaurant Pinguino, at the front of the property, offers tables overlooking the sidewalk and beach and a big bar in back. Live bands perform during the high season, when Pinguino's becomes the town's hottest dance spot. The hotel rooms are a/c and some are very comfortable. Ask about good low-season discounts and special weekly rates.

Cabañas María del Mar, Av. Carlos Lazos 1 (on Playa Norte), tel. (987) 7-0213 or 7-0179, fax (987) 7-0173, began providing visitors with simple bungalows many years ago. It has since grown into one of the island's larger complexes. You have a choice from simple bungalows or more upscale hotel rooms. Most of the rooms are on the beach and have two double beds, ceiling fans, a/c, terraces, refrigerators, and purified water. Ask to see your room before you pay—some are nicer than others. Facilities include a pool, restaurant, bar, and game room. Rates include continental breakfast.

Expensive

Hotel Belmar, Av. Hidalgo at Abasolo (above Pizza Rolandi), tel. (987) 7-0430, fax (987) 7-0429, offers 10 nicely decorated rooms with a/c, tile floors, and satellite TV; the master suite even has its own hot tub and kitchenette.

Called the "star" of Isla by some visitors, **Nabalam,** on Calle Zazil at Playa Norte (just up the road from Cabañas María del Mar), tel. (987) 7-0279, fax (987) 7-0436, U.S. tel. (800) 552-4550, offers comfy rooms and a superb location on the white-sand beach. Its two-story white stucco buildings face the sea, and all rooms are junior suites with sitting areas, dining tables, a/c and fans, and patios or balconies. Folk art and photographs from Chiapas, along with Maya carvings, decorate the rooms and public spaces; landscaped trails lead to the restaurant and beach. Hammocks hang under the palms beside comfortable lounge chairs in a small garden facing the beach. The hotel's restaurant, Zacil Ha, is one of the island's best, and the *palapa* bar is a popular happy-hour hangout for tourists as well as local expats.

Premium

Though Isla Mujeres has long been known for its low key, glitz-free atmosphere, a couple of flashy resorts have now been built here. Both are on the island's south end; either take a taxi back and forth to town, rent a golf cart, or ride a bike.

Puerto Isla Mujeres, U.S. tel. (800) 952-4550, is a small marina tucked away where you'll never see it unless you go looking for it. Along with slips for luxury yachts, it offers beautiful hotel/condos sprawled along the shore. The atmosphere is tranquil and private. Sun worshipping is the favorite pastime of most guests, and meals are served at tables next to the large circular pool. The bungalows are luxuriously furnished. In high season, prices are in the premium range, but in low season, this is one of the best bargains in the Yucatán. One drawback: no beach. Call for off-season rates.

La Casa de los Sueños, on Carretera Garrafón, tel. (987) 7-0651, fax (987) 7-0708, U.S. tel. (800) 551-2558, is a small, colorful, nonsmoking resort with its own beach, "infinity" pool, nine rooms and suites, and graceful surroundings. Breakfast and bikes are included in the rates. Light lunches are available. Each room has a terrace or balcony with an ocean view, marble bathrooms, and a/c. The modern Mexican architecture sings with bright colors and beautiful pottery; an art gallery is planned. This is a really lovely place.

Condos

Expensive: At **Condo Nautibeach,** the large pink structure at the west end of Av. Rueda Medina, the condos have full kitchens and eclectic decor chosen by the individual owners, who rent out their places to tourists. The pool is particularly attractive; it's backed by the sea and bracketed by *palapa* bars. The restaurant here, Chez Magaly, is one of the island's fanciest.

For the visitor who plans to stay a week or two, two-bedroom apartments are available on the beach at **Cristalmar Resort and Beach Club,** south of town on the Cancún side of the island, U.S. tel. (800) 552-4550, Mexico fax (987) 7-0007. The apartment-suites have one or two bedrooms. Each is a/c and comfortable, with lots of tile and a color TV. Breakfast, lunch, and dinner are served by the pool near the *palapa* bar, which stays open all day. Taxis to town are about US$4. You can snorkel, sun, and swim; fishing and scuba diving can be arranged through the front desk. Hacienda Gomar is next door and the snorkeling is great under Gomar's dock—large schools of colorful fish enjoy the shade. Prices go down in the low season.

Note: Cristalmar is a family resort par excellence. We recently observed a wonderful family gathering here that included an 83-year-old great grandma, grandparents, eight siblings, and their brood of kids ages 3-17, lots of them—35 people in all. The gentleness shown by the entire hotel staff was remarkable, even when the little ones were dashing about, maybe yelling a little too loud, splashing in the pool, or bringing in their day's catch of fish for the chef to cook . . . "please." Even the pool-cleaning guy interrupted his chores to help the little city kids, who had never seen coconut trees and thought coconut came out of a package. He helped them climb the tree and capture the big yellow nut, then he split the coconut, explained the juice, and showed them how to clean it. During the holidays, Cristalmar puts out piñatas for the kids to attack and demolish, releasing the shower of candies and confetti inside. No wonder this is a favorite destination for families, year after year.

Premium: Between Laguna Makax and Bahía de Mujeres, **Villas Hi-Na-Ha,** Cancún tel. (98) 84-7074, U.S. tel. (800) 552-4550, offers pleasant two-bedroom, three-bathroom a/c villas with full kitchens overlooking the sea. Amenities include a beach, pool, and fishing pier. Breakfast is included in the rates.

FOOD

As always, seafood is the highlight of most restaurant menus on Isla Mujeres; the fish is caught right in the front yard. Dozens of simple, informal indoor and outdoor cafes and a number of small fast-food places sell *tortas,* tacos, and fried fish.

Arriba

Vegetarians and health-food fans are in luck at this great second-story restaurant on Hidalgo between Abasalo and Matamoros. The salads of fresh veggies and cucumber-dill dressing are worth celebrating, as are the vegetable kabobs and tempura served with wasabi and soy sauce. Fish and poultry dishes are prepared with a minimum of oil; potatoes are sauteed with jicama, onions, and herbs; and the Caribbean rice with ginger, vegetables, and egg is a meal in itself. Try the watermelon margarita or avocado pie for a real change of pace. Look for the blue-and-white trim and narrow stairway on Hidalgo. Open for lunch and dinner.

Cafecito

As the name implies, Cafecito, on Calle Juárez at Matamoros, serves great cappuccino and espresso, along with wonderful crepes filled with fresh fruit and ice cream. Breakfast choices include fresh waffles, fruit plates, and eggs—you may find yourself starting every day here!—while at dinner the chef goes all out with specialties that include a sublime shrimp curry (good, but expect to wait for your food). Glass-topped tables cover pretty arrangements of sand and shells, and soothing soft jazz plays in the background. Part of this small cafe's charm is its status as a gathering place for world travelers of all ages. Open 8 a.m.-noon and 6-10 p.m.; closed Thursday and Sunday nights.

Pinguino

Sunset watching is superb from the porch tables looking out to sea at Pinguino, the Posada del Mar's restaurant on Av. Rueda Medina, tel. (987) 7-0300. The chef does marvelous things with lobster here; if you're going to splurge, this is the place to do it. Plan on spending the evening and start with an appetizer of nachos or a seafood cocktail, then move on to the feast. Bands perform inside Pinguino during the high season, and at times it seems as if everyone in town partakes in the party. Pinguino is also good for huge breakfasts of *huevos rancheros,* yogurt and granola, and toasted homemade whole wheat bread.

El Mesón del Bucanero

On Hidalgo, this large outdoor cafe serves good seafood and Yucatecan specialties for breakfast, lunch, and dinner. Prices are reasonable— a breakfast of bacon, eggs, beans, and toast runs about US$3.50. Good fried fish and *chilaquiles.*

Miramar Restaurant

It's always nice to discover a cafe with good food, good service, and a nice ambience. That's the Miramar. It's nothing fancy, but the open-sided, *malecón* cafe provides great views of the harbor. You can see the ferries come and go and watch the fishermen cleaning their catch and tossing scraps to the waiting pelicans. Seafood dominates the menu; try the whole fried fish, about US$7.

Sol Dorado

A newish little place on Av. Madero, a couple of doors down from the Caribe Maya Hotel, the Sol Dorado features a nice garden behind the bar and pool table. Occasionally there's live music, and the food is good and reasonably priced (entrees start at about US$8).

Pizza Rolandi

This small cafe, on Av. Hidalgo between Madero and Abasolo, tel. (987) 7-0430, has good food and a usually efficient staff. It's one of the few places in town with a satellite dish, which they are willing to tune to such luxuries as NFL playoff games. The cafe serves beef, great fish, pastas, calzone, and pizza. Be sure to try their garlic bread; it's great with beer.

Bistro Francaise

Superb seafood is the hallmark of this cafe on Matamoros, and for good reason: Diane, the owner, hails from Montreal and is a former fish broker who inspects every fish and shrimp that comes into her restaurant. Breakfasts here are also tasty; try the excellent crepes or the french toast made with fresh bakery bread. Among the dinner specialties are filet mignon and shrimp curry.

Chez Magaly

Caribbean food with a European flavor is the specialty of Chez Magaly, on Av. Rueda Medina at Playa Norte's Nautibeach Condos, tel./fax (987) 7-0436. Sit by the sea and enjoy tender steaks, superb shrimp and lobster, authentic Caesar salad, and outstanding service. Sipping a tequila sunrise while watching the sunset is the *only* way to end a tropical day—or to begin a romantic candlelight dinner. Closed Monday.

Zacil Ha

This newish restaurant at the Nabalam hotel, on Calle Zazil at Playa Norte, tel. (987) 7-0279, is one of the island's best. Check out the popular happy hour in the *palapa* bar.

Others

Restaurante El Sombrero de Gomar, on the corner of Hidalgo and Madero, tel. (987) 7-0142, gives visitors an ice cream parlor on the street floor and colorful Mexican patio ambience on the second floor. The food is good, especially the barbecued meats. Everyone, even the waiter, seems to be having a good time—it's a real Mexican party. A little pricey but worth it; open 7 a.m-11 p.m.

On Playa Norte, try **Las Palapas Chimbo,** an open-air beach cafe serving simple but tasty fish dishes. As the evening goes on the music can get hot and last all night. **Café Mirtita,** on Av. Rueda Medina near Morelos, serves great brewed coffee and good simple food. A small fan mounted at each table ensures your comfort. This old standby consistently puts out good hotcakes, egg dishes, sandwiches, and hamburgers with all the trimmings (US$4). It's very clean and reasonable, and features friendly, quick service.

Check out the **Cafe Las Flores,** Av. Rueda Medina near Calle Matamoros, where you'll find such specialties as hummus with toasted pita chips, along with outstanding salads and delicious breakfast specials. If you want a box lunch to take to the beach, here's the place. Open daily 10:30 a.m.-4 p.m.; dinners in the offing.

Anyone who likes crepes with mushrooms and hollandaise better check out **El Nopalito,** Av. Guerrero 70 (near Matamoros), tel. (987) 7-0555, a small cafe attached to the folk art shop, El Nopal. You'll find homemade bread, yogurt, muesli, and lots of good sandwiches. The cafe is run by Anneliese Warren, who speaks English, German, and Spanish and who loves to talk about her island. The cafe is open daily for breakfast, and Mon.-Fri. for dinner.

Robert's, tel. (987) 7-0451, is a pretty pink and blue Caribbean-style house right on the main square—a good spot for lunch and peoplewatching.

Off the Beaten Path

For an unbeatable eating adventure, go inside the *mercado* and look for the sign on the wall that says *Don Nacho Beh, rey del taco* (Señor Beh really is "king of the taco" makers). Early

AISLINN RACE

Sunday mornings he prepares his prize recipe, *tacos de cochinita pibil.*

Best *licuados* and ice cream in town are at **La Flor de Michoacana,** across from the playground.

Groceries

If you prefer to cook your own meals, you can buy groceries at several places in town. The *mercado municipal* opens every morning till around noon; it has a fair selection, considering that everything must come from the mainland. Well-stocked supermarkets with liquor and toiletries include: **Mirtita,** Av. Juárez 14, tel. (987) 2-0127, open 6 a.m.-noon and 4-6 p.m.; and the larger **Super Betino,** Av. Morelos 5 (on the plaza), tel. (987) 7-0127, open 7 a.m.-9 p.m. **La Melosita,** Av. Hidalgo 17 (at Abasolo), tel. (987) 7-0445, is a mini-supermarket open 10 a.m.-midnight, with candies, piñatas, film, sundries, cigarettes, gifts, and snacks. **Panadería La Reina,** on Av. Madero, makes great *pan dulce.* It's open 6 a.m.-noon and 5-8 p.m. Fresh pastries appear on the shelves at 5 p.m.

ENTERTAINMENT AND SHOPPING

Nightlife

Little Isla Mujeres isn't the nightlife capital of Mexico. Those who need to be "entertained" will not find the clubs, shows, fireworks, and other glitzy coddling that is everywhere in Cancún. In fact, the reason many folks come to Isla Mujeres is to avoid all that—instead to stroll around the plaza, watch the moon reflect off the water, buy hot *elote* (corn) and sweets from the vendors, and watch families at play, observing the respectful relationships between the very young and old. This is the real Mexico.

Evening activities here might include taking in a Spanish-language movie at the theater (on Morelos near the plaza), dancing in the plaza during special fiestas, or listening to the military band that occasionally comes to the navy base. You might check out the **Casa de la Cultura** on Av. Guerrero, where classes are offered in a variety of subjects, including folk dancing, aerobics, and drawing. The Casa also has a library with a book exchange.

Those who must "party" will find a lively group of people and live or canned music at **Ya Ya's,** Av. López Mateos at Rueda Medina. It goes on late into the evening and there's a pool table and satellite TV. Breakfast, lunch, and dinner are served.

A Great Event

The free, 12-day **Isla Mujeres International Music Festival** takes place on the plaza beginning the second weekend in October. The island rocks with bands and dancers from everywhere. Hotel reservations are suggested. The plaza comes alive with music, and housewives set up tables to sell all kinds of homemade goodies from savory to sweets.

Massage

We found a fabulous masseuse in Isla Mujeres. Her name is Lane and she learned her profession while working at rehab centers in California. The ambience certainly adds to your experience; her small house is on the edge of a cliff overlooking the sea, and you hear the waves crashing on shore while you're being lulled into a somnolent state. Her massage lasts about an hour and a half and costs about US$45-50. For an appointment call (98) 45-2724.

Shopping

You'll find several excellent folk-art shops on Isla Mujeres. **La Loma,** Av. Guerrero 6 (near La Perla del Caribe Hotel), sells carved wooden masks from Guerrero, wooden animals from Oaxaca, lacquered boxes and trays, textiles from Guatemala, and a huge display of handcrafted jewelry. **El Nopal,** at the El Nopalito restaurant, has some beautiful embroidered dresses and shirts, as well as crafts from all over Mexico. Several shops along Calle Matamoros were filled with Guatemalan bags, vests, and jackets when we last looked, with a great selection at **Qué Bárbara.** Here you'll find *artesanía típica,* designer clothing, and art. T-shirts bearing the images of Maya gods are featured by the hundreds at **Casa del Arte México** on Av. Hidalgo; check out the fine limestone carvings as well. Gorgeous jewelry and precious gems are displayed at **Van Cleef & Arpels** and **Rachat & Rome,** both near the ferry pier.

SERVICES

Money

Banco Atlántico, on Rueda Medina between Madero and Morelos, tel. (987) 7-0005, will change money Mon.-Fri. 10 a.m. The bank also offers one ATM machine at the front of the bank and another on Av. Hidalgo at Madero. Money is returned in pesos, up to an equivalent of around US$200. It's not unusual for the machines to run out of cash, so get money during banking hours. Though banks always give the best exchange rate, many *casas de cambio* are reasonable, perhaps charging an extra US$0.60 per US$100 over the bank rate. You'll see signs here and there; an easy one to find is across the street from Banco Atlántico near the ferry (frequently their rate is comparable to the bank).

Many stores, hotels, and restaurants in Isla accept credit cards, but ask first.

Medical Services

For medical treatment, call Dr. Greta Shorey, tel. (987) 7-0443, a Briton in charge of the Red Cross on the island. We've never had occasion to use her but have heard great reviews from a couple of readers. Another local doctor, Dr. Salas, also has a good reputation.

You'll find well-stocked *farmacias* at Av. Juárez 2 and on Av. Francisco Madero at Hidalgo.

Travel Agencies

While on Isla Mujeres, for all of your travel needs contact **Club de Yates de Isla Mujeres.** They can fix you up with side trips to the mainland or fishing trips from Isla Mujeres. Even if you don't want a ticket but have a problem while you're on the island, stop in and ask for help—they'll do their best. To get to Club de Yates coming off the

---

**ISLA MUJERES
TELEPHONE NUMBERS**

city hall	(987) 7-0098
police station	(987) 7-0082
customs office	(987) 7-0189
chamber of commerce.	(987) 7-0132
office of tourism	(987) 7-0188

---

dock, turn left and walk about 150 meters; their office is on the left, tel. (987) 7-0086 or 7-0211.

In the U.S., for good guidance in choosing a hotel or purchasing airline tickets, and for local transportation information, call Isla Mujeres specialists at tel. (800) 552-4550 or (608) 297-2332, fax (608) 297-2272. They will design a trip to fit your needs.

Other Services

A limited selection of **newspapers and magazines** can be found on the corner of Juárez and Bravo. The **post office** is at Av. Guerrero 13; open weekdays 9 a.m.-9 p.m., Saturday, Sunday, and holidays 9 a.m.-noon. **Tim Pho** on Av. Juárez, does laundry by the kilo. Bring it in separated or all your white socks might come back pink.

GETTING THERE

Passengers-Only Ferries

Two types of passenger boats travel from Puerto Juárez to Isla Mujeres. The modern, a/c, enclosed ferries charge about US$3.50 one-way and make the crossing in less than half an hour. The older open ferries charge about US$1.75 each way and make the trip in 45 minutes. Buy your ticket on board for either boat. At least one boat leaves every hour from Puerto Juárez to Isla Mujeres 6 a.m.-8 p.m., and from Isla Mujeres to Puerto Juárez 5 a.m.-6 p.m. At the foot of the dock in Puerto Juárez you'll find a tourist information center sponsored by the municipal government, with bilingual employees and a restroom (small fee). The office is open sporadically, and during the off season it's hard to find someone.

From Playa Linda Pier in the Cancún hotel zone, a more comfortable boat, the **Shuttle Express,** tel. (98) 83-3448, leaves four times a day for the island. The fare is about US$13 roundtrip. This may not be as costly as it sounds when you consider that taking a taxi from the hotel zone to Puerto Juárez can cost almost as much roundtrip as the shuttle. (You could catch a bus to Puerto Juárez—Ruta 8 from Av. Tulum—for a lot less, although that could be recommended only if you're traveling light.)

Note: Be aware of the time the last passenger boat leaves Isla Mujeres. If you haven't got a

Isla Mujeres Port

hotel reservation you might have to sleep on the beach, and it can rain any time of year.

Car-and-Passenger Ferries
A car ferry leaves Punta Sam (five km north of Puerto Juárez) daily and carries passengers and cars to Isla Mujeres. You really need a good reason to bring a car, though; the island is short, with narrow, one-way streets. RVs can travel on the ferry, but there are very few places to park once you're there and no hookups.

The trip on the ferry from Punta Sam takes 45 minutes. Arrive at the ferry dock an hour before departure time to secure a place in line; tickets go on sale 30 minutes in advance. The ferry departs from Punta Sam six times daily 7 a.m.-8 p.m., and from Isla Mujeres six times daily 6 a.m.-7 p.m. Fare for an ordinary passenger car is about US$6 (more for RVs) and about US$2 for each passenger. Walk-on passengers are permitted. The car-ferry schedule tends to run on time.

Those traveling the Peninsula by bus will find it easier to make ongoing connections in Puerto Juárez than in Punta Sam.

GETTING AROUND

Mujeres is a small and mostly flat island, and in town you can walk everywhere. The eight-km (five-mile) distance from one end of the island to the other is a fairly easy trek for the experienced hiker. Other options include taxis, bicycles, rental cars, golf carts, motorcycles, and municipal buses.

Cars, Carts, Mopeds, and Bicycles
If you want to see the outer limits of the island, bicycles and mopeds are the most popular ways to go. The newest trend in transportation is the golf cart, which travels at a top speed of about 15 km per hour. The carts are safer for novices than mopeds and provide more shelter from the sun. Rental cars are beginning to appear on the island as well. Most hotels can arrange rentals, or you can check with the shops scattered all over downtown. Rental carts cost about US$60 per (24-hour) day, US$50 per eight-hour day, or US$14 per hour. Mopeds are about US$35 for 24 hours, US$23 for eight hours, or US$8 per hour. Bike rentals run about US$7-10 for eight hours.

By Taxi
Taxis are plentiful and easy to get; fares are posted at the taxi stand. The main taxi stand is on Av. Rueda Medina next to the ferry dock; service is available 24 hours, tel. (987) 7-0066. Taxis deal strictly in pesos, and fares double after midnight. A two-hour tour around the island in a taxi—including stops to watch the lighthouse keeper making hammocks and to inspect the Maya temple on the south tip—will cost around US$15 per trip, for up to three passengers.

MAYA RIVIERA

For centuries after the Spaniards came, the ancient Maya structures at Tulum, Cobá, Akumal, and Xcaret were mostly deserted, serving as jungle-gyms for the thorny iguana in the middle of the bush. After centuries of tropical rains the stone ruins were covered with vines, ferns, and tall trees growing from nooks and crannies in the stone. Historians believe that in pre-Cortesian times, Tulum and Xcaret were used as nautical lookouts along the turquoise coast. Today the same locations welcome busloads of curious tourists.

Now called the Maya Riviera, the stretch of coast between Cancún and Tulum is reached via paved Hwy. 307 (soon to be four lanes) paralleling the Caribbean. In addition to the ruins, travelers will find myriad resorts, beautiful beaches, and growing villages—not to mention the aqua sea that edges this flamboyant part of the world.

PUERTO MORELOS

Puerto Morelos, 17 km south of Cancún, is the first small village on the north end of the Maya Riviera. The town has limited accommodations and few attractions to detain most people. At one time its only claim to fame was the vehicle ferry to Cozumel. But more and more people are beginning to notice Puerto Morelos's peaceful mood, lack of tourists, and easy access to the sea. As with some of the other towns on the Caribbean coast, divers are bringing low-key attention to Puerto Morelos, using the town as a base to explore the rich coastline. Another interesting development is the availability here of many forms of yoga and meditation; check with the hotels.

A short walk through town reveals a central plaza, shops, and a cantina; a military base is nearby. For years the little plaza has been relatively uninspiring. However, the village is proud of two new (ecological) dry-compost public restrooms on the small plaza, and who knows what other changes will have occurred by the time you get there! During the winter season the town holds a Sunday *Tianguis* (market) on the plaza—fun things to browse through, a gathering place for locals and visitors alike.

Puerto Morelos's most spectacular attraction is its reef, which begins 20 km north of town. Directly in front of Puerto Morelos, 550 meters offshore, the reef takes on gargantuan dimensions—between 20 and 30 meters wide. For the scuba diver and snorkeler this reef is a dream come true, with dozens of caverns alive with coral and fish.

This tranquil dock offers good fishing.

OZ MALLAN

Jardín Botánico
On the way to Punta Bete, just a couple of km south of Puerto Morelos, you'll find a lovely botanical garden, study center, and tree nursery spread over 60 hectares (150 acres). Three km of trails wind under a canopy of trees, past specimens (labeled in English, Spanish, and Latin) of the Peninsula's plants and flowers. Habitats range from semievergreen tropical forest to mangrove swamp. Look for the epiphyte area, with a variety of orchids, tillandsias, and bromeliads. As you wander around you'll also find a re-creation of a Maya *chiclero* camp (showing how chicle was harvested to be used in chewing gum), some small ruins from the Post-Classic period, and a contemporary Maya hut illustrating day-to-day life—from cooking facilities to hammocks. Be prepared: wear good walking shoes, cover up your arms and legs, and use bug spray—the jungle is full of biting critters at certain times of year.

The garden is open daily 9 a.m.-5 p.m. Admission is US$2 and includes a map of the area. You can hire a guide for an additional US$5.

CrocoCun
About 1.6 km north of town, look along the seaward side of the highway for the turnoff to this fascinating little crocodile farm. Here you'll observe crocs—from babies to full-grown adults—and learn how they breed, hatch, and lots more. Hang onto the kids!

Snorkeling and Scuba Diving
Snorkeling is best done on the inland side of the reef, where the depth is about three meters; expect visibility up to 25 meters. The reef has long been a menace to ships; early records date losses from the 16th century. One wrecked Spanish galleon here is a boon for divers; its coral-crusted cannons are clearly visible from the surface five meters above. Another exciting dive destination is **Sleeping Sharks Caves,** eight km offshore.

Scuba divers will get good service at the PADI-affiliated **Wet Set** dive shop at the Caribbean Reef Club Hotel, tel. (987) 1-0198. The shop also offers snorkeling, fishing, and other water sports.

Fishing
Onshore fishing is only fair off the pier. Deep-sea fishing can be arranged at the hotel Posada Amor.

QUEEN CONCH

A popular, easy-to-catch food beautifully packaged—that's the *problem* with the queen conch (pronounced "conk"). For generations inhabitants of the Caribbean nations have been capturing the conch for their sustenance. The land available for farming on some islands is scant, and the people (who are poor) have depended on the sea—especially the conch—to feed their families. Even Columbus was impressed with the beauty of the peach-colored shell, taking one back to Europe with him on his return voyage.

The locals discovered a new means of making cash in the 1970s—exporting conch meat to the United States. The shell is also a cash byproduct sold to throngs of tourists looking for local souvenirs. An easy way to make money, except for one thing: soon there will be no more conch! In recent years the first signs of overfishing have become evident; smaller-sized conch are being taken, and fishermen are finding it necessary to go farther afield to get a profitable catch.

It takes three to five years for this sea snail to grow from larva stage to market size. It also takes about that long for planktonic conch larvae carried into fished-out areas by the currents to replenish themselves. What's worse, the conch is easy to catch; large (shell lengths get up to 390 cm) and heavy (about three kilograms), the mollusk moves slowly and lives in shallow, crystalline water where it's easy to spot. All of these attributes are contributing to its demise.

Biologists working with various governments are trying to impose new restrictions that include closed seasons, minimum size of capture, a limit on total numbers taken by the entire fishing industry each year, limited numbers per fisherman, restrictions on the types of gear that can be used, and most important—the cessation of exportation. Along with these legal limitations, technology is lending a hand. Research has begun, and several mariculture centers are now experimenting with the queen conch, raising animals in a protected environment until they're large enough for market or grown to juvenile size to be released into the wild.

A new research center at Puerto Morelos is in operation and recently released its first group of juvenile conchs to supplement wild stock. This is not always successful. Sometimes one group of larvae will survive, and the next 10 will not—for no clear-cut reason. In the wild, not only does the conch have humans to contend with, it also has underwater predators: lobsters, crabs, sharks, turtles, and rays.

The conch is not an endangered species yet, but it must be protected for the people who depend on it for life.

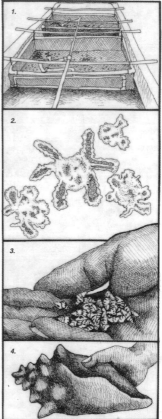

1. These tanks hold juvenile queen conch.
2. conch larval stage
3. From these tiny shells . . .
4. . . . grow these beautiful large mollusks.

DIANA LASICH HARPER

Day-Trips

Local resident Sandra Dayton, tel.(987) 1-0136, leads trips into the jungle for a glimpse of the Maya culture. You'll first visit the Jardín Botánico to learn about medicinal plants and traditional remedies, then trek to a Maya village as a guest. Lunch and a swim at a secluded cenote are all part of the day.

Hotels

Budget/Inexpensive: Simple, 20-room **Posada Amor,** tel. (987) 1-0033, fax (987) 1-0178, is a friendly, family-run hotel with ceiling fans, shared baths (some private baths) with hot water, and a patio where you'll meet other independent travelers. The lighthearted decor is mosquito-netting tropical. Nonguests can take a hot shower for US$3. Try the all-day Sunday buffet in the family-run restaurant in front.

Inexpensive: Hacienda Morelos, one block south of the plaza, tel. (987) 1-0015, overlooks the beach. The upstairs rooms are especially nice, offering a great view of the sea. All rooms have cooling ocean breezes, mini-refrigerators, immaculate white decor, and bathtubs as well as showers—a rarity in these parts. A small pool and sunbathing area sit right above the beach and an enclosed parking lot is out front. The main entrance is at the Daisy restaurant, one of the best in town.

Hotel Playa Ojo de Agua, tel. (987) 1-0015, offers modern rooms overlooking a beautiful beach just north of town center. The rooms have kitchens and ceiling fans; other amenities include a dive shop and pool. For information or reservations contact Ernesto Muñoz, Calle 12 #96, Colonia Yucatán, Mérida, Yucatán 97000, Mexico, tel. (99) 25-0293.

Expensive: Rancho Libertad, tel. (987) 1-0181, U.S. tel. (888) 305-5224, is a *palapa* hideaway south of the ferry dock, next to Caribbean Reef Club. Its charming two-story cabañas sit right on the sand, and offer private baths with hot water, ceiling fans, suspended beds, and great beachfront shade *palapas.* Rates include a continental-breakfast buffet. Adults only.

Premium: South of the ferry dock on an isolated stretch of white-sand beach, the **Caribbean Reef Club at Villa Marina,** tel. (987) 1-0191, fax (987) 1-0190, U.S. tel. (800) 3-CANCUN, offers spacious rooms and suites with fans

and a/c, cool tile floors, cozy living areas and terraces, and kitchen facilities with microwave ovens. Guests will find satellite TV, a pool, a friendly bar, and a beachfront restaurant where you get not only great fresh seafood but good Cuban-style cooking as well. Diving equipment is available on the premises at the **Wet Set** dive shop, and guests receive free use of Windsurfers, Sunfish sailboats, tennis courts, and more. This great getaway spot is also just a few minutes' walk from a "European-style" beach.

Yoga Retreat

Expensive: At **Villa Shanti,** owners Jack and Jean Loew have created a secluded, comfortable yoga retreat in their eight-apartment villa just a block from the beach. Jean Loew offers yoga classes twice a week and week-long yoga retreats in the high season. Guests are treated to the classes as well as to shiatsu therapy. Each apartment has a bedroom, modern bathroom, kitchen, a/c, and fan; outside there's a barbecue area, swimming pool, and large *palapa* strung with hammocks. The Villa is also used by groups for yoga, rebirthing, channeling, and healing retreats. For information on reservations and upcoming retreats, contact the Loews 1 May-30 Nov. at P.O. Box 464, Glen, New Hampshire 03838-0464 USA, tel. (603) 383-6501; 1 Dec.-30 April at Apdo. Postal 789, Cancún, Quintana Roo 77500, Mexico, tel. (987) 1-0040, fax (987) 1-0041.

Rental Properties

Several private houses and apartments in Puerto Morelos are available for rentals of a week or more. Bill and Connie Bucher have two properties for rent: **Cabañas Puerto Morelos,** which consists of three one-bedroom units with sitting areas and kitchens; and **Villa Amigos,** a two-bedroom, two-bath house (the master bathroom has a bathtub, rare in these parts) with a full kitchen and outside patio. For rates and information call or fax (612) 441-7630 in the U.S., or (987) 1-0004 in Puerto Morelos.

Vicki Sharp also offers two rentals: **Los Arrecifes,** consisting of eight nicely furnished apartments, each with separate bedroom and full kitchen, on a great windswept beach north of town; and **Casa Miguel,** a beautiful guesthouse closer to town. For rates and information contact Sharp at Apdo. Postal 986, Cancún, Quintana

Roo 77500, Mexico, tel. (987) 1-0112, fax (98) 83-2244; she also knows about other rental properties in the area.

Villas Clarita is a two-story, Spanish-style building five blocks from town. It offers four one-bedroom apartments—each with kitchen and either a balcony or patio—as well as separate one and two bedroom cabañas set around a swimming pool. For rates and information call (508) 535-4869 in the U.S., or (987) 1-0042 in Puerto Morelos. **Villa Latinas,** tel.(987) 1-0075, has seven furnished apartments for rent by the week or month.

Camping

No one minds if campers spread their sleeping bags north and south of the lighthouse away from town, houses, and hotels. The beach is free and this is a relatively safe, peaceful town. Choose a high spot sb you'll stay dry. It can get gritty if the wind freshens, and if it's very still be prepared for mosquitoes.

Food

Several good budget cafes serving typical Mexican food and good seafood circle the main plaza. The **Posada Amor Restaurant** can be depended on for outstanding *mole poblano* and other regional dishes at moderate prices. **Los Pelicanos** serves good hamburgers. And the waterfront **Restaurant Las Palmeras** serves excellent fresh seafood in a pleasant atmosphere; the *pulpo Mexicano* (octopus) is delicious, as is conch in garlic sauce.

Palapa Pizzeria is a popular hangout by the plaza. **Daisy Restaurant,** on the beach south of the plaza at the Hacienda Morelos hotel, is the fanciest in-town restaurant. Its large brick dining room faces the sea and holds fountains and folk art. The seafood is excellent, as are the Mexican dishes, and the staff is most accommodating. **Horizantle** is a neat little coffee shop near the plaza.

For all-out feasting, one of the best restaurants in town is at the **Caribbean Reef Club,** where a talented Cuban chef prepares steaks, ribs, and burgers imported from the United States.

Shopping

Puerto Morelos has a supermarket called **Autoservicio Marino**—look for a red-brick front and a big sign with Popeye and Olive Oyl next to the Posada Amor. They carry almost everything in a shopping-cart atmosphere.

Stop at **Arte Maya** to see unique artwork being created. The finished product consists of brightly painted metal cut-outs in a variety of sizes and designs—bracelets, wall hangings, etc. Started some 17 years ago by the late Armando Fernández in his home, the shop now has a staff of craftspeople. You'll see Fernández's work in upscale shopping centers in Cancún. The prices are better here!

Services

The **bank** is open to cash traveler's checks Mon.-Fri. 9:30 a.m.-1 p.m. **Marand Travel** (opposite Posada Amor) also cashes traveler's checks. A liquor store, pharmacy, and car repair are within walking distance of downtown. Ask at the pharmacy about the laundromat; last we checked it was a few km away, near UNAM.

Puerto Morelos has one of the best gas station/rest areas along Hwy. 307. Though gas availability has become more reliable and stations are placed reasonably close to each other (others are at Tulum, Playa del Carmen, and Felipe Carrillo Puerto), top off your tank whenever you can. The Puerto Morelos station also has two markets, a public Ladatel phone, restrooms, and a restaurant.

Getting There

Buses from north and south stop at Puerto Morelos frequently. From Cancún it's about a 40-minute drive, from Chetumal about five hours. Hitching is reasonably easy from the larger towns (Chetumal, Cancún, Felipe Carrillo Puerto, Playa del Carmen); try Hwy. 307 where the service roads enter the towns.

Ferry to Cozumel

The vehicle ferry to Isla Cozumel departs Puerto Morelos daily beginning at 6 a.m. Check the schedule the night before. Be at the dock two or three hours early to get in the passenger-car line. It also expedites things to have correct change and the car's license number in hand when you approach the ticket window. The ticket office is open 5 a.m.-6 p.m. The trip takes two hours and can be a rough crossing, so take your Dramamine if you tend to get seasick. Light snacks are sold on the passenger deck. This ferry does not have a "cruise-ship" ambience.

Note: If you happen to be in Puerto Morelos on Christmas Eve, be sure to drop in at the vehicle ferry. Every year the company throws a typical Christmas party—big buffet dinner, drinks, piñatas for the kids—and it goes on until the last dog leaves. Of course it's all free!

PUNTA BETE

Continuing south on the highway, you'll soon come to Punta Bete. Not a town, at least not yet, it's just a four-km stretch of beach that's a complete tropical fantasy. Swaying palms hover along the edge of pure white sand, with gentle blue crystal waves running across the shore. Getting in and out of the water here can be hazardous to your feet, thanks to rocks and coral scattered on the sea floor. Shoes or sandals help. If you have diving booties, use them. The rocky bottom makes a perfect snorkeling area 10-20 meters offshore.

As recently as 1965, no tourists visited this part of the coast. At that time Quintana Roo was only a federal territory and there wasn't even a road to this fine white-powdered beach. Family groups, mostly descendants of the Chan Santa Cruz Indians, tended their small, self-sufficient *cocales* (miniature coconut plantations). In recent years, yellowing disease destroyed most of the tall coconut palms. A new species of palm, resistant to the devastating disease that began in Florida, has now been planted. Today, most of the old *cocales* are small tourist centers.

Cabañas Capitán Lafitte

This all-inclusive resort draws a large repeat clientele with fine service, good food, and a wonderful beach location. The stucco oceanfront cabañas have double- and king-sized beds, hot water, ceiling fans, and private bath. Along with daily maid service, each room is provided with a handmade reed broom to help keep the sand out. Other amenities include a swimming pool, game room, and coffee delivered to your room each morning. Every afternoon between 5 and 6 p.m., a flock of small, colorful parrots flies over the pool.

A full dive shop on the premises has a good selection of rental equipment, including sailboards. The management provides transportation by skiff to nearby Lafitte Reef, an exciting snorkeling destination. Here, a lazy day of floating on the clear sea will bring you face-to-face with blue chromis, angelfish, rock beauties, and often the ugly grouper—it's a great place to use your underwater camera.

Successful anglers can have their catch prepared by the restaurant chef. Hands off the large, handsome turtles you may see, and don't expect to find turtle soup or conch ceviche on the menu; the management makes it clear that they support the preservation of these endangered species.

Rates, including breakfast and dinner: US$85 pp double occupancy, children 4-10 US$38 per night, children three and under free. There's an extra US$10 charge per room for a/c, and a US$20 per room surcharge on holidays. During high season it's best to have reservations. Ask about Casa Olé and El Cofre, large two-story beachfront duplexes for families. No credit cards or personal checks are accepted; cash and traveler's checks only. Car rentals are available.

For information and reservations contact Turquoise Reef Group, P.O. Box 2664, Evergreen, CO 80439 USA, tel. (800) 538-6802 or (303) 674-9615, fax (303) 674-8735.

Shangri-La Caribe Resort

On its own entry road 62 km south of Cancún, Shangri-La Caribe is an almost-luxurious resort and a perfect perfect place to kick back. Exotic stucco-and-*palapa* bungalows, each with private bath, hold comfortable beds, fans, tile floors, hot water, and balconies or patios with hammocks. The beachfront bungalows are just steps from the sea. Other amenities include a swimming pool, a poolside bar and grill, a dive shop, gift shop, and car-rental desk. A large, circular *palapa* serves as a gathering place during the cocktail hour and is a great place to meet fellow travelers. Breakfast and candlelit dinner are served in a lovely indoor/outdoor dining room; the food is great.

The dive shop, **Cyan Ha,** is open seven days a week, offers rentals and lessons, and has a PADI-certified divemaster. Beginners should ask about trips to the shallow reefs of Chenzubul—a perfect place to enjoy a secure but exciting introduction to the Caribbean underwater world and its exotic inhabitants. All swimmers will enjoy exploring nearby Cenote Jabali.

Rates, including breakfast, dinner, taxes, and tips: US$130-180 d (depending on proximity to the beach), children 4-10 US$38, children three and under free. No credit cards. For reservations contact Turquoise Reef Group, P.O. Box 2664, Evergreen, CO 80439 USA, tel. (800) 538-6802 or (303) 674-9615, fax (303) 674-8735.

Las Palapas Cabañas

Just south of Shangri-La Caribe, lovely Las Palapas Cabañas Resort, tel. (987) 3-0582 or 3-0584, fax (987) 3-0458, is nearly idyllic. Its 50 units (in two-story *palapa*-roofed buildings) are comfortable, clean, and upscale. Hammocks hang on the front porches and small desks face windows looking out to landscaped walkways or the beach. The large pool is great for swimming laps, while the white-sand beach seems to go on forever—you can easily walk to Playa del Carmen along the shore. Gourmet meals are served in the large *palapa*-covered dining room and often feature German dishes for the frequent German tour groups that stay here. The management and staff go out of their way to make your stay comfortable; many guests spend a week or more.

Rates, including breakfast and dinner, tax, and tip: from US$130-184 d, depending on time of year and room location. No credit cards—cash or traveler's checks only.

Xcalacoco

Budget travelers can skip the all-inclusive resorts and head straight to Xcalacoco; follow Hwy. 307 south until you see the "Punta Bete" sign, then turn east onto a white single track road leading 2.2 km to the sea. Here you'll find an area to camp (about US$5, bring bug repellent and mosquito netting), as well as **Novelo's**, eight simple cement cabañas on the lovely white sand. Each of the budget-priced cabañas offers a tile floor, king bed, private bathroom, and front-porch hammock; candles and kerosene in place of electricity provide a romantic atmosphere. A *palapa* restaurant on the beach serves good Mexican specialties. For reservations contact Ricardo and Rosa Novelo, Xcalacoco, "Punta Bete," Apdo. Postal 176, Playa del Carmen, Quintana Roo, 77710 Mexico. No phone.

Getting There

A taxi from Cancún will cost approximately US$45-55 for up to four passengers. From Playa del Carmen taxi fare is less. Heading south from Puerto Morelos, Capitán Lafitte is the first of the Punta Bete resorts you'll come to; watch for the signed turnoff on the highway. From there it's approximately eight km farther south to Shangri-La and Las Palapas. A couple of good mini-buses run from Cancún to all the resorts along the Maya Riviera, leaving from the ADO bus station. Ask for directions when making reservations.

PLAYA DEL CARMEN

Not too many years ago, your stroll through Playa del Carmen would have been escorted by children, dogs, little black pigs, and incredibly ugly turkeys; you might even have seen the milkman delivering milk from large cans strapped to his donkey's back. No more. The small town that we writers used to describe as a "sleepy fishing village" has today exploded into a large Caribbean resort.

With its population increasing nearly 20% annually, Playa del Carmen is the fastest-growing area in Quintana Roo. Tourists crowd the streets, and the milkman has been replaced by mini-markets with modern refrigeration. Ferries from Cozumel come and go all day, and luxury cruise ships anchor close by in the bay.

Though high-rises are so far absent, the town is sprawling farther north as more and more visitors return for a permanent stay. And classy hotels and condos are spreading along the beach south of the dock; in fact, there you'll find a whole new community called **Playacar,** which holds an 18-hole golf course, **Aviary Xaman Ha,** Maya ruins, a few restaurants, several new hotels, and even a small private school.

Nature endowed Playa del Carmen with a broad, beautiful beach—one of the Peninsula's finest. It's filled with jet-setters when ships are in port. The rest of the time it plays host to a conglomeration of independent travelers: archaeology buffs, students of Maya culture, backpackers, adventure seekers, and sun-lovers. The cooler early hours are best for walking along the beach. Warm afternoons are perfect for swimming and snorkeling, snoozing on the sand, or watching the magnificent frigate bird make silent circles above you, hoping to rob another bird of its catch.

The waterfront has been greatly improved with the addition of a brick-lined pedestrians-only *malecón*, whose low wall makes a perfect perch for evening peoplewatching or stargazing. Avenida 5, the main street running parallel to the *malecón* one block west, has also been turned into a pedestrian walkway, where new cafes and shops are opening at an amazing rate. Though not as inexpensive as it once was, the town is still a bargain compared to Cancún or Cozumel.

Note: The persistent old rumor that there will be an international airport in Playa has been heating up lately. Who knows, it may come to pass, but I hope they finish building Hwy. 307 first!

Accommodations

Shoestring: Playa del Carmen's **CREA youth hostel** can't be beat. Follow the signs off the main street about one kilometer (about a 15-

This relaxed family enjoys living out of their camper on the beach for several months each year.

OZ MALLAN

minute walk from the bus station). Bunks in fairly new, clean, single-sex dorms cost US$8 pp, and simple cabañas (most sleeping up to four) rent for US$17 per night. Amenities include a dining room with reasonably priced food, a basketball court, and an auditorium. Too bad it's not closer to the beach.

Budget: Mom's Hotel, Av. 30 at Calle 4, tel. (987) 3-0315, combines a bed and breakfast with rooms and apartments. It offers simple pleasant accommodations, secure parking, a pool, restaurant, bar, and lots of books.

Inexpensive: Tree Tops Hotel, Calle 8, tel. (987) 3-0351, has a jungly patio and simple rooms, some with private bath and some shared. **Hotel Alejari,** on Calle 6, tel. (987) 3-0374, fax (987) 3-0005, is a hidden gem set in a garden environment. The duplexes and studios are clean and simple, with a/c or fan, tile floors, hot water, and private bathrooms; some have kitchenettes. Beach access is available through the back gate, and the reception office has a public phone.

Moderate: Bed and Breakfast Bal Na Kah, on Calle 12 just off Av. 5, occupies a delightful two-story building a short walk from the beach or town. Mino, the proprietor, serves a simple breakfast each morning and keeps a bowl of fruit handy all day long. In addition, the kitchen and refrigerator are open to guests to prepare meals, and every once in a while Mino throws an impromptu potluck supper. Lots of fun, interesting people seem to be attracted to Bal Na Kah. Binki is the favorite house parrot. Reservations are advised; this well priced hostel stays pretty full. For information and reservations, contact Turquoise Reef Resorts, P.O. Box 2664, Evergreen, CO 80439 USA; tel. (800) 538-6802, fax (303) 674-8735.

Albatros Royale, three blocks north of the plaza at Calle 6 and Av. 5, tel. (987) 3-0001, is one of the nicest hotels along this stretch of beach. Owner Sam Beard, an American expat, knows how to offer his guests comfort without exorbitant rates. The Royale's two-story buildings face each other across a landscaped pathway leading to the beach. Hammocks are strung by the front door or on the balcony of each room, and guests tend to congregate on patios for card games and conversation. Tile floors and fans keep the 31 rooms cool and comfortable. Call (800) 538-6802 (Turquoise Reef Resorts) or the hotel for reservations.

Expensive: Mosquito Blue, at Av. 5 between Calles 12 and 14, tel./fax (987) 2-1245, offers a pool, a big outdoor movie screen, and well-kept, attractive rooms with a/c, modern bathrooms, and cable TV. **Chichan Baal Kah,** Calle 16 Norte, U.S. tel. (800) 538-6802 or (303) 674-9615, is a charming hotel in a shady residential neighborhood—a welcome change from the hustle and bustle of downtown Playa. The quiet little hotel offers seven kitchen-equipped suites, each sleeping three people (no children under 16 allowed). The kitchens all have juicers—there's almost always a basket of oranges around—and table service for six. Full maid and linen service are provided; other amenities include a small swimming pool, a sun deck with barbecue facilities, and an honor bar. Early-bird coffee service and bikes are available. This is a honey!

Mayan Paradise, Av. 10, tel./fax (987) 3-0933, is a newer hotel offering 40 rooms with kitchen, a/c, TV, and *palapa* ambience. Amenities include a great pool, beautiful landscaping, and a terrific restaurant. Though not on the beach, the hotel has its own beach club; ask at the desk.

On the outer edge of the busy town center, **Hotel Da Gabi,** Calle 12 just off Av. 5, fax (987) 3-0048, is a fine little hotel with fan-cooled rooms, 100 meters from the beach. The excellent Italian restaurant on site serves homemade fettuccine, ravioli, and brick-oven baked pizza.

The white stucco, Spanish-style **Pelicano Inn,** U.S. tel. (800) 538-6802, is a real treat. Each room has a private bathroom, a hammock, and a balcony to watch the sea. King size beds are available, and rates include a breakfast buffet. No a/c, but there are fans.

Expensive/Premium: Near the Continental Plaza Playacar, **Playacar Condominiums** are beautifully designed and either right on the beach or a short walk away. A five-minute stroll from town, each unit has one to three bedrooms, a fully equipped kitchen, washer and dryer, and living room. Some units have balconies, and the complex has a swimming pool. These are great for families or small groups. Prices begin at about US$110 per night for a one-bedroom condo, depending on time of year. For more information write to Apdo. Postal 396, Cancún, Quintana Roo 77500, Mexico.

Premium: Continental Plaza Playacar, tel. (987) 3-0100, fax (987) 3-0105, U.S./Canada tel. (800) 882-6684, was the first hotel built south of the dock. The five-floor hotel is occupied by 188 rooms and 16 suites, all with a/c, satellite TV, private terraces overlooking the Caribbean, tile bathrooms and floors, and comfy beds. Common-area amenities include a beautiful pool and lounging area, several dining rooms and bars, and a spacious, attractive lobby (check out the striking painting of the birds and animals of Quintana Roo). Scattered around the grounds are many Maya ruins that

Continental Plaza Playacar

OZ MALLAN

were carefully preserved while the hotel was being built. If you need luxury, this is the place. Reservations are a must, since the hotel is often filled with large tour groups. Ask about good package deals.

Premium (All-Inclusive): Diamond All-Inclusive Resort, tel. (987) 3-0341, fax (987) 3-0348, U.S. tel. (800) 858-2258, is part of the Di-

amond all-inclusive chain. Rooms are upscale, with lovely decor, a/c, modern bathrooms, and comfortable beds. Rates include almost everything: meals, snacks, drinks, taxes, tips, and most activities, including diving, snorkeling, tennis, volleyball, scuba lessons, bikes, and aerobics. It's one big party with theme nights, live entertainment, and excellent food.

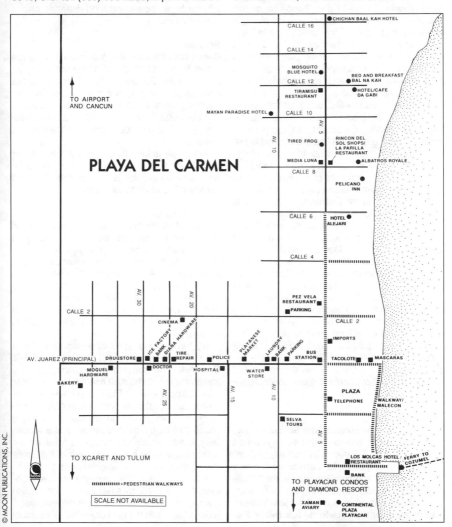

PLAYA DEL CARMEN

TO AIRPORT AND CANCUN

CHICHAN BAAL KAH HOTEL
CALLE 16
CALLE 14
MOSQUITO BLUE HOTEL
BED AND BREAKFAST BAL NA KAH
CALLE 12
TIRAMISU RESTAURANT
HOTEL/CAFE DA GABI
MAYAN PARADISE HOTEL
CALLE 10
AV. 5
AV. 10
TIRED FROG
RINCON DEL SOL SHOPS/ LA PARILLA RESTAURANT
MEDIA LUNA
ALBATROS ROYALE
CALLE 8
PELICANO INN
CALLE 6
HOTEL ALEJARI
CALLE 4
PEZ VELA RESTAURANT
PARKING
CALLE 2
AV. 30
AV. 20
CINEMA
CALLE 2
ICE FACTORY
BANK
DIANA HARDWARE
IMPORTS
AV. JUAREZ (PRINCIPAL)
DRUGSTORE
TIRE REPAIR
PLAYANESE MARKET
LAUNDRY
BANK
BUS STATION
TACOLOTE
MASCARAS
MOGUEL HARDWARE
DOCTOR
POLICE
HOSPITAL
WATER STORE
BAKERY
AV. 25
AV. 15
AV. 10
PLAZA
TELEPHONE
WALKWAY/ MALECON
SELVA TOURS
AV. 5
TO XCARET AND TULUM
LOS MOLCAS HOTEL/ RESTAURANT
FERRY TO COZUMEL
BANK
TO PLAYACAR CONDOS AND DIAMOND RESORT
IIIIIIIIII = PEDESTRIAN WALKWAYS
XAMAN AVIARY
CONTINENTAL PLAZA PLAYACAR
SCALE NOT AVAILABLE

Food

New restaurants are springing up even faster than hotels in Playa del Carmen. Around the central plaza several small cafes serve a variety of good inexpensive Mexican, Italian, and seafood dishes.

For Yucatecan food or good fresh seafood at moderate prices, try **Pez Vela,** on Av. 5 near Calle 2; open 8 a.m.-11 p.m. **Tacolote,** on the first block off the beach, across from the plaza, is modeled after a cafe of the same name in Cancún (but has different owners). Beloved for its many varieties of tacos and heaping platters of fajitas, it gets very noisy—especially when all the restaurants along that road decide to turn up their music to outdo each other.

Máscaras, on the first block off the beach across from the plaza, is an excellent Italian restaurant serving delicious pizza and pasta—most everything is baked in a brick, wood-burning oven. Try the spinach cannelloni—marvelous! Máscaras makes good fresh limeade, served in bulbous glasses with lots of purified ice. You can also get *big* margaritas and cold beer.

Nuestra Señorita Carmen, on Av. 5, is a popular budget spot serving grilled fish and Yucatecan meals priced under $5. **Karen's Pizza,** on Av. 5, has a huge courtyard dining area that gets packed at dinner. **Media Luna** is a popular vegetarian hang out. For a real Mexican experience, try **La Parilla,** on Av. 5 at Calle 10; expect live music and great Mexican food. Just north of the Hwy. 307/Playa del Carmen intersection, **Faisán y Venado** restaurant is one of the few places around for Yucatecan cuisine. It's clean, with good food and friendly service.

Near the Mosquito Blue hotel you'll find the excellent Italian restaurant, **Tiramisu,** where the pasta is great but the tiramisu dessert is not what an Italian would expect. It's open for breakfast and lunch.

Shopping

In the colonial-style **Rincón del Sol** center, Av. 5 at Calle 8, are several shops selling carved masks, T-shirts, Guatemalan textiles, and resortwear. Among them, **La Catrina** is filled with shells, figurines, and *papeles picados,* the tissue-paper cutouts Mexicans string up for fiestas; **Luna Maya** features one-of-a-kind jewelry from Guadalajara; and **El Vuelo de los Niños Pá-**

jaros carries handcrafted papers made from bark, as well as a good selection of Latin American CDs and cassette tapes.

La Playense, on Av. Juárez (Principal), offers gifts of all kinds—check out the woodcarvings. Get your photo supplies at **Omega** on Av. Juárez across from the bank. If you need to send a fax, go to **Computel,** Av. Juárez at Av. 5, which offers copies and long-distance phone service as well.

Services

Banco del Atlántico, Av. Juárez at Av. 10 (three blocks from the ferry dock), and **Bancomer,** Av. Juárez at Av. 25, both cash traveler's checks and advance cash on credit cards. Money-changing hours are Mon.-Fri. 10 a.m.-12:30 p.m. The **post office** is on Av. Juárez in a small building between the police station and the mayor's office.

At **La Palma** laundry on Av. 5 you can either do it yourself (after 6 p.m.) or have it done for you. Laundry service is provided all day, and usually takes three to four hours.

Transportation

By Taxi: A taxi from Cancún International Airport to Playa del Carmen will cost about US$40-50. If there are several passengers, you can make a good deal—bargain with the driver before you start your journey. A taxi from Carmen to Tulum (with three passengers) runs about US$25-30 roundtrip. Nonmetered taxis meet the incoming ferry at Playa del Carmen and are available for long or short hauls; again, make your deal in advance.

By Ferry: Two types of passenger ferries travel between Playa del Carmen and Isla Cozumel. The faster **MV Mexico** is a/c and makes the trip in about 30 minutes; fare is about US$7.50 pp one-way. The slower open-air boats take about 45 minutes; fare is about US$3. Between the two, ferries depart just about every hour 6:30 a.m.-8 p.m. You can request a specific ferry, but invariably you will get a ticket on the next boat out. (This is a way to keep all the ferries in business, including the older ones.)

The ferry crossing is usually a breeze. However, the calm sea does flex its muscles once in a while. If you're prone to seasickness, delay your departure till the next day—the sea seldom stays angry for long. Young boys with imaginative homemade pushcarts or men with three-wheel *triciclos* meet incoming ferries at the dock to carry luggage for a small fee. Because of the ferry traffic, this is also a good place to try **hitchhiking** north or south.

By Bus: Three bus lines provide this small town with the best bus transportation on the coast. Buses going north to Cancún travel the 65 km in 50 minutes. **Autotransportes del Caribe** carries passengers to and from Cancún in a small bus that makes six daily trips. Seats are reserved; buy your ticket a half hour in advance. **ADO** bus company offers one first-class reserved bus daily between Playa and Cancún. **Playa Express** mini-buses run throughout the day to Cancún nonstop, with minimal room for luggage. Check at the bus station for the current bus schedule from Playa del Carmen to Cancún.

ADO operates three luxury express buses to Mérida daily; the buses have a/c, bathrooms, and refreshments. Other buses travel to and from Chetumal and other points south. If you're sightseeing on the bus to Chetumal, just a word to the driver and he'll drop you off at the turnoff to Tulum, Xelha Lagoon National Park entry road, or one of the small beaches south along the coast. Ask what time his schedule brings him back, since you must be on the highway waiting to return to Carmen.

Getting Around Town: The road going to the dock is closed to all vehicle traffic; watch the signs and follow the traffic to the parking lot north of the *malecón* and the plaza. Most other streets are one-way in a confusing system. Parking is severely limited. Street signs are beginning to appear, but most locals give directions by using landmarks. Once you're off the main paved entry road into town, you'll find the streets still bumpy, but they improve a little each year. In short, park wherever you can and rely on your feet to get you around town. Remember, don't park too close to a corner or the cops will remove the license plate; to get it back you'll have to pay a large fine. If you're taking the ferry to Isla Cozumel for the day, park your car at the public parking lot by the bus station; fees are posted.

XCARET
ECOARCHAEOLOGICAL PARK

Xcaret is about an hour's drive south of Cancún and one km off the highway toward the sea. The small port, called Pole during the Post-Classic period (A.D. 1200-1500), was an important trading center and Maya ceremonial center. Maya pilgrims en route to Isla Cozumel to worship the goddess Ix Chel used Xcaret as a jumping-off point; historians say the Maya would spend several days here praying for a safe crossing before boarding their wooden canoes.

Today, the site draws pilgrims of another sort: fun-seekers coming to frolic at Xcaret's natural-history oriented theme park. Though some visitors have compared Xcaret to Disneyland (and the crowds can often feel comparable), park developer Miguel Quintana says it's much more. Here the family fun centers around some decidedly serious endeavors.

Maya Archaeology

Archaeologists under the direction of the Instituto Nacional de Antropología e Historia continue ex-

It's fun to spend an entire day at Xcaret.

cavating the site, which is rich with Maya history. Several ruins in the park's developed area have been restored, and according to archaeologist Tony Andrews, dozens more structures are scattered throughout the surrounding bush; so far 60 buildings and remnants of hundreds of platforms have been found. The work will probably take another six or seven years to complete.

Natural History Studies

Other scientists here are studying the region's fauna, including turtles, manatees, bats, and butterflies. Their study areas are all open to the public and hold educational exhibits. The immense screened-in butterfly enclosure, for example, offers exhibits explaining how the butterfly develops and illustrating different varieties and the plants they prefer.

Swimming with Dolphins

Of all the natural-history programs here, the most popular involves the chance to swim with the park's dolphins. A limited number of visitors each day are given the opportunity to pay about US$65 to swim with the graceful animals. Trainers supervise the entire event, first showing a video to all "swimmers," then providing instructions on in-the-pool interaction. There's something really special about touching and talking to these creatures while looking them straight in the eye. I've heard this is a wonderful therapy for children and adults who suffer from hard to treat mental illnesses. Perhaps these animals sense a problem.

Swimmers must reserve a time slot for their swim, and the reservations are taken on a first-come, first-served basis starting first thing in the morning at the dolphin area. This means when the park gates open there's a mad rush to get there. If you're not a good runner or get turned around in the park, you're liable to be disappointed. And note that if you take the Xcaret bus from Cancún, you'll arrive too late to sign up. If you're staying in Cancún and want to swim with the dolphins, rent a car and get to Xcaret early, before the 9 a.m. opening.

Underground River

What used to be an underground river here has been made into a "floating adventure." Openings were made in the earthen ceiling of an underground cavern to let in light and circulate air (a couple of cenotes were destroyed in the making). People are given life jackets and, starting at the entrance of what was once considered a sacred cenote, they spend 20-30 minutes floating along the underground river, admiring coralline deposits and unusual little fish until they reach the other end, 1,000 feet south. Many visitors say the float alone is worth the price of park admission.

Snorkeling

The *caleta* (small bay) at Xcaret provides beginning snorkelers, especially children, with a

Float for 20-30 minutes on the surface of an underground river at Xcaret.

perfect learning spot. The water is shallow and there's little current, though to enter the water you must either climb over rocks or jump off a small wooden platform. But it's not necessary to go much beyond the limestone shoreline to discover colorful denizens of the sea. Resident schools of parrot fish and blue and French angelfish almost always put in an appearance. About the only problem is fighting off the tourists; come early in the day and you might have the small bay almost to yourself.

Entertainment
In addition to the recreation activities, the park offers a variety of first-class entertainment. A living-history presentation takes you on a mystical trip through a tunnel where you'll view ancient Maya ceremonies. A *charreada* (Mexican rodeo) is presented daily in late afternoon, and at night, the park puts on an incredible show in the stone amphitheater. The nightly show changes frequently—it might include classical music, ballet, or just about anything—but it's always a marvelous show in an exotic setting. Transportation is provided from Cancún.

Around the Park
Trails meander throughout the lushly landscaped park, past orchid-covered trees, a large variety of tropical plants, and ferns from all over Southern Mexico. A stroll along the breakwater gives you a view of the regal dolphins. Large, informative plaques placed about the park explain just about everything.

Facilities include a dive shop offering equipment rental and lessons, restaurants, a gift shop, clean restrooms, and a stable with some fine rental horses for riding through the jungle surrounding the beach.

Information
Tickets: You have several options to choose from. If you arrive after 4 p.m. for the evening entertainment, you must pay the full amount, but this ticket will get you in the next day for the entire day. If you think you'll be coming back more than once, ask about their multiple entrance tickets. A single ticket price right now is about US$32, and is good for entry to the living-history presentation, picnic areas, good snorkeling spots, and a lovely sandy beach adjacent to placid aqua water—everything except swimming with the dolphins.

Sunblock: Do *not* apply any type of sunblock before coming to Xcaret. When you arrive and pay for your ticket, they will ask you for your sunblock and in place of it give you a special sunblock that won't pollute the water.

Hours and Directions: The park is open Oct.-March 9 a.m.-9 p.m., April-Sept. 9 a.m.-10 p.m. If you're driving, look for the only high hill on Hwy. 307 (at Km 72, six km south of the Playa del Carmen turnoff), where you'll find the park entrance. Bus tours to Xcaret from Cancún are available (see the Cancún section, above). For more information, call (98) 83-0654 or 83-0743.

CALICA DOCK

Just south of Xcaret is the dock used for decades by the large Calica company to ship limestone products to the United States. The dock has now been pulled into use by cruise ships. Usually the ships stay docked for the day, and taxis and tour buses take passengers to sightsee on this part of the Maya Riviera. It's feasible to hire a taxi for the day and visit many of the sights along this coast. You can try haggling over price before you take off, but the taxis are really "unionizing" their fee schedule.

PAMUL

A small beach worth exploring—beachcomb here for shells, coral, and interesting jetsam—Pamul is in some places steep and rocky, in others narrow and flat. The south end of the beach is sandy, but the shallow water along here harbors the prickly sea urchin—look before you step, or wear your shoes while you're wading.

The Quintana Roo coast offers miles and miles of pristine dive spots, and the waters here at Pamul are pretty ideal. The water is crystal clear, allowing you to examine the fascinating life within the shallow tidepools cradled by rocks and limestone. Snorkeling is better the closer you get to the reef 120 meters offshore. On the way the sea bottom drops off to about eight meters, and its colorful underwater life can absorb you for hours.

Turtles

If it's a bright moonlit night in July or August, you may be treated to the unique sight of large turtles lumbering ashore to lay eggs in the sand. If you're here 50 days later it's even more exciting to watch the tiny hatchlings (about eight cm in diameter) make their way down the beach to begin life in the sea. Much has been written about protecting the turtles of the Caribbean from humans, but nature in the form of egg-eating animals provides its own threat to this endangered species. On the beach of Pamul, more than half the eggs are scratched up from the sand and eaten by small animals that live in the adjacent jungle. However, marine biologists are taking a larger part in protecting the eggs and hatchlings by digging them up and burying them in a protected area until they hatch.

Accommodations

Inexpensive: Cabañas Pamul, a small hotel on the beach, offers simple but clean cabañas with electricity between sunset and 10 p.m., hot and cold water, and shared bathrooms.

Camping

The campground at the south end of the hotel has room for 15 RVs. All spots have electricity and water; eight are large pads with sewer hookups (US$13), and seven will accommodate

GIANT TURTLES

At one time the giant turtle was plentiful and an important addition to the Indian diet. The turtle was captured by turning it over (no easy matter at 90-100 kilograms) when it came on shore to lay its eggs. Any eggs already deposited in a sandy nest on the beach were gathered, and then the entire family took part in processing this nourishing game. First, the parchmentlike bag of unlaid eggs was removed from the body, then the undeveloped eggs (looking like small, hard-boiled egg yolks). After that, the meat of the turtle was cut into strips to be dried in the sun. The orange-colored fat was put in calabash containers and saved for soups and stews; it added rich nutrients and was considered an important medicine. The Indians wasted nothing.

Today CIQRO, a protective organization, along with the government, keep a sharp lookout along the coast for egg poachers during the laying season. Turtle-egg farms are being developed to ensure the survival of this ancient mariner. Sadly, today's poacher travels the entire coast, and each beach is hit night after night. The turtle can lay as many as 200 eggs in an individual nest or "clutch." One beach may be the instinctual home for hundreds of turtles (at one time thousands) that return to the site of their own hatching each year.

Turtles can live to be a hundred years old, which means they can lay a lot of eggs in their lifetime. But as the poachers steal the eggs on a wholesale basis, the species could eventually be wiped out entirely. If caught, poachers are fined and can be jailed—though the damage has been done. When released they usually return to their lucrative habits.

DIANA LASICH HARPER

In most Mexican marketplaces a ready market for these eggs exists among superstitious men who believe the eggs are an aphrodisiac.

The survival of the giant sea turtle lies within the education of the people—locals and visitors alike. Shoppers will see many sea turtle products offered for sale: turtle oil, tortoise-shell combs, bracelets, rings, buttons, carvings, and veneer inlaid on furniture and jewelry boxes, plus small stuffed, polished hatchling paperweights. **Note:** It is against the law to bring these products into the U.S. and other countries. If discovered they will be confiscated. Sadly, many travelers are not even aware of the law, and often the products get by the inspectors. If tourists refused to purchase these products, the market would dry up—a big step toward preserving these gentle lumbering beasts.

small trailers (US$5). You can use the showers and toilets in the hotel. Camping fee is about US$4 pp, which includes bathroom privileges.

Food
Los Arrecifes, the cafe/bar on the beach, is quite nice, and a great place to watch the sunset in the bar-swings. The kitchen offers fresh-caught seafood, good breakfasts, and hamburgers and such at reasonable prices. The menu explains that all water and ice is purified and the veggies and fruits are bathed in *Microdin*. It's open 8 a.m.-8 p.m.

Other Practicalities
A small cenote nearby use to provide water for Pamul; to be safe, other than at the restaurant, boil the water before drinking. Otherwise, buy bottled water here; you'll find a mini-super across the highway from the entrance road. Los Arrecifes cafe has a dive shop (also called Los Arrecifes) on the premises, where you can arrange a three-hour snorkeling trip to the reef for US$30 pp. The shop's mailing address is Apdo. Postal 1681, Cancún, Quintana Roo 77500, Mexico.

PUERTO AVENTURAS AND VICINITY

One of the most ambitious developments on the Maya Riviera, Puerto Aventuras—a few minutes south of Akumal—includes residential housing, time shares, hotels, all sorts of resort amenities, and a large marina.

Boating
At the marina, yachtsmen will find everything they need: gas and diesel, marine supplies and minor repairs, purified water and ice, bait, 24-hour radio monitoring and medical services, restrooms and showers, car rentals, travel agencies, a shopping center, yacht club, hotels, and restaurants. Boat access into the marina is through a carefully planned channel, well marked for navigation and ready with an escort service through the reef 24 hours a day. Some of the marina's waterways are left from the days of the Maya, simply improved and opened to the sea. In other cases they are totally man-made. The marina can hold almost 300 boats with a maximum length of 120 feet and a maximum draft of 10 feet.

Diving
Puerto Aventuras is a favorite spot for world-class diving. Ten different well-known dive sites are just minutes away, and the beauty of the Caribbean along this coast is legendary. The water is crystalline and full of curious marine creatures who look back at the diver.

Mike Madden's Dive Center, Apdo. Postal 117, Playa del Carmen, Quintana Roo 77710, Mexico, tel. (987) 3-5129 or 3-5131 (also at the Diamond resort in Playacar and at Club Aventuras Akumal), offers scuba instruction, night dives, daily reef dives, cavern trips, snorkeling, and cenote diving (as well as jungle adventures and deep-sea fishing). Trips are available to little-known dive spots such as Canyonland Reef, Chanyuym Reef, Xpu-Ha, Xaac, and Xaac Chico.

Madden has been involved in some unusual adventures that have placed his name in the *Guinness Book of World Records.* In 1987 he was the leader of the expedition that discovered and surveyed Nohoch Cave, the world's longest known underwater cave system. Today, visitors can explore Nohoch (whose name means "huge" in the Maya language) with Madden's dive guides or other area guides. Permanent guide lines have been placed along over 13 km of passageways to ensure that divers will be able to find their way out of the cave, as well as to provide a baseline for further surveys. Some of the cave's vast chambers are as much as 300 meters wide and are majestically beautiful, with sparkling columns, rimstone pools, stalagmites, stalactites, cave pearls of pristine white limestone, and blue passageways channeling off in all directions. One room has six feet of airspace overhead, allowing even beginning snorkelers to view the breathtaking visions of this marine wonder.

Another cavern trip offered by Madden's Dive Center is called the Indiana Jones Adventure. The trip goes to **Nohoch Nah Chich** ("Giant House of the Birds"), named for the bats that lived in the cave. Part of the giant cave system can safely be reached from a cenote on the property of a local farm family. A jeep takes you within three km of the cenote; from there you hike in. Trekkers have a chance to visit with the family; they still get their water from the cenote. There's about a 15-minute guided tour of the cenote for snorkelers (after which snorkelers can go back in and spend as much time as they wish). This is a fascinating trip for snorkelers since you have the opportunity to see some of the sparkling wonders of the underwater caves, usually accessible only to scuba divers. The group departs at 9:30 a.m. and returns at 2:30 p.m. Cost is about US$38; no children under 10. You can find a short article and photo on one of the caves in the September 1990 issue of *National Geographic* magazine.

Note: Cavern diving is dangerous and different from open-sea diving. It requires highly specialized training. The danger of getting lost within this subterranean and subaquatic world is very real; hundreds of untrained divers have lost their lives in underwater caves over the years.

Golf and Tennis

Puerto Aventuras has several tennis courts and a nine-hole, tournament-quality golf course. Golf carts are available for rent.

CEDAM Museum

Artifacts recovered from the sunken ship *Mantanceros* can be seen at the CEDAM Museum on the waterfront. CEDAM (an acronym for Conservation, Ecology, Diving, Archaeology, and Museums) is a nonprofit organization. The *Mantanceros* was a Spanish merchant ship that left Cadiz, Spain, in 1741, headed for the New World. Loaded with trade goods, it foundered and sank on the reef two km north of Akumal. No one knows for certain why the ship sank, since there were no survivors. Research suggests the ship probably engaged in battle with a British vessel and then drifted onto the treacherous reef now known as Punta Mantanceros. For more detailed information on the finds of the *Mantanceros,* read *The Treasure of the Great Reef* by Arthur C. Clarke. Beginning in 1958, CEDAM spent several years salvaging the *Mantanceros.* Artifacts retrieved and on display here include belt buckles, cannons, coins, guns, and tableware.

Accommodations

Premium: The **Omni Puerto Aventuras,** tel. (987) 3-5100, fax (987) 3-5102, formerly Club de Playa, has undergone a massive renovation. The luxurious but intimate 30-room hotel faces the marina on one side and a shimmering white beach and the translucent water of the Carib-

bean on the other. All rooms have tile floors, king-size beds, beautiful colors, regional decor, and first-class amenities. The first floor rooms have private patios with jacuzzis; the second- and third-floor rooms have balconies with private jacuzzis and marina and partial ocean views. Each room has a "magic" box in the wall where complimentary breakfast is delivered to your room each morning. All types of watersports equipment are available. Other amenities include a swimming pool, pool bar, lobby bar, beach *palapa* bar, and the excellent **Da Vince** dining room.

Premium (All-Inclusive): Club Oasis is a great all-inclusive destination. The grounds are large, with the sea and the marina nearby and pools right at hand. All rooms are nicely appointed, with comfortable beds, a/c, and balconies. Several dining areas are available, and the breakfast buffet—including fresh eggs cooked to order—just doesn't quit.

Food

Papaya Republic is a desert-island-type restaurant, far from the madding crowd on a beach a short distance from the central part of Puerto Aventuras. After you turn off Hwy. 307 onto the main entry road, take the right arm through the golf course and start looking for the signs. You want to wend your way to the beach. Of course there's no phone or address; this is a desert island! But it's well worth the hunt, whether you lunch on the chilled fresh gazpacho, shrimp in wine sauce, dorado almendrado, or quesadillas and cold beer. This is gourmet heaven on a little bit of sand with a *palapa* roof and the gorgeous sea at its front door. Stop by here even if you're on your way farther south. It's only five minutes off the highway.

Several cafes are at the marina. **Solo Mío** makes good Italian food, including pizza. What used to be Carlos'n Charlie's is now **One For The Road,** offering good Mexican food. Need a cigar? Or a good cuppa coffee? Try **Coffee Bar & Tobacco Shop. Richard's Steak House** serves the best (imported) beef steaks and brochettes around. For ice cream check out **Mexico Lindo.**

Shopping and Services

Along the walkway by the marina channels you'll find most everything you need, including cafes, a laundromat, a small medical service for emergency first aid, a beauty parlor, a travel agency, a money changer, a taxi stand, **Videorama** (what would the kids do without video games for a week?), and several markets that carry sundries as well as groceries, ice, and drinks. You can rent a car for a day at your hotel; also ask about bike rentals.

Katenah Bay
Continuing south, the highway soon passes Katenah Bay, a curved slice of white sand washed by crystal clear aqua water. Here you'll find the beautiful premium/all-inclusive **El Dorado Resort and Spa,** U.S. tel. (203) 459-8678. Guests at the El Dorado are pampered with good service and have a choice of three restaurants (Italian, Mexican, and Continental) and a couple of bars. Rates include use of the pool, tennis court, sea kayaks, paddleboats, bicycles, and snorkeling equipment, as well as all gratuities. The rooms are really junior suites; some have jacuzzis on their balconies or patios, some have ocean views. The "Spa" part is a little misleading, but the resort does offer a beauty and nail shop, massage, and aromatherapy, all for an extra fee. Taxis and car rentals are available. The resort has a dive service on the premises and good snorkeling just offshore. Rates begin at US$97-190 pp double occupancy, depending on season and room (best rates run April 5-Dec. 19). No children under 18 permitted.

AKUMAL AND VICINITY

About 100 km (60 miles) south of Cancún, the crescent of intensely white sand at Akumal Bay is home to an ever-growing resort that survives nicely without the bustling activity of Cancún (although it gets busier each year). The traveler desiring the tropical essence of Yucatán *and* a dash of the good life will appreciate Akumal, which offers a good range of hotel rooms, dining, and activities. During the off-season you'll have little difficulty finding a room here. However, if you travel 1 Dec.-15 April, make reservations.

The barrier reef that runs parallel to the Quintana Roo coast protects Akumal Bay from the open sea and makes for great swimming and snorkeling. Proximity to the reef and easy access to the unspoiled treasures of the Caribbean make it a gathering place for divers from all over the world. For the archaeology buff, Akumal is 10 km (six miles) north of Tulum, one of the few walled Maya sites on the edge of the sea. In Maya, Akumal means "Place of the Turtle," and from prehistoric times the giant green turtle has come ashore here in summer to lay its eggs in the warm beach sand.

History
Akumal was a small part of a sprawling working coconut plantation until 1925, when a *New York Times*-sponsored expedition along the then-unknown Quintana Roo coast stumbled on the

Akumal beach

OZ MALLAN

tranquil bay; it was another 33 years before the rest of the outside world intruded on its pristine beauty. In 1958, Pablo Bush and others formed CEDAM, a renowned diver's club, and introduced Akumal as the "diving capital of the world." Soon the word was out. The first visitors (divers) began making their way to the unknown wilderness. At that time, the only access to Akumal was by boat from Cozumel. A road was built in the 1960s. Since then, Akumal has continued to grow in fame and size each year. Though many people come here, it still remains a beautiful, tranquil place to study the sea and stars.

Flora

Akumal is surrounded by jungle. In March, bright red bromeliads bloom high in the trees, reaching for a sun that's rapidly hidden by fast-growing vines and leaves. These "guest" plants making homes in established trees are epiphytes, not parasites. They don't drain the sap of the host tree, but sustain themselves with rain, dew, and humidity; their leaves absorb moisture and organic requirements from airborne dust, insect matter, and visiting birds. The bromeliad family encompasses a wide variety of plants, including pineapple and Spanish moss. The genus seen close to Akumal is the tillandsia, and the flame-red

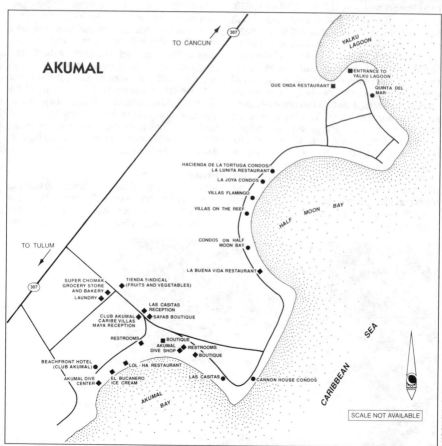

AKUMAL

TO CANCUN 307

YALKU LAGOON

ENTRANCE TO YALKU LAGOON

QUE ONDA RESTAURANT

QUINTA DEL MAR

TO TULUM

307

HACIENDA DE LA TORTUGA CONDOS/ LA LUNITA RESTAURANT

LA JOYA CONDOS

VILLAS FLAMINGO

VILLAS ON THE REEF

HALF MOON BAY

CONDOS ON HALF MOON BAY

LA BUENA VIDA RESTAURANT

SUPER CHOMAK GROCERY STORE AND BAKERY

TIENDA SINDICAL (FRUITS AND VEGETABLES)

LAUNDRY

LAS CASITAS RECEPTION

CLUB AKUMAL CARIBE VILLAS MAYA RECEPTION

SAYAB BOUTIQUE

RESTROOMS

BOUTIQUE

AKUMAL DIVE SHOP

RESTROOMS

BOUTIQUE

BEACHFRONT HOTEL (CLUB AKUMAL)

LOL - HA RESTAURANT

AKUMAL DIVE CENTER

EL BUCANERO ICE CREAM

LAS CASITAS

CANNON HOUSE CONDOS

CARIBBEAN SEA

AKUMAL BAY

SCALE NOT AVAILABLE

© MOON PUBLICATIONS, INC.

CEDAM AND THE BIRTH OF AKUMAL

In 1958 a small group of Mexican divers was salvaging the *Mantanceros,* a Spanish galleon that sunk off the Palencar reef in 1741. These men, originally Mexican frogmen active during WW II, were first organized in 1948 and called themselves CEDAM (Club de Exploración y Deporte Acuáticos de Mexico—a nonprofit organization). This was not the typical fun-and-games type of dive club; its members were dedicated to the service of country, science, and humanity.

While diving the *Mantanceros* they camped on the beaches of Akumal, two km south of the dive site. This bay, part of an enormous copra plantation owned by Don Argimiro Arguelles, was (and still is) a deserted crescent beach of white sand edged by hundreds of coconut palms. Then the only way in and out of Akumal was by ship. As owner and captain of the ship leased by the divers as a work boat, Don Argimiro spent much time with the group. It was during one of those relaxed evenings around the campfire that Akumal's destiny was sealed. Arguelles sold Pablo Bush (organizer of the charter group of CEDAM) the bay and thousands of acres of coconut palms north and south of Akumal.

Pablo Bush's tropical lagoon had no airstrip nearby, and even if there had been one, there would have been no road to reach it. So for 12 years the creaky vessel, SS *Cozumel,* plied the waters between the island of Cozumel and Akumal carrying divers, drinking water, and supplies. The only change to the environment was the addition of typical *palapa* huts built for the divers.

The CEDAM organization, in the meantime, was gaining fame and introducing Cozumel and the Yucatán to the diving world. Visiting snorkelers and scuba divers were entranced, and the word soon spread about the exotic Mexican Caribbean coast.

In 1960 the idea of promoting tourism began to circulate, but Quintana Roo was still a territory. Pablo Bush and other movers and shakers began

talking road and airport. The government began listening. But governments move slowly, and it was three governors and two presidents later that the road was finally completed. In the meantime, Cancún was born, Quintana Roo became a state, and finally Akumal bloomed. The beautiful bay continues to grow. Today several hotels, restaurants, dive shops, and many other services make visitors (not only divers) welcome.

In 1966, CEDAM International was born and gave new meaning to the initials: Conservation, Ecology, Diving, Archaeology, and Museums. Akumal is the main headquarters for both CEDAM groups in the Caribbean and international symposiums and seminars are still held here for the active divers of the world. CEDAM has had an active part in archaeological exploration in several cenote dives during which early Maya artifacts were retrieved.

In 1968 (before Cancún), the owners of Akumal formed the Club de Yates Akumal Caribe, A.C. (A.C. means Civil Association, nonprofit). They turned over 5,000 acres of land to the government and donated the Cove of Xelha for a national park. The aim was to open the isolated area to tourists, and in so doing jobs became available to the local residents. CEDAM provided housing, food, electricity (added in 1982), running water, a school for the children, and a first-aid station with a trained nurse. Till this time, the sparse population lived in the shadow of their ancient ancestors—few were ever exposed to modern civilization—and hauled in water from deep wells eight miles inland.

In 1977 a fire destroyed one of the original large *palapa* structures built on the beach; the closest fire protection then was in Cancún. The only communication even today is by shortwave radio. Although it's still rather primitive (who knows for how long), all who visit Akumal fall in love with its slow, rustic way of life and tropical beauty. Houses are springing up, and though many more visitors come today, the wide beaches are still never *too* crowded.

---

flower that blooms on the tops of so many of the trees here is only one variety of this remarkable epiphyte. While searching for bromeliads, you undoubtedly will see another epiphyte, the orchid.

Dive Shops

Akumal was born because of the interest of divers so it's natural that here you'll find two of

the best dive shops around. Both rent excellent equipment and offer a good selection of gear for sale.

Akumal Dive Shop (Apdo. Postal 1, Playa del Carmen, Quintana Roo 77710, Mexico), tel. (987) 2-2453, U.S. tel. (800) 777-8294, is owned by Dick Blanchard and Gonzalo Arcila, who have been taking divers from Akumal to pristine dive spots like La Tortuga and The Nets for more than 15 years; dive lessons are available.

Akumal Dive Center offers a three-day dive certification course as well as a four-hour resort course that culminates in one escorted dive on the reef. If you decide to take a resort course from any dive shop, check to make sure that you'll be making the dive one-on-one with a divemaster. The Akumal Dive Center is fully PADI certified. For advance dive information, contact Akutrame Inc., P.O. Box 13326, El Paso, TX 79913 USA, tel. (915) 584-3552 or (800) 351-1622, Canada tel. (800) 343-1440. The shop also rents kayaks and sailboards.

Snorkeling

Akumal Reef protects the bay from the open sea, providing calm swimming areas ideal for snorkeling. A good spot within wading distance is the rocky area on the north end of the bay. Floating along the surface of the water and looking through your private window into the unique world below can be habit-forming along this coast. Take it slow and easy, and you won't miss anything. Search the rocks and crevices that you'll drift over, even the sandy bottom—what may look like a rocky bulge on the floor of the sea may eventually twitch an eye and turn out to be a stonefish hiding in the sand; hands off, it's deadly.

Within walking distance of Akumal, **Yalku Lagoon** is worth a snorkel for the many fish you'll see in a quiet hideaway. Parrot fish gather here in numbers and make a multicolored glow just below the surface. A current of fresh water flows into this small lagoon, which is at most three meters deep; the visibility is about five meters. To care for the lagoon and lessen the impact of an increasing number of visitors (30,000 in 1996), a neighborhood organization of Akumal residents (Vecinos de Akumal) have taken on the task of protecting and maintaining the entrance to Yalku. Stone paths are now in place and there is an ecological toilet on site. Guards are on duty to instruct and ensure that suntan lotions and trash do not contaminate the waters. Plans are for biological studies and monitoring of the lagoon. This is a fine example of how a caring community can safeguard its local treasures and preserve their beauty for future generations. Admission to the lagoon is US$5 adults, US$2.50 children.

Accommodations

The hotels in Akumal proper are all on the beach. A few villas and condos are also available for rent on Half Moon Bay, just a short distance north of Akumal Bay.

Expensive: The old thatch huts once used by the CEDAM diving club now form the core of **Club Akumal Caribe Villas Maya.** The cottages have been spruced up with private baths, tile floors, fans, small refrigerators, and a/c; even the lighting has been improved for readers. Plenty of water sports are available, along with tennis and basketball courts. Nearby is the Club's three-story **Beachfront Hotel,** which offers 21 rooms,

Quinta del Mar is a beautiful villa on Half Moon Bay.

OZ MALLAN

each with full bath, compact refrigerator, and small porch or balcony. The rooms look out on the Caribbean and the garden area, which has a swimming pool and pool bar. They're also just a few steps from the sea, Lol Ha restaurant, and all the other facilities of Akumal.

Premium: Club Akumal also offers a couple of higher-priced options. Its **Cannon House condos** lie on a separate beach around the point north of Akumal Bay. Each has two bedrooms, two bathrooms, a fully equipped kitchen, and a living room with two sofa beds. The Club's **Villas Flamingo** consists of four smashing villas on Half Moon Bay. Each villa has an enormous living room, fully equipped kitchen, dining room, one or two upstairs bedrooms, an ocean view, tasteful furnishings, a large terrace with barbecue grill, daily maid service, laundry facilities, and a/c; a swimming pool is shared by the four individual villas. For reservations and information on all of Club Akumal's facilities, including dive packages with a room and some meals, contact Akutrame Inc., P.O. Box 13326, El Paso, TX 79913 USA, tel. (915) 584-3552 or (800) 351-1622, Canada tel. (800) 343-1440.

Near the entrance to Yalku Lagoon, **Quinta del Mar** is a striking villa that faces the sea and can accommodate six or eight people. The beautiful white stucco structure is set in a garden with cooling breezes and is decorated with colorful weavings, paintings, and pottery. Daily maid service is provided by Mercedes and her husband, Alejandro, caretakers who live in a small cottage on the property. If you wish, Mercedes and Alejandro will prepare meals (extra fee). The villa has four bedrooms, four and a half baths, a living room, dining room, fully equipped kitchen, tile floors, and lots of windows to bring in the luxuriant outdoors. A comfortable terrace on the ground floor offers stunning views of the Caribbean. Quinta del Mar is within walking distance (one km) of the dining rooms and shops of Akumal Beach. Rental fees vary widely depending on time of the year and number of guests, but as an example, for three bedrooms and three and a half baths the weekly rate begins at US$1,550 in the low season and goes up from there. For more information, contact Terry, U.S. tel. (908) 446-1548; e-mail: pargot@mail.caribe.net.mx.

Las Casitas Akumal, at the east end of Akumal Beach, U.S. tel. (800) 5-AKUMAL, has airy, furnished condominiums with two bedrooms, two baths, living room, kitchen, and patio; daily maid service included. These casitas are really looking great. They're walking distance to restaurants, a grocery store, dive shop, sandy beach, and beach bar; the bay is right at your front door.

Villas on the Reef and **La Joya** are small, secluded condos on the beach of Half Moon Bay. Each condo has a view of the sea and includes one or two bedrooms, a fully equipped kitchen, one or two bathrooms, a living room, and dining room. All are fully screened, fan cooled, and nicely decorated with art and weavings from the Yucatán and Guatemala. Maid service is provided daily; a local cook can be hired on request. Ask about the beach-level suite offering **handicap access.** Divers should inquire about good-value dive packages; other seagoing day-trips are also available. For information and reservations contact Akumal Vacations, P.O. Box 575, Conroe, TX 77305 USA, tel. (800) 448-7137.

Camping

No camping is permitted at Akumal, but you can camp—at least for a little while longer—just a few km south at Xcacel (sha-SELL) and Chemuyil (shem-oo-YEEL). Both of those beaches are nice and have camping facilities, but they're also both slated for major hotel development (sigh!).

Food

Regulars to Akumal know that the old **Lol Ha** Restaurant burned to the ground a while back. Now it has reopened with a stunning new structure, still with a romantic *palapa* ambience looking out on the sea. You can expect excellent seafood and Mexican and American specialties; at breakfast time the basket of homemade sweet rolls still comes immediately when you sit down, and the orange juice is still fresh-squeezed. Good sandwiches, and yes, Lol Ha still prepares a Thanksgiving turkey. It's open for breakfast and dinner-by-candlelight. Ask about the box lunches.

Adjacent to Lol Ha is the **Snack Bar Lol Ha,** serving lunch from noon to 5:30 p.m. With the best hamburgers on the beach, really good guacamole, and the tasty Maya treat *tacos cochinita,* this is one lively place most of the day, but especially at happy hour 4-5 p.m. (half-price drinks).

The bar serves drinks 11 a.m.-11 p.m. Nearby, try the **Lol Ha Pizzeria,** which serves pizza and other tasty Italian specialties.

Around the bend on Half Moon Bay, look for **La Buena Vida Restaurant,** a two-story *palapa* offering a tropical atmosphere. The sandy first-floor bar has swinging seats and a fun happy hour. The upstairs dining room makes a delicious hamburger, and the flan is always firm and tasty with fresh coconut. Also on the menu are turkey and fish dishes. La Buena Vida is on the beach south of Vista del Mar condos; open 7 a.m.-11 p.m.

Also on Half Moon Bay you'll find **La Lunita,** a fine little dinner house on the ground floor of the Hacienda de la Tortuga condos. It serves good lobster and tasty fish, inside or out. Closed Sunday.

If you're in the mood for Italian, try the neat little **Que Onda** restaurant one block from the entrance to Yalku Lagoon. It's an outdoor cafe run by *real* Italians preparing *real* Italian food. The lasagna is very tasty, as is the bruschetta, and the pastas are served with light sauces. Prices are not cheap, but everything is well-prepared. Open for dinner.

Kids discover great ice-cream cones at **El Bucanero Ice Cream Parlor.** Just before the main entrance arch to Akumal, a small general store called **Super Chomak** sells a good selection of groceries, cold drinks, liquor, beer, ice, sundries, fresh fruit, vegetables, meat, frozen chicken, and fresh-baked *pan dulce* (get here early in the morning for the baked breads). Attached to the store is a small fast-food window selling tacos and *tortas.* Open 7 a.m.-9 p.m.

Shopping

Two gift shops, the **Akumal Bazaar** and **Boutique Sayab,** sell a little of everything: typical Maya clothing, leather sandals, shawls, postcards, pottery, original Maya art and reproductions, black coral and silver jewelry, and a good selection of informative books (in English, French, and German) about the Peninsula and the Maya.

In Plaza Ukana (near the arch entrance) you'll find a couple of stores: **La Rosa,** selling women's clothing and accessories, and a **camera store** selling film, processing, and camera equipment.

Services

Laundry service is available around the corner from Super Chomak—leave clothes before 9 a.m. for next-day pickup. The closest **bank** is 36 km north at Playa del Carmen. A convenient **gas station** is at the junction of Hwy. 307 and the Tulum ruins road, 24 km south. Stations are also found in Playa del Carmen and Puerto Morelos. Remember, the gas stations are just that, with no mechanics. However, there's a good **mechanic** in the village of Tulum on Hwy. 307. He doesn't have a sign but is easy to find (on the left side of the road going south) by the many cars parked under a large metal awning; prices are reasonable.

Stamps are sold at the Villas Maya lobby, and mail is taken from there to the post office every day except weekends and holidays.

Transportation

By Taxi: Taxis will bring you to Akumal from Cancún or from the ferry docks at Playa del Carmen. Arrange the price before you start. The average fare from Cancún to Akumal is around US$45-55 (up to four passengers; they say this price is controlled by a taxi drivers' union). From Playa del Carmen it's approximately half that.

By Car: From Cancún, it's an 80-km, one-hour drive south on Hwy. 307 to Akumal. From Mérida take Hwy. 180 east to Cancún and turn south on 307 (both good two-lane highways), which passes the entrance road to Akumal. Car rentals are available in Cancún and Mérida, and at the Capitán Lafitte, Shangri-La, and Puerto Aventuras resorts, all fairly close to Akumal. Highway 307 is good, and the side roads (though rough and potholed) are drivable.

By Bus: Local buses frequently pass the Akumal turnoff, going both north and south throughout the day. Ask the driver to drop you off (it's not a regular stop); from the highway it's about one km to town—a hot haul if you're carrying luggage. The bus from Playa del Carmen to Tulum makes the trip several times each day. Ask the driver what time you must be on the highway to be picked up.

Chichén Itzá Tours

Mayaland Tours offers tours from Akumal to Chichén Itzá. Tour buses pick you up at your hotel and take you to and from the ruins. Lunch is provided at the Mayaland Hotel, where you can also use the swimming pool. Free beer, wine, and soft drinks are served on the bus back to your hotel. The tours run on Monday, Wednesday, and Friday and cost US$66 pp. For information contact Mayaland's Cancún office, tel. (98) 87-2450, fax (98) 87-2438, U.S. tel. (800) 235-4079.

Aventuras Akumal

Just south of Akumal, Aventuras Akumal is an isolated, upscale resort on a breathtaking turquoise bay ringed by white-sand beach. Modern, comfortable villas, condos, and hotels perch along the water's edge.

One of them, **De Rosa Villa** (Expensive/Premium), tel./fax (987) 4-1271, offers condos or villas with one and two bedrooms, all lovely, right on white sand with the sea just steps away. You can snorkel, literally, in your front yard. The accommodations are upscale and comfortable, with spacious living quarters and modern amenities including a sauna, rooftop bar, and in most units a fully equipped kitchen. The resort has no restaurant, but proprietors Nancy and Tony offer an extra-charge "food package" that includes a do-it-yourself breakfast, buffet or box lunch, and gourmet Yucatecan dinner. Units are available by the night or week. Make sure your first meal is taken care of before you arrive. It's really a must to have a car for this area.

An additional attraction is that Tony is an avid diver and offers cenote dive packages as well as conventional scuba and snorkeling trips; all include accommodations.

CHEMUYIL AND XCACEL

The beaches just keep coming, one right after the other—and all beautiful! Until now this coastal area really hasn't been discovered by most of the world; many who have found it return year after year. But how long will it last? Resort hotels are planned for both Chemuyil (shem-oo-YEEL) and Xcacel (sha-SELL).

Chemuyil

This tranquil beach boasts natural attributes of powder-fine sand, a turquoise sea, and crowds of shady coconut palms. The water is calm, thanks to the reef, and snorkeling and fishing attract many day visitors. The entrance fee (US$7 per car) is paid at the front gate after you turn off Hwy. 307.

If things haven't changed, you'll find a shaded beach cafe (serving *típico* Mexican food, beer, and cold sodas), as well as a few basic, moderately priced rooms at the north end of the beach (inquire at the restaurant). A few budget-priced hammock *palapas* with shared bathrooms and cold water are also available.

Chemuyil can get crowded during the busy winter season. Day-trippers from Cancún drive their rental cars to this beach, but only occasionally does it appear to be overcrowded with overnighters. Camp on the south end of the beach to avoid the day-trippers. Trailers can park in the lot for about US$8 per night (plus the entry fee)—no hookups, but use of showers and bathrooms is included in the parking fee.

Anyone can be a successful fisherman in this bay; it takes little more than throwing a baited hook into the surf five or six meters off the beach.

Xcacel

You can count on meeting some fascinating people here: day-trippers from Cancún, people in camper-vans, on cycles, or on foot. A few pack everything they can in campers and RVs and spend an entire exotic winter among Xcacel's palms for very little a month. About US$10 pp per night provides a campsite and use of a clean shower and toilet; no hookups or electricity. The space gets crowded fast. For about US$7, day-trippers can use the beach, showers, and restrooms. The small restaurant here has gotten pricey, and is open only noon-4 p.m. A hamburger is about US$6; fish is less. On certain days groups from cruise ships anchored in Playa del Carmen or Cancún are bused to Xcacel for lunch at this little restaurant and the whole place gets a bit congested. If you're cooking your own meals, bring plenty of food and water; it's a long trek to the local Safeway.

Surf and Sand

The sea directly in front of the campgrounds can be rough, but only a few hundred meters north the reef blocks large waves, producing calm water again—great swimming, fishing, snorkeling, and scuba diving on the reef. When beach-combing, wear shoes along this strip of beach to protect your feet from sharp little bits of coral crunched up in the sand. This is a good place to find shells, especially in front of the campgrounds after a storm. All manner of treasure can be found, from masses of dead coral to sea urchin shells, keyhole limpets, maybe even a hermit crab carrying an ungainly shell on his back.

Hiking

If you're a hiker or birdwatcher, take the old dirt road that runs parallel to the shoreline from Chemuyil to Xelha, about five km in all. The road edges an old coconut grove now thick with jungle vegetation. Just after dawn, early birds are out in force looking for the proverbial worm or anything else that looks tasty. If at first you don't see them, you'll surely hear them. Look for small, colorful parrots or brilliant yellow orioles; you may even see a long-tailed motmot. If you decide to hike to the mouth of Xelha National Park, bring your snorkeling gear, especially if you get there before all the tour buses. Remember: don't wear sunscreen or bug repellent into the water.

PARQUE NACIONAL XELHA

Snorkeling

By midday the body count grows—many, many bodies lying face down in the turquoise sea, floating in the lagoon, plastic air tubes at attention. These are snorkelers at Xelha (shel-HAH) Lagoon, where the warm clear water invites you to don mask and fins and experience a remarkable undersea world inhabited by rare and beautiful tropical fish.

Xelha is protected by the 250-km-long Honduras Reef, longest reef in the western hemisphere. Open to the sea only through a small opening in the reef, the multifingered lagoon is a safe harbor for many species of fish. Vast schools of inch-long silver stripers sail gracefully in and out of the reefs in large clouds. The rainbow parrot fish spends a lot of time grazing on the reef—that's the crunching sound you often hear when diving or snorkeling close by. Yellow striped sergeant majors dart here and there, always looking for a handout. The lagoon is strictly off-limits to fishermen.

In addition to the fascinating fish, the lagoon holds other features of interest. Many underwater caverns punctuate the lagoon's edge; in one you'll see the remains of a decaying Maya temple altar. Little islands, narrow waterways, and underwater passages make for marvelous snorkeling amid the beautiful coral formations and fish. This is truly a diver's paradise.

Everything needed to snorkel is available for rent: masks, fins, large floating tubes, and underwater cameras. Life jackets are loaned to children (and adults who want them). Guided water tours are available.

Other Activities

You don't dive or snorkel? Don't despair. Sparkling white sand has been brought in to cover the sharp coral that edges the lagoon, creating a sunbathing beach along part of the shoreline. Sun chairs and showers are available. In addition, small platforms extend over the turquoise sea, providing convenient observation points. You can spend a lazy hour or three in the sun, lying on these platforms and enjoying the myriad colors undulating just below the surface of this natural aquarium.

Another attraction at Xelha is the river adventure. Hop a small tram that takes you to the head of the river about a kilometer inland; from there you can snorkel or tube back to the lagoon, watching plentiful birdlife along the way.

Others might prefer just strolling the grounds; one path leads to *palapa* sunshades and beach chairs on the sand overlooking the open sea. Another area holds a hammock grotto under a shady *palapa*—a perfect place for a snooze.

Certain areas of Xelha are off limits for swimming, but not for looking. The lagoon is surrounded by tropical vegetation and palm trees here and there; the place is swarming with many varieties of birds, butterflies, iguanas, and lizards.

Practicalities

Sunscreen: Despite its commercial aspects, the park is wholly devoted to saving the lagoon's natural treasures. Marine biologists have been working for almost two years to clean up the lagoon and revitalize fish reproduction. Because the lagoon is surrounded by reefs and shoreline, it takes longer for the ocean to wash out the impurities of civilization. The management insists that you do not wear your own tanning lotions; they provide you with their own formula, which is ecologically safe for the lagoon's sealife.

Facilities: Five restaurants are scattered about the property; one specializes in seafood, another in Mexican cuisine. You'll also find ice cream stands and gift shops.

Hours: Xelha is open daily 8 a.m.-6 p.m. Buses from Cancún are available. The best time to explore Xelha and have it all to yourself is promptly when the gate opens, before large tour buses arrive carrying loads of cruise-ship passengers.

RUINAS DE LA XELHA

Across the highway and about 200 meters south of Xelha lies a small group of archaeological ruins. Be prepared for a bit of a stroll from the entrance. The structures are mostly unimpressive except for the **Templo de Pajaros** ("Temple of the Birds"). Protected under a *palapa* roof, one wall still shows remnants of paintings and it's possible to make out the tails and outlines of the original art depicting birds and Chac (the Maya rain god). A young boy is always available to guide you around; certainly worth a dollar or so.

Continuing along a dirt path farther into the jungle, you'll find an enchanting cenote surrounded by trees covered with bromeliads, orchids, and ferns. A few swallows put on a graceful ballet, swooping and gliding low over the water, stealing a small sip each time. Thick jungle

and vines surround the crystal-clear water and it's a perfect place for a swim.

PLAYA TANKHA

Between Xelha and the turnoff to the Tulum ruins is Playa Tankha, where you'll find **Casa Cenote,** a special restaurant that shouldn't be missed. As its name suggests, Casa Cenote sits between a large cenote and the sea. The cenote, Tankha, is one of the deepest along the Caribbean coast. Just offshore, the snorkeling is superb; you'll discover the fresh-water bubbles where the cenote empties into the sea, and you might spy a family of shy manatees—they once visited regularly but now come back only occasionally. The white-sand beach here is a great place to spend the day.

An American runs the restaurant, which has one of the most spectacular *palapa* roofs around. Sunday-afternoon barbecues are a big hit with visitors as well as expats living around Tulum and Akumal. All settle in for the afternoon over heaping plates of barbecued ribs, steaks, or lobster shish kabob. The regular menu features homemade potato chips, nachos with all sorts of toppings, great burgers, and marinated chicken.

Casa Cenote is open Tues.-Sun. noon-sunset. The plan is to open for dinner soon. Some bungalows are also planned. Look for the Casa Cenote sign between Xelha and Tulum, then follow the dirt road east along the coast until you spot the *palapa*.

ISLA COZUMEL

Lying 19 km (12 miles) offshore from the Maya Riviera, the Caribbean isle of Cozumel is the largest of the three islands off the east coast of Quintana Roo. Surrounded by water the color of imperial jade, and edged with white-sand beaches and craggy black castles of limestone and coral, Cozumel ("Land of the Swallow") once drew Maya noblewomen, who came in large dugout canoes to worship Ix Chel, goddess of fertility; today the island draws pilgrims of a different sort—divers and sunseekers enjoying the sun, sand, and sea.

The island has something of a split personality. The lee (west) side faces a calm sea ideal for swimming, diving, water-skiing, sailboarding, beachcombing, or relaxing in the sun. This is the island's developed side, where the small seaside town of San Miguel de Cozumel (the island's *only* town) concentrates offices, shops, banks, markets, hotels, and restaurants. The island's east coast is another world, relatively devoid of people but dotted with isolated coves and beaches—some with placid water, others with spectacular crashing surf. Clear water and the proximity of at least 20 live reefs make snorkeling a must, even for the neophyte. Between the coasts, the island's overgrown interior holds Maya ruins ripe for exploration and accessible by motorcycle, bike, car, or foot.

The people of Cozumel, in their quiet way, are accepting and friendly to the growing number of visitors who come each year. The island's lively discos and steady influx of divers and cruise ships make it a more upbeat place than Isla Mujeres, yet Cozumel still lacks the jet-set feeling of Cancún—perhaps because it's a real town where fishing and diving flourished long before outsiders arrived. But guess what else has arrived? A traffic light! There goes the town.

Land and Climate

Cozumel is 47 km (29 miles) long and 15 km (nine miles) wide. The island's high point measures a scant 14 meters (45 feet) above sea level. Temperatures are warm year-round, with daytime highs averaging 27° C (81° F). The heaviest rains begin in June and last through October. It's possible for rain to fall almost every day during that time, but the usual afternoon shower is brief and causes minimal interruption of travel or activities. Occasionally, however, the skies can open up and let loose torrents. During wet months, expect high humidity. November through May is generally balmy, with daytime highs averaging 25° C, lower humidity, and an occasional cool evening. But remember, tropical climes can change from mellow to miserable and back again very quickly.

Fauna

Iguanas and other lizards skitter through Cozumel's jungles. The iguana, more visible than the others because of its size and large population, is often seen sunning atop rocks along the east shore or even in the middle of the warm paved

Hummingbirds are seen everywhere in the Yucatán bush. The tiny bird was an important part of Maya art and religion.

DIANA LASICH HARPER

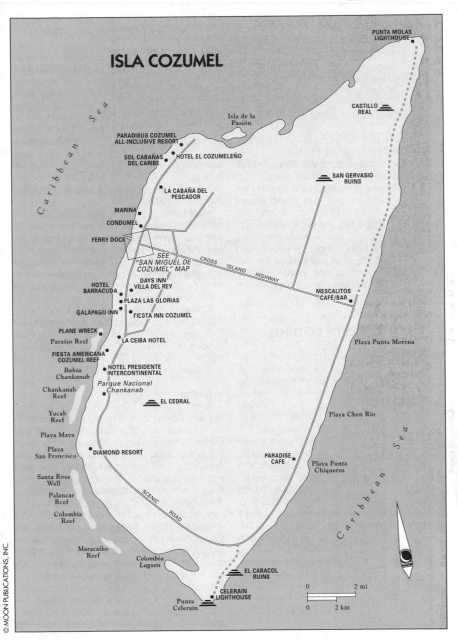

ISLA COZUMEL

PUNTA MOLAS
LIGHTHOUSE

Caribbean Sea

Isla de la
Pasión

CASTILLO
REAL

PARADISUS COZUMEL
ALL-INCLUSIVE RESORT

SOL CABAÑAS
DEL CARIBE   HOTEL EL COZUMELEÑO

SAN GERVASIO
RUINS

LA CABAÑA DEL
PESCADOR

MARINA

CONDUMEL

FERRY DOCK

SEE
"SAN MIGUEL DE
COZUMEL" MAP

CROSS ISLAND HIGHWAY

HOTEL
BARRACUDA

DAYS INN
VILLA DEL REY

MESCALITOS
CAFÉ/BAR

PLAZA LAS GLORIAS

GALÁPAGO INN   FIESTA INN COZUMEL

PLANE WRECK

Paraíso Reef

LA CEIBA HOTEL

Playa Punta Morena

FIESTA AMERICANA
COZUMEL REEF

Bahía
Chankanab

HOTEL PRESIDENTE
INTERCONTINENTAL

Chankanah
Reef

Parque Nacional
Chankanab

Yucab
Reef

EL CEDRAL

Playa Chen Río

Playa Maya

Playa
San Francisco

DIAMOND RESORT

Santa Rosa
Wall

PARADISE
CAFE

Playa Punta
Chiqueros

Palancar
Reef

Colombia
Reef

SCENIC ROAD

Caribbean Sea

Maracaibo
Reef

Colombia
Lagoon

EL CARACOL
RUINS

Punta
Celerain

CELERAIN
LIGHTHOUSE

0   2 mi

0   2 km

© MOON PUBLICATIONS, INC.

road that parallels the beach. Though the iguana is said to move slowly, the traveler with a camera has to be lightning fast to capture it on film; once it spots a human, the timid iguana slips quickly into its underground burrow or up the nearest tree. The iguana found in Cozumel is commonly shades of dark green. It can grow up to two meters long, including its black-banded tail, and has a comblike crest of scales down the middle of its back.

Armadillos, deer, small foxes, and coati also call the Cozumel jungle their home.

Marinelife is abundant in the waters surrounding the island. Brilliantly colored fish—from tiny silver bait fish traveling in cloudlike schools, to the grim, thick-lipped grouper—lurk in and around graceful, asymmetrical formations of coral with names like cabbage, fan, and elk. You'll see rainbow-hued parrot fish, yellow-and-black-striped sergeant majors, French angelfish, yellow-tailed damselfish, and shy silver-pink squirrel fish with their big, sensitive-looking eyes. In shallow coves, daring Bermuda grubs come up out of the water to eat from your hand; watch the teeth!

SAN MIGUEL DE COZUMEL

San Miguel has a relaxed, unhurried atmosphere, though it's no longer the sleepy fishing village it once was. The town offers a good selection of restaurants from budget to gourmet, as well as hotels in every price range. Grocery stores, curio shops, banks, a post office, telegraph office, dive shops, and anything else you might need are available. The main street, known either as the *malecón* or Av. Melgar, extends 14 blocks along the waterfront. The main dock is at the foot of Av. Juárez, in the center of town.

Plaza del Sol, the large central plaza, boasts modern civic buildings and imposing statues of the late Mexican president Benito Juárez and a great general named Andrés Quintana Roo. The surrounding streets are closed to vehicular traffic, making the plaza a pleasant place to stroll, shop, and enjoy the island's tranquility. In spring, masses of orange *framboyán* (poinciana) flowers bloom on the surrounding shade trees, under which local townspeople gather for festivals, religious celebrations, and friendly chats. Cafes and gift shops surround the plaza.

ARCHAEOLOGICAL SITES

Cozumel was one of the most important ports-of-trade for the Post-Classic Putún Maya seafarers. The island was a major producer of honey and contained the most important pilgrimage destination on the Peninsula's east coast. Women from throughout Mesoamerica traveled to Cozumel to worship at the shrine of Ix Chel ("She of the Rainbow"), goddess of childbirth and medicine. Twenty-four archaeological sites have been discovered on the island, which was occupied from A.D. 0 on. The island's indigenous population grew significantly after A.D. 800 and reached its peak in 1400.

Most ruins on the island are of the "oratorio" type: small square buildings, low to the ground, with short doors that led early Spaniards to believe the places were once inhabited by dwarfs (a now discredited myth). El Cedral is the exception; though the temple is small, major ceremonies were probably held on this site. Several of the ruins are easily reached by car or motorbike.

Cozumel Archaeological Park, on Av. 65 Sur a few blocks inland from the International Pier, contains reproductions of Mexico's most famous archaeological finds and an exhibit of a typical Mayan home. The park is open daily 8 a.m.-6 p.m.; admission US$3.

El Cedral

Just beyond Playa San Francisco on the main highway leaving town, a paved road takes off to the left and ends 3.5 km (2.1 miles) further at El Cedral. Small and not enormously impressive, this is the oldest Maya structure on the island. Amazingly, it still bears a few traces of the paint and stucco applied by the original Maya artist. But the deterioration indicates that hundreds of years have passed it by. A tree grows from the roof, its thick, exposed roots tangled in and around the stones. Fat iguanas with bold black stripes tracing their midsections guard the deserted, mold-covered site, where sounds of cows blend with the songs of countless birds and the resonant buzz of unseen insects.

Located in what is now a small farm settlement, El Cedral was once used as a jail in the 1800s. Right next to it is a rustic, modern-era stucco church painted vivid green. Go inside and take a look at two crosses draped with finely embroidered lace mantles—a typical mixture of Christianity and more ancient belief, which some believe is associated with the Talking Cross cult.

San Gervasio

San Gervasio is a well-preserved and recently reconstructed group of structures. Travel east on Av. Juárez (the cross-island highway), then turn left (north) on a dirt road (look for the San Gervasio sign) and follow it approximately 10 km (six miles) until it dead-ends at the site's entrance. The silence of these antiquities looming in the midst of dense brush, with only birds singing in the tall trees, overwhelms the visitor with an image of what it must have been like centuries ago when only the Maya visited.

Three building groups are visible at San Gervasio; these are connected by trails built along the old Maya causeways. The structures are mainly small temples and shrines built on platforms around a plaza. In the middle of one causeway is the Témple of Ix Chel, a small but well-preserved building that was probably a shrine, although the connection to the goddess is not certain. Archaeologists at San Gervasio have recently found a grave containing 50 skeletons as well as some Spanish beads, leading them to believe that these were victims of a European disease brought by the conquistadors.

San Gervasio is open 8 a.m.-5 p.m.; admission is US$4.50. A snack bar sells cold drinks. Be prepared; guides will offer their services for about US$10-12 for two people. That's a bit pricey considering you can do just as well in this small area by first getting solid information and a site map at Cozumel's museum (downtown).

ALONG THE PERIMETER ROAD

Following the scenic road south from San Miguel will take you past many beautiful beaches and sights of interest. The road loops back up the east side of the island and meets the cross-island highway, where a left turn will take you back to San Miguel. The following points of interest are listed in that order: north to south down the west side of the island, then south to north up the east side.

Parque Nacional Chankanab

Chankanab, nine km (5.5 miles) south of San Miguel, is a national park centered around a lagoon containing more than 60 species of marinelife, including an assortment of fish, crustaceans, turtles, and coral. The lagoon is shallow, and at one time swimmers could go from the lagoon to Chankanab Bay (on the sea) through underwater tunnels; the tunnels have collapsed and no longer assure safe passage. Swimming in the lagoon is now prohibited.

As you stroll the grounds of the wonderful, shady park, you'll discover lovely stone Maya reproductions. A small pond—a crystal-clear natural aquarium—is surrounded by a botani-

OZ MALLAN

Chankanab Lagoon

cal garden of 352 species of tropical and sub-tropical plants from 22 countries, as well as those endemic to Cozumel.

Also within the national park boundaries, Chankanab Bay is a popular beach for sun-bathers, swimmers, divers, and snorkelers. The snorkeling here is excellent—the bay's showy sea creatures have no fear of humans, and lime-stone caves near the shoreline make for great exploring. A sunken boat, rusty anchors, coral-crusted cannons, and an antiquated religious statue all make for eerie underwater sightsee-ing. Adventurous scuba divers can check out the coral reef, close offshore at depths of 2-16 meters. Note that the word Chankanab means "little sea" in Maya, probably because the bay can get surgy.

Park facilities include a floating barge that al-lows swimmers a place to haul out and catch the rays; a well-equipped dive shop offering rentals, air, sales, and instruction; several gift shops; a snack stand; and two *palapa* restau-rants. The park is open daily 9 a.m.-5 p.m. Most people come to spend the day—it's a great place for the kids. Park admission is about US$8, which includes use of shade *palapas*, freshwater showers, dressing rooms, and lockers.

Playa Corona
South of the national park, Playa Corona makes a pleasant place to spend an afternoon. Here you'll find a white-sand beach, workout equip-ment, good swimming and snorkeling, and an outdoor cafe serving fresh fish and cold *cerveza*.

Playa San Francisco
Continuing south, you'll soon come to Playa San Francisco. This 3.5-km (2.1-mile) stretch of busy beach has two open-air restaurants, dressing rooms, a bar, gift shops, a volleyball net, wood-en chaise lounges, and snorkeling equipment rental (US$7 per day). During the week it's rela-tively quiet, but during busy seasons and on weekends it's inundated with tourists, many brought by bus from cruise ships that anchor in the downtown harbor. San Francisco is also a popular Sunday destination for local citizens. Fresh fish and Mexican specialties are served to the accompaniment of loud, live music, romp-ing kids, and chattering adults. The bay is usually filled with dive boats attracted to nearby San Francisco Reef.

South to Punta Celerain
Continuing south, between Playa San Francisco and Punta Celerain you'll find several other beach clubs, among them **Playa Sol Beach Club** (snorkel shuttles US$15/hour), **Diamond Resort, Playa Mac,** and **Punta Francesa,** which lies on a lovely tip of land by the sea and serves a buffet noon-4 p.m.

Punta Celerain
At the southern end of the scenic road, you'll come to a dirt road turning south off the pave-ment. This dirt road meanders parallel to the coast behind sand dunes and eventually ends at **Punta Celerain Lighthouse,** on Punta Celerain (the southernmost tip of Cozumel). All along this road, turnoffs lead east to beautiful isolated beaches.

Part way down the road is El Caracol ruins, where a small, conch-shaped structure has been restored. According to archaeologists, it was built A.D. 1200-1400 as both a ceremonial cen-ter and navigational guide; the Maya keeper used smoke and flames in the equivalent of a modern-day lighthouse. One of the docents at the town museum explains how the small open-ings at the structure's top act as a foghorn when the wind blows through them. Behind this small building, a dirt path over a sand dune goes to an-other beach great for swimming, sunbathing, and beachcombing.

The lighthouse is four km (2.4 miles) from the main road. From a distance it appears white, tall, and regal; up close it needs a paint job. Next to the lighthouse is a small army base with sol-diers on guard. Wander around the point to view strong surf crashing over an irregular black lime-stone shore in great clouds of misty surf, spray-ing tall geysers through jagged blowholes. The family at the lighthouse is friendly; ask to climb to the top for a spectacular 360-degree view of the island (leaving a tip wouldn't hurt).

Back on the paved road and turning up the east shore, a large sign warns of the conse-quences of taking turtle eggs. The turtles are protected species, and they come to shore here in large numbers during the summer to lay their eggs. You'll often find a soldier (with tent) sta-tioned by the sign; in addition to guarding against poachers, this coastal watch keeps tabs on the boating activity between Cozumel and the Yucatán coast—boatloads of illegal drugs are frequently picked up along here.

Playa Punta Chiqueros to the Cross-Island Highway

Swimming is idyllic at Playa Punta Chiqueros, a protected cove with crystalline water and a white-sand beach. A small restaurant/bar, the **Paradise Cafe,** sits on the edge of the lovely crescent bay. You can camp on the beach—with a tent or a vehicle—but there are no facilities. If driving an RV, check with the restaurant owners before you park.

A bit farther north, at **Playa Chen Río,** you might find space for a tent and a few camping vehicles on a broad flat area next to the beach (ask around).

At the east end of the cross-island highway you'll find the tiny **Mescalitos Café** facing the sea. Expect a couple of daily seafood specials. You can rent a horse here if you like.

North of the Cross-Island Highway

To visit beaches on this part of the east shore, you'll need a motorcycle or 4WD for the unpaved sandy road. If you rent a jeep for this trip, make sure that the 4WD hasn't been disengaged by the rental agency (almost all agencies do this to conserve gas). Because of its condition, the 24.5-km (14.7-mile) road is seldom used, and few people see these beautiful beaches. If you decide to hike along this coast, you'll make better time in many areas walking on the road rather than on the rocky shore in between sandy beaches.

The first two beaches north of the cross-island highway, **Playa Santa Cecilia** and **Playa Bonita,** are good beachcombing spots, and Playa Bonita is a good camping beach (no facilities). Hardcore adventurers can follow trails west from the road to various little-known Maya ruins, abandoned cenotes, and caves; this kind of jungle trek requires carrying all essentials. From the Maya site at **Castillo Real** to the north, there are no more sandy beaches before the lighthouse on Punta Molas. Many ships have sunk along this violent shore: cannons and anchors are occasionally found to prove the legends.

SNORKELING

Snorkeling and diving are the most popular outdoor activities on Cozumel. If you can swim but haven't tried snorkeling, Cozumel is a great place to begin. It's easy to find a fascinating marine environment close to shore; in many cases you need only step from your hotel. Along the lee side of the island almost all the beaches are ideal snorkeling sites. If it's your first time, practice with a snorkel and mask while sitting in shallow, calm surf with your face underwater, breathing through the snorkel that protrudes above the surface. (Or use your bathtub to learn before leaving home.) Once you're accustomed to breathing with the tube, the rest is simple. And wear fins, which make it easier to maneuver in the water.

A few easy-to-reach snorkeling sites include Bahía Chankanab, Playa San Francisco, and

The reefs make Cozumel a favorite divers' destination.

OZ MALLAN

the beaches at the Hotel Presidente Interconti- nental and La Ceiba Hotel (where there's an un- derwater plane wreck). One other spot that's seldom used any more is north of town at **Isla de la Pasión.** This tiny island in Bahía Abrigo offers secluded beaches and a rocky shoreline good for underwater exploring. It's now a state reserve without cafes, restrooms, or other facilities. Ask at a dive shop for information.

Rental equipment is available at hotels and dive shops. Dive shops also offer boat trips to off- shore reefs.

SCUBA DIVING

If you've always wanted to learn to scuba dive, here's the place to do it. A multitude of dive shops and instructors offer certification, or in- struction sufficient for one dive. Make sure to find a qualified instructor; ask for his or her qual- ifications and accident record, and ask around town for more information about the person (try the harbormaster). It's your life.

Offshore fringing reefs make good simple dives for the neophyte; caves and crevices line the shore, and coral heads rise to within three meters of the surface. Experts can find boat trips geared to wall diving, night diving, and deep div- ing. In winter, a wetsuit top is suggested; the rest of the year a bathing suit will suffice.

Note: Since 1980, a refuge has protected marine flora and fauna on the west coast of Cozumel from the shore up to and including the Drop-Off (El Cantil). It is illegal to fish or to re- move any marine artifacts, including coral, from the area. And all divers should be aware that even touching a delicate coral reef kills it. Take care not to scrape your equipment or push off from the coral with your feet. Do your part to protect and save the area for future generations of divers to enjoy.

Some of the more popular dive spots are list- ed following.

Plane Wreck

A 40-passenger Convair airliner—engines re- moved—reposes upside down on the seabed, 100 meters off the La Ceiba Hotel pier. It was purposely sunk in 1977 for the Mexican movie production of *Survive II,* and now it affords

schools of fish shady hiding places on the white sandy bottom. The water's clarity allows a clear view of the wreck, as well as multicolored sponges and huge coral heads. A 120-meter trail has been marked with underwater signs pointing out the various types of marinelife on La Ceiba reef. The visibility is up to 30 meters, and the average depth is 9-17 meters.

Paraíso Reef

About 200 meters off the beach just south of the International Dock (between the Presidente and the dock), North Paraíso Reef can be reached ei- ther by boat or from the beach. It averages 9- 17 meters deep and is a site of impressive star and brain corals and sea fans. The south end of the reef, farther offshore, is swarming with sea life. This is a good spot for night diving.

Chankanab Caves and Reef

For easy-access diving, go to Chankanab La- goon Park; along the bayshore, steps are carved from coral for easy entry. Three large under- ground caverns here are filled with hundreds of fish of all varieties. Striped grunt, snapper, sergeant majors, and butterfly fish are found in all three caves. Dives average 5-12 meters.

A boat is needed to dive Chankanab Reef (sometimes referred to as Outer Chankanab Reef), several hundred meters offshore south of Laguna Chankanab. Night diving is good here at depths of 8-15 meters, where basket starfish hang out with octopi and jail-striped morays. At the drop-off, stunning coral heads are at a max- imum depth of 10 meters; in some spots coral is within three meters of the surface. Coral heads are covered with gorgonians and sea fans; striped grunt and mahogany snapper slowly cruise around the base. This is a good location for snorkelers and beginning divers.

Tormentos Reef

This medium-depth reef features innumerable coral heads in 8-12 meters of water above a sandy bottom. The heads are decorated with fans, gorgonians, and sponges. With little current, you can get excellent photos. Great numbers of invertebrates prowl the sandy bottom; look for flamingo tongue shell, arrow crab, black crinoid, coral shrimp, and sea cucumber. The farthest section of the reef drops to 21.5 meters, where you'll see deep-sea fans, lobsters, and immense groupers.

Yucab Reef

One km south of Punta Tormentos, Yucab Reef is fairly close to shore, shallow (good for beginners), and alive with such beauties as queen angelfish, star and brain corals, sponge, and sea whip. The coral reef is about 120 meters long, with an average depth of nine meters, and coral heads about three meters from the floor. When there's a current it can be two or three knots.

Tunich Reef

A half km south of Yucab—directly out from Punta Tunich—this deeper reef (15-24 meters) has about a 1.5-knot current or more, and when it's stronger you could be swept right along to Cuba! The reef is loaded with intricately textured corals, and the water activity attracts manta rays, jewfish, and barracuda. It's a good reef to spot shy moray eels. Just south of here you'll find **Cardona Reef.**

San Francisco Reef

Another popular boat-dive site, San Francisco Reef is one km off Playa San Francisco. The abbreviated (half-km) coral reef runs parallel to shore and is teeming with reef fish of many varieties and brilliant colors. Depths average 17-19 meters.

Santa Rosa Wall

This sensational drop-off, which begins at 22 meters and just keeps going to the black bottom of the Caribbean, really gives you a feeling for the ocean's depth. Strong currents make this a drift-dive and a site for experienced divers only (watch your depth gauge). You'll discover tunnels and caves; translucent sponges; stony overhangs; queen, French, and gray angelfish; white trigger fish; and many big groupers.

Paso del Cedral

This flat reef with 22-meter, gardenlike valleys is a good wall dive. In some places the top of the reef begins 15.5 meters from the surface. Sea life includes angelfish, lobster, and thick-lipped grouper.

Palancar Reef

The reef most associated with Cozumel is actually a five-km series of varying coral formations about 1.5 km offshore. Each of these formations offers a different thrill. Some drop off dramatically into winding ravines, deep canyons, passageways, or archways and tunnels with formations 15 meters tall—all teeming with reef life. Depths vary; at the south (deep) end, the top of the reef begins at 27 meters.

Horseshoe, considered by some to be the best diving in the Caribbean, is a series of coral heads forming a horseshoe curve at the top of the drop-off. The visibility of 66-86 meters, plus a solid bronze, four-meter-tall, submerged modernistic sculpture of Christ, make this a dramatic photo area. The statue, created especially for the sea, was sunk on 3 May 1985 with great pomp and ceremony and the presence of Ramón Bravo, well-known TV reporter and Mexican diver. The much-discussed reef lives up to its good press. Just south of here find **La Francesa Reef.**

Colombia Reef

Several km south of Palancar, Colombia Reef is a deep-dive area, with the top of the reef at 25-30 meters. In addition to undersea canyons and ravines, here the diver may encounter giant sea turtles and huge groupers hiding beneath deep coral overhangs. Water temperature averages 23° C (73° F) in winter and 27° C (81° F) in summer; when the water cools down, you'll see spotted eagle rays here. This reef is best for experienced divers, as there's usually a current. Visibility is 50-66 meters.

Maracaibo Reef

At the island's southern tip, this reef offers an exhilarating experience for the experienced diver. It's considered by most to be the ultimate challenge of all the reefs mentioned. At the deepest section, the top of the wall begins at 37 meters; at the shallow area, 23 meters. Unlike at many other reefs, coral formations here are immense. Be prepared for strong currents and for who-knows-what pelagic species, including shark. Dive boats do not stop here on their regular trips and advance reservations are required for this dive.

Other Good Diving Areas

North of San Miguel, **Barracuda** and **San Juan Reefs** are for experienced divers only—currents can be as fast as six knots. In that kind of current a face mask could be ripped off with the wrong move. It's definitely a specialty dive (somewhat like a roller coaster!). Check with Aqua Safari for more information; reservations are necessary for their trips to these reefs.

Dive Trips and Lessons

Many of the reef dives mentioned may be arranged through one of the many dive shops in town, through the boatmen's co-op, or by some of the hotels that have their own equipment and divemaster. All equipment is provided and sometimes lunch and drinks. Shop around to find an outfit that suits your needs, level of diving experience, and pocketbook (prices vary). Scuba lessons for certification or a resort course for one-day dives are available at most of the same shops. Be sure to check the qualifications and track record of the dive shop and divemaster you choose.

Aqua Safari, Av. Melgar at Av. 5 Norte, tel. (987) 2-0101, and in the Plaza Las Glorias hotel, tel. (987) 2-3362, enjoys an excellent reputation for safety, experience, good equipment, and happy divers who return year after year. Aqua has its own fleet of boats and offers two-tank morning dives, one-tank afternoon dives, and evening dives; they operate daily except Sunday, Christmas, and New Year's Day. Aqua Safari Dive Shop hours are 8 a.m.-1 p.m. and 4-6:30 p.m.

Other reputable Cozumel dive shops include: **Blue Bubble Divers,** tel. (987) 2-1865; **Caribbean Divers,** tel. (987) 2-1080; **Del Mar Aquatics,** tel. (987) 2-1833; **Scuba Du,** tel. (987) 2-1379; **Dive Paradise,** tel. (987) 2-0017; and **Fantasia Divers,** tel. (987) 2-2840.

Underwater Photography

The clear waters around Cozumel allow outstanding photographs. Underwater camera rentals are available at **Island Foto-Video Center,** at the La Ceiba Hotel, tel. (987) 2-0379, and at some dive shops. You might also check out **Tony Tate's Cozumel Underwater Video Service,** tel. (987) 2-1444, fax (987) 2-1850. Tate accompanies divers on their dives and shoots a video of their underwater adventure for a great souvenir.

Dive Safety

Because of the growing influx of divers to Cozumel from all over the world, the small island continues to increase safety services. All reputable shops require divers to show their certification card and state the date of their last dive. If they don't require a card, I'd question their integrity. Some shops require divers who haven't been in the water for a while to go through a checkout dive so divemasters can ascertain their ability.

At affiliated dive shops, US$1 per dive day is added to divers' fees to help support the **SSS** (Servicios de Seguridad Sub-Acuática). This donation is like having an insurance policy; it enti-

Aqua Safari boats wait for passengers for an all-day dive trip.

OZ MALLAN

tles the distressed diver to make use of Cozumel's hyperbaric chamber, marine ambulance, and fully trained round-the-clock personnel (each facility offers 24-hour service). All divers are welcome to use these services, but nonparticipants pay regular commercial rates, so inquire about affiliation before choosing a dive shop. The recompression chamber is on Calle 5 Sur near Av. Melgar, tel. (987) 2-2387.

FISHING

Cozumel boasts good deep-sea fishing year-round. Red snapper, tuna, barracuda, dolphin, wahoo, bonito, king mackerel, and tarpon are especially plentiful March through July, also the high season for marlin and sailfish. You can hire a boat with tackle, bait, and guide for anywhere from US$125 to US$825, depending on length of excursion, size of boat, number of people, and season. Arrangements can be made at the boatmen's co-op, tel. (987) 2-0080, or by contacting Club Náutico de Cozumel at Marina Puerto de Abrigo Banco Playa (Apdo. Postal 341, Cozumel, Quintana Roo 77600, Mexico), tel. (987) 2-0118. You can also just visit the marina in midafternoon when the boats are returning from the day's fishing trips; talk with boat captains and their customers, choose a boat to your liking, and negotiate the fee on the spot. The main marina is just north of town; a smaller one is by the Presidente Cozumel hotel.

TOURS

In the Saddle
Sea Horse Ranch, tel. (987) 2-1958, offers horseback expeditions into the Cozumel bush, where you will see off-the-beaten-track Maya ruins and even the Red Cenote. English-speaking guides explain island flora and fauna. Regular tours are offered Mon.-Sat.; reservations necessary.

Glass-Bottom Boats
Even non-divers can get a close-up view of Cozumel's flamboyant underwater realm on a glass-bottom-boat tour. Small boats cruise along the lee side of the coast, and bigger motorized launches travel farther out to the larger reefs.

Prices vary accordingly. Ask at your hotel, one of the dive shops, or Fiesta Cozumel, tel. (987) 2-0831, whose *Nautilus IV* is the island's newest tour boat. Called a floating submarine, the boat actually has a glass-enclosed area below deck for viewing shallow reefs.

ACCOMMODATIONS

Inexpensive
For 20 years, the Anduze family has been running the fine old **Hotel El Marqués,** Av. 5 Sur on the plaza, tel. (987) 2-0677, fax (987) 2-0537, a great downtown option. Rooms have eclectic furnishings, a/c, and small in-room refrigerators; the third-floor rooms have good views. Los Cocos Restaurant is on the premises.

Hotel Aguilar, Av. 3 Sur 98 (one block from downtown), tel. (987) 2-0307, fax (987) 2-0769, is another oldie still serving the traveler well. The simple rooms have a/c and fan; no credit cards accepted.

Hotel Posada Cozumel, Calle 4 Norte 3, tel. (987) 2-0314, is another basic low-cost accommodation. All rooms are doubles with bathroom and hot water; some have a/c, others a fan. The simple, clean hotel has a swimming pool.

Hotel Flamingo, on Calle 6 Norte about five blocks north of the *malecón,* tel. (987) 2-1264, U.S. tel. (800) 806-1601, offers large, clean rooms, some with balconies, and a pleasant Mexican ambience. Good value here, ask about packages.

Moderate
Villas Ix Chel, 55 Av. Bis 1033 (between 15 and 17 Sur), tel./fax (987) 2-4435, is for the visitor who doesn't mind being away from downtown. It's a fine newish little apartment complex with patios and hammocks, private bathrooms, and daily maid service, about a 15-minute walk to the plaza. Accommodations range from single rooms to nicely furnished, kitchen-equipped apartments sleeping three.

Hotel Mary Carmen, Av. 5 Sur 4, tel. (987) 2-0581, is a small, pleasant, simple hotel just a stone's throw from the plaza, discos, restaurants, shops, and all other downtown activities. The 28 rooms are clean and surround a nicely tended garden.

SAN MIGUEL DE COZUMEL

PIZZA HOLANDI

PANCHO'S BACKYARD CAFE/ CINCO SOLES

CALLE 10 NORTE

5 AV. NORTE

10 AV. NORTE

15 AV. NORTE

CALLE 8 NORTE

20 AV. NORTE

MUSEO DE LA ISLA DE COZUMEL

GRAL. R. MELGAR

CALLE 6 NORTE

BAKERY ZERMATT

CARLOS'N CHARLIE'S

CALLE 4 NORTE

MEXICANA AIRLINES

SPORTS PAGE RESTAURANT

LOS ALMENDROS RESTAURANT

HARD ROCK CAFE

EL PORTAL RESTAURANT

MAIN DOCK AND FERRY

CALLE 2 NORTE

LAS PALMERAS RESTAURANT

NIÑOS HEROES MONUMENT

BENITO JUAREZ PARK

PLAZA DEL SOL

SAN MIGUEL CHURCH

25 AV. NORTE

AV. BENITO JUAREZ

ARTS AND CRAFTS MARKET

MARY CARMEN HOTEL

COCINA ECONOMICA MI CHABELITA

HOTEL EL MARQUES

LA CUCCINA ITALIANA

ALFALFA RESTAURANT

CALLE 1 SUR

PEPE'S GRILL

LOS COCOS

TELEPHONE OFFICE

LA CHOZA RESTAURANT

DR. A. ROSADO SALAS

25 AV. SUR

CALLE 3 SUR

5 AV. SUR

10 AV. SUR

15 AV. SUR

20 AV. SUR

SAFARI INN

WAFFLE HOUSE

VILLAS LAS ANCLAS

SCALE NOT AVAILABLE

POST OFFICE

RECOMPRESSION CHAMBER

© MOON PUBLICATIONS, INC.

At **Club del Sol,** tel. (987) 2-3777, fax (987) 2-2329, U.S. tel. (800) 228-6112, you stay across the road from the waterfront (and a small snorkeling area) for a good price. The hotel offers few frills but has a pleasant low-key Mexican ambience. Hammocks hang about the heavily landscaped property, which features a swimming pool, dive shop, and an open-air cafe with good food. The a/c rooms are simply furnished; a few have kitchenettes. Many of the guests return annually.

Playa Azul, tel. (987) 2-0043, fax (987) 2-0110, is a fine family-oriented destination on the north side of town.

Expensive

A half mile from town, **Hotel Barracuda,** tel. (987) 2-0002, fax (987) 2-0884, is another old standby. A favorite with divers, the hotel is right on the beach and boasts its own pier, dive shop, and restaurant. The 50 simple rooms have a/c and balconies.

Villas Las Anclas, Av. 5A Sur 325, tel. (987) 2-1955, fax (987) 2-1403, is another small well-priced complex with seven efficiency apartments. Each has a/c and nice furnishings; the complimentary coffee is excellent. No credit cards.

Days Inn Villa del Rey, Av. 11 Sur 460, U.S. tel. (800) DAYS INN, Mexico fax (987) 2-1692, is a simple, clean, downtown hotel with 43 a/c rooms (some with kitchenettes) and a pool. It's four blocks from the ocean and five blocks from the plaza.

Fiesta Inn Cozumel, on the Chankanab road at Km 1.7, tel. (987) 2-2899, fax (987) 2-2154, U.S. tel. (800) FIESTA1, offers 180 well decorated rooms across the street from the beach. Amenities include a large pool away from the road and a *palapa* on the beach serving drinks and snacks. Room service is available until 11 p.m., and the hotel's Los Arcos dining room serves a breakfast buffet for US$9 and a dinner buffet for US$12.

North of town, **Sol Cabañas del Caribe,** Carretera San Juan, Km 4.5, tel. (987) 2-0411, fax (987) 2-1599, U.S. tel. (800) 336-3542, offers nine simple little cabanas in addition to standard hotel rooms. It's pricey but not glitzy. Each unit has a/c, simple furnishings, and comfortable beds, and there's a pool. The windsurfing shop at the hotel is operated by one of Mexico's top windsurfing champions and is a great place to learn; kayaks are available for rent as well.

Also on the north side of town is **Coral Princess Resort,** tel. (987) 2-3200, fax (987) 2-2800, U.S. tel. (800) 253-2702, with fully equipped condos overlooking the beach.

Premium

The bright pink, upscale **Plaza Las Glorias,** on Chankanab road at Km 1.5, tel. (987) 2-2200, fax (987) 2-1937, U.S. tel. (800) 882-6684, is right on the beach, and features in-house diving service through Aqua Safari Dive Shop. Amenities include a/c, a pool, a private dock for divers, good entry into the ocean for snorkelers, and a fine dining room.

Hotel Presidente Intercontinental, tel. (987) 2-0322, fax (987) 2-1360, U.S. tel. (800) 447-6147, is probably the island's nicest hotel and sits on one of the best beaches on the San Miguel side. Visitors find a relaxed happy atmosphere, 260 a/c rooms, a pool, beautiful grounds and public rooms, and several dining rooms that serve delicious meals with music. Be sure you try El Caribeno, the open-air *palapa* cafe overlooking the sea. Rooms are well decorated in pastel colors and priced according to location; some are upstairs with a "partial" view of the sea, others have a full view, some have private balconies, and some (the most expensive) offer private patios opening onto the beach. All sea sports are available. Snorkeling is great here and just a few steps from the hotel. Easy car rentals and taxi service.

Fiesta Americana Cozumel Reef, just south of town on the Chankanab road (at Km 7.5), U.S. tel. (800) 343-7821, Mexico fax (987) 2-2688, is one of the island's newer hotels. It sits on the landward side of the street, but beach access is simple—a pedestrian bridge leads from the hotel over the road to a beach club, which has a pool, restaurant, dive shop, and boat dock.

Hotels for Divers

Inexpensive: Some hotels go out of their way to accommodate divers. One such hotel is the 12-room **Safari Inn,** downtown on Av. Melgar, above Aqua Safari Dive Shop and across from the Safari boat dock (Apdo. Postal 41, Cozumel, Quintana Roo 77600, Mexico), tel. (987) 2-0101,

fax (987) 2-0661, e-mail: dive@aquasafari.com. The hotel is modern, simple, and clean, has a/c, and is very convenient for diving expeditions, though still close to downtown activity. Dive/hotel packages available.

Galápago Inn, tel. (987) 2-0663, a dedicated divers' hotel, offers a great dive shop, hammocks hanging by the beach, and a very good restaurant (stop by even if you're not staying here). The inn is often full with groups from U.S. dive shops. For information on dive packages at the Galápago contact Aqua-Sub Tours, tel. (800) 847-5708, or the hotel.

Expensive: La Ceiba Hotel, on the edge of town, U.S. tel. (800) 435-3240, Mexico fax (987) 2-0065, welcomes divers, and what could be nicer? A sunken airplane lies just offshore in front of the hotel—it's a popular site for shore dives. The hotel offers comfortable rooms, a pool, a/c, and an on-site dive shop.

All-Inclusive Hotels

Expensive: El Cozumeleño, at Playa Santa Pilar, tel. (987) 2-0344, fax (987) 2-0381, U.S. tel. (800) 437-3923, is a multistory hotel right on the sand, with the blue Caribbean at its feet. The rooms are nicely decorated, and have a/c and private balconies. Keeping cool is easy; in addition to the sea, guests have use of two pools, sailboats, and Jet Skis. Deep-sea fishing nearby can be arranged in-house. Dining is a delight on the beautiful sea-view terrace. US$109 pp, double occupancy.

Premium: South of Playa San Francisco, **Diamond Resort,** tel. (987) 2-3433, fax (987) 2-4508, U.S. tel. (800) 858-2258, offers rooms in modern, two-story, *palapa*-roofed villas. Everything is included in the daily price—meals, drinks, gratuities, tennis, and a host of water sports. Dive packages are available at the dive shop, and great dive spots are just minutes from shore. Guests enjoy all the splash-sports, plus Sunfish sailers, pedal boats, and one free scuba lesson in the pool. Daytime and nighttime activities include aerobics, cocktail parties, and theme nights. Town is a US$10 cab ride away. The hotel is often filled with tour groups; US$170 pp, double occupancy.

Paradisus Cozumel All-Inclusive Resort, tel. (987) 2-0412, fax (987) 2-1599, U.S. tel. (800) 336-3542, is a five-star hotel at the far north end of the leeward side of the island, about a 15-minute drive to town. Amenities include marble tile floors, pastel decorated rooms, private balconies, 24-hour room service, direct-dial phone service, a/c, satellite TV, mini-bar, tennis, two pools, and a dive shop. Dining is exquisite, with a choice of continental haute cuisine or typical Yucatecan specialties. At this one, all-inclusive *really* includes everything. US$350 double.

Condominiums

Premium: Condos have not taken over the Cozumel shoreline—yet! One of the finest is the small and intimate **Condumel,** a 20-minute walk or five-minute cab ride north of town (Attn. Sara, Apdo. Postal 142, Cozumel, Quintana Roo 77600, Mexico), tel. (987) 2-0892, fax (987) 2-0661, U.S. tel. (800) 262-4500. Condumel has its own beach and swimming dock where iguanas sunbathe with the visitors.

The condos are outfitted with a/c, one bedroom with king bed, and a kitchen ready for the cook. A few basic food items, including beer and purified water, are thoughtfully chilling in the fridge in case you don't want to go shopping right away. Owner Bill Horn also manages Aqua Safari dive shop and will arrange diving trips and equipment.

Bed and Breakfast

Inexpensive: Tamarindo, Calle 4 Norte 421 (between Avs. 20 and 25), tel./fax (987) 2-3614, is a pleasant B&B about five blocks from the plaza and four from the ocean. Breakfast is served on the patio; some rooms have a/c, and there's a community kitchen.

Moderate: B&B Caribo, 799 Av. Juárez, U.S. tel. (800) 830-5558, is another nice little place away from downtown, about eight blocks from the sea. The house was the former home of a Mexican doctor, and the proprietors—a couple of American expats—have really fixed it up. Some rooms have a/c, some have fans, a couple have kitchens, and a couple share a bathroom. A lovely fountain and colorful flowers contribute to a charming atmosphere, and the breakfast is good. Along with everything else, the B&B offers "special" weeks when stays are coupled with seminars by experts on a variety of topics; call for the upcoming program.

Island Camping

Cozumel has no campgrounds with facilities. However, hidden coves and isolated beaches on the island's east side make great primitive campsites. Bring everything needed to camp, including water. Don't expect even a tiny *tienda* at which to buy forgotten items. If you ask the tourist office about beach camping, they'll tell you to get permission from the navy, which occupies the large building south of town (on the ocean side across from the Costa Brava cafe and hotel). You can also request permission for camping at **Mescalitos Bar, Balneario Popular,** and **Paradise Cafe,** all on the east side of the island. None of these places have camping facilities of any kind, but they might let you stay on their property.

FOOD

Cozumel holds fast-food stands and restaurants to fit all budgets. Seafood is exquisite and fresh, and Yucatecan specialties simply must be tasted! *Camarones con ajo* (shrimp with garlic), *caracol* (conch), and tangy ceviche (fish or conch marinated in lime, vinegar, chopped onions, tomatoes, and cilantro) are all tasty treats. *Huachinango Veracruz* (red snapper cooked with tomatoes, green pepper, onions, and spices) is popular, and snapper is caught off the reef year-round; eat it a few hours after it's caught. Fresh seafood is sold in most cafes.

Inexpensive Cafes

Budget-class **La Cocina Económica Mi Chabelita,** two blocks from the plaza heading inland on Calle 1 Sur to Av. 10 Sur, offers ample servings of *pescado frito* (fried fish) and *carne asada* (grilled meat) for about US$4. **Casa Denis,** the yellow house just up Av. Juárez from the plaza, has a few tables set out by the street and more in a back garden. Have a cold beer and empanadas stuffed with fish for under US$4. **Comida Casera Toñita,** on Rosado Salas, is a great find for its *comida corrida,* the fixed-price afternoon meal that covers both lunch and dinner and fills you up for about US$6.

Prowl around on the back streets away from the sea toward the middle of the island—more and more small cafes are opening up, and prices

are usually cheaper than at those near the ocean. **Las Tortugas,** Av. 10 Norte 82, serves good tacos.

El Portal, an open cafe facing the waterfront, serves tasty family-style food. A sturdy breakfast of bacon, eggs, beans, and toast costs about US$5. Open for breakfast, lunch, and dinner. **Las Palmeras,** at the foot of the pier in the center of town, has been serving good food for many years and is always busy; moderate prices.

Mexican and American Entrees

Once you discover **Los Cocos,** Av. 5 Sur one block from the plaza, you'll probably return frequently. It's open for breakfast and lunch. Cream cheese muffins? Oh yes.

La Misión, Av. Juárez 23, is beloved by hungry divers who devour huge portions of fresh fish, *carne asada,* and fajitas—all prepared in the open kitchen by the front door. **Mr. Papa's,** Av. Melgar at Calle 8 Norte, is another favorite for hearty eaters, especially on the nights they offer the all-you-can-eat barbecued chicken dinners.

For the zany crowd, **Carlos'n Charlie's,** north of the plaza on Av. Melgar, tel. (987) 2-0191, is a lively restaurant specializing in fun; beer-drinking contests held nightly. **El Capi Navegante,** on Av. 10 Sur, tel. (987) 2-1730, serves good seafood, and you can usually find a coupon for a free margarita in the tourist brochures.

Yearning for an American hamburger and a football game? Go to the **Sports Page,** a video bar/restaurant (usually a good money exchange also) on the corner of Calle 2 Norte and Av. 5, tel. (987) 2-1199. Try a taste of "Americana" with hamburgers, steaks, or sandwiches; if you happen to be in Cozumel in January, rest easy, you'll be able to watch the Super Bowl right here.

Mexican food lovers pack **La Choza,** on the corner of Av. 10 Sur and Rosado Salas. The simple little cafe with oilcloth-covered tables, painted cement floor, and Mexican wood furniture is always crowded with returning aficionados. Lately we've been hearing mixed reviews on the food.

In an old building on the waterfront, **Pancho's Backyard,** Av. Melgar 27, offers a gracious atmosphere reminiscent of vintage colonial Mexico. The tableware is *típico* pottery, but guaranteed to be lead-free. The *carne asada* is tasty, as is the shrimp brochette, served at the table on a unique charbroiler. The jicama salad is served with a delicious orange-and-coriander dressing, refreshing on a hot summer night.

More Expensive

Pepe's Grill, a half block south of the plaza on Av. 5 Sur, has long been noted for its relaxed atmosphere and sunset view from the nautical-style second-story dining room. If you're in the mood for a good prime rib and salad bar, this is the place. It's open for dinner only, with main courses (à la carte) running US$12 and up. The service is excellent.

Lobster, lobster, and more lobster is what you'll find at **La Cabaña del Pescador,** north of town. Diners choose their lobster at the front counter; then it's weighed and the meal priced accordingly—about US$15-20 for a hefty lobster tail served with bread, potato, and vegetables. There's nothing else on the menu except drinks, and the place is packed in the high season. Recent remodeling has added a little more space. Outside, geese mill about the garden

OZ MALLAN

Food is performance art at many Cancún restaurants.

and pond. The restaurant is open for dinner only; full bar, no reservations.

A half km south of town, **Acuario Restaurant,** Av. Melgar at Calle 11 Sur, serves elegant fish and lobster dinners with cocktails. Walls are lined with huge aquariums filled with tropical fish, including a few brightly colored eels. It's open noon-midnight.

Planet Hollywood is a hulking presence across from the waterfront. It's a popular place, usually crowded with tourists having FUN. **Hard Rock Cafe** on Av. Melgar is another trendy choice for fun and food.

Gourmet

For a romantic, candlelight dinner go to **Arrecife** at the Hotel Presidente Intercontinental. The lusciously elegant dining room serves scrumptious lobster, savory beef, immense shrimp, and other delectable entrees in an elegant linen-and-crystal atmosphere.

Italian

At **La Cuccina Italiana,** on Av. 10 Sur between Rosado Salas and Calle 1, owner Paolo and family offer delicious authentic Italian food and a variety of wines, all at good prices. **Prima Trattoria,** Rosado Salas 109, specializes in northern Italian seafood dishes and handmade pastas, served in a charming rooftop garden. **Pizza Rolandi,** Av. Melgar 22, offers Swiss-Italian specialties, as well as good pizza, lasagna, calzone, and salads, plus beer and great sangria. The outdoor patio/dining room is a pleasant place to be on a balmy Caribbean evening; indoor dining is also available.

Yucatecan

If you yearn for a taste of ancient Yucatán, go to **Los Almendros** (yes, of Ticul and Mérida fame), Calle 2 Norte at Av. 10. In the garden the señora makes tortillas by hand—¡*Sabroso!* (tasty). Try favorites such as *pok chuk* and (on some Sundays) *puchero*. Great food, lovely atmosphere.

For Vegetarians

Alfalfa's, on Calle 1 Sur in the garden of the Casa San Miguel B&B, serves breakfast, lunch, and dinner, offering vegetarian dishes and other healthy meals. Try the scrumptious veggie tacos. Open Mon.-Sat. 9 a.m.-9 p.m.

Breakfast Time

The Waffle House is on the *malecón,* next door to Aqua Safari Dive Shop. The made-to-order waffles are a real treat, even replacing tortillas as the base for the savory *huevos rancheros.* Other breakfast options include eggs, hash browns, and homemade whole wheat toast. The restaurant also serves great cold coffee drinks, tasty pastries, lunch, and excellent linen-napkin dinners.

Coffeehouses and Bakeries

How times have changed! Ten years ago in Cozumel it was hard to find any coffee except instant. Today the town is overrun with fine coffeehouses. The **Coffee Bean,** in Plaza Orbi on Calle 3 Sur, offers gourmet coffees, pastry, and lunch. **Esquisse,** Rosado Salas 200, serves tasty Mexican coffees, hot and cold, and great French pastries. It also holds a Mexican art gallery and a shop with magazines, postcards, posters, and crafts. Between 8 and 11 a.m. it offers two-for-one coffees.

 Bakery Zermatt, Calle 4 Norte at Av. 5, serves great Mexican pastry, bread, and pizza by the slice. You'll find another bakery a block north of the plaza at Calle 2 Norte, and a third on the corner of Calle 3 Sur and Av. 10. If you notice the aroma of roasting beans, follow your nose to **Cafe Caribe,** Av. 10 Sur 215, the original coffee shop in town and still great. It's a good place for a pastry and a basic cuppa joe or a superb cappuccino, Irish coffee, mocha, or other concoction.Open 8 a.m.-noon and 6-9 p.m.

ENTERTAINMENT

Discos are popular in Cozumel; at night the town jumps with lively music. Dancing continues till morning at **Neptuno,** Av. Melgar at Calle 11 Sur, and **Scaramouche,** Av. Melgar at Rosado Salas. The **Presidente, Plaza las Glorias, La Ceiba,** and **Melía** hotels have music at cocktail hour and often during dinner. **Joe's Lobster Pub,** Av. 10 Sur 229, presents live salsa and reggae after 8 p.m.

Special Events

The **Billfish Tournament** is held every year in May, bringing fishing enthusiasts from all over—especially boaters from the U.S. who cross the Gulf of Mexico to take part in the popular event. **Carnaval,** a movable fiesta usually held in February, is a great party with street parades, dancing, and costumes—all with a tropical flavor. Another popular event is the celebration of the patron saint of San Miguel, held the last week of September.

Cinemas

Cinema Cozumel is on Av. Melgar (the *malecón*) at Calle 4 Norte; **Cine Cecilio Borgues** is on Av. Juárez at Av. 35; showtime 9 p.m. at both. Sometimes an American film is screened with its original soundtrack intact and Spanish subtitles added, but the majority of films shown are Spanish-language productions.

Cozumel's museum

Museo de la Isla de Cozumel

The town's small nonprofit museum is on the waterfront north of the plaza in an old building that once housed a turn-of-the-century hotel. Informative exhibits cover island wildlife, coral reefs, and artifacts of historic Cozumel. The museum also offers a bookstore, library, and a pleasant outdoor cafe overlooking the sea. It's closed on Saturdays. A small admission fee is charged.

The Plaza

On Sunday evenings local citizens and tourists meet in the central plaza. Families—sometimes three generations—gather around the white gazebo to hear Latin rhythms and the tunes of the day played by local musicians. A few women still wear the lovely white *huipiles,* while men look crisp and cool in their traditional *guayaberas* and best white hats. Children, dressed as miniatures of their parents, run, play, and chatter in front of the band. It's hard to say who does the best business—the balloon man or the cotton-candy vendor. This is a nice place to spend an evening under the stars, meeting the friendly folk of Cozumel.

SHOPPING

You can buy almost anything you want in Cozumel. Gift shops are scattered all over town. You'll see black coral jewelry, pottery of all kinds, and typical Mexican clothing and shoes. A few trendy fashion houses carry the latest sportswear, T-shirts, and elegant jewelry. Take a look at **Los Cincos Soles,** in the same building as Pancho's Backyard restaurant on Av. Melgar, for handsome tableware and glassware.

Talavera, Av. 5 Sur 141 near the plaza, sells gorgeous handpainted dishes. **The Flea Market,** Av. 5 Norte between Calles 2 and 4, sells a conglomeration of unique souvenirs and artwork; you'll find Cuban cigars, old coins, weird sculpture, Xtabentun (you can taste-test this Yucatecan liqueur), and good English-language books. Farther down the street, at the corner of Av. 5 Norte and Calle 4, is the home of **Manuel Azueta,** who weaves gorgeous multi-hued hammocks on his front porch. The prices are higher than in the souvenir shops, but the quality is far better.

The gift shops of some hotels carry a limited selection of English-language reading material. **La Belle Ondine,** Av. Melgar at Calle 4 Norte, has an unpredictable selection of English-language books and also sells maps of the coastal area. Several excellent jewelry shops line Av. Melgar; check out the stunning selection of precious and semiprecious gems at **Casablanca** and **Van Cleef.**

INFORMATION AND SERVICES

Tourist Information and Consulates

The tourist office has moved back to Plaza del Sol, 2nd floor, facing the plaza; tel./fax (987) 2-0972. Open Mon.-Fri. 8:30 a.m.-3 p.m. An information booth in the plaza, tel. (987) 2-1498, is an on-again, off-again affair. When open it's a font of information, usually staffed by someone who speaks English. A complete list of hotels in every price bracket is available, along with maps of the island and any general information you might need. The closest U.S. Consular Office is in Cancún, tel. (98) 84-2411.

Money

The four banks in town—Bancomer, Banpaís, Banco Serfín, and Banco Atlántico—are all near the main plaza; exchange dollars or traveler's checks 10:00 a.m.-12:30 p.m. Since the advent of the cruise ships, almost everyone in town will accept dollars. But there have been complaints that cruise-ship passengers often are taken advantage of with the exchange; know your rates and count your money.

Communication

The Calling Station, Av. Melgar 27, corner of Calle 3 Sur, tel. (987) 2-1417, offers good services. Come here to make long distance calls in private a/c booths, send faxes, or rent videos, VCRs, or video cameras. The long-distance phone office is on Calle 1 on the south side of the plaza; open 8 a.m.-1 p.m. and 4-9 p.m. Several new Ladatel phone booths are in town near the plaza; dial 09 to place collect calls with an international operator. Long-distance calls can be made from many hotels as well. Calling collect will save you a good part of the added tax. The **post office** is on Melgar close to Calle 7; open Mon.-Fri. 9 a.m.-1 p.m. and 3-6 p.m. The **telegraph office** is in the same building, tel. (987) 2-0106 or 2-0056, and open Mon.-Fri. 9 a.m.-8:30 p.m., Sat.-Sun. 9 a.m.-1 p.m.

Laundromats
Lavandería Mañana, Av. 11 #101, tel. (987) 2-0630, charges by the kilo; open Mon.-Sat. 7 a.m.-8 p.m., usually one-day service. Pickup service on request. A self-serve laundry, **Margarita Laundromat,** is at Av. 20 #285, tel. (987) 2-2865. **Express Laundry,** on Av. Salas between Avenidas 5 and 10 Sur, tel. (987) 2-2932, has self-service machines and dry-cleaning service.

Medical Services and Pharmacies
In the event of a medical emergency, contact your hotel receptionist for an English-speaking doctor. **Hospital y Centro de Salud,** Av. Circunvalación, tel. (987) 2-1081, is a small clinic with a doctor on duty; open 24 hours a day. The **Medical Specialties Center of Cozumel,** Av. 20 Norte 425, tel. (987) 2-1419, has a 24-hour clinic and access to air ambulance services. Pharmacies include **Los Portales,** on Calle 11 Sur, tel. (987) 2-0741; **Farmacia Joaquín,** on the plaza in front of the clock tower, tel. (987) 2-0125, open 9 a.m.-1 p.m. and 5-9 p.m.; and another in Centro Comercial on the north side of the plaza. If still in need of help, call the U.S. Consular Office in Cancún, tel. (98) 84-2411. Three dentists are listed in Cozumel's Blue Guide: Z. Mariles, tel. (987) 2-0507; T. Hernández, tel. (987) 2-0656; and Escartín, tel. (987) 2-0385.

SAN MIGUEL DE COZUMEL EMERGENCY NUMBERS

Police.	(987) 2-0092
Red Cross	(987) 2-1058
Ambulance.	(987) 2-0639
Air Ambulance	(987) 2-4070, 2-3545, or 2-3370
Hospital	(987) 2-0140
24-Hour Medical Service. . .	(987) 2-2387 or 2-1081

GETTING THERE

By Boat
Passenger ferries come and go to Playa del Carmen from the downtown dock in San Miguel. Two types travel between Playa del Carmen and Cozumel. The faster **MV *Mexico*** is a/c and makes the trip in about 30 minutes; fare is about US$6 pp, one-way. The slower open-air boats take about 45 minutes; fare is about US$3. Between the two, there is a ferry departing just about every hour 6:30 a.m.-8 p.m. Check the schedules posted at the ferry pier. Car ferries use the international pier across from the Fiesta Americana Sol Caribe Hotel, where cruise ships dock. Arrive a few hours early and be prepared with exact change and your car license number when you approach the ticket window or you may lose your place in line and not get on the often-crowded ferry. The car ferry departs once a day for Puerto Morelos on the mainland. Check the schedule at the international pier or call (987) 2-0950.

By Air
Air travel from various points on the Yucatán Peninsula is becoming more common. Close by there are flights from Mérida and Cancún to Cozumel (Aerocaribe). It may be possible to fly between Cozumel and Playa del Carmen when you visit; the service is inconsistent. Check with your hotel tour desk. International flights arrive from the U.S. via several airlines. Remember that schedules change with the season. Airlines serving Cozumel include: Aerocaribe/Aerocozumel, tel. (987) 2-3456; American Airlines, U.S. tel. (800) 433-7300, Continental, tel. (987) 2-0847; Mexicana, tel. (987) 2-2945; and Taesa, tel. (987) 2-4220. Charter flights are available from major U.S. gateways in the high season; ask your travel agent for information.

Cozumel International Airport is approximately three km from downtown San Miguel. Taxis and minibuses meet incoming planes. Taxi fare to town is US$5-7 pp in a *colectivo* that will take you to your hotel; it's more for the return trip in a private taxi. When departing, an airport-use tax (about US$12) is collected. This tax applies to all international Mexican airports, so hang onto US$12 for each international airport city where you plan to stay 24 hours or more. Although there's a *casa de cambio* (moneychanger) at the airport, change your money in town, as banks and some shops (when you're making a purchase) give the best exchange rates, with hotels notoriously giving the worst. Cozumel airport has many small duty-free shops with a good selection of gifts. Reading materials, especially English-language pictorial books about the area, are found here and there. The airport has a dining room upstairs, and on the ground level a snack bar, but they're usually not open before the earliest flight departs.

Travel Information in the United States
For a knowledgeable travel agent, call **Four Seasons Travel** from anywhere in the U.S., tel. (800) 552-4550. They specialize in Mexico's Caribbean coast and will work with you to create a vacation that best suits your needs, whether it's to Cozumel, Cancún, Isla Mujeres, or low-key resorts along the entire Quintana Roo coast and Yucatán Peninsula.

GETTING AROUND

Getting around on the island is easy; it's flat and the roads are maintained. It's easiest in the city of San Miguel. The roads are laid out in a grid pattern with the even-numbered *calles* to the north of the town plaza, odd-numbered *calles* to the south; numbered *avenidas* run parallel to the coast. There is now a public bus running along Av. Melgar and to the hotels north and south of town on the leeward side. The schedule was erratic on our last visit; ask about it at your hotel. All of downtown San Miguel is easily reached on foot.

Several transportation options exist for exploring the outlying areas of the island on your own—which everyone should do! Escorted tours around the island are available through any travel agency or your hotel. Avenida Juárez begins in downtown San Miguel at the dock and cuts across the middle of the island (16 km), then circles the south end. The road around the north end of the island isn't paved. Walking the flat terrain is easy, but distances are long.

By Bicycle or Motorbike
The 70 km of paved island roads are easily explored by bicycle— about US$15 per day at most hotels and at **Ciclissimo,** tel. (987) 2-1593.

Mopeds and 125cc motorcycles are the most popular vehicles on the island, but some risks are involved. Helmets are now required by law on the island, a definite improvement that helps prevent serious injury. Be conscious of the vehicles around and behind you when on a motorbike, and get out of the way of impatient taxi drivers. Mopeds and motorcycles are available for rent at most hotels and at rental shops all over town; rates are around US$25-30 a day. Remember to bargain; at certain times of the year you'll get a discount.

By Car
Cozumel has one gas station, five blocks from downtown at Av. Juárez and Av. 30; open daily 7 a.m.-midnight. Cozumel has government-sponsored Green Angel motorist assistance. If your car should break down on the coastal highway, stay with it until they come by with gas, parts, or whatever help you need to get you on your way. The Green Angels cruise only on paved roads and only during daylight hours.

Car rentals run about US$45-80 daily and are available at: AutoRent at La Ceiba Hotel, tel. (987) 2-0844; Budget at the airport, tel. (987) 2-0903; Hertz at the airport, tel. (987) 2-1009; Rentador Cozumel, Av. 10 Sur, tel. (987) 2-1120; and National Inter Rent, Av. Juárez 10, tel. (987) 2-1515.

By Taxi
Taxis will take you anywhere on the island and are available by the day; agree on a price before your tour begins. Expect to pay in the neighborhood of US$60 for four hours. Traveling with a local cabbie is often a real bonus since drivers know the island and its hidden corners better than most guidebooks (other than this one of course!). Remember, when the cruise ships arrive, many of the taxis are busy with cruise passengers at the ferry pier and the international pier, leaving the rest of the visitors high and dry. Ask at your hotel for ship times if possible and plan your movements around it. The same goes for the larger shopping centers; they are jammed when the ships are in port.

For taxi service it's usually a matter of standing on the sidewalk and waving your arm, or waiting on Av. Melgar at the foot of the downtown dock—taxis queue along the sidewalk on the waterfront. The taxi office is on Calle 2 Norte, tel. (987) 2-0236 or 2-0041, and any hotel will call a taxi.

TULUM, COBÁ, AND THE SOUTHERN CARIBBEAN COAST

TULUM ARCHAEOLOGICAL ZONE

Seven km south of Akumal on Hwy. 307, Tulum is one of Mexico's most well-known archaeological sites, largely due to its seaside location. Perched on a cliff 12 meters above the sea, Tulum was part of a series of Maya forts, towns, watchtowers, and shrines established along the coast as far south as Chetumal and north past Cancún. Measuring 380 by 165 meters, it's the largest fortified Maya site on the Quintana Roo coast, though it's small compared to other archaeological zones. Tulum means "Wall" in Mayan; the site is enclosed by a sturdy stone wall three to five meters high and several meters thick. Within its confines, 60 well-preserved structures reveal an impressive history.

History

Originally called Zama ("Sunrise"), the site was occupied from A.D. 1200 on, when Mayapán was the major power and this part of Quintana Roo was the province of Ecab. Many of Tulum's buildings—none especially elegant—show late Chichén Itzá, Mayapán, and Mixtec influences.

The Spanish got their first view of this noble, then-brightly-colored fortress when Juan de Gri-jalva's expedition sailed past the Quintana Roo coast in 1518. This was the Spaniards' first encounter with the Indians on the new continent, and according to ships' logs, the image was awe-inspiring. One notable comment in the log of the Grijalva expedition mentions seeing "a village so large, that Seville would not have appeared larger or better."

Tulum evidently outlasted the conquest; the Temple of the Frescoes contains several fine wall paintings, one of which portrays a rain god astride a four-legged animal that is almost certainly a horse. Horses only arrived with the Spanish.

In 1850, Tulum was inhabited by a group of Maya known as the Chan Santa Cruz, members of a "Talking Cross" cult. The Spanish had taught the Indians Catholic rituals, many reminiscent of Maya ceremonies; even the cross reminded the Maya of their tree of life. They believed that the gods spoke to the Maya priests through idols.

In order to manipulate the Indians, a clever revolutionary half-caste, José María Barrera, used an Indian ventriloquist, Manuel Nahual, to speak through the cross. At a cross in a forest shrine called Chan, near what is now known as Felipe Carrillo Puerto, a voice from the cross urged the Indians to take up arms against the

El Castillo, Tulum

Mexicans once again. Bewildered, impressed, and never doubting, they accepted the curious occurrence almost immediately. The original cross was replaced with three crosses that continued to "instruct" the guileless Indians from the holy, highly guarded site.

The political-religious Chan Santa Cruz group grew quickly and ruled Quintana Roo efficiently. These well-armed, jungle-wise Indians successfully kept the Mexican government out of the territory for 50 years. Even the British government in British Honduras (now known as Be-

lize) treated this group with respect. Around 1895 the Indians requested that the Territory of Quintana Roo be annexed by British Honduras, but the Mexican government flatly refused and sent in a new expeditionary force to try once again to reclaim Quintana Roo.

The Mexican army was doomed from the outset. They fought not only armed and elusive Indians but constant attacks of malaria and the jungle itself. The small army managed to fight its way into the Indian capital of Chan Santa Cruz, where they were trapped for a year. The stand-

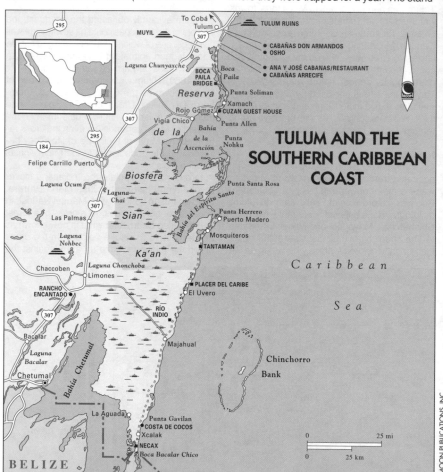

TULUM AND THE SOUTHERN CARIBBEAN COAST

© MOON PUBLICATIONS INC

off continued until the Mexican Revolution in 1911, when Pres. Porfirio Díaz resigned.

Four years later the Mexican army gave up and the capital was returned to the Indians, who continued to rule Quintana Roo as an independent state—an embarrassment and ever-present thorn in the side of the broadening Mexican Republic. This small, determined group of Indians managed to keep their independence and culture intact while the rest of the world proceeded into the 20th century. But life in the jungle was tough, and with famine, a measles epidemic, malaria, and 90 years of fighting, the Chan Santa Cruz population was reduced to 10,000. Weary, in 1935 they decided to quit the fight and were accorded the recognition given to a respected adversary. When their elderly leaders signed a peace treaty, most of the Chan Santa Cruz agreed to Mexican rule. This was one of the longest wars in the Americas.

One of the few pure Chan Indian villages left in 1935 was Tulum, and today many residents are descendants of these independent people. Even after signing the treaty, the Indians still maintained control of the area and outsiders were highly discouraged from traveling through. They say a skeleton imbedded in the cement at the base of one of the temples at Tulum is the remains of an uninvited archaeologist—a warning to other would-be intruders.

All of this has changed. With foresight, the Mexican government in the 1960s recognized the beautiful Quintana Roo coast as a potential tourist draw, and the new state entered the 20th century. The advent of roads and airports has paved the way for the rest of the world to visit the unique ruins of Tulum—the most visited of all the Maya ruins.

The Structures
Tulum is made up of mostly small, ornate structures with stuccoed gargoyle faces carved onto their corners. In the **Temple of Frescoes,** looking through a metal grate you'll see a fresco that still bears a trace of color from the ancient artist. Archaeologically, this is the most interesting building on the site. The original parts of the building were constructed around 1450 during the late Post-Classic period, and as is the case with so many Maya structures, it was added to over the years.

Across the compound, a small *palapa* roof protects the carved **Descending God.** This winged creature is pictured upside down and is thought by some historians to be the God of the Setting Sun. Others interpret the carving as representing the bee; honey is a commodity almost as revered on the Peninsula as maize. Visitors are no longer allowed to climb this ruin to view the carvings.

El Castillo is the site's most impressive structure; the large pyramid stands on the edge of a 12-meter limestone cliff overlooking the sea. The building, in the center of the wall on the east side, was constructed in three different phases. A wide staircase leads to a two-chamber temple at the top; visitors are no longer allowed to climb this

Tulum

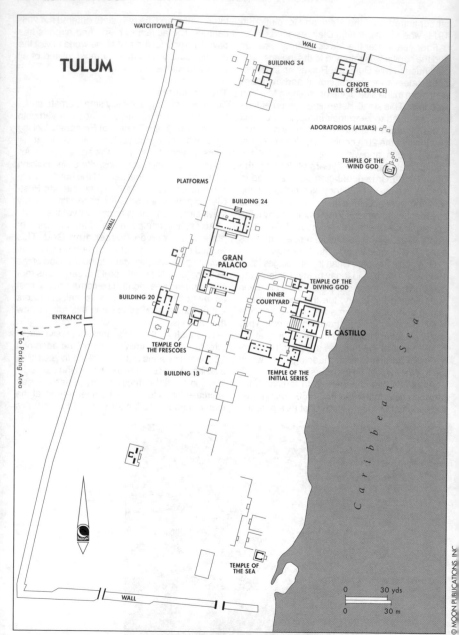

TULUM

WATCHTOWER

WALL

BUILDING 34

CENOTE
(WELL OF SACRAFICE)

ADORATORIOS (ALTARS)

TEMPLE OF THE
WIND GOD

PLATFORMS

BUILDING 24

GRAN
PALACIO

TEMPLE OF THE
DIVING GOD

INNER
COURTYARD

BUILDING 20

EL CASTILLO

WALL

ENTRANCE

To Parking Area

TEMPLE OF
THE FRESCOES

BUILDING 13

TEMPLE OF THE
INITIAL SERIES

C a r i b b e a n   S e a

TEMPLE OF
THE SEA

0   30 yds

0   30 m

WALL

© MOON PUBLICATIONS, INC.

stairway, but the view from the hill on which the Castillo stands encompasses the sea, the surrounding jungle (with an occasional stone ruin poking through the tight brush), and scattered clearings where small farms are sprouting up.

Entrance and Visitors Center
The new Tulum Center houses a restaurant, restrooms, museum, bookstore, and a ticket office for the Inter-Playa bus. The bus brings visitors to Tulum from Cancún and Playa del Carmen starting at 7:30 a.m.; the last bus leaves Tulum on the return trip at 4:40 p.m.

At the entrance, you can catch a shuttle to the ruins (US$1.50 roundtrip), thereby avoiding the 10-minute walk, or hire a guide from the Licensed Guides' Organization. The guides cost about US$20-25 for four people and come well recommended.

The site is open daily 8 a.m.-5 p.m. At 8 a.m., most tour buses have yet to arrive, making the cooler early hours a desirable time to explore and photograph the aged structures. Admission costs US$3.50 pp (plus about US$5-10 to bring in your camcorder; the price changes). Parking is available; US$1.50.

Accommodations: Most of the Tulum-area accommodations and campgrounds are in the Tulum Archaeological Hotel Zone, which is at the north end of Boca Paila/Punta Allen Rd., a few km south of the ruins (see "Boca Paila/Punta Allen Road," below).

Two budget-priced hotels lie at the intersection of Hwy. 307 and the old Tulum access road (just north of the new entrance), a 10-minute walk from the ruins. The elderly **El Crucero Motel** offers spartan, usually clean rooms, each with private bathroom, fan, and hot water—*sometimes.* Check your room before you pay. Restaurant on premises. Nearby, the **Hotel Acuario,** tel. (98) 45-1181, Cancún tel. (98) 86-5106, is newer and again, pretty simple. Most of the 27 rooms have a/c; there's a pool, but often it's not filled. Some rooms are large enough for six persons. This hotel can get really noisy and busy with large tour buses stopping in the parking lot. Car rentals and restaurant on premises.

Village of Tulum
Tulum pueblo is on Hwy. 307, just south of the turnoff to the archaeological zone. The village has always been the home of stalwart Maya people with the courage to preserve their ancient traditions; today they've chosen to enter the world of tourism, but only with tiny steps.

The stretch of Hwy. 307 that parallels the pueblo now has a row of glaring streetlights down its middle, while its shoulders are crowded with ramshackle storefronts. A plaza and kiosk have been built a bit north of the traditional center but seem barren most of the time. Dirt roads extend ever farther into the jungle as additional humble homes are built to house workers for the nearby resorts. Restaurants are popping up, open-air gift shops selling Mexican handicrafts are multiplying, and food stores now have sophisticated refrigerators and freezers. Many small markets, fruit stands, trinket shops and *loncherías* line the highway.

COBÁ AND VICINITY

Northwest of Tulum, roughly midway between Tulum and Nuevo X-Can, the early Maya site of Cobá covers an immense area of some 50 square km. The ancient city was begun in A.D. 600, and thousands of Maya are believed to have lived here during the Classic period. Only in recent years has the importance of Cobá come to light; now archaeologists are convinced that in time it will prove to be one of the largest Maya excavations on the Yucatán Peninsula. More than 5,000 mounds have yet to be uncovered.

Distances between groupings of structures are long (in some cases one to two km), and each group of ruins is buried in the middle of thick jungle. All along the paths are mounds overgrown with vines, trees, and flowers. Watch for signs and stay on the trails.

The fact that the jungle hasn't been cleared away here nor all the mounds uncovered adds a feeling of discovery to your visit. But you should come prepared with comfortable shoes, bug repellent, sunscreen, and a hat. Water is a necessity.

Ancient Highways
The remains of more than 50 *sacbe* (roads) have been found crisscrossing the entire Peninsula, and there are more here than in any other location. The roads pass through what were once outlying villages and converge at Cobá—an in-

dication that this was the largest city of its era. One such *sacbe* is 100 km long and travels in an almost straight line from the base of Nohoch Mul (the great pyramid) to the town of Yaxuna. Each *sacbe* was built to stringent specifications: a base of stones one to two meters high, about 4.5 meters wide, and covered with white mortar. However, in Cobá some ancient roads as wide as 10 meters have been uncovered. Archaeologists have also discovered the mines where the inhabitants excavated the sand used to construct the roads, and a massive stone cylinder that was used to flatten the roadbeds.

The Pyramids

Cobá's tallest pyramid, **Nohoch Mul,** is the tallest pyramid on the Peninsula (42 meters, a 12-story climb!). The view from the top is spectacular, and a small temple there bears a fairly well preserved carving of the Descending God. **La Iglesia,** the second highest pyramid at the site (22.5 meters), also offers splendid views of the surrounding jungle and Lake Macanxoc from its summit. Many offering caches of jade, pearls, and shells have been found in La Iglesia and other temples.

Scientists conjecture there may be a connection between the Petén Maya (who lived hundreds of km south in the Guatemalan lowlands) and the Classic Maya who lived in Cobá. Both groups built lofty pyramids, much taller than those found in Chichén Itzá, Uxmal, or elsewhere in the northern part of the Peninsula.

Other Highlights

Numerous carved stelae dot the site; some are covered by *palapas* to protect them from the elements. One temple is named **Conjunto Las Pinturas** because of the stucco paintings that once lined the walls. Minute traces of the paintings, in layers of yellow, red, and blue, can still be seen on the temple's uppermost cornice. This small building is well preserved, and bright green moss grows up the sides of the gray limestone.

Flora and Fauna

Cobá in Maya means "Water Stirred by the Wind." Close to a group of shallow lakes (Cobá, Macanxoc, Xkanha, and Zacalpuc), some very marshy areas attract a large variety of birds and butterflies. The jungle around Cobá is good for viewing herons, egrets, and the motmot. Once in a while, even a stray toucan is spotted. Colorful butterflies are everywhere, including the large, deep-blue *morphidae,* as well as the bright yellow-orange barred sulphur.

If you look on the ground, you'll almost certainly see long lines of cutter ants. One double column carries freshly cut leaves to the burrow, and next to that another double column marches in the opposite direction, empty jawed, returning for more. The columns can be longer than a kilometer, and usually the work party will all carry the same species of leaf or blossom until the plant is completely stripped. It's amazing how far they travel for food! The vegetation decays in their nests, and the mushrooms that grow on the com-

ruins at Cobá

OZ MALLAN

COBA ARCHAEOLOGICAL ZONE

post are an important staple of the ants' diet. The determined creatures grow up to three cm long.

People

Cobá today holds a fraction of the population it had at its peak. Because of its (up till now) isolation from outsiders and low profile, traditional Maya ways are still common in the area.

The locals live in communities on both sides of the lake, planting their corn with ceremony and conducting their family affairs in the same manner as their ancestors; many villages still appoint a calendar-keeper to keep track of the auspicious days that direct them in their daily lives. Residents by the ruins operate small artisans' shops and restaurants and typically speak a smattering of Spanish. The community on the far side of the lake has a small clinic and a basketball court that serves as the town plaza. The communities have electricity, but no telephone service; the only phone in the area is the cellular

one at the Villa Arqueológica. But things are changing rapidly.

Accommodations

Budget: A couple of modest inns are on the highway, south of the turnoff to the archaeological zone on what could be called the main street of Cobá. **Bocadito's** cabins on Calle Principal are simple and clean; each has a private bathroom, cold water, tile floors, two double beds, and a place for a hammock. This is a popular stop, so get here early to ensure a room. Bocadito's has a good restaurant and is popular with tour groups.

Moderate: There's one upscale hotel in Cobá, the **Villa Arqueológica,** tel. (800) 258-2633, part of a chain that has placed hotels at various archaeological zones in Mexico. Each hotel has a well-equipped library with many volumes containing histories of the area and the Maya people. This little sister of the Club Med resorts has an entirely different personality from what you might think. First of all, you pay for everything separately, and the food is more costly than at any other restaurants around—some say a lot better, some don't agree. The decor is a pleasant white-stucco and red-tile Mexican.

The villa has small but attractive rooms, a/c, a shallow swimming pool, outdoor bar and dining, good *típico* and French food, and a gift shop that carries quality reproductions of Maya art. It's hard to predict seasonal highs since groups from Europe are bused in all year long; reservations could be important even though the hotel is often quiet.

Food

All time favorite **Bocadito** (at the hotel) offers good typical inexpensive food, simplicity, and pleasant surroundings. The bus stops here, offering bus tickets for sale and a schedule of departures and prices. Close by, a small market carries purified water, cold sodas, and a few groceries and sundries.

A number of outdoor cafes are springing up near the entrance to the ruins. In Cobá you'll find the cafes at the inns clean and pleasant. The food, though limited in choice, is *típico* and can be quite good.

Near the Villa Archaeológico, look for **Nicte Ha,** a small cafe that serves a good toast and

OZ MALLAN

A roof has been placed over this carved stela to help preserve it from nature's constant attack.

coffee breakfast starting at 8 a.m. But what's fun about this little cafe is proprietor Victor Kinil's occupation of feeding the crocodile that floats in the nearby lake. Nicte Ha means "flower of the water," and the flowers of this water are the eyes of the croc, who drifts along with only his open-eyes showing. Victor calls him a cannibal because his favorite food is raw chicken and chicken bones. The croc gets fed every few days on the beach near the water.

Shops and Services
Small gift shops carry the usual, including carved wooden jaguar statues, hammocks, and pottery depicting the Maya gods. One gift shop advertises their available bathroom (there's a public restroom across from the entrance to the ruins site).

Tourist services are beginning to appear along the 13-km road from Tulum to Cobá. There are small markets with cold drinks at most settlements, and a full-blown rest stop called **Lolche.** You can't miss it—look for the wooden statue of a rifle-bearing campesino next to a large parking lot. Designed with tour groups in mind, Lolche has a small snack bar with cold soda, bottled water, and sandwiches; clean restrooms; and a huge souvenir shop with rows and rows of pottery, masks, hammocks, and woodcarvings. Check out the carved wooden jaguars with glass eyes. Open daily during the daylight hours.

Transportation
Getting to Cobá is easiest by car. The road between Tulum and Cobá is good all the way. North of the site, a new 31-kilometer road provides a good fast **shortcut to Valladolid,** Chichén Itzá, and Mérida; from Cobá look for the signs that say Chemax where the intersection gives you the choice of Cancún or Valladolid..

If traveling by local bus, your schedule is limited to two or three buses a day. Northwest-bound buses run to Cobá (en route to Nuevo X-Can and Valladolid) from Playa del Carmen and Tulum; make sure the bus actually goes in to Cobá along its route. Some buses go to the entrance of the ruins; most stop on the main road by Bocadito's restaurant where schedule and tickets are available. Some southeast-bound buses from Valladolid to Tulum and Playa del Carmen stop at Cobá; again, make sure the bus actually goes into the town. (If you're planning to spend the night, make sure you have reservations or get there very early in the day.) You'll often run into travelers on the trail at the Cobá ruins who are willing to give you a ride. Organized bus tours are available from hotels and travel agencies in Cancún, Playa del Carmen, and Cozumel.

Punta Laguna
Fifteen km northeast of Cobá on the road to Nuevo X-Can, you'll pass Punta Laguna, a forested area where spider monkeys can occasionally be seen and howler monkeys occasionally heard. The local Maya have built a small *palapa* on the side of the road as well as on the side of a lagoon. At either place, for a small fee a Maya guide will take you through the forest to look for the monkeys; the rough trail passes small deteriorating stone structures built by the Maya. In-

creasing tourist activity in the area is sure to drive the monkeys away eventually. For now, however, few people stop here, and the monkeys can be seen in the early morning and at dusk. At those times of day, birders will also be in heaven here.

At the roadside hut where you pay to see this very natural park, the Maya sell jars of honey from their own hives—another way they're trying to help their economy.

BOCA PAILA/PUNTA ALLEN ROAD

This road intersects Hwy. 307 across from the Cobá turnoff and in three km comes to a T intersection. Here a cluster of signs marks the area on either side of the intersection as the **Tulum Archaeological Hotel Zone.** If you turn left (north) you'll find a few hotels and campgrounds fairly close to the ruins. If you turn right you can follow this road all the way to Punta Allen, past a string of simple cabana/campgrounds.

If you're planning to drive south to Punta Allen on Boca Paila Rd., first fill your gas tank at the brand new Tulum Pemex station since there's not another one to be found on the 57-km coastal road. Start out early in the morning so that if it's not for you, you'll have time to go back. It takes 2.5-3 hours to reach Punta Allen from Tulum. The challenging road passes through Sian Ka'an Biosphere Reserve, an enormous nature reserve. At the end of the peninsula you'll come to Rojo Gómez, a tiny fishing village. (In a pinch you can buy a little drum gas in Rojo Gómez; ask at Socorro's Store.)

This route holds few attractions for tourists looking for a glitzy Caribbean vacation. But explorers, naturalists, bird watchers, artists, snorkelers, scuba divers, kayakers, and fishermen love the ragged beaches, beautiful sea, humble accommodations, bird-filled wetlands and islets, and the mysterious canals where the Maya left their mark. Pilgrims will revel in the area's isolation and lack of commercialism.

Though the first part of the Boca Paila Rd.—where many beachside hotels are located—is paved and smooth, don't be fooled. It soon becomes potholed, ridged, and rugged even before you pass the last hotels. Though it's slow-going, bumpy, and uncomfortable, any vehicle can han-

dle this road when it's not raining. Four-wheel drive may be necessary if the rains have been particularly heavy. RV's are not permitted on the road.

Tulum Hotel Zone and Vicinity

If you turn north at the T intersection, you'll come across **Cabanas Don Armando,** a simple compound with small rooms , shared toilet facilities, a restaurant, and a wide beach often frequented by topless Europeans. It's run by a large friendly Mexican family. Shoestring/budget rates. Camping with your own gear is about US$2.35 pp.

Also north from this intersection you'll find two popular, usually full combination cabana/campgrounds. **Santa Fe** and **El Mirador,** sit side by side on the beach immediately south of the Tulum ruins. The cabins are tiny, and toilets and showers are shared. Shoestring rates. Bring drinking water, bug repellent, and mosquito netting. If you're camping it helps to have a tent; when the wind blows it gets mighty gritty on this beach. The Santa Fe has a cafeteria, and its popular Bar Marley is reggae central.

Right next door is **El Mirador,** a simple, pleasant sit-down restaurant up some steps; diners overlook the Caribbean Sea. There's also a dive shop along here, and a reef lies just offshore.

South of the T intersection are more simple cabanas and basic hotels on the beach. All are much beloved by travelers seeking seclusion and tranquility; none accept credit cards. Many don't have public power and depend on gas lanterns or small generators for part of the day. (Although they had power for a while, it was knocked out by a hurricane; they expect to have it soon again.) A few have freshwater showers. Some sell bottled water (water from all other sources here must be boiled or otherwise purified).

Piedra Escondida, tel./fax. (987) 1-2092, is a small resort right on the beach offering eight clean rooms in two-story cabanas. It's simple but pleasant, with a full-service bar and restaurant on the premises and hot and cold water. Inexpensive/moderate rates.

La Perla (Apdo. Postal 77, Tulum, Quintana Roo 77780, Mexico), is a surprise on this isolated beach. It boasts lovely white tile bathrooms and showers, hot water, and a generator that runs 5-11 p.m. A bar and restaurant are on the premises. Inexpensive rates.

JUAN VEGA

Local legend has it that during the height of the post-Caste War conflict, Juan Vega was kidnapped by the Maya Indians as a young child. His entire family and young companions were put to death, but, because he was carrying religious books and could read, he was spared. The Maya had a curious acceptance of the Christian religion. Because of certain similarities, they managed to weave it into their own beliefs and would listen attentively to Juan Vega's preaching.

Although Vega was a captive, he was given tremendous respect and spent his entire life in the village, marrying a Maya and raising a family of mestizos in the village of Chumpon. Vega (nicknamed "White King of the Maya") operated a chicle business at Muyil. Chumpon is referred to by knowledgeable outsiders as the "Jungle Vatican." Vega saved the lives of many captured Mexican soldiers. They were doomed to death by the Maya, until he stepped in and read the laws of the Christian God from his worn books.

In 1961, Quintana Roo was still a no-man's land without roads and Vega was seriously ill; through a fluke, archaeologist Pablo Bush heard about Vega. Bush, acting quickly, used a small plane to spot the hidden jungle village and a helicopter to pick up the sick man (by foot it was a three-day expedition into the village). Juan Vega was rescued—but only after he asked the chief's permission to leave. After surgery and a long stay in a Mexico City hospital, the newspapers gave an account of Vega, and a soldier who had once been saved by Vega came to visit him. A recovered Vega had one request while in Mexico, to visit Abuelitas (the Virgin of Guadalupe). When able, he made his pilgrimage to the shrine and then happily returned to his isolated village and family in Chumpon. Juan Vega lived in Chumpon until his death a few years later.

In the same area, rustic **Zamas,** U.S. tel. (800) 538-6802, is a low-key, thatched-hut resort manned by low-key Americans. The rooms have electricity for lights, but no other appliances. They're on both sides of the road, which means some rooms are not right on the sea. The restaurant and bar are open 7:30 a.m.-9:30 p.m., according to need.

Osho Oasis (Apdo. Postal 99, Tulum, Quintana Roo 77780, Mexico), tel. (987) 4-2772, U.S. tel. (415) 381-6746, is really a meditation center, but anyone is welcome. You'll find simple cabanas with hanging double beds, mosquito netting, and screenless shutters. A few offer private bathrooms; the others share community bathrooms and hot showers. The dining room is a striking building that serves mediocre meals but overlooks a beautiful bay. The entrance to Reserva de la Biosfera Sian Ka'an is just across the street. Moderate/expensive rates.

SIAN KA'AN BIOSPHERE RESERVE

About six km south of the Tulum ruins on Boca Paila Rd. is the entrance to Sian Ka'an Biosphere Reserve. From here to road's end at Punta Allen, you'll be entirely within the reserve. In the Maya language, Sian Ka'an means "Where the Sky is Born."

You'll usually find a guard at the reserve entrance; ask him about road conditions ahead (RVs are not permitted). Admission to the reserve is free, but you're supposed to sign yourself in and then back out when you leave. The guard will offer to sell you a short but informative book about the reserve. Continuing south from the entrance gate, you'll encounter an army checkpoint with a small group of soldiers. Stop and smile—they're just kids doing their job, looking for drug and arms runners. They may ask you to get out of the car and open your trunk—or not.

No matter what you decide to do in the reserve, it's a good idea to always travel with a flashlight, bug repellent, sunscreen, hat, and walking shoes that will survive in the water.

Flora and Fauna

A wide variety of plants thrive in the reserve, including four species of mangrove and many medicinal plants. Birdlife is abundant—over 300 species at last count. Toucans and parrots reside in the jungle year-round, and bird-watchers flock to **Laguna Chunyaxche,** a watery stopover for migrating flamingos, herons, and egrets.

Bird Island, a small island in Laguna Chunyaxche, hosts two species of crocodile, which are found in estuaries throughout the preserve. Another notable reptile here is the boa constrictor, which can grow to lengths of over four meters (13 feet). Mammals that live in the jungle include monkeys, raccoons, foxes, and various rodents.

Local waters are lobster rich, and not too long ago, wildlife groups in association with the local lobster cooperative and the Mexican equivalent of the National Science Foundation studied the way the Yucatecan fishermen handled the spiny crustaceans. The Rojo Gómez villagers don't use lobster traps as we know them, but instead create artificial platform habitats from which the lobsters can come and go. The lobsters grow sheltered in these habitats, and when they reach a predetermined size, the fishermen take them by hand.

Fishing

This area is considered the hottest fly fishing grounds in Mexico; Bahía Ascensión is one of the Caribbean's richest permit and bonefish fishing grounds (all catch and release). In May and June the target is tarpon, along with barracuda and snook. In years past, visitors looking for fishing guides had to ask local fishermen to take them fishing. Today many small fishing-guide outfits are found in the area. Ask around Rojo Gómez or check with Cuzan Guest House.

Hiking

For the hardy type with lots of time, walking the 57-kilometer road from Tulum to Punta Allen

can be high adventure. Plan at least two weeks (that is if you take time to smell the flowers and float in the silky sea). Along the way, the sea sometimes disappears behind sand dunes, but it's never that long a trudge through the bush to dozens of fine beaches where you might be seduced into staying awhile. Here and there you'll find coconut trees on which to sling your hammock—a tropical paradise. Be sure to carry mosquito netting for your nights under the stars. And be prepared for long stretches with nothing but empty beach and an occasional small ranchito surrounded by thick jungle. Several large luxury homes are going up along this coast, all with heavy duty fences; take the hint.

Restaurants are *nada* until you reach Rojo Gómez; come prepared with your own victuals and water. Before you start out remember that once you reach the end of this peninsula, you either have to hoof it back, make arrangements with a villager for a ride, or catch the irregularly scheduled bus between Rojo Gómez and Felipe Carrillo Puerto.

Muyil

One of the larger Maya sites within the Sian Ka'an biosphere reserve is Muyil, also known as Chunyaxche. Situated near Laguna Chunyaxche on the edge of the karstic limestone shelf, the site was an ancient Maya seaport. It has been the subject of a study conducted by Tulane University and the Quintana Roo Regional Center of INAH. Along with mapping the site to determine its size and settlement pattern, grad-

Trekkers find many campsites along Quintana Roo's Caribbean coast.

uate students from Tulane and villagers from Chumpon have been excavating for ceramics in order to ascertain the settlement's dates of occupation.

The potsherds dug up at the area indicate that Muyil was settled about A.D. 1 and occupied continuously until the Spanish conquest began. The report's author, archaeologist Elia del Carmen Trejo, notes that since no Spanish ceramics have been identified and because there is no mention of a settlement at Muyil in books from the period, the population of Muyil likely perished in the 40 years following the conquest. A large *sacbe* (roadway) at Muyil runs at least a half kilometer from the site center to near the edge of the lagoon. The western half of the road runs through mangrove swamp.

Six structures are spaced along the roadway approximately every 120 meters. They range from two-meter-high platforms to the large *castillo,* one of the tallest structures on the Yucatán Peninsula's east coast. All but the westernmost of the structures face westward, away from the lagoon. The Maya always oriented their structures with precise reference to the positions of the sun and Venus. Orientation of the roadways between the structures suggests that the residents were always supposed to pass these structures along their north side; no one knows why.

The *castillo,* at the midpoint of the *sacbe,* stands 21 meters above the lagoon's water level. At the summit is a solid round masonry turret, which is unique to ancient Maya structures. From the summit it's possible to see the Caribbean.

Muyil is about 25 km south of Tulum; look for the signs. The ruins are open daily 8 a.m.-5 p.m. Entrance fee is about US$3.

Tours

Amigos de Sian Ka'an, tel. (98) 84-9583, fax (98) 87-3080, offers an eco-tour into the reserve—by car on unpaved roads and by boat through the coastal lagoons. The tour takes you through tropical forest to the ancient Maya seaport remains of Muyil-Chunyaxche and to Boca Paila fishing village.

Jim Holzman, tel. (983) 4-0358 (answering machine in English), fax (983) 4-0383, e-mail: cuzan@mpsnet.com.mx, offers guided weeklong boat and kayak tours of the reserve's estuaries, lagoons, and caves. Trips can be tailored to suit your particular interests, and might focus on mangroves, manatees, or Maya canals. Jim also rents kayaks by the day. His business is in Rojo Gómez just south of Cuzan Guest House.

Accommodations North of Rojo Gómez

Heading south through the reserve, you'll come to several resorts. **Cabanas Ana y José** (Apdo. Postal 15, Tulum, Quintana Roo 77780, Mexico), tel. (98) 80-6022, fax (98) 80-6021, is one of the nicest of the small cabana groups along the entire Boca Paila Road. Its two-story tile-roofed stone buildings house a variety of accommodations, all with private tile bathrooms, tile floors, and freshwater showers (with hot water in the planning stages). A colorful screened-in sand-floored *palapa* restaurant overlooking the sea serves three meals a day. Lights are on from sunset until 10 p.m. Moderate rates.

Down the road from Ana y José's at Km 9, **Las Ranitas,** tel. (98) 80-6022, fax (98) 80-6021, is a new upscale version of the rest of the small bungalow resorts along this dirt road. It has a

Maya construction using chit *palm*

dining room, all sea-view rooms, a swimming pool, and some luxurious touches. It should be completed by the time you read this, and according to the manager it will be "100% ecological." Expensive rates.

Also along this road travelers will see several other budget-priced bungalows worth checking out. **Cabañas Arrecife** is reasonably modern and very clean, with well-kept grounds and (usually) an abundant water supply (boil your drinking water or use bottled). **Cabañas Tulum,** tel. (98) 25-8295, offers 18 small cabanas with beds, bathrooms, ceiling fans, and electricity from sunset until about 10 p.m. There's a restaurant on the premises and a white beach that now hosts topless sunbathers.

About 25 miles south of Tulum, **Pelican Point Lodge,** U.S. tel. (800) 550-1383, Mexico fax (987) 1-2092, run by Gernot and Anna Woods, offers an opportunity for fishermen to try their luck at Bahía Ascensión. Gernot offers packages that include fishing, meals, and accommodations in their lovely lodge set on the edge of a cliff overlooking the sea. Anna Woods is an artist and founder of *Sian Ka'an Artistas,* an art co-operative and international arts exchange. She spends time in Maya villages in Mexico, Guatemala, and Honduras, and offers **Yucatecan Art Education Seminars** several times a year; subjects have included batik, collage, painting, and cooking.

The lodge offers comfortable accommodations in several different buildings. Designed for low environmental impact, it uses the sun and the wind to generate electricity; 12-volt halogen lights are used throughout. Moderate rates.

Rojo Gómez

Rojo Gómez (also called Punta Allen) is a small fishing enclave on a finger of land overlooking Bahía de la Ascención. The village offers what a lot of the Quintana Roo coast has lost: an end-of-the-road ambience. Only a few simple businesses operate, and the sand streets are easy to mistake for beach with palm trees scattered here and there.

Accommodations: Old-timer **Cuzan Guest House** has held firm through hurricanes, a bad entry road, and now modernization. The simple but charming stucco and wooden *palapa* cabanas each have private bath and solar hot water

and electricity. The bungalows can be very hot during the warmer times of the year. Perhaps when electrical service is improved, fans will be installed? Moderate rates; bargain fishing packages. Kayaks and bikes available for rent. For information contact Sonia Lilvik, Apdo. Postal 24, Felipe Carrillo Puerto, Quintana Roo 77200, Mexico, tel. (983) 4-0358 (answering machine in English), fax (983) 4-0383, e-mail: cuzan@mp-snet.com.mx. Allow a week or so for answers.

Food: A few small cafes in town serve basic Mexican meals with the freshest fish and lobster as the centerpiece. **Tres Reyes** is a combination grocery store, tortilleria, and cafe. The **Cuzan Guest House Dining Room** (open to the public) is a laid-back *palapa* hut in the sand that serves an à la carte menu of pretty good food. Just remember where you are: don't order the steak, but the seafood and Mexican food are great!

Several markets in town offer a fair selection of grocery items, and **Panaderia Lupita,** about a block from the town square, makes good bread.

FELIPE CARRILLO PUERTO

Highway 307 from Tulum to Chetumal passes through Felipe Carrillo Puerto, a small colonial city with some of the richest history in Quintana Roo. When the Caste War was going badly for the Maya, three clever Maya leaders—one a ventriloquist—reintroduced the "Talking Cross" to the Indians near Felipe Carrillo Puerto (see the History section of the Introduction chapter). The talking cross dictated tactical orders to cult followers—who called themselves the Chan Santa Cruz ("People of the Holy Cross")—and predicted victory in the Maya fight against the Spanish. Felipe Carillo Puerto became the capital of the Chan Santa Cruz; at that time, the city, too, was named Chan Santa Cruz.

When the war was over, the fathers and grandfathers of many of today's *antiguos,* or old-timers, rejected the peace treaty negotiated between their leaders and the Mexicans. They took their families into the jungle and began new villages, continuing their secretive lifestyle and calling themselves *separados.* Here in Felipe Carrillo Puerto, many *antiguos* still cling to the belief that one day the Maya will once again control the Quintana Roo coast.

THE "TALKING CROSS" WAR

1847: The beginning of the Caste War.

1849: The Caste War goes against the Maya and they retreat, getting lost in the thick jungles of Quintana Roo.

1850: The "Talking Cross" appears at the cenote and delivers commands for reviving the war against the whites.

1850-58: The Maya warriors have their ups and downs, but life goes on for the Indians as they manage to hold off their adversaries.

1858: The Maya capture the fortress of Bacalar (just outside of Chetumal) and begin building a ceremonial city complete with church, palaces, barracks, and schools. This is the beginning of their total independence from the rest of Mexico.

1863: The British at Belize recognize the Indian state and engage in arms trade with them.

1863-1893: The Maya lose great numbers of people due to epidemics and internal conflicts.

1893: Mexico and Britain wrangle a peace treaty; the Indians no longer have their important source of arms.

1901: Under General Ignacio Bravo, the Mexican federal army takes over the stronghold city of Chan Santa Cruz and renames it Felipe Carrillo Puerto.

1901-15: While the Mexicans occupy the Maya city with brutality, the Maya in the jungle continue to raid and harrass the Mexicans, virtually isolating them from the rest of Mexico.

1915: The Mexicans give up and return Quintana Roo to the Maya.

1917-20: Influenza and smallpox epidemics decimate the Indians.

1920-29: Chicle boom. General May, the Indian leader, accepts a peace treaty with Mexico, distressing the more militant Indians.

1929: These militant traditional Maya disclaim May's "sell-out" and revive the cult of the "Talking Cross" at X-Cacal Guardia.

Little English is spoken in Felipe Carrillo Puerto, and other than its historical significance, the town holds nothing in the way of tourist attractions. Whether you're driving north or south, you should fill up at the **Pemex station** here. It sells Magna Sin unleaded gas, and the next station with unleaded is 98 km distant.

XCALAK PENINSULA

This low-lying limestone shelf—bounded by Bahía Espíritu Santo on the north, Bahía Chetumal on the south, and the Caribbean Sea on the east— holds a mosaic of savannas, marshes, streams, and lagoons, dotted by islands of thick jungle. The coastline is a series of sandy beaches and dunes interrupted by rocky promontories, some of which connect with the offshore Belize Reef. The shore is dominated by still-healthy coconut plantations planted in the early 20th century.

Maya sites have been discovered on the peninsula's shores and in its jungles, but little is known about the area's preconquest history; the peninsula was already abandoned when the Spaniards unsuccessfully tried to settle Bahía Espíritu Santo in 1621. Later, however, the peninsula became a sanctuary for Indian refugees fleeing Spanish control in the interior, as well as a haven for pirates, British logwood cutters, and Belizean fishermen.

In 1910, the village of Xcalak ("shka-LAK"), at the peninsula's southern tip, held a population of 544; a few additional people were scattered among the *cocales* (small coconut plantations) and ranchos along the coast. In the ensuing years, the population fluctuated. The major industries—*cocales* and fishing—have been disrupted several times with the onslaught of major hurricanes, and more recently, the yellowing disease that has decimated the state's coconut trees.

Only in recent years has a rough dirt road opened the isolated peninsula to home builders and a few (so far) small resorts. Tracts of land along the coast are rapidly being bought up by large- and small-scale developers and private individuals seeking a last bit of undisturbed paradise. In 1993, the government of Quintana Roo began working with a major tourism developer to study the peninsula and ways it could be enhanced by tourism without destroying its fragile ecology.

The rumor is that the Xcalak Peninsula is going to be the "new" but controlled Playa del Carmen, with a marketing label of "La Costa Maya." The government is taking precautions to stem what could be runaway development. Hotels will not be allowed higher than the palm trees, septic systems will be tightly regulated, and a limit will be imposed on the number of rooms allowed to be built at each resort. Hopefully the authorities will stick to their guns, and everyone will cooperate to keep this area pristine for generations.

Overland to Xcalak

Just south of Limones, a paved road breaks off Hwy. 307 and meanders east for 57 km through varied scenery. It's currently a dead-end road; car-ferry service from Xcalak to Chetumal was once offered, but now only a passenger ferry makes the run.

Much of the land along the road has been cleared of jungle, and small ranchitos are scattered about. In some areas mangrove swamps line the highway and are home to a large variety of birds, including hundreds of egrets and the graceful white heron. However, in drought years so little rain falls that many of the swamps dry up and the birds go elsewhere. The remaining trees are covered with green and red bromeliads, orchids, and ferns. Colorful flowers brighten the landscape in spring.

After about 55 km on this paved road, there's a turnoff to the left (north) going to Uvero and Placer. Many getaway houses are springing up along that part of the coast and a few small diving destinations are becoming popular. If you continue east down the pavement another couple of km, you'll come to Majahual on the sea, a geographic point on the map but no town. A military camp guards the point, but again, they're just a bunch of kids trying to decide who might be a drug runner. Here turn right on the new paved road (south) to reach Xcalak, another 66 km. The road parallels the coast, and the jungle along this stretch hasn't been disturbed much; it's teeming with animals and noisy birds. Along the

way you'll discover miles and miles of isolated beach and few facilities. Don't expect gorgeous white-sand beaches à la Cancún—just the turquoise sea, sea grasses, transparent white crabs, a variety of fish waiting to be caught for your dinner, and curious birds checking out the newest visitor to their deserted paradise. It's all free—so far. But development is coming. A 4,500-foot runway is in place; commuter flights will soon begin on a limited basis. And a new cruise dock is going to be built near Majahual within the next year.

Xcalak Village

The tiny fishing village of Xcalak lies just a short distance from a channel that separates Mexico from Belize's Ambergris Caye. It was founded in 1900 as a military base for a project to dredge a canal across the southern end of the peninsula. The project never got off the ground, and instead a small rail line was laid between Xcalak and La Aguada on Chetumal Bay.

Visitors will find a few hotels, small grocery stores, and simple cafes. **Commacho's** cafe has been around forever and serves simple meals for lunch and dinner. **Adolfo's** also serves lunch and dinner and maybe breakfast by now. It's a simple sand-floored cafe with good seafood and Maya specialties.

Electricity in the village is wind-generated and can be iffy, but generators take up where the wind stops. Bring flashlights and batteries to get around after dark.

Ferry to Chetumal: A *panga*-type, passengers-only ferry carries about 30 passengers across the bay to Chetumal on Monday and Friday. The trip takes an hour and a half. Car-ferry service was originally attempted but didn't work out, so while backpackers on foot can make use of this short-cut, drivers will have to backtrack to Hwy. 307.

Diving and Fishing

Diving is the most popular activity along this coast, and locals say Tom Biller is *the* diving captain of Xcalak. He takes divers across the reef to breathtaking **Chinchorro Bank,** 26 km off the coast. Scuba divers designate this world-class diving, with crystal-clear water and a huge variety of colorful fish, delicate coral, and three sunken ships clearly visible from above. Ask for

Tom at either Costa de Cocos or Sand-Wood Villas (see "Peninsula Accommodations," below).

Fishing for tarpon, bonefish, barracuda, and snook (all catch and release) is also popular around here. Both Costa de Cocos and Sand-Wood Villas offer fishing trips in their boats.

Peninsula Accommodations

Inexpensive/Moderate: Sin Duda, U.S. tel. (888) 881-4774, is a pleasant little inn next door to Sand-Wood Villas. Its twin two-story buildings are connected by walkways and imposing stairways to a roof deck providing a 360-degree view of jungle, lagoon, sea, and reef. Three of the rooms are double rooms, and the fourth is a combo room: kitchen, living, bedroom. Families are welcome. Tranportation is available into Xcalak for dinner.

Expensive: The peninsula's first resort was **Costa de Cocos,** U.S. tel. (800) 538-6802, U.S. fax (303) 674-9615, a fine little resort catering to divers. From Majahual, drive south exactly 52 km and you'll see the sign for Costa de Cocos on a gravel road. The resort features a dining room and eight beautiful bungalows—each with a shower, hot water, and lots of comfortable touches—set on palm-studded, tropical-paradise oceanfront. It's a diver's dream, with a safety-conscious PADI-trained divemaster, a 30-foot custom dive boat *(El Gavilan),* and a new boat due to arrive imminently. Chinchorro Bank, a one-hour boat ride away, is a favorite dive destination. Guided trips to hidden caves and rich fishing grounds are also offered. And kayakers interested in nature should ask about a naturalist-led kayak trip to the "back-water."

Breakfast and dinner are included in the room rates, which start at US$75 s, US$120 d. Diving, fishing, snorkeling, and all other excursions are extra. It is suggested that guests bring along a supply of favorite snacks, since shopping in town is limited. Beer and soft drinks are sold on site; liquor isn't, but feel free to bring your own.

Sand-Wood Villas, tel. (983) 8-0404, U.S. tel. (800) 247-5330, is a comfortable and immaculate four-plex. Each unit has a living room, kitchen, two bedrooms, two bathrooms, hot water, and ceiling fans. You can bring your own food or buy it from a grocery truck that comes four times a week. Purified water and ice are supplied, and meals are available on request.

On the back side of the villas there is great fishing in Laguna San Julia. Diving is provided by **Adventures Chinchorro.**

BACALAR AND VICINITY

Back on Hwy. 307, heading south from Limones, you'll come to Bacalar, a small enclave beside beautiful, multihued Laguna Bacalar. The lagoon is enjoyed by locals, and a couple of other interesting sights are nearby.

Fuerte San Felipe

This 17th-century fort was built by the Spanish for protection against the bands of pirates and Maya that regularly raided the area. It was destroyed in 1858 during the brutal Caste War. The star-shaped stone edifice has been restored, and cannons are still posted along the balustrades overlooking Laguna Bacalar. Originally, the moat was filled with sharp spikes; today it's filled with flowers and plants. The fort has a diminutive

Rancho Encantado

museum displaying metal arms used in the 17th and 18th centuries. A token assortment of memorabilia recalls history of the area. The museum is open daily except holidays and charges a small entry fee.

Cenote Azul
A circular cenote, 61.5 meters deep and 185 meters across, filled with brilliant blue water, this is a spectacular place to stop for a swim, a canoe ride, or lunch at the outdoor restaurant (where the adventurous gourmand can taste the jungle creature called *tempescuinkle*). Children in the area may request an admission fee to visit Cenote Azul and will make quite a fuss until you give them a few pesos. In many remote areas, locals (most of whom live at a subsistence level) are beginning to seek their share of the tourist dollar.

Accommodations
Moderate: Near Cenote Azul, built into the side of a hill overlooking Laguna Bacalar, is **Hotel Laguna** (Av. Bugambilias 316, Chetumal, Quintana Roo 77000, Mexico), Chetumal tel. (983) 2-3517, Mérida tel. (99) 27-1304, with clean rooms and private baths. Each room has a fan and a beautiful view. The dining room serves tasty Mexican food at moderate prices. A small pool (filled only during high season) and outdoor bar look out across the unusually hued Lagunas de Siete Colores ("Lagoons of Seven Colors"). A diving board and ladder make swimming convenient in the lagoons' sometimes blue, sometimes purple, sometimes red water; fishing is permitted, and you can barbecue your catch on the grounds. Ask about a bungalow including kitchen facilities. Reserve in advance during the high season and holidays. To find the hotel, turn left off Bacalar's main street and follow the shore south.

Expensive (All-Inclusive): Rancho Encantado (P.O. Box 1256, Taos, NM 87571, USA), tel./fax (983) 8-0427, U.S. tel. (800) 505-MAYA, U.S. fax (505) 776-2102, is an enchanting miniresort on the edge of Bacalar Lagoon. The 12 attractive, comfortable *casitas* feature native hardwoods and Mexican tile, and each holds a small sitting room, ceiling fan, coffee pot, bathroom, and a small porch with a hammock and a view of the garden or lagoon. Facilities include a lagoonside spa and massage area, kayaks for guest use, and a large *palapa* where visitors enjoy a tropical buffet breakfast and candlelit dinner, both included in the room rates. Also available is a private villa with three bedrooms, 2.5 baths, and private dock, on the waterfront a short distance away.

Encantado is a favorite of bird lovers. The grounds are a lush Eden of tropical shrubs, coco palms, and fruit trees—all just a few steps from the lagoon shore. Flocks of parakeets and a huge variety of other birds flit from tree to tree. Bird-watchers should talk to Luis, the manager, who keeps a list of birds you can expect to see and hear on the grounds. He's a font of information and an excellent nature photographer.

Other activities that can be arranged include archaeology and sightseeing tours of the area and scuba trips to Chinchorro Banks.

Camping
On the edge of the lagoon, **Laguna Milagros Trailer Park** accepts both RVers and tent campers; about US$7 pp. Amenities include restrooms, showers, sun shelters, a narrow beach, small store, and open-air cafe.

CHETUMAL AND VICINITY

Chetumal is the capital of Quintana Roo and the gateway to Belize. The city lacks the bikini-clad, touristy crowds of the north, instead presenting the businesslike atmosphere of a growing metropolis. Still, the largest building in town—housing government offices—rises just three stories.

The population is a handsome mixture of many races, including Caribe, Spanish, Maya, and Anglo. Schools are prominently scattered around town. Though sea breezes help, the climate is generally hot and sticky. The most comfortable time to visit is the dry season, Nov.-April. Copious rainfall in the region creates dense jungle with vine-covered trees, broad-leafed plants, ferns, and colorful blossoms. The forests here are noted for hardwood trees, such as mahogany and rosewood. Orchids grow liberally on the tallest trees. Deer and javelina roam the forests.

Those interested in Maya archaeology will find several Maya sites off Hwy. 186, within day-trip distance west of Chetumal.

A Walk through Town

Chetumal is a good city to explore on foot; a 10-minute walk takes you from the marketplace and most of the hotels to the waterfront. Wide, tree-lined avenues and clean sidewalks front small variety shops. Modern sculpted monuments stand along a breezy bayside promenade, while the back streets harbor pastel-colored, worn wooden buildings with an old Central American/Caribbean look.

At the city center, note the **Monument to the Mestizo,** an interesting sculpture symbolizing the joining of Spanish shipwrecked sailor Gonzalo Guerrero and a Maya princess—the birth of the Mestizos. Heading down Av. de los Héroes

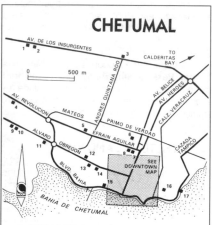

CHETUMAL

1. Xul-ha bathing resort
2. hospital (I.S.S.S.T.E.)
3. Payo Obispo Zoo
4. airport
5. Javier Rojo Gomez Public Library
6. Conasuper market
7. health center (S.S.A.)
8. civil hospital
9. El Palmar bathing resort
10. La Laguna de las Milagros bathing resort
11. Paradise Restaurant, Bar & Nightclub
12. Han Dal Gas Station
13. Consulate of Guatemala
14. city hall
15. EXPOFER Fair Installation
16. House of Culture (C.R.E.A.)
17. Quintana Roo Social Club

© MOON PUBLICATIONS, INC.

toward the bay, you'll pass **Altamirano Market,** a typical Mexican market place and a great place to practice your bargaining techniques, and **Museo de la Cultura Maya,** a fine large museum where leafy jungle penetrates half the spectacular main exhibit hall.

Numerous small shops and a few upscale department stores line Av. Héroes. At the southern end of the street near the sea you'll come to the walkway to **La Bandera Square,** where Sunday concerts and city celebrations are held, and the newly renovated **Palacio de Gobierno.**

The waterfront lacks beaches, but Boulevard Bahía makes for a fine bayfront stroll; along it you'll find cafes, monuments, a lighthouse, and, hopefully, a cooling breeze. The modern shell shaped structure you'll see is the **Palacio Legislativo.** Just northwest of the Palacio in a wooden colonial-style building is a handmade model of **Payo Obispo,** as Chetumal was called in the 1930s.

Accommodations

Although Chetumal is not considered a tourist resort, its status as the state capital and its location on the Belize border make it a busy stopover for both Mexicans and Belizeans. Arrive as early in the day as possible to have your choice of hotel rooms. During the holiday season it's wise to reserve in advance. Most of the hotels are within walking distance of the marketplace, downtown shops, and waterfront.

Inexpensive: The low-priced hotels are for the most part friendly. All have hot water and some have a/c (most are fan-cooled). Some are clean, some aren't; look before you pay. **Hotel Caribe Princess,** Av. Alvaro Obregón 168, tel. (983) 2-0520, is very clean and offers rooms with a/c and TV.

Moderate: Hotel Los Cocos, Av. Héroes 134 (at Calle Chapultepec), tel. (983) 2-0544, fax (983) 2-0920, has pleasant a/c rooms, a pretty garden, a large, clean swimming pool, a bar with evening disco music, and a quiet dining room with a friendly staff and a varied menu. The lobby holds a car-rental desk and one of the best travel agencies in Chetumal. **Holiday Inn,** Av. Héroes 171, tel. (983) 2-1100, fax (983) 2-1607, is probably the nicest hotel in town. Amenities include a/c, swimming pool, a good restaurant, and a bar with evening entertainment.

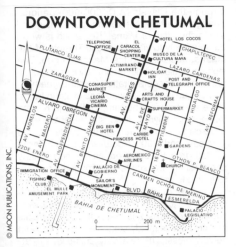

fices and cafe at the airport seem to be open only when flights are expected. An airport van provides transportation to hotels or downtown. **Aviacsa** provides service between Mexico City and Chetumal. **Taesa** offers daily flights from Chetumal to Cancún, Mexico City, and Mérida. **Aerocaribe, Aeroméxico, Bonanza,** and **Mexicana** serve the city less frequently.

By Bus: First- and second-class buses from points all over Mexico arrive throughout the day at the new, modern Chetumal bus station, Salvador Novo 179 (on the highway, 20 blocks south of town). Taxis to town are available from the station. With the expanding road system, bus travel is becoming more versatile and is still the most inexpensive public transportation to the Quintana Roo coast.

Buses run between Chetumal and Mérida (5.5 hours), Mexico City (22 hours), Cancún, and Campeche. Check with a travel agent for pickup point in Chetumal, usually at one of the hotels. Fares and schedules change regularly.

Food
Emiliano's, Av. San Salvador 557 (at Calle 9), tel. (983) 7-0267, is easily comparable to the best seafood houses in Cancún. Start with the shrimp or conch pâté, followed by shark empanadas, then the freshest ceviche, *pulpo en su tinto,* and *chiles rellenos* stuffed with seafood. It's the perfect spot for a long lunch or celebratory dinner. A three-course meal will run about US$20-30, though you can get by much cheaper (e.g., a heaping platter of *arroz a la marinera,* rice mixed with seafood, runs about US$8). Open for lunch and dinner.

Several fast-food cafes line Av. Alvaro Obregón. For seafood try **El Pez Vela,** and for chicken go to **Pollos Sinaloa.**

Events
Chetumal hosts an **auto road race** in December. Open to drivers from all over the globe, it's gaining prominence in the racing world. Hotel reservations should be made well in advance.

Windsurfing is popular on both Bahía Chetumal and Laguna Bacalar; state competitions are held in both areas yearly. For more information, write to the Secretaría de Turismo, Palacio de Gobierno 20, Chetumal, Quintana Roo 77000, Mexico.

Transportation
By Air: Chetumal's small modern airport still has only a few flights each day. The rental-car of-

children's parade on the first day of spring, Chetumal

To Cancún costs about US$17. **Omnibus Caribe Express,** tel. (983) 2-7889, offers deluxe service to Cancún and Mérida.

Batty Bus and **Venus Bus** offer frequent buses into Belize; US$2-7. You will have to get off the bus when you go across the border into Belize. Have your passport handy, sometimes this takes a while.

By Car: Paved road connects Mérida, Campeche, Villahermosa, and Francisco Escárcega with Chetumal. The cross-peninsula highway from Chetumal to Escárcega can be filled with potholes. Highway 307 links all of the Quintana Roo coastal cities. There's little traffic, and the route's four gas stations are well spaced (top off at each one).

Kohunlich

Sixty-seven km west of Chetumal on Hwy. 186, turn left and drive eight km on a good side road to this unique Maya site. The construction lasted from the Late Preclassic (about A.D. 100-200)

one of the giant masks of Kohunlich

through the Classic (A.D. 600-900) periods. Though not totally restored nor nearly as grand as Chichén Itzá or Uxmal, Kohunlich is worth the trip if only to visit the exotic **Temple of the Masks,** dedicated to the Maya sun god. The stone pyramid is under an unlikely thatch roof (to prevent further deterioration from the weather), and unique gigantic stucco masks stand two to three meters tall. The temple, though not extremely tall as pyramids go, still presents a moderate climb. Wander through the jungle site and you can find 200 structures or uncovered mounds from the same era as Palenque. Many carved stelae are scattered throughout the surrounding forest.

Walking through luxuriant foliage, you'll note orchids in the tops of trees, plus small colorful wildflowers, lacy ferns, and lizards that share cracks and crevices in moldy stone walls covered with velvety moss. The relatively unknown site attracts few tourists. The absence of trinket sellers and soft-drink stands leaves the visitor feeling that he or she is the first to stumble on the haunting masks with their star-incised eyes, moustaches (or are they serpents?), and nose plugs—features extremely different from carvings found at other Maya sites. The site is well cleared, and when we last visited, archaeologists from INAH were excavating a burial mound. Like most archaeological zones, Kohunlich is fenced and open 8 a.m.-5 p.m.; admission is US$3.50. Camping is not allowed within the grounds, but you may see a tent or two outside the entrance.

If you're driving, Kohunlich is an easy daytrip from Chetumal or Bacalar; in Chetumal check with local buses or travel agencies or your hotel for information about organized tours to Kohunlich and the nearby ruins at Xpujil, Becán, and Chicanná in the state of Campeche (see "Río Bec Archaeological Sites" in the Campeche chapter).

CROSSING INTO BELIZE

Across the Río Hondo from Chetumal lies the country of Belize, which makes an easy side trip for the explorer, archaeology buff, diver, or the just-plain-curious. Belize is easily reached from Chetumal by taking a Batty or Venus bus or taxi over the Río Hondo bridge.

a camping tour

OZ MALLAN

There's rarely a problem crossing the border if you show a valid passport. It's best to be prepared to show money or proof of onward travel. If driving, you must buy insurance with Belizean dollars; moneychangers are waiting for you as you cross the border. Their rates seem comparable to bank rates. U.S. citizens and most others don't need visas, but citizens of a few countries do; check with your embassy before leaving home.

Tours
Henry Menzies Travel and Tours, Box 210, Corozal Town, Belize, tel. (42) 2725, takes visitors back and forth across the border all the time. Henry is a good, honest guide/driver who knows the border-crossing ropes and will take you anywhere in Belize.

International Expeditions, One Environs Park, Helena, AL 35080 USA, tel. (800) 633-4734 or (205) 428-1700, offers several good theme trips with small groups. The 11-day **Naturalist Quest** expedition is led by a knowledgeable naturalist who takes the group into the country's Jaguar Sanctuary and Howler Monkey Sanctuary. Other expeditions visit the country's Maya archaeological sites, offshore cayes, or nearby Costa Rica.

Further Reading
For details about traveling in Belize, including accommodations, restaurants, attractions, diving, and everything else you ever wanted to know about the country, pick up a copy of Moon Publications' ***Belize Handbook.***

KATHY ESCOVEDO SANDERS

THE STATE OF YUCATÁN

INTRODUCTION

Yucatán is a Mexico that clings to its past. It embraces intriguing prehistoric archaeological sites as well as an ancient history well displayed in libraries and museums. Some of these museums are located at the sites themselves. Today's visitors come to bathe in the light of this antiquity, to climb the old stone pyramids, to observe the unique hieroglyphs that archaeologists have begun to understand. Foreigners are intrigued with the stories of adventurous Spaniards and the brave Indians who fought with their bare hands against an army of four-legged animals carrying men with exploding sticks—never before seen on this continent. It's no wonder that the Indians were intimidated and at first believed the horse and rider were one creature.

The Yucatán Peninsula is brimming over with wealth. Not the wealth of gold or power, but a prosperity that includes nature, history, and the Maya of today who exude an aura that we believe existed hundreds of years ago. Because the Yucatán Peninsula was ignored for so many years, nature was left on its own; birds and animals freely multiplied, fish were taken as needed, trees grew tall, and thick vines hid a special minutia from the tiniest insect to the most colorful lizards and blossoms. Not only do travelers find the ancient remains of the Maya, but also an introduction to colonial history from the days of the Spaniards.

Today a new history is being written by modern travelers from all over the world. The visitor makes startling discoveries, whether trekking among mys-

ARCHAEOLOGICAL ZONES OF YUCATÁN

Acanceh	Izamal	Sayil
Ake	Kabah	Uxmal
Calcetok	Labná	Xlapak
Chichén Itzá	Mayapán	
Dzibilchaltún	Oxkintok	

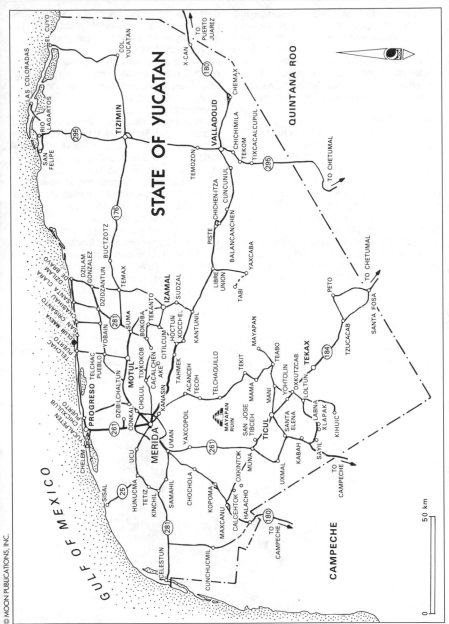

STATE OF YUCATAN

50 km

© MOON PUBLICATIONS, INC.

terious old structures of the Maya, or studying fine Spanish architectural styles and fresco images that have melded into the outstanding *Mexican* art tradition. For further meditation on stunning impressions of the Yucatán, it is *so* easy to make a quick trip to white beaches of choice; either on the Gulf of Mexico or on the Caribbean Sea, where life moves as slowly or as quickly as you wish.

Land and Climate

Yucatán is a triangle-shaped area bordered by the Gulf of Mexico on the north, the state of Quintana Roo on the east, and the state of Campeche on the west. It occupies 38,508 square km (14,868 square miles) and boasts a population of over 1.5 million. The state has no lakes or rivers; it depends for its water supply upon underground rivers and natural wells called cenotes (from the Maya word *dzonot*).

The climate is hot and humid in summer; most of the rain falls between May and October. The average daytime temperature during these months is 37° C (96° F). Fortunately a breeze blows during most of the year and the drier winter months seem much cooler.

Flora and Fauna

Yucatán's verdant coastal estuaries are the only ones in the world fed by underwater springs. The estuaries serve as a haven for many exotic resident birds and for thousands of wintering migratory birds. El Cuyo, the wildlife refuge at Río Lagartos, protects the world's largest colony of nesting American flamingos; close-by Celestún also plays host to the striking pink bird. Yucatán is also home to one of the continent's most beautiful orchids, the *Rhuncholaelia digbuana*.

Economy

Yucatán's main industries are tourism, fishing, and commerce. Tourism is at the top of the moneymaking list; major tourist draws inlude the state's numerous archaeological zones and its abundant wildlife. Fishing has been a way of life for centuries along the coast; only in recent years has the activity become mechanized and organized to a point where exporting fish (mostly to the U.S.) is now big business.

At the turn of the century and into the early 1900s, Cordemex employed thousands of locals to work the thorny henequen fields caring for and harvesting with simple machetes the sword-shaped, spiked fronds. These campesinos (farm workers) were paid with housing and an inadequate charge account at the company store—a tie that effectively chained workers who could never find their way out of debt. Other important industries in Yucatán are salt, honey, and building materials (including cement, blocks, and lime). The Oxkutzcab area is booming with citrus fruits.

giant anteater

DIANA LASICH HARPER

MÉRIDA AND VICINITY

INTRODUCTION

With a population of around 650,000, Mérida is the largest city on the Yucatán Peninsula. The colonial capital of the state of Yucatán, the city combines the appeal and grace of old Europe (as it should, since much of it was patterned after Paris) with a large dose of modern, cosmopolitan culture. Museums, old churches, beautiful government buildings, monuments, and shady, tree-lined plazas fill the city, and music is everywhere. Heady Latin rhythms and modern dance steps share billing with Maya and Spanish folkloric songs and dances, and free concerts and other gatherings throughout the week are well attended by local citizens as well as visitors.

"The White City," as Mérida has been called for centuries, is very clean. Sewage problems have been eliminated and potable water plants are scattered all around town. However, it is still recommended that you drink bottled water if it's provided by the hotel. Some of the hotels have purification plants on-site. To be sure, ask hotel personnel. If there's a bottle of water in your room, you can be certain the water out of the tap is only for washing.

If there's a flaw in Mérida, it's the traffic in the narrow streets. But as the city is one of the loveliest old colonial towns on the Peninsula, it's possible to overlook the rush of cars and buses.

History

Mérida was originally called T'ho or Ichcansiho by the Maya (depending on which chronicle you read). The first Spaniards to arrive found a large Maya commercial center with ornate stone structures that reminded them of the Roman ruins in Spain's city of Mérida—hence the name.

The city was founded 6 January 1542 by Francisco de Montejo "El Mozo" (The Younger) to celebrate his victory over the Indians after 15 years of conflict. The Maya, by then slaves of the Spanish invaders, were forced to dismantle their temples and palaces and use the materials to build homes, offices, cathedrals, and parks they were not permitted to enjoy. Mérida be-

came the capital and trade center of the Peninsula and the seat of civil and religious authority. The Spaniards lived in fine houses around the central plaza in downtown Mérida, while Indian servants lived on the outer edges of town. Todays residents are an even mix of Indians, ladinos, and mestizos, and the enmities of the past are nowhere to be seen.

SIGHTS

Domingo en Mérida

Sunday is a wonderful day in Mérida. The streets in the heart of the city around the plazas are closed to all vehicular traffic. Regulars visit a mini-flea market in the Plaza Santa Lucía (on Calle 60), which is followed by a band—often the well-known Mérida Police orchestra—playing

The heart of Mérida is the central plaza.

typical Yucatecan music. Around 11:30 a.m., a marimba concert begins in Hidalgo Park (also known as Cepeda Peraza, at Calles 60 and 59). At 1 p.m., the City Hall Folkloric Ballet performs the mestiza wedding dance at the Palacio Municipal. The music goes on all day.

Everyone in the city (or so it seems) dresses in their Sunday best and comes downtown. Sidewalk cafes do a lively business, as do the dozens of pushcarts selling drinks, *tortas* (sandwiches), *elote* (corn on the cob), and sweets. In the evening some families take in the cinema; others meet with friends, listen to the music, and chat. Whatever the activity, loud, smelly cars are gone for the day and a glorious freedom turns the clock back in time to a more gracious period.

Central Plaza Area

Surrounded by aristocratic colonial buildings, the large green central plaza (Plaza de la Independencia) is an oasis in the middle of this busy town. Friends gather here all day and late into the night. This is a city where people stroll the streets after dark and feel safe and comfortable. In the old custom, sweethearts sit on *confidenciales* (S-curved cement benches) allowing intimate tête-à-tête—oh so close!—but without touching. White-sombreroed men gather early in the morn-

MÉRIDA

FIESTA AMERICANA

HYATT REGENCY MÉRIDA

HOTEL EL CONQUISTADOR

PALACIO CANTÓN/ANTHROPOLOGY

RAILROAD STATION

EL CENTENARIO PARK AND ZOO

To Celestún

To Valladolid and Chichén Itzá

To Airport and Campeche

SEE "DOWNTOWN MÉRIDA" MAP

0   1 mi

0   1 km

© MOON PUBLICATIONS, INC.

ing; visiting mestizas in colorful *huipiles* sit in the shade and share lunch with their children, enjoying the sights of the big city.

Sidewalk cafes edge the park, and in the cool of evening locals and tourists enjoy music and song. As Philip Terry said in his 1909 guide: "In Mexico singing is almost a disease. Bus drivers, mule skinners, your cook and your maid sing all day; songs burst out of taverns; pilgrims afoot on the road sing."

The *Calesa*

Mérida's narrow streets were originally designed for *calesas* (horse-drawn buggies), and you can still ride a *calesa* through the old residential neighborhoods. From 9 a.m.-9 p.m. on Sunday a major downtown section surrounding the central plaza is closed off to vehicular traffic. This is the ideal day to tour the city in a *calesa* and see beautiful old mansions built at the turn of the century or earlier. Like taxis, the horse-drawn buggies are not metered, so arrange your fee and route before starting out. Average price is around US$15 per hour; on Sunday a ride through the quiet downtown streets will cost a little less.

"SIGN" LANGUAGE

John Stephens brings to life the period 1839-1842 in his book, *Incidents of Travel in the Yucatán Peninsula*. Reading it, especially after visiting the region (or even better—while there) brings the reality of his words to life.

According to one of his little vignettes on life in Mérida, most of the city's Indian population could not read, so the city fathers came up with the plan to sign the streets so that everyone would know how to find an address. On each corner building before the street stood a painted wooded carving of a familiar figure, e.g., a flamingo on *street of the flamingo*, a bull for *street of the bull*. One figure was an old woman with spectacles on her nose; that street became known as the *street of the old woman*. The early Méridanos were much more clever than today's street authorities, who have named the streets mostly by numbers. This can be confusing to many of us who *can* read, but would still prefer to see the fine painted carvings designating the streets.

This sculpture of Spaniards with their feet firmly planted on the heads of the Maya depicts the dominance the Spanish had over the Maya.

The *calesas* have regular routes for their one-hour tours, among them Paseo de Montejo Drive, Old Mérida Neighborhoods, Centenario Park, and Park of the Americas.

The Cathedral

The most prominent building on the plaza is the cathedral. Built from 1561 to 1598 with stones taken from Maya structures on-site, it's one of the oldest buildings on the continent. If you search, you'll find an occasional stone with a Maya glyph still visible. The architecture prevalent in Spain at the time is reflected in the Moorish style of the two towers. Surprisingly, the interior is stark in comparison to some of the ornately decorated churches in other parts of Mexico—during the Caste War and the 1910 revolution, the church was stripped of its valuable trimmings. Note the impressive painting of the meeting between the nobles of the Maya Xiu clan and the Spanish invaders in 1541. This solemnly portrays the Xiu tribe joining the Spaniards as allies—a trust that was violated, marking the beginning of the end of the Maya regime.

In the church, a small chapel houses a revered image of Christ called El Cristo de las Ampollas ("Christ of the Blisters"), carved from a tree in Ichmul that is said to have been engulfed in flames but remained undamaged. Reportedly the wooden statue then went through another fire in a church, this time developing blisters as living skin would. Though the statue is honored with a fiesta each fall, every Sunday sees the devout crowding around to touch the statue and sigh a brief prayer.

Palace of the Archbishop

Just south of the cathedral facing the plaza, this once-elaborate building was the home of the archbishop. Since the revolution, when the church's power was restricted, the large struc-ture has housed the local military post. The building has been remodeled and now houses the Museo MACAY. Exhibits by Yucatecan artists are changed frequently. Open Tues.-Sun. 8 a.m.-5 p.m.; admission US$3.

Casa Montejo

Facing the south edge of the central plaza is the Banamex Bank building, once the home of Francisco de Montejo. The Casa was con-structed in 1542 by Montejo's son, Francisco de Montejo "El Mozo" (The Younger), using tal-ented Maya craftspeople and recovered stone. The unique carvings of Spaniards standing at attention with their feet planted firmly on the heads of the Maya remain in place today—a blatant reminder of their tyranny at the time. These works of art were also rendered by Maya slaves. It's said that 13 generations of Montejos lived in the house until it was sold to Banamex in 1980. Today the bank takes up the entire struc-ture, including a large second floor. You can see the enormous patio during business hours (9 a.m.-1 p.m.).

Los Palacios ("The Palaces")

Opposite the northeast corner of the central plaza is the **Palacio de Gobierno.** Striking ab-stract murals painted by Fernando Castro Pacheco in 1978 decorate the interior walls and

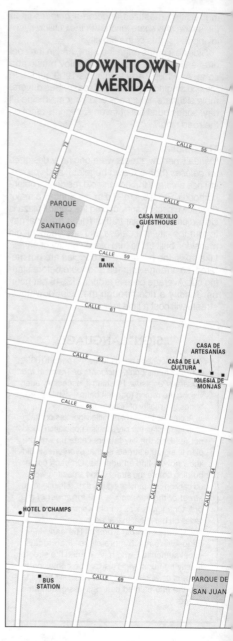

DOWNTOWN MÉRIDA

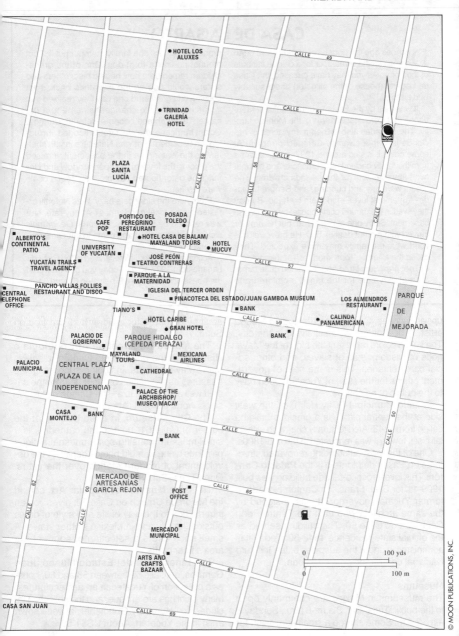

CASA DE LAGARTO

Decades ago the houses of Mérida were often named for the owners, or for a unique attribute of the home. As you may have guessed, the Casa de Lagarto (house of the alligator) has a suitably wild history.

It was built by the Laviada family, affluent Méridanos that were descendants of the Montejo family. The Laviadas also owned many acres of hacienda land in a swampy Campeche region. At some point, it is said around 1937, a visitor came from the family hacienda in Campeche and brought two baby alligators for the Laviada children. The gators were tiny and cunning, and Señora Laviada—an animal lover—fed them by hand. By day they lived in the garden of the house, by night in the basement. Sadly one of them died, but his brother thrived with a great deal of TLC. He grew well beyond what the family may have expected. They called the alligator Toot, short for Tutenkahmen.

Toot grew very large and remained quite tame; a great playmate for the family's children and grandchildren. As one family member put it, Toot thought he was a (big) dog. One of the grandchildren remembers how he and his brothers and sisters would ride on the alligator's back. Toot continued to grow, and one day they realized that it was necessary to change *his* name to a *her* name; Tutenkahmen became Nefertiti. During a violent hurricane, the city streets flooded, including the basement that was Nefertiti's inside shelter. As the water rose in the basement, it raised the gator to the level of the open window and Nefertiti the gator floated out into the street. Locals were terrified.

From here the story gets hazy. Was Nefertiti arrested by the local gendarmes? At any rate, she *was* rescued by the family. *National Geographic* picked up on the story and came to interview reptile and owner.

According to legend, Nefertiti lived in the Casa de Lagarto from 1937-1970. Today you can walk past the house; it's on Calle 61, between 62 and 64.

upper galleries. Castro, an outstanding Mérida artist, is now elderly and still living in the city. The subtle colors represent the birth of the Maya, gods of wisdom, sale of slaves, and other social commentaries. This is the seat of government offices for the state of Yucatán; open daily to the public at no charge.

Palacio Municipal ("City Hall"), on the west side of the central plaza, is a gracious building dating from 1543. Architecturally charming with its tall clock tower, it was renovated in the mid-1800s.

One of the most outstanding renovated structures on Paseo de Montejo is the **Palacio Cantón.** This lovely rococo-facade building was built 1909-11 for Gral. Francisco Cantón Rosado, a former Yucatán governor. It was designed by the same architect who built the Teatro Peón Contreras on Calle 60. The building served as the official state residence 1948-60. Today it is administered under the auspices of the Instituto Nacional de Antropología e Historia.

Museums

The museums in Mexico are commonly open to the public Tues.-Sat. 8 a.m.-8 p.m., Sunday 8 a.m.-2 p.m. Some charge a small admission for adults (no charge for children); all are free on Sunday.

The **Museo Regional de Antropología e Historia,** in the old Palacio Cantón, displays many Maya artifacts, including such intriguing treasures as antiquities brought up from the sacred well at Chichén Itzá. The Cantón building itself is worth the visit.

The **City Museum,** in a red building at the corner of Calle 61, next to the cathedral, is a small museum housing some unusual antique paintings along with old photos depicting the development of modern Mérida over the years. Open Tues.-Sun. 8 a.m.- 8 p.m.

The large **Museum of Popular Art,** behind the Mejorada Church on Calle 59, gives you an introduction to the way of life and style of dress outside the city and in Mexico's other states. A small shop offers a selection of some of the area's finer crafts.

The **Pinacoteca del Estado/Museo Juan Gamboa,** on Calle 59 between 58 and 60, houses a collection of Yucatecan art and sculptures. Many paintings are antique, and the collection includes sculptures by Gottdiener, a well-known artist in the Yucatán. About US$1.50.

Museo de Historia Natural, Calle 59 at 84, gives a look into the area's natural history. It's open Tues.-Sat. 9 a.m.-6 p.m. All musicians will enjoy a look around **Museo de la Canción Yucateca,** in the Casa de la Cultura on Calle 63 between 64 and 66. The museum houses a collection of music and instruments, some very old. Open Tues.-Sat. 9 a.m.-8 p.m.

Museo MACAY, on Calle 60 next to the cathedral, houses a permanent exposition of Yucatán art. Open Wed.-Sun. 8 a.m.-5 p.m. The **Museo Numismático de Mexico,** Calle 60 #469 (between 53 and 55), holds a neat coin collection. Open Mon.-Sat. 9 a.m.-1 p.m. and 4:30-8:30 p.m., Sunday 9:30 a.m.-1:30 p.m.

Biblioteca Carlos Menéndez

Anyone interested in old books and history, take a minute to look in this large library of really antiquated works. If you can speak Spanish, talk to director Juan Francisco Peón Ancona, a longtime Mérida resident and the city historian. He has a world of knowledge to share about the city. The library is on Colón at Calle 22.

ACCOMMODATIONS

Budget

Although there's no youth hostel in Mérida, numerous small hotels near the plaza offer economical shelter. **The Trinidad Galería,** Calle 60 #456, tel. (99) 23-2463, is an old residence that has been transformed into a captivating hotel with modern touches, including a swimming pool, green garden, ceiling fans, and a/c. It's difficult to describe this museum-cum-hotel. The owner, Manolo, is a collector of unusual art—be it modernistic or just bizarre, it's always fun to cogitate. Around every corner, a new discovery awaits; could be a wooden horse, or a modern painting that might rival a Dali (or not). Pieces display contemporary names you may never have heard of. There are nudes, cracked renaissance statues, and who knows what else you'll find. The rooms are simple, most with private bath, and there's an off-and-on coffee bar on the premises. None of the tile matches—but in a very artistic way. Look carefully before you pay to see if it suits your style. Rooms with a/c are a little higher.

Hotel Mucuy, Calle 57 #481, tel./fax (99) 23-7801, is in a quiet neighborhood northeast of the plaza. The 10-room hotel is spotlessly clean and has a relaxing patio where guests can lounge in the sun and read books obtained from an amply stocked shelf of English-language paperbacks. Ask about low-cost tours to the ruins.

Facing the municipal bus station, **Hotel Rodríguez,** Calle 69 #478, tel. (99) 21-4300, is plain—except for its beautiful tile floors and bathrooms. The rooms in the back of the building are the quietest. Handy location, pleasant staff. Ask for purified water at the desk.

Another little gem to check out is **Casa de Huéspedes,** near the courtyard at Calle 62 #507. A home from a time when Mérida had many such mansions, it has high ceilings, spacious rooms, and a charming courtyard with surrounding balconies. Unfortunately, only one small bathroom with toilet and shower serves all the rooms. This is a popular place with the hip European crowd.

Inexpensive

Certainly not fancy, but with a lot of four-star features, three-star **Hotel Caribe,** Calle 59 #500, tel. (99) 24-9022, fax (99) 24-8733, U.S. tel. (800) 826-6842, is a good buy. The location is ideal—on Hidalgo Park (Cepeda Peraza), near everything, and just one block from the main plaza. The old three-story colonial residence has been renovated and has a swimming pool and a marvelous view from the roof. Take your choice of two dining areas, inside El Rincón or at the few tables outside on Hidalgo Park.

Hotel D'Champs, Calle 70 #543 (near 67), tel. (99) 24-8655 or 24-8829, fax (99) 23-6024, is one block from the main bus station and six blocks southwest of the main square. It has 100 rooms, a large shady patio, and a garden with a variety of big trees that make it cool and quiet; a great escape from the downtown area. All rooms are clean and have a/c, telephones, and bathrooms.

Posada Toledo, Calle 58 #487 (at the corner of Calle 57), tel. (99) 23-4355, used to be one of the best budget hotels in Mérida, but price increases have put it in the inexpensive range. Still, it's a charming place in a huge old mansion. Travelers tend to congregate in the central hallway and courtyard; some rooms open onto this busy hallway, which can be a drawback if you enjoy an afternoon siesta. The 15 rooms have high ceilings, wood floors, and antique furnishings. Check out the fancy blue and violet master suite—two enormous rooms elaborately decorated and with two air-conditioners and a bathroom as big as some of the other bedrooms. Fans or a/c.

Moderate

A lovely colonial hotel to check out is the **Gran Hotel,** Calle 60 #496 (on the lively Parque Cepeda Peraza, across from the cathedral), tel. (99) 24-7730 or 23-6963, fax (99) 24-7622. The turn-of-the-century Italianate building has recently been restored, but a little bit of the good old days lingers on in the high-ceilinged loggias, Corinthian columns, arches, shiny tile floors, and dark woods. Anyone who appreciates old elegance should take a look; obviously Cuba's Fidel did. Credit cards okay. The clean restaurant serves good food and offers tables inside the dining room or on the hotel's inner courtyard.

Expensive

A few blocks' walk from the central plaza, **Los Aluxes,** Calle 60 #444, tel. (99) 24-2199, fax (99) 23-3858, is a multistoried hotel providing courtesy valet parking for its guests. The hotel has a friendly staff, the kind that remembers your name as you come and go. Rooms are comfy and have carpet and satellite TV; suites, with individual terraces and tropical plants, are a good buy—especially #317, #417, and #517. Credit cards okay. Excellent food is served in the lobby dining room, and an intimate bar/lounge emanates mellow late-night music; room service available. Other amenities include a pool and tropical garden.

Calinda Panamericana, Calle 59 #455, tel. (99) 23-9111, fax (99) 24-8090, U.S. tel. (800) 228-5152, has a lovely entrance and large central courtyard that were once part of a gracious turn-of-the-century mansion. The hotel offers spacious high-ceilinged rooms—each with a/c and private bath—furnished in early-1900s simplicity. Other amenities include elevators, a swimming pool, patio bar/coffee shop, dining room, and live entertainment. Credit cards okay.

Hotel Casa del Balam, Calle 60 #488, tel. (99) 24-8844, fax (99) 24-5011, U.S. tel. (800) 235-4079, has received high ratings for years.

The large, clean rooms have heavy, dark-wood, colonial-style furniture. On the lower floors you may not wish to open the windows because of the traffic noise outside. The shady courtyard is filled with lush tropical plants; comfortable chairs sit under wide arches along tiled corridors. Enjoy a drink from the lobby bar in the company of a splashing fountain. There's a small pool, and a pleasant restaurant faces the street.

Hotel El Conquistador, on Mérida's broad Paseo de Montejo at Calle 45, tel. (99) 26-2155 or 26-2690, fax (99) 26-8829, is one of the city's nicer hotels. The 170 rooms and suites are newly refurbished and offer a/c, lovely tiled bathrooms, telephone, and TV. The dining room is done in rich colors and modern design with a splash of Yucatecan art; the food is outstanding, including a breakfast buffet overflowing with freshly baked pastries, rolls, tropical fruits, and typical cuisine (ask for the cheese rolls-mm-mm!). Good service (ask for Juan). Other amenities include a cheerful staff, indoor pool, rooftop pool, solarium, restaurant, bar, parking lot, car-rental desk, and travel agency. The hotel is about a 10-minute taxi ride to the main plaza.

Premium

The neighborhood around Paseo de Montejo and Av. Colón is rapidly becoming a deluxe tourism center. The 17-story **Hyatt Regency Mérida,** Calle 60 #344 (at Av. Colón), tel. (99) 42-0202, fax (99) 25-6700, U.S. tel. (800) 228-9000, is the city's tallest building. The Hyatt has 300 comfortable rooms with all amenities including personal safes. Two floors of rooms are set aside as the Regency Club, whose guests receive complimentary continental breakfast, evening cocktails and hors d'oeuvres, and special concierge service. A bit costly, but regal. The complex includes the Restaurant Peregrina, a swim-up bar at the landscaped pool, and all the services you expect in a five-star hotel.

The **Fiesta Americana** is one of the newer hotels on the Paseo de Montejo, tel. (99) 42-1111, fax (99) 42-1112, U.S. tel. (800) 343-7821. The rooms are modern and comfortable with luxurious amenities. An add-on to an old colonial structure, the hotel begins on the second level, reached by way of a modern escalator. The first level is a snazzy shopping mall with all sorts of fine shops, including a **Sanborn's** with its eclectic mixture of books, gifts, bakery delights and wonderful confections, along with a good pharmacy. The hotel offers excellent food, a pool, and club rooms where a fine continental breakfast and afternoon cocktails are served. The service is great!

Bed and Breakfast Guesthouses

Inexpensive: One of the best deals in Mérida, **Casa San Juan,** Calle 62 #545A (between 69 and 71), tel. (99) 23-6823, U.S. tel. (800) 555-8842, is an intimate little inn with Old World charm. It occupies an antiquated townhouse built in 1850 and renovated in 1905; ask Pablo, the owner, to tell you the history of the place. Breakfast is a simple continental spread in the dining room. A small patio outdoors offers shade and lounges for reading. The Casa San Juan is just a few blocks from the center of town, plazas, cafes, and shopping.

Inexpensive/Moderate: Four blocks from the main plaza, **Casa Mexilio Guesthouse,** Calle 68 #495 (between 57 and 59), tel. (99) 21-4032, fax (99) 28-2505, U.S. tel. (800) 538-6802, U.S. fax (303) 674-8735, is a bit different than most. Another old colonial residence, this inn is owned and operated by hosts who speak English, Spanish, and Maya. They are dedicated to providing personal touches in eight charming rooms, all decorated with Mexican and Guatemalan folk art. Two deluxe rooms have private terraces and a/c—check out the rooftop room with its great view of the city. Relax in the second-floor living room, complete with piano, or cool off in the tiny swimming pool, or soak in the jacuzzi. Check out the lush plants on the shady patio. A tasty breakfast is provided, as is a refrigerator for guest use. Roger and Jorge also arrange special tours of Yucatán and Quintana Roo.

Outlying Haciendas

The countryside surrounding Mérida holds numerous haciendas on large plots of land. Many have gradually been decaying, even falling down, but others have been prized by families that have owned them for hundreds of years and now use them as holiday getaways and places to celebrate special occasions. Still others have been or are in the process of being renovated and transformed into either hotels, bed and breakfasts, or restaurants. Anyone interested in

the history, architecture, or the art of the past should look into these old buildings. Many have their own wells, some of which were cenotes. Most have ancient trees inhabited by generations of birds. And at many, you can arrange a ride on the old henequen rails or a trip to nearby Maya sites.

Moderate: About 10 km out of Mérida through the rural countryside, the intimate **Hacienda Tanil,** tel. (99) 25-9194, fax (99) 25-3646, was once part of a plantation covering thousands of acres. The history of this old house has the intrigue and romance of all of the old properties. The present owners can trace the history of the hacienda back to 1607, when it was owned by Diego Solis Osorio, mayor of the Yucatán Province (long before there were states). Diego's wife was the granddaughter of Francisco de Montejo the elder, an important player in settling the area. Originally, the hacienda was an ordinary farm. Later it specialized in cattle, and then became a prosperous henequen plantation.   A stay at the hacienda brings you into the gracious atmosphere of Mérida's past. Antique carvings complement the thick-walled architecture typical of the time. Broad archways around a lovely patio provide shady spots to read. You can swim in the pool (obviously a latter day addition) or ride one of the beautiful horses. The three guest rooms are comfortable, and every place you look you see bright blossoms and brilliant color. Up a flight of stairs the original stone chapel is still in use, this is where many of the owners' family were baptized and married. The owners are delightful, and guests are pampered.

To top it all off, the food here is tasty. Homemade tortillas are made by the village ladies who take care of the kitchen. We had the most wonderful *botana* (appetizer) of chunks of jicama and oranges sprinkled with ground chile piquin sprinkled with lime juice.

If you yearn for something different, want a little rest, or a change of pace as you whiz through the Yucatán Peninsula, stop at Tanil. Ask about the weekend special.

Expensive: Hacienda Katanchel (Tixkokob, Yucatán 97470, Mexico), U.S. tel. (800) 223-6510, U.S. toll-free fax (888) 882-9470, e-mail: hacienda@mail.mda.com.mx, is a gracious spot with 741 acres to roam and enjoy. Built in the 17th century as a cattle ranch, it was converted

HENEQUEN

Henequen grows easily in the northern section of the Yucatán Peninsula, especially in the area surrounding Mérida. At one time hundreds of sprawling haciendas grew the thorny crop in this sparse, rocky soil—precisely what this type of agave requires. Field factories stil dot the coutnryside. Henequen requires seven years of growth before its first harvest. Each man works close to the land, using a scythe to cut one selected tough leaf at a time. These are brought into the field factory in bundles, then shredded and allowed to dry into pale yellow, strawlike sheaves of individual fibers. These sheaves are then processed, dyed, woven, braided, reshaped, and reworked into a multitude of forms by sophisticated machinery. The end product may be wall coverings, twine of many thicknesses and colors, floor mats, interior car cushions, burlap bags, or simple Yucatán hammocks. One of the more recent by-products is animal food. Adding blood meal (from nearby packing houses) and protein (from soy beans) to plant residue produces a nourishing (they say) pellet for dogs, chickens, and other animals.

A visit to the grounds of the Cordemex factory (a huge complex covering many acres of large buildings) will take you past the nursery starts of thousands of henequen seedlings. Also interesting to see are mature experimental plants. The result of years of hybridizing are the first thornless leaves—much easier to handle. In one of the field factories called San Francisco, on the road to Chichén Itzá, stop and take a look around (if you're lucky you'll miss the tour buses that also stop here). A little old man clad in sparkling white cotton will hand you a small sheaf of bleached henequen. While you hold one end, he quickly twists and manipulates the threads, finally handing you a neat piece of woven twine. Your souvenir is *Mayan* twine, for the Maya worked entirely by hand.

It's quite obvious to a visitor that OSHA doesn't exist in Mérida; workers wear shorts and kerchiefs across their mouths to repel thick dust emanating from the machinery. Some are barefoot or wear sandals. On the highway to Progreso, new cottages house the workers.

to a henequen plantation in the 19th century. Henequen ranchers realized huge profits for decades and took pleasure trying to outdo themselves in the grandeur of their haciendas. But nothing lasts forever, and when nylon was developed, the henequen market took a big plunge. Many fine old haciendas, including this one, were abandoned.

Recently, however, Hacienda Katanchel was renovated and miraculously returned to its original splendor. The 39 suites today cater to travelers who delight in this historical grandeur. While exploring the property, owners Anibal González and his wife Monica Hernández discovered a preclassic astronomical observation site dating from the 3rd century. And while clearing the jungle they found the platforms of what were once 33 workers' dwellings. These have been transformed into stunning deluxe pavilions for guests.

A hacienda was a "little city." Each had a *casa de maquina* (machine house) where the henequen was processed; today at Katanchel it is a wonderful dining room. Each had a chapel and a combination general store/pay office called a *tienda de raya*. Today the *tienda* is a boutique

featuring crafts, herbs, and souvenirs. The main house and its public rooms are beautifully decorated, a pool was built, and guests have the opportunity to explore many villages scattered about the countryside.

FOOD

Cafes of every description are found in Mérida. Yucatecan as well as Mexican food is included on most menus, and the "hot stuff" is served on the side, so you needn't worry about the infamous *habanera* chiles making a sneak attack. Be sure to try Yucatecan salsa made from the usual chiles, cilantro, tomatoes, spices, and one addition—a dash of citrus fruit and rind (mostly sour orange). If your palate is ready for a change from Yucatecan gourmet, Mérida offers excellent Arabic, Chinese, and European food.

For those traveling on a budget, it's a simple matter to find filling economical meals in Mérida. As always, the park vendors sell good tamales. Also check out the supermarkets (lots of new ones) for good hot lunches to go (some have small cafeterias), the mercado, and the big new department stores, where small budget cafeterias are available. Finally, note that in some cantinas in Mérida, when you order a cold beer in the middle of the afternoon, you'll be served tasty snacks (a more than ample lunch!).

Cafes
La Prosperidad, Calle 56 #456, tel. (99) 28-5283, is a popular spot; locals crowd into the large cafe daily for drinks, snacks, and good live music. Try it either for cold beer or for a large *típica comida corrida* (typical meal of the day) including a variety of dishes: *pollo pibil, panuchos, pollo escabeche,* tortillas, *rellenos,* cold chicken, and avocado—a big meal for a reasonable price.

At **Pórtico del Peregrino,** Calle 57 #501, tel. (99) 28-6163, gourmets should taste the *berenjenas al horno* (slices of eggplant layered with chicken and cheese), a specialty prepared at this low-key, charming cafe next door to Cafetería Pop. Dining out on the intimate, vine-covered patio or inside the a/c dining rooms. The kitchen staff is very cooperative with vegetarians; the chef will happily fix something that fits into your diet plan.

Just outside the tourist office, the **Café Peón Contreras,** Callejón Congreso at Calle 60, offers outdoor tables overlooking the Parque de la Maternidad (more tables inside). It's a lovely setting, but the food wasn't up to par when we visited. Unless you hear otherwise, stick with coffee and a slice of carrot cake while you rest your feet.

Mexican and Yucatecan
On Parque Hidalgo, **Tiano's** presents a full-out Mexican fiesta with marimba musicians playing through the afternoon and evening, and festive banners and piñatas hung above the outdoor tables. Mexican and regional dishes are well prepared and the margaritas are considered first-rate. Unlike the other restaurants around the park, Tiano's serves drinks only with meals, except when business is slow or late at night.

For the purist whose mouth waters for hand-made tortillas, **Los Almendros Restaurant,** at Calles 50 and 59 off Mejorada Square, is one of the few places where you can still watch them being made. Enjoy *poc chuc,* a zesty marinated meat dish. Now open for Sunday buffet, noon-5 p.m. The newest branch restaurant of the Almendros family is **Gran Almendros,** Calle 57 #468 (between 50 and 52), tel. (99) 23-7091. It features the same delicacies in a new "Gran" style.

If you're in the mood for classic Yucatecan cuisine, spend an evening at **Tulipanes,** Calle 83, tel. (99) 24-3313, or **La Ciudad Maya.** Both serve *típico* Yucatecan food and put on exotic shows. At La Ciudad, there are three shows a day: Cuban at 4 p.m., Maya at 8 p.m., and International at 11 p.m. We've been told costumes are great, and the Maya show offers light and sound, fire, and interesting narrated stories of the Maya. The classical *jarana* dancers do five traditional dances including the May pole. Get ready for a colorful hour and forty-five minutes. Touristy? Perhaps. Tulipanes has been importing a great Cuban show nightly during the high

---

MUKBIPOLLO

Día del Muerte ("Day of the Dead") is probably a bigger celebration than Christmas in some parts of Mexico. Everyone hustles and bustles for special foods, gifts, and plants, and every street corner and the markets are overflowing with orange flowers called *cempasuchil,* which are like marigolds with long stems.

The popular dish to serve on this holiday is *mukbipollo,* which in essence is a large tamale baked as a pie. The *masa* (corn dough) is pressed into a large square pan, filled with a saucy mixture of pork or chicken and many spices and other preferred ingredients, then topped with more dough. The whole pan is carefully wrapped in banana leaves then buried in an underground oven (a hole in the ground where the fire has been burning a special wood for some time). It is then covered with more leaves, a piece of corrugated metal, and finally dirt. This creates a steam oven. The dish is cooked for about two hours, then dug up and served for the big dinner of the day. Many other specialties are served as well. One favorite appetizer is sliced sweet oranges mixed with sliced jicama, all gently sprinkled with chile powder.

season, however, they still do a Maya sacrifice around their own cenote.

El Tucho, Calle 60 #482 (near Parque Santa Lucía), tel. (99) 24-2289, looks touristy from the entrance and is totally Yucatecan inside. Order a drink and you'll be served a plate of *botanas* or appetizers; order another drink and you'll get another appetizer, and on and on until the afternoon is gone. Or, order their combination plate of Yucatecan specialties—a good introduction to regional cuisine. Open noon-9 p.m., with live Yucatecan and Cuban shows in the afternoon.

International

Well worth an evening's visit, **Alberto's Continental Patio,** Calle 64 #482, tel. (99) 28-5347, serves excellent Lebanese cooking, plus continental and Yucatecan dishes. For a refreshing supper, try the Lebanese salad: mixed greens covered with a light blend of olive oil, vinegar, a hint of garlic, and a smidgen of fresh chopped mint leaves—perfect for a warm tropical evening. The atmosphere is delightful—old Mexico in your most romantic dreams. The building dates from 1727; picture 1.5-meter-thick walls surrounding the patio, with plants and vines providing dappled shade. Here and there are astounding pieces of ancient stonework and antique furniture. At night it's magical, with shimmering candles reflecting on delicate crystal. Moderate to expensive prices.

Outdoor cafes surround the Parque Cepeda Peraza (also called Parque Hidalgo), one of the best spots in the city for peoplewatching. Italian food lovers try **Giorgio,** for heaping platters of pasta, good pizzas, and sandwiches stuffed with ham, salami, and cheese. It's beside the Gran Hotel.

Hong Kong, Av. Colón at Calle 14, serves outstanding Chinese food.

Vegetarian

Amaro, Calle 59 #507 (between 60 and 62) is a fine vegetarian restaurant. Try one of their unusual drinks, or great Yucatecan specialties. Another veggie place is **Govinda Gopala,** Calle 55 #496 (between 58-60). Closed Sunday.

Breakfast and Sandwiches

Cafetería Pop Restaurant, Calle 57 #501 (between 60 and 62), tel. (99) 28-6163, is still the solid standby for a good, economical continental breakfast (fresh orange juice, toast, and coffee for about US$3.50). Don't let the word "cafeteria" throw you; Pop is a sit-down cafe with a waiter to take your order. It's clean, modern, and always cool. They serve fine sandwiches, great chocolate cake, pies, ice cream, and malts. Reasonably priced simple dinner entrees are served nightly. This is a gathering place for both locals and visitors. Open Mon.-Sat. 7 a.m.-midnight.

Goodies

Pan Montejo is one of the city's best bakeries, with one location by the main plaza at Calle 61 between 60 and 58, and several others throughout the city.

outdoor cafe, Mérida

OZ MALLAN

SHOPPING

Mérida offers great shopping for local arts and crafts. Prices at the **Mercado Municipal** are hard to beat and you'll find a selection of quality crafts from all parts of Yucatán. Even if you're not interested in a shopping spree, take a trip through the busy *mercado* for a wonderful social and cultural experience. You'll see many women from the rural villages of Yucatán state wearing *huipiles* (we-PEE-lays). Calle 60 from the main plaza to Los Aluxes hotel is filled with shops and galleries displaying souvenirs and treasures. At Parque Hidalgo, artisans frequently display their work, including some gorgeous handcrafted amber jewelry.

The Malls

Shopping malls are opening all over Mérida. Most have modern, slick architecture, unique full-service shops, trendy restaurants, movie theaters, and everything else you find in the most upscale malls in the United States. But one of our favorites is unique; **Plaza Internacional,** on Calle 58 at 59, occupies a stone colonial mansion that has been hurled into the 20th century. The plaza has two stories, a central courtyard, shops all around and on the ground floor, and pleasant little cafes. It's a great place to stop and study the wonderful old architecture that never seems to lose its charm.

Check out a fine shopping and dining complex near Casa Montejo on Pasaje Pichete— Calle 61, midway down the same block as the Palacio de Gobierno. The facade of this handsome colonial home has been remodeled and the inside completely transformed into restaurants and shops. You'll also find clean public restrooms (admission) on the second floor.

Mercado Municipal

Euphoric pleasures of color—bundles of brilliant flowers and rainbows of neatly stacked fruits and vegetables—and a steady stream of people make a visit to the bustling *mercado* great entertainment. Here are foods of all description— cooked tamales, raw meat, live chickens—and pungent odors wafting from mounds of unusual-looking herbs, spices, and fruit. The candyman offers delicate sugar flowers, shoes, and Day of the Dead skulls (if it's near the holiday) for just a few pesos. Be sure to stop by the *tortillería*. Upstairs, tiny fast-food windows serve the cheapest meals in Mérida: tacos, tamales, *tortas,* and *licuados*.

Chattering merchants invite you to inspect (and bargain for) their colored woven hammocks, huaraches, and gleaming chunks of clear, amber-colored copal (incense), in use since the days of the Maya. Narrow little "gold stalls" hold thousands of dollars' worth of gold earrings along with charms and bangles of every description stored in small glass cases.

You'll see the common and the uncommon, the ordinary and the extraordinary. The ordinary seems always in demand: straw baskets of every shape, pottery bowls for every use, Panama hats in the final stages of manufacture, *guayaberas* (wide-lapel, pleated cotton shirts), and white *huipiles* with thickly embroidered flow-

mercado municipal

ered borders in every color. Some things you may not want to see, such as *mecech*, jeweled lapel beetles—the crawly kind outlawed in the United States. The market is at Calles 56 and 67.

The nearby **Mercado de Artesanias Garcia Rejon**, on Calle 65 between 60 and 58, is devoted to local arts and crafts. Some of the items are machine made, while others are the real thing. This is a good spot to compare the two and get an idea of prices and quality.

Huipiles

The *huipil* is a lovely type of dress first worn by Indian women at the insistence of hacienda *patrones*. The squared neckline and hem are edged with brightly colored embroidery, and a lace-finished petticoat peeks out at the bottom. The similar, long *terno* is more elaborately decorated than the *huipil* and is worn at fiestas and celebrations.

Most Mérida women are fashion-conscious and vitally into modern clothing. *Huipiles* are worn almost exclusively by women from small rural communities surrounding Mérida who have come to market for the day. The *huipil* is a unique remembrance to take home and a cool *típico* garment to wear in warm weather. Unfortunately, machine embroidery on synthetic fabrics is the norm in most shops. All-cotton, handembroidered garments are available, but you must search them out and the cost is much higher. The thick embroidered designs (usually brilliantly colored flowers) are often symbolic to the woman who is wearing them.

If the price of the handembroidered garments (which can be US$150 and up) discourages you, shop around for good-quality machine work (US$45). Try the *mercado,* the small shops that line the streets around the plazas, and hotel gift shops like the boutique at the **Casa del Balam**, Calle 60 #488. Also try **Agoras Fonapas Crafts Center**, Calle 63 #503 (between 64 and 66). Here many *huipiles* are cotton, but they're seldom handembroidered.

Guayaberas

Yucatecan men wear the *guayabera* in place of a white shirt with tie and jacket. This shirt is perfectly acceptable for any dress occasion you may encounter in Mérida or any other part of Mexico. The most common color is white, but they're also available in pastel tones. They're found in most of the shops, but for a large selection and made-to-order *guayaberas* go to **Jack's**, Calle 59 #507, tel. (99) 23-1592. The **Camisería Canul**, Calle 59 #496-B, is another popular place to buy or order the Yucatecan shirt. Prices range from about US$18 up to US$60 for made-to-order. Visitors on tour buses are brought to these shops so they're apt to be crowded, Both have large selections and a great variety of sizes.

Panama Hats

If you're in the market for a hat, look for a local *jipi* shop and pick up a Panama hat. They're made in several towns in the states of Yucatán and Campeche, and the finest are made of the *jipi-japa* fiber; ask for *finos* for the most supple. They can be folded and stuffed in a pocket and then will pop back into shape when needed. But buyer beware, many cheaper "palms" are used as well and these will not take that kind of treatment. Browse around **La Casa de los Jipis**, Calle 56 #526, where you'll see the hat in many qualities. Ask questions; they'll educate you on the subject of Panama hats. Not cheap here, the *finos* may cost US$65, but if you want classic design and the best quality that should last forever, it's worth it. For a simple sun hat, try the street vendors seen near every plaza and at the entrances of many hotels—bargain!

Hammocks

Yucatán is noted for producing the best hammocks in Mexico. Street vendors try to induce tourists to buy them, which is okay as long as the buyer knows what to look for. Many shops sell them, including **La Casa de los Jipis**, Calle 56 #526 (near Calle 65). Don't hesitate to ask the vendor to stretch out the entire hammock while you inspect it carefully. To judge whether a hammock will be long enough for you, hold one end of the body of the hammock to the top of your head and let it drop. The other end of the body should be touching the floor for you to be comfortable (a little extra on the floor is even better). Ask what it's made of, and don't be afraid to bargain.

Arts and Crafts

On Calle 63 between 66 and 64, the **Fonart** center for arts and crafts (look for the sign reading "Casa de Artesanías") sells silver, gold, leather, ceramics, onyx, and typical clothing from the 31 states of Mexico. The selection of folk art in this restored monastery is excellent, and the back courtyard has been turned into a gallery featuring rotating art and folk art exhibits.

YUCATÁN HAMMOCKS

Yucatán hammocks have the reputation of being the best in the world. Many local people sleep in them and love it. *Hamacas* are cool and easy to store, make wonderful cribs that babies cannot fall from, and come in a variety of sizes.

It's important to know the size you want when shopping. The Yucatecans make a *matrimonial* one that is supposed to be big enough for two people; for even more comfort, get the *familia*—weavers say the whole family fits. A good hammock stretches out to approximately five meters long (one-third of which is the woven section) and three to five meters wide. Check the end strings, called *brazos;* there should be at least 100-150 triple loops for a *matrimonial.*

A variety of materials is used: synthetics, henequen, cotton, and linen. It's a toss-up whether the best is pure cotton or linen. The finer the thread the more comfortable; the tighter the weave the more resilient. Experts say it takes eight km of thread for a *matrimonial.*

OZ MALLAN

Occasionally you'll see good reproductions of Maya images that were made in Ticul under the supervision of the late artist Wilbert González. González used Maya techniques to create his pottery. His work is so extraordinary and authentic that it fooled police, who accused him of stealing original art. He sat in jail for three months while the "expert archaeologists" studied the pieces and found them to be original Maya art. Only when his friend Victor Manzanilla Schaffer (ex-governor of the state of Yucatán) returned from an extended trip to Japan was the matter clarified and González released. He shrugged the incident off with a wry smile and the comment, "That's my Mexico." After that incident he began inserting a hidden code or a dime in each piece to protect himself. Note the striking wall of Maya reproductions designed by González in the Casa de Artesanías.

Each Sunday, 10 a.m.-3 p.m., a **Bazaar of Arts and Crafts** is held in Centenario Park and Zoo. See artists and their paintings, sculpture, and crafts, and—to add a little zing—watch chess instructors go knight to rook with students. Also on Sunday, 10 a.m.-2 p.m., an **Antique and Crafts Bazaar** is held at Santa Lucía Park. Sellers bring worn books, antique bric-a-brac, old stamps, furniture, typical clothing, and lovely artwork—good browsing! A large handicraft market at the corner of Calles 65 and 62 usually has a good selection of crafts.

Maya Feather and Shell Art: The Maya created lovely art in a variety of forms. Using shells and feathers was considered a lost art for years, but this form is again surfacing in bazaars and tourist shops. The ancients used brilliantly colored feathers to weave elegant garments from the richly hued birds of the Yucatán Peninsula, especially the blue-greens of the now-seldom-seen quetzal. Some fine examples of this art can be seen at the Anthropological Museum in Mexico City and at Mérida's Museum of Popular Art.

Antique Shops

A few antique shops are scattered throughout Mérida. The "junk shops" are the most intriguing! At Manolo Rivero's **Ridecor,** Calle 60 #456, the dusty shelves are full of rare old books (if you can read Spanish, you're in luck), chipped 17th- and 18th-century religious art (a large collection), empty rococo frames, odd pieces of bric-a-brac, and delicate glass—all complete with resident cobwebs. Rivero runs an art gallery next door.

Art Galleries

The art buff interested in the world of modern art should visit **Galería Manolo Rivero,** Calle 60 #456, which shows works of such outstanding avant-garde artists as Jos, or Alberto Lenero, Roberto Turnbull, and the controversial Gustavo Monroy. **Galeria Casa Colón,** Av. Colón #507, offers contemporary art by Latin American artists.

Books, Magazines, and Newspapers

As usual, the large hotel gift shops carry a good supply of English-language books, including fiction, nonfiction, and pictorial, about the area. American magazines and often the *News,* a Mexico City-published English-language newspaper, are available. The Rocketeria on the corner of the Parque Hidalgo has a good selection of reading material, tapes, and CDs in English.

EVENTS AND ENTERTAINMENT

Music

Music is heard all over Mérida. Informal free concerts and other entertainment are regularly presented for Mérida's residents and visitors at parks and plazas throughout the city. Families and friends gather under the stars in the warm tropical night for a variety of music each evening year-round, beginning at 9 p.m. And on Sunday you'll likely have your choice of marimba, classical, or folkloric concerts. See the accompanying weekly events schedule.

This is casual entertainment, so don't hesitate to speak to your benchmate—very often you'll make friends with a great Meridano who will take delight in showing off the city, or will at least give you the opportunity to ask questions or practice Spanish.

Teatro Peón Contreras

This theater, at Calles 60 and 57, was built in 1908 during Mérida's rich period and is patterned after a European design. The lovely old building continues to host concerts and other entertainment, but it's worth visiting just to see the classic interior. During the busiest seasons (winter and spring), colorful folkloric dances are presented

---

MÉRIDA'S WEEKLY CULTURAL EVENTS

SUNDAY

Santa Lucia Square: popular art and antiques bazaar; 11 a.m., live music

Park of the Mother: "Children in Culture" (arts and crafts)

Cepeda Peraza Square (also known as Hidalgo Square): 11:30 a.m., live marimba music

Plaza Independencia: handicraft bazaar; 11 a.m., concert at Hall of History in the Governor's Palace, 2nd floor; 1 p.m., Mestizo Wedding (folkoric dance)

Centenario Park: 10 a.m., Children's Festival; zoo is open all day

MONDAY

Palacio Municipal: 9 p.m., Yucatecan Regional Dance

TUESDAY

Santiago Square: 9 p.m., live band music and dancing

Teatro Peon Contreras 9 p.m., University Folkloric Ballet

THURSDAY

Santa Lucia Square: 9 p.m., Yucatecan Serenade (folkloric music and dance)

FRIDAY

University of Yucatán (Central Patio): 9 p.m., University Serenade

---

every Tuesday night. For a list of attractions at the theater, call (99) 24-9290 or 24-9389. The tourist information center is in one corner of the theater building.

For Children

Sunday is family day in Mexico, and Mérida is no exception. The tree-shaded parks are popular for picnicking, playing ball, and buying giant colorful balloons and other fanciful goods sold by vendors. Children's movies are offered from 8 a.m. throughout the day at **Pinocchio's Movie House,** just across from El Centenario Park. On Sunday, festivals are held at **El Centenario Park Zoo** and **La Ceiba's Park** at 11 a.m., and at **Mul-**

say's Park at 6 p.m. Here children (and parents) are entertained by magicians, clowns, puppets, and theater groups. Organized games are open to even the smallest child and offer prizes to winning participants. The Mérida zoo is outstanding and a popular stop for both children and adults. Also on Sunday at the **Parque a la Maternidad**, children take part in drawing classes.

Bars, Discos, and Live Music
Choices for spirited disco nightlife are the **Holiday Inn** disco, or Mérida's biggest, **Bim-Bom-Bao Disco,** 20 minutes north of downtown by car or taxi (the taxi drivers know where it is). **Freeday Restaurant and Video Bar,** formerly Amarantus, has good food and is upbeat, while **Tequila Rock** is rowdier—both are in the same building at Paseo de Montejo 250. **Xtabay** nightclub, next door to El Tucho restaurant, opens when the restaurant closes, and features live salsa music.

INFORMATION AND SERVICES

Tours and Travel Agencies
Taking a guided city tour is a good way to get the lay of the land when you first arrive in Mérida. **Discover Mérida** company, tel. (99) 27-6119, offers two-hour city tours in open-air buses. Cost is about US$30 and includes lunch, sometimes at an outlying hacienda. Buses depart from Parque Santa Lucía daily at 10 a.m. and 4 p.m.

Yucatán Trails, Calle 62 #482 (between 57 and 59 in the heart of town), tel. (99) 28-2582 or

---

MÉRIDA EMERGENCY NUMBERS

U.S. Consulate:	(99) 25-5011
Fire Department:	(99) 24-9242
Immigration:	(99) 28-5823
Green Angels:	(99) 83-1184
Police:	(99) 25-2555
State Police:	(99) 46-1203
State Judicial Police:	(99) 28-2553
Red Cross:	(99) 28-5391 or
	29-7998
Tourism Department:	(99) 28-6547
Tourism Police:	(99) 25-2555

28-5913, fax (99) 24-4919, is a reliable travel agency where English is spoken. The helpful staff can make or change reservations for airlines, hotels, or group tours. A daily city tour (pickup at your hotel) is available for about US$30 pp; other tours are also available. Ask for company president Denis Lafoy (from Canada) for more complete information and updated schedules. Denis also heads up the city's once-a-month get together of resident expats. Give him a call if you're getting homesick and would like to get together.

Turismo Aviomar, Calle 58 #500-C, tel. (99) 20-0444, fax (99) 25-5064, is another dependable travel agency offering good trips to all the Maya ruins around the Peninsula.

Mayaland Tours, Av. Colón #502, tel. (99) 25-2246, fax (99) 25-7022, U.S. tel. (800) 235-4079 (also in the Casa del Balam hotel, tel. (99) 24-6290), specializes in travel to the entire Peninsula. Now associated with Grey Line, the company offers good package deals and a fleet of modern, a/c buses, including a few double-deckers. Among the tours offered: an eight-hour tour to Chichén Itzá, including transportation, admission to the ruins, and lunch, for US$43; a similar tour to Uxmal and Kabah for US$40; a tour to Uxmal's ruins and the sound and light show for US$43; and a tour to Dzibilchaltun and Progreso. Travelers interested in visiting the Maya ruins at Chichén Itzá and Uxmal should ask about a super package deal that includes a room at the Hotel Mayaland at Chichén Itzá or the Hotel Hacienda Uxmal (minimum one-night stay) and a Volkswagen beetle with unlimited mileage; all you have to pay is the insurance. Your car will be delivered to any hotel in Cancún or Mérida, to the Mérida International Airport, or to any Mayaland Resort.

Mayaland has also started a transfer shuttle service between Uxmal, Mérida, and Chichén Itzá. The shuttle departs from the Hacienda Uxmal at about 7:30 a.m., arrives in Mérida and departs for Chichén at about 9 a.m., then returns to Mérida at about 3:30 p.m., and departs for Uxmal at 5 p.m. Cost is about US$28 for the Uxmal-Mérida segment and about US$30 for the Mérida-Chichén leg. They also have a VIP lounge at the Mérida airport, where clients are offered refreshments and assistance with their travel itineraries.

Ecoturismo Yucatán conducts some wonderful ecological tours of Southern Mexico, Belize, and Guatemala, along with tours emphasizing culture, natural history, and birdwatching. Their trip to Celestún is great. They pick you up at your hotel, drive through the countryside, then board a boat to cruise on the estuaries and observe the flamingos and many other beautiful birds. The boat winds into the mangroves where you discover a freshwater cenote. All the guides know their birds, and it's obvious they're into conservation. For information contact Roberta and Alfonso Escobedo at Calle 3 #235 (32-A to 34), Col. Pensiones, tel. (99) 25-2187, fax (99) 25-9047.

Tourist Information Centers
Several tourist information centers are found in Mérida. One is at the Teatro Peón Contreras on Calle 60, tel. (99) 24-9290 or 24-9389, where you'll usually find someone who speaks English. It's open daily 8 a.m.-8 p.m. Another office is at the Palacio Gobierno (facing the north side of the main plaza). Both offices gives out information, maps, and tourist literature.

Money
Banks are everywhere you look in Mérida; you'll find five of them on Calle 65 alone. Hours are Mon.-Fri. 9 a.m.-1:30 p.m. Get there early during the busy seasons as there's usually a line to exchange money. Changing traveler's checks at a bank is usually more advantageous than at a hotel. Often shops will give an even better exchange than the bank (with a purchase); usually a sign is posted—if not, ask. *Casas de cambios* are a good choice when the banks are closed; many are scattered about town.

CONSULATES IN MÉRIDA

Belgium	(99) 81-1099
Belize	(99) 28-6152
Cuba	(99) 44-4216
England	(99) 28-6152
France	(99) 25-2886
Germany	(99) 81-2976
Switzerland	(99) 27-2905
USA	(99) 25-5011

Communications
The **post office** is at Calles 65 and 56, near the *mercado*. Business hours are Mon.-Sat. 9 a.m.-7 p.m. If you need to send a fax, ask at the post office or your hotel. The cost of a fax can be exorbitant, as much as US$5 per page.

Ladatel Direct Dial USA telephone booths are everywhere in the plazas, parks, and newer shopping malls; calling from one of these booths is cheaper than at your hotel, where the service charge could be as high as 100%.

Consulates
In case of lost passports, legal problems, or emergencies, get in touch with your consulate. The **U.S. Consulate** is at Paseo de Montejo, Av. Colón 453, tel. (99) 25-5011 or 25-5009. Office hours are 8:30 a.m.-5:30 p.m.; for emergencies after working hours, call (99) 25-5039. There's also a U.S. consular agency in Cancún, open 10 a.m.-2 p.m. The **British Consulate** (which also handles Belize business) is at Calle 58 #450, tel. (99) 28-6152. The Canadian Consulate no longer has a Mérida office; for emergencies call Mexico City, tel. (99) 254-3288 (calls will be answered 9 a.m.-5 p.m.; an answering machine accepts after-hours messages and your call will be returned).

Language School
The **Centro Idiomas del Sureste** is a great place to perfect your Spanish while living with a local family. The school is a favorite with Spanish teachers from the U.S., archaeologists, and Maya scholars, who get intensive training in the language with classes geared to their area of interest. Classes are held at two locations: one in the downtown historical district and another in a residential area north of downtown. For further information, contact Directora Chloe Conaway de Pacheco, Calle 14 #106 y Calle 25, Col. Mexico, Mérida, Yucatán 97000, Mexico, tel. (99) 26-1155, fax (99) 26-9020.

GETTING THERE

By Air
Planes fly into **Mérida International Airport** from most cities in Mexico and from a few outside the country. Airlines serving Mérida are listed

below; check with the airlines or a travel agent for prices and schedules. Remember, there is a US$12 departure tax when you fly out of Mexico.

Continental Airlines, U.S. tel. (800) 525-0280, provides good service to Cancún, and Cozumel. **Mexicana Airlines,** Calle 58 #500, tel. (99) 24-6676 or 24-6633, U.S. tel. (800) 531-7921, offers direct flights to Mexico City and Miami and connecting flights to Cancún, Oaxaca, Monterrey, Chetumal, Cozumel, Tijuana, Guadalajara, Puerto Vallarta, Houston, New York, Miami, San Francisco, and Los Angeles. **Aerómexico,** tel. (99) 24-9455 or 27-9000, U.S. tel. (800) 237-6639, offers direct service to Miami and Mexico City, and connecting flights to other cities in Mexico. **Aviacsa,** tel. (99) 26-9173 or 46-1344, flies from Mérida to Cancún, Monterrey, Ciudad Juárez, Villahermosa, Tuxtla Gutiérrez, Oaxaca, and Mexico City. **Aviateca,** tel. (99) 25-8059, flies to many cities in Guatemala. **Aerocaribe,** tel. (99) 28-6786, and **Taesa,** tel.(99) 23-6553 or 46-1826, fly from Mérida to Cozumel.

To and From the Airport: The airport service road is on Av. de Itzes (Hwy. 180), seven km southwest of town. A cafe, post office, long-distance phone, moneychanger, car rental counters, and several gift shops are inside. The cafe and food stands usually don't open until 8 or 9 a.m.; you may want to grab something to eat at your hotel if you have an early flight out. You'll also find a hotel reservation desk; most of these folks don't speak much English, and if you don't speak much Spanish, everyone will have to be a little patient. If you have already chosen a few hotels from this book, they can check for you to see if there's room at the inn.

Taxis charge about US$12-15 *to* the airport, but *from* the airport you can get a *colectivo* cab to your downtown hotel for about US$8; buy your

ticket at a counter in front of the air terminal. Hang onto your ticket until all packages, baggage, purses, and carry-ons are accounted for at your destination. The cabbies in Yucatán have had a great reputation for honesty, but lately a few Mexico City-types have been inching into Mérida; there's no point in pushing your luck.

For bus transportation from the airport into the downtown area, look for bus #79. Figure on the trip taking 30 minutes. The fare is less than US$0.50. This is an economical way to and from the airport, but the bus can be crowded; if you are carrying more luggage than you can put in your lap, you might consider a cab.

By Train
Mérida's train station is on Calle 55 between Calles 48 and 50, eight blocks northeast of the central plaza. Look for the sign that says "Ferrocarriles Unidos del Sureste." At the station you'll find an information booth, tel. (99) 27-7701 or 27-7501; it's open daily 7 a.m.-10 p.m. and also sells bus tickets. Trains departing from Mérida have no dining cars; bring a lunch or plan on buying from the food vendors at each stop. To walk downtown from the train station, turn west (right) from the main entrance along Calle 55 and go five blocks to Calle 60; turn south (left) and it's three blocks to the plaza.

By Bus
The second-class bus terminal (Camionera Central) is on Calle 69 between 68 and 70, tel. (99) 21-9150. The new first-class terminal is behind it on Calle 70. The **Progreso Bus Station,** on Calle 62 between Calles 65 and 67, has departures for Progreso every half-hour 5 a.m.-7 p.m., as well as three buses to Dzibilchaltún. Bus transport on the Peninsula is excellent, with routes going to all parts of Mexico. Several lines now offer deluxe service, a great improvement and well worth the extra pesos for long trips.

Caribe Express offers deluxe service on a/c buses including movies shown en route. Nine express buses leave to Cancún daily for about US$12; two departures daily to Playa del Carmen and Tulum for US$12; and five to Chetumal for US$15.

Autotransportes Peninsulares offers deluxe service to Campeche, Ciudad Carmen, Escárcega, Villahermosa, and Cancún, and first-class service to Ticul and Oxkutzcab twice daily. Another fine service is with **Clase Elite** in the new terminal on Calle 65; tickets also for sale at Calle 69. **ADO** line has deluxe and first-class service throughout Mexico. ADO also has 12 daily departures to Villahermosa, six to Campeche, two to Chetumal via Ticul, and two first-class buses (US$20) and one second-class bus (US$18) daily to Palenque. **Expreso de Oriente** has its own a/c waiting room next to the main terminal and offers deluxe service to Cancún, Valladolid, and Playa del Carmen. You can reserve your tickets in advance by calling (99) 26-0031 or 26-5562.

Autotransportes del Sureste has the best coverage for out-of-the-way destinations, with daily service to the Guatemalan border, Palenque, and San Cristóbal de las Casas at 6 p.m. It's also the best line for reaching Uxmal, with departures from Mérida at 6 a.m., 9 a.m., noon, and 3 p.m.; the last bus departs Uxmal on the return trip at 7:30 p.m.

By Car

Good highways approach Mérida from all directions. Be prepared for one-way streets and avoid arriving on Sunday—a large area in the center of town is closed to vehicles. If you don't know the city, it can be a real headache to drive to your hotel, since many are downtown. If you should land in town on Sunday, flag down a cabbie and pay him to lead you to your hotel. He'll know how to get around the detours—worth the few pesos.

A *periférico* traffic loop surrounds the city, making it possible to bypass the congested downtown streets if you're headed from Chichén Itzá to Uxmal, for example. Unfortunately, the *periférico* is not well marked, and it takes a few attempts before you can figure it out.

The eight-lane toll highway (180D) from Mérida to Cancún cuts the driving time by 30-60 minutes. The highway, called an *autopista,* begins about 16 km (10 miles) east of Mérida at Kantunil; from Mérida take Hwy. 180 toward Valladolid. Tolls to Chichén are about US$6, to Cancún about US$20. The toll road to Cancún is nearly empty since most bus and trucking companies find the tolls prohibitive. The road is in great condition, with rest stops, gas stations, and clearly marked exits to major sights.

GETTING AROUND

Mérida is laid out in a neat grid pattern of one-way numbered streets. The even-numbered streets run north and south, the odd east and west. The central plaza is the center of town and you can easily walk to most downtown attractions, shops, and marketplaces. Buses provide frequent service in and around the city and outlying areas. Bus stops are at almost every corner along the main streets and buses go to any destination in the city. During the day, it's never more than 10 minutes between buses; they run less frequently at night. Unfortunately, no public buses run directly from the main plaza and nearby hotels to the bus station, and some taxi drivers in Mérida are beginning to treat tourists with the same cheating style as in some of the larger cities, like Mexico City.

On Foot

The best way to see Mérida is on foot. Granted, some of the sidewalks are narrow, and the traffic can be thick, but the city is cozy to wander. Look up for street names, which are usually found at the intersection on the building corners, high up.

Car Parts

If you should have a problem with your car while in Mérida and need parts, head to Lubcke Repuestos del Golfo y Caribe, Calle 58 #471, tel. (99) 24-1545 or 23-0485. Ask for Jaime (pronounced "HI-mee") Lubcke; he speaks English and is a friendly, helpful guy. Using his fax machine, he can get parts quickly (for Mexico).

Car Rentals

Cars are available from several agencies in the airport terminal building, downtown Mérida, and most of the larger hotels. Advance reservations are advised during the busy winter months.

Avis has offices: one mile from the airport, tel. (99) 84-2020; at the three major hotels (Hyatt, Fiesta Americana, Holiday Inn); and close to the main Plaza, tel. (99) 28-0045. Their leader is the VW convertible for US$29 per day. Rates flex with supply and demand. **Budget** is also at the airport, tel. (99) 46-1308, and on Calle 60 at 57, tel. (99) 28-1750. **Dollar** is at the airport, tel. (99) 46-1323, and at the Mission Park Inn, tel. (99) 23-9500. **Hertz** is at the airport, tel. (99) 84-0028.

Check with **Mayaland Resorts** if you intend to make overnight visits to Uxmal and Chichén Itzá. With a three-night minimum in summer and a five-night minimum in winter, you can get *free* use of a VW sedan with unlimited mileage, and they'll deliver to your hotel in Cancún, to Mérida International Airport, or to any Mayaland Resort. Contact Mayaland Resorts in Mérida, tel. (99) 25-2122 or 25-2133; in Cancún, tel. (98) 87-5411 or 87-2450; or from the U.S., tel. (800) 235-4079.

Taxis

Taxis are generally found at taxi stands in most neighborhoods and there's almost always a queue at any one of the parks. If it's late, any hotel, cafe, or disco will call one for you. Some taxis are metered and some are'nt, so establish your fare in advance. Make sure you understand the amount before you get in, even if you have to hold your fingers up. The average fare around town is about US$3-5.

Calesas

At one time, a *calesa* (horse and buggy) was the only means of getting around the city; today it's a pleasant alternative. From near the plaza, *calesas* are a relaxing, slow way to see aristocratic old houses with carved facades, marble entries, stone gargoyles, etched glass, and wrought-iron fences, some with their elegance slipping, others well maintained over several generations in this European-flavored residential district.

Sunday is the best day to tour by *calesa.* The rest of the time, the main streets are so busy and noisy that it's rather hectic. As with everything else, you should bargain with the driver, but expect to pay about US$15 per hour for a tour of Mérida.

SURROUNDING MÉRIDA

CELESTÚN

On the northwest shoulder of the Peninsula, a narrow finger of land separates the estuaries of Río Esperanza from the Gulf of Mexico. At the tip of the one-kilometer strip is the small fishing village of Celestún (pop. 17,000). The town's biggest attraction is Celestún Biosphere Reserve, which offers birdwatching extraordinaire. Other than birds, estuaries, and sea, Celestún offers little entertainment.

The plain central plaza, flanked by a market and a simple pink stucco church, is a gathering place for townspeople, but everything moves in slow motion. The clean, white beach on the north edge of town meanders for miles—a beautiful place for a morning walk. In the afternoon, the

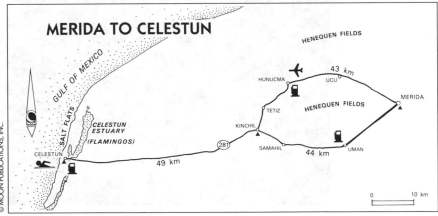

MERIDA TO CELESTUN

choppy water gets silty with the rising wind. A few small cafes spill out onto the sand; parents sit at white tin tables, enjoy fried fish and beer, and watch their children play on the beach close by. Except during July and August, you and the fishermen have the beach to yourselves. For the artist and photographer, the harbor, with its hundreds of boats, fishermen, curious traps, and mended nets stretched out to dry, provides endless and colorful subjects. Photographers: Protect your lenses from sand blowing on this coast.

Celestún Biosphere Reserve

The Mexican government declared the Celestún estuary a national park and ecological reserve in 1979, setting aside some 146,000 acres in the states of Yucatán and Campeche. The area has since been upgraded to a biosphere reserve and is monitored by several ecological groups, including Pronatura.

This is one of the few breeding areas in the northern hemisphere for the American flamingo, and hundreds of other birds and waterfowl breed in the wetlands and mangrove forests. Some 250 of the 509 identified bird species in the Yucatán Peninsula can be spied here. It's not unusual to see a blue heron or an anhinga perched on a tree stump with wings stretched to dry in the sun.

The area includes a series of intriguing habitats: mangrove forests, coastal dune vegetation, savannas, low deciduous forest, and hummocks (small islands of mangroves in the wetlands), and of course seashore and the Celestún estuaries. According to Pronatura specialist Joann Andrews and trained expert David Bacab, "the Yucatán Peninsula's mangrove forests are more extensive than those found in Florida and much less explored."

Programs have been set up in the local schools to educate Celestún's residents about the importance of preserving the estuary's fragile ecology. Similar educational programs address the importance of the sea turtles that lay their eggs on the beaches in May and June.

Taking a tour with a knowledgeable guide is a must. A variety of trips are available, and the true nature lover hangs around Celestún for a couple of days and takes them all in. There's much to do in the area: bicycle tours, kayak tours, crocodile tours, shelling tours, a flamingo boat ride (seasonal), and jungle tours, even at night. Most snorkelers never think of swimming in the Gulf of Mexico, but there are some good snorkeling and scuba diving spots as well.

Birdwatching

Anyone who takes pleasure in studying birds will want to stop and stay a few days here. In winter, when birds are migrating from the cold climates of the north, many pause at Celestún on their way to South America. Others make their home here until nature directs them back north. One of the most startling (in hue) of the many winged inhabitants here is the American flamingo, whose color ranges from pale coral to flame

Yucatán flamingos

OZ MALLAN

Celestún beach cafe

red with black wing tips. It is an amazing color-high to see thousands of birds; some congregating in great flocks on the shore, others flying in formation across the blue sky. When a group of flamingos is seen standing on a beach, the vibrant colors melting together provide a wonderful stroke to the senses.

The best time for birdwatching is in the early morning before the day warms up. Protect yourself from the sun—wear a hat and use sunscreen if you plan on spending a few hours in a boat on the estuary. Fishing boats along the Río Esperanza can be hired to go into estuaries to see the birds. One kilometer before you reach town, launches are available for hire at the dock under the bridge that spans the river. The old vessels are rickety, and some make so much noise they scare off the birds. Today there are many newer boats, most with sun covers, and most boatman are willing to stop frequently for pictures (if that's your wish). The captain will turn off the motor and quietly pole the boat as close as possible without scaring off the flock. Expect to pay approximately US$30-50 per boatload of about four-six persons.

Tour Guides

Don't hesitate to call one of these folks to get an in-depth look at the beauties of Celestún. These people know what they're talking about. In Mérida, call **Ecoturismo Yucatán,** Calle 3 #235 (32A-34), Col. Pensiones, tel. (99) 25-2187, fax (99) 25-9047. Alphonso carries his clients in good vans and boats and hires only the most knowledgeable guides. In Celestún, contact local-boy-made-good David Bacab's **Celestun Expeditions,** tel./fax (99) 16-2049. David has myriad suggestions and tours that highlight the rich nature of Celestún. He also leads tours for Ecoturismo Yucatán. Both companies have guides fluent in both English and Spanish; and they all know their birds.

Everyone associated with the flamingos is very protective. They will not take you to the breeding grounds during brooding season for fear the pink birds will be frightened and kick their lone egg out of the mud nest. Check with Ecoturismo for exact dates of restrictions.

Accommodations

The jet set has yet to discover Celestún. Living is simple here, which, keeps most of the hotels in the budget category. The local police do not object to people sleeping on the beach, but a combination of wind and sand causes gritty discomfort. Those driving vans and campers are welcome to park on the beach, but pick a spot close to the road where the sand isn't so soft that you get stuck.

Budget: Hotel María del Carmen is the nicest place in town; each of the nine rooms has good window screens, two double beds, and private bathroom. The hotel is on Calle 12 parallel to the beach, tel. (99) 28-0419 or 28-0152. To get there, look for the sign for Restaurant Vista del Mar.

In the heart of downtown Celestún, on the seafront, **Hotel San Julio,** Calle 12 #92, tel. (99) 1-8589, is constantly blown by the wind, but maintains clean, simple accommodations with private bathrooms. You'll have easy access to the beach through the hotel patio.

Another smaller hotel right on the beach is **Hotel Gutiérrez,** Calle 12 #22, tel. (99) 28-0419 or 28-6978. Each of its 18 spartan yet comfortable rooms has two double beds, a private bathroom, and tile floor. The three-storied stucco hotel is cooled by ceiling fans and sea breezes, especially the front rooms. The rooms are clean (if you don't count the constant, inevitable, blowing sand). Purified water and cold soda are sold in the lobby. On the same street (which faces the beach) is the simple, reasonably priced **Posada Martín,** Calle 12 #76.

Inexpensive: The 12-room **Hotel Aguilar,** on Calle 12, is also acceptable.

Expensive: A few km down the road, a fine new hotel has opened that was designed to respect the ecology of the area. The **Hotel Eco Paraíso Xixim** (pronounced "shee-sheem") is right on the beach, tel. (99) 16-2100, fax (99) 16-2111. The hotel was designed with nature in mind, from the water usage to the bungalows set up to take advantage of every breeze. The *palapa* bungalows right on the beach are really lovely junior suites; each has a sitting area, comfy beds, and a hammock-hung patio right outside the door. The colors are mellow, and a short walk brings you to a modern pool, an immense shade *palapa*, a good dining room, and a tall lookout platform that gives views of the sea and coast for miles. No question, it's a long way from city zing. But this is a perfect hub for visiting the Maya sites and a great place to commune with nature in great comfort, enjoying the sun, white sand, and aqua sea.

Food

A few small seafood cafes edge the beach. **Playarita** and **Restaurant Celestún** are the old standbys and both serve good seafood. **Restaurant Vista del Mar** at the Hotel María del Carmen is a good choice for any meal. Try a generous fresh shrimp cocktail for about US$3 or a succulent ceviche that ranks with that of any restaurant in the Yucatán. This is fish country; the closer you get to Campeche, the bigger the shrimp!

You can get great crab claws here. Meet the incoming fishermen if you want to buy the freshest. The market is active with a good supply of fresh fruit and vegetables; it opens early and closes at 1 p.m.. The *panadería* makes good bread, and the *tortillería* opens by seven in the morning.

Services

When visiting any small town on the Peninsula, it's best to arrive with enough cash in pesos to cover your visit. Hotel Gutiérrez has a public phone in the lobby and will place calls for a charge. The town has a gas station. If you need a policeman, your best chance is to try the Palacio Municipal on Calle 7.

Getting There

Celestún is west of Mérida on the Gulf of Mexico. From Mérida, buses go direct to Celestún, departing from a terminal at Calle 71 #585 (between 64 and 66), tel. (99) 24-8480. The one-way trip takes about 90 minutes. From Mérida by car, follow the signs out of town marked Sisal-Hunucma. At Hunucma go to Kinchil and pick up Hwy. 281 to Celestún. **Note:** There is no coastal road from Sisal to Celestún, though some old maps show one.

DZIBILCHALTÚN

Traveling north from Mérida, a straight shot on Hwy. 261 leads to Progreso and the Gulf of Mexico. On the way, you might want to pull off the road and take a look around Dzibilchaltún ("dzee-beel-chawl-TOON"), a very old Maya site. The turn-off road to the site is about 21 km from Mérida.

Dzibilchatún's Temple of the Seven Dolls

To the layperson, Dzibilchaltún doesn't offer the visual displays of the Peninsula's more fully reconstructed sites. To the archaeologist, however, the site represents a valuable piece of history; it's the oldest continuously used Maya ceremonial and administrative center on the Peninsula. The map of the site shows close to 8,400 fallen structures. The **Temple of the Seven Dolls** and the cenote are long time favorites. Now there is a fine new museum. The site is open daily 8 a.m.-5 p.m.; admission is less than US$3. Worth a stop.

PROGRESO

On the Gulf of Mexico, Progreso (pop. 45,000) is Mérida's closest access to the sea—an easy 33-km drive from the state capital on a wide highway. Meridanos flock here in summer to escape the intense heat and sticky humidity.

The town was founded in 1856. During the halcyon days of the henequen industry, ships were a regular part of the scene along the calm Progreso waterfront and its then-amazing two-kilometer-long wharf. Expansive mansions built by henequen entrepreneurs still line the water's edge just east of town; now they're vacation homes for Mérida's well-to-do. Many are used for rentals—an adaptation to the town's burgeoning new tourism industry.

With Yucalpetén taking over as the more important fishing port, Progreso leads a subdued existence most of the year. However, during the two weeks of Easter holiday and in July and August, most of Mérida arrives at this beach. The whole town comes to life; all the restaurants are open, usually-quiet shops hustle, the beaches are filled with families enjoying the surf and sun.

The gracious walkway along the shore, called the *malecón,* is taking on a new look. A tourist center in the middle of town was built to accommodate the many more visitors anticipated when cruise ships are able to dock offshore (who knows when or even *if* this is coming to pass).

What *has* come to pass is an increasing influx of American, Canadian, and European visitors who spend their winters enjoying Progreso's warm seaside clime. Many fine, fully furnished condos have sprung up north of town; anyone interested in a longer-than-usual stay can get more information from **Mar-Mex de Yucatán,** Calle #248, Progreso, Yuc. 97320, Mexico, tel./fax (993) 5-3257.

El Faro
Built 1885-91 on the site of an earlier lighthouse, today's 40-meter-high El Faro was originally lit with kerosene. It was converted to electricity in 1923; a 1,000-watt lightbulb and a series of amazing reflectors create all the light seen far out to sea. A backup generator ensures that there's always light to lead the *marineros* through the shallow Gulf waters and into Progreso. Even Hurricane Gilbert couldn't knock this old-timer down! Visitors: Tip the keeper after a visit.

On the same property, pay a visit to the **Casa Cultural,** a small museum with a few artifacts and often a good local, art exhibit. Open to the public 8 a.m.-4 p.m.

The Wharf
At the turn of the 20th century, Progreso's two-kilometer-long wharf was the longest stone wharf in the world. With a recently completed addition, it may still be the longest in the world. The new extension and small island (seven km total) was created to enable luxury cruise ships to pull into Progreso for short visits. The wharf is in place, but the water is still too shallow for the big cruise ships. Even the proposed new ferry from Florida—promised for so long—looks like a zilch.

The bay is shallow at Progreso because it sits (as does most of the Yucatán Peninsula) on a limestone shelf that gradually drops off into the Gulf. (Geographers conjecture that at one time Yucatán, Cuba, and Florida were all one long extension of land.) The end of the original wharf sat in only six meters of water.

For 100 years Progreso's wharf was the scene of heavy international shipping—the days when the henequen industry was in its prime. Today, only a small percentage of henequen products is shipped. In addition, the wharf has lost some of its impact since the 1968 construction of the protected Yucalpetén harbor, six km west of Progreso. However, some ships still tie up at the Progreso wharf to pick up honey, cement, sisal products, fish, salt, and steel—Mexican products going to foreign ports. The wharf is open to the public, either by foot or in a vehicle (as long as you don't try to park).

Pier fishermen will find lots of company with abundant local advice and fish stories—in Spanish. They say early in the morning or late in the afternoon you only have to throw out your hook to catch a string of fish!

Beaches

Travelers just returning from the Caribbean side of the Peninsula will find the Gulf coast very different. The water doesn't have the crystalline clarity and flamboyant shades of blue that make the Quintana Roo coast famous. But the beach at Progreso is nothing to apologize for; it's open and broad with clean sand. Except for the stormy season (June-Oct.), the warm water is calm. It's possible to walk a kilometer from shore into the sea and still have dry ears. A paved road and inviting palm-lined promenade wind along the breezy *malecón* waterfront. The beach is dotted with *palapa* sun shelters and a few cafes.

For the energetic it's an invigorating seven km walk east along the shoreline from the wharf to Chicxulub. Don't expect fascinating flotsam and jetsam, but you'll see shells aplenty—plus gangs of people in midsummer. In winter, the beach is practically deserted except on weekends.

Accommodations

Progreso has a limited selection of accommodations. However, the choice for travelers is growing daily. Economy-minded travelers can usually find rooms to fit any budget if they're not too fussy; it's a little harder in July or August.

Some backpackers claim they use the beach for overnight sleeping; if you ask the town authorities for permission, they make it clear that camping is not allowed and that they'll check you into their "free" hotel involuntarily if you're caught. Beaches east and west of town are more likely places to camp than in the center of the promenade, which the town is trying to dress up to attract more tourists.

Budget/Moderate: Tropical Suites, just across from the beach, tel. (993) 5-1263, offers standard rooms at budget prices, as well as suites with stove and refrigerator at moderate prices.

Inexpensive: Hotel San Miguel, on Calle 78 between 29 and 31, tel. (993) 5-1357, is close to the sea and close to the center of town. It's simple but a/c. At the west end of town is the small, clean **Playa Linda,** tel. (993) 5-1157, offering rooms with private bath. **Sian-Ka'an,** Calle 17 s/n (Carretera Yucalpetén-Chelem), tel./fax (993) 5-4017, is a fine little hotel/beach club just out of Progreso at Yucalpetén-Chelem. It also offers local and International food at its restaurant/bar, **Yikil-Ha.**

Food

Progreso's cafes are typical of Mexican seaside resorts: if you like sweet, fresh-caught fish you're in luck—but it's hard to find much else.

Pricey by Progreso standards, **Capitán Mariscos** is preferred by some. The restaurant serves excellent seafood in an airy, open-porch atmosphere at the far east end of the *malecón*. Dressing rooms and showers are provided for guests who wish to swim. While strolling along the *malecón,* look for **Le Saint Bonnet** for some of the best International food in Yucatán; open for break-

---

CHICXULUB CRATER

In the late 1940s, scientists from Pemex (Mexico's national oil company) doing exploratory oil drilling on the Yucatán Peninsula discovered gravitational anomalies near the town of Chicxulub. The core samples they drilled, and subsequent research by scientists from all over the world, confirmed evidence of a huge meteor crater here.

The immense crater is at least 180 km across and even deeper than that. Half of the crater is on land and the other half is in the sea. The crater is invisible to the eye; it's buried under a thick layer of sediments deposited after the meteorite's impact. A line of caves lines up with the outer ring of the crater, leading scientists to speculate that the massive impact created the many cenotes scattered about the Peninsula. You don't find such dense numbers of cenotes in other parts of the world.

Most scientists believe the undoubtedly huge Chicxulub meteorite fell to earth 65 million years ago; one theory says this impact plunged the entire world into darkness for a lengthy period and resulted in extinction of the dinosaurs—events that created the period in geologic time known as the KT (Cretaceous-Tertiary) boundary.

fast, lunch, and dinner. At the public market—busy for such a small city—you'll find a fine little ice cream store selling good frozen bars.

Information and Services

Three **banks** are open Mon.-Fri. 9 a.m.-1:30 p.m.; Bancomer accepts Canadian dollars. A Pemex **gas station** is on the main street one block south of the plaza; another is on the one-way entrance road from Mérida. Both stations are open daily 5 a.m.-midnight.

A **tourist information office,** Calle 30 #176, tel. (99) 5-0114, is open Mon.-Sat. 9 a.m.-1 p.m. and 3 p.m.-7 p.m.. The **post office,** tel. (99) 5-0545, is open Mon.-Fri. 9 a.m.-7 p.m., Saturday 9 a.m.-1 p.m..

Transportation

By Bus: From Mérida, buses leave the depot (on Calle 62 between Calles 65 and 67) every 30 minutes daily 5 a.m.-9 p.m.; allow one hour for the trip. You'll be dropped off at the bus station in Progreso, Calle 29 #151 (between 30 and 32), a few blocks from the center of town and a short walk from the *malecón.* Buses depart the Progreso station for Mérida about every half-hour 5 a.m.-9 p.m., and also go to Yucalpetén, Chicxulub, and Dzilam del Bravo.

By Car: Driving from Mérida, take Calle 60 at the central plaza and go north, following the Progreso signs out of the city. Do not try to reach Progreso from Sisal or Celestún on a coastal road; you must return almost all the way to Mérida.

EAST OF PROGRESO

Chicxulub Puerto

The coastal road from Progreso (east of the wharf) wanders behind a long string of summer houses for seven km to Chicxulub Puerto, a small fishing village on a broad, white-sand shore. Worn fishing boats often lie beached along the sand here, adding a picturesque touch to the scene.

Many of the houses along the road from Progreso are available as rentals. Summer is high season, with prices in the stratosphere. In the winter months the rental fees are quite reasonable, US$150-300 monthly depending on the size of the house. Real estate offices in Mérida can

help you out, or just ask around town at the beach.

Strolling around the small fishing village, you'll run into a *panadería* (bakery) where you can buy a tasty small loaf of French bread for about US$0.50 and *pan dulce* for less. You'll also find a small Conasuper market, and seasonal fruit and vegetable stands by the side of the road.

La Parilla Mexicana, Calle 27 near 50 (on the Progreso/Chicxulub road), serves good char-broiled meats, pizza, pasta, and salads. **Las Palmas** advertises itself as the first restaurant in Chicxulub to change from sand floors to tile floors, and besides, the food is good. Just order a beer or drink and they'll bring you enough snacky things to make a meal; good seafood. Next door is **Dino's Disco.** On Friday nights a video bar comes to life; Saturday night is dance night. **Moctezuma/Chicxulub** is a local hangout painted with fluorescent colors so it's easy to see in the dark; good seafood, and liberal snacks served with drinks.

Telchac Puerto

Continuing along the coast east from Chicxulub Puerto, the road parallels the sea for 75 km to Dzilam de Bravo. Along the way are several small villages, all tuned in to life on the sea. Forty km past Progreso is Telchac Puerto, the largest of these villages. On the road going into town, a large coconut grove shelters **Los Cocos,** a *balneario* (day-use swim resort) with dressing rooms, *palapa* sun shelters, and a restaurant that serves fried fish, beer, and soda pop. The prices are reasonable and the surroundings tropical. Investigate the lighthouse and the small flotilla of fishing boats—great photo possibilities.

Telchac Puerto is the site of **Nuevo Yucatán,** a planned megaresort area that's having a hard time getting off the ground. Nuevo Yucatán's one major hotel has been through several management changes.

Between Telchac Puerto and Dzilam de Bravo the road passes three small villages. On this section of the coastal road you'll see copra drying in the sun and a salt works. Just beyond the small village of **Chabihau** is a narrow strip of sandy beach good for camping. About 10 km farther is **Santa Clara,** located on the inland side of a small lagoon and crossed by many causeways. Strolling around these areas, you'll discover several good beaches.

Club Maeva

On the Progreso-Telchac road, 26 km (16 miles) from Progreso and 76 km (47 miles) from Mérida's international airport, this large complex is a beautiful resort with 163 a/c rooms. The view from the front is the white sand and blue-green water of the Gulf of Mexico; in the rear the scene is a pink lagoon with dozens of species of birds. The only problem is it must be hard to fill since it's so far out. Everytime we visit, it's either changed hands or is closed. The hotel has gone from being Paraíso Maya to Maeva and at this point I don't know. But, if you're in the neighborhood looking for something nice, check it out—you might luck out.

Dzilam de Bravo

The coastal road from Progreso ends at Dzilam de Bravo. In order to go farther around the Peninsula to San Felipe or Río Lagartos, you must first return south on any one of the paved roads from the small towns, then catch another northbound road. All the paved roads return to Mérida. About 13 km before Dzilam de Bravo, there's a small village cemetery where a wooden grave marker was found with the name Jean Lafitte. Historians question the validity of his burial here, since after his departure in 1826 there's no record of his return. But Pierre Lafitte, his brother, is known to be buried in the cemetery. The Yucatecan fishermen held both brothers in great esteem because of the brothers' good treatment of local sailors. Jean's marker, authentic or not, was moved to the museum at Puerto Aventuras on the Caribbean coast of Quintana Roo. If you decide to spend the night in Dzilam de Bravo, check out the simple **Hotel Dzilam,** about US$10 d.

IZAMAL

Izamal, north of Hwy. 180 between Mérida and Chichén Itzá, is a fine old colonial town (pop. 13,500) with Maya origins. Arriving Spaniards were determined to squelch the importance of Izamal as a Maya pilgrimage destination. Led by Friar Diego de Landa, they lost no time tearing down most of the religious Maya ceremonial centers. Spaniards (as was their custom) used the same stones to construct their own city buildings and churches. The original Maya city that the Spaniards destroyed was called Itzamna (variously translated as "City of Hills" or "Dew from Heaven"). Two archaeological sites in town—**Itzamna** and **Kinich Kakmó**—are worth a look.

Izamal received a much-needed popularity boost when Pope John Paul II visited in August 1993. As might be expected, the town underwent a massive beautification project in preparation for the pope's visit. The plaza itself was remodeled (some say destroyed), with benches and trees removed for the crowds and not replaced. A charming colonial city with much to offer, Izamal was beginning to attract more attention from tourists even before the pope arrived, and has now become a popular stop en route to Chichén Itzá.

During the colonial period the city must have been a shiny jewel in New Spain's showcase. Today, the entire city is painted yellow and is often referred to as Ciudad Amarilla ("Yellow City"). The plaza is surrounded by buildings all of the same color, condition, and arched design, with massive porticoed stone pillars and sheltered walkways. The lovely, large tourist center at the entrance to town was built colonial style, around a courtyard, with places for eating and folkloric dances.

Convent of Saint Anthony

The most imposing structure in the small town is the yellow Convent of Saint Anthony de Padua, a church-convent complex built on what looks like a broad hill. Actually, the hill is the base of what was once a Maya temple, Popul-Chac, destroyed in the 1500s. The immense base measures 180 meters long and stands 12 meters high. The current church was designed by Fray Juan de Mérida; construction began in 1533. Wander through the church grounds, and in one of the stark stone cells you'll see a huge caldron, metal tools, and a hanging rack still used to make candles for church use. The buildings surround a grassy courtyard (8,000 square meters, the largest in Mexico) with 75 arches.

Accommodations

Most travelers to Izamal just pass through, stopping long enough to take a look around; even with a climb to the top of local pyramid Kinich Kakmo, that should take no more than a couple of hours. However, if you decide to spend the night, you'll find a couple of places to check out. All are budget priced.

The **Green River Hotel** is on Av. Zamna—a new, tree-lined boulevard parallel to the main road through town. The hotel is simple but has tile floors and private bathrooms, and though the grounds are a little ragged, the rooms are generally clean. Look for signs at the entrance to town.

For something a little nicer, check out the pleasant **Mecan-che Guest House,** Calle 22 #305, tel./fax (995) 4-0287, e-mail: macanche@pibil.finred.com.mx. It offers 12 bungalows with private baths and hot water, as well as a lovely garden with lots of birdsong. Each room has a fan and screened windows, and most have their own covered patios. The dining *palapa* holds an honor system bar. Breakfast (included in the rate of US$20 s/d) consists of fresh fruits, juice, brewed coffee, cereals or eggs. Part of the same complex, **Rancho Santo Domingo** is two blocks away and welcomes campers (US$5) and RVs (US$20)—water hookups only. Facilities include a swimming pool, public toilets, and showers.

Diane Boyle, owner of Mecan-che and Rancho Santo Domingo, is part of a group that is restoring **Hacienda San Antonio de Chalante** to its turn-of-the-century glory. The hacienda is in Sudzal, about 11 km south of Izamal, and has a few rooms available. Rates of US$35 include breakfast, lunch, and a light supper; coke, beer, and wine available. Amenities include a swimming pool and rental bikes. Tours can be scheduled to nearby ruins and cenotes. Reservations requested.

Food

The restaurant situation in Izamal is improving. Near the ruins, the restaurant **Kinich Kakmó,** Calle 27 #299 (between 28 and 30), is a pretty courtyard affair serving regional dishes, including a full meal of *poc-chuc* (marinated grilled pork), beans, salad, and tortillas for US$5. It's open daily 11:30 a.m.-5:30 p.m. The **restaurant** by the plaza is a good place for a cool drink and a plate of tacos, and there are several other small cafes under the arches of the buildings around the plaza.

Services

A few small stores sell minimal basics. The bank doesn't cash traveler's checks. Don't leave town without visiting **Hecho a Mano,** a fine folk-art shop on Calle 33 across from the church. Owners Hector Garza and Jeanne Hunt display their collectibles and Hunt's gorgeous photographs in the tiny shop. These two are a great source of information about the area.

Transportation

If driving, take Hwy. 180 from Mérida, turn left (north) at Hoctun and continue 24 km to Izamal. Highway 180 is a well-used road and hitching is comparatively simple during daylight hours. Along the road from Hoctun, any second-class bus will stop for you at a wave of your arm. The bus station is near the plaza; buses depart for

Izamal taxi stand

Mérida hourly 4:30 a.m.-7:30 p.m. and for Valladolid and Cancún three times daily.

Once in Izamal, any hour of the day you'll find a queue of *calesas,* here more commonly referred to as *victorias,* parked in front of a broad stairway leading to the church and courtyard or the visitor center. These tiny, horse-pulled buggies do an active business carrying locals (often whole families) around town. The *calesas* are not impractical bits of nostalgia for the tourists to admire (though you will); they're the only transportation some families have.

SOUTH TOWARD UXMAL

Yaxcopoil

A fine old turn-of-the-century hacienda, Yaxcopoil ("yawsh-koe-poe-EEL") is right off Hwy. 261 between Mérida and Uxmal and is clearly marked. A half-hour visit gives a great insight into what life must have been like in the days when Mexican haciendas operated like small fiefdoms. Hundreds of Indians provided the labor necessary to grow and harvest the thorny henequen plant which, until after WW II, made the owners of these small kingdoms millionaires. At Yaxcopoil you'll see remnants of the 1890s' and 1900s' furniture used in the drawing rooms and dining rooms, hinting at the gracious life the *patrones* enjoyed. Take a look into the kitchen with its unique woodstove made from white tile, pictures of the family, framed documents showing dates of events, even the old safe. This is a stroll into the past. With luck you may have Ernesto Cuitam Yam as your guide. A Maya, he was born in Yaxcopoil. His parents told of life on the hacienda when they worked there—under

much different conditions than now. The hacienda is open Mon.-Sat. 8 a.m.-6 p.m., Sunday 9 a.m.-1 p.m.; admission is about US$3.50.

Muna

Hwy. 261 passes through the rustic city of Muna, where lovers of 17th-century architecture might enjoy a look at the large Franciscan church. In the late afternoon sun, the facade with its lacy belfries glows a mellow gold, almost hiding the decay that adds to its appeal. Early in the morning on the edge of the plaza, women sell small quantities of fresh fruits and vegetables. Opposite the plaza, a series of open stalls offers cold drinks and Yucatecan snacks, including good *panuchos* (mini-burritos); for the big appetite, go for the *tortas* or tamales.

Oxkintok

The ruins of Oxkintok have attracted much attention in the past few years, as archaeologists uncover an urban center at least three square miles in size. The ruins sit in a fertile plain at the edge of the hilly Puuc region, and may have been connected to Uxmal by a limestone *sacbe.* Large pyramids have been uncovered, all including tombs with some remaining treasures (though there was considerable looting in the past and many relics have been lost). Reconstruction is far from complete, and you're likely to be the only person at the site. Still, it's fascinating to see such a large center on the verge of discovery. To reach Oxkintok follow the signs in Muna for Oxkintok and Calcehtok (a left turn); once in Calcehtok, turn right at the sign just past the small town and drive down a dirt road about half a kilometer to the ruins, which are about 30 km northeast of Uxmal.

UXMAL AND VICINITY

Uxmal is a must-take journey from Mérida while you're in the state of Yucatán. This is the area Stephens and Catherwood told us so much about during their 1840s' visit; many people carry John Stephens's popular book, *Incidents of Travel in the Yucatán Peninsula,* and refer to the proper chapters while sightseeing in this area. We do this all the time, and recently while visiting old haciendas, found many references to the old compounds. Even more amazing, many descendants of the people that he mentions still own these once lovely haciendas.

Eighty km south of Mérida (a one-hour drive) in a range of low hills covered with brush, Uxmal is the greatest Maya city of the Puuc region. Some believe it was founded by Maya from Guatemala's Petén in the 6th century. Others contend it dates back even further, perhaps to the Preclassic period.

Unlike most of northern Yucatán, the Puuc region has good soils, allowing for greater population density than other areas. The city is believed to have been the hub of a district of about 160 square km encompassing many sites, including Kabah, Sayil, Labná, and Xlapak. These Maya sites all reached their apogee during the Late to Terminal Classic eras (A.D. 750-925).

Uxmal was probably the largest of the Puuc sites. It emerged as the dominant city-state between A.D. 850 and 900, when the House of the Magician, the Great Pyramid, and the Nunnery were built. Uxmal's control may have encompassed Kabah, because a *sacbe* (raised causeway) extended to that nearby city. Few stelae have been found at the site, but we know the name of at least one ruler, Lord Chac, who could have ordered the monumental construction.

In the mid-10th century, Uxmal was abandoned, probably after being defeated by Chichén Itzá's armies. During the Postclassic era, the Xiu clan based in the nearby town of Mani spuriously claimed to be descended from Uxmal's rulers and occupied the ruins.

Puuc Architecture
The Maya word Uxmal (oosh-MAHL) means "Thrice Built," referring to the number of times this ceremonial center was rebuilt—in fact, it's believed that Uxmal was built five times. In many instances structures were superimposed over existing buildings; all are examples of the purely Maya "Puuc" style.

Puuc architecture is one of the major achievements of Mesoamerica; hallmarks of the style include thin squares of limestone veneer, decorated cornices, boot-shaped vault stones, rows of attached half columns, and upper facades heavily decorated with stone mosaics and sky-serpent monster masks.

Precious Water
Because of the almost total absence of surface lakes or rivers in Yucatán, the collection of water was of prime importance in the survival of the Maya. Unlike most Maya centers in Yucatán, Uxmal was not built around a cenote, since there are none in this arid part of the Peninsula. Rainwater was collected in *aguadas* (natural holes in the ground) as well as in man-made *chultunes* (cisterns) built into the ground, sometimes right inside a house or under a patio.

Most of the Maya religious ceremonies and idols were devoted to the worship of Chac, the rain god. The constant threat of drought inspired the people to build great centers of worship, with hundreds of carvings and mosaics representing Chac and his prominent long hooked nose.

EARLY EXPLORATIONS

Father López de Cogulludo explored the ruins in the 16th century, long after the Indians had abandoned the site. Without any facts to go on, he referred to the Nunnery Quadrangle (Las Monjas) as the dwelling of the Maya "Vestal Virgins," who kept the "Sacred Fire."

Cogulludo was followed by Jean-Fredric de Waldeck in 1836, who published a handsomely illustrated folio showing the structures of Uxmal peeking over thick brush. He compared them with the ruins of Pompeii. In 1841, the adventurous "dynamic duo" of John L. Stephens and Frederick Catherwood began their well-docu-

FROM MERIDA TO UXMAL AND THE PUUC RUINS

© MOON PUBLICATIONS, INC.

mented journey through the Peninsula. By that time, the Indians must have cleared plots of land around Uxmal to plant corn, since Stephens commented that "emerging from the woods we came unexpectedly on a large open field strewn with mounds of ruins and vast buildings on terraces and pyramidal structures grand and in good preservation"—shown beautifully by Catherwood's sketches.

The first real excavations, led by the noted Danish archaeologist Frans Blom, began in

1929. Blom was involved in many archaeological digs in the Maya hinterland.

Since Blom's time, many other archaeologists have worked with the Mexican government at Uxmal; the result is a fine reconstructed site open for the enjoyment of the public. The small area (700 by 800 meters) of Uxmal presents some of the finest examples of pure Maya design, without Toltec influence.

THE TEMPLES OF UXMAL

House of the Magician/ House of the Diviner

This "pyramid" is the tallest on the grounds, rising 38 meters. It's shaped in a distinctive elliptical form, rather than a true pyramid. The west staircase, facing the Nunnery Quadrangle, is extremely steep (a 60-degree angle). Before you begin your climb do some leg stretches to loosen your muscles! Under this west stairway you can see parts of the first temple built on the site; a date on a door lintel is A.D. 569. On the east facade, the stairway has a broader slant, and though it's still a steep incline, it isn't nearly so hard on the legs.

In the upper part of the east staircase you can enter an inner chamber which is **Temple Two. Temple Three** consists of nothing more than a small shrine at the rear of Temple Two. Climbing the west stairway brings you to **Temple Four** and an elaborate Chac mask with an open mouth large enough for a human to pass through. **Temple Five** dates back to the 9th century and is reached by climbing the east stairway. From this viewpoint you'll be able to see the entire site of Uxmal and the surrounding brush-covered Puuc hills. These five temples were built one over the other!

Nunnery Quadrangle

The Nunnery, northwest of the House of the Magician, is a courtyard covering an area of 60 by 45 meters, bounded on each side by a series of buildings constructed on platforms of varying heights during different periods of time. The buildings, which contain numerous small rooms, reminded the Spaniards of the nunneries in Spain.

House of the Turtles

A path leads south from the Nunnery to the House of the Turtles. This simple structure is

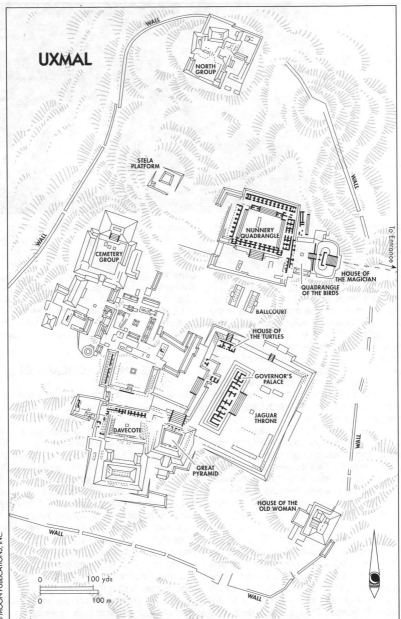

UXMAL

WALL

NORTH
GROUP

STELA
PLATFORM

CEMETERY
GROUP

NUNNERY
QUADRANGLE

WALL

To Entrance

HOUSE OF
THE MAGICIAN

QUADRANGLE
OF THE BIRDS

BALLCOURT

HOUSE OF
THE TURTLES

GOVERNOR'S
PALACE

JAGUAR
THRONE

DAVECOTE

WALL

GREAT
PYRAMID

HOUSE OF THE
OLD WOMAN

WALL

WALL

© MOON PUBLICATIONS, INC.

0   100 yds

0   100 m

*House of the Magician,
Uxmal*

OZ MALLAN

six by 30 meters. The lower half is very plain, but the upper part is decorated with a frieze of columns; a cornice above that has a series of turtles along its facade. The turtle played an important part in Maya mythology.

Governor's Palace

Just south of the House of the Turtles is the Governor's Palace. Its facade is even more elaborate than those found at the Nunnery, culminating in a portrait-relief over the central doorway that may represent Lord Chac, Uxmal's most powerful ruler. The palace is considered by some to be the finest example of pre-Hispanic architecture in Mesoamerica. It sits on a large platform, measures almost 100 meters long, 12 meters across, and eight meters high, and has 11 entrances. The lower facade is plain, but the upper section is a continuous series of ornate carvings and mosaics of geometrical shapes and Chac masks. Two arrow-shaped corbel arches add to the delicate design of this extraordinary building. A double-headed jaguar in front of the palace (presumed to be a throne) was first found by John Stephens in 1841.

The Great Pyramid

Another large structure is the Great Pyramid (30 meters high), originally terraced with nine levels and a temple on the top. According to early explorers, at one time four small structures sat on each of the four sides of the top platform, described as palacelike. The top story is decorated

in typical Puuc fashion, with ornate carvings and stonework depicting flowers, masks, and geometric patterns.

Others

Walking through the grounds, you'll find many other structures and a ball court. Visit the **Dovecote, House of the Old Woman, Phallic Collection, Temple of the Phallus,** other small structures, and as-yet-unexcavated mounds.

TIPS AND PRACTICALITIES

Uxmal is not a city; don't expect much in the way of services. The few hotels have restaurants, but not much else is close by. To do justice to this fascinating antiquity, plan at least a full day to explore thoroughly. Because Mérida is only an hour away, it's easy to make this a day-trip by bus or car. Or continue on and spend the night in Ticul, 65 km (one hour) farther.

You can pick up a guide (or he'll try to pick you up) at the entrance to the ruins. If you feel a need for this service, be sure you agree on the fee before you begin your tour. Also something to remember: every guide will give you his own version of the history of the ruins, part family legend (if you're lucky) and part fairy tale. And let's face it, no one really knows the history of this obscure culture shrouded by the centuries. Many good books are available on the archaeological ruins of the larger sites (see "Booklist").

The grounds are open 8 a.m.-5 p.m.; admission charge is about US$6.50, parking is about US$1.50, use of a video camera is about US$8 extra. A sound and light show is presented each evening (see "Entertainment," below). The restaurants and shops in the visitor center and the artisan stands on the grounds are open until 9 p.m.

ACCOMMODATIONS

Inexpensive/Moderate
Rancho Uxmal is at least a 45-minute walk from the ruins, but the manager, Don Macario Cach Cabrera, will give you a ride if he can, or will flag down a bus for you. Buses returning from the ruins to Mérida will stop at the hotel. Twenty rooms have fans, hot-water showers, and comfortable beds; six more rooms have a/c. The long swimming pool is well filtered and clean, and the restaurant is great. Try the *poc chuc* with onions, cabbage, and tortillas; it's the best in the area. The owners also have a small, very rustic campground next door.

Moderate
About one km from the ruins is **Hotel Misión Uxmal,** U.S. tel. (800) 437-7275. Transportation to the ruins is available. This hotel has all the modern amenities, including a pool, bar, dining room, and nice rooms with private bath and a/c. Credit cards accepted; US$80, including breakfast and dinner.

Expensive
Hotel Villa Arqueológica, U.S. tel. (800) 258-2633, is the newest of Uxmal's hotels and is owned by a branch of Club Med. A clone of its sister hotels in Cobá and Chichén Itzá, the hotel has small, attractive, and functional rooms, with twin beds on built-in cement platforms, a/c (a few readers have complained that the a/c can be noisy), and private bathrooms with shower. Both floors look out onto a tropical courtyard.

The flower-covered patio has a sparkling (shallow) pool, outside bar and table service, a covered cabana area, and a complete library on the history and culture of the Maya. You'll find some French dishes along with local specialties in the large dining room. Lunches and dinners average about US$25 pp, breakfast US$12—à la carte menu only. Credit cards are accepted.

Premium
An older colonial-style favorite, **Hotel Hacienda Uxmal,** Mérida tel. (99) 25-2122 or 25-2133, fax (99) 25-7022, U.S./Canada tel. (800) 235-4079, has undergone some renovations in the past few years. Air-conditioning and cable television have been added to some rooms, and a spacious wooden deck has been built around the pool. Other features include tile walkways and floors, large old-fashioned rooms with heavy carved furniture, pathways through tropical gardens, and a gift shop and bar. Credit cards are accepted.

A spacious dining room serves typical Yucatecan food and some continental dishes in fixed-price meals. There are usually four entree selections at dinner, plus a fruit salad or soup and dessert for about US$18. Snacks and lower-priced meals are available at the cafe Nicte-Ha, next to the hotel's second pool, just across from the road to the ruins (open 1-8:30 p.m.).

FOOD

The hotel dining rooms welcome visitors for lunch. Expect to pay about US$12-16 for a complete three-course lunch; ask what light meals are available. The hotels used to allow those who paid for a meal to swim in their pools, but that practice seems to have been stopped. Ask before you dive in. The exception is the Nicte-Ha cafe at the Hacienda Uxmal; diners are allowed to use the pool by the cafe, but not the pool by the main hotel buildings.

At the Uxmal Visitors Center at the entrance to the ruins, a small restaurant serves cold drinks and light meals, and a kiosk just outside the entrance to the ruins offers cold drinks. If you're driving, another alternative is to take the road back toward Mérida (Hwy. 261), 18 km north to Muna where there are small cafes in the villages and a few on the road.

ENTERTAINMENT

Every evening a **sound and light show** is presented in Spanish (7 p.m.) and English (9 p.m.)

learning to embroider

at the ruins overlooking the Nunnery Quadrangle. Escorted tours to the shows are available from Mérida. If you've never seen one of these shows, check it out. It's mood-altering to sit under the stars in the warm darkness surrounded by stark stone remnants and listen to Latin-accented voices and a symphony orchestra echo in stereo from temple to temple, narrating the (so-called) history of the Maya while colored lights flash dramatically on first one and then another of these stark structures.

Sometimes Mother Nature adds her own drama: the rumble of thunder from a distant storm, or jagged streaks of luminous light in a black sky. The already eerie temples reflect a supernatural glow evoking the memory of the Maya, their mysterious beginnings and still unsolved disappearance.

Admission is about US$1.50 for the Spanish show and US$2 for the English show; reserve and buy tickets either at hotels in Uxmal, or at government tourist offices and travel agencies in Mérida.

SHOPPING

The visitor center at the entrance to the Uxmal site is modern and beautiful. With the visitor in mind, the center offers clean restrooms, gift shops, a small museum, an auditorium where a short film promoting the Yucatán Peninsula is shown, a bookstore with a good supply of English-language books about the various ruins on the Peninsula, an ice-cream shop, and a small cafeteria.

Outside the entrance are kiosks where local women sell the *huipil* (Yucatecan dress). Their prices can be much better than in gift shops; frequently the garments are made by the saleswoman or someone in her family. Some dresses are machine-embroidered or made of polyester, though many are still handmade of white cotton with bright embroidery thread. Be sure you get what you want. The *huipiles* worn by Maya women always look snow white with brilliant colors. Don't forget to bargain.

The only other shopping at Uxmal is at the small gift shops adjoining the hotels near the ruins. Most of them sell the usual curios, clothing, tobacco, postage stamps, and postcards. The exception is the **Villa Arqueológica,** where high-quality Maya reproductions depicting ancient idols are displayed. Here, the prices reflect the excellent workmanship. Note: If you're driving or on a tour bus (not a local bus), you'll have the opportunity to stop at some little shops selling *huipiles* and crafts along the highway close to the ruins. Usually the tour buses make a stop or two for shopping.

GETTING THERE

Local **Autotransportes del Sureste** buses leave Mérida's main bus station (Calle 69 #544) daily, with departures at 6 a.m., 9 a.m., noon, and 3 p.m.; the last return bus to Mérida departs Uxmal at 7:30 p.m. Check at the bus station in advance, since schedules are apt to change. Allow at least one hour for the trip (79 km)—be sure to check the return time to Mérida. Buses to Uxmal leave Campeche from the ADO station (Gobernadores 289).

Buses do not go directly onto the ruins road, but instead stop on the side of the highway at the turnoff to the ruins. The highway (261) from Mérida to Campeche city passes close to the Uxmal ruins and is a well-maintained road. From Mérida the drive to Uxmal takes about one hour; from Campeche allow two hours (175 km southwest). Travel agencies in Mérida offer tours of the ruins at Uxmal. Check with the government tourist office at Teatro Peón Contreras on Calle 61 in downtown Mérida for more information.

PUUC RUINS

An entire day could be spent making a loop from Uxmal to the smaller Puuc sites of Kabah, Sayil, Xlapak, and Labná, lying in the jungle-covered hills southeast of Uxmal. For the most part these are small sites and easy to see or photograph quickly, and the ornate Puuc design is well worth the time and effort. The government has re-

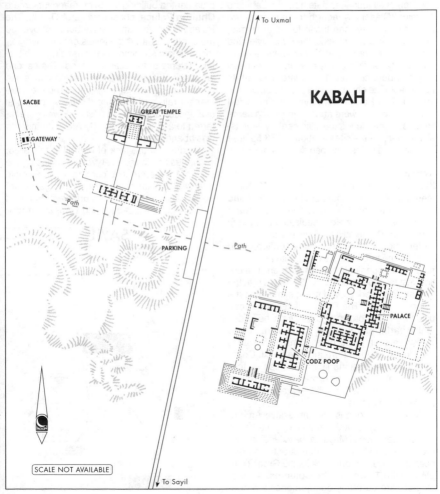

To Uxmal

KABAH

SACBE

GREAT TEMPLE

GATEWAY

Path

PARKING

Path

PALACE

CODZ POOP

SCALE NOT AVAILABLE

To Sayil

© MOON PUBLICATIONS, INC.

opened the ruins to anthropologists and archaeologists, and some excavation and renovation is underway. The countryside for some 15 km around Uxmal and the Puuc sites is now a national preserve, and some of the indigenous animals and birds are beginning to multiply.

The politics of the smaller Puuc sites were certainly dominated by their larger neighbor. Kabah was settled as far back as the Late Preclassic (300 B.C.-A.D. 250), but the ruins we now see at all four sites date from the Late and Terminal Classic. Although the buildings are generally smaller than those found at Uxmal, they are all fine examples of the Puuc style, and some, like the temple at Xlapak, have a gemlike beauty. Sayil, the only one which has been fully mapped, covered 1.7 square miles at its Late Classic height and had a population of over 10,000. The Puuc must have been crowded then! These sites were abandoned at the same time as Uxmal during the 10th century. Admission to each of the sites is about US$3.50, free on Sunday; all sites are open daily 8 a.m.-5 p.m.

Kabah

Kabah was constructed in A.D. 850-900. Nineteen km south of Uxmal, structures are found on both sides of Hwy. 261. The most ornate building is the **Codz-Pop,** dedicated to the rain god, Chac. This temple is 45 meters long and six meters high. Part of the original rooftop comb (at one time three meters high), with its uneven rectangular openings, can still be seen. The entire west facade is a series of 250 masks with the typical elongated, curved nose, some almost a complete circle. The Puuc architecture is colored beige, rust, brown, and gray from the oxides in the earth that engulfed the building for so many years. Small pits on each mask are said to have been used to burn incense or oil; Codz-Pop must have shone like a Chinese lantern from great distances throughout the rolling countryside. Inside the building are two parallel series of five rooms each.

West of the road is the impressive Arch of Kabah. It is presumed that this arch marks the end of a ceremonial Maya *sacbe* extending from Uxmal to Kabah. A few more structures have been partially restored—look for the **Great Temple** and the **Temple of the Columns.** Archaeologists are currently doing intensive recon-

struction work at Kabah; when finished, it will be a truly impressive site.

Sayil

A short distance brings you to a side road to Oxkutzcab (Hwy. 184); follow the side road first to Sayil (in Maya this word means "anthill"). This is probably the most imposing site of the loop. Several hundred known structures at Sayil illustrate a technical progression from the earliest, unornamented building to the more recent, ornate **Chultun Palace,** constructed in A.D. 730. The Palace is a large, impressive building, over 60 meters long, with three levels creating two terraces, again showing the outstanding architectural talents of the Classic period. The second level is decorated with Greek-style columns and a multitude of rich carvings, including the ever-present rain god and one distinctive portrayal of a descending god (an upside-down figure referred to as the bee god). By A.D. 800 this site was abandoned.

Because of the lack of rainfall in this area, *chultunes* are found everywhere, including the sites of the ceremonial centers. One example of a *chultun* that holds up to 7,000 gallons of water can be seen at the northwest corner of the Palace. The fast-decaying **Temple Mirador**

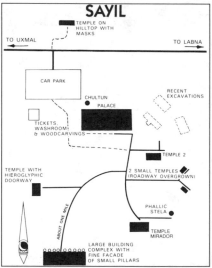

arch at Labná

(on a path going south from the Palace) and the monument of a human phallic figure lie beyond.

Xlapak

Six km farther on the same road (east of Sayil) is the Xlapak turnoff. Though this Puuc site is small, do stop to see the restored building with its curious carvings: tiers of masks, curled Chac noses, and geometric stepped frets. It's easy to pick out the light-colored areas of restoration compared to the darker weathered stones that were covered with bushes and soil oxides for so many years. The word Xlapak in Maya means "Old Walls."

Labná

Another Maya arch of great beauty is at Labná, located three km beyond Xlapak. More correctly the arch should be referred to as a portal vault. Be sure to examine the northeast side of this structure to see two outstanding representations of thatched Maya huts, one on each side of the portal. This arch is one of the largest and most ornate built by the Maya; the passageway measures three by six meters.

The Puuc-style **Palace** was built at the end of the Classic period, about A.D. 850. The elaborate multiroom pyramid is 135 meters long by 20 meters high and sits on an immense platform 165 meters long. A *chultun* is built into the second story of the Palace; according to archaeologist George Andrews, at least 60 *chultunes* have been located in the Labná area, indicating a popula-

tion of about 3,000 residents within the city.

The stark, square **El Mirador** building stands on a tall mound with a roof comb gracing the top. The comb on the small temple was originally decorated with a carved seated figure and a series of death heads. The carvings were still in place in the 1840s when John Stephens traveled through the Peninsula. The elements and time continue to wreak their destruction on the ancient structures of the Maya.

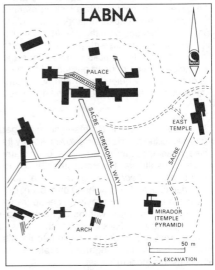

LABNA

OXKUTZCAB AND VICINITY

OXKUTZCAB

The small village of Oxkutzcab is known by outsiders because of its proximity to the caves of Loltún. The town is smaller and easier to navigate than Ticul and is a nice place to stop for a visit. Land in the area is fertile. Approaching Oxkutzcab, you travel through acres of healthy tall cornfields, giving you the same feeling you would have in a farm town near Kansas City, Missouri. Suddenly you're surrounded by citrus groves, bananas, and coconut palms. Then you remember—you're in the tropics!

Oxkutzcab is the orange capital of the entire Peninsula. The two-week-long Orange Festival, celebrated in late October or early November, is renowned throughout Yucatán; be sure to stop by if you are in the area at that time, but don't expect to find an empty room.

A large Franciscan church faces a central plaza with painted cement benches, a strange gazebo, and a painted plaster statue of a woman carrying a load of oranges on her head. A graceful arched building along one side of the plaza is the government center. While looking around, you find more examples of stark 16th-century Spanish-influenced architecture. In the morning, the streets bustle with people coming to market; big and little trucks parked hither and yon unload crates of fresh produce. At 1 p.m. all of this activity quiets down and, with commerce completed, folks pack up and go home.

Triciclos

Be careful crossing the streets—you might get run down in the bicycle traffic or overtaken by its three-wheeled cousin, the *triciclo,* seen in many small towns all over the Peninsula. Similar to an Indonesian *becak,* the *triciclo* has a more utilitarian look and no overhead protection. But the result is the same: providing cheap transportation for the family, with dad (or paid "cabbie") pedaling in the back, mom and the kids sitting up front. When not filled with people, it's used for hauling anything from a crate of live chickens to a modern TV set.

Accommodations and Food

La Cabaña Suiza, at the Los Tucanes Hotel, is one of the best restaurants in the area. To reach Los Tucanes drive one and a half blocks toward town from the Pemex and turn left. The owner has a fondness for birds, and keeps parrots, parakeets, and a few squirrels in cages by the tables. They make pretty music, but also attract bugs, so sit as far from them as possible. The restaurant specializes in grilled pork, chicken, and beef served with tortillas and beans; the Yucatecan specialties are also good, and the prices are very reasonable—less than US$5 for a complete meal.

Rooms at the hotel are about US$20.

LOLTÚN CAVES

Seven km southwest of Oxkutzcab, Loltún's underground caverns are the largest known caves in Yucatán. In addition to being a fabulous natural phenomenon, Loltún is an important archaeological find.

The Loltún caves were not only a crucial source of water but an important ceremonial space for the ancient Maya. They also contain evidence of humans' earliest presence in Yucatán. Researchers have found a midden of bones belonging to extinct mammals, including mammoths, dated 9000-7500 B.C. They were obviously dragged to the cave by Early Hunters. Early Preclassic ceramics (2000-1250 B.C.) have also been discovered here. One of the most interesting Maya relics is a Preclassic relief of a lord carved in the style of southern Maya cities like Tikal. Caves were important pilgrimage spots for the Maya; they represented fertility and riches, as well as entrances to the underworld.

The most important archaeological find here is the relief called "The Warrior," which is carved on a rock face just outside the Nahkab entrance to the cave. Researchers believe that it was carved in the Izapan style of Kaminaljuyú, the enormous Preclassic city near Guatemala City. The last room holds strange rock carvings that may be models of temples.

Maya art by Wilbert González

On many of the walls are decorated handprints, either in silhouette or negative outline, whose meaning remains a mystery. The earliest inhabitants of the area used the caves as a source of water and of clay for pots; their function as a religious site probably developed during the Classic era.

Loltún means "Rock Flower" in Maya and in the caves are carvings of small flowers. Hieroglyphic inscriptions on the walls are guesstimated by the guides to be more than a thousand years old. Throughout, *chultunes* are placed strategically under the dripping roof to catch water. This saved water was called "virgin water," important in ceremonies that Maya priests directed to the rain god.

A Guided Walk

No one is allowed to visit the caverns without a guide—and with good reason. Loltún is immense, and it would be very easy to get lost in the meanderings from grotto to grotto, up and down, in total darkness. (Select caverns have been wired for lights, which are turned on and off by the guide as the group moves through.) If you understand Spanish you'll enjoy a few giggles at the stories and anecdotes the guide weaves into his commentary as you stroll through chambers once lived in by thousands of Maya Indians.

Along the way the guide points out common artifacts used by the Indians, such as stone metates (corn grinders) in the "kitchen." Numerous natural formations bear startling resemblances to certain persons (like the Virgin of Guadalupe) and animals (such as the distinct head of an open-mouthed tiger). Giant columns stand from floor to ceiling and when tapped give out a resonant hum that echoes through the darkened passageway. You'll see the stone-carved head now referred to as the Head of Loltún, found by two Americans, Jack Grant and Bill Dailey, during an archaeological dig in the caves in 1959-60.

Toward the end of the two-hour tour you come to an opening in the roof of an enormous two-story-high cavern. The sun pours into the room, creating dust-flecked shafts of golden light. The gnarled trunk of a towering tree grows from the floor of the cave reaching hundreds of feet up through the sunny opening, and flocks of birds twitter and flit in and around the green leafy vines that dangle freely into the immense chamber from above—breathless sights and sounds of nature not soon to be forgotten.

Practicalities

Wear walking shoes in the caves. For the most part it's an easy two-km walk; however, it's dark and damp, and in a few places the paths between chambers are steep, rocky, and slippery. Buy your tickets (about US$3.50) at the office next to the clean restrooms (no restrooms in the caves). Tours begin daily at 9:30 a.m., 11 a.m, 12:30 p.m., 2 p.m., and 3 p.m. Have five or six pesos ready for the guide at the end of the trip (he'll ask for it). Lectures are *usually* given in Spanish only, but ask for an English-speaking guide when you buy your ticket; you might get lucky.

If you arrive early or need lunch or a cold drink after walking through the caves, stop at the small cafe next to the cave exit. The owner is friendly, the beer is cold, the food is good and moderately priced; *poc chuc* (barbecued pork fillet) with bean soup and handmade tortillas hits the spot. Escorted tours are available from Mérida; contact Trails Travel Agency, Calle 62 #482, tel. (99) 28-2582 or 28-5913, fax (99) 24-4919.

TICUL

Northwest of Oxkutzcab, the busy small city of Ticul (pop. 20,000) is an agricultural center, pottery town, and shoemaking center. An elaborate, high-domed 18th-century cathedral faces the plaza; next to it is a Franciscan monastery built 200 years earlier. Shoes are offered for sale in many small shops lining the streets, and according to some Meridanos the prices for good leather *zapatos* are a bit cheaper here than in Mérida.

Ticul is growing, and the traffic through town is horrendous. All the cycles, buses, and trucks

**TICUL TO
LOLTUN CAVES**

vie for space in narrow lanes on potholed streets. The town now has one traffic light, and a system of one-way streets is emerging, but it hasn't eased the congestion much. Try to arrive in Ticul before 10 a.m. or after 3 p.m. to avoid the worst traffic, and no matter when you arrive, park far away from the market and do your sightseeing on foot.

Local Pottery

All around town you'll see signs—complete with location directions—extolling local pottery *fábricas* (factories). At these small *fábricas* you'll see the artist at work and can buy pottery direct from the potter.

Probably the most famous *fábrica* is **Arte Maya,** Calle 23 #301 (on Hwy. 184 as you approach town from Muna). This small factory/instruction center on the west side of town specializes in unglazed terra-cotta reproductions of classic Maya art. From the highway it's easy to spot; look for two-meter-tall "miniatures" of pyramids and idols, as well as an awe-inspiring wall covered with masks of the Maya era. Begun by the late artist Wilbert González, the gallery provides a selection of work—from beginning pieces to outstanding one-of-a-kinds done by the most talented. These pieces are crafted in terra-cotta and jade. They aren't cheap, but can be museum-quality art. González's work bears a special mark identifiable by him and Mexico's Anthropological and Historical Art experts, which prevents mistaking his work for original Maya art.

The Marketplace

Visit the popular marketplace in Ticul—the earlier in the morning the better—for a good choice of fresh produce, including some unusual fruits. In July and August try the *guaya,* a cousin of the litchi nut, which grows on trees in clusters. From a distance, *guayas* resemble green grapes, but on closer examination the fruits are much larger, and have the same texture, size, and color of the outer green skin of a walnut. Crack the skin and eat the refreshing sweet jelly around the seed—tasty!

Food

One of the best *típico* eateries in town is **Restaurant Los Almendros,** just past the market on Calle 23, Ticul's main street. Only Maya specialties are served. This restaurant is reputedly the originator of *poc chuc,* a very popular meat dish served all over the Yucatán Peninsula. Branches of the cafe (same name) are in Mérida, Cozumel, and Cancún. Open 9 a.m.-7 p.m.

MANI

This small town east of Ticul was the scene of early surrender by the Xius (prominent Maya rulers with descendants still living in the state of Yucatán). Montejo the Elder quickly took over, and by the mid-1500s a huge church/monastery complex had been built; 6,000 slaves working under the direction of Fray Juan de Mérida completed the structure in only seven months. This old building, still with a priest in residence, is huge and in its day must have been beautiful, with graceful lines and pocket patios. Fray de Mérida also designed and built similar structures at Izamal and Valladolid.

Historians believe it was in Mani that Friar Diego de Landa confiscated and burned the books held in reverence by the Maya. These codices, the first books produced in North Amer-

ica, were handlettered on fig bark carefully worked until it was thin and pliable, then coated with a thin white plaster sizing and screen folded. According to Landa they were filled with "vile superstitions and lies of the devil." Since that time, only four more codices have been found. The most recent one found, though its authenticity was doubted at first, is gaining more and more credibility among archaeologists. The remaining three books are in museums in Dresden, Paris, and Madrid. Replicas can be seen at the Anthropological Museum in Mexico City. The destruction of the codices was a monumental tragedy not only for the Maya—the loss to the world is incalculable. Only a little progress toward learning the mysterious glyphs has been made; who knows, the destroyed books may have been the lost key to their language, their history, and their mystery. It is hoped that other codices exist and will some day turn up—perhaps in an unexcavated tomb still buried in the jungle. Many villages still practice the ancient rituals of their ancestors and appoint keepers of the sacred records. However, these people have learned from the experiences of their ancestors and tell no outsiders of their task.

CHICHÉN ITZÁ AND VICINITY

Chichén Itzá is one of the finest Maya archaeological sites in the northern part of the Peninsula. Largely restored, the site is about a three-hour drive from Cancún and about two hours from Mérida.

Restoration, begun in 1923, continued steadily for 20 years. After a hiatus, workers are again uncovering and reconstructing buildings on the site, and there are enough unexcavated mounds to support continued exploration for many years.

HISTORY

Two distinct styles of architecture—now known as "Old Chichén" and "New Chichén"—are represented at the site. According to scientific consensus, the Old Chichén buildings were constructed by the Maya between the 5th and 12th centuries (Late Classic period). Scientists disagree, however, on the origin of the New Chichén structures.

Because these newer buildings bear a remarkable similarity to those in the ancient Toltec capital of Tollan (today called Tula), 1,200 km away in the state of Hidalgo, some scientists believe the Toltecs invaded and ruled Chichén Itzá for 200 years, building new structures and adding to many already in place. Most researchers, however, concur that the Toltecs never ruled at Chichén Itzá, and that the people who built the "Old Chichén" and the "New Chichén" were the same: Maya.

Topiltzin Quetzalcoatl

The traditional theory formulated by Ralph Roys holds that in the 9th century, Chichén Itzá was a typical Late Classic city of the northern region, featuring Puuc-influenced architecture and hieroglyphs commemorating important political events. The remnants of this era may be seen in structures like the Nunnery and the Akab Dzib in the "Old Chichén" part of the site. During the 10th century, when Yucatán was embroiled in

Terminal Classic wars and political strife, a king named Topiltzin Quetzalcoatl in the far-off Toltec capital of Tula (just north of Mexico City) was expelled from his realm after a power struggle with the warrior caste. He was last seen departing from the Gulf coast on a raft of serpents headings west.

In A.D. 987, the same year as his departure, The Books of Chilam Balam recorded the arrival on Yucatán's shores of a king named Kukulcán, identifying him, like Tolpiltzin Quetzalcoatl, with the Feathered Serpent. Kukulcán gathered an army that defeated the Puuc city-states of northwestern Yucatán and made Chichén Itzá his capital, rebuilding it in a mixed Toltec-Maya style. These Toltec traits include reclining chac mool figures, warrior columns, skull platforms, feathered serpents, and the cult of Tlaloc. As in Tula, hieroglyphs were absent from the art. Relief carvings showed bloody battle scenes celebrating the Toltec victories. After dominating northern Yucatán for more than two centuries, Chichén Itzá was abandoned in 1224, perhaps after an invasion.

Putún Maya
Another theory holds that Chichén Itzá was first settled by the Itzá, a tribe of Putún Maya seafarers. In the 9th century, they fought and defeated the Puuc cities centered around Uxmal and the eastern power of Cobá and carved out a territory in central Yucatán. The Itzá gave the city its current name, "The Well of the Itza." They settled around the sacred cenote and built monuments to commemorate their victories and legitimize their rule. The sacred cenote's depths received not only human sacrifices (male and female, adults, and children) but offerings from throughout Mesoamerica.

The city-state of Chichén was ruled by a Putún Maya-style joint government. In other Maya cities, hieroglyphs are always associated with a sole ruler who needed to legitimize his claim to power; they are absent at Chichén Itzá, because the form of government is different, not because they were Toltecs. The Putún Maya were far-ranging traders and probably built the Central Mexican cities of Cacaxtla and Xochicalco, thus Chichén's Central Mexican connection. There was a Toltec influence, but Chichén Itzá probably influenced Tula more than the other way around. Perhaps the traits we regard as definitively Toltec—chac mools, warriors columns, etc.—actually came from Yucatán. It is certain that Chichén Itzá was a more grandiose "Toltec" city than Tula itself.

After an internal revolt toppled the Itzá, Chichén Itzá was abandoned for good.

Later At Chichén Itzá
Though Chichén Itzá was most likely abandoned toward the end of the 13th century, Maya were still making pilgrimages to the sacred site when Montejo the Younger, the Spaniard who played a role in ultimately subjugating the Maya, settled his troops among the ruins of Chichén Itzá in 1533. Although they placed a cannon on top of the pyramid of Kukulcán, the Spaniards were unable at that time to conquer the elusive Indians, and after a year left Chichén Itzá for the coast. The pilgrimages continued.

Today, a different breed of pilgrim comes to Chichén Itzá from all over the world to walk in the footsteps of great rulers, courageous ball players, mysterious priests, and simple peasants.

In 1988, UNESCO declared Chichén Itzá a **Heritage of Humanity** site.

SIGHTS

So far 18 structures have been excavated, and many of those have been restored. The former uses for those buildings are not truly understood. Archaeologists can only study and guess from the evidence that has been found.

Temple of the Warriors
On a three-tiered platform, the Temple of the Warriors stands next to the impressive **Group of a Thousand Columns**—reminiscent of Egypt's Karnak. The number of columns actually gets closer to 1,000 each year, as archaeologists continue to reconstruct. Many of the square and circular stone columns have carvings still in excellent condition. In 1926, during restoration, a subtemple found underneath was named **Chacmool Temple.** The former color on the columns of the inner structure is still slightly visible.

Close to the Thousand Columns on the east side of the plaza is a cleverly constructed sweat house with an oven and a channel under the

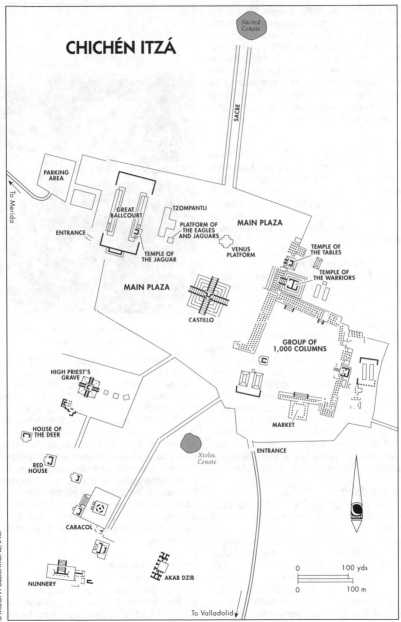

CHICHÉN ITZÁ

Sacred Cenote

SACBE

To Merida

PARKING AREA

GREAT BALLCOURT

ENTRANCE

TZOMPANTLI

PLATFORM OF THE EAGLES AND JAGUARS

TEMPLE OF THE JAGUAR

VENUS PLATFORM

MAIN PLAZA

TEMPLE OF THE TABLES

TEMPLE OF THE WARRIORS

MAIN PLAZA

CASTILLO

GROUP OF 1,000 COLUMNS

HIGH PRIEST'S GRAVE

HOUSE OF THE DEER

RED HOUSE

Xtoloc Cenote

ENTRANCE

MARKET

CARACOL

NUNNERY

AKAB DZIB

To Valladolid

0   100 yds

0   100 m

© MOON PUBLICATIONS, INC.

floor to carry off the water thrown against the hot stones. Indian sweat houses are a combination religious and health-giving experience still used today throughout North America. Archaeologists are working behind this area, uncovering structures buried by jungle mounds. Within this area is the Market, with a rectangular courtyard surrounded by columns. Some speculate this courtyard was covered with palm thatch and used as a marketplace.

The Platforms
Strolling the grounds, you'll find the **Platform of Venus** and **Platform of Eagles and Jaguars.** The flat, square structures, each with low stairways on all four sides, were used for ritual music and dancing, and, according to Diego de Landa (infamous 16th-century Franciscan bishop), farce and comedy were presented for the pleasure of the public.

Temple of the Bearded Man
At the north end of the ball court sits the handsome Temple of the Bearded Man. Two graceful columns frame the entrance to a small temple with the remains of decorations depicting birds, trees, flowers, and the earth monster. It's doubtful whether anyone will ever know if the unusual acoustics here were used specifically for some unknown display of histrionics, or if it's accidental that standing in the temple you can speak in a low voice and be heard a good distance down the playing field, well beyond what is normal (much like in the dome of St. Peter's Cathedral in Rome). Was this the "dugout" from which the coach whispered signals to his players downfield? Some believe that only the upper class actually watched the game, and that the masses remained outside the walls and listened.

Great Ball Court
Of several ball courts at Chichén Itzá (some archaeologists say nine), the most impressive is the Great Ball Court, the largest found yet in Mesoamerica. On this field, life-and-death games were played with a 12-pound hard rubber ball, in the tradition of the Roman Colosseum. The playing field is 135 meters by 65 meters, with two eight-meter-high walls running parallel to each other on either side. On these walls, note the reliefs that depict the ball game and sacrifices.

Group of a Thousand Columns viewed from atop of Temple of the Warriors

The players were obliged to hit the ball into carved stone rings embedded in the vertical walls seven meters above the ground using only their elbows, wrists, or hips. The heavy padding they wore indicates the game was dangerous; it was also difficult and often lasted for hours. (In Diego de Landa's book, written in the late 1600s, he mentions in two different places, "The Indians wore padding made of cotton with salt padding.") The winners were awarded jewelry and clothing from the audience. The losers lost more than jewelry and valuables, according to the carved panels on the site—they lost their heads to the winning captain! Another theory is that the *winners,* too, were granted the "privilege" of losing their heads.

Temple of the Jaguar
On the southeast corner of the ball court, the upper temple was constructed A.D. 800-1050. To get there you must climb a steep stairway at the platform's south end. Two large serpent columns,

with their rattlers high in the air, frame the opening to the temple. The inside of the room is decorated with a variety of carvings and barely visible remnants of what must have been colorful murals.

Sacred Cenote

Today's adventurer can sit in the shade of a *palapa* terrace and enjoy a cold drink near the sacred cenote (say-NO-tay). This natural well is 300 meters north of Kukulcán. The roadway to the sacred well is an ancient *sacbe* that was constructed during the Classic period. The large well, about 20 meters in diameter with walls 20 meters above the surface of the water (34 meters deep), is where the rain god Chac supposedly lived; to con him into producing rain, sacrifices of children and young adults were made, evidenced by human bones found here. On the edge of the cenote is a ruined sweat bath, probably used for purification rituals before sacrificial ceremonies.

In 1885, Edward Thompson was appointed United States consul in nearby Mérida. A young writer greatly interested in the archaeological zones surrounding Mérida, he eventually settled in Chichén Itzá and acquired the entire area, including an old hacienda (for only US$75). For many years he had studied Diego de Landa's account of human sacrifice still going on at the time of the Spanish conquest. Stories of young virgins and valuable belongings thrown into the well at times of drought, over hundreds of years, convinced him there was treasure buried in the muddy cenote bottom. During 1903-07, with the help of Harvard's Peabody Museum, he supervised the first organized dive into the well. Fewer than 50 skeletons were found, mostly those of children, male and female. Precious objects of jade, gold, and copper, plus stone items with tremendous archaeological value, were also dredged from the muddy water.

Thompson set off an international scandal when he shipped most of these important finds to the Peabody Museum by way of diplomatic pouch. He was asked to leave, and for years (1926-44) a lawsuit continued over the booty. Ironically, the Mexican court ruled in favor of Peabody Museum, claiming that the Mexican laws concerning archaeological material were inadequate. After the laws were toughened up, the Peabody Museum, in a gesture of friendliness, returned many (but not all) of the artifacts from Chichén Itzá's well of sacrifice.

The next large-scale exploration of the well was conducted in the 1960s and sponsored by the National Geographic Society with help from CEDAM (a Mexican organization of explorers and divers noted for having salvaged the Spanish ship *Mantanceros* in the Caribbean). As Thompson suspected before his untimely departure, there was much more treasure in the cenote to be salvaged. Hundreds of pieces (including gold, silver, obsidian, copper bells, carved bone, and other artifacts, plus a few more skeletons) were brought to the surface. In order to see in this well, thousands of gallons of chemicals were successfully used to temporarily clarify the water (an unusual experiment by the Purex Co.). The chemicals destroyed many of the blindfish and shrimp in the cenote.

Observatory

One of the most graceful structures at Chichén Itzá is the **Caracol**, a two-tiered observatory shaped like a snail, where advanced theories of the sun and moon were calculated by Maya astronomers. Part of the spiral stairway into the tower/observatory is closed to tourists in an effort to preserve the decaying building. The circular room is laid out with narrow window slits facing south, west, and toward the summer solstice and the equinoxes. The priests used these celestial sightings to keep (accurate) track of time in their elaborate calendrical system.

Kukulcán

The most breathtaking place to view all of Chichén Itzá is from the top of Kukulcán, also called El Castillo. At 24 meters it's the tallest and most dramatic structure on the site. This imposing pyramid, built by the Maya on top of another, smaller pyramid, was probably constructed at the end of a 52-year cycle in thanksgiving to Maya gods for allowing the world to survive the elements—maybe even Halley's comet! Halley's swept by this part of the earth in A.D. 837 (and most recently in 1986); the construction of the second temple was in approximately A.D. 850.

Kukulcán was built according to strict astronomical guidelines. Giant serpent heads repose at the base of the stairs. Each of the four sides has 91 steps. Including the platform on top, that makes for a total of 365 steps—one for each day of the year. On 21/22 March and September (equinox days) between noon and 5 p.m., the sun casts an

the observatory

© MAIIAN

eerie shadow darkening all but one bright zigzag strip on the outside wall of the north staircase. This gives the appearance of a serpent slithering down the steep north-facing steps of the pyramid, giving life to the giant heads at the base. It seems to begin at the bottom in the spring and at the top in the fall. This was first noticed only a few decades ago. In the days when there were only a few people on the grounds watching, you could not only observe the serpent slithering down the steps, but also watch the shadow on the ground move toward the road to the sacred well—maybe looking for a sacrifice? Today the ground is covered with people. A visit during the dates of the equinox is a good time to observe the astronomical talents of the Maya, but be prepared for literally thousands of fellow watchers. Note: Some scientists have serious questions as to whether this effect was deliberately created by the Mayas or just a fluke caused by recent reconstruction. Whichever, it's still fascinating to watch the eerie effect on those particular days!

Be sure to make the climb into the inner structure of Kukulcán where you'll see a red-painted, jade-studded sculpture of a jaguar, just as it was left by the Maya builders over a thousand years ago. Check the visiting hours since the inner chamber is not always open.

Others

The largest building on the grounds is the **Nunnery,** named by the Spaniards. From the looks of it and its many rooms, it was a palace of some sort built during the Classic period. **Tzompantli,** meaning "Wall of Skulls," is a platform decorated on all sides with carvings of skulls, anatomically correct but with eyes staring out of large sockets. This rather ghoulish structure also depicts an eagle eating a human heart. It is presumed that ritualistic music and dancing on this platform culminated in a sacrificial death for the victim, the head then left on display, perhaps with others already in place. It's estimated that the platform was built A.D. 1050-1200.

A much-damaged pyramid, **Tomb of the High Priest,** is being taken apart piece by piece and rebuilt. The ruin is intriguing because of its inner burial chamber. Sometimes referred to as **Osario** (Spanish for "ossuary," a depository for bones of the dead), the pyramid at one time had four stairways on each side (like El Castillo) and a temple at the crest. From the top platform, a vertical passageway lined with rock leads to the base of this decayed mound. There, from a small opening, stone steps lead into a cave about three meters deep. Seven tombs were discovered containing skeletons and the usual funeral trappings of important people, in addition to copper and jade artifacts. Archaeologists are working all around this area (commonly called "Old Chichén Itzá") and have several partially exposed ruins roped off. Work is expected to continue for several years and should result in significant findings about the Maya.

TIPS AND PRACTICALITIES

You can easily walk the 10-square-km grounds. Wear walking shoes: climbing around in sandals can be uncomfortable and unsafe. Arrive early to take advantage of the weather (it's much cooler in the early hours) and the absence of the crowds that arrive later in tour buses.

For some, a short walk around the grounds is enough to say they've "been there." The site *can* be done in a day—not thoroughly, perhaps, but you will come away with a good idea of what Chichén Itzá is about. With two days, you can study these archaeological masterpieces at your leisure, have a chance to climb at your own pace, and be there at the odd hours when the inner chambers open (only for short periods each day).

For a ruins nut, the best advice is to spend the night either at a hotel adjacent to the ruins, where you can be up and on the grounds as soon as the ticket taker is there (usually 8 a.m.), or at the nearby town of Piste with a good shot at getting to the site as early as you wish. This also allows time to return to your hotel for a leisurely lunch (maybe a swim), a short siesta, and an afternoon return visit (free with your ticket).

The ruins are open daily 8 a.m.-5 p.m., although some of the structures have special hours (posted on the buildings, or ask at the entrance). Admission is US$6.50 pp, US$8.50 additional if you bring in a video camera, plus a small fee to use the parking lot. The visitor center offers clean restrooms, a cafe, small museum, auditorium (where short, informative films are shown), bookstore, gift shop, and information center. You'll also find restaurants in the hotels near the site; check the hours since they're usually open for lunch, 12:30-3 p.m. only.

The ruins puts on a high-tech nighttime sound and light show; it's presented in English at 9 p.m. and Spanish at 7 p.m. French, Italian, German, and Maya versions may also be added. The fee is about US$5.

ACCOMMODATIONS

Only a few hotels are close to the ruins. Other hotel options are in nearby Piste (see below).

Inexpensive
Hotel Dolores Alba, 2.2 km east of the ruins , is comfortable, small, and clean, with a swimming pool, dining room, and private baths. Free transport to the ruins is available. For reservations and information, write Calle 63 #464, Mérida, Yucatán 97000, Mexico, tel. (99) 28-5650, fax (99) 28-3163. Be sure to designate that you want a room in the Chichén Dolores Alba, since this address also takes reservations for its sister hotel, the Mérida Hotel Dolores Alba.

Expensive
Villa Arqueológica, owned by Club Med, is a pleasant hotel with a lighthearted ambience. "Almost" deluxe, small-though-functional rooms have private bath and a/c (some rooms have noisy air-

Mayaland dining room

OZ MALLAN

conditioners; listen to yours before you sign the register). Amenities include a *shallow* swimming pool, a delightful garden and pool area, a bar, covered patio, and the best restaurant on this side of the ruins. Don't forget to bring along your receipt, voucher, or any other communication that says you have reservations and have paid. This hotel has been known for overbooking. Prices drop slightly in the summer. Reservations are suggested; from the U.S. call (800) 258-2633.

Expensive/Premium

The **Hotel Mayaland** is in the heart of the archaeological zone surrounded by over 100 acres of tropical fruit and flowering trees filled with unique species of birds. The lovely colonial hotel has 164 rooms with private baths, as well as a restaurant, bar, swimming pool, and tropical gardens. It's been around since the early 1930s and provides visitors with an ambience of beauty and tranquillity. A long, winding staircase in the lobby, ornate leaded-glass windows in the original dining room, tile floors, tall ceilings, and overhead fans lend an exotic look.

Many of the rooms have been renovated, with TVs and a/c added to those in the main building. The hotel offers a variety of accommodations; from standard rooms, to villas, to suites. Prices vary with the season. Reservations suggested. From the U.S. call Mayaland Resorts, tel. (800) 235-4079; ask about their package deals, including a family plan.

Note: Many people remember how convenient it once was to walk from Mayaland to the archaeological zone; as we go to press, the gate from Mayaland to the Chichén Itzá grounds is not open—you must go to the main entrance.

Premium

Hotel Hacienda Chichén Itzá, tel. (99) 24-2150, U.S. tel. (800) 223-4084, is another historic place to stay. Once a working hacienda, it was the site of the archaeologists' original bungalows. The narrow-gauge railroad tracks used in the 1920s for transportation and hauling still go through the outlying hotel grounds. The old mule train is also still in its place, but not used today. This hotel has lots of history, plus private bathrooms, a pool, dining room, and the main building of the original hacienda. Recently the hotel was renovated and modernized; it's a lovely place to stay. Reservations suggested.

TRANSPORTATION

By Car

Chichén Itzá lies adjacent to Hwy. 180, 121 km east of Mérida, 213 km west of Cancún, and 43 km west of Valladolid. An eight-lane *autopista* connects Cancún and Mérida; exit at Piste. Tolls from either Mérida or Cancún are about US$12. The regular roads to Chichén Itzá are in good condition, as long as you slow down for the *topes* (traffic bumps) found before and after every village and school. Hitchhiking at the right time of day will put you in view of many autos on Hwy. 180, but be at your destination before dark or you may spend the night on the roadside; there's little traffic on this road after sunset.

By Bus

Local buses leave for Piste from Cancún and Puerto Juárez (three-hour trip), and from Mérida (less than two hours). Ask about the return schedule.

By Plane

Small planes offer commuter service to Piste from Cancún, Cozumel, and Chetumal. For information and reservations check with **Aerocaribe,** tel. (98) 84-1231 in Cancún, tel. (987) 2-0877 in Cozumel. Expect to pay around US$60 one-way between Piste and Cancún.

Escorted Tours

Escorted tours on modern a/c buses leave daily from Mérida. Check with your hotel or one of the many travel agencies in the city. A variety of tours and prices are offered; check around before you make a decision. **Yucatán Trails,** in downtown Mérida at Calle 62 #482, tel. (99) 28-2582 or 28-5913, fax (99) 24-4919, offers a short trip to Chichén Itzá on the way to Cancún. A scheduled 9 a.m. bus stops at Chichén Itzá for a couple of hours, and again in Valladolid for lunch, then drops you off in Cancún, arriving approximately 6 p.m. Your luggage is safe in the same bus for the entire trip. So, although you don't spend a great deal of time at the ruins, you have the opportunity to make a brief visit en route while transferring from Mérida to Cancún. Fare is about US$70 pp including lunch, a tour of the ruins, and continuing transportation to Cancún; if you just go from Mérida to Chichén Itzá and back it's US$38 roundtrip.

Check with your travel agent either in the U.S. or in Cancún or Cozumel; some agencies in Mexico provide a pickup service for travelers who wish to spend the night at the archaeological zones.

THE BALANKANCHE CAVES

Only six km east of Chichén Itzá, take a side trip to the Balankanche Caves. Here you'll descend into the earth and see many Maya ceremonial objects that appear to have been just left behind one day, 800 years ago. Discovered in 1959 by a tour guide named Gómez, the site was studied by prominent archaeologist Dr. E. Wyllys Andrews, commissioned by the National Geographic Society. What he saw, and what you can see today, is stirring: numerous stalactites, and a giant stalagmite resembling the sacred "Ceiba Tree," surrounded by ceramic and carved ceremonial artifacts. This was obviously a sacred site for the Maya—a site that perpetuates the mystery of the ancient people: Why did they leave? Where did they go? Who were they? Where did they come from in the very beginning? And what is the secret of their complex hieroglyphics?

At the entrance you'll find a parking lot, a cool spot to relax, a small cafe, a museum, interesting photos of Maya rituals, and guides; a sound and light show is offered nightly. The entrance fee is about US$6.50, sound and light show is under US$4. The caves are open 8 a.m.-5 p.m. Guided tours are offered in Spanish at 9 a.m. and noon; in English at 11 a.m., 1 p.m., and 3 p.m.; and in French at 10 a.m. Surrounding the site you'll find a botanical garden with a variety of (identified) plants native to the areas around the Yucatán Peninsula.

Note: Remember that all museums and archaeological sites in Mexico are free on Sundays and holidays, and children under 12 are always free.

PISTE

Piste, 2.5 km west of Chichén Itzá, has a unique tradition of providing the workforce for the site's archaeological digs. Originally the men were chosen because they were the closest; now it's a proud tradition of the people.

Piste is growing up. The once-quiet village is becoming a viable addendum to Chichén's services. More hotels and restaurants are available each month as the number of tourists interested in Chichén Itzá grows. Be sure to look around at the many cafes and gift shops as well.

Puebla Maya
This pseudo Maya village is set up as a tourist attraction and rest area. Once inside the entrance, you walk along man-made rivers and lagoons to a large *palapa*-covered restaurant, often filled with tour bus groups. The US$10 buffet lunch is a good deal, especially since Piste's restaurants are typically overpriced, with only mediocre food. Live musicians play in the restaurant, while artisans give pottery and hammock-weaving demonstrations in small Maya huts. Puebla Maya is open daily 11:30 a.m.-4:30 p.m.

Accommodations
Budget: Posada Olalde is a pleasant, modest place that's very convenient to the ruins, about a half-mile walk or 10 minutes on the bus. It's a little complicated to find, so ask in town for directions. **Posada El Paso** is another simple, clean inn with screened windows, fans, a locked parking area, and (sometimes) hot water. Look for the cafe Posada El Paso; the hotel is right next door. The cafe is inexpensive and the food is good.

Moderate: The **Piramide Inn Hotel,** U.S. tel. (800) 262-9696, offers a swimming pool and peaceful, grassy, tree-shaded grounds. The 44 pleasant rooms have baths and a/c. Unfortunately, the hotel has done away with its campground, but may allow RVs to park in the lot, without hookups. The dining room is open to both hotel guests and the public. Add 10% to the rates if you use a credit card.

Expensive (All-Inclusive): The **Hotel Misión Chichén,** just a few km west of the ruins on Hwy. 180 and just outside Piste, U.S. tel. (800) 223-4084, has a pool, a/c, and a dining room. The rate of US$85 pp includes breakfast and dinner; credit cards accepted. Rates drop slightly in the summer. Reservations suggested. Note: If you have stayed at the **Uxmal Misión Hotel,** don't expect this one to be nearly as nice.

EASTERN YUCATÁN

VALLADOLID AND VICINITY

Once a major colonial city, Valladolid still centers its social life around the zócalo, officially named **Parque Francisco Cantón Rosado.** Young couples sit in the park and hold hands, parents enjoy the cool shade on a Sunday afternoon while their kids play hide-and-seek amid the trees; this is a great place to meet the friendly Valladolidans. During fiestas, such as Candelaria Day, the park comes alive with music, and the cool walkways are lined with stalls selling balloons, pottery, leather goods, and all manner of prepared goodies straight from mamacita's kitchen.

Valladolid is gaining attention from tourists as an alternative to staying at Chichén Itzá or in Piste. It's an easy bus or car ride from here to the ruins, restaurants and hotels are less expensive, and you have the advantage of staying in a traditional Mexican town. Shopkeepers and hoteliers are responding to the attention by sprucing up their properties and providing more tourist services. If you're en route between Cancún and Chichén Itzá, consider spending a night here.

History
The valiant townspeople fought off Francisco de Montejo and his nephew when they attempted to capture the city in 1544. However, Francisco's son, Francisco "El Mozo" (The Younger), was tougher. After finally conquering the city in the 16th century, he built large churches in Valladolid as a reminder to the indigenous people that the Spanish were now in control and would not let up until they totally crushed the people's ancient beliefs—just as they had already crushed many of their temples. To the outsider it may look as though this was accomplished, but anyone who has the opportunity to witness a religious event will recognize that the Maya didn't give up their beliefs—they just blended them with the Catholicism forced upon them.

Churches
Valladolid has many churches. Some are no longer used for services but instead offer exhibits on the city's history (San Roque, for instance, at Calles 41 and 38). Most of the ornate decorations that once lined the altars were removed during either the Caste War or the revolution.

The architecture of these structures is graceful, powerful, and quite remarkable. The most well known are the **Church of San Bernardino de Sienna** and the **Ex-Convent of Sisal,** built in 1552. The oldest churches in the Yucatán, they're on Calle 41-A, three blocks southwest of the parque. Other architectural notables include the churches of **Santa Ana,** Calles 41 and 34; **La Candelaria,** Calles 35 and 44; and **Santa Lucía,** Calles 27 and 40.

Cenote Zaci
On Calle 36, between Calles 37 and 39, Cenote Zaci still attracts tourists, both local and national. This particular lake always has a green surface scum that the Mexicans call lake lettuce (supposedly excellent feed for ducks and chickens). You see few gringos swimming in this water. The cave itself is dark, very large, and littered—a sign of tourism.

When you climb back up the often-slippery stairs, stop at the museum (small thatched huts that house interesting exhibits of the area). You'll find a cafe and bar on the grounds. Open 8 a.m. till dark; a small admission is charged.

Dzitnup
On Hwy. 180 about four km west of Valladolid, you'll see a small handmade sign that says Dzitnup. Turn off at the sign and follow the road about two km to a delightful underground cenote. Wear comfortable walking shoes and your swimsuit in case you decide to take a swim. After a reasonably easy descent underground (in a few places you must bend over because of a low ceiling; there's a hanging rope to help), you'll come to a beautiful, circular pond of crystal-clear water. It's really a breathtaking place, with a high dome ceiling that has one small opening at the top letting in a ray of sun and dangling green vines. Often an errant bird or fluttering butterfly can be seen swooping low over the water before heading to the sun and sky through the tiny opening.

Cenote Dzitnup

You'll see dramatic stalactites and a large stalagmite; catfish and blindfish swim in the placid water. This place is typical of the many underground caverns and grottoes common around the Peninsula, and well worth the small admission. When returning to Hwy. 180, at its intersection with the Dzitnup road check out the southeast corner, where you'll find another cenote on private property. For a few pesos they will take you down some steps to an open-air area with a scum-covered cenote. The sight of tree roots reaching down into the cenote far below is unusual.

Accommodations
Valladolid offers a good choice of simple hotels. If you're looking for real luxury you won't find it, but with a little searching you can discover satisfactory lodging. Being close to the *parque* is convenient, since that's where most of the action takes place.

Budget: The **Hotel María de La Luz,** on Calle 42, tel./fax (985) 6-2071, gives a good and accurate first impression, with a swimming pool and curved, sweeping stairway to the second floor. The 33 rooms have been renovated with a/c, tiled baths, TV, and good mattresses. **Hotel María de Guadalupe,** Calle 44 #198 (between Calles 39 and 41), is reasonably clean, within walking distance to the *zócalo,* and close to the bus station.

Inexpensive: Just across from the plaza by the cathedral is the **Hotel San Clemente,** Calle 44 #206, tel. (985) 6-2208. The 60-room hotel has a/c or fans, private bathrooms, good food, and a pool.

Inexpensive/Moderate: The nicest and most expensive hotel in town is probably the **Hotel El Mesón del Marqués,** Calle 39 #203 (across the street from the plaza), tel. (985) 6-2073 or 6-3042, fax (985) 6-2280, which offers a/c, a pool, outdoor and indoor eating, and a gift shop. The building is said to have been the home of an old prominent family. The proprietress is most helpful and can assist in arranging tours to Río Lagartos. The hotel's restaurant is one of the best in town. Several food stands next door in a courtyard serve lunch to most of the town.

Food
Probably the best place to eat is at Hotel El Mesón del Marqués. A reader tells of good food at **Café de Los Arcos Restaurante,** Calle 39 #200A, a couple of blocks from the parque. The economical *comida corrida* was said to be excellent.

About four km outside Valladolid on the road toward Chichén Itzá, look for **Restaurante La Choza Viajero,** an open, palm-thatched cafe on a small hill. The selection is good; regional chicken, pork, and beef meals for US$3-4.50.

Services
Most businesses and shops are on the streets surrounding the *parque.* **Banks** are open Mon.-Fri. 9 a.m.-2:30 p.m. The **post office** is at Calle 40 #195-A.

Transportation

Valladolid is on Hwy. 180, easily reached by bus from Mérida, Cancún, Tizimín, and other connecting points.

The city is easy to get around. It's laid out in a grid pattern with even-numbered streets running north to south, odd-numbered streets running east to west. The *parque,* at the center of the city, is bordered by Calles 39, 40, 41, and 42. Seeing the city on foot is simple; maps of the area are available at the tourist office in the Palacio Municipal or at most of the hotels that surround the plaza.

RÍO LAGARTOS

A little more than 100 km north of Valladolid, on the northernmost point of the Yucatán Peninsula, the isolated town of Río Lagartos is a small picturesque fishing village only gradually catching up with the rest of Yucatán State. Rows of wooden clapboard houses line narrow streets where there are still few autos. But television has now come to town, cable and all.

Río Lagartos is best known for the colonies of flamingos that return here each year to nest. In April, May, and June, thousands of pink and cerise *Phoenicopterus ruber* flamingos throng to the area's shallow lagoons and estuaries, which wind for many km in and around small islets and sandbars. In addition to the flamingos, birdwatchers will spot plover, white egret, heron, cormorant, and pelican.

Like the flamingos, the town's residents build their homes in swampy water that seems to flood a good bit of the land. While visiting, you might see a cement foundation being poured right into the water. A pleasant promenade meanders along the waterfront, from where you can watch the fishing boats and the activities of the fishermen who have been making their living plying the seas for generations.

Besides fishing, tourism is beginning to contribute to the local economy; birdwatchers are flocking to town, but tourist visitation here is still infinitesimal compared to most other cities on the Peninsula. Many folks also work 16 km east at Las Coloradas salt factory, which has been in operation since Maya days; even today, most of the factory's employees are Maya.

Flamingo-Watching

The locals are very protective of the flamingos; during the April-June brooding season, visitors are not allowed to approach the nesting area for fear they will disturb the birds, who guard the mud nests that protrude above the surface of the shoreline. The sounds of outsiders cause them to rise in flight, often knocking fragile eggs from the nests.

The rest of the year, it's an easy matter to rent a boat and guide. Through Hotel Nefertiti you can arrange an early-morning boat tour to the flamingos. For about US$40-45 you can hire an open launch to take one to four people on a three-hour trip from the boat dock near the hotel through the estuaries to find the birds (if you're going to see crocs, it's in these estuaries that you'll find them). As you meander through the estuaries, you'll see flocks of the startling pink birds covering the white beach or standing one-legged in the shallow water. The combination of colors—blue sky, white sand, green water, pink birds—is breathtaking. The sandy beach is often tinted a soft coral, covered with silky flamingo feathers.

A good captain/guide motors you out quickly, but when the birds are spotted he knows all the right methods to get as close as possible without scaring them into the air and onto another (farther) sandbar. He cuts the motor at just the right moment, pulls out his long pole, lets the current help, and if you have a camera he tries to keep the sun at your back.

In addition to your camera, bring binoculars, protection from the sun (many are open boats), water, and a snack. Serious photographers should bring a long lens (a tripod helps, too), since many of your pictures will be taken with the birds in flight, seldom closer than 300 meters (unless you get lucky). If you can, start out before breakfast—the best time to begin the day when flamingo hunting.

It's best to make arrangements the day before. Get all particulars straight before you begin your trip: how long it will last and where you will be going. Be sure you settle your price early on. Even for one person, the charge is the same. During the heavy tourist season (December, March, April, July, and August), expect the price to be higher.

The busiest times are July (especially the feast day of Santiago on the 20th) and Easter

Flamingos lay one egg in a cone-shaped mud nest.

DIANA LASICH HARPER

week. Starting in May and through June and July, the flamingos fly to a distant cove and build their mud nests. They are kept under close scrutiny by the Ministry of Ecology and Urban Development. From November to March there aren't as many birds, but the young are just beginning to color; at hatching, flamingos are mostly white, and at three months the black feathers along their wings begin to grow.

Locals are well versed in the habits of flamingos, and willing to tell you how the birds build their nests; how, if a storm hits at nesting time, the usually calm water sweeps away their one egg; and how some shady characters (not locals) steal eggs and young birds to sell on the black market—illegal since this is a national park. But don't forget to bring your Spanish dictionary, because most of the local guides speak little English.

Accommodations

Budget: The **Hotel Nefertiti,** on the waterfront, is the only hotel and the only multistory building in Río Lagartos. The rooms are spartan and not noted for cleanliness, but have bathrooms and (usually) hot water. The first-floor rooms seem to have constantly wet floors from moisture oozing through the cement; ask for a second-floor room and inspect it carefully. An open-air *palapa* dining room doubles as a disco some nights.

An alternative is to inquire at the cafe on the plaza; there may be a place where you can hang your hammock for a reasonable fee.

Food

The **Hotel Nefertiti Restaurant** is about as good as it gets. The one thing for sure: the seafood is always fresh. Though the decor is garish, the prices are moderate, and you'll come away satisfied. For something cheaper, try the **Restaurant Negritos** on the plaza; it serves mostly seafood. The small market has a limited selection but will keep body and soul together nicely. If you have transportation, a pleasant surprise is the food at **Restaurant El Payaso** in San Felipe, 12 km west of Río Lagartos.

Transportation

By Public Bus: From Valladolid, it's a two-hour bus trip to Río Lagartos. There are no direct buses; the bus stops over in Tizimín, where you have time to look the town over as you wait for your transfer. In Río Lagartos, the bus drops you off in front of the Restaurant Negritos, which also sells bus tickets.

By Car: Río Lagartos is 103 km north of Valladolid on Hwy. 295. You'll find **Pemex** stations at Valladolid, Tizimín, and Río Lagartos.

Tours

In Mérida, **Yucatán Trails Travel Agency,** Calle 62 #482, tel. (99) 28-2582 or 28-5913, fax (99) 24-4919, offers a two-day birdwatching excursion from Mérida to Río Lagartos, including an overnight stay at the Hotel Nefertiti.

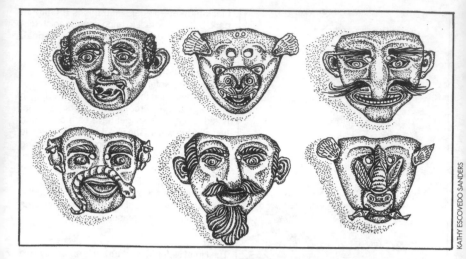

KATHY ESCOVEDO SANDERS

THE STATE OF CAMPECHE
INTRODUCTION

The Land

Occupying the southwest section of the Yucatán Peninsula, the state of Campeche is bordered on the north and east by the state of Yucatán, on the northwest by the Gulf of Mexico, on the southeast by the state of Quintana Roo, on the southwest by the state of Tabasco, and on the south by Guatemala. Campeche covers 50,952 square km, and is occupied by a population of over 600,000. In the north, the land is dry; however, just a few km south of the Campeche/Yucatán border, rivers begin to run, and the land becomes green and tropical. Several fine harbors are nestled along the Gulf coast, and just a few km inland, rolling hills rise to low, jagged mountains.

Climate

Though only a few hundred km apart, the northern and southern parts of the state exhibit vastly different climates. The arid north stands in stark contrast to the thick, lush rainforest of the southern and eastern parts of the state, which re-

ceive as much as 1,500 mm (60 inches) of rain each year. While the north has little water, in the south abundant lakes and rivers flow into the Laguna de Terminos. The farther south, the more humid the weather. Even here, some areas become parched after a long dry period.

Fauna

Campeche harbors a variety of animals, including peccaries, jaguars, tapirs, armadillos, ocelots, and deer. For a closer look at these creatures, take a hike into the bush. Bird hunting is a popu-

ARCHAEOLOGICAL ZONES OF CAMPECHE

Edzná	Río Bec	Becán
Dzibilnocac	Haltunchen	Xpujil
Xcalunkin	Hochob	Isla Jaina
Hormiguero	Nocuchich	
Chicanná	Calakmul	

lar sport supported by quantities of wild duck, turkey, and pheasant. Other more beautiful birds (for watching only) include flamingos, parrots, and herons. The coastal waters along the Gulf are thick with barracuda, swordfish, dolphin, tuna, and snapper, as well as lobster and shrimp from the tiniest to the largest.

History

Several Maya towns in various pockets of the state are believed to have been trade centers between central and Southern Mexico, as well as important crossroads between the north and east part of the Peninsula. During pre-Hispanic times the Campechean coast bore the title of La Ruta Maya ("The Mayan Route"), a main artery for traders traveling by land and on the sea in their sturdy canoes. Until 22 March 1517, when the first Spaniards arrived here, the Maya had never seen people that were so different. It took 25 years of both Spanish and Indian bloodshed to end the Maya power in Ah Kim Pech (Campeche). Despite the difference in arms (Spanish guns versus the Indian lance),

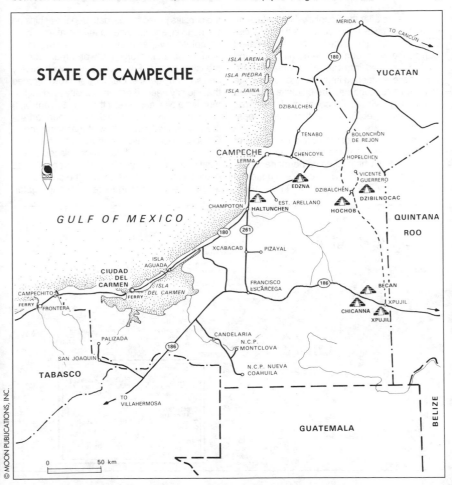

a deadly determination to repel the intruders motivated the Maya to resist the Spanish for an entire generation.

Economy

Lack of roads and communication systems isolated Campeche (along with the rest of the Peninsula) from the development of the rest of Mexico. Only since the beginning of the 1950s has Campeche really begun to enter the 20th century and join the outside world. Good highways have been built; agriculture is starting to thrive; fishing has grown from a family industry to big business; and the greatest economic boon of all has been the discovery of offshore oil. As some fine archaeological sites attain fame, the tourism industry is also developing within the state.

CAMPECHE CITY AND VICINITY

Twenty years after the Spaniards' first attack on Campeche, it was finally conquered by Francisco de Montejo. The state's capital, also called Campeche, was founded on 4 Oct. 1540 and soon developed into the state's major port. Campeche is steeped in pirate lore. During the 16th and 17th centuries the city was attacked repeatedly by vicious European pirates—it was destroyed and rebuilt several times over a period of many years.

From 1558, for almost two centuries the city of Campeche was harassed, burned, and sacked by buccaneers who'd taken up permanent residence on the Island of Tris, today's Ciudad del Carmen—only 208 km away. On 9 Feb. 1663,

the corsairs joined forces, gathered their ships on the horizon, and launched a furious attack. They completely wiped out the city, killing men, women, and children—the worst massacre in the city's history. Finally, after so much misery and so many deaths, the Spanish crown agreed that the city needed protection. City leaders formulated a plan and quietly the work began. On 3 January 1686 builders laid the cornerstone of the new walled city. The wall that surrounded Campeche was of stout stone construction, from three meters thick with four gates placed strategically around the city. Indeed, in an effort to make this bastion impregnable, the builders extended the wall into the sea, with huge gates

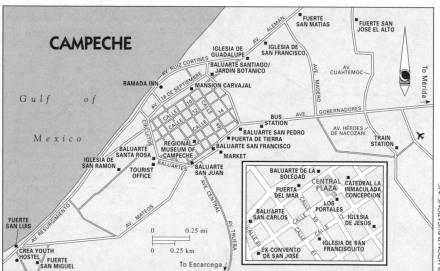

that allowed ships to swiftly unload their cargo into the protected fort, often with a brigantine in pursuit. Though finishing touches weren't made until 1704, the completion of the sturdy bastion finally gave Campecheans a security that would ultimately end the era of invasion. Still, isolated attacks upon the coastal cities south of Campeche continued from the pirates' notorious island base. In 1717, determined to wipe the bandits out, Captain Don Alonso Felipe de Aranda led a sneak attack that routed or killed all the pirates and burned their ships. Once and for all, peace reigned over the Gulf coast. For even more protection the Puerta de Tierra ("Land Gate") was built in 1732.

Campeche spent the next 200 years developing a peaceful society, including the growth of an economy not dependent on the shipment of silver and gold. Even after the Independence in 1821, Campeche, isolated from much of greater Mexico's turmoil, suffered from its own problems of development.

Before the Mexican Revolution, Campeche city was inhabited almost exclusively by descendants of colonial Spaniards. During the early glory days after the wall was built and the pirates were routed, life was good for the landowners. The Indians were slaves and suffered the same indignities as their fellows in the rest of the land. In the 1820s, with the coming of Mexico's independence, slavery was abolished. Campeche soon settled into an era of humble existence, an oblivion that brought few changes for decades. For years Campeche was part of an alliance with Mérida, but several years after the Caste War in 1842, it seceded and became part of the Federal Republic of Mexico as the independent state of Campeche. For decades, little was heard about this old city until oil was found to be a lucrative money maker, and simple fishing developed into a major industry. The city continues to change and tourism is building.

SIGHTS

The Walled City

The old city within the ramparts of the ancient wall is well laid out, and once you figure out the numbering system for the 40 square blocks, walking is a piece of cake. The streets that run southeast to northwest, perpendicular to the sea, are odd-numbered from 51 on the north to 65 on the south. Streets running northeast to southwest are even-numbered beginning with Calle 8 on the west through Calle 18 on the east. Most of the more popular sights and services lie within these ancient boundaries, set off by the seven remaining *baluartes,* (bastions) built by Spanish settlers. This old part of the city is surrounded by Circuito Baluartes on three sides, and by Av. 16 de Septiembre on the seaward side (a filled-in area). The city outside the wall is creeping ever outward toward the mountains, north and south, up and down the coast.

The City Center

Near the sea, Campeche's **Central Plaza** is bordered by Calles 8, 10, 55, and 57. This charming spot provides a resting place between walking tours around the city. Park renovations in 1985 added contemporary wrought-iron fences and benches. But even with its modern gazebo in the center, the plaza's feeling of antiquity is overwhelming. Campeche is endowed with the charm of 1700s architecture, and the city has recently been involved in revitalizing the oldest buildings, renovating old stone facades, painting where needed, bringing back its colonial charm. Sunday concerts are held in the plaza; the band looks as if it stepped out of a Norman Rockwell painting, black shiny-brimmed hats and all. Don't be surprised to hear an oompah band—with French horns, flutes, violins, and bassoons—blaring forth with the excitement of a great orchestra. The plaza is the heart of the city: families gather, friends meet, and children run and play.

The central plaza is bordered on one side by **Catedral La Inmaculada Concepción,** one of the oldest Christian churches on the Yucatán, constructed 1540-1705. On Calle 10, the plaza faces **Los Portales,** another aging structure with a graceful facade and arcaded passageways.

The modern square glass building near the waterfront with the colorful mosaic is the **Palacio de Gobierno.** The concrete building next to it that resembles a flying saucer is **Congressional Hall.**

The **Regional Museum of Campeche,** on Calle 59 between 14 and 16, is housed in a lovely old building with a colorful history. Its exhibits are a combination of colonial and archaeological/anthropological artifacts. Among other things, you'll see the famous jade mask from Calakmul. When Mexican archaeologists found the mask

detail of the beautiful tilework of the Ex-Convento de San José

years ago it was in many pieces; it has since been put together. On display upstairs are many of the arms used in the days of the marauding pirates. Small admission.

Ex-Convento de San José, at Calle 10 at 65, was the first lighthouse in Campeche, raised in 1864 and built on the front of this former church. The original part of the structure, the ex-convent, was built by Jesuits in 1700; the adjacent building, a Jesuit college, was constructed in 1756. The baroque church, impressive with its quixotic Talavera tile facade, provides an artisans' exhibit and shop. The history of the building is as varied as that of the city of Campeche: it's gone from church to army post to warehouse to art museum. The paintings on display present a striking contrast: two giant religious murals are placed next to a modern artist's violent portrayal of what was wreaked upon the Maya in the name of God.

The **Mansion Carvajal** is another old mansion that has been restored to its original beauty, and is perhaps even more beautiful now. The building has a checkered history: formerly owned by a rich family named Carvajal, it was used as Hotel Senorial until the mid-1970s. Today it houses the government offices. It's well worth a visit; note the Moorish-style architecture.

The *Baluartes* and Forts of Campeche

Many remnants of the city's bastions remain more or less intact. Though neglected for years, and even with sections destroyed to make way for trolley tracks, the remaining ramparts have managed to survive modern architects and violent storms and to lend a wonderful old-world ambience to Campeche. What was formerly the seawall and shipyard within the gate was filled in some years back to make way for a wide avenue and new buildings on the modern waterfront. You can visit seven of the eight original bastions—San Francisco, Soledad, Santiago, Santa Rosa, San Pedro, San Juan, and San Carlos— and several forts, all now used as public buildings. The Circuito Baluartes is the trail where once the wall stood—a bus tour is available that circles the old city and takes you to each bastion.

Fuerte San Miguel: This 18th-century fort 2.5 km southwest of town includes moat and drawbridge. You can feel the terror that motivated inhabitants to build such sturdy protection—so sturdy that it has survived 200 years. This fort houses Campeche's archaeological museum, or as the tourist office refers to it, the **Maya Museum.** The collection here is not large, but you'll get just a small taste of the fine pieces found on Isla Jaina, which apparently was used as the cemetery of the noble Maya. To get to the fort, follow the coastal road south until you come to the large statue of a man with a raised arm, a work titled *The Resurgence of Campeche,* and then follow the signs.

Baluarte Nuestra Señora de la Soledad: This is the site of many stelae found in Campeche, now in a hall called Dr. Roman Pina Chan. Many of the carved stones are said to be 1,000 years old. This is the largest bastion on the city's seaward side. See the Mayan fountain close by. It's easy to find near the waterfront on Calle 8 across from the central plaza.

Baluarte Santiago: Here you'll find the **Jardín Botánico Xmuch Haltum,** a small garden with many species of plants native to the arid plains in the north and the green jungle of the wet southern region. This walled garden is a short but worthwhile trip. The offices of ecotourism are here, and they are worth checking out if you are touring the state. Santiago is on Av. 16 de Septiembre near the waterfront. Each of this garden's ancient gates is a wonder of architecture that shouldn't be missed.

Fuerte San José, one of Campeche's two remaining forts, complete with cannons and rifle slits and thick walls, houses a museum that shows the arms used during the pirate era.

Baluarte San Carlos: On the west corner of Circuito Baluartes between Calle 8, the Progress Fountain, and Av. 16 de Septiembre, it was one of the first fortresses built, today flanked by the Governor's Palace and the State Congress building. The *baluarte* now contains a city museum, with photographs, drawings, and models of the city's development. It's open daily 9 a.m.-2 p.m., 4-8 p.m.

From **Puerta de Tierra** ("Land Gate"), Calle 59 at Av. Gobernadores, visitors experience how the forts and walls protected the city parameters. This inland wall, a long stone fortification, seems impenetrable even today. If someone is minding the fort you'll get an escorted tour atop the stone walls, from where you can spot the corresponding wall across town that protects the city from the sea. A **Sound and Light Show** takes place every Friday evening at 8:30 p.m. at the Puerta de Tierra. The 30-minute show transports visitors back into the past via lights, music, and drama. The presentation tells of the romance and the tragedy of the Indians, the pirates, and the Spaniards. Who knows if it's historically accurate, but attending is a good experience; US$3 admission. For more information, check at the tourist office or at your hotel.

ACCOMMODATIONS

In a city the size of Campeche, you might expect a larger number of hostelries, but there aren't

that many. Still, you should be able to find something to suit you in your price categories, and Campeche offers a youth hostel to boot.

Shoestring

The **CREA Youth Hostel** (IYHF) in the university area is very clean and offers segregated dorms with bunk beds. It charges a US$5 deposit for blankets, pillow slips, and towels. These articles are changed every three days; the deposit is refunded when you leave. The well-laid-out grounds are neatly kept and roomy, with a swimming pool, ballpark, and cafeteria. Meals are very inexpensive here. Breakfast is served 7:30-9:30 a.m., lunch 2-3:30 p.m., dinner 7:30-9:30 p.m. To get to the YH from the center of town, take the bus marked "Campeche Lerma" going south along the coastal highway to the corner of Agustín Melgar. Look for the sign that reads Centro Cultural Deportiva Juvenil. Several budget cafes and food stands are nearby. If you're so inclined, it's about a 20-minute walk from the central plaza.

Budget

Another good value for your peso is **Hotel Castelmar,** Calle 61 #2, tel. (981) 6-2886, in a colonial building three blocks south of the plaza. The large rooms have ceiling fans, private bathrooms, and hammock hooks; if you're lucky and have a choice, ask for a front room with a balcony. When we last checked, maintenance had deteriorated at the Castelmar; some bathrooms lacked toilet seats, and some rooms had only a curtain blocking the bathroom from view. If you don't like the first room you see, ask to see another. The management is friendly and willing to answer all questions.

Inexpensive

A good bargain is the **Hotel Colonial,** Calle 14 #122, tel. (981) 6-2230. From the outside it looks new, painted a soft beige and white. Inside you'll find everything spotlessly clean, tile everywhere (although none of it matches), 1920s simple painted wooden furniture, sheets so white they might glow in the dark, hot water, bathroom, ceiling fans, a few a/c rooms (extra), purified water available downstairs, and a central area for reading or relaxing. Cash only, pay daily, and the landlady means business.

Hotel Reforma, Calle 8 #287, tel. (981) 6-4454, is centrally located, very humble, and fairly clean (but check).

Posada del Ángel, next to the cathedral at Calle 10 #309 between 53 and 55, tel. (981) 6-7718, offers 15 rooms with a/c, hot water, and private bathrooms. It's clean and has a refrigerator for guest use.

In the colonial setting of an old three-story mansion, the **Hotel América,** Calle 10 #252, tel. (981) 6-4588, offers usually clean rooms with hot water, private bathrooms, ceiling fans, marble floors, and colonial touches. It has 52 rooms, 38 with telephones.

In a modern setting, friendly, family-run **Hotel López,** Calle 12 #189, tel. (981) 6-3342, has (usually) clean rooms simply furnished with ceiling fans (a/c extra), hot water, and bathrooms; the upstairs restaurant has a TV. The colorful old hotel is beginning to show its age.

Expensive

You'll find the **Ramada Inn** at Av. Ruíz Cortínes 51, Apdo. Postal 251, tel. (981) 6-2233 or 6-4611, telex 75519, U.S. tel. (800) 228-2828. Credit cards accepted. The pleasant hotel has 120 modern rooms, most with small balconies and ocean views, a/c, tile bathrooms, and double or king beds. The Ramada is simply but well-decorated with tile floors and pastel colors, and has a pool and friendly staff. **Cafetería Poquito** is a moderately priced coffee shop where a hamburger or enchilada plate costs about US$6. **El Grill** dining room serves a pricier, but very good, dinner. This is a really lovely place to dine, with stained-glass windows, nouvelle Mexican cuisine, and fine piano music adds to the atmosphere. The **Piccolo Bar** and **Atlantis Disco** offer nightly entertainment. Reservations are a must for December.

At the **Hotel Debliz,** Av. Las Palmas 55, tel. (981) 1-0111 or 6-1611, the rooms are comfortable, with tile and natural wood. The Debliz is outside of town, on the northern extension of Av. Ruíz Cortínes called Av. Barranda (en route to Mérida). It's a good choice if you have a car and want to bypass town, and it's popular with large tour bus groups. A large meeting room is available for business meetings. The restaurant is large, with a linen-and-crystal atmosphere. Pool, disco, and six suites with separate bedrooms are available.

Hotel Baluartes, on Av. Ruíz Cortínes, tel. (981) 6-3911, fronts the promenade that runs along the water across the street from the Ramada Inn. It's clean, has 104 well-furnished rooms, swimming pool (nonguests can swim for a small charge), sidewalk cafe, bar, dining room, and banquet facilities.

FOOD

A number of budget, fast-food-type cafes sell *tortas,* or if you yearn for a hamburger try the **Pinkus** cafes (Parke Pinkus on Campeche-Hampolol, or Pinkus Burger at Av. Francisco I. Madero 269). For real budget food, the food stands in the **marketplace** serve *típico tortas,* beans, tortillas, *panuchos,* and tamales. Fruit lovers—try the unusual fruits you'll see at the markets, or sample the buys of the season. Avocados, for instance, sell for about a nickel each. The **Nueva España Panadería** makes great egg breads and sweet breads. Be there 12:30-1 p.m. and again at 5 p.m. to get them hot and fresh! Locations: Calle 10 between 59 and 61, and Calle 12 between Calles 59 and 57 near **Helados Bing**—good for a refreshing guava ice cream cone.

Remember, this is seafood country, so for a little more money take advantage of it. Try the shrimp, excellent though expensive, the stone crabs, or the fish specialty of the day, which is usually sweet and fresh. Try other regional specialties, too. Though the **Miramar** restaurant (Calles 8 and 61) has been operating for many years, it has the flavor of today's Campeche and is always busy with visitors and residents alike, all putting away excellent seafood. Try the *arroz con mariscos,* a large, tasty dish of rice with clams, shrimp, and conch, served with bread and butter, about US$6. Grilled shrimp, on the other hand, is about US$10.

La Pigua, Miguel Alemán 197-A, is great at lunchtime, when it fills with professionals and couples taking long breaks. The long dining room has glass walls backed by lush gardens—it's like eating in a greenhouse! All the seafood is excellent, and the ambience is worth appreciating for hours. **Barbillas,** on Av. Lázaro Cárdenas, prepares good fish and meat dishes. If you're waiting at the ADO bus station, the food is not bad at all and very reasonable. For about US$3,

the marketplace

OZ MALLAN

you can get *tortas*—chicken and cheese, or ham and cheese. Or for about US$5, you get fillet of fish, chicken *pibil,* stuffed peppers, or the local specialty, *pan de cazón* (a dish made of layered tortillas, black beans, and shark). The bus drivers say the food is good.

The small, vegetarian-friendly **La Perla,** Calle 10 #345 near the university, is a student hangout with low-priced, filling meals and great *licuados* and fruit salads. **Balneario Popular** on the beach serves good seafood at reasonable prices. For great *tortas* and luscious desserts, try **Maxim's** on Av. López Mateos. **Video Taco,** on Av. Francisco I. Madero, two blocks south of Av. Gobernadores, has incredibly cheap prices, a youthful atmosphere, and videos thrown in. It opens at 6:30 p.m.

Restaurant La Parroquia, on Calle 55 between 10 and 12, is open 24 hours, serves *típico* food, sandwiches, and a wide variety of other dishes. There is also a nightly "show folklórico." Another good eating place is the **Cafetería Continental** at Calles 8 and 61. At **Restaurant**

Maranganzo you can get good regional dishes, both seafood and *típico;* moderate prices. Look for it at Calle 8 #261. For good tacos and *flautas,* try **La Carreta** on Calle 8.

INFORMATION AND SERVICES

Tourist Information
The **State of Campeche Office of Tourism** has moved back to the office at Plaza Moch Couoh, Av. Ruiz Cortines, tel./fax (981) 6-6767. You'll usually find at least one English-speaking staff member. The staff hands out good street maps and hotel and restaurant information. They'll make local calls for reservations if you have trouble speaking Spanish and are always immensely helpful. Since Campeche is changing more these days, you might want to stop by even if you don't have a question just to see what's new. It's open Mon.-Fri. 9 a.m.-9 p.m., Saturday 9 a.m.-7 p.m., Sunday 9 a.m.-1 p.m..

Other Services
The two banks below give good service: **Banamex** at Calle 10 #15 is open Mon.-Fri. and will change money 10 a.m.-noon, tel. (981) 6-5252; **Bancomer** at Calle 59 #2-A (across from Baluarte de Soledad on Av. 16 de Septiembre) is open Mon.-Fri. and will also change money 10 a.m.-noon, tel. (981) 6-2144.

Edificio Federal, at Av. 16 de Septiembre and Calle 53, tel. (981) 6-43-90, is open for both telegraph and postal business. For medical emergencies, ask the hotel to refer you to an English-speaking doctor, or call **Seguro Social,** tel. (981) 6-1855, on López Mateos on the south side of the city. Another choice is the **Clínica Campeche,** Av. Central 65, tel. (981) 6-5612.

Important numbers: **Fire Department,** tel. (981) 6-2309; **police,** tel. 06; **Red Cross,** tel. (981) 6-0666 or 6-5202.

TRANSPORTATION

Campeche is on the Gulf coast, 190 km southwest of Mérida and 444 km northeast of Villahermosa (across the Tabasco state border). On the main highway, Campeche is a natural stopover for the trip between these two capitals.

By Plane

Campeche is serviced by **Aeroméxico,** U.S. tel. (800) 237-6639, once daily from Mexico City, and by small commuter airlines, which offer only a few flights. Ask about shuttle flights from Mérida. Though small, the airport is modern, two km northeast of the city, and taxis meet most flights. Check with your Mexican travel agent for flights within Mexico.

By Train

The train station is two km east of town center on Av. Héroes de Nacozari; taxi fare is about US$6 from downtown. The bus marked "China" passes in front of the station and you can catch it at the market or Av. 16 de Septiembre downtown. The state tourist office has the most recent schedules, prices, and information. Trains to Central Mexico or Mérida run daily. Get to the station at least an hour early to buy tickets and recheck departure time; no sleeping cars are available, and travelers report unpleasant conditions and thievery on the trains.

By Bus

Campeche has a good bus system covering the entire city, inside and outside the wall, and the price is right for everybody—cheap. Bus stops are on most corners or, as is so convenient in Mexico, the buses will stop most anyplace. Remember that in Campeche west is always towards the water, and east is inland.

Four blocks northeast of the city at Gobernadores 289 between Calle 47 and Calle Chile, the bus station houses both first and second-class buses. The **ADO** (first-class) terminal has a restaurant, waiting room, and baggage check-in facing Gobernadores; the second-class terminal is on the opposite side (enter through first class or Calle Chile). ADO offers more frequent service to Ciudad del Carmen, Villahermosa, and Mérida. Check the schedule at the terminal for departure times to the Caribbean coast, Chetumal, Mexico City, and all other destinations throughout Mexico.

Camioneros de Campeche, the second-class line, has five buses daily to Uxmal, to Edzná daily at 8 a.m. and 2:30 p.m. (this bus drops you off and picks you up one kilometer away from the ruins), and to Dzibalchén, near the sites of Dzibilnocac and Hochob; figure two hours one-way. You'll see countryside, with frequent stops in small towns along the way. Archaeology buffs: Ask the tourist office to help you arrange a trip to Calakmul, the site where the jade mask was found. It's difficult to reach, but worth it to see the important structures if you're a fanatic. At your hotel or travel agency ask about tours to the ruins.

Express bus service is appearing in many parts of Mexico. The vehicles are modern, clean, and a/c, with airline-type seats and bathrooms. An attendant will serve you coffee and cookies, and some buses have earphones for music—these

Campeche rainwater salesman making deliveries

OZ MALLAN

are the 747s of the road. Campeche is a stop for express buses. The deluxe **Omnibus Caribe Express** buses depart from the Plaza Super Díaz on Av. Ruíz Cortínes for Cancún and Mérida at 10 p.m.; fare to Cancún is US$25, to Mérida US$9. The departure point for this bus changes; check with the tourist office for the latest information.

By Car
Two good highways link Campeche and Mérida: Hwy. 180 *via corta* (the short route) and Hwy. 260 *via larga* (the long route). If you're traveling roundtrip by car to or from Mérida, try both roads to see more of the countryside (traveling time is almost the same both ways: two to three hours). Highway 180 runs south parallel to the coast (and also parallel to a new toll road from Campeche to Champotón), and crosses a bridge that brings you to Isla del Carmen; to continue south, you must travel on a series of ferries from Isla del Carmen to the mainland. Staying on Hwy. 180 brings you to the state of Tabasco. To Chetumal it's 421 km from Campeche; north to Cancún it's 514 km.

Travel Agencies
If you're on foot and wish to see more of the city or to tour the Maya site at Edzná, contact the nearest travel agency. A daily city tour will take you to most of the museums and sites in the city, with pickup at your hotel about 4:30 p.m. and return at 8 p.m.. (Remember, most of the museums are closed on Monday.) Fare is approximately US$10. Tour pickups for Edzná depart at 8 a.m. and return around 1 p.m. after a two-hour trek through the site. This is probably the most time-economical way to see Edzná if you don't have your own transportation; fare is approximately US$30.

Car Rentals
Getting around within the city is quite simple either on foot or by bus. But if you wish to visit the outlying areas at your leisure, car rental is recommended. Prices fluctuate daily with the season and the peso, so shop around for your best buy. Car rentals are available in the lobbies of two hotels. At the Ramada Inn ask for **Jaina Rents,** tel. (981) 6-2233; **Hertz** is at Hotel Baluartes. Both hotels are on Av. Ruíz Cortínes.

Taxis
You can flag down taxis in most parts of the city. Taxi stands are at these intersections: Calle 55 and Circuito, close to the market; Calles 8 and 55, left of the cathedral; Gobernadores and Chile, close to the bus terminal; Costa Rica and Circuito Baluartes; Central and Circuito Baluartes. To request a cab by phone, call (981) 6-1113, 6-2363, or 6-5230.

ARCHAEOLOGICAL ZONES

ISLA JAINA

Isla Jaina is not open to the public, although rumors of development persist. Most visitors, except for the devoted archaeology buff, will find little of interest here. What is interesting about the small island is the historical background discovered in the contents of the old graves.

Burial Grounds of the Elite
North of Campeche city, near the coast, the swampy island of Jaina has the largest known Maya burial ground on the Yucatán Peninsula. According to archaeologist Sylvanus Morley, who discovered the impressive site in 1943, Jaina was used for burial ceremonies for the Maya elite since A.D. 652. The most important and powerful dead were carried in long, colorful processions to this small island. Bodies were interred in burial jars in crouching positions, with statues resting on the folded arms. Some were found with a jade stone in the mouth; the skin was often stained red and then wrapped in either a straw mat or white cloth. Plates with food, jewelry, weapons, tools, and other precious items to accompany the dead to the other world were placed on their heads.

In 1950, more than 150 skeletal remains were discovered along the banks of Jaina rivers after flooding. Thousands have been looted and are part of private (underground) collections.

The dead were buried with Isla Jaina's signature offering, the famous Jaina figurines—

OZ MALLAN

Statues found on Isla Jaina at burial sites show anatomical realism and minute details indicative of everyday living. This man is wearing a false nosepiece, which was considered a sign of class.

one of the high points of Mesoamerican art. (The best Jaina figurines are on display in Mexico City's Museo Nacional de Antropología.) These are small (4-10 inches), finely crafted ceramic sculptures that were obviously portraits of the deceased, many with facial scarification. They are dressed in ritual costumes, like those of warriors and ball players, and frozen in ritual positions, including as captives being tortured. Their function may have been to show the dead in the guises of the Maya gods. A quarter of the sculptures were female, almost all representing the bare-breasted goddess Ix Chel. The Jaina figurines often doubled as rattles, with clay balls rolling around the hollow interiors. The dead of

Isla Jaina may have been Puuc nobility, because that is the nearest major Maya area.

The ancient Maya outdid themselves in developing this offshore island. Jaina's low elevation was raised by platforms made of *sascab* (limestone material) brought from the mainland in canoes. This material covered the brittle coral of the island and allowed the Jaina Indians to build two imposing pyramids, **Zacpool** and **Sayasol,** as well as altars and other ceremonial structures on the island.

HECELCHAKÁN

About 75 km north of Campeche on Hwy. 180 toward Mérida, stop at Hecelchakán's **Museo Arqueológico del Camino Real.** Some fine examples of Jaina burial art are displayed here. Hecelchakán is a small city; the museum is easy to find near the center of town north of the church. The museum's hours are erratic; it's supposed to open at 10 a.m., but is usually open when someone is there. You can check at the small market next door for more information. The next time you visit Mexico City, go to Museo Nacional de Antropología at Chapultepec Park to see a superb exhibit of Maya art, including the best of the Jaina graves—or at least what's not in private collections.

EDZNÁ

Edzná was settled as an agricultural village by the Middle Preclassic (600-300 B.C.). During the following centuries, a network of drainage and irrigation canals 13.75 miles long was dug around the settlement's center and extended into agricultural zones. The canals were used as highways to transport canoe-borne goods and probably played a double role serving as defensive moats as well. Edzná's most ambitious building program began in the early 7th century and continued for about 200 years. The site contains some of the earliest examples of the Puuc style, as well as examples of southern Maya influence that may have arrived here via Cobá. Edzná was abandoned during the 10th century, most likely because of wars with Chichén-based armies.

As you approach Edzná (about 60 km southeast of Campeche) on the road from Cayal, a tall pyramid rising from thick vegetation on the valley floor is visible from quite a distance. The site covers an area of six square km in the midst of a wide valley of cultivated land and scrub forest bordered by a low range of mountains. This Maya city is remote but easy to get to from Campeche.

The Temple of Five Stories

This is the grand sight of Edzná. People lived at this site as early as 600 B.C., and the existing structures are dated from around 300 B.C. to A.D.

200. The city grew and prospered until A.D. 900, when it (along with many other Classic centers) was suddenly deserted for reasons yet to be discovered. The largest structure is on the east side of a large open area called **Plaza Central.** This five-story pyramid has an open comb on top (seen only on some Maya structures) to give the impression of more height and to bring the temple closer to the sun. At one time this comb was covered with ornate stucco carvings, and the rest of the building's stones were coated with smooth stucco and painted brilliant colors. Over the centuries the elements have worn away the stucco coating, exposing the rough stones beneath.

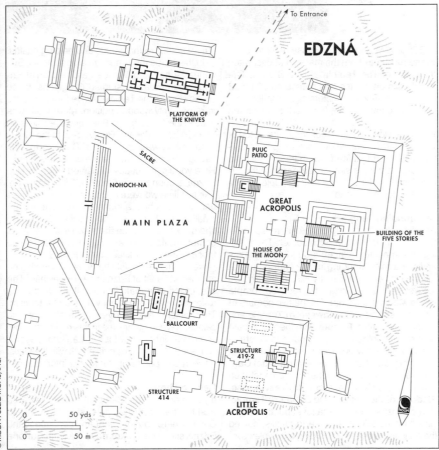

The unimaginatively named Temple of Five Stories sits on Plaza Central.

OZ MALLAN

Edzná in Maya means "House of Grimaces"; the name comes from the masks that decorated the comb of The Temple of Five Stories. The temple sits on a base that measures 60 by 58 meters and stands 31 meters high. The four levels of living quarters are believed to have been used by Maya priests; a shrine and altar are on the highest level and the roof comb sits on top of that. Under the first-floor stairway is a corbel-vaulted tunnel that leads to an inner chamber. The architecture is simple compared to the ornate facades of the Puucs only a couple of hundred km down the road.

Surrounding Temples

At Edzná you can't help but be impressed with the elegant planning of each center. The buildings are gracefully placed around open plazas and platforms, blending nicely with nature. It must have been the Beverly Hills of its day. On the west side of the plaza is the restored **Temple of the Moon** (Paal u'na). On the two corners of the plaza stand the **Southwestern Temple** and the **Northwestern Temple,** with the sweat bath next door. Another plaza surrounded by structures not yet excavated (or previously excavated and overgrown again) is called **Grupo del Central Ceremonial.** Here beneath the vegetation you'll see the **Great Acropolis, Great House, Platform of the Knives,** and **Southern Temple.** Part of Edzná is below sea level but the Maya, with their incredible engineering skills, solved the drainage problem by building a complex sys-

tem of underground canals and holding basins.

In the 1920s the American archaeologist Sylvanus Morley and Mexican archaeologist Enrique Juan Palacios studied the glyphs; those on the stairs of the Temple of Five Stories are still in remarkably good condition. More work was done in the 1940s by the Palenque specialists Alberto Ruz l'Huillier and Raul Abreu. In the 1980s a ball court was uncovered. Be sure to look through the barbed-wire fence under the *palapa.* Here you'll see a couple of carved stone masks. Edzná is open 8 a.m.-5 p.m., US$3 admission. The last time we were in Edzná, its new facilities had not been built and the toilets were dirty. A small *palapa* hut sells snacks; stick with the bottled drinks here! Once the new visitor center is complete, its services will be comparable to those of the larger sites on the Peninsula.

Note: Archaeologists have begun working on another site east of Edzná near Hopelchén. The site, called **Xtampak,** lies about 30 km down a rough dirt road, and is not yet ready for tourism. The workers have uncovered a three-story-high palace. Several other sites in this region may become highlights on a tour of La Ruta Maya. If you're a dedicated ruins buff, check with the tourist office in Campeche city for further information.

Getting There

If you're driving from Campeche, take Hwy. 180 east to Chencoyil, then go east on Hwy. 261 to Cayal, where you turn right and continue to the Edzná site. The 60-km drive takes about one hour. From the bus station in Campeche a second-class bus leaves twice daily at 8 a.m. and 2:30 p.m. **Note:** The bus drops you off and picks you up about one km from the site. Unless you have great faith in your hitchhiking skills, forget the 12:30 p.m. trip since the only return bus passes the ruins between 11:30 a.m. and noon. Allow one hour for the trip. Campeche hotels will line you up with an escorted tour to the ruins, or check with any of the travel agencies in the city. The tourist office in Campeche runs tours to Edzná from Baluarte San Carlos daily at 9 a.m. The tour lasts five hours, and costs US$15 pp including transportation, guide, and admission to the ruins. Contact the tourist office to make sure the tours are still running.

ON THE ROAD TO RÍO BEC

Escárcega

Visitors would probably bypass Escárcega on the Peninsula sightseeing route except that is the quickest crossing point from Campeche City to the Caribbean side of the Peninsula. It lies 149 km south of Campeche at the junction of Highways 186 and 261 and is most often used as a gas stop on the way to the Río Bec area (about 150 km), Chetumal (270 km), and the east coast of the Peninsula. Mérida is 355 km north, and Villahermosa is 297 km southwest.

However, it's growing from a grubby little railroad stop (where you formerly thought twice before stepping off the train) to a fairly respectable village of 15,000. While far from being a tourist town, it sees many adventurers passing through each year on their way to explore the surrounding jungle. As outsiders come, services increase. I'd still lock my car before leaving it parked on the street. Travelers have reported holdups on the roads in this area, and you should definitely not travel at night. If you find it necessary to overnight, expect very spartan hotels in the budget class.

The town lies one and a half km west of the highway. If driving, follow the signs into town. The **ADO bus station** is at the intersection of Hwy. 261 and Justo Sierra. The **second-class bus station** is at Justo Sierra and Calle 31. The **Caribe bus station** (for buses east to the Caribbean coast) is on Hector Perez Martínez three blocks west of the plaza. The **train station** is a half kilometer up the tracks, north of Mendez. Two trains pass through daily headed for Campeche and Mérida, and two run in the opposite direction toward Coatzacoalcos and Mexico City. There are no first-class trains on this run.

If You're Driving

Drivers shouldn't be surprised or frightened of the soldiers and the stops they will encounter in this area. Usually you're stopped near the Quintana Roo border in Xpujil. This has become a major check point for the army looking for drug smugglers. These soldiers are looking for drugs of any kind, so if you have none, you have nothing to worry about. They'll ask to see in your trunk and in your glove box; cooperate and you should have no problems.

RÍO BEC ARCHAEOLOGICAL SITES

Driving east on Hwy. 186 from Escárcega will ultimately bring you to Chicanná, Becán, and Xpujil, the most accessible sites of south-central Yucatán's Río Bec culture. They share the distinctive Río Bec architectural style, whose hallmarks are "palaces" with flanking towers that appear on first glance to be Classic pyramids with temples on top. When you look more closely, you realize that the "pyramid's" steps are actually reliefs and that the temple is just a solid box with a phony door. It is as if they wanted the look of a Tikal-style temple without going through the trouble of building one. The towers are usually capped with roof combs, and sky serpent masks are frequent decorations on all ceremonial buildings.

The earliest occupation of the Río Bec area occurred between 1000 and 300 B.C. The great earthworks at Becán, which were probably defensive, were built around A.D. 150. Shortly afterward, the distant city of Teotihuacán's influence appears at the site in the form of ceramics and other evidence. Researchers believe that during the Early Classic, Becán was ruled by trader/warriors from that great culture. Most of the existing structures in the Río Bec region were built between A.D. 550 and 830. Then the population gradually dwindled and by the time of the Spanish conqest the sites were completely abandoned. The Río Bec sites were rediscovered early in the 20th century by chicle tappers.

The sites of Chicanná, Becán, and Xpujil are well worth the visit and are easy to get to from the main highway (186) crossing from Escárcega to Chetumal in southern Quintana Roo. To further develop the Mundo Maya project (also called La Ruta Maya), the Mexican government has recently agreed to spend big bucks in this area of Campeche where some of the most interesting archaeological sites have been fairly well ignored until now. Water has always been a stumbling block for tourist development, but rumors say there will soon be plenty of water and electricity with which to begin upgrading the area. INAH (the archaeological arm of the Mexican government) has begun work on some of the main structures, and many more structures and caves in the jungle continue to be "found." Because of the proximity to Calakmul, one of the largest Maya sites found thus far, and the concentration of sites (though at present not fully developed), there will be many tourists coming through this part of Campeche.

The adventurous may also want to explore the sites of Río Bec itself and El Hormiguero, which lie south of the road and are reachable only during the dry season along poor dirt roads.

Chicanná

Roughly 145 km east of Escárcega and 199 km southeast of Campeche city, the Maya site of Chicanná is about a half kilometer off Hwy. 186. The small city included five structures encircling a main center. An elaborate serpent mask frames the entry of the main palace, **House of the Serpent Mouth**—it's in comparatively good repair. Across the plaza lies **Structure I,** a typical Río Bec-style building complex with twin false-temple towers. Several hundred meters south are two more temple groups, though they're not as well preserved. Throughout the area are small and large ruins. If you're curious to compare the subtle differences of design and architecture of the ancient Maya throughout the Peninsula, the group is worth a day's visit.

Accommodations: Near Chicanná note the sign that says "hotel." Turn off onto a deserted limestone road and in the middle of nowhere you'll find a wonderful oasis/hotel, the **Chicanná Ecovillage,** tel. (981) 6-2233. Here one- and two-story solar-powered stucco villas are beautifully decorated and well landscaped. The lodge offers a small, inviting pool, and good food in a small dining room; the staff can arrange tours to the nearby ruins, including Calakmul. This place has a special ambience—no city sounds, just the song of the birds and the rhythmic swish of the broom, constantly cleaning the stone walkways. The hotel's entire operation functions according to stringent ecological rules. Moderate rates.

Becán

Another two km along Hwy. 186 (202 km south of Campeche city) is the turnoff to Becán. Dating from 500 B.C., Becán offers archaeology buffs some of the largest ancient buildings in the state. Excavation is proceeding according to schedule. **Structure VIII,** just off the southeast plaza, offers a labyrinth of underground rooms, passageways, and artifacts, indicating this to be an important religious ceremonial center. You'll see an unusual waterless moat—15 meters wide, four meters deep, and 2.3 km in diameter—surrounding the entire site. Archaeologists believe this protective-style construction indicates that warring factions occupied this part of the Peninsula during the 2nd century. Historians claim that the residents were constantly at war with Mayapán, in what is now the state of Yucatán.

Xpujil

Six km east of Becán, past the nearby small village of Xpujil, is this classic example of Río Bec architecture: the remains of three false towers overlooking miles of jungle. On the back side of the central tower, check out what's left of two huge inlaid masks. Xpujil is one of the best-preserved Río Bec-style structures, unique for having a taller central tower in addition to the flanking twin towers. If you're in a vehicle that can handle a primitive jeep road, you can reach Río Bec by taking the road south of the gas station near Xpujil.

Just before you get into the small town of Xpujil, you'll see a large, circular *palapa* restaurant called **Maya Mirador.** This is an okay lunch stop, serving simple Mexican fare and cold drinks (no wild game sold here). Behind the cafe, a few small spartan rooms are available. Ask about a van that takes passengers from Chetumal to Tikal. Public restrooms are available.

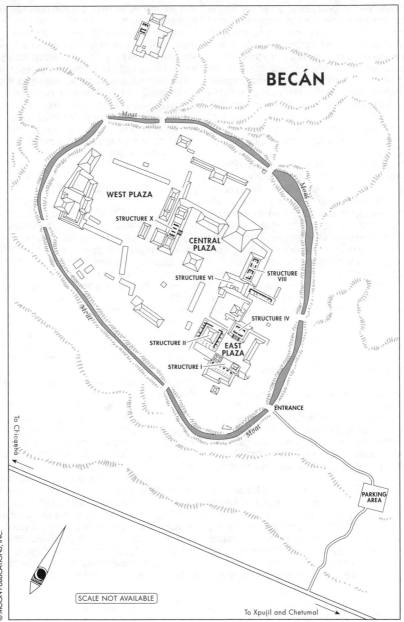

BECÁN

Moat

WEST PLAZA

STRUCTURE X

CENTRAL
PLAZA

STRUCTURE VIII

STRUCTURE VI

STRUCTURE IV

STRUCTURE II

EAST
PLAZA

STRUCTURE I

Moat

ENTRANCE

To Chicanná

PARKING
AREA

© MOON PUBLICATIONS, INC.

SCALE NOT AVAILABLE

To Xpujil and Chetumal

This is also an ideal place for birdwatching in thick jungle with little or no tourist traffic. Don't forget your binoculars and bug repellent! If you're traveling by bus to Chetumal, check with the tourist office or a travel agency for bus trips to these sites. Not fully restored, the ruins will give you an indication of what archaeologists find when they first stumble upon an isolated site. You will have renewed wonder at how they manage to clear away hundreds of years of jungle growth, figure out a puzzle of thousands of stones, and end up with such impressive structures.

Note: Although you should be careful of those few strangers who are always looking to rob and steal, the majority of the people in the Yucatán Peninsula are friendly, kind folks. On a recent visit to Belize, we took a day-trip into Mexico to the ruins of Xpujil, and our car gave up without warning. There we were, stranded—it was almost dark, no phones, or much of anything else. We eventually flagged down a pickup truck, and a kind-hearted farmer agreed to drive us to the Mexico/Belize border (as long as we didn't mind riding in the back with various and sundry animals). We were grateful, animals and all, for the friendly helping hand.

Zoh Laguna

Zoh Laguna village is 10 km north of Xpujil. In the midst of the forest, it was created in the 1930s as a mill town to house Maya workers, 35 years before archaeologists uncovered Xpujil. The mahogany veneer mill is no longer in full operation.

The small, tree-shaded town is laid back and slow moving, and unlike the typical Maya village, the houses are all built of whitewashed wood planking. This makes a comfortable hub to explore the Río Bec and Calakmul archaeological regions.

The village houses the **Calakmul Model Forest,** part of an international network of Model Forests helping the locals diversify their economy and adjust to the extreme changes taking place in their lives—in this case the increasing numbers of tourists eager to visit the ruins close by. In 1994, Becán—best known archaeological site in the area—welcomed about 30-40 visitors per month. In 1997, the numbers had risen to 300 per month.

Visitors have very little choice of hotels in the area; however that may all change. Right now, visitors will find the fine little **Hotel Bosque,** which offers just six simple rooms, each with washbasin, towels, large window, tiled floors, mirror, desk, and small dresser. Bathrooms (toilet and shower) are shared between two rooms (no hot water); hammocks are available to rent. The hotel has a nice breezy common room at the entrance. Budget rates; all the proceeds go to sustainable forestry work in the region.

CALAKMUL RESERVE

Calukmul, in the Petén region in the southern area of Campeche 35 km from the border with Guatemala, has given its name to one of the newest, largest biosphere reserves in Mexico. This site was once home to more 60,000 Maya. What may turn out to be the largest of all the structures built by the Maya, a massive pyramid, looms 53 meters (175 feet) over a base that covers two hectares (five acres).

An archaeological team from the Universidad Autónoma del Sudeste in Campeche has mapped 6,750 structures; uncovered two tombs holding magnificent jade masks, beads, and two flowerlike earcaps; excavated parts of three ceremonial sites; and found more stelae than at any other Maya site. From the top of pyramid two, it's possible to see the Danta pyramid at Calakmul's sister site, El Mirador, also part of the Calakmul reserve on the Guatemala side of the border. Both of these sites predate Christ by 100 years.

Heading the archaeological team at Calakmul, William Folan has made startling discoveries, but even more important, he has been instrumental in pushing through the concept of the biosphere reserve. Today it has become a reality. Calakmul is not yet on the usual itinerary because of the difficulty reaching it; if you'd like more information contact the tourist office in Campeche city. See the October 1989 issue of *National Geographic* magazine for color photos of the Calakmul archaeological site.

THE STATE OF TABASCO
INTRODUCTION

Technically, only three Mexican states make up the Yucatán Peninsula: Campeche, Yucatán, and Quintana Roo. However, to provide continuity for anyone studying the Maya culture or tracing La Ruta Maya (the route of the Maya people), it would be a mistake not to include the classic past of the Olmec culture, which flourished in the nearby jungles and hills of what is today the Mexican state of Tabasco.

THE LAND

Geographically, there's a vast difference between Tabasco and its northern neighbors. In Tabasco the land is flat near the sea, and only swells into gentle hills as it nears the border of Chiapas. Water is everywhere: swampy marshland, lakes, small brooks, spectacular waterfalls, and two large navigable rivers (Usumacinta and Grijalva) as well as smaller ones (including the San Pedro and the Chacamax, which begins in Chiapas). The soil is rich and fertile,

with so few rocks that the Olmecs had to travel many miles to find the material to carve their colossal heads.

Much of the land is covered with thick rainforest, rich stands of coconut, healthy banana groves, and cacao plantations. The state occupies 25,337 square km. Most of the 1,065,000 inhabitants are mestizo or Chontal Indians, with the greatest density of people in and around the capital, Villahermosa.

Climate
Tabasco is tropical—hot, humid, more sticky than its neighbors in the north. Most of the ap-

---

**ARCHAEOLOGICAL
ZONES OF TABASCO**

La Venta	San Miguel
Comalcalco	Jonuta

STATE OF TABASCO

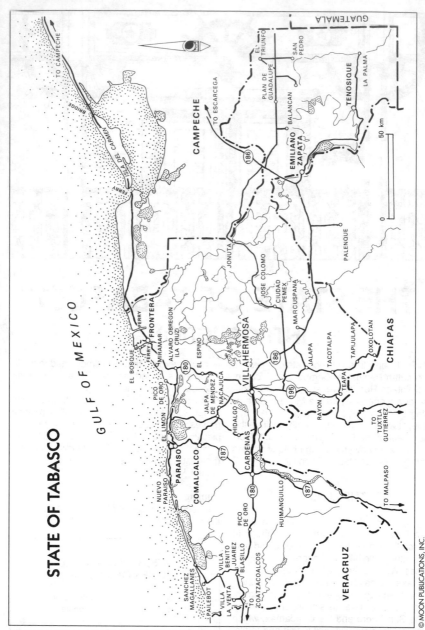

© MOON PUBLICATIONS, INC.

proximately 1,500 mm (60 inches) of yearly rainfall occurs between May and October. The driest season, when most visitors come, is 15 Dec.-15 April. But don't be surprised by showers at any time of the year in the tropics.

HISTORY

This was the first land of the Olmecs, predecessors of the Chontal Maya. Historians have determined that the Olmecs preceded all others; their society is considered the mother of Mesoamerica. The Olmecs flourished about 1200-400 B.C., and they were the first progressive society in the Americas. More than likely they were the first to begin carving in stone and building ceremonial centers.

For the most part, their centers had been long deserted by the time the Spanish first stepped on Maya land. Arriving on the coast of Tabasco in 1519, Cortés faced his first battle with the Maya on the Gulf coast and established a city called Santa María de la Victoria in honor of his initial victory. But his success was short-lived, as the Indians fought it out for 20 years more before Francisco de Montejo really gained control of the land. As the Peninsula developed and the riches of the New World began flowing from the Gulf ports to Spain, pirates attacked often enough to make living on the coast a day-to-day gamble. In 1596 the city was moved inland and renamed Villahermosa de San Juan Bautista.

Life went on with little agitation. An oblivion settled over the colony until the 1821 break from Spain, which was followed by chaos in the rush for positions of leadership. Internal conflict continued until the 1863 French invasion. This act was the catalyst that finally brought Tabascans together, and the French were ousted.

The age of President Porfirio Díaz (1876-1911) was the longest period of peace in Mexico during its first 100 years of independence. But though modernization and economic advances began throughout most of the country, Tabasco and the other southern states barely felt this wave of progress. Foreign capital was welcome; British and U.S. oil industries saw the potential, and the seed of Tabasco's future growth was planted. The country mopped up after the bloody revolution (1910-20) and began putting its economic life together. Nationalization of foreign industry slowed things down, but ultimately the government-sponsored Pemex oil company brought Tabasco into the 20th century.

ECONOMY

In the last few decades, Tabasco has made some rapid strides in modernization—all due to the oil industry. A side effect is the upsurge of agriculture with the introduction of modern machinery and improved methods, enabling the state to become a viable world-class producer of the excellent Tabasco banana and cocoa bean products.

This giant Olmec head weighs more than 15 tons.

OZ MALLAN

The state is growing into a center for culture as well as for big business. Although the present economic conditions in Mexico have slowed progress, many of the state's inhabitants have benefited from the oil boom—with better-paying jobs, improved housing, upgraded roads, and a higher standard of living. The cities have discovered the "new" industry: tourism. Tourists are attracted by modern hotels, restaurants, and an advertising campaign extolling the natural beauty and archaeological attractions of this green state.

VILLAHERMOSA AND VICINITY

The Olmecs, Mexico's oldest culture, left a rich legacy of unusual stone heads; travelers interested in the ancient past should not leave the Yucatán Peninsula without a visit to Villahermosa. Its two most important archaeological sites are Comalcalco, the largest and most important Maya site in Tabasco, and La Venta Park.

Today, Villahermosa combines the sophisticated look of a big city with the friendly atmosphere of a small town (pop. over 500,000). You can't help but notice a happy, independent feeling among the Villahermosans. The cafes, parks, and shops are alive with chattering, bustling people who seem content with their present lifestyle and proud of their ancient heritage. Walking the streets of Villahermosa, you'll notice an abundance of museums, public buildings, schools, and more recently, union buildings with long lines of men waiting for jobs and doctors' offices everywhere.

SIGHTS

La Venta Park

The actual site of La Venta, one of the greatest Olmec communities, is 129 km (80 miles) east of Villahermosa on an island in the swamps of the Tonalá River. La Venta was probably founded after 900 B.C. and functioned primarily as a ceremonial center. The main structure was a 34-meter-high pyramid made of clay that may still contain royal tombs. An incredible cache of jade figurine burial offerings found here are now in Mexico City's Museo Nacional de Antropología. La Venta was abandoned by 300 B.C. The site itself has largely been destroyed in service of Mexico's oil industry, and its major monuments were moved to this park-museum.

La Venta ("The Marketplace") ruins were first investigated by Frans Blom in 1925; however, it was the intrusion of the Pemex oil drills that brought the Olmec ceremonial center back to national attention. With oil development in the region threatening to destroy the site, the entire complex was moved to the outskirts of Villahermosa and today occupies a park laid out in the precise configuration in which the site was found by petroleum engineers. Called La Venta Park Museum (a must-see!), it contains colossal basalt heads weighing thousands of pounds and unusual sculptures not found anyplace else on the Peninsula. However, the true-blue archaeological buff should visit the original site. Near the original site, archaeologists have discovered a series of large heads made from wood (a first!). They are terribly decayed and filled with fungus, but scientists are trying different methods of treating the wood.

The park, three km from the center of Villahermosa, is on the lovely Laguna de las Ilusiones. (The lagoon is a relaxing place with a high-flying jet of water that shoots rainbow spray toward the hot midday sun.) It is a combination outdoor museum and wildlife preserve, with small animals running freely and others in cages or, as in the case of the crocodiles, within their own muddy moat. (Next door visit the children's zoo and park. A large, greenery-filled, walk-through aviary contains a marvelous array of tropical birds, including colorful toucans.) The complex was conceived by Carlos Pellicer Cámara, poet and much-revered Tabasco statesman. A self-guided tour (brochures with explanations are available at the entrance for a small fee) leads you by way of concrete footprints through the trees and tropical foliage past five giant heads more than two meters tall and weighing more than 15 tons each. No one has yet figured out how the Olmecs (without the wheel) managed to move these giant basalt heads and altars weighing up to 30 tons, since the raw material comes from an area almost 100 km distant.

The Olmec culture left a diverse collection of carvings at La Venta. Along with the giant carved heads wearing war helmets and facial features displaying thick down-turned lips (typifying the jaguar), other more delicate carvings are scattered about. Dwarfs coming out of doorways, or framed within structures, along with a mammoth altar and an arrangement of stone pillars called the **Jaguar's Cage,** are part of this outstanding collection. You'll see stone carvings of animals, including the unusual manatee, along with stelae depicting various unique scenes such as the bearded man, all placed in appropriate settings.

The park also houses a cafe and bookstore. Every evening except Wednesday, a good sound and light show is presented at 7 p.m., 8:10 p.m., and 9:15 p.m. for a small fee. The park is open Tues.-Sun. 8 a.m.-4 p.m.; admission is about US$2. A tourist information booth at the entrance to La Venta is open the same hours as the park, which is at the intersection of Blvd. Grijalva and Paseo Tabasco. From Madero near the city center, buses marked Tabasco 2000, Circuito 1, Foviste, and Parque Linda Vista go to La Venta (ask the driver when you board). Taxis are reasonable and easy to flag down. After visiting the park, if you're still in the mood to explore, from La Venta it's an enjoyable walk along a busy boulevard (Paseo Tabasco) to two more parks, Tabasco 2000 and Parque La Choco.

Tabasco 2000

This series of new buildings is developing into an impressive cultural center. It includes a modern Palacio Municipal; a convention center with facilities for large groups, often presenting plays and other entertainment; and a planetarium that offers permanent exhibits and occasional special shows. Lovely fountains and walkways make a pleasant stroll. Take a look at Tabasco's most modern shopping mall, the Tabasco 2000 commercial center. The mall is unusual for this part of Mexico, with its polished marble floors and glass-enclosed shops that carry everything from camera equipment to the latest in fashions and the newest in electrical appliances.

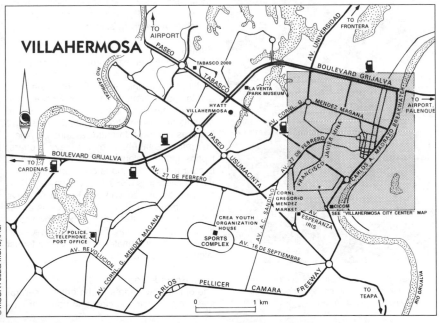

© MOON PUBLICATIONS, INC.

Parque La Choco

A little beyond Tabasco 2000 is Parque La Choco. During Villahermosa's artisan festival in May, this park comes to life, with hundreds of booths presenting a wide variety of crafts and cuisine from regions throughout the state. If you feel the need for a refreshing swim, La Choco has a large, clean swimming pool open Mon.-Sat. 7 a.m.-9 p.m.. There's a fee, and you must pass inspection by the pool doctor. Check with the tourist office for particulars.

CICOM

Another well-laid-out complex of interest to the visitor along the Río Grijalva is CICOM (Centro de Investigaciones de las Culturas Olmeca y Maya), dedicated to studying the Olmec and Maya cultures. One of the main attractions is the **Museo Regional de Antropología Carlos Pellicer Cámara,** a well-designed museum dedicated to Carlos Pellicer Cámara. Documentation of the history of Tabasco and the Olmec, Toltec,

CICOM museum has artifacts such as this exhibit, which shows bodies buried in large clay pots in a fetal position.

and Maya cultures is beautifully presented throughout four floors. You'll see Olmec and Maya pottery, clay figurines, stone carvings, and delicate pieces of carved jade, along with explanatory photos showing the sites where they were discovered. One exhibit is devoted to Carlos Pellicer Cámara and his life. This poet, also an anthropologist, is much respected by Villahermosans and is remembered and honored in many ways throughout the city.

On the grounds of the CICOM complex is a complete and efficient installation dedicated to the study of the ancient cultures, including offices, laboratory, workshops, auditorium, classrooms, and lecture halls for special seminars. This is also a growing business center with a cafe, Ministry of Education office, handicrafts center, and the very impressive **Teatro Esperanza Iris.** This beautiful theater presents entertainment throughout the year; check with the theater office for upcoming events. However, people are welcome to look into the building most times during the day. Designed as an opera house, it seats 1,300 people. The **Casa de Artes,** part of the complex, offers classes in art, handicrafts, music, drama, and classical and folkloric dancing—everyone is welcome. Performances and exhibits are presented regularly by students.

Yumka

Villahermosa's newest park is quite an ambitious project. The name Yumka means "He Who Watches the Jungle" in the Chontal language, and the park resembles a zoo or African safari where animals live in natural habitats. View the animals from hiking trails, monorail cars, and boats as you travel through savannas, jungles, and marshes inhabited by monkeys, jaguars, hippos, giraffes, elephants, and birds. The park is near the airport and is open daily 9 a.m.-5 p.m.; admission is US$3. On Saturday and Sunday vans depart from La Venta Park to Yumka at 8 a.m., returning at 3 p.m.; the fare is about US$1.50. A taxi to the park from downtown costs about US$10 each way. For the most up-to-date schedule and information, check at the tourist information desk at La Venta.

Zona Remodelada

The old narrow streets of the original central areas, nicely tiled and closed to traffic, are re-

OZ MALLAN

ferred to as Zona Remodelada or Zona Luz. The tree-lined streets bring you past small shops and tiny cafes bustling with people. The **Plaza de Armas** is a pretty park surrounded by government buildings on a slight rise above the zone, and it boasts the area's newest attraction, **El Puente de Solidaridad.** This footbridge, which opened in 1993, spans the Río Grijalva and allows the residents of Colónia Las Gaviotas on the other side of the river to cross to the town center. A tall lookout tower atop the bridge is open to the public and is a fine spot for surveying the city.

Deportivo Ciudad/Sport Complex

This impressive layout offers blocks and blocks (south of the main part of Villahermosa) devoted to sports. Here Tabascans take part in baseball, basketball, aerobics, football, tennis, volleyball, soccer, and swimming. For the children it offers a huge playground and even (what looks like) a resident circus. The grounds are well landscaped with monuments, fountains, and wide walkways. There's a large CREA building (youth organization house, day use only) where many activities are planned for Villahermosa's young people. The city leaders are to be commended for creating such a fine sports complex open to everyone for a token fee. No doubt oil money had something to do with this.

Museum of Popular Art

This small museum at Calle Zaragosa 810 displays the culture of the people of more recent history, between the time of the Spanish occu-

pation and the discovery of oil. In the former home of noted sculptor Angel Enrique Gil Hermida is the room of Indian Music and Dances. Here you can see the dresses, masks, and musical instruments used since the time of the Spanish conquest. A changing exhibit introduces you to whatever custom is practiced at the time of year you happen to visit. For example, 31 Oct.-15 Nov. you'll see typical displays as they appear in homes to commemorate **El Día los Muertos** ("Day of the Dead"). Skeletons are dressed in an article of the deceased's clothing and set on a shrine in a prominent place in the home. Also at the shrine, favorite foods are arranged along with candles and a religious picture or symbol. According to belief, eternity opens its doors during this time and the deceased are allowed a visit home to enjoy earthly pleasures. Cemeteries overflow with visitors, and cart vendors do a thriving business selling skeleton and skull candies, flowers, and soft drinks. It's not a gloomy time, just a melancholy holiday that the people take very seriously; it's celebrated graveside all over Mexico.

A Spanish-speaking guide takes you through the very small museum. On its premises are a library, a bookstore, and a small shop selling typical handicrafts. Open daily 9 a.m.-8 p.m.

Marketplace

Visit the José María Pino Suárez market for an introduction to some exotic foodstuffs. Besides small stalls displaying mounds of herbs and spices with piquant aromas and colors of ochre, sienna, saffron, and rust, there are rows of dewy

Washtubs like this one have been in use for centuries.

OZ MALLAN

fresh vegetables and fruits, and game animals not usually seen in the grocery store back home. Right out of the jungle, hanging up in front awaiting a buyer, are iguana, peccary, pheasant, and paskenkly, some already skinned; you'll also see chicken, beef, pork, and fresh fish.

ACCOMMODATIONS

Budget

The best selection of budget hotels is on Madero or in the Zona Remodelada. Inconveniently, it's about a 20- to 30-minute walk to these areas from the ADO first-class and second-class bus stations. Luckily, taxis are easy to find and economical. Overnight camping and trailer parking are allowed at the Sports City complex, also a considerable distance from the bus depots. Keep in mind that Villahermosa is a busy city and the best-value rooms are taken quickly, which makes room hunting a first priority upon arrival. To all hotel prices add 12% tax.

A few humble hotels are mentioned only because of their budget value. **Hotel Malecón,** Calle Lerdo 106 and the *malecón,* offers ceiling fans, private bathrooms, and no hot water, and it's not too clean. Its only saving grace is its price.

The **Hotel Providencia,** Constantinople 216 between Reforma and Lerdo, six blocks south of Fuentes, tel. (93) 12-8262, is spartan, noisy, and not always clean (look first), with small rooms.

Hotel San Rafael, Constitución 240, tel. (93) 12-0368, is another simple hostelry that offers a living room with a TV, hot water, private bathrooms, and ceiling fans; you'll find a restaurant and bar next door.

Hotel San Miguel, Calle Lerdo 315, tel. (93) 12-1500, is one of the better choices in the Zona Luz, more for the friendly management than the comfort of the rooms. Still, the location is ideal, without too much traffic noise yet in the center of the action, if you can cope with painfully thin mattresses.

Inexpensive

Hotel Palomino, Av. Mina 222, tel. (93) 12-8431, is right across the street from the bus station and is quite acceptable, with blue tile bathrooms, shelves for your clothes, fans, and hot water; ask for a room at the back for less street noise.

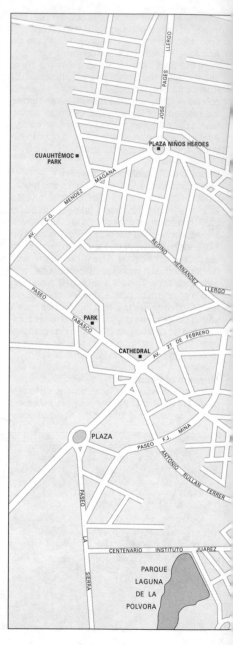

VILLAHERMOSA
CITY CENTER

2D CLASS
BUS TERMINAL

RUIZ CORTINES

BLVD.

HOTEL MAYA
TABASCO

LA ARBOLEDA

ADO BUS
TERMINAL

PEMEX
HOSPITAL

PASEO

FRANCISCO JAVIER

MINA

EUSIBIO

CASTILLO

JUAN

ALVAREZ

JOSÉ MARÍA
PINO SUÁREZ
MARKET

COTP

BREAKWATER

AV. C.G. MENDEZ

MAGAÑA

MADERO

I. MARÍA SUÁREZ

CHOCO'S
HOTEL

MADRAZO

Río   Grijalva

BREAKWATER

FRANCISCO

JOSÉ

CONSTITUCIÓN

VICENES

SALDIVAR

DE ABRIL

GEN. IGNACIO ZARAGOZA

TOURIST
INFORMATION BOOTH

POST AND TELEGRAPH
CENTRAL OFFICES

LERDO DE TEJADA

TELEPHONE
CENTRAL OFFICE

REFORMA

A. CARLOS

AV.

CAPITÁN
BUELO

ALFONSO

MEXICANA AIRLINES

PLAZA
DE
ARMAS

IGNACIO ALLENDE

HOTEL PLAZA INDEPENDENCIA

PASEO TABASCO

Río   Grijalva

LAS

GAVIOTAS

LOS PELLICER CAMARA FREEWAY

CICOM

| 0 | | 500 yds |
| 0 | | 500 m |

© MOON PUBLICATIONS, INC.

Choco's Hotel, Av. Lino Merino at Constitución, tel. (93) 12-9044, is between the bus station and the Zona Luz. It has larger, more comfortable rooms than other hotels in this category.

Hotel Madan, Pino Suárez 105, tel. (93) 12-1650, has simple rooms above one of the Zona Luz's most popular restaurants.

Moderate

The **Hotel Don Carlos,** near city center, Av. Madero 418, tel. (93) 12-2499, fax 14-0986, is comfortable with clean rooms, bathrooms, a/c, TVs, telephones, dining room, cocktail lounge, travel agency, and car rental.

Look at **Hotel Miraflores,** also near city center at Reforma 304, tel. (93) 12-0022, very old and starting to chip apart, but clean.

Hotel Plaza Independencia, Av. Independencia 123, tel. (93) 12-7541, fax 14-4724, is close to the Plaza Las Armas, the Zona Luz, and the *malecón,* but sheltered from traffic noise. The small rooms have a/c, phones, and TVs; those on the top floors have a good view of the river.

Expensive

The **Hotel Cencali,** at Juárez and Paseo Tabasco, tel. (93) 15-6600, is comfortable and within easy walking distance of La Venta.

Hotel Maya Tabasco, Ruíz Cortínes 907, tel. (93) 14-4466, is the nicest hotel close to the bus station and is definitely worth checking out if you're just passing through town. La Venta is about a 10-minute walk away.

The **Calinda Viva Villahermosa** is on Paseo Tabasco and Blvd. Ruíz Cortínes 1281, tel. (93) 15-0000, fax 15-3073, U.S. tel. (800) 4CHOICE. It's the most moderately priced of the city's fancier hotels and is very popular with tour groups.

As Villahermosa quickly grows, more and better hotels are being built all the time. The area along Av. Ruíz Cortínes at Paseo Tabasco has become a hotel zone. **Hyatt Villahermosa,** Av. Juárez 106, Col. Linda Vista, is nicely furnished, with room service, a/c, restaurant, coffee shop, disco, large swimming pool and patio area, sauna, laundry, tennis court, car rental, and nine meeting rooms with audiovisual equipment available. You can also stay on the hotel's Regency floors, which include continental breakfast and afternoon drinks along with a private lounge; tel. (93) 13-4444, fax 15-1235, U.S. tel. (800) 233-1234.

FOOD

You can get as exotic with your food as you wish in Villahermosa. A few cafes specialize in pre-Cortesian recipes. For instance, how about *tamales de chipilin, pejelagarto* (lizard meat), *chirmol de congrejo* (a spicy rabbit stew), *mondongo en ajiaco* (tripe and vegetables), or just plain iguana stew? For a drink that's native to the area, try *pozol* (made of corn and raw cacao beans); *cacawada* is another tasty drink (sweetened cacao beans mixed with water though it doesn't taste anything like chocolate). Before roasting, the flesh around the beans has a tart fruity flavor—very refreshing.

For baked goods, **La Baguette,** Av. Juárez 301, has French bread.

Restaurants

Choosing a restaurant can be tough since there's a large selection. The Plaza Las Galas just down Av. Mina from the bus stations is a great place to get a snack or meal if you're stranded between buses. The best restaurant near the plaza is **Ric's Coffee Shop,** similar to a Denny's, immaculately clean and comfortable, with full breakfasts costing about US$4, and full meal specials including drinks costing about US$5-8. Ric's is open daily 8 a.m.-10 p.m., and it is the best place in the neighborhood to linger over a meal while you wait for your bus. The plaza also has a branch of La Baguette, a larger bakery called La Hogaza, and La Michoacana ice cream shop. The cheapest meals are available at the market, off Pino Suárez near Zozaya. Lots of supermarkets are scattered throughout the city.

Los Tulipanes, Periférico Carlos Pellicer Cámara 511, tel. (93) 12-9209, serves *típico* regional food, with a seafood dinner costing about US$25. Live music and a Sunday show mark this restaurant. Closed Monday.

In the Zona Luz there are many small, clean, cheap restaurants. Look also for more upscale cafes; **El Matador** is open 24 hours, convenient for after hours at the discos, and serves good but expensive (US$10) taco dinners. **El Guarayguao** restaurant, also the name of a bird, is a small place but is excellent, serving Tabasco cuisine. Dinner here will cost about US$25.

Restaurant Galerías Madan is one of the most popular Zona Luz restaurants, filled night and day with groups of businesspeople clustered over never-ending cups of coffee. Try for a table by the front windows, where you can watch the action on the street. The daily special *comida corrida* is a good deal, with soup, salad, entree, dessert, and drink for about US$8.

If you're looking for an outstanding (pricey) continental meal, have dinner at Hyatt's **Bugambilia.** The food is exquisite, the ambience is romantic, and the entertainment is mellow jazz. It's well worth the splurge, about US$60 for a complete meal for two including wine. The **Tukan Room** at the Hotel Cencali serves a good *comida corrida*—or four-course set lunch—for about US$9. It's pretty good but nowhere near the luxury and upkeep of the Hyatt.

For a change of pace from Latin food try **La Pagoda,** Niños Héroes 167. And if you like window shopping, you'll find many more cafes all over the city serving both *típico* and exotic cuisines, along with black beans and spicy mole sauces.

Sea Fare

For something a little special, take a lunch or dinner cruise along the Río Grijalva onboard the small restaurant-ship *Capitán Beulo.* The lunch trip is a breezy tour with a peek into life on the busy river. The food is nicely served, with fresh fish the specialty. If you order the shrimp cocktail, don't be surprised when it's served to you "naked"—it's accompanied by many bottles of interesting condiments and fresh lime, all meant to be added by the diner. The shrimp is so fresh and sweet it's delicious au naturel.

At night, the small ship takes on a sparkling dimension. For the most part you sail along black banks, so your attention turns to the linen decor, the food, or perhaps a special companion with whom to share the stars reflecting on the quiet river. This is not a cheap dinner, but with the boat excursion included it's good value, about US$25 (get the current price at your hotel or tourist office). The trip is made daily (except Monday) at 1:30 p.m., 3:30 p.m., and 9 p.m.; catch the floating restaurant at the pier on the Madrazo Breakwater at the foot of Lerdo de Tejada. During winter's high season reservations are suggested, tel. (93) 12-3137.

**VILLAHERMOSA
EMERGENCY NUMBERS**

Fire Department	(93) 13-1900
Highway Patrol	(93) 13-2214
Red Cross	(93) 13-3593
Social Security Hospital	(93) 13-1199

INFORMATION AND SERVICES

Tourist Information

The **State of Tabasco Tourism Office** is in the Tabasco 2000 center in the SEFCOT building across the street from the Liverpool department store. The office, Paseo Tabasco 1504 on the second floor, is difficult to find; it's open Mon.-Fri. 9 a.m.-4 p.m., tel. (93) 16-3648 or 16-3633. You're better off checking with the tourist information booth at La Venta Park, open daily 9 a.m.-4 p.m., or at the airport, staffed when flights are due.

Money

Traveler's checks can be cashed 10 a.m.-1 p.m. at **Bancomer** on Av. Zaragoza at Juárez, **Banamex** in the Centro Financiero at Tabasco 2000, and **Banco de Atlántico** at Av. Méndez 747.

TRANSPORTATION

Considered a gateway to Central Mexico, Villahermosa is easily reached by many means. A fine transportation network connects it with Mexico City, Chiapas, Guatemala, the Quintana Roo coast, and the rest of the Yucatán Peninsula, although to link up with the national train service you must travel 58 km to Teapa.

By Plane

Villahermosa has a busy airport. Flights arrive daily from many cities in Mexico, as do connecting international flights from Madrid, Paris, London, Rome, the U.S., and several points in Asia. You can make direct flights to Mexico City, Oaxaca, Mérida, Tuxtla Gutiérrez, and other large cities, as well as to special destinations in small air taxis: Bonampak, Ciudad del Carmen, Emiliano Zapata, and Palenque. **Mexi-**

cana Airlines, tel. (93) 16-3785, Aeroméxico, tel. (93) 12-1528, Aerocaribe, tel. (93) 14-3202, and Aerolitoral, tel. (93) 13-3614, fly in and out of Villahermosa.

When you arrive at the airport, tel. (93) 12-4386, you have the choice of a taxi or *combi* service to your hotel or the center of town. It's at least a 45-minute walk to town center. The *combi* service is erratic here and only travels if there are three or more passengers going to the same destination. A taxi to the downtown hotels costs about US$15. You may want to talk with other passengers while waiting for your luggage to see if you can share a cab. Numerous auto rentals are within the a/c air terminal, plus a coffee shop, restaurant, and several gift shops. The staff at the state tourist information booth in the terminal is very helpful and provides detailed city maps; there's almost always someone who speaks English as well as other languages.

By Bus

Buses from all over Mexico arrive frequently. The ADO first-class bus station, at Mina and Merino in the northeast section of the city, is one of the nicest in Mexico, very clean and orderly. Autotransportes Cristóbal Colón has first-class and deluxe service to Mexico City, Mérida, Campeche, Chetumal, San Cristóbal de las Casas, and Tuxtla Gutiérrez. Regular first-class buses travel to Palenque seven times a day on ADO, which also has deluxe Mercedes-Benz buses to Palenque twice daily. UNO has the most luxurious buses, with a/c, refreshments, and movies en route to Mérida and Mexico City. The dreadful second-class bus station, called Central de Autobuses de Tabasco, is on Ruíz Cortínes Blvd. near the Maya Tabasco Hotel. Buses to Comalcalco on Servicio Someliera depart from here.

By Car

Highways into Villahermosa are easy driving from both north and south. From Campeche and points east take Hwy. 186. From Campeche along the coastal route take Hwy. 180. From Veracruz along the coast take Hwy. 180 east. From San Cristóbal de las Casas and points south take Hwy. 190. These all converge in Villahermosa. If driving from the airport into downtown Villahermosa, have a few pesos ready for

the toll. Local taxis take a roundabout detour to eliminate paying, but make sure you know where you're going before trying it.

COMALCALCO ARCHAEOLOGICAL SITE

The Ruins

A beautiful pastoral site of green rolling hills and plains, Comalcalco was probably the westernmost outpost of the Classic Maya world (excepting the far-flung settlements of the Putún Maya). The existing structures were built during the Late Classic at the same time as Palenque. Some archaeologists believe that Palenque's last rulers actually built Comalcalco and moved here after the collapse of their native city. They see Palenque's influence in the building structures, the vaulted masonry tombs, and the use of stucco for commemorative reliefs and sculptures that covered the important buildings. Other researchers believe that the site may predate Palenque, and

Comalcalco's kilned-brick construction is evident here.

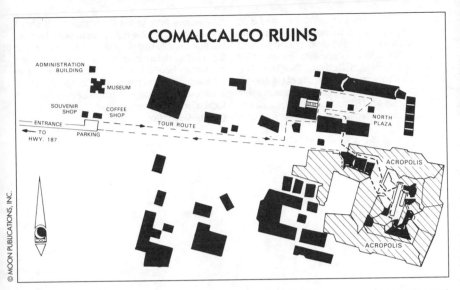

COMALCALCO RUINS

ADMINISTRATION BUILDING

MUSEUM

SOUVENIR SHOP

COFFEE SHOP

ENTRANCE

← TO HWY. 187

PARKING

TOUR ROUTE

NORTH PLAZA

ACROPOLIS

ACROPOLIS

© MOON PUBLICATIONS, INC.

that all the influence flowed in the other direction. Because the city lies on a stoneless coastal plain, Comalcalco was constructed of kiln-fired brick slabs rather than stone. Many of the bricks were incised with designs, including animals, humans, glyphs, and patterns.

Most of the site's artwork is barely visible now after centuries of exposure to the elements. The stucco surface is almost totally gone, exposing the bricks that so closely resemble those made today. **Note:** The bricks are fragile and you are not permitted to climb on the pyramids wherever the signs read No Subir.

Several mounds are now bare; the original structures were built of wood and have long since deteriorated. **Temple No. 1,** the immense structure on the left as you walk from the entrance, has the best remaining example of the stucco high relief that once covered most of the structures. Today these valuable remnants of history are covered with glass and have been roofed over to deter any further deterioration. The facial features of these figures are unique, with thick, strangely shaped lips, somewhat resembling the colossal heads in La Venta, yet vastly different in style. The Palenque site in Chiapas flourished at the same time as the Chontal Maya site here in Comalcalco, and arti-

facts indicate there was communication and trading between the two sites. At the entrance to the ruins is a small museum, a gift/book shop that doesn't have much to sell, and a snack stand. You pay a small admission to the site, open 8 a.m.-5 p.m..

The walk up a hill to the **Palace** reveals a lovely view of the green countryside below and mounds scattered here and there but not yet excavated. From the top of the hill you'll see cattle, animals unknown to the Maya, living in the shadows of the ancient structures. While wandering you'll discover a sunken courtyard, many pieces of the traditional corbel arch, and the remains of small display niches all through the structures. The Chontal Maya were as talented and creative as the rest of the Maya throughout Mesoamerica.

The entomologist might enjoy observing the giant beetles often visible in the trees near the buildings at the entrance. The insect is the size of a hand and about three inches thick, shiny black, and apparently common in this rural part of the state.

Getting There

You can reach Comalcalco from the Villahermosa ADO first-class bus station at Mina and

Merino on daily buses at 12:30 a.m. and 8:30 p.m., and on **Servicio Someliera** buses every half-hour from the second-class station on Ruíz Cortínes. Be sure to check with the driver for return-trip information. If driving, take Hwy. 180 west from Villahermosa to the city of Cárdenas, and when you come to the junction with Hwy. 187, continue on 187 to Comalcalco. Just beyond the ruins is cacao bean country. A choco-late factory (ask at the Comalcalco gift shop) gives a tour if it's the right time of year; harvest season usually begins around 15 October, but the weather determines the exact date and when the factory begins operating. Travel agencies in Villahermosa sometimes offer Comalcalco tours if there are enough interested people (at least four). For information contact Viajes Agma, tel. (93) 12-9866, fax 14-3849.

KATHY ESCOVEDO SANDERS

THE STATE OF CHIAPAS
INTRODUCTION

Chiapas is a state shrouded in mystery with a prehistoric culture that has survived for centuries. The area has passed from rags to riches to rags—and who knows what the new millennium will bring? Though one of Mexico's most impoverished states, it harbors cities with the trappings of once-wealthy strongholds that date from colonial era of the New World. But in contrast, the poverty-stricken indigenous people weave and wear rich clothing of opulent colors and sumptuous designs that in the cities of the "material world" sell for enormous prices. The Indians who live in arcane villages still sustain their secrets and keep them well-hidden from the outside world. They give a half-hearted welcome to outsiders—only since they discovered that money came along with the concession. They sell their crafts in hopes that trade will help pull them out of their cycle of poverty. Though it may "take a village to raise a child," it's going to take the help of

the Mexican government and a new slant on education, medical care, etc. to change the lifestyle of the indigenous Chiapanecans—and it must be on their terms. Perhaps *that's* their secret; though they would like to raise their level of living, they won't share their cultural exile, and if reaping the benefits of the modern age means giving up their independent thinking and falling in line with a world that they don't respect, it may be generations before things change much in the Indian world of Chiapas. Once they join the ranks of those Tzeltales and Tzotsiles who have already capitulated, the rich culture of the region will begin to die.

In the meantime, visitors are largely unaware of or unconcerned about the plight of the Indian. Instead they are enthralled with a peek into an earlier time. They love strolling the streets lined with colonial buildings, and because Chiapas was such a favored location for the early settlers from Spain, convents and churches proliferate. Even if structures are no longer used as churches (though many are), the rest are used for other purposes: libraries, museums, government offices, and they're open for all to enjoy. Other notable and oft-visited places are impressive Maya archaeological sites scattered across the state, which boasts what some consider the most magnificent of all Maya ruins, Palenque.

THE LAND

The southernmost state of Mexico, Chiapas is bordered on the west by Oaxaca and Veracruz, on the north by Tabasco and Campeche, and on the east by Guatemala. Covering 74,415 square km, it has a population of two million.

Forests and Mountains

While the low-lying coast and jungle areas are typically tropical, a large part of Chiapas is in the rugged mountains of the Sierra Madre del Sur "highlands." The thick rainforest offers innumerable lakes, grand rivers, and uncountable waterfalls. The Sierra Madre del Sur rainforest, together with the Petén rainforest in Guatemala, becomes the Lacandón rainforest. The *Montes Azules Biosphere Reserve* is a tract of 330,000 hectares in the heart of the Lacandona and forms more than half of the viable tropical rainforest in Mexico. Much of the Lacandona is at sea level, but the mountains, often crowned with thick clouds, average 1,500 meters in elevation, and some peaks are as high as 3,000 meters.

El Chichon, one of the region's few volcanoes, in 1986 turned day into night. For 35 hours, there was no sun or light, just an eerie blackness. The eruption deposited tons of ash (no lava) on an area encompassing 200 km surrounding the volcano. My first thought was of the massive cleanup job that would have to be done on Palenque; however, not so. Winds blew the structures clean. Another Chiapanecan volcano, dormant for many years, is the 3,000-meter peak of Tacaná overlooking Mexico's southern Pacific coast and the city of Tapachula. This bustling, German-influenced business center—complete with smog—is a popular stop on the way to or from Guatemala. Tapachula is one of the Mexican gateways into the **El Triunfo Biosphere Reserve.**

El Triunfo Biosphere Reserve is smaller than other reserves, but it is a one of a kind in Mexico. Here in breath-taking cloud forest is one of the world's few remaining habitats of the quetzal. Almost extinct, the bird is startlingly green, with two tails that measure up to 24 inches long. The quetzal's is the plumage valued so highly by the nobles of both the Maya and Aztec, who used it in clothing and headdress.

Caves and Canyons

Wherever in Mexico you find limestone mountains, they will be riddled with caverns that were used by the ancient Maya for burials, rituals, and ceremonies; many remain unexplored by outsiders and are difficult to reach. Recently, archaeologists discovered an impressive collec-

CHIAPAS TRAVEL ADVISORY

Personal security in Chiapas continues to be unpredictable, as highlighted by the massacre of 45 peasants by an unknown paramilitary group at the small village of Acteal in December 1997. As a local resident of San Cristóbal de las Casas reported: "This horror arose from infighting that has gone on for hundreds of years. Unfortunately, the press wants to make it political and Bishop Ruiz and Subcommandante Marcos [of Zapatista fame] are fanning the flames." This same resident says she still feels safe walking the streets of San Cristóbal alone at night, where Mexican police are quite visible.

The countryside is a different story. Traveling in groups of two or three is no longer a guarantee of safety. We recently received a letter from a woman who went for a short walk in the jungle with her boyfriend and a taxi driver in broad daylight and ended up being beaten and raped by a gang of men dressed in army fatigues and ski masks. We suggest sticking to the most well-traveled routes wherever possible.

Traveling between Chiapas cities after dark, whether in a bus or a car, is asking for trouble. In the past year several vehicles have reportedly been stopped and the passengers robbed.

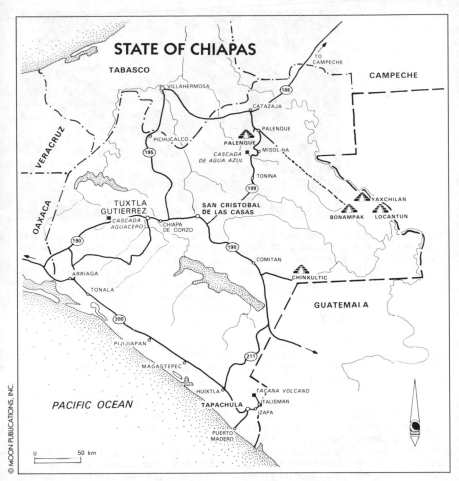

tion of Maya artifacts in a cave called **Tepesco del Diablo** in the La Venta Canyon area. If you wish to see the artifacts they found, go to the Regional Museum of Tuxtla Gutiérrez.

Though they're not on the usual tourist route, visitors may explore the caves. The caves are in their natural state, and only true spelunkers should attempt to explore them; even then, you must be accompanied by local guides with proper equipment. The best way to reach these massive geological formations is to travel by car; often you must switch to a boat, since the steep, rugged canyons in which the caves lie are cut by rivers. Rumors tell of many abandoned caves in this vast area that still hold archaeological and anthropological treasures. Remember, taking any artifacts, even a pottery shard, carries a large fine.

Climate

The tropical Chiapas lowlands are hot and humid, especially May-October, the rainy season. Although rainfall can be as high as 4,000 mm (160 inches) in the mountains, it's somewhat less in

Palenque

OZ MALLAN

the lowlands. Be prepared for chilly weather in the highlands in November, December, January, and February; bring a light wrap just in case. Occasional hurricanes from the Gulf and the Caribbean pass over Southern Mexico.

HISTORY

The earliest inhabitants of the Chiapas area are presumed to be the Olmecs. The Maya settled in during the Preclassic period and during the Classic age created their most outstanding structures. The actual Chiapanecan territory was occupied by many groups and cultures that mostly spoke a Maya tongue. The Choles inhabited the jungle; the Tojolabales lived in the plains between the valley of the Chiapas River and jungle; the Chiapanecans occupied the central part of the valley; the Mames lived along the coastal regions; the Zoques lived on the hillsides of the highlands; and the Tzotziles and Tzeltales cultivated the highlands. Today the largest of these linguistic groups are the Tzotziles

and Tzeltales, and they are familiarly referred to as the Chamulans, Zinacantecos, Oxchuqueros, and San Pedranos.

After the intrusion of the Spaniards in 1519 many years of fighting ensued. It took numerous Spanish soldiers to finally defeat the brave warriors of Chiapas (the Chiapanecans were described by Bernal Díaz, conquistador who fought with Hernán Cortés, as "the most courageous warriors they encountered in the new world.") The first Spanish army, a mix of Spaniards and their Mexican allies the Tlaxcaltecans, arrived in 1524 and were soon driven off by the Chiapanecans. In 1527, a Spanish army from Guatemala tried to take over but it too was sent running. Only in 1530, when Diego de Mazariegos arrived, were the outsiders able to assume control of the area and, as in all Spanish conquests, the Indians were soon subjugated and made virtual slaves on their land.

When he became bishop in 1544, Bartolomé de las Casas tried to abolish slavery and managed to convince the Spanish crown to provide legal protection for Indians throughout the New World. Although marginally successful, it was a first step. Bishop de las Casas was and is held in great respect by the local Indians. On and off in the 16th and 17th century, Chiapas came under the legal jurisdiction of the Spanish in Guatemala. Repeated Indian uprisings against the Royalists and then the Republic continued until 1911 in a gallant though futile effort by the Tzotzil and Tzeltal groups.

ARCHAEOLOGICAL ZONES OF CHIAPAS

Palenque	Izapa	Corzo
Yaxchilán	Bonampak	Toniná
Chinkultíc	Chiapa de	

CACAO BEANS AS CURRENCY

Along with quills filled with gold dust, the ancient Maya considered cacao beans "precious." John Stephens points out that as late as the 1840s in isolated Maya villages, the locals were still using cacao beans as currency among themselves.

ECONOMY

After the Independence in 1921, Chiapas plodded along with little economic growth and generally was isolated from the world, but that's all changing. Along with cattle ranching, oil, silver, gold, and copper mines, tourism is bringing new money into state coffers. This is providing a base to build more roads, extend advertising, and improve facilities for tourists. All of this should mean more money for Chiapanecans, even though the current overall economic condition in Mexico makes it slow going. In the past couple of years, the increased attention has focused on the Zapatistas' call for more economic help for Chiapas's highland Indians. Ironically, instead of scaring away tourists, the rebel uprising on 4 January 1994 has sparked an intense curiosity about the area and its indigenous people. Because of this spotlight, the Mexican government has been (in small ways) helping the people. The Mundo Maya (Maya World) Program is becoming very popular, especially with Europeans. Repairing and building roads has become a priority, enabling easier access to the isolated locations of some of the ancient Maya cities. While before only the real adventurer would investigate such faraway places as Bonampak and Yaxchilán, now a good road allows the more timid visitor to reach them by bus or car.

For these roadbuilding projects and others, many Mexicans were put to the task, and despite the minimal wage, it has at least provided some jobs. For the indigenous people, life is hard—their "economy" is almost nonexistent. In Chiapas, 80% of the population is of Maya origin and the average income is about US$5 per month, with one interesting exception, Zinacantán. This village has developed a fine industry raising hothouse flowers, exporting them all over

Mexico and the world; the United States is the village's top foreign customer. The whole village of Zinacantán benefits.

Timber/Forest

For years in Chiapas, the chief industry was timber harvesting and exportation, leading to the destruction of many acres of essential rainforest. The Chiapas rainforest is the second largest rainforest (South America's Amazon has the largest) in the Americas. Many outspoken groups want the timber industry stopped altogether in Latin America to preserve the rainforest, but so far the ecologists have been unsuccessful. The timber industry provides minimal wages to some. But for a few isolated Indian cultures, such as that of the Lacandón, the forest provides the backdrop for their unique way of life. Once the forest is gone, their ancient lifestyle will be destroyed.

Cattle Ranching

Cattle ranching began in the colonial period, and immense haciendas were built in the then-isolated areas of the New World. At the time of the conquest, no more than half of this state's territory was populated. The densest populations lived in the state's southeastern corner, where the cocoa bean was a major product for the indigenous people. By 1890 the demographics had changed. On formerly empty land, 50,000 hectares were under the control of only six haciendas. Today, cattle ranches continue to grow at the expense of the rainforest but provide minimal jobs for the people—a double-edged sword.

PEOPLE

The people in the communities of Chamula, Zinacantán, Larrainzar, Zoque, Chol, and Lacandón, among others, still speak their native tongue; most speak Tzotzil and Tzeltal (some of the men speak Spanish as a second language) and practice their ancient traditions. Many of their villages are in the outlying areas of the Chiapas Highlands—the fringe of civilization. Most of these people live a very simple life with no material "things." For example, while Chiapas produces immeasurable quantities of electricity at Chicoasan Dam, most indigenous people do not have that luxury, nor do they have paved roads, running water, or in-

THE TUMPLINE

*Like the deity of his Maya
ancestors, this man carries his
heavy load with the help of
a tumpline around his head.*

OZ MALLAN

door plumbing. Adults die young, most villages
have a high infant mortality rate, for the most part
the people are illiterate, and they suffer from poor
health care—many are alcoholics.

Indian Traditions

The Indians have survived over many centuries
doing things in much the same way as their ancestors did, and each small village has hung
onto its ancient traditions. For example, each
group carries a stick of authority. Originally these
sticks were used for protection; today they're
symbols of hierarchy within the group. The car-
rier always wraps a kerchief around the stick
where he touches it in respect for this object.

Each village wears separate clothing styles,
practices a craft specialty, and even raises or
produces separate items—some villages sew
trousers, some make bread, and they trade with
other villages or coops. Villages grow different
crops, such as peanuts, cotton, cacao beans,
and of course they all raise corn for their subsistence. They use the few animals they have in

special ways. The Chamulans would *never* think
of eating their sheep; they treasure the wool the
sheep provides. The women card the wool and
weave clothes; the small animal also provides
the black shaggy raincoats that keep their wear-
ers dry in the area's horrendous rainstorms.

Every village wears clothing distinct in weaving style and color, and if a woman marries into
another village, she must change not only her al-
legiance, but her clothing style as well. These
fashions vary greatly. The Oxtuc men wear
miniskirts and their wives wear long *huipiles;*
their raincoats are made from palm fronds. It
takes a Magdalena woman eight months to
weave a *huipile* of complex design on her backstrap loom. Married Lacandón men wear *tucan*
feathers; single Lacondon men wear no feathers.

The Lacandón villages use certain mind-altering substances for their religious ceremonies
and use monkey skulls to make drums and rattles. Today the Lacandón sell their arrows for
souvenirs; not too long ago they dipped them
in poison to hunt. The tip of each arrow point is

made from a different material depending on the intended prey.

The Simojovel villagers (Zoque Maya) work in caves deep in the earth mining amber. The miners don't necessarily then produce great art; they sell the petrified resin to artists who turn the yellowish material into often lovely pieces of jewelry. The Zoque makes little money from his dangerous foray into the black caves lit only by candlelight.

These examples just hint at the customs of these people, and all the many different linguistic groups carry their traditions in their souls.

Music of the People
Music is and has always been used for religious rituals. Greatly valued are the wooden harps, marimbas, and violins that are handed down from father to son. These music makers might appear primitive when compared to symphonic instruments, but many of them are uniquely fashioned—they're often crafted from the bones and skin of a deer, the hard shell of an armadillo, or the skull of a monkey. The music they produce may not be melodious as we think of melody, but it performs a sacred function.

TUXTLA GUTIÉRREZ AND VICINITY

As early as 400 B.C., small ceremonial centers were scattered about the valley of Tuxtla. However, the real birth of Tuxtla took place much later in a Zoque village called Coyatoc. Subsequently, Nahua intruders translated the name to Tochtlan, which was changed further when the Spanish tried to wrap their tongues around the Maya language; then it became Tuxtla. Coyatoc, Tochtlan, Tuxtla: all of these versions mean the same thing, valley of the rabbit, or more literally, house of the rabbit (house=coya, toc=rabbit).

In 1768, the province of Chiapa was separated into two municipalities and in due course they were both made cities. In 1892, the whole area was merged and officially proclaimed the capital of the state, as Tuxtla Gutiérrez.

Tuxtla is a modern city. Visitors will find little evidence of colonial occupation on the surface. Government buildings, museums, theaters, parks, and even San Marcos church on the Plaza Cívica are a modern interpretation of what once was a colonial church. However, as modern as the city is, the undercurrent of ancient tradition is strong in its foods, myths, legends, beliefs, and crafts, including fine textiles.

Tuxtla Gutiérrez has been the state's commercial center since it replaced San Cristóbal de las Casas as capital of Chiapas in 1892. The Tuxtla airport makes the city a gateway to the rest of the state and the busy hub reflects the city's brisk growth. The center of a thriving coffee-growing zone, it has a population numbering approximately 250,000. Although Chiapas is one of the most picturesque states in the Mexi-

can Republic, its capital is a large, busy city that could be anywhere. But don't let that stop you from looking around. The modern city is definitely worth a one- or two-day stopover to see a few outstanding sights and to use as a springboard for some fascinating outlying areas.

SIGHTS IN AND AROUND THE CITY

Plaza Cívica and San Marcos Cathedral
The Plaza Cívica includes the main square and government buildings. A governor of Chiapas gave the Plaza Cívica area a makeover not too many years back. It's a shady, tree-lined square surrounded by streamlined government buildings and the San Marcos Cathedral. The cathedral, white with modern lines, has a stark beauty. Its German-made clockwork mechanism (a carillon with 48 bells) sends 12 carved apostles in and out of the tower every hour to the chimes of a medley of international music. The church was originally built in the second half of the 16th century as a Dominican convent. Today the central part of the front arch is the only piece that remains from the colonial era. The church has been redesigned many times over the centuries. Even the main altarpiece is new.

The plaza has become a gathering place for angry people with complaints, many of them justified. At almost any given time you'll find large groups of Indians demonstrating for their rights. These are 99% peaceful demonstrations and much more common since the Zapatistas stretched their muscles in 1994.

Parque Marimba

This popular gathering place is another park with shade trees and walkways, along with a charming kiosk where musicians frequently play a variety of music. By comparison with the plaza, this is a much happier place to relax and people watch. Vendors sell snacks and drinks, but people come for the music. The music program varies among the police band, a

woodwind band, marimbas, and visiting musicians. The common denominator is the dancing! No matter what the beat, the whole family, young and old, gets up and dances; every night, free, 7-9 p.m. Visitors are warmly welcomed here, a great place for fun in the center of this busy city. Lots of cafes are nearby, and within the park various events take place throughout the year. On our last visit, a book fair in the park continued for two weeks. Small booths lined up along the edge of the park selling all varieties of books. Several booths offered kid-size tables with crayons, and paper, and children's books with supervised play times to keep the small ones happy while mom and dad browsed. The park's at Av. Central between 8 and 9 Poniente.

San Pascualito Church

As far back as 1601, the Spanish padres denounced a group that worshipped a skeleton called San Pascual. Apparently to avoid the wrath of the padres, the worshippers went underground. They remained there until 1892, when a group in the neighborhood of San Roque and Calvario formed a brotherhood and built a hermitage where they venerated a *wooden* skeleton. In 1934, while fighting the power of the Catholic church, a group of fanatics burned all the statues of saints they could find. However, devotees protected the wooden skeleton by moving it from house to house. As with most legends, there are many versions. Some believers are convinced the wooden skeleton you see today is the original; others have doubts.

The cult continues to grow. In the 1950s, a church was erected for its many followers. It was and is especially prevalent among the *mercado* healers and spiritualists. A popular myth in Tuxtla tells how the coffin-cart passes through the city and San Pascualito picks up the dead amidst a wail of agony. Today's skeleton is kept in a coffin-cart in the church and is displayed once a year on 14 May, when a grand festival is held at the church, 5A Poniente Sur, down the street from the main square and San Marcos Cathedral.

El Calvario and the Old Market

El Calvario church dates to the end of the 19th century. The entrance is a modest neo-Gothic style and inside you'll find a sculpture of a reclining Christ that attracts a stream of the devout. Next to the church is the old *mercado* (dating from 1942). As you will notice, there really isn't much in this city that dates back very many years. In this market we first saw the delightful little birthday crowns made of wire and paper flowers that are ordinarily presented to and worn by the celebrant; they're especially popular with children

City Museum

The museum was created in an old home in the San Roque district. Typical exhibits trace the history of the city from its inception as the state capital. Visitors get a taste of the revolution as it affected Tuxtla, politics, herbalism, and most interesting, a re-creation of a Zoque home in the patio, complete with chicken coop. The museum is open Tues.-Sun. 10 a.m.-2 p.m., 5-8 p.m. Nearby in San Roque district is the Institute of Arts and Sciences.

House of Arts and Crafts

A combination sales room and museum, the House of Arts and Crafts, Blvd. Dr. Belizario Dominguez #950, tel. (961) 2-5509, is open Mon.-Sat. 9 a.m.-2 p.m. and 5-8 p.m., Sunday 9 a.m.-2 p.m. You'll find a good selection of textiles, pottery, leather, lacquerware, baskets, stone crafts, filigree jewelry, and amber. We've been told you can trust the authenticity of the amber here; however, caveat emptor! The museum has created scenes representing the multiethnicity of the state of Chiapas.

Joyyo Mayu and Cana Hueca Parks
Two parks at the edge of the city attract those interested in relaxing in a green environment. At Joyyo, on an inlet of the Sabinal River, ducks and other wildlife frolic in a pastoral scene with placid water and great chestnut trees along the shoreline. This is a good place for a picnic. Or, close by at Cana Hueca, bikers and runners occupy paths that meander through lush vegetation. To get to the parks, go west on Avenida Central from the center of town until you come to the junction and Central becomes Av. Belizario Dominguez. Turn right, and before you cross the Sabinal River you will see Cana Hueca, and just after crossing you'll see the entrance to Joyyo.

Calzada de Los Hombres Ilustres
The Calzada de Los Hombres Ilustres, a parklike area along the banks of the Rio Sabinal near downtown, contains several of the city's main attractions, including the Regional Museum of Chiapas. The **Xiloteca** offers an exhibit of the types of wood found throughout the forests of Chiapas. It's easy to see why this area has attracted lumber interests from all over the world for four centuries. Don't miss the **Botanical Garden,** green, cool, and a relaxing place to wander (all 4.4 hectares) if you're interested in the state's flora or just a quiet afternoon with only the songs of the birds to accompany you. You'll discover a variety of flora. Walkways are clearly marked with names of vegetation , what (if anything) the plant is used for, where it grows—highlands, lowlands, etc. Admission is free.

Regional Museum of Chiapas
The museum building, also in the same green area, in itself is quite lovely. Designed and built in 1984, it is a modern mix of shiny gray marble and white and black parallel planes. The architect, Juan Miramontes Najera, won first prize for his design at the *Third Biennial of Architecture,* held in Europe in 1985. Two rooms are engaged in a permanent display of prehistory dating from 10,000 B.C.: preclassic and pro-

toclassic—the time of the Olmec expansion and the development of Chiapa de Corzo till 300 A.D.; the classic period, characterized by the consolidation of social classes and the era of the classic Maya and Zoque; and the postclassic period, after the so-called "fall" of the notable Maya cities in 900 A.D. The postclassic exhibit demonstrates the expansion of the highland communities and their movement and disbursement into small, isolated villages, along with the establishment of the Chiapanecans in the central areas. Check out the upper floor, where you'll find a very good exhibit of the colonial and republican era from the 16th century, including artistic, ethnographic, and historical; there's a great collection of Chiapanecan colonial art.

City Theater
Another of Tuxtla's modern buildings, dating from 1984, this is a good example of the high-tech theaters going up in Mexico. Compared to the charming old colonial theaters that were quite small and intimate, it has a large stage and will hold 1,200 spectators, plus an art gallery in the vestibule. Check with the tourist office for current presentations.

Tuxtla Gutiérrez Zoo
On the southeast side of the city, in a forest called El Zapotal, is the must-see Miguel Alvárez del Toro Zoo. Built in 1980, this is probably the finest zoo in Central America, filled with animals and birds that are found in the wilds of Chiapas. A 2.5-km-long trail meanders up and down the side of a hill under tall trees with hanging vines. The animals are housed in surroundings as natural as possible. Note the unusual *aarpia* (harpy eagle)—a very large bird (about one meter tall) with deep, thick feathers around its eyes and feet—and other unusual birds, including the brilliant South American macaw or the *guacamaya*

ocelot

roja and the *pavon,* the Chiapas state bird. Don't miss the large cats. A puma named Mustafa responds when called. Sleek, healthy jaguars pace within their enclosure, including the black jaguar—the delicate jaguar pattern shows through the ebony-shaded fur. Look for ocelots, javelina, coatimundi, and raccoons. Families of spider monkeys swing high in the trees to the roar of their neighboring howler monkeys. The active, spinning, swimming nutria (semiaquatic rodent) puts on a great show. It's easy to watch through an outdoor underwater viewing window.

Don't miss the nocturnal room. Here, separated from the outside world by a piece of glass and a special light, industrious little animals think day is night and vice versa. It's fun to watch them go about their business, which otherwise remains hidden in evening shadows. The zoo is open Tues.-Sun. 8:30 a.m.-5:30 p.m. Admission is free but donations are most welcome. Note: Catch buses to the zoo along Av. Central. A tourist information booth at the zoo is open during zoo hours.

Not Just for the Kids
The **Infantile Center** in the eastern zone of the city is divided into two sections. One contains a walk-around museum that shows life in the colonial era, and the second includes fun and game things that kids enjoy (even a giant brontosaurus). Both sections are in a lovely wooded area with a small train for transportation.

In the same complex you'll find the state library and archives (with excellent bibliographical information from the 16th, 17th, and 18th centuries), the Convention Center, State Auditorium, and a park with a lake and beautiful plants and trees. If you trek through all of this, plan on at least an hour or two. It's open Tues.-Sat., 10 a.m.-8 p.m.

ACCOMMODATIONS

Tuxtla has a good selection of hotels. Be sure to check out the rooms before you pay; some in the budget class can be grim, but for the most part are just old, clean and very simple.

Shoestring
The **CREA Youth Hostel (IYHF)** is on 16 de Septiembre, tel. (961) 1-1201. The entrance is at the left of the youth center and cafe. Spotlessly clean dormitories (single sex) are furnished with bunk beds, and the price includes a towel, pillowcase, and sheets. Curfew is 9 p.m., and the doors are locked 9 p.m.-6 a.m. The 52 rooms have fans, TVs, and telephones.

Budget
Hotel Plaza Chiapas, 4A Sur Poniente #210, is simple, low-priced, clean, and in the center of town; it is walking distance to the plaza, shops, and restaurants.

For other budget hotels, either walk around the downtown area, or talk to the staff at the **State of Chiapas Tourism Office** on the first floor of the Secretaría de Fomento Económico building across from the Hotel Bonampak, Dr. Belisario Domínguez #950, Tuxtla Gutiérrez, tel. (961) 2-5509 or 2-4535. An information booth just inside the building is open Mon.-Fri. 8 a.m.-8 p.m. Other information booths are at the airport (open when flights are due),

Inexpensive
Hotel Maria Eugenia, Av. Central Oriente #507, tel. (961) 3-3767 fax 3-2860, in the center of town, has a pool, bar, restaurant, satellite TV, parking, A/C, and it accepts credit cards. This is a pleasant hotel, and part of the time someone at the desk speaks English.

Moderate
Hotel Bonampak, Blvd. Dr. Belisario Domínguez #180, tel. (961) 3-2050, fax 2-7737, U.S. tel. (800) 585-1234, is a modern hotel across the boulevard from the State Tourism Office. It offers nicely furnished clean rooms, tile bathrooms, TV, telephones, and cushy beds. But look further: there's a pool close by that dates from the '50s. In the front building is a good coffee shop for breakfast; in the back, the dining room (again, at least 40 years old) is a gracious old room with elegant architecture and sculptured, plastered domed ceilings. Formal ambience, wine list, and a great filet mignon.

For something fancier, try the **Hotel Flamboyant,** with restaurants, cafes, bars, and all services. Really a nice hotel, it's farther out of town at Blvd. Dr. Belisario Domínguez Km 1081. For reservations write to Apto. Postal 640, Tuxtla Gutiérrez, Chiapas 29000, Mexico; tel. (961) 5-0888.

Expensive
Hotel Camino Real. Blvd. Belisario Dominguez, tel. (961) 7-7777, fax 7-7779, U.S. tel. (800) 722-6466, is the newest and most modern hotel in town. The 210 rooms are luxurious, the dining areas are very attractive, and as in all of Tuxtla its design is in the modern vein. The lobby/dining/atrium area is open, airy, and pleasant. All of the amenities that you would expect in a luxury hotel are available at a moderate price. The hotel is on a hill overlooking the city, 15 minutes from the airport, and a comfortable walk to the central district of town.

FOOD AND ENTERTAINMENT

Regional Food and Dance
The indigenous culture and cuisine of Chiapas aren't readily evident in Tuxtla, which makes a visit to **Las Pichanchas,** Av. Central Oriente #837, tel. (961) 2-5351, a must, especially for first-time visitors. The *palapa*-roofed courtyard restaurant is decorated with local pottery and long streamers of *papeles picados,* a perfect setting for the folk dancers performing in the traditional costumes of the villages around San Cristóbal de las Casas. The menu is difficult for the uninitiated to decipher. For a good sampling of dishes from the countryside, try an assortment of tamales and the appetizer plate of local cheeses and sausages. Marimba musicians perform 2-4 p.m., the perfect time for a leisurely lunch Mexican style; folkloric dancers perform nightly at 9 p.m. It's open daily except major holidays 12:30 p.m.-midnight.

Cheap Eats
At **Super Tacos,** on Calle Central and 3 Sur, you'll find only tacos, but it's a clean, gracious, and budget friendly operation. (Note: across the street you'll find the *Mexico News* for sale.)
Domino's Pizza and **KFC** are also in town.

Music
At the **Parque Marimba** every evening, 7-9 p.m., there's a party; music, dancing, and fun. Some nights the city police band plays, on other nights it's marimbas and wind instruments, and the variety of music encourages everyone to get up and dance. This is a park for the whole family.

We noticed that there was an absence of "dissenters" at this park.

Tuxtla has a couple of lively discos, **Baby Rock** and **La Uno.** Both charge a cover; however, there are many "special" nights—ladies (free) night, Thursday night one-peso beer, etc. So check them both out; they open about 9 p.m. and close at 3 or 4 a.m., or when everyone is gone.

Days at the Races
At the annual Tuxtla road race, modern, high-tech automobiles from all over the world take part in a road rally that continues for seven days and 3,000 km along the Pan American Highway. The event takes place in the fall of each year; for more information, call the Tourist Office, tel. (961) 2-5509, 2-4535.

SHOPPING

Tuxtla is an excellent place to shop. The modern look belies the fine Indian handicrafts to be found in the city. Shops in Tuxtla are generally open daily 9 a.m.-2 p.m. and 5-9 p.m. except Sunday. For native crafts, look around the *mercado.*

A visit to the city *mercado* is always fun and filled with bright colors. *Típico* crafts as well as mounds of exotic fruits and vegetables and cold glasses of *tazcalate,* a tasty sweet drink made from local chocolate, cinnamon, and *pinole* (roasted corn), are sold here. The main market is three blocks south of the main plaza.

Indian weavers from outlying areas often sell their wares in the shade across from the main plaza next to the "white" cathedral. A stop at **Casa de las Artesanías** will give you an overview of crafts from the entire state of Chiapas. About six blocks from the government tourist office at Belisario Domínguez #2035 (see House of Arts and Crafts above), the two-story purple shop is operated by the government. You'll discover fine embroidery, wooden carvings, pottery, leather products, jewelry, and weaving. These products are a good representation of both the indigenous and the mestizo culture of the state. The shop is open Mon.-Sat. 9 a.m.-2 p.m. and 5-8 p.m., Sunday 9 a.m.-1 p.m. Note: Vendors offering amber in a plain brown wrapper can be found on most street corners. But it takes

AMBER

Amber comes from the resin of different kinds of pine trees that covered various regions of the earth 40 or 50 million years ago. Over time, natural catastrophes altered the earth's crust and entombed within it forests of now-extinct varieties of conifers. Among those classes of trees buried was the succinifer pine which, judging by the size of some pieces found, had the capacity to secrete great quantities of resin. The resin was transformed into amber through an extremely long process of petrification.

A hard and brittle substance, amber is generally yellowish, although it can have many different tones such as white, pink, red, wine, brown, or black, among others. It can be opaque, transparent, or marbled, depending on its degree of purity, and it emits a unique aroma when burned.

Primitive civilizations attributed magical properties to amber, and numerous references have been made about its importance since time immemorial. Its distribution has helped determine the commercial routes of Maya traders across Central America in ancient times.

There is evidence of amber's existence in the state of Chiapas as far back as 250 B.C. Subsequently it was distributed throughout the Yucatán Peninsula, Oaxaca, and what is now Central Mexico by two Maya tribes of Southern Mexico (Zoques and Zinacantecos). Until the arrival of the Spaniards, amber was principally used to make adornments such as nose and lip rings, earrings, and beads for necklaces.

Amber was first mined near Simojovel, a small town in northern Chiapas. Throughout the years new veins have been discovered. Unfortunately for the amber miners, they have always been found in hard-to-reach places where landslides are a constant danger. To find amber deposits, miners begin by searching for layers of coal, a highly risky job because of the condition of the loose, shaky terrain. Once coal is located, a tunnel is drilled and large blocks of coal are cut away until the "hearth of amber" is found.

Generally the raw amber is sold to the artisans of Simojovel, who, with the help of sandpaper and files, polish the pieces, giving them a beautiful finish. Once the amber has been polished, the artisans create pieces in a great variety of imaginative forms such as vine leaves (which were made even before the Spanish conquest), feet, hands, hearts, crosses, red currant berries, feathers, raindrops, fangs, triangles, leaves, flowers, and tears. Amber is also found in earrings, rings, bracelets, necklaces, and in multifaceted pieces that look like geometrically carved gems.

Sometimes trapped insects are found in amber, which considerably raises its value. Samples found have enabled entomologists to classify almost 75 insect species from the Tertiary or Cretaceous periods. The advantage of studying an insect specimen preserved in amber is that the insect's molecular structure has remained intact, without a substitution of minerals for its organic tissues. These specimens offer excellent study conditions to biologists and archaeologists.

In Chiapas, tradition has endowed amber with magical properties. Certain Maya groups put bracelets hung with small pieces of amber on their children to protect them from the "evil eye." With the passage of time, the mestizo population adopted this custom and added more modern attributes of *good luck* to the use of the amber.

Amber has had many names. The Greeks called it *electron* due to its capacity to accumulate electricity. Because of its resinous origins the Romans called it *succo* or juice and, due to its similarity to water bubbles with the reflection of sun rays within them, the Aztecs called it *apozonalli,* or water foam.

a trained eye to tell the difference between real amber and an imitation. The government shop or a reputable jeweler might be the better place to buy it to ensure its authenticity. Amber is found in the state of Chiapas and it is seen in many shops.

The city is filled with modern shops, including glitzy department stores, trendy dress shops, and beauty shops. Shoppers have access to all high-tech appliances and equipment.

SERVICES

The area code for Tuxtla Gutiérrez is 961.

The **State of Chiapas Tourism Office** is on the second floor of the Secretaría de Fomento Económico building across from the Hotel Bonampak, Dr. Belisario Domínguez #950, Tuxtla Gutiérrez, tel. (961) 2-5509 or 2-4535. An information booth just inside the building is open Mon.-Fri. 8 a.m.-8 p.m. You'll find other information booths at the airport (open when flights are due), the zoo (open during zoo hours), and the Casa de las Artesanías (open during shop hours).

GETTING THERE AND AROUND

Tuxtla's main airport, **Aeropuerto Llano San Juan,** is about a 30-minute drive from town; a taxi from town costs about US$15. **Mexicana** airlines flies from here, and an airport transport service takes Mexicana passengers to the airport, departing the downtown office about two hours before the flight and costing about 30 pesos; the same trip from the airport to town is just double, 60 pesos—I don't know why! For information, contact the Mexicana office at Av. Central Poniente #206, tel. (961) 2-5402. **Aerocaribe,** tel. (961) 2-2032, also flies from here. You may be able to have the minivan pick you up at your hotel if you make arrangements.

Several bus lines serve Tuxtla. If you're traveling to Chiapa de Corza, go to the bus station at 2A Oriente Sur, and if you're heading to the docks for a boat trip through Sumidero Canyon, tell the driver you want to get off at "la launcha," US50 cents OW. **Cristóbal Colón** is one of the main bus lines, with first-class and deluxe service to Mexico City, Oaxaca, Palenque, San Cristóbal de las Casas, and other points. The station is at 2 Norte Poniente #268, tel. (961) 2-1639, 2-3624. Another good line is **Maya De Oro Plus. Autotransportes de Oriente** has first-class and deluxe service to most destinations from Av. 5 Sur at Calle 9 Poniente Sur, tel. (961) 2-8725. Going to Chiapa de Corzo on a local bus takes about 40-60 minutes with stops along the way, and costs about 10 pesos. The bus to San Cristóbal de las Casas takes two hours by bus (about one and a half hours by car), and the fare is about 25 pesos. The new luxury buses (often with the word "plus" attached) will cost a little more.

BEYOND TUXTLA

The Chiapas countryside is beautiful. Adventurous travelers who drive, or who hire a car and driver from Tuxtla or Chiapa de Corzo, will find the area well worth exploring. Before you take off with map in hand, make sure you understand the road signs. In Chiapas the highway numbers can be confusing, since federal highways and state highways often have the same numbers. Please note the different shapes of the signs.

SUMIDERO CANYON

A drive into the mountains 22 km northeast of Tuxtla presents a dramatic view of the rugged Sumidero Canyon. This spectacular perspective of the canyon includes the 14.3-km-long gorge with sheer cliffs that drop 1,800 meters into the Grijalva River. As you ascend into the mountains you'll find five lookout points with a diverse vista from each: La Ceiba, La Coyota, Las Tepehuajes, El Roblar, and at the end of the road Los Chiapas. At Los Chiapas you have a breathtaking look at the canyon and at the river zigzagging far below.

Here you'll find a small cafe, selling regional tamales and the favored local drinks—*pozol, tazcalate,* or a steaming cup of excellent Chiapas-grown coffee. No instant coffee here!

A persisting "Tepechia" legend tells that the Chiapas Indians refused to be taken prisoner when it was apparent they would suffer defeat at the hands of the Spanish invaders. Men, women, and children chose instead to jump to their deaths from the top of these Sumidero cliffs. *Combis* leave Calzada de los Hombres Ilustres in Tuxtla daily (as they fill up), taking passengers to the Sumidero Canyon. Ask at your hotel or at the tourist office. **Transportes al Cañon,** Av. 1 Oriente and Calle 7 Sur, tel. (961) 3-3584, has minibuses to the canyon and information on boat tours. Anyone who has the time and inclination will find both views of the canyon fascinating, from the river by boat and from the road by car.

A CAVE COUNTRY LOOP

Caves can be found in all of Mexico and the mountainous regions especially offer numerous

OZ MALLAN

Sumidero Canyon

to the west from 195) are along a road that's not much more than a dirt track. For more information about guides and transport contact the tourist office in Tuxtla, or in Suchiapa or Villaflores. No one should go into the caverns alone, let alone without a local guide who knows his way around and who has the proper equipment. These caverns are still in their native state, pitch black, and would be interesting mostly to devoted spelunkers. The formations within are beautiful, with stalactites and stalagmites creating odd and mysterious shapes. Even for those of us who are not spelunkers, the area surrounding the caverns is breathtaking. Large chestnut trees mingle with myriad other trees loaded with orchid plants, bromeliads, delicate ferns, and generations of birds. Coffee trees hide the entrance to Guaymas. Local guides know the way to many more caves in the area: Belen, El Nilar, La Calavera, El Jaragual, El Encanto, and the Crystal Caverns. The limestone plateau is rich in caves small and large and smothered in lush tropical growth. Don't expect much commercial tourism of any kind near Guaymas.

caves. You can make a loop on State Hwy. 195 (a small road) beginning in Tuxtla. Going south from Tuxtla, you'll pass many little villages; these are not tourist destinations, just the Chiapan countryside. This entire agricultural valley region is referred to as La Frailesca, which indicates padres from the Dominican era who came in and began "evangelizing." After about 18 kms, you'll reach the pleasant little town of **Suchiapa.** It's worth a stop to stroll the town and to look at San Esteban Church on the main square, built at the end of the 16th century. Suchiapa was a stronghold of the Chiapa Indians and most of the populace today are descendants of those ancient people. Continue on 195 until you see a small sign at the cutoff to Guaymas Caverns, or keep going south and you will come to another small Chiapanecan town, Villaflores.

Guaymas Caverns

Caves were sacred to the early Maya. The Maya believe that all life began from caves. Guaymas is 61 km from Tuxtla, and the last 14 km (a cutoff

Villaflores

The Dominican padres traveled far and wide evangelizing the Chiapanecans. The villages of this region—previously known as Cutilinoco and Matacapana—are pre-Hispanic towns.Villaflores grew from the ex-hacienda Santa Catalina. The town is mainly an agricultural village founded in 1876 by Julian Grajales. Nothing remains from the old hacienda, except its traditions. Several other nearby towns grew from one-time haciendas at about the same time: **Villa Corzo** grew from ex-hacienda Trinidad La Ley, and **San Pablo Buenavista,** 22 km farther, from the ex-hacienda of the same name (here there are still remnants of the old buildings). If you remain on the road toward Domingo Chanona, you'll find the ruins of another hacienda, but it's not really worth a special trip to drive there.

Villaflores is the farming center of the region, producing mainly corn and cattle. Many farmers drive pickups, but you'll still see cattle pulling aged wooden corn carts with wooden wheels. Running alongside the road the Angostura waterway reveals tranquil inlets and islands. If you feel the need, there are a few very humble rooms available in Villaflores.

If you follow the "loop" all the way back to just west of Tuxtla, continue southwest on Hwy. 190 and cut south when you reach Hwy. 195, which will dead-end into Hwy. 200.

ON THE WAY TO TAPACHULA

Parallel to the ocean, Federal Highway 200 runs southeast from the Oaxaca border all the way to Tapachula at Mexico's border with Guatemala. The road meanders through the mountains and through an arid area with breathtaking views. The road passes small towns, abandoned archaeological sites, and the remains of former haciendas. Most of the haciendas have little left to show from their 17th- and 18th-century beginnings. The exceptions are the chapels.

Over the years the small houses once used by the hacienda workers became villages. And even though the owners' "big houses" or "main houses" and the business end of the haciendas were abandoned when the government broke up the large tracts of property, the hacienda chapels continued to be used and cared for; in most cases they became the village chapels. Of course there are a few exceptions and an occasional big old house still stands; if you see a tall chimney you can be reasonably sure it marks the spot where a sugarcane plant was once in business.

Tuxtla to Tonalá
On the way to Hwy. 200, you'll pass several historical settlements. Near the town of Jiquipilas the landscape offers what is believed to be an ancient Maya platform and temple. Near the Soyatenco River, check out the hill called Cerro de la Chumpa, once believed to be the dwelling of the Maya goddess Jantepusi-llama. At one time the entire area was an important ceremonial center of the Zoque Indians.

For the most part, the landscape is agricultural, its beginnings traced to ex-hacienda Santa Lucia. On its way to Cintalapa the road passes through the Valley of Cintala, another area of sprawling ex-haciendas. Some of the shells of these old estates stand here and there: Las Cruces, with a beautiful old chapel; Macuilapa; El Rosario; and La Valdiviana with its tall chimney. Crossing the Sierra Madre Sur, the road winds through the dramatic pass of La Sepultura and eventually reaches Tonalá and Hwy. 200.

Puerto Arista
Here a little jog takes you to the coast at Puerto Arista, 185 km from Tuxtla. Puerto Arista is the most important beach community along this coast. In the 19th century the plan was to develop this as a major port for international commerce. However, it never happened, and most Chiapanecans are happy to have this lovely undeveloped beach to themselves. Tourism hasn't really taken hold here, so life moves at an easy pace. Scenic surroundings offer lacy waves breaking over broad beaches; the surf is quite heavy here and lifeguards are on duty only on weekends and holiday time.

The favorite swimming spot is Boca del Cielo, a small lagoon formed by a peninsula. Everywhere you look you'll find a lovely photo-op. Views of cloud-capped mountains back a white lighthouse. At La Joya Lagoon bright-colored boats cut through the blue water. Canoes are great for bird watching, and it's easy to make your way to see the great bird population close by. If you fancy sunsets, get ready for some of the best, often with horseback riders silhouetted against an orange sky.

Accommodations: If you plan to spend the night, you'll find several small *posadas* in nearby Tonalá. Check out the **Hotel Del Rey,** Av. Joaquin Miguel Gutiérrez, tel. (966) 3-1969, nothing fancy, with a/c, and it takes American Express. Budget. Another small hostel is **Hotel Farro,** 16 de Septiembre and Matamoros 360, tel. (966) 3-0033, simple, clean, with a/c. Budget.

Southeast from Tonalá
Another stop along the way is **Pijijiapan** (pee-hee-hee-ah-PAN), 240 kms from Tuxtla. Lined with houses of crayon-colored facades and tile roofs, the streets of this old town present a whimsical look. On the outskirts of town look for archaeological remnants on large granite stones with carvings from ancient Olmecs. The largest is called **Los Soldados,** which shows a group of Indian warriors. Signs are few, so don't hesitate to ask in town. From here dirt roads meander through marshlands and salt flats.

DIANA LASICH HARPER

A variety of monkeys, including the spider monkey, live in the rainforest.

Beyond Pijijiapan on the main road, **Mapastepec** is one gateway for hikers into El Triunfo Biosphere Reserve. This is a difficult entrance and special permits and equipment are required. Mountain climbers can hire a local guide and it's unwise for anyone desiring to visit El Triunfo to go without one. If you prefer to have reservations, then check with the Tuxtla Gutiérrez Tourism Office or the Natural History Institute for guide information. Triunfo is also accessible from Guatemala.

El Triunfo Biosphere Reserve

A visit to Mexico's cloud forest brings you up close to myriad mountain streams, waterfalls, and lush tropical flora, including immense trees, some with aboveground tormented roots, magnificent 30-foot-high tree ferns, delicate vines that creep from tree to tree, and a mixture of tiny-to-large blossoms. All of this is punctuated by bird song and flitting hummingbirds, forest falcons, and the brilliant blues, greens, and reds of such stars as the tanager, trogon, and most spectacular, the quetzal. The quetzal was revered centuries ago for use by Maya nobility. The color is brilliant green, and it sports two tails up to 24 inches long. The bird is nearly extinct, and lives only in the misty cloud-forest regions of Mexico, Guatemala, and Honduras. All of these dazzling birds are experts at fading into the leaves and vines of the forest, so bring your binocs and study long and hard. Good photographs are hard to come by in the often vaporous atmosphere of the cloud forest, but your personal microchip will long remember the look, the scent, and the aura of the unspoiled forest and its delicate features.

This is a trip for the hardy hiker since you will be hiking up the side of the (dormant) volcano, there are no roads, and depending which entry you take, it's at least an eight-mile hike, often on muddy trails since this is, remember, a cloud forest, with constant mists and rains that make it the greenest section of Mexico.

Beyond El Triunfo

Acacoyagua is the home of a dynasty begun at the turn of the 20th century. Japanese immigrants, known as the Enomoto colony, put down roots here. At the central plaza in town, a handsome memorial commemorates these people. Even today you will see many folks with the physical characteristics of these long-gone ancestors or hear the last names of their predecessors. The countryside around Acacoyagua is reminiscent of the mountainous countryside of Japan: an intense green, with fern-lined streams, tall fir trees, all with the beauty of a Japanese watercolor. In nearby Tapachula, it's common to find restaurants serving Japanese-inspired dishes.

Highway 200 ends at the busy border hub of Tapachula.

CHIAPA DE CORZO

Many years before the Spanish conquest, Chiapa de Corzo was inhabited by Indians from Nicaragua. The settlement was on the Kandelumini River (today called the Grijalva River). The Chiapanecos were courageous warriors and only after two invasions did the Spaniards get them under control. Conquistador Luis Marin led the first foray in 1524. His troops were forced to turn back in failure. In 1528, Diego Mazariegos attacked and was brutally successful conquering the Indians. On 3 April of that year, the town was named Villa Real and dedicated under a large ceiba tree. Like most Spanish settlements in those early years, it was given as an *encomienda* to the conqueror Mazariegos. This lifestyle made vassals of the Indians who built the city under the direction of the Spanish. Fortunately, the Indians had a hero in Bishop Bartolomé de las Casas. He began making changes from the time of his arrival years later, and by 1552, the *encomienda* was dismantled. The city was then called Villa Real Corona. The name of the settlement continued to change as it grew; it was called Chiapa Español and then and Chiapa de los Indios. According to legend it was named for the *chia,* a small fruit that once grew abundantly

in the region. The city's present name, Chiapa de Corzo, was given in 1888 in honor of the president of the municipality, Angel Albino Corzo.

It's an easy one-hour trip (10 km) from Tuxtla to Chiapa on a local bus. If you're driving there's a big Pemex gas station just before the turnoff to San Cristóbal de las Casas.

SIGHTS

The once vibrant, important city inhabited by influential Spaniards is today small and laid-back and home to many Indians. Signs of change are imminent with the construction of new highways and the influx of Mundo Maya tourists; the pace is quickening. The city even boasts a charming little hotel.

La Pila

The centerpiece of the small city is the largest colonial fountain in the state. Set regally under an elegant Moorish-style brick structure in the center of a grassy park, it illustrates the strong Moorish influence over the Catholic kings of Spain. The fountain was built by Fray Rodrigo de Léon in the middle of the 16th century and was completed in 1562. This was not just the village water supply; it was a gathering place where women did their laundry, collected water in *calabasas* for drinking, but maybe more important, the gathering was a social event: even the animals had their own water troughs. The striking building is built of red bricks cut in unusual three-dimensional diamond shapes in a typical Muhadin style, or as some say, as a replica of the Spanish king's crown. Take time to read the informational plaques around the fountain for a thumbnail history of the city and the fountain.

Note: In October and November, a little chewing bug called the *chanquista* is particularly annoying. One bite draws blood and then becomes a large ugly-colored welt that hangs on for days. So when in grassy areas in the city, wear bug repellent and long pants; the insects seem to go for the skin nearest the ground. Of course if you're in the countryside do the same thing.

ESCRITO PÚBLICO

Not too many years after the conquest of Mexico, there grew a need for the general populace to write letters. Most didn't know how to write. So in every village there would be tucked under an arch on the main square a man sitting at a little table with a sign, *Escrito Público.* For a peso or two, the most uneducated could come to have a letter written. Some of these were love letters, but most were letters that involved mistreatment by one party or another. And from early in the 16th century, the lowest citizen could be represented by an attorney. But, it all had to be put in writing. Even today, in small villages and large, you'll find the public writer somewhere near the square ready to write a letter for those who cannot.

The Plaza

La Pila sits in the town plaza, and a variety of small shops and businesses lie across the road. Here you'll find a pharmacy, an *escrito publico*, the town letter writer, and at least one shop that sells the locally made wooden masks and other crafts. Not too far away the **El Companerio Café,** Av. Coronel Urbina 5-B, serves good food, average entree US$3-4.50.

Santo Domingo Cathedral

Santo Domingo Cathedral is a huge, though simple, white building that stands next to the town soccer field. Its huge bell was cast in gold, silver, and copper in 1576, and when it tolls it can be heard for miles around the countryside. Vendors set up shop near the church and among other things sell "black" and "white" *pozol* in large (maybe a liter), round-bottomed tin cups. This thick drink is made from hominy, chocolate, and cinnamon. It serves as a "fast-food" lunch for workers on the go in Chiapas. Eat your heart out, McDonald's. One family drives up in a truck every day and unloads tables, buckets, and everything needed to prepare the *pozol*. This same family has been selling *pozol* from this corner under the trees for more than a decade. Some diners make the trip all the way from Tuxtla to lunch or breakfast on this tasty *pozol*. Nearby you'll find women selling pottery from Amatenango, and across the street the flower lady always has a glorious variety of colors; you'll first notice the sweet aroma and then the splash of color.

Ex-Convent
of Santo Domingo—Centro Cultural

The convent was built in 1554 in the usual design of the friars, with thick walls and broad archways edging once-lovely patios. Tile floors and wooden stairways lead to a multitude of rooms. Wandering through the old convent is worth the time to see the lovely old architecture. The Spaniards really knew how to build to last. Some of the old walls are eight feet thick. No matter how hot the day, it's always cool in the shadows of the arched corridors.

Today a few of the rooms on the second floor are used as a museum. Displays show elegant lacquerware, another fine craft brought from Europe by the padres and mastered by the Indians under their tutelage. You'll see wonderful examples of this precision craft—from tiny, delicate jewelry boxes to enormous wooden chests, each covered with bright colors and intricate designs.

Artist Doña Martha Vargas puts on a lacquer-painting demonstration *almost* every day; if this is important to you, check with the tourist office in Tuxtla for her regular schedule. Her work is amazing. Also displayed in the museum are wooden masks depicting the Spanish conquistadors with those vivid blue eyes. Here and there on the patio you'll spot a marimba or two.

Embarcadero

It's a short walk from the town center to the embarcadero (city dock), where passengers board launches to go up the Grijalva River through Sumidero Canyon. The docks are a bustling hub; try one of the outdoor *palapa* cafes for a cold beer or snack with a good view of life on the river.

Small boats give you the opportunity to view the steep canyon walls from the level of the river. This awesome waterway was formerly a roaring series of mighty rapids that literally cut their way through the massive towering stone. In 1960 it took a team of surveyors nine days to travel through the hazardous, rushing white water of the canyon. In 1981 the water was harnessed with construction of the **Chicoasén Dam,** one of Mexico's largest. As a result, the tranquil riverway serves as a favorite recreational area for locals and visitors alike—a trip in a small boat to the dam and back takes about three hours. Along the water's edge the cliffs present interesting rock formations, caves (some large enough for a small boat to pull into), waterfalls (during the rainy season), and an ever-changing vista of plants and trees. In one area at certain times of the year, you'll see a plant formation that looks like a Christmas tree hugging the cliff; perfectly shaped bright green moss or low-growing plants with a sprinkling of colored growth.

Most of these small launches are open (bring water, hat, and sunscreen). Price of the trip varies depending on the number of passengers. Figure about US$60-80 per boat RT, and most boats hold 6-10 people. Check with the Tuxtla Gutiérrez tourist office or one of the travel agencies.

El Calvario Church

This old church shows its age in at least part of the structure. In the San Pedro District, it was

OZ MALLAN

pozole *vendor*

built in the 17th century on a hill next to one of the revered ceiba trees.

San Sebastian Ruins

This 17th-century church was obviously a grand building in its day. Built on the hill of San Gregorio, it represents a history of great wealth and the one-time importance of the city of Chiapa. The church had three naves, and the remaining walls echo the influence of the Muhadin, Renaissance, and baroque architecture that Spain brought to the New World. The structure has been used in a variety of ways over the centuries. During the battle of 21 October 1863, it served as a fort during the fight for Independence. Not a great deal is left today, just a few walls and fine arches, and many memories—but the view remains. From here visitors gaze down on the urban development that covers the landscape of the Río Grande.

ACCOMMODATIONS AND FOOD

With the growing attraction of Chiapas and the interest in Mundo Maya, Chiapa de Corzo has added to its tourist services. Overnighters are few, so accommodations in the city are limited. The most economical are very simple, usually clean, but not much more.

Hotel Los Angeles, Julian Grajales #2, tel. (968) 6-0048, has an old charm, large rooms, tiled bathrooms, and windows that look out onto the street. Shoestring.

The **Hotel Marisa,** Av. Domingo Ruiz #300, tel. (968) 6-0773, fax 6-0389, is on the road to Tuxtla. Shoestring.

The nicest hotel is **La Ceiba,** three blocks west of the plaza. It has an Old World look but the shiny flavor of New World products; pool, parking garage, lobby bar, a/c, dining room that serves fine local specialties, and 42 rooms with private bath. Budget.

ENTERTAINMENT AND EVENTS

Historical Parachicos

Imagine an army of wooden-faced (real wood), blue-eyed Spaniards wearing mustaches and bright bushy yellow hair—many of them only three feet tall, others man-size; this is the beginning of a great fiesta in Chiapa. On 15 January the biggest celebration of the year, the Festival of St. Sebastian, is held in the park around *la pila* (the fountain). The main characters are boys and men dressed in special costumes. Various legends relate how this party first began. A favorite tells about a rich Spanish woman,

María dc Angulo, living in Central America with her crippled son. She prayed to St. Sebastian and searched for the special doctor who would cure the boy. After many false leads, she was told of a powerful herbalist in Namandiyugua near Chiapa de Corzo; she came to the village as soon as possible, praying that her son would be cured. The herbalist instructed her to bathe the boy in a small lagoon called Jaguey ("where the wild pig swims"). She continued to bathe him in the lagoon and also continued to pray to St. Sebastian, just in case. The boy was cured, indeed a miracle. She gave credit to both the herbalist and St. Sebastian. The herbalist suggested that the boy needed time to recuperate and proposed that a little fiesta would distract him. Doña Angulo organized her servants, who put on costumes with wooden masks, serapes, and whips. And so the first Parachico (*para* for, *chico* small one) celebration was born.

Over the years the Parachico costume evolved into today's colorful representation. For both men and women, it consists of a headdress of a bushy, yellow fiber (like an old-fashioned scrub brush) and an artfully painted wooden face mask. This blond, blue-eyed (with real-hair eyelashes), pink-skinned Spaniard carries a rattle and wears pants and shirt of "good" quality, a belt of richly embroidered satin, and brightly colored serape from the city of Saltillo. Women and girls wear the typical dress of embroidered tulle (in honor of Doña Angulo).This design of this costume is prescribed and they faithfully adhere to it. Parachico is the biggest event of the year in Chiapa de Corzo.

Purists disagree with the accuracy of this version of the legend. Several authors/historians have their own ideas about the origin and even the evolution of the costume. Some believe that the birth of the festival emanates from war dances of the pre-Hispanic era; others that the origin lies in a particular dance by Arabs and Christians brought from Spain during the colonial period. So the argument continues—but so does the celebration. Whatever the origin, if you happen to be in the area, visit on 15 January to take part. Shoppers, note: these quality masks are handcrafted by special artisans in Chiapa de Corzo and though you'll see the masks all over Mexico, this is the originating point and you will find them in gift shops around the city.

The Marimba

Anyone who has spent any time in San Cristóbal or Tuxtla, or just in a plaza or an outdoor cafe, is familiar with the sound of the Chiapa marimba; this is *tropical* music! The marimba appears to have originated in Chiapas with the dense settlement of Spaniards in Chiapa de Corzo. It is believed that a small version of the instrument was originally brought from Africa's Angola with the slaves accompanying the Spanish. In no time the instrument was adopted and adapted by Mexicans and Central Americans. A change here, an adjustment there, and Chiapas produces some of the finest marimbas in the country. In Chiapa de Corzo area, it is constructed from the "singing" wood, *hormiguillo,* which gives the marimba its brilliant sound. Sticks made from the strong but flexible *guisisil* wood are wrapped at one end with natural rubber to make mallets that fly across the keys.

The marimba is no longer the step-sister of concert instruments; it lacks only two octaves to equal the range of a concert piano. More and more fine music is being written for the marimba by classical and popular musicians all over the world.

The Nandayapas are an extended family of extraordinary Maya musicians. They are creators of the country's finest marimbas, still patterned from the 100-year-old templates of the first generations of the Nandayapa family. The keys function like the parts of a string quartet, says the elder Zeferino Nandayapa. You hear a violin, second violin (contralto voice), the viola, and the cello. The Nandayapas play Bach, Mozart, Sambas, Sones, and lively Mexican music. Their marimbas come in all sizes, but their "concert" size can be up to eight feet long, waist high, and can range up to six and a half octaves.

If you're lucky enough to attend a concert of the Nandayapa Orchestra at Carnegie Hall in New York, you're apt to hear selections such as Franz Liszt's *Rhapsody #2* or Manuel Falla's *Fire Dance,* both played like you've never heard them before. Marimba music is an art form, an art form that lives in the heart of Mexicans, especially the Chiapanecans. Award-winning Mexican poet Oscar Oliva said, "In all religious and sacred ceremonies, the marimba is there. With music from the marimba, we bury our friends, our parents, our brothers." The marimba is the soul of Chiapa life, at birth, at death, in happiness, in sadness.

SAN CRISTÓBAL DE LAS CASAS

San Cristóbal is an appealing old colonial city. One-story pastel buildings with wrought-iron covered windows and tile roofs line the hilly streets, lending a special charm to this historic city. For centuries, behind paint-deprived walls antiquated colonial buildings held hidden courtyards filled with plants and flowers, bits and pieces of another life, memories of the past. But now, as more and more tourists discover San Cristóbal, the old colonial buildings are opening up. Art galleries, restaurants, and trendy malls selling beautiful clothing, crafts, and antiques attract visitors by the droves.

A more important reason to visit is San Cristóbal's Indian culture. This is the Indian center of the Mexican highlands—a place to watch the people, whose diverse clothing styles date back hundreds of years. Those in the know can identify villagers by the clothes they wear, since each village uses its own central color and particular style when weaving the textiles to make their garments. Each year we return we find more and more people on the narrow streets, both locals (all turned vendors of something) and visitors from all over the world. Tourism officials continue to talk about building a large airport nearby, and if it comes to pass, expect even more people to come and explore.

HISTORY

In 1528, life drastically changed for the Indians who had settled in the Hueyzacatlan Valley centuries before. On 31 March of that year Diego Mazariegos founded the city called Villa Real de Chiapas (today's San Cristóbal de las Casas). It began a conflict of cultures that still has not been resolved. By 1538 a neat grid of streets had been cut into the hilly valley, and the Spanish had taken over. They built large churches and houses of authority around a central plaza, and their one-story red-tile-roofed houses displayed wrought iron fences. Spanish padres took seriously their task of preaching the gospel and proselytizing Indians, who also took their gods seriously. The city was laid out with barrios in the corners and on the edges of the growing town, each with a church and a priest who looked after the souls and bodies of his flock, often in extreme ways. In 1544, Bishop Bartolomé de las Casas arrived and he was shocked at the way the Indians were used by the rich and powerful. He tried to make humane changes, but he was like a leaf blown into the wind.

Villa Real de Chiapas was the most important city in the highlands and became the state capital, until 1892, when Tuxtla Gutiérrez took over. In 1943 the city name was changed to San Cristóbal de las Casas in honor of the patron of the Indians.

In the early days, the barrios were industrious centers of specific industries. Barrio Cerrillo was known for its blacksmiths, Barrio Guadalupe for its carpenters, La Merced was the candle-making center, Santa Lucia was a center for handcrafts, and San Felipe was the laundry center. Today each barrio has its church and plaza, and the barrios all celebrate their feast days with parties that last through the night with loud cannons, music, dancing, and traditional food.

The Spaniards introduced wheat growing and for centuries it was a common crop on the outskirts of San Cristóbal. From the 16th century and into the beginning of the 20th century wheat mills sat near the mouths of the great rivers in the valley. Eventually high-tech methods took over and most of the mills disappeared. A few remnants of these large haciendas survive; northeast of the city on the Río Amarillo you'll find the mills of **Utrilla** and **Los Arcos;** more are scattered about, but none are functioning.

What makes this city unique is the way the ethnic groups have held onto their ancient be-

SAN CRISTÓBAL DE
LAS CASAS CENTRO

COLONIA

EDGAR ROBLEDO

REVOLUCIÓN

HONDURAS

MERCADO
JOSÉ
CASTILLO

PRIMERA CALLE

ARGENTINA

COLOMBIA

BARRIO DE

MEXICANOS

COSTA RICA

CALZ

LÁZARO CÁRDENAS

AV. 16 DE SEPTIEMBRE

NICARAGUA

AV. B. DOMÍNGUEZ

YAJALÓN

DIAGONAL

ARRIAGA

ECUADOR

REAL DE MEXICANOS

CONVENTO DE
SANTO DOMINGO

SNA JOLOBIL

SIMOJOVEL

COLÓN

AV. CRISTÓBAL COLÓN

TONALÁ

BARRIO EL CERRILLO

CANADA

BELICE

BRASIL

VENEZUELA

GUATEMALA

CHIAPA DE CORZO

IGLESIA
SANTO DOMINGO

COMITÁN

EL
JACARANDAL

CHILÓN

TUXTLA

AV. PICHUCALCO

HUIXTLA

NA BALOM
MUSEUM/HOTEL

MUSEUM OF
REGIONAL DRESS

TAPACHULA

ESCUADRON

201

AV. 5 DE MAYO

CASA
MEXICANA

AV. GRAL. UTRILLA

DR. NAVARRO

DUJELAY

HOTEL RINCÓN
DEL ARCO

28 DE AGOSTO

HOTEL
FLAMBOYANT
ESPAÑOL

EJERCITO

NACIONAL

AV. DIEGO

AV. VICENTE GUERRERO

ISABEL LA CATÓLICA

PRIMERO DE MARZO

TALLER
LENATEROS

FLAVIO A. PANIAGUA

12 DE OCTUBRE

5 DE FEBRERO

AV. 20 DE NOVIEMBRE

HOTEL POSADA
DIEGO DE
MAZARIEGOS

INSTITUTO
JOVEL

MA. ADELINA FLORES

NICOLAS RUÍZ

CAFE
ALTURA

CATHEDRAL

HOTEL
SAN MARTÍN

POSADA
MARGARITA

HOTEL POSADA
DON QUIJOTE

BARRIO DE

LA MERCED

HOTEL
CATEDRAL

GUADALUPE

VICTORIA

PALACIO
MUNICIPAL

REAL DE GUADALUPE

BARRIO DE

GUADALUPE

PLAZA DE
GUADALUPE

DIEGO DE MAZARIEGOS

PLAZA 31
DE MARZO

PIZZE Y MASS

HOTEL POSADA
LOS ANGELES

AV. ORTIZ DE DOMÍNGUEZ

FRANCISCO I. MADERO

LA PARED BOOKS
AND GIFTS

MATAMOROS

EMILIANO'S
MOUSTACHE

STATE
TOURISM

HOTEL
CIUDAD
REAL

HOTEL SANTA
CLARA

POSADA SAN
CRISTÓBAL

AV. JOSEFA ORTIZ DE DOMÍNGUEZ

AV. J.M. SANTIAGO

DR. JOSÉ F. FLORES

LA PALMA

CUAUHTÉMOC

CAFE LA
SELVA

POSADA FRAY
BARTOLOMÉ DE
LAS CASAS

FRANCISCO LEÓN

SCENIC
VIEWPOINT

NIÑOS HÉROES

AV. CRESCENCIO ROSAS

AV. MIGUEL HIDALGO

AV. INSURGENTES

AV. BENITO JUÁREZ

LA ALMOHONGA

AV. J.M. ROJAS

IGLESIA SAN
CRISTÓBAL

IGNACIO ALLENDE

HNOS DOMÍNGUEZ

JULIO M. CORZO

BARRIO DE

BARRIO SAN

RAMON CORONA

SANTA LUCIA

ANTONIO

ALVARO OBREGÓN

HOTEL
POSADA
VALLARTA

SOSTENES

ESPONDA

SCALE NOT AVAILABLE

PEDRO MORENO

To First Class Bus Station,
Omnibus Cristóbal Colón, La
Coleta Bullring, and Municipal
Park of San Cristóbal Caves

RESTAURANT TIKAL/
PEPE'S PIZZA

To Chamula

14 DE SEPTIEMBRE

© MOON PUBLICATIONS, INC.

liefs; each group is different, each with its own mystery, color, and tradition. And though most of their villages lie on the outskirts of San Cristóbal, the city draws them together, bolsters their belief in their separate existence. Despite the intrusion of the Pan American Highway bringing outside influences and the seduction of material temptations from visitors from all over the world, San Cristóbal seems to be the ship that carries these ethnic groups unchanged through *centuries* of change. After 500 years, will life change for these groups?

THE PEOPLE

Visitors to San Cristóbal should know that the Chamulans, Zinacantecans, and Lacandóns do *not* like to be photographed, and they like it even less when you produce a camera inside their churches. In Chamula you can buy a permit at the city hall to take pictures in the square as long as it isn't a special holiday. For photographers intent on coming home with pictures of the locals, go to the public market in San Cristóbal (any morning except Sunday, which is market day in the villages). If you use a long lens and stand in an inconspicuous spot, it's possible to get pictures of the people while they're busy shopping. If they see you they'll turn away. You can ask permission from your subject, and if he/she asks for payment—well, that seems fair. But, don't expect too much cooperation.

Despite the influx of tourists (mostly European), little change has taken place here. You'll still find no high-rise hotels, no Denny's, but always thousands of Indians dressed in their traditional clothing, bustling to the rhythm of San Cristóbal's public market. The outside world has introduced a few variations in the lifestyle of the indigenous people. More and more men wear factory-made straw cowboy hats or even baseball caps, and among city-dwelling mestizos polyester clothing is becoming popular. The people in the outlying villages such as San Juan Chamula and Zinacantán still make their own flat-crowned hats, and women still use the backstrap loom to weave the colorful fabric for their blouses and *huipiles.*

THE PLAZA AND NEARBY

Main Square

The official name of the square is Plaza de 31 de Marzo. Green iron benches are scattered along the wide walkway under tall shade trees. The centerpiece is a two-story kiosk with table and umbrellas where cold drinks and snacks are served; I've never seen anyone but tourists there. The square has had many faces. During the colonial era it served several functions; a large fountain supplied water for the village, it was the gathering spot of the public market, and it was the scene of punishment during the years of the Inquisition. More recently, the Zapatistas rebelled against poverty and governmental neglect. Today it has resumed its tranquil appearance most of the time, though crowds of indigenous people showing their displeasure in front of the Palacio Municipal often spill out onto the square. Yet, it's a happy gathering place for fiestas, especially for Christmas and the Fiesta of San Juan.

If you decide to sit awhile (it's a great place to rest your feet after a long morning exploring the city), expect to be inundated by Chamulan women and children selling woven bracelets and belts, small wooden Zapatista dolls in all sizes, and Chiclets gum. Young entrepreneurs, boys 9-10 years old, carry boxes of candy and lollipops, younger brothers sell newspapers, and older teens hawk amber of questionable origin. Most of the women carry babies in their *rebozos,* many of the children are unkempt with skin rashes, women and children are dirty, and most of them chew on big brother's candy. Of all the Indians from the outlying villages, the Chamulans seem to be the ones who need help the most, the ones who seem to be the "welfare cases" (if Mexico had welfare!).

Look for the very aged leather-faced man who uses a long palm frond to sweep and clean one long side of the stone-lined walkway before he moves to the next side of the square.

Casa Sirena

Across from the square sits the oldest house in town. Constructed around 1555, it is quite a lovely old building, and you can still see a stylized version of what looks likes two serpent women, and over the corner of the building, a carving of a sea nymph that gives the house its name. Look for the carved lions, an indigenous craftsman's interpretation from some medieval representation. The insignia on the coat of arms over the door has been destroyed, so although the house is most often ascribed to be the original home of Luis de Mazariegos (the conqueror of Chiapas), some believed it may have been built another, Andres de la Tobilla.

Palacio Municipal

This structure, on the west side of the main square, has been rebuilt many times since the first stone was laid in 1885. Rebel troops led by Juan Ortega burned the previous building to the ground in 1863 during a skirmish between royalists and republicans. When construction of this building began, the city was still the capital of the state and the plan included a much larger edifice, but before it was completed fate stepped in and San Cristóbal lost its rank. Construction was halted with only 25% of the building completed. It's a lovely neoclassic design with columns painted a pale blue. The columns and lower arches present a show of dignity due a structure that takes care of state business. Frequent demonstrations take place here, and this building bore the major damage during the Zapatista uprising in 1994. Behind the palace lies a plaza where civic ceremonies are held.

Law School Auditorium

A few blocks south of the plaza is another old building with a fanciful history, the ex-church and monastery of the Jesuits. At one time it was an exclusive school, San Francisco Javier School. Once the Jesuits were expelled in 1767, the school no longer functioned. It was converted to the Tridentine Seminary of Nuestra Señora de la Concepcion until the beginning of the 19th century, when part of the church was reconstructed. Today it houses the Universidad Autonoma de Chiapas Law School, and the old structure of the church serves as the auditorium.

CHURCHES AND MUSEUMS

You don't have to be a "church person" to enjoy the marvel of architecture and art gathered in

---

HETZMEK

The Maya woman took the infant, who was about six months old, and spoke slowly and reverently to him as she placed a gold bracelet on each tiny wrist. The young mother and father watched the "godmother" intently as she introduced the infant to his future. On a table between them lay a book, a coin, a weeding blade, a gun, and a pair of scissors. *"Koten, Antonio Cuitok, ten kin mentik hetzmek tech—* Come Antonio Cuitok, I make the *hetzmek* for you." She went on, "I give you all these things to hold, so that you learn them when you grow up." She picked up the book, a Catholic missal, and read several prayers from it, then placed it in the baby's tiny, grasping hands. "I give you this book so that you will learn to read." Then the blade—". . . that you will learn to farm"—the gun, etc., until all of the items were given and explained.

Then the godmother placed the baby astride her left hip, a signal that he'd passed from infancy to babyhood. She circled the table counterclockwise nine times. Though the godmother was dressed in a beautiful white *huipil*, embroidered with bright flowers, the baby was dressed 20th-century style: a blue nylon romper suit.

The ceremony was complete, the baby's future now ensured. The "nine lords of the night" would protect him; the bracelets pledged good health during his first two years.

In each community, *hetzmek* is carried out in a slightly different manner. Some must call in a friend from another village because no one at home remembers all of it. Though the ceremony might differ from village to village, the child is always shown his potential future and placed astride the hip for the first time on this day.

San Cristóbal. Just take a stroll to investigate these beautiful structures—some are more than 450 years old.

Iglesia Santo Domingo

In 1547, the first Santo Domingo Church was a simple adobe. The present church is probably the most impressive of the many churches in the city. Santo Domingo offers a baroque facade that glows a delicate rose. The structure is covered with ornamented mortar with intricate carvings, Solomonic columns, statues tucked into ornate niches—and that's just the outside. The interior houses a sensational pulpit with gold carvings everywhere. You'll see many nostalgic *retablos* (religious paintings frequently offered in place of money donations, or in thanks for favors; the painters were not always professionals). It's not unusual to find an Indian healer (often a female *curandera*) performing rituals in the Catholic environment: touching the stricken pilgrim with flowers, surrounding him with smoking copal, murmuring incantations in the guttural Maya language while passing burning candles over and around the "patient"—all in front of the church altars. These ceremonies originate from a mix of Maya and Catholic rituals.

Outside the building, Indian artisans set up tables and sell their crafts. This is larger than most public markets. Also on the grounds is Sna Jolobil, a co-op of craftsmen from villages in the highlands. Some of the finest weavings are found here.

Santo Domingo cathedral

Cathedral

The main plaza of the cathedral was constructed in 1528 on the north side of the main square. Originally dedicated as the *Nuestra Señora de la Anunciación,* it was rededicated a few years later to San Cristóbal. The facade is a standout, its bright yellow-ocher contrasting with 17th-century white mortared niches and geometric designs. Some call it austere, but the simplicity of it presents an outstanding backdrop for the hordes of colorfully dressed Indians and tourists who constantly crowd into the church plaza. On the inside, note the elaborately carved wooden pulpit. Those interested in religious art will see much from the colonial era. The church and church plaza come to life during festivals, especially the celebration of the feast day of Corpus Christi.

Iglesia San Cristóbal

Up many steps, high on a hill looking over the entire town, you'll find the Iglesia San Cristóbal.

It's open just once a year, July 17-25, during the celebration of the feast of St. Christopher. During this celebration, pilgrims stream up and down the steps to the church; a road leads to the church as well. Built in the 17th century , it now has a neoclassical facade.

Museum of Regional Dress

Anyone who is entranced with the ethnic history of the Mexican Indians will enjoy a visit with Sergio Castro. You must make an appointment to visit his museum, where you will find a gentleman who knows the anthropological history of all the communities in the Chiapas highlands. Along with the displays of clothes that play such an important role in the "togetherness" of each village, he tells anecdotes and legends of the people. He will answer your questions, not always with the answer you want, but you will come away feeling that you know the highlands and its people. Ask at the tourism office in the Palacio Municipal for information about entrance to the museum.

Na Balom Museum

Visitors should not miss Na Balom Museum. The late Swiss-born Gertrude Duby Blom, known to everyone as Trudy, and her husband, Danish archaeologist Frans Blom (also deceased), arrived in San Cristóbal in the 1920s to excavate Moxviquil, Maya ruins outside of town. Frans had been involved over the years with the archaeology of the Maya in several locations on the Yucatán Peninsula, including Bonampak (Lacandón land). Both Frans and Trudy became very interested in the highland Lacandón Indians and worked to preserve their culture and the rainforest. The Bloms' San Cristóbal home (cum museum/research center/library/guesthouse) is named Na ("House") Balom ("Jaguar"), from the Tzotzil language; not as many suppose from the Lacandón tongue, whose word for jaguar is *barum*.

San Cristóbal Catholic
Church Archival Office
is a treasury of history
of the area.

OZ MALLAN

Though the Lacandón are usually associated with the Bloms, they gained their first notoriety after a visit in 1933 by French anthropologists Jacques and Georgette Soustelle. Jacques Soustelle told the world of Lacandón hunting techniques involving bows and poison-dipped arrows. They generally hunted monkeys, wild pigs, and wild turkeys. More intense contact with the outside world began during the last half of the 20th century, when loggers began to harvest mahogany trees, which they dragged to the river and then floated to Tenosique. The Lacandón worked for these loggers and earned money for the first time; logging still goes on in the area. The Lacandón men continue to wear the traditional white dress and long black hair. (Amazingly, some of these very old Indians have not a sign of gray in their black tresses.)

The entire house (and garden) is a museum of Maya artifacts. An old chapel and several rooms offer extraordinary exhibits showing life in the jungle. The gardens cover a large area and include vegetables, trees, flowers, and plants of the area. At one time, thousands of sapling trees were grown here from seed and given to the Indians to encourage them to replant areas of rainforest destroyed over the years by logging and slash-and-burn farming. In fact, Na Balom still gives away 15,000 trees each year.

Although the Lacandón did not allow anyone else to photograph them, they posed for thousands of pictures for Trudy over the years, and marvelous black and white portraits of these people are displayed throughout the house. The extensive library has books and articles covering all of Central America and attracts social scientists and students who come every year to intern at Na Balom.

About a dozen rooms are available for guests, though it's rare to get a room without a reservation.For information on becoming a volunteer, to be part of the artist-in-residence program, or for room reservations, write to Na Balom, Av. Vicente Guerrero #33, San Cristóbal de las Casas, Chiapas 29220, tel./fax (967) 8-1418.

Na Balom is open for guided tours daily at 4:30 p.m.; tours include a film on Trudy's work with the Lacandón; the fee is US$2.50. The library is usually open to the public weekdays 9 a.m.-2:30) p.m.

ACCOMMODATIONS

San Cristóbal is one of the colonial gems of Mexico. Old homes—most of which from the outside look the same—have recently been opened up to visitors who are intrigued with the beauty and the sense of the past the old structures impart. Many visitors to this colonial city would much prefer to stay in these one-of-a-kind masterpieces sporting walls five to eight feet thick, some smothered in colorful blossoms, with a central patio that might have a working fountain encircled with greenery and bright flowers attracting birds and butterflies. Many enjoy examining wall niches holding intricately painted pottery and antiquated woodcarvings, tile floors, and sometimes antique furniture that belonged to the original family. As a result, hotels are opening up within the walls of these lovely old homes. Granted, tastes vary, and if you happen to prefer the modern glitz of glass and stainless steel, expect little evidence of that in San Cristóbal—at least so far. Some talk of a modern resort on the outskirts of town. But for now, visitors still come to see what has been in San Cristóbal for literally centuries.

Accommodations in San Cristóbal range from very nice with fireplaces and private bathrooms to simple *posadas* with spartan rooms and shared baths. It can get very cool at night in these mountains, so be sure you have enough blankets before the desk clerk goes to bed. If there's a fireplace in your room, make sure you have enough firewood to keep it going. The nicer hotels fix a fire for you at the first chill. In some of the less expensive places, you must pay for the firewood. If you plan to stay at one of the more upscale hotels, reservations are a good idea since many tour groups stay in them, especially during the high season 15 Dec.-15 April, and in July and August when the town is filled with European travelers. Rates are highest at Christmas and Easter, and in July and August. Expect prices to go down 10-20% when tourism is low. Check with your travel agent, though many of the budget hotels aren't available through an agency.

Note: If you decide to write directly to Mexico, address your letter to the hotel, either street or box number, San Cristóbal de las Casas, Chiapas 29300, Mexico. Don't forget, look at your room before you pay your money, especially at the budget hotels, and ask if there's hot water and when.

Budget

The traveler on a budget should have no trouble finding cheap rooms in San Cristóbal de las Casas; this is one of the most economical tourist areas in Mexico—so far! If none of the rooms described below fits your requirements, check with the tourist office on the main square at the corner of the city hall, catercorner from the cathedral. The staff is helpful and someone there usually speaks English. Other good places to get information are the popular cafes, such as Madre Tierre at Insurgentes #19, or El Puente Cafe at Real de Guadalupe #55, where you'll find fellow travelers who have been around here for a while. Calle Real de Guadalupe is also a good street to look for inexpensive accommodations. Remember, low budget and budget generally means simple; always look at the room before you decide.

Joaquín Hernanz Humbrias owns the charming three-story **Don Quijote,** Av. Colón #7, tel. (967) 8-0920, fax 8-0346, built within a narrow colonial building decorated with costumes of the region's indigenous groups and photographs of the area. Each of the 22 carpeted rooms has a modern tile bathroom and two double beds. There's a rooftop terrace as well.

Hotel Posada Vallarta, Hermanos Pineda #10, tel. (967) 8-0465, lies just off Av. Insurgentes, close to the Cristóbal Colon bus station and within walking distance of the downtown area. You can expect a balcony, no heat but plenty of warm blankets, hot water, towels, private bathroom, Spanish TV. It's very clean and nice.

Posada Las Morales, five blocks from the plaza at Ignacio Allende #17, tel. (967) 8-1472, has bungalows for rent by the day or week, with fireplaces and stoves.

Hotel San Martín, Real de Guadalupe #16, tel. (967) 8-0533, is another budget *posada;* this one offers 26 small rooms, large bathrooms, peach and rust decor, and two single beds in each room. The owners keep it very clean, and have large bottles of purified water in the hallways.

Posada Margarita, Calle Real de Guadalupe #34, tel. (967) 8-0957, offers dorm rooms and private rooms, all with shared baths. A *típico* courtyard and small cafeteria make for good sociable evenings, and a helpful tour desk has information on horseback riding and tours to the surrounding villages. Ask about (cheap) laundry service. Check the bulletin board by the reception area for good information.

Posada San Cristóbal, Av. Insurgentes #3, tel. (967) 8-1900, offers 10 simple, pleasant rooms, and a cafeteria is open all day.

Posada Fray Bartolomé de las Casas, Niños Héroes #2, tel. (967) 8-0932, fax 8-3510, is near the plaza at Insurgentes. All 26 smallish rooms are heated, have baths, are usually clean, and have hot water all day long. The courtyard is a pleasant place to smell the flowers, and a simple breakfast is served in a small dining room.

El Paraíso, Calle 5 de Febrero #19 close to the plaza, tel./fax (967) 8-0085, opened in 1993. It's one of the few hotels in a totally new building, with stunning modern architecture that reflects the city's character. Heavy wood beams and textured ochre and blue walls reflect the regional traditions, with glass skylights covering corridors filled with sculptures and plants. The 13 rooms have sloping wood ceilings, wood-framed windows facing the courtyard or street, and Guatemalan spreads on the beds (you have a choice of king-size or two doubles). Owners Daniel and Teresa Sutter are from Switzerland and Mexico and speak four languages between them—Spanish, English, German and French. Their European tastes are reflected in the hotel's restaurant, where the Swiss chef prepares excellent cheese and beef fondues, mushrooms sautéed in garlic, and several salads.

Hotel Real del Valle, Real de Guadalupe #14, tel. (967) 8-0680, fax 8-3955, is possibly the friendliest hotel in town, with owners who do everything they can to keep their guests happy. They have 40 rooms in all, 20 in the older front section and 20 in a newer back section, all with tiled baths and small desks. The rooftop solarium is a great spot for sunning, and in colder times there's a fire in the fireplace by the lobby and in the upstairs dining room. Laundry service is inexpensive. You can even arrange to take Spanish classes while you're here.

The **Hotel Plaza Santo Domingo,** Av. Utrilla #35, tel./fax (967) 8-1927, is just across the street from the back of the church of the same name and a few short blocks from the market, making it convenient for die-hard shoppers. The 29 rooms are set back from the street behind the courtyard and restaurant, cutting down on traffic noise. All are carpeted and have TVs, tiled baths with the sinks outside the bathrooms, and small desks; US$3.50 is added to your bill if you use a credit card. The management is eager to please and helpful with information on the area. The restaurant and bar are great places to take a break even if you're not staying here, since there are few such places around the market.

Inexpensive

One of our personal favorites and one of the most charming hotels, **Hotel Palacio de Moctezuma,** Av. Juárez #16, tel. (967) 8-0352, fax 8-1536, is just two blocks from the center of town. This is a cozy place with 42 rooms, mini-courtyards, greenery, fresh flowers everywhere, and intimate salons. Old, though modern, the clean hotel offers pleasant vistas with arched entrances, tile floors, and a delightful dining room with a fireplace and good food. Rooms are small and carpeted, some newly added, others remodeled with modern bathrooms, telephones in most rooms, and one or two double beds in each.

Hotel Santa Clara, Insurgentes #1 Plaza Central, tel. (967) 8-1140, fax 8-1041, on the plaza, is well worth checking out, even if you decide you don't wish to stay—the hotel is the former home of conquistador Diego de Mazariegos. It's quite simple but has lovely 16th-century touches such as wooden beams and carvings, and all 42 rooms can get as cold as any old castle in the winter. It has a pool, courtyard tables with umbrellas, and a restaurant and bar on the premises.

Another favorite is **Hotel Rincón del Arco,** about a 10-minute walk from town center at Ejercito Nacional #66, tel. (967) 8-1313, fax 8-1568. The easiest way to get here the first time is by taxi. At one time a private home, the building has been in the same family for several generations. The original structure was built in 1650, with some additions and renovations over the centuries. The architecture is stunning with lots of tile, brick-arched doorways, white stucco, wooden beams, and greenery-filled inner patios. Each of the 36 rooms has a clay fireplace, ready with wood to light on a cold night. The rooms are modern and comfortable with carpeting, tile, and spotlessly clean bathrooms. The upper rooms have terrific views of the city and its churches. Rates stay the same throughout the year. On the premises, **Restaurante Maya** serves tasty food either in the dining room or on the terrace. It specializes in regional and local cuisine. A large warehouse-type room in the hotel houses old handoperated wooden looms, expertly operated by weavers who produce lovely fabrics. General manager Señor José Antonio Hernanz, a member of the family that owns the hotel, told us that this business has been providing fabrics to Chiapas shops and to other hotels for years. Ask at the shop called **La Segoviana** at Av. Real de Guadalupe #26 if you would like to see the bedspreads; be sure to take the exact measurements you need if you are interested in buying.

Hotel Ciudad Real, Plaza 31 de Marzo #10 in the heart of the town, tel. (967) 8-0187, fax 8-0464, offers a wonderful ambience of the past. Probably the best part of the hotel is its colonial design with high ceilings, archways and columns, and a courtyard dining room two floors high. The rooms are old but comfortably furnished.

Hotel Posada de los Angeles is a little charmer at Francisco I. Madero #17, tel. (967) 8-1173, fax 8-2581. Small, it has just 20 pleasant rooms, with two double beds in each room. A patio has been covered with a wooden roof, but it has a multitude of skylights. The fountain in the patio has pretty little clay doves and tiny pocket gardens. Ask for a second-floor room; those on the first floor have an "old" smell. You'll find a restaurant and a bar on the premises.

Another favorite if you can get in is **Na Balom Museum.** The rooms have private baths, are colorful and earthy, each furnished with the crafts of a different village, and most have fireplaces that keep the rooms cozy on chilly nights. Dinner (US$7) can be a stimulating event. Guests, seated together around an immense table that fills the dining room, are often journalists, anthropologists, and archaeologists from all over the world, adventurers with a keen interest in the Maya culture, and the volunteers. Trudy had many opinions and was outspoken on many subjects, all making for lively conversation. Everyone who knew Trudy misses her brash loyalty and unique personality. If you're not staying here, you can still come for dinner, but you must make reservations; write or call Av. Vicente Guerrero #33, San Cristóbal de las Casas, 29220, Chiapas, Mexico, tel./fax (967) 8-1418. About a dozen rooms are available for guests, though it's rare to get a room without a reservation. For information on this delightful house see "Na Balom Museum," above.

Moderate

Opened in 1993 three blocks from the town center is the **Hotel Arrecife de Coral,** Av.Crescencio Rosas #29, tel. (967) 8-2125, fax 8-2098, e-mail: arrecife@sancristobal.podernet.com.mx. The hotel offers 50 modern rooms (38 carpeted, 12 tiled), with TV and telephone. The light and airy rooms are arranged around a large grassy area filled with a riot of flowers and topiary. Chaise longues are provided for enjoying sunny days. The restaurant seats 150. Peek into the kitchen—

all stainless steel and gleaming white tile, a friendly invitation to sample the wide range of regional dishes or international foods. The *chiles rellenos* are a house specialty. The **Delfin Bar** has live music every weekend. Off-street parking.

Moderate/Expensive

Hotel Catedral, Av. Guadalupe Victoria #21, tel. (967) 8-1363, one and a half blocks from the central plaza, is one of San Cristóbal's newest and finest hotels. It opened in 1995 with 84 sumptuous rooms, heated indoor swimming pool, and underground parking, all very upscale for San Cristóbal. The luxurious suites are carpeted, and feature jacuzzis and minibar/fridges. All rooms have satellite TV and telephone. The hotel's graceful colonial Spanish architecture blends perfectly with the surrounding structures that are several hundred years old. Many rooms open onto the three-story atrium/courtyard, which can be very noisy when tour groups gather for an early morning departure, or after a late night of festivities. Interior rooms are also available. The fine restaurant offers excellent beef dishes along with international and regional foods. Comfortable rattan chairs and lots of greenery make the bar overlooking the street a relaxing place to unwind after a day filled with shopping or visiting nearby villages.

Expensive

Casa Mexicana, 28 de Agosto #1 at Utrilla, close to Santo Domingo church, tel. (967) 8-0698, fax 8-2627, also opened in 1993 and is a charming old-style hotel with a good dining room. Floor tiles lead from the entryway to an atrium courtyard featuring a stone-edged pond filled with tropical plants and sculptures, all covered with a multiangled skylight. New architecture again reflects local traditions, with burnished terra-cotta-colored walls, lots of pillars and arches, and skylight-covered courtyards leading to the rooms. The 29 simple rooms have angled wood-beam ceilings, carved wooden headboards;two junior suites have in-room whirlpool tubs; and the hotel also offers three two-bedroom villas. On the premises is **Los Magueyes** restaurant, with outdoor and indoor tables covered with peach linens, Talavera china, and candlelight. In keeping with the hotel's cosmopolitan ambience, the menu offers *coq au vin,* stroganoff, goulash, and *mole* *poblano;* dinner for one with one cocktail costs about US$20. All in all, Casa Mexicana is one of the nicer hotels in town.

An old favorite in town was one of the first places to go deluxe, reopening in 1992 as the **Hotel Flamboyant Español,** three blocks northwest of the plaza at 1 Marzo St. #16, tel. (967) 8-0045, fax 8-0514. The colonial-style house, built in 1917, was known to longtime San Cristóbal fans simply as the Español. The Flamboyant's owners (who also have hotels in Tuxtla Gutiérrez and Huatulco) closed the hotel for many months and completely remodeled the rooms and public spaces, filling the 51 rooms with handcarved furnishings and handwoven textiles made by local artisans. The walls throughout are painted in warm, glowing rust and gold and face glass-covered courtyards. A large, open-air courtyard separates the rooms from the street, cutting down on traffic noise. Rates are 50% less in low season.

Hotel Posada Diego de Mazariegos, in two buildings across the street from each other at 5 de Febrero #1 and María Adelina Flores #2, tel. (967) 8-1825, 8-0833, fax 8-0827, was for years considered the finest hotel in San Cristóbal—it now has lots of competition. Many of the rooms have fireplaces; specify that you want one when you make reservations and again when you check in (the rooms are cold in the winter). The rooms have nice wood touches and the bathrooms are quaint with handpainted tiles and bathroom sinks. The courtyards are filled with plants, and both are covered with plastic so they can be used year-round, rain or shine; it can get stuffy. A few suites are available, but the fireplaces are in the living rooms and some nights it gets chilly enough to want the fire as near the bed as possible! A good restaurant has a warming fire going when needed, coffee shop, bar, laundry service, car rental, travel agency, and often "imported" Indian women weaving and selling their textiles on the spot. Frankly, the hotel is aging and looked a bit drab at the latest visit but it is a popular destination for tour groups, many from Europe, so it is often very busy and mealtime gets hectic in the dining room.

Five minutes from downtown and handy for people who are driving is **Hotel Bonampak,** Calzada Mexico #5 (just past the monument), tel. (967) 8-1621 or (800) 528-1234, fax 8-1622, is a Best Western hotel, relatively upscale, and modern in design. It's very American with 50 clean rooms with private bathrooms, room service, restaurant and bar, and miniature golf. The hallways in the hotel are heated, but the rooms can sure get cold!

Premium

In the upscale category is a truly special guesthouse, **El Jacarandal,** near the market and Santo Domingo Church at Calle Comitán #7, tel. (967) 8-1065. Owners Percy and Nancy Wood have taken a rambling colonial home and turned it into a lovely retreat, with only four rooms filled with folk art, fireplaces, and lovely bathrooms with sunken tubs. Private patios face a collage of plants and flowers. Guests frequent the formal living room and library filled with books on Latin America and plenty of cozy chairs by the fireplaces. The Woods maintain a stable of eight horses ready for rides to remote villages and into the forest. A cordial staff and excellent cook serve meals family-style. Guests are treated as visiting friends. Although a stay is costly, all three meals, open bar, laundry, horseback rides, and tips are included in the rates, which are available upon request. Make reservations well in advance.

FOOD

Restaurants

To get to **La Parilla,** Belisario Domínguez #32 in the Cerillo neighborhood, tel. (967) 8-220I, walk north on Domínguez until it runs into Dr. Navarro, about five blocks from the plaza. The restaurant is a big hit with meat lovers, and can keep vegetarians happy as well with its half-dozen variations of *queso fundido* (melted cheese served with tortillas), baked potatoes with a variety of toppings, and *chiles rellenos*. A cowboy theme prevails in the paraphernalia and paintings of horses, but the big attraction is the meat. Grilled steaks, smoked chicken, pork chops, and sausages are served on sizzling metal platters atop wooden cutting boards; order the whole grilled onion and a bowl of beans or a baked potato as side dishes, and you have a bountiful meal. Guests order dinner by checking off boxes on a list of selections—ask for the English version if your Spanish is shaky. A full dinner with side dishes and two beers costs about US$15-20. La

Parilla is open Mon.-Sat. 6:30-11:30 p.m., Sunday noon-midnight.

Normita, Av. Benito Juárez and Calle José Flores, serves good local specialties (try the *pozole*). The tiny cafe has a fireplace and unusual wooden tables. It's not fancy, but is good and reasonable; no credit cards. The prices can't be beat, however, and you can fill up on a steaming bowl of *pozole* and tortillas for under US$5.

Fogón de Jovel, Av. 16 de Septiembre #11, tel. (967) 8-1153, is a semitrendy restaurant, which is something different for unpretentious San Cristóbal. Designed for the tourist (expect busloads), the selection of dishes is large, the waiters are costumed, and you might catch a marimba band/folkloric show. The Chiapan food is outstanding, especially served in the delightful colonial atmosphere of a lovely old home with patio and rooms decorated with folk art. Try the Chiapan tamales and the thick, creamy corn soup. This is a good place to try local liquors, including *posh,* mixed with orange or pineapple juice; and *cervecita dulce,* a sweet ginger ale. Ask for the English menu, which describes the local dishes and their ingredients. The restaurant is open daily 1-5 p.m. and 7-11 p.m., and it accepts credit cards.

Pizzas and Tacos
Restaurant Tikal/Pepe's Pizza, on Calle Insurgentes #77-A, (967) 8-6383, is one block from the first-class bus station. It's best known for the most popular pizza in town; the pizzas are baked in an old-fashioned clay oven. Phone orders usually are delivered within 30 minutes and the pizzas are piping hot. Restaurant Tikal has a large economical menu. One of its best meals is a large plate of *enchiladas suiza* for only $2. Pizzas cost from $3.75 for a small four-slicer to $11.75 for a family-size pizza of 16 generous slices; you have four standard varieties to choose from or create your own from 14 different ingredients.

A close second or maybe even a tie with Pepe's Pizza is **Pizze y Mass** at Calle Real de Guadalupe #9, tel. (967) 8-6556. The music blares and it is usually smoky and crowded with groups of Europeans loudly discussing the merits of their home soccer teams. You can buy pizza by the slice or whole. Most weekends you can buy freshly made lasagna, cannelloni, or other mouth-watering pasta dishes at about $6.25 for a large portion.

Emiliano's Moustache, Crescencio Rosas #7, is where the locals go for tacos. The aroma of *tacos al pastor* hits you about a half-block away. As you walk in you see the rotating spit and the two women who make and bake fresh tortillas by the hundreds. The Emiliano's Special is an artery-hardening delicacy composed of several meats, melted cheese, green peppers, mushrooms, and whatever else the cook has on hand at the moment, served with a never-ending supply of tortillas made on the spot. One portion is enough for two hungry people. It comes with three types of salsa, chopped cilantro, and onions. At the other end of the spectrum is a vegetarian special. Daily *comida corridas* are about US$2.25. Usually you have four choices of entrees, one always vegetarian. Portions are generous and include a small appetizer, soup, entree, dessert, and beverage. Service is fast and friendly. You'll find a full bar upstairs, two dining rooms, and live easy listening music on Thursday, Friday, and Saturday evenings.

The Arts and Gastronomy
More and more funky little cafe/coffeehouse/art gallery/bookstore combinations are opening in San Cristóbal. For something more upscale visit the **Café La Selva** on Av Crescencio Rosas #9 at the corner of Cuautemoc. Opened in 1996 as a branch of a Mexico City chain, this is actually a cooperative of coffee growers who proudly serve the full-bodied coffee grown in Chiapas. Choose from a simple cup of café Americano or work your way through 25 combinations of coffees and liqueurs. Mouth-watering cakes and cookies are baked fresh daily. Flaky croissants come with real butter. Available for takeout on any day are at least 10 types of coffee and the only fresh decaf in San Cristóbal. Gourmet coffee supplies tempt you from display cases at the entrance. Be sure to try the chocolate-covered coffee beans. A separate room houses a gallery featuring fine art of well-known artists from throughout the world. The exhibit changes frequently.

For good Italian and French cuisine, try **El Teatro Café,** Calle 1 de Marzo #8, serving fresh-made pastas and crepes.

Tuluc, Insurgentes #5, tel. (967) 8-2090, a fine little cafe, is gaining a reputation for both good food and economical prices. It's a narrow place with some fine indigenous crafts from the

Coop Sodam displayed at the entrance. It has a casual atmosphere and serves regional specialties. The best bargain is the *comida* (US$5.50), which includes plenty of food. The first offering is usually a tropical drink, followed by a hearty soup served with home-baked rolls, entree platter with rice and your choice of fish or chicken, dessert, and coffee or tea. Tuluc accept dollars and traveler's checks.

Vegetarian Dining

Casa de Pan, at the end of Belisario Domínguez across from La Parilla, tel. (967) 8-0468, has a bakery in front worth visiting all by itself for its chocolate chip cookies, brownies, croissants, even bagels, and homemade jams. The back dining room is painted a pretty soft peach with bougainvillea climbing one wall and a peaked glass-and-wood roof. For breakfast offerings include homemade granola, whole wheat muffins, and yogurt; lunch and dinner feature steamed rice and veggies, curried vegetable-filled *empanadas,* homemade soups, and quesadillas. Travelers heading out on long bus trips should remember that Casa de Pan will prepare great sandwiches "to go" on their tasty wheat rolls. Be sure to ask that they be wrapped in foil; otherwise you'll get them in a paper bag. Some travelers complain of long waits for their pizzas. Casa de Pan is open Tues.-Sun. 7 a.m.-8 p.m.

Vegetarians are well taken care of in San Cristóbal. You'll find vegetarian dishes on many menus, such as at funky **El Trigal,** 1 de Marzo #13, tel. (967) 8-3928; it's in an offbeat neighborhood, but the food is good and the prices fit the budget pocketbook. Each day it serves a special vegetarian platter, but the homemade yogurt is really worth bragging about. *Comida corrida* available daily; it's open 7 a.m.-10 p.m.

You'll now find **Café Altura** on Plaza Xaman, 20 de Noviembre #4, half a block from the cathedral. The cooks make soy burgers, big salads, and all sorts of coffee drinks. They also have granola, rice, and grains for sale, and two-for-one coffee during happy hour 4-5 p.m.; the cafe is open daily 7 a.m.-9 p.m.

Las Estrellas, Calle Escuadrón 201 #6, serves pasta with vegetables and several types of quiche near the Santo Domingo church.

Madre Tierra, Av. Insurgentes #19, is another really great place to sample vegetarian food (as well as good meat and chicken). The cafe is in a colonial house with heavy beams, high ceilings, and archways that lead to a patio where you'll often catch great live folkloric music. The ambience is peaceful, with mellow recorded classical music when the patio musicians don't appear. This is a great place to meet over a cappuccino, a healthy salad, or a sinfully rich brownie! Each day the menu varies a bit, and you can expect such delicacies as green gnocchi (every Italian knows about these tasty little dumplings), chicken curry, moussaka, ratatouille, spinach crepes, and soups from cream of spinach to carrot to lentil to onion. Also on the menu are good salads, tasty pastries from its bakery next door, and of course whole wheat bread. Note: when you see *pan integral* on the menu, it means whole wheat bread. A set dinner *(comida corrida)* with multiple courses is about US$8. The restaurant is open daily 8 a.m.-9:45 p.m; the bakery is open Mon.-Sat 9 a.m.-8 p.m., Sunday 9 a.m.-noon.

Mall Food and Coffeehouses

Some not-to-be-missed malls have opened around town, and almost all of them boast a cafe or two. In the **Plaza Calle de la Real Mall,** look for **Plaza Real Restaurant** at Calle Real de Guadalupe #5; you can't miss it in the center of the mall. It's a good place for breakfast with fresh-squeezed orange juice and eggs any way you want them. The big omelette platter includes potatoes and beans; here also is good American coffee plus a cappuccino machine that steams up a storm, perfect with the homemade apple strudel. This is rather a trendy place and the prices reflect it, but it's attractive and very clean and has a lively atmosphere with the comings and goings of shoppers.

Wandering through the city, you'll find a number of small cafes and coffeehouses. Remember, this is coffee country, and it usually plays host to many student travelers from around the world—who often like San Cristóbal so much that they stay for a month or a year. The coffeehouses become pleasant, vibrant gathering places for these adopted citizens. Most of the cafes in San Cristóbal are tiny and serve regional food, though with the increase in tourists more are changing their menus to include continental style food. But until there's a jet-sized airport, San Cristóbal will maintain its unique ambience.

San Cristóbal street

OZ MALLAN

SHOPPING

Shops can be found on every corner of San Cristóbal; most carry the handwoven textiles and *típico* clothing of Chiapas (as well as of Guatemala), handwoven straw hats festooned with ribbons, and bows and arrows made by the Lacandón Indians (without the poison), as well as leather goods and other souvenirs of the state. Bargain—the people expect it—except at the trendiest.

Strolling the streets will uncover a plethora of small malls. The old colonial houses were naturals for malls; all the rooms were arranged around a central courtyard. Now these rooms have become shops and offices, and in many courtyards tiny cafes are growing up. Check out antique stores; you'll find some marvelous old prizes, maybe even an antiquated wedding gown. The real bargain hunter can't miss sniffing out a precious remembrance from San Cristóbal's past.

Sna Jolobil

For fine regional crafts, visit Sna Jolobil (in Tzotzil Maya it means "House of Weaving") at the ex-Convento de Santo Domingo at 20 de Noviembre. This co-op is made up of 700 weavers from 20 Tzotzil- and Tzeltal-speaking villages in the highlands of Chiapas. The creation of Sna Jolobil encouraged a revitalization of Maya art and gave a new dignity to preservation of the ancient designs. The younger generations are mo-

tivated to study old methods of dyeing wool and cotton as well as ancestral weaving techniques. Each weaver creates her original designs with unique symbols and values related to her ancestors. Sna Jolobil is also a study center for the technique of brocade, in which the designs are woven directly into the cloth. Brocaded designs portray gods, animals, flowers, fertility symbols, and the Maya vision of the cosmos. This is a true incorporated profit-sharing co-op ("Sociedad Civil"). Outstanding textiles are displayed with set prices, most of which are quite moderate for the work each piece requires. Sna Jolobil is open daily 9 a.m.-2 p.m. and 4-6 p.m; it accepts credit cards.

Taller Lenateros

You'll find more Maya craftsmen and their colorful work at Taller Lenateros, Av. Flavio A Paniagua 54, tel. (967) 8-5174, fax 8-6367. An award-winning press is operated by Maya men and women who produce beautiful handmade paper made of such diverse materials as flower petals, carnations, gladiolas, vines, stems, moss, recycled paper, and rags. Along with unique art cards, notebooks, photo albums, etc., you'll find wood block prints representing both ancient and current Maya artistic themes. Check out the limited editions of children's books, poetry, art, and a wonderful guide to natural dyes. This is a Maya cultural center in action, and it helps the individual artists come into their own while preserving this fragile old culture. Paper-making and book-binding classes cost about US$6. Taller Lenateros is open Mon.-Sat., 9 a.m.-6 p.m. Free English/Spanish tours are given daily except Sunday; ask for Andrew, Ambar, or Doña Mari.

Mercados

The public market on Av. Utrilla is large but mostly devoted to the needs of the locals. This is a lively gathering spot for the *indígenes* every morning except Sunday, which is the day that most of the outlying villages have their own markets. It's at these village Sunday-markets that you will see outstanding woven textiles and leather goods. Market days are perfect peoplewatching days. **Note:** Be careful with your camera if you are in one of the outlying villages, where people strongly object to having their photos taken.

All week the plaza around Santo Domingo church is filled with craftspeople selling their wares, including *huipiles,* embroidered placemats, woven belts, and dolls. Guatemalan textiles are in great supply these days, with piles of shirts, shorts, and pants of Guatemalan fabrics and rows of leather and fabric belts. Some treasures are to be found, if you look hard enough.

More Arts and Handicrafts

Scattered about San Cristóbal are religious shops selling candles and all sorts of religious art, including the small *milagros* or miracles: tiny metal reproductions of arms, legs, etc. For some striking pieces of modern art covered with these small "prayers," check out **Arte Religioso** at Guadalupe Victoria #26.

La Segoviana, Real de Guadalupe #26, tel. (967) 8-0346, is a fine shop offering a great selection of loom-woven textiles, sweaters, and beautiful bedspreads. Bring your measurements for whatever you wish to buy. This is a family-run operation that's been in San Cristóbal for decades.

Balum-Canan, Calle Real de Guadalupe #2B, offers some striking indigenous-made clothing. Looking for a hammock? Stop at **Hamaca'tik** at Av. General Utrilla #33B in Casa Utrilla, a blue colonial home turned into a small shopping arcade. Also look at the replicas of Maya huts at the Coop Sodam, the same as those displayed at the restaurant Tuluc. You'll find amber and handmade batik as well.

Two blocks from the marketplace, check out the handicrafts at **Yaxal Vinajel,** Calle Tonalá #3A, usually with a good selection of masks and other Maya crafts. The government-sponsored **Casa de Artesanías DIF,** Av. Niños Héroes at Hidalgo, has a small museum on the clothing, crafts, and lifestyles of the different villages; textiles are sold in the front part of the building; it's open daily 9 a.m.-2 p.m. and 4-8 p.m.

El Encuentro, just up the street from El Puente cultural center at Real de Guadalupe #63, is a great place for excellent quality regional folk art, including embroidered *huipiles,* ceremonial hats, and bolts of woven cloth. **Citlali** jewelers has a staggering display of silver and amber at Real de Guadalupe #27 and in Plaza de la Calle Real.

RECREATION AND EVENTS

Ecological Tours

Pronatura, a private nonprofit ecological organization, is based in San Cristóbal studying the cloud forest, a haven for migratory birds. Tours to the cloud forest reserve of **Huitepec** above town are available, with hikes through the forest where 100 species of birds and 600 species of plants have been discovered. For information go to the Pronatura office at Adelina Flores #21, tel. (967) 8-0469. To reach the reserve on your own, take the road to Chamula; the turnoff is at Km 3.5. The reserve is open daily 9 a.m.-5 p.m., tel. (967) 8-1883.

Horseback Riding

Horseback riding is popular throughout the hills surrounding San Cristóbal. Check with your hotel; several have horses available or can tell you where to go to find them. Ask about horses *and* guides at the tourist office. Having a guide is really a good idea if you plan to ride through the villages in the countryside. Make arrangements and/or reservations a day in advance. We've heard rave reviews about the horseback riding tours to Chamula and the mountains and caves run by Oliviero Frances and Susanna Scheid; you can make reservations with them at La Galería or call (967) 8-1547.

Fiestas

This is a very colorful city all year round, but during religious holidays San Cristóbal comes to life with a passion. The cannons blast, every church has a fiesta, and people come in droves from villages and surrounding areas.

GETTING THERE

The majority of travelers to Chiapas fly into Tuxtla Gutiérrez and drive or take a bus or taxi to San Cristóbal de las Casas.

By Air

The small San Cristóbal Airport is newly opened. Airline passengers still stop at Tuxtla Gutiérrez first. Direct flights are planned and perhaps will have begun by the time you have this book in your hands. In the meantime, Mexicana Airlines flies from Mexico City, Acapulco, Oaxaca, Mérida, and Villahermosa to Tuxtla. **Aviacsa** flies between Huatulco, Minatitlán, Oaxaca, Tapachula, and Villahermosa; **Aerocaribe** flies from a few smaller cities; and **Taesa** flies between Tuxtla and Tapachula. Don't take anything for granted; the schedules and airlines make constant changes. Check with your travel agent.

By Car

It takes time to reach 2,200-meter-high San Cristóbal de las Casas. Thankfully, the roads are continuously being improved. Only 45 years ago you could figure a trip from Tuxtla Gutiérrez was 12 hours by mule. Today it's a one-and-a-half hour drive on a good road. However, if you plan to drive, be prepared for steep, winding, hairpin curves with many switchbacks and dramatic canyon drops. From Villahermosa expect the drive to take about two hours through beautiful green forest with spectacular views of the valleys below on highways 190 and 195. From Palenque to San Cristóbal, figure about five to six hours on another winding road, especially if you plan to stop along the way.

By Bus

Buses from Villahermosa, Palenque, and Tuxtla Gutiérrez to San Cristóbal de las Casas are available several times a day. From Palenque check out **Auto Transportes Tuxtla**—they make the trip in six hours, four times daily. From Tuxtla go to the first-class bus station, **Cristóbal Colón**, where you have a choice of 12 departures to San Cristóbal daily. Several new bus lines with deluxe, first-class buses serve the area. From Palenque and Tuxtla, both **Transportes Dr. Rudolfo Figueroa** and **Transportes Mundo Maya** stop in San Cristóbal en route between Palenque and Tuxtla, and have new buses with comfy reclining seats; the Figueroa buses show movies. In San Cristóbal several deluxe lines, including **ADO Gran Lux** and **Cristóbal Colón**, have headquarters in the **Cristóbal Colon** bus station on Insurgentes, with first-class and deluxe service to Tuxtla, Palenque, Villahermosa, Mérida, Oaxaca, Cancún, and Mexico City. Smaller second-class lines are scattered around the city. Unless you must scrimp every penny, the deluxe buses are a great bargain, not just with comfort, but also in time saved and safety.

By Taxi

There's always a taxi. Expect to pay about US$35-40 from Tuxtla; bargain and try to find a group to share the cost. Some travel agencies also offer a transfer service from Tuxtla hotels or the airport, costing about US$40 for four peoples; call the agencies for reservations.

GETTING AROUND

The best way to see the city is on foot. Driving around the narrow crowded streets of San Cristóbal is nerve-racking. For the outlying areas a car is a big advantage. *Colectivos* (small buses) travel on Utrilla between the *zócalo* and the market. **Taxis** can be found on the *zócalo* and will take visitors to outlying villages as well as to Tuxtla Gutiérrez. **Tour buses** make a variety of excursions; check with local travel agencies or the tourist office. **Bicycles** are available for rent at Gante, Av. 5 de Mayo #10B. Rental bikes and bike tours are available at Rent a Bike, Av. Insurgentes #57, tel. (967) 8-4157.

You'll find a **Budget Rent-A-Car** office at M. Adelina Flores #2, tel. (967) 8-1871. If flying into Tuxtla Gutiérrez, rent a car at the airport.

Travel Agencies

Travel agencies abound in San Cristóbal, most offering identical tours. These include tours within the city; tours to the villages, mountains, and caves; horseback riding; and longer tours to the

Montebello Lakes, Comitán, Palenque, and the ruins of Chinkultíc. Some agencies use public transportation for their tours; check this out if comfort is important. One of the largest and most reliable agencies is **ATC** on Av. 5 de Febrero at 16 de Septiembre, tel. (967) 8-2550, fax 8-3145. It has offices in Palenque and Guatemala City as well, and it offers well-organized tours to all the villages and ruins, shuttle service from Tuxtla to San Cristóbal, and intensive tours throughout La Ruta Maya, including Guatemala. Other agencies in San Cristóbal are: **Jovel,** Calle Real de Guadalupe #26-G, tel. (967) 8-2727; **Lacantun,** Calle Madero #19-2, tel. (967) 8-2587 or 8-2588; and **Viajes Marabasco,** the local American Express representative at the Hotel Flamboyant Español, 1 de Marzo #15, tel. (967) 8-0726.

SERVICES AND INFORMATION

Grupo de Mujeres is a woman's center that offers a variety of services—including medical treatment. It has an excellent reputation and is serviced by professionals who volunteer their talents. Contact Marita Figueroa, Calle Rivera #5, Barrio Tlaxcala, San Cristóbal, Chiapas 29220, Mexico, tel. (967) 8-4347. This is probably a good medical emergency center for women visitors.

Laundromats: Try Lava Sec, Crescencio Rosas #12, or **Lavorama** Guadalupe Victoria #20A, both open daily 8 a.m.-9 p.m.

Communication: The post office is at Cuauhtémoc and Crescencio Rosas. Long-distance telephone and fax service is available at storefronts and hotels all over town. Ladatel public phones using Ladatel cards are near the tourist office and telephone office on Hidalgo; cards are available for sale at the Hotel Santa Clara and at the money exchange office on Real de Guadalupe. The area code for San Cristóbal de las Casas is 967.

Tourist Offices

If you stand facing the front of the City Hall (Palacio Municipal), turn left to the next block and find the State Tourist Office, or Sedetur, tel./fax (967) 8-6570. This is a very helpful office, English speaking and offering all the most up-to-date information about what's going on in Chiapas. The

staff has answers to most questions and will direct you to accommodations for budget or otherwise, bus schedules, and tours.

San Cristóbal has a friendly local tourist office, on the plaza in the municipal building, across from the cathedral. Plenty of staff members are on hand, including at least one English-speaking person, Mon-Sat. 8 a.m.-8 p.m., Sunday 9 a.m.-2 p.m. Information on tours, new tourist services, restaurants, and happenings is posted on the large bulletin boards outside the office; another board inside holds messages from travelers to each other. Stamps are sold here, and there's even a mail box.

Language School

Travelers staying in San Cristóbal for two weeks or more can learn Spanish at the **Centro Bilingue** in El Puente cultural center at Real de Guadalupe #55, tel. (967) 8-4157, tel./fax 8-3723, which has been in operation since 1986. Director Roberto Rivas Bastidas has developed a program that combines three hours of one-on-one instruction and three hours of independent homework five days a week along with complete immersion in the language by a stay with a local family; he says that after two weeks, students are comfortable and proficient in Spanish. Students are evaluated as to their level of proficiency at the beginning of the course and can combine their language classes with study of the local cultures as well.

Another school to look into is **Instituto Jovel** language school, Calle Maria Adelina Flores #21, San Cristóbal de las Casas, 29201, Chiapas, Mexico, tel./fax (967) 8-4069, e-mail: jovel@sancristobal.ppodernet.com.mx. Students can make arangements for homestays here, enjoy group or individual instruction in Maya weaving and cooking, as well as hear guest speakers who are knowledgeable in sociology, anthropology, archaeology, and current events involving Chiapas. Homestay is included along with three meals a day, about 15 hours a week is the average time spent in class, and the cost is about US$100 per week.

Bookstores

You'll find several bookstores around the city. A good shop to check out is **La Pared Bookstore,** tel. (967) 8-6367, e-mail: lapared@sancristobal.podemet.com.mx. About 20 steps from the Palacio Municipal, La Pared is a little shop jammed with wonderful surprises. To start with, it offers new and used books, more than 1,500 books in English, including guidebooks and many economical classics for sale or trade, and books in Spanish and many other languages. Now for the surprises: amber jewelry or carved pieces by a talented local artist. Some of the amber features embedded insects dating from 35 million years ago. Other local forms of art include masks of papier-mâché and other materials, paintings by indigenous artists—an ever-changing exhibit of one-of-a-kind pieces. American ex-pat/owner Dana Gay also offers a telephone/e-mail ser-

vice. And if you miss your pet, drop in to visit Samson, the shop's friendly Yorkshire terrier. There's an English speaker in the shop every day. Dana is a font of good tips about the city.

Librería Chilam Balam, Casa Utrilla #33, tel./fax (967) 8-0486, across from Santo Domingo Church complex, has a fine selection of travel books and others of interest. Stop by and say hello to English-speaking Gerard, and he can help you find what you are looking for, whether it's a guidebook or anything else—in Italian, English, French, German. The shop also sells maps, tapes, CDs, videos (some with English subtitles), and a little local art. Chilam is open seven days a week, all day.

INDIAN VILLAGES
BEYOND SAN CRISTÓBAL

Transportation to the outlying villages is becoming more easily available. Look for *colectivos* near the market in San Cristóbal that go to the nearby towns. Buses go to the Montebello Lakes, but the schedules can change from season to season so check at **Transportes Montebello,** at 5A Av. Sur.

THE PEOPLE AND THEIR CUSTOMS

Indian children begin learning their life's work at an early age. As infants they're carried around in their mothers' rebozos until they can walk or until there are other infants to take their place. It's not much longer before they begin trailing after mom or dad. Mom and kids usually look after their small flocks of sheep grazing on bushy hillsides. The animals are well-cared-for, their flesh is *never* eaten, and they are shorn regularly. All little girls learn the art/craft of cutting wool from the sheep, carding, spinning, weaving, and embroidering. Each community is trapped by tradition into a certain craft and design and type of clothing; only the rebels try to change the system.

Indian men are obligated to spend a year helping run the government. The political year is spent in the village parliament or as a policeman. During that time the rest of his village helps to keep his milpa (family corn field) watered and cared for while he leaves his barrio and lives near the city hall. Men have little choice. All seven districts of the highland Indians know this is a duty that is expected of them, and it generally involves the whole family one way or another. In addition, for one or two years a family also becomes the caretaker of patron saint. Family members wash the statue and its clothes, change it from everyday to fiesta clothing, make offerings of candles and *posh* (Indian brandy made from sugarcane). It is the family's responsibility to pay for fireworks and food and to see that there is music at the appropriate times.

Many Chamulan families have refused on economical and moral grounds to continue to finance these practices when they barely have enough money to sustain themselves. Many Chamulans have moved to the city, and as a result a whole community of Chamulan people has slapped housing together along the *periférico* of San Cristóbal.

SAN JUAN CHAMULA

Note: It's becoming more difficult to visit Chamula on your own. More and more vendors excessively harass visitors; some visitors have reported that they have been cursed and hit if they refuse to buy. We have not witnessed this ourselves. But there is no question about it, the Chamulans are poor, usually dirty, and they have refused any kind of help from the Mexican government—they value their independence. They are an interesting cultural part of the highland people, so if you wish to visit, look for groups to join from San Cristóbal. Apparently they don't bother the groups as much.

The People of Chamula

The women are noted for their beautiful weavings, and visitors to San Cristóbal will recognize Chamulan women by their dress: white *huipiles* with simple flowers embroidered around the necklines and black or brown wool skirts with red belts and sky-blue wool *rebozos* wrapped around their shoulders; there's almost always a baby tucked into the folds of the shawl. These garments are not only handwoven on a waist loom, but they are generally made of wool that has been carded by the women from animals raised on the family plot. Their craft brings in real pesos that add to the family coffers. While they weave most of the clothes the family wears, more and more they sell their beautiful weavings to tourists who come to Chiapas' cities and villages.

The women of Chamula have few rights and work very hard. It's common to see women plodding up and down the hills, firewood stacked high on their backs with the help of a tumpline

A CEREMONY FOR CHAC

Maya rituals are still practiced for many occasions, but usually within the confines of the village or the home—seldom when outsiders are around. These rituals are a fascinating marriage of Catholic and Maya mysticism.

At a *Chachaac* rite, a Maya priest and the people beseech the rain god Chac for help. The altar (often set up in a clearing in a jungle) is made of poles and branches. With four distinct corners (with a tall candle at each), the altar has been dedicated to the four cardinal points—sacred in the Maya religion. In the center is a crucifix with a figure of Christ dressed, not in a loincloth, but in a white skirt embroidered with bright red flowers, like a *huipil.*

The priest is a revered village elder and is brought offerings of cigarettes, soda pop, sometimes food, maybe a raw chicken. Onlookers (usually only men) find stones and sit down in front of the priest for the ceremony.

The cigarette offerings are placed on one end of the altar next to small gourd bowls. On the ground nearby lies a plastic-covered trough made from a hollowed log. At the beginning of the ceremony (dusk), the priest lifts the plastic sheet and drops something into the log. Kneeling on an old burlap sack with a young helper beside him, he pours water into a bucket, adds ground corn and mixes it with a small bundle of leaves. The two of them pray quietly in Maya dialect to Chac for quite a while. At some unseen signal, one of the men in the group throws incense on a shovel of hot coals. As the exotic aroma spreads, the priest begins praying in Spanish. Everyone stands up and chants Hail Marys and Our Fathers. The priest dips his sheaf of leaves in a gourd and scatters consecrated water in all directions—now the ceremony begins in earnest.

Young boys sit under the altar and make repetitive frog sounds (a sign of coming rain) while gourds of

the sacred corn drink *zaca* are passed to each person. Christian prayers continue, and more *zaca* is passed around. The ceremony continues for many hours, with occasional rests in between. Bubbling liquid sounds come from the log trough. It's a mixture of honey, water, and bark from a balche tree.

As the evening passes the priest takes intermittent naps between rounds of prayers. The men occasionally stop and drink beer, or smoke cigarettes from the altar. The young acolyte gently nudges the napping priest and the praying starts again. Each round of prayers lasts about 45 minutes, and nine rounds continue throughout the night. No one leaves, and the fervor of the prayers never diminishes.

At dawn, after a lengthier-than-usual round of prayers, the priest spreads polished sacred divination stones on a burlap sack and studies them for some time. Everyone watches him intently and after a long silence, he shakes his head. The verdict is in: Chac has communicated and there will be no rain for the village this planting season.

The sun comes up and the men prepare a feast. Chac must not be insulted despite the bad news. Thick corn dough cakes, layered with ground squash seeds and marked with a cross, are placed in a large pit lined with hot stones. The cakes are covered with palm leaves and then buried with dirt. While the bread bakes and the gift chicken stews in broth, blood, and spices, gourds of *balche,* Coca-Cola, or a mixture of both are passed around to all—for as long as they can handle it. The mixture is not fermented enough to be as hallucinogenic as it is proclaimed, but enough to make a strong man ill. The rest of the morning is spent feasting and drinking. Chac has spoken, so be it.

The priest accurately forecast the weather. No rain fell the rest of that spring or summer, and the villagers didn't raise corn in their milpas that year.

(strap) across their foreheads. Women and little girls are generally barefooted; men and little boys wear shoes. Legend says that women become fertile from the earth through their feet. In the highlands few women from the outlying villages speak Spanish; depending on their village, they speak a dialect of Maya such as Tzotzil or Tzeltal.

The men of Chamula are known to drink excessively; it's not unusual to see men lying by the

side of the road on Sunday mornings, or to see a woman half carrying or helping her husband stagger along the road after a Saturday night of drinking. Unless a woman is very clever and sly, every penny she earns is taken from her and is spent as the man sees fit. The man definitely calls the shots in the family and his wife is little more than a chattel.

Chamulan men wear machine-made hats, western-style pants and shirts, leather boots, and long, woolen tunics; most men wear white tunics and the village leaders wear black tunics. Generally there are three outfits in an Indian's adult life: wedding outfit, fiesta, and everyday. A man also wears a special official dress of authority during the time he fulfills his obligation to help run the government.

By day the men work their fields of corn accompanied by their sons. It's hard work, modern tools are non-existent, and many must carry water in heavy metal cans up and down steep hillsides to their milpas. In some cases the men must travel quite a distance to find work or a field to raise the family corn. Life is not easy for men or women in this traditional time warp.

Central Chamula Sights

Visitors are welcome in Chamula as long as they understand the *rules* set forth by the villagers. One of the favorite attractions is the colorful blue and white St. John the Baptist Church and the huge plaza in front. To go inside, get the necessary permit at the government building cater-corner from the church on the side of the plaza (3 peso charge pp)—hang onto the permit because you may be asked to produce it. Remember, bring no cameras in the church. Don't even carry one where it can be seen. Tuck it in your backpack, purse, pocket, hide it somewhere—and if you use it, you lose it, literally—and maybe your life. These people mean business.

The large plaza facing the church is the center of village life. On Sundays huge crowds come for market day. Theatrical celebrations mark feast days. This is the place to observe the Chamulan people in their native surroundings. Large green crosses nearby have special meanings.

St. John the Baptist Church

An exotic aroma greets you as you walk in the door of the church: a mixture of fresh pine, flowers, incense, and candles. You may witness people prostrated before their favorite saints. During special celebrations, groups of two or three musicians dressed in colorful ancient garb are scattered about the church adding a low-pitched tintinnabulation of ancient sounds. Hundreds of tapers placed reverently on the floor in front of each penitent glow in the dim light, and families kneeling together reverently pray—pausing now and then for a swig of *posh* (sugarcane brandy). Visitors

are expected to come to church only to pray. Strangers are requested to stay at the back of the church and not to disturb the congregation. Seventy-five thousand Chamulans from these hills consider the church their own.

The church is a precious, sacred space for the villagers. This is no longer a Catholic church; there are no clergy and haven't been for many years since the Chamulans kicked all mestizos out of their village. The rituals used today are the Indians' interpretation of traditional Catholic rituals—even baptism, which is performed by the godfather and godmother with prayers and candles. Candles are everywhere; lines of them are waxed to the floor where entire families come to pray. Red candles burn for someone who is ill, black candles announce death, but most are white. At first glance the church may look Catholic, but very soon even non-Catholics will notice a difference.

The floor is covered with pine needles; fresh bundles are carried from the forest every Saturday. The statues of the saints are dressed in many layers of brilliantly flowered clothes with mirrors hung around their necks. Most of the statues are now kept in glass boxes because villagers occasionally sought revenge when a request to the saint was not fulfilled. It wasn't unusual for them to break a statue's finger off, turn the statue backward to face the wall, or even to take the statue outside and stick its head in the ground. The Chamulans do not think of the statues as statues, but rather as real people with whom they can interact. Beware the wrath of the believer! Some anthropologists say that the innermost layer of clothing on the statue is woven with the secret symbols of the ancient Maya.

The villagers take turns being the *cargo holder,* caretaker of a saint's statue for one to two years. The caretaker and his family are responsible for anything the saint might "need." On the feast day and special occasions, the statue is carefully undressed, washed scrupulously clean, and reverently robed in freshly washed or even new handwoven garments. Washing the statue's clothes is still another ritual of celebration. The clothes are laundered in a sacred pond according to a specifically prescribed rule. A small wash is performed 15 days before the fiesta and the large wash eight days before the cele-

THE SEARCH FOR CHAMULA

Village life is obscured in mystery and legends. Chamulans tell a tale about the discovery of their present location. As the story goes:

The ancestors gathered their animals and left their highland homes (and their beloved church bells) in a place today called El Bosque, where life was unpleasant—where it was difficult to farm and raise sheep, where they continually struggled with ants and biting insects. The ancestors included St. Peter, St. Andrew, St. Paul, St. Michael, St. Sebastian, and St. Catherine, all led by St. John the Baptist.

The journey was long, and they roamed the hills and valleys for days. At a hill called Holchu Mtik they stopped and spent several days; after many discussions the ancestors decided the hill wasn't their destiny because it just wasn't big enough to support their many traditional festivals and religious ceremonies. They made another foray into the hilly countryside to Kuchumlutik, where they found the earth full of thorns; however, St. John discovered a good quality clay here and he marked the place for future potters. They continued, and eventually St. John climbed to the top of a hill with a view of the valley, where he saw a distant reflection flashing in the sun.

With great ceremony St. John led his throng, and when they reached a lake, he pronounced that this was their future home, saying, "Brethren, I think we have arrived." But at that moment a serpent-man appeared and said, "Who are you people? My name is Vashakmen and this is my land." St. John told him of their search and posed to the odd creature a curious question. "Would you allow me to build my house in the middle of the lake?" Vashakmen was dumbfounded and asked how that would be possible, and then said, "Even if it were possible, where would I live?" St. John answered, "I will dry up the lake and you can live forever on the top of my house."

And so according to the Chamula legend, it all happened. The saint parted the mountains, drained the lake, leaving only the springs that would be needed to sustain life. Houses were built in the dried lake bed. Chamulans refer to today's Chamula as the earth's navel.

The Chamulans believe that Vashakmen took the form of a beam across the bell tower of the church. The beam is not of wood, they say, but of a serpent. If you scratch the beam, it feels like a serpent's skin, at least to some. The locals celebrate the creature Vashakmen with a song in the Tzotzil language sung at special ceremonies.

---

bration. The majordomos drink the wash water and then the celebration begins. They bring in musicians, have a glass of *posh*, and then dance. Chamulans approach these religious duties with great seriousness, and drinking *posh* is required in most rituals.

Chamulan Holidays

The Chamula church is a scene to be experienced, especially during a holiday. *Carnaval* is one of the biggest celebrations and goes on for a week. Shrove (or fat) Tuesday, the day before Ash Wednesday is especially colorful. Ceremonies take place on the days leading up to it, and the final event takes place around the church *atrium* and central plaza. It includes the men from all three Chamulan barrios, San Juan, San Sebastian, and San Pedro. The men gather into their three groups, much like army platoons preparing to attack. They dress in special costumes, including "rooster foot" (high-backed

huaraches), knee-length pants, red-tasseled white scarves, brilliantly striped cummerbunds, and tall cone-shaped hats. The hats, covered with monkey fur, strap around their chins like beards and are topped with colorful ribbons springing from the point of the cones. Some carry a cane made from the penis of a bull; others wave flowered cloth banners on tall poles.

Tooting horns and clouds of incense signal the time to run. Little boys join into the festivities, running behind the men and learning their futures. At an unseen signal they stop, slowly wave the banners over the incense and then begin running again. The *casiques* (head men) of the different villages crowd together on a second-floor balcony of the government building wearing straw, flat-crowned, beribboned hats, each holding under his arm a silver-headed cane (sign of his authority). What a colorful scene, and you can't take even one picture! Good Friday brings another time of great ceremony.

Two of the most important factors in Chamulan celebrations (and there are many) have always been the presence of *posh* (the potent sugarcane liquor) and the pyrotechnics that go on throughout the nights of merrymaking, the cost for which is shared by the community.

Church on the Hill

On the top of the hill overlooking the village are the remains of an early Christian church. Built in 1526, it was intentionally destroyed in a 16th-century fire. The Chamulans were quite set in their notion of keeping outsiders out even back then. Today it's used as a cemetery and is often filled with people tending the graves of their families. The building itself is just a skeleton of old stone. Across the dirt road an entrepreneur set up a small portable "museum" of a few artifacts in a thatch structure.

ZINACANTÁN

In nearby Zinacantán, life moves at a different pace. Though they too are dedicated to their culture and traditions, the villagers are more enterprising, their village is very clean, and it seems that everyone works. They have a thriving business exporting hothouse flowers. As you drive through the countryside you'll see their large hothouses dispersed in hills and valleys. All children go to school, and the last time through we heard the sounds of a band practicing in the schoolhouse. You seldom see the villagers selling or begging on the plaza in San Cristóbal. You *will* see them at their roadside stands along the highway displaying their weaving.

The men are probably the most colorful of the area Indian groups. You recognize them by their short white pants (the story goes that the men think their legs are beautiful), tunics woven of red and white threads that appear pink from a distance, with bright-colored flowers or designs embroidered atop the woven cloth and fuchsia tassels hanging loose, and handwoven straw hats with semiflat crowns and bright ribbons streaming from the edges. The women, on the other hand, wear dark skirts and white blouses trimmed with a minimum of color, topped with a beautiful blue *rebozo* (shawl). The Zinacantecans have been merchants since the early

1600s and still travel around the region selling their homegrown vegetables, fruit, and flowers.

Textiles

Try to visit a weaver's home. Extended families practice these home industries. The Zinacantecans' textiles are noted for their colorful embroidery in flamboyant reds, pinks, cerise, purples, and navy blues. The work is done outdoors in a family yard with most of the women attached to a waist loom. They create tablecloths, bedspreads, placemats, and of course the men's tunics. If you're looking for things such as placemats, don't expect to find eight exactly alike. Perhaps the design and color will be similar, but they might be an inch longer or wider, adding to the charm.

As we passed through a weaver's house, we noticed a "wedding gown" hanging on the wall. It was quite lovely. Mostly white, the woven fabric was lighter than most, almost, but not quite, sheer. A small cross was embroidered just below the neckline. But the really unusual part was the bottom third of the dress, embroidered with lovely white feathers (which turned out to be chicken feathers) trimmed in rather subtle colors. Historically, the Aztecs used feathers in their weaving, but this group obviously was exposed to this tradition early on by the Tlaxcaltecans (from near Mexico City) who accompanied Mazariegos when he conquered the Chiapas highlands in the 16th century.

SAN ANDRES LARRAINZAR

This Tzotzil-speaking municipality consists of about 54 villages with 17,000 inhabitants scattered across the hilltops of the Chiapas highlands. A few of the more well-known villages are Sts. Marta, Magdalena, and Santiago. This area has about 32 primary schools, many of which go only to the fourth grade. The quality of education is inferior, and many children do not attend because they are needed at home to work. Within their culture, women have always been considered inferior and have no voice in the community; this is gradually changing. Most of the Larrainzars do not speak Spanish, especially the women. Alcoholism is a major problem with the men (and some of the women). Several years ago the Larrainzars voted that cantinas will not be tolerated within *some* of the villages; the city fathers were strongly influenced by various religious outsiders.

Village Life

These people are very poor. Their dirt-floor one-room homes are made of adobe (mud slapped onto stick frames) with either thatch or corrugated metal roofs. A few have tile shingles; none have indoor plumbing. The women cook over an open fire in the yard or in bad weather in the single room; the smoke *eventually* escapes through the roof. If you wonder, when you buy a piece of cloth while traveling through this area, why it smells of smoke, more than likely the portable waist loom was hooked up to the center post of the weaver's house or to a tree in the yard, close to the cooking smoke.

Can you imagine finishing daily chores if you must supply each need by making it from scratch, including cloth? No wonder the people seldom have more than two changes of clothing. Most of their days are spent doing simple things that we take for granted. They bathe, shampoo, and wash their clothes in cold water carried from the community faucet and search the surrounding hills for firewood for the cookfire (a constant job).

Medical care is nonexistent and a small group of Catholic nuns have brought in *indígenes* from other villages to teach the villagers about their illnesses and cures with herbal medicines, *curandero* style. Healing is a lost art to many of the Indians, and since there are no doctors among them, they are relearning how to prepare salves, tinctures, syrups, capsules, and soaps from the herbs and roots available to them in their environment.

The villagers continue to eke a living from poor soil in a cold climate atop tall mountains. Farming is their only way of surviving and corn is their main crop. Traveling through the highlands, you see milpas (cornfields) planted up and down the vertical mountainsides; in many cases water must be hand-delivered to the crop. Corn tortillas and beans are the staples of their diet. Often the only means of bringing cash into the house is selling what other few vegetables they grow, as well as chickens, eggs, and sometimes a pig.

Textiles

Again, weaving is an important part of life and brings in some extra pesos. The municipality of San Andrés Larrainzar is known for its unusual weaving style. This group is very involved in the Sna Jolobil co-op in San Cristóbal. Not only are the women selling their weavings for an economic advantage there, but they are learning and preserving more of their traditions. The women eagerly study old textiles and take classes in the ancient art of natural dyes. The Larrainzars are well-known for adding colored bits of yarn into the warp and weft of their backstrap looms to create special designs. One product is the brocade, an ancient design that incorporates traditional symbols such as the snake, diamond, flower, and the "trickster monkey." The background color is usually bright red with many

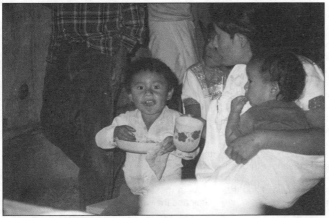

Larrainzar
Indian family

OZ MALLAN

colors woven in. The symbols tell a story that's handed from mother to daughter.

Competition to sell textiles to tourists is fierce. All the women from San Cristóbal's outlying villages weave, and there are more than 200,000 Indians living in the "neighborhood." Since most Indians do not have transportation, bringing their crafts to market is especially difficult for those living in isolated mountainous areas. Often buyers representing city stores from other parts of Mexico travel into these villages and offer prices that are simply not fair, and then sell them in their trendy shops (far from Chiapas) at inflated prices. (We all like a bargain, but it's high-handed robbery to pay US50 cents for an intricate weaving that took five days to produce and then to sell it for US$25-50.)

Village Co-ops

The villages are beginning to learn to work together—it's probably their only chance of survival. Fourteen villages have community co-op stores. Awhile back, a benefactor from Switzerland donated a heavy-duty commercial treadle sewing machine to each of five Larrainzar communities to help with the co-op program. He also provided a couple of bolts of fabric to each village to "seed" the operation. Two men from each village traveled to San Cristóbal weekly for four or five weeks to be trained as tailors. Making their own trousers cuts the price by about half.

Each village specializes in one "product": five villages produce trousers and shirts, two more raise bees, four raise rabbits, five raise chickens, two make bread, and one village is organizing to weave the cloth for the women's skirts. Probably one of the biggest pluses is the Sna Jolobil in San Cristóbal, where someone is always there to sell the textile at fair prices to the tourists.

To the Villages

The trip to many of the villages is tough. The good paved road ends just after the turnoff to Chamula and Zinacantán (tour buses don't go past this point). Beyond the pavement are dirt roads, and it's best to have a 4WD vehicle. The dirt roads, not much more than dirt tracks, are potholed, ridged, and rough, although they do meander through beautiful scenery with green mountains and along a lively river. Occasional heavy rains flood the roads, turning them into rivers of mud.

Eventually a dirt track to the village of Vayalem stops at the foot of a mountain (many villages sit at the top of mountains). From here it's a hike on a narrow path straight to the top. The air is clear and crisp, the sky blue, and the green trees incredibly beautiful. At the crest of the hill sits the village. A small group of houses is constructed of adobe with red tile roofs. As usual, all the women and little girls of the village are barefoot; their most formal attire consists of a dark wool skirt, a crisp white cotton blouse with colorful red woven designs trimming the neck and sleeve cuffs, and a white wool shawl that is worn in a variety of ways, but mostly bulging with a baby. The men wear Western trousers and shirts, machine-made straw hats, and generally cowboy boots; little boys are dressed just like their dads.

The dirt track leads beyond the path to Vayalem to other mountains and other villages, but it is not recommended that you just "show up" at one of these villages. The people are suspicious of strangers, with good reason; outsiders have interfered with their lives as far back as any legend goes. Larrainzar has been the scene of many of the meetings between the Mexican government and the Zapatistas. If you're interested in visiting a village, contact the tourism office in San Cristóbal and ask someone there to recommend a guide who knows the people and takes visitors there regularly.

SOUTH OF SAN CRISTÓBAL DE LAS CASAS

Amatenango del Valle

The Pan American Highway, Hwy. 190, takes you past the cutoff to Amatenango del Valle. At this pottery-making village you will find Tzeltal craftsmanship—immense jars up to 3-4 feet tall and often 20-30 inches in diameter—and marvelous doves, from tiny carry-along size to tall, graceful, and almost as big as the jars. All of these are made without a wheel. Stacks of hundreds of natural gray pottery is sun-dried in large heaps, and then fired in the traditional open fire on the top of the ground rather than in a kiln. Don't expect the pottery to be as durable as some, but the pieces are a wonderful *típico* souvenir.

As in most home industries, this is a family affair and the women do their work in the yard of the house with a few shady spots under a thatch overhang. The women wear folded cloth on the top of their heads that they can quickly drop to protect them from the sun, a rather unusual "hat"—it also comes in handy to drop in front of their faces when gringos start to take their pictures without permission. They are, however, willing to be photographed with a few pesos. The extended family working on the pottery consists of daughters, grandmothers, and aunts, and lots of little kids and small animals. We were fortunate to meet Juliana Lopez, a well-known matriarch of Amatenango who has been making pottery for decades. She proudly told us that the small, sharp, metal scraping tool that she held in her leathery hands was given to her in the U.S. Several years ago Juliana was part of a group of Chiapas craftspeople who visited the U.S. to exhibit their pottery and their ancient work methods. Their colorful traditional clothing in bright reds and brilliant yellows made a big hit. While telling us of her adventures Juliana never missed a beat, smoothing and scraping until she had a fine even surface.

No men were to be seen. We ran into them later pulling their carts on the Pan American Highway. The men trudge up the broad highway and into the woods early in the day pulling their handmade wood-carts, complete with oil cans and machetes. Once the carts are completely loaded and the wood tied securely, they climb on behind (usually a young boy or two is along as well) and go full speed down the highway. A rope is the steering wheel and the braking system is primitive. The carts are about six feet long and these men are all daredevils— Chiapanecan style! It's about a five-hour trip up and down the hill, wood-cutting session included.

Children and women set up shop on roadsides selling their pottery and the children will try to sell you their own handmade crafts—small primitive animals that more than likely have not been fired. The price is right, and they are cute remembrances to take home to a child.

Comitán

It's a 76-km drive to Comitán from San Cristóbal, but some consider the town—along with the Montebello Lakes beyond—well worth the trip. If driving, you'll travel south on Hwy. 190 (Pan American Highway), which takes you very close to the Guatemalan border. It's not unusual to see jeeps or trucks filled with Guatemalan soldiers and guns.

Comitán is a town built on a roller-coaster site with steep hills. It's often used as an overnight hub and gateway for a day of exploring the lakes beyond. Comitán also makes a dynamite local liquor called *comitecho* from sugarcane and it is really fiery!

Few sights in town are worth the stop. **La Casa de la Cultura** is a small museum (next to the church on the *zócalo*) with curious regional Maya artifacts from nearby archaeological sites such as Chinkultíc. Archaeologists are working on the ruins of Tenan Puente southeast of the city; ask for information in town. The Comitán *zócalo* is pleasant, with a historical monument and colonial ambience.

This bustling city has lots of traffic and limited accommodations. Take a look at the budget **Hotel Lagos de Montebello** (on the highway) if you're traveling with limited funds. The tourist office in San Cristóbal lists other hotels in the area.

Take the opportunity to fill your gas tank before you leave town.

Lagunas de Montebello National Park

The lakes are about a 60-minute drive from Comitán (51 km). This setting in the Lacandón Forest was made for photos. The lakes reflect myriad colors from pale blue to lavender, deep purple, and reddish black, covering an area of 13,000 square miles. The official slick brochure from the Mexico City tourist office says that there are 16 lakes in all. In Chiapas, the local tourist office says there are 59, with access to 50 by way of a paved road. The lakes are beautiful and look like Lake Tahoe.

A few km off the main highway, a dirt road leads to Lake Tziscao, where you'll find single-sex dormitories, 33 bunks in all, as well as a small cafeteria and a camping area. These are very spartan accommodations—it is not recommended that you spend the night here. And you'd be wise to check with the San Cristóbal tourist office before you go to make sure if it's safe to travel here. Do not go alone. Go in a group. Off the paved road you'll find the turnoff to the Maya site of Chinkultíc, with a pyramid standing guard over the Guatemala/Mexico border. You may even see the Guatemalan army.

Parador Museo Santa Maria

Another way to enjoy the lakes and Chinkultíc is to spend a night at a small parador, part of what once was a hacienda. You really are spending the night in a museum; only the curious need "apply." This is far from a glitzy hotel, but rather a look back into life in a hacienda. The first family to live in this hacienda came from Germany in 1830. Later Mexicans bought it for 35,000 pesos, paid in silver coins. Originally the hacienda was 1,757 hectares, and today it totals about 3.8 hectares. The help and their children still use the simple old chapel, where a candle is usually always burning.

The present owners have been renovating for several years. Notice the beautiful burnished wood columns that line the walkway; apparently they had been painted bright green by some early "decorator" and since have been stripped and restored to their natural wood finish. And although there's a small indoor kitchen with a few modern appliances such as a refrigerator, the old outdoor kitchen is still used. Outside a large stone oven roasts whole pigs for special occasions. The *comal* sits on a fire made of wood till it burns into glowing coals. Handmade *masa* dough is shaped by hand into round flat cakes, cooked just right on both sides, and voila! You have tasty tortillas. In the outside kitchen under a wide, wood roof, baskets scattered about the rough counters hold fresh picked beans and chiles, drying before they go into the pantry. Most meals are served in the lovely garden if the weather is nice, and it is said to be springlike year-round. Lots of birdsong accompanies garden meals. However, a formal dining room serves if the weather is bad.

Lovely old paintings, unusual clocks, and bric-a-brac fill the living room. The bedrooms are simple, though furnished in antique pieces with a distinct European look. Most of the rooms have a private bath and a small sitting area. The beds are not the softest. The grounds are well-kept with views of green fields and a lake, and the mountains rise in the distance. For reservations write to Apto. Postal #137, Comitán, Chiapas, Mexico. Inexpensive. From here it's not very far to go to either Chinkultíc or Montebello Lakes.

coatimundi

BOB RACE

PALENQUE AND VICINITY

Palenque is a *do-not-miss* attraction on any itinerary of Maya ruins. The setting, on a lush green shelf at the edge of the Sierra de Chiapas rainforest, adds to the serenity of this noble archaeological compound of ornate carvings and graceful design. In the west part of the Peninsula about 150 km southeast of Villahermosa and 10 km from Santo Domingo (also called Palenque Village), the site continues to undergo changes. The modern visitor's center with folk art shops, a restaurant, and a museum opened in May 1993 on the main road just before you reach the ruins. Next to the visitor center, check out the Merle Green Robertson Library.

When traveling from town, the *colectivo* might stop first at the museum, but it will continue to the ruins. Entrance to the museum is included in the admission price to the ruins, so it's smart to go to the ruins first and then the museum on the way back. One entry into Palenque is a steep 1 km pathway between the museum and the ruins through the forested jungle, past waterfalls and the rushing river. Eventually there will be a ticket booth and entryway for the ruins at the foot of this path. For now, you pay your fee at the top of the hill by the main parking lot. After you visit the ruins, either walk the one-km path to the museum, or catch a *colectivo* at the entrance (about US55 cents) and ask the driver to stop at the complex. If you then take the *colectivo* from the center into town, it will cost you another fare.

The ruin site is open daily 8 a.m.-5 p.m. The most recent admission price was roughly US$2.30 (hang on to your ticket, it gets you into the museum), US$8.50 video camera fee, and a small parking fee; admission is free on Sunday. The museum is open Tues.-Sun. 10 a.m.-5 p.m. You'll see a cold-drink stand and souvenir stall at the entrance of the site. The tomb in the Temple of the Inscriptions is supposed to be open (which means the light is on) 10 a.m.-4 p.m. Ask about this when you buy your ticket. It is not always open. Lacandón Indians, content for so many years to stay hidden, now can be found near the entrance selling their arrows and other handmade crafts. The men still dress in their white sacklike dresses, wear their black hair long, and smoke their handmade cigars. You seldom see Lacandón women, usually only men and young boys. As women and men wear the same hair style, the only way to tell them apart is the color of the dresses; women wear flowered dresses and the men wear all white.

The structures at Palenque are continually being excavated and restored. It may be several lifetimes before all of the still-buried ruins are revealed. But those structures that have been freed from the jungle offer a mysterious, awe-inspiring vision of great pomp and opulence. Experts say 8-11 km of unexcavated buildings surround the present site.

Scholars have been able to decipher enough of the many glyphs to construct a reasonable genealogy of the Palenque kings, from the rule of Chaacal I (A.D. 501) to the demise of Kuk (A.D. 783). But it was during the reign of Lord Pacal and his son, Chan Bahlum (A.D. 615-701), that Palenque grew from a minor site to an important ceremonial center. Again we see the brilliance of the Classic period through beautiful sculpture, unusual life-size carvings, and innovative architectural design. These buildings are outstanding even when compared with other sites of the same period constructed throughout the Peninsula, Guatemala, Belize, and Honduras.

Passed By

Somehow the conquistadors missed Palenque completely, even though Cortés passed within 35-45 km of the site. By that time, however, Palenque had been long abandoned. The earliest Spanish-recorded comments on Palenque were made by a Spanish army captain, Antonio del Río, who passed through in March 1785. He drew maps and plans and excavated by royal order for one year. The Spaniard was highly criticized by archaeologist J. Eric Thompson for "bulldozing" the ruins. Captain del Río broadcast wild and fantastic assumptions about the beginnings of the Maya. After visits by a few other laypeople who took home strange drawings, it wasn't long before Europeans envisioned Palenque as the lost city of Atlantis or part of Egyptian dynasties. When Americans John L.

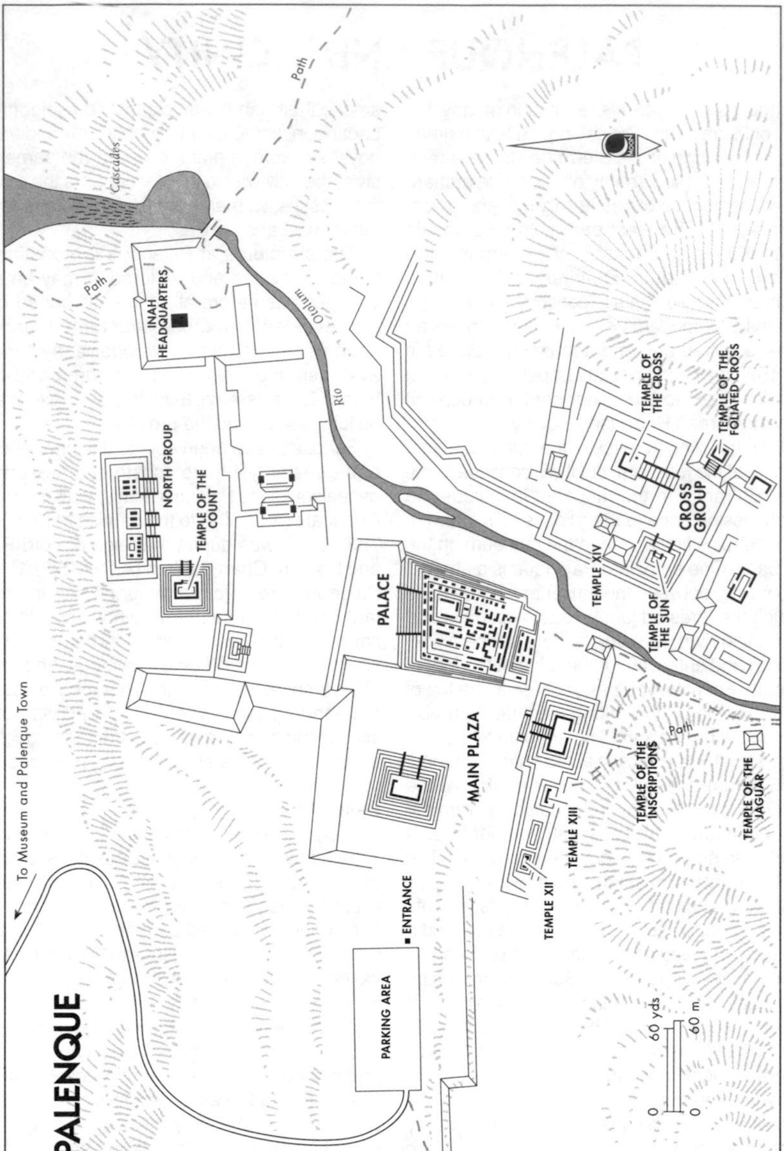

PALENQUE

To Museum and Palenque Town

PARKING AREA

■ ENTRANCE

MAIN PLAZA

TEMPLE XII

TEMPLE XIII

TEMPLE OF THE INSCRIPTIONS

TEMPLE OF THE JAGUAR

Path

PALACE

TEMPLE XIV

TEMPLE OF THE SUN

CROSS GROUP

TEMPLE OF THE CROSS

TEMPLE OF THE FOLIATED CROSS

TEMPLE OF THE COUNT

NORTH GROUP

INAH HEADQUARTERS

Rio Otolum

Cascades

Path

Path

Path

0   60 yds
0   60 m.

© MOON PUBLICATIONS, INC.

Stephens and Frederick Catherwood wrote about the site and drew outstanding realistic reproductions in the mid-1800s, a true picture of Palenque began to emerge.

Everywhere on the grounds you'll see reminders of the great leader Lord Pacal. Carvings of him and his family, as well as some of the finest examples of Maya funerary art, are found in many of the structures. Palenque is renowned for its extraordinary stucco bas-relief sculpture. Rather than work in smaller figures, typical of much Maya art, the Palencanos often created figures as tall as three meters.

TEMPLE OF THE INSCRIPTIONS

At the entrance you can hire a guide; the price for a two-hour tour for a group of one to seven people is about US$25. Walk through the entrance and past Temple XII (also known as Temple of the Skull—look for the carved skull on the lower right corner) and XIII on the right side of the road. Temple XIII is now open to the public; it's a small though interesting little ruin. Just beyond XIII you'll come to the Temple of the Inscriptions, also on your right. This 24-meter-high pyramid kept a secret burial site hidden within its depths for more than a thousand years, until 1952. At the top of the eight-stepped pyramid is the temple, where magnificent tablets of glyphs tell the ancestral history of the Palenque rulers.

The rear gallery of the Temple of the Inscriptions is divided into three chambers. Here, Mexican archaeologist Alberto Ruz L'Huillier (in 1949) first uncovered a stairway filled with rubble, cleverly hidden under a stone slab floor of the center chamber.

Untouched Crypt

At the foot of the stairs another sealed passage was found, in front of which were clay dishes filled with red pigment, jade earplugs, beads, a large oblong pearl, and the skeletons of six sacrificial victims. When the final large stone door was removed, Ruz experienced the lifetime dream of every archaeologist: before him was the untouched crypt of Lord Shield Pacal. On 15 June 1952, after three years of excavating the steep passageway, Ruz entered the small room for the first time.

The centerpiece of the chamber is the sarcophagus topped by a flat, four-meter-long, five-ton slab of stone. The magnificent slab is beautifully carved with the figure of Pacal in death, surrounded by monsters, serpents, sun and shell signs, and many more glyphs that recount death and its passage. The walls of the chamber are decorated with various gods, from which scientists have deduced a tremendous amount about the Palencanos' theology.

Working slowly to preserve everything in its pristine state, Ruz didn't open the lid of the sarcophagus for six months. It took a week of difficult work in the stifling, dust-choked room to finally lift

Temple of
the Inscriptions

OZ MALLAN

the five-ton slab. On 28 November 1952, the scientists had their first peek into the sepulcher. In the large rectangular sarcophagus they found another, body-shaped sarcophagus (a first in Maya history), within which was Pacal's skeleton, with precious jewelry and special accoutrements to accompany him on his journey into the next world. A jade mosaic mask covered the face, under which his own teeth had been painted red. (The mask was exhibited at the Anthropological Museum in Mexico City until 24 December 1985, when it was stolen along with several other precious historical artifacts. The mask was recovered in 1989.) It is estimated that Pacal was taller than the average Maya of the time. A disagreement between scientists stemming from different methods of deciphering the number-glyphs has given various ages at death. Some say he was 80-100 years old, while others say he was 60 at the most.

Too bad Ruz didn't live long enough to learn about DNA. The current buzz is that Pacal's tomb will be reopened and his remains will be put through DNA testing to see if in fact he was the son of the red queen as is believed. Ruz would have been fascinated to have such definitive scientific results.

This excavation began a new concept in Maya archaeology. It was formerly believed that the pyramids had served a single function, as a base for temples brought closer to the heavens. But now it's known that other pyramids were used as crypts for revered leaders as well. All of this bears a resemblance to the culture and beliefs of the Egyptians, and imaginative students of history have tried to link the two cultures—so far unsuccessfully.

The Climb

The Temple of the Inscriptions is probably the most difficult climb at Palenque, but don't let that stop you. To reach the temple as the Maya did, you walk up the front of the structure, 69 very steep steps. Take it slowly! At the top, while catching your breath, study the fine panels and carvings in the temple, and then begin your trip down the stairs into the depths of the pyramid. Occasionally the lights of the abrupt stairway leading down into the crypt are off; check with the ticket-taker before you make the climb. The steps can be slippery, and without light it's pitch black,

so it's always a good idea to travel with a small, powerful mag-lite. An iron gate allows you to view the burial chamber without entering the room. The magnificent carved slab is suspended several centimeters above the sarcophagus.

Note: You can make an easier climb to and from the temple from ground level on the back side of the structure up a path of earth and stone. The small structure sitting cater-corner from the Temple of the Inscriptions entrance is a memorial to Alberto Ruz L'Huillier.

OTHER SITES

The Palace

Palenque's Palace is one of the most unusual structures on the Yucatán Peninsula. Directly in front of you as you walk up the main pathway with the Temple of the Inscriptions on your right, the Palace occupies the unusually large space of a city block. The four-story tower, another rarity of the Classic Maya, will immediately catch your eye. Archaeologists believe that the tower was constructed to give a good view of the winter solstice (22 December), when the sun appears to drop directly into the Temple of the Inscriptions. It was also used to make astronomical calculations—an important part of their daily lives. Larger-than-life panels are still clearly recognizable throughout the site; various glyphs that line steps and walls give insight into the life of the Maya during the reign of Pacal. The Palace sits on a platform 10 meters high, and you can explore a labyrinth of underground passageways and tunnels.

Discoveries

Palenque was a minor center during the Early Classic era (A.D. 250-600). Later kings dated the foundation of their dynasty from A.D. 431. Pacal (603-684) ascended the throne at age 12. He spread Palenque's influence throughout the western Maya lowlands. Before he died, he built the Temple of the Inscriptions to house his elaborate tomb, which was decorated with deifications of his life and his glorious ancestors. He was succeeded by Chan Bahlum, who was noteworthy for having six digits on his hands and feet. Chan Bahlum reigned for 18 years and built the temples of the Cross, Foliated Cross, and

OZ MALLAN

Palenque Palace

Sun to prove the pre-ordination of his rule. After he died in 702, his younger brother, Kan Xul, took the reins of power. His rule was Palenque's apogee; the Palace was enlarged and the city's power reached its greatest extent. Kan Xul's heirs were less successful, and Palenque's prominence and glitter gradually dwindled. The last historical record found in the city is dated A.D. 799; it is a blackware vase from Central Mexico that with crude hieroglyphs celebrates the accession of a king named 6 Cimi to Palenque's throne.

Just east of the Temple of the Inscriptions, you come to the South Group, which includes the Temple of the Cross, the Temple of the Foliated Cross, and the Temple of the Sun, all built around a plaza on the edge of the jungle. The Temple of the Sun is the first of these, with tablets at the top depicting Lord Pacal and Chan Bahlum. The Temple of the Cross is the largest of this group and contains tablets of Chan Bahlum wearing the full paraphernalia of royalty after his accession and accompanied by the cigar-smoking God L, a Lord of the Underworld, in an owl-feather headdress. The small Temple of the Foliated Cross against the jungle wall to the right holds more tablets celebrating the succession of Chan Bahlum. A major excavation under way is centered on the South Group. A team of Mexican archaeologists recently found a major tomb at the base of the Temple of the Cross. A headless body of an official, perhaps the governor of a neighboring city, and 630

pieces of jade were discovered here. They have also found five perfectly preserved incense burners and some extremely fine ceramic figurines. One of these figurines, on display in the museum, is already considered one of the finest Maya sculptures yet found; it depicts a man seated on square bench. His head has been broken off, but his helmet, in the form of a bird, was found nearby.

Restoration is also taking place in the northern area, which includes the Ball Court and the Temple of the Count. Archaeologists continually uncover more buildings in this area, and estimate another 400 undiscovered structures.

Walking past these structures to the east, you'll reach the park's original small museum, now used to store artifacts discovered in the restoration. A stone bridge crosses the river here—signs ask that you not wade or swim here. Don't worry, more cool pools lie along the way. The bridge marks the beginning of the pathway down the hill to the museum. Though some use this path as an entrance to the site, it is better to save it for the end, when the downhill walk in the cool shade is most gratifying. The pathway is marked by rocks along the sides that are sometimes difficult to see, as evidenced by the lost wanderers following trails leading nowhere. After about 10 minutes, you reach a cascading waterfall and several small pools perfect for cooling weary feet. Several small structures are being reconstructed here, and though none have the size and stature of the main ruins, they do provide shaded resting areas. If you walk this path at closing time, keep an eye out for birds and monkeys. When there are few humans around, these creatures come out of their hiding places and crash and soar through the trees. The pathway ends at the main road, a short distance from the museum.

The Visitor Center

Inaugurated in May 1993, Palenque's visitor center is a welcome addition well worth visiting. The complex includes an architecturally impressive museum containing artifacts and replicas of the carvings and murals from the ruins. Two excellent folk art shops are in a separate building with a small cafe selling sodas and snacks. If San Cristóbal de las Casas isn't on your itinerary (or even if it is), take the time to browse through these shops, and don't forget

your credit cards! The displays include Lacandón arrows; intricate weaving, embroidery, and pottery from various Indian groups from throughout Chiapas; and a good selection of books and postcards. The shops and cafe are open daily 10 a.m.-5 p.m. The *colectivos* will stop here as well; plenty of parking space is available.

SANTO DOMINGO DE PALENQUE

The community of Santo Domingo de Palenque, referred to as Palenque Village, is eight km from the archaeological site. The small town bulges at its seams with the influx of tourists interested in the Palenque ruins. Hotels, cafes, curio shops, a large shady plaza, and a tourist information office help make the traveler feel welcome. Again, ask

SANTO DOMINGO DE PALENQUE

© MOON PUBLICATIONS, INC.

before you take pictures of the people anywhere in Chiapas.

Santo Domingo de Palenque has matured over the years from a dirt-road village to an amiable small town. It is the seat of the surrounding municipality of about 60,000 residents, about 16,000 of them living within the town limits. Much of the surrounding area has been cleared of trees and jungle (to the consternation of ecologists) and converted to cattle-grazing land. Some of the small farms are growing into large agricultural complexes. Fine mahogany forests have been destroyed by outside lumber companies who have bought the timber rights from local Indians. Many say this will ultimately destroy the lush rainforest and the culture of the Indians that has survived in this isolated world for centuries.

Tourism is the biggest moneymaker for the city, and locals are now learning to work in tourist services through a local vocational training program. The largest numbers of visitors come in tour buses and pass through quickly, leaving the town's 900 hotel rooms full one day and empty the next. However, for years Palenque has been a gathering place for backpackers from all over the world—and for psilocybin seekers. The wise pilgrim will not ask *just any* local about the mushroom trade, since the government has offered good rewards for information on 'shroom activity.

VILLAGE ACCOMMODATIONS

For such a small town it's amazing how many hotels are scattered about. Most are simple inns in the budget category, but more upgraded hostelries are springing up each year. Look at your room before moving in (or paying), and make sure you have ample blankets (this can be cold country in the winter). For reservations check with your travel agent, or contact the hotel (write to the street address or Apto. Postal number, Palenque, Chiapas 29960, Mexico). Allow about six weeks for return mail. Once in the city, if you have any problems, ask for recommendations at the local tourist office, Calle Jiménez at Casa de la Cultura. The area code is 934.

Budget to Inexpensive

Palenque has a large selection of budget hotels, but few stand out as exceptional bargains, especially when cleanliness and comfort are considered. Your best choice is **La Posada** (see below). Still, the budget hotels fill up fast; if you're traveling during high season, reservations are advised. Next to/around the corner from the ADO bus station, **Hotel Santa Elena** Prolongacion Nicolas, La Canada, tel. (934) 5-0437, fax 5-0193, is *clean* with two double beds, private bath, fan, modest furnishings, TV in the lobby, and always with a crowd of Mexicans watching. This little hotel locks the doors at curfew, so check on the hours. Right in town, **Hotel Avenida**, Av. Juárez #173, tel. (934) 5-0116, fax 5-0435, is an option only when you want to be right above the bus station.

Hotel Misol-Ha, Av. Juárez #14, tel. (934) 5-0092, is also very basic, closer to the plaza. **Hotel Lacroix**, just up from the plaza Calle Hidalgo #10, tel. (934) 5-0114, has potential, though it could use a major cleaning and renovation. Still, it's popular with the backpack set.

Others to check out are the **Posada San Francisco**, Calle Hidalgo at Allende (no phone); **Posada Charito** at Av. 20 de Noviembre #15-B, tel. (934) 5-0121; **Hotel San Antonio** at Independencia #42, no phone; and **Hospedaje San Juan** on Tercera Sur, tel. (934) 5-0616. The **Hotel Palenque**, overlooking the plaza at Calle 5 de Mayo #15, tel. (934) 5-0188, also shows promise and could be a great choice if maintenance improves.

La Posada, in La Cañada sector off Calle Merle Green behind Maya Tulipanes, tel. (934) 5-0437, fax 5-0193, is the best bargain at Palenque, with very friendly management and staff. Owner Lourdes Chavez de Grajalves is active in the local hotel association and is well-informed about buses, restaurants, and all the other questions tourists tend to ask. The hotel's eight rooms are set far back from the road, away from restaurant and traffic noise. The downstairs rooms have one double bed on a concrete platform, good-sized bathrooms with plenty of hot water, portable fans, and shelves for clothing. Eight new rooms were almost complete when we visited; each will have two beds. Purified water, sodas, beers, snacks, and sundries are sold in the main building, its walls decorated with written testimonials from past guests. Tables and chairs are set out on a wide lawn in front of the rooms, where travelers (many European) share notes. Lourdes reports that three monkeys have made appearances in a tree on the lawn—keep an eye out!

The **Hotel Kashlan,** on Calle Allende at 5 de Mayo, tel. (934) 5-0297, fax 5-0309, is a longtime favorite near the plaza, with well-maintained rooms, most with windows on the inner hallway, and a good travel agency in the lobby.

Hotel Mallorca, tel. (934) 5-0838, is another simple hotel on the road to Pakal-Na. Rooms have two double beds.

Inexpensive

Hotel Chan Kah Centro, on Av. Indepencia, is clean, modern, and reasonable. (It has the same owners as the Chan Kah Resort Village on the road to the ruins.) It offers small rooms with bathrooms, fans, restaurant on the first floor, and terrace bar on the second floor (try to get a room away from the bar). Some guests have complained about lost reservations, less than cordial service, and inflated rates when business is good. For reservations write to Apto. Postal 26. Be sure to indicate "Hotel Chan Kah Centro." Or call (934) 5-0318, fax 5-0486.

On the main highway coming into town from Villahermosa (about one km north of the plaza), you'll see the **Hotel Tulija,** tel. (934) 5-0104, fax 5-0163. The rooms are simple, with a/c, private bath, swimming pool, and a/c dining room that serves a big lunch for about US$5.

Another moderate hotel in Santo Domingo is the **Hotel Casa de Pakal,** Av. Juárez #18. It's in the central part of town and offers 16 clean (though small) rooms (often closed during off-season).

Maya Tulipanes, at Merle Green #6, tel. (934) 5-0201, fax 5-1004, has 33 rooms with baths. Most have fans and a few have a/c. It's a rambling old place under the trees but often is filled with groups.

The **Hotel La Cañada,** Apto. 91, Calle Merle Green #14, tel. (934) 5-0102, fax 5-0392, has been around for quite a while, with cottages and rooms secluded by tall shade trees. The rooms are simple; all have private bathrooms. Be sure to specify if you want a/c since only some of the rooms are equipped. This is a peaceful tropical spot but it also has a lively disco close by. Because it's often filled with groups, reservations are suggested, The hotel's restaurant is the most dependable one in the neighborhood, though the quality of the food is erratic. The nearby Fogon de Pakal restaurant had closed when we last visited, and was being used as a music club on weekend nights.

Hotel Xibalba, in the same complex as the Hotel La Cañada, is actually made up of rooms that once were a part of Hotel La Cañada, and they're some of the nicest ones in La Cañada sector. Four rooms have bathtubs, almost unheard of here, and a/c; four more have showers and fans. The hotel is run by the owners of the Xibalba travel agency just up the road. Also in the area is the moderate **Hotel Chablis,** tel. (934) 5-0446, fax 5-0870.

Closer to the ruins, **Villas Kin-Ha,** Carretera Palenque Ruinas Km 2.7, tel. (934) 5-0533, fax 5-0544, has cabanas spread through a landscaped clearing surrounded by thick trees. The oval-shaped huts with *palapa* roofs each have two rooms with king-sized or double beds, tile floors, and some nice touches such as wicker lamps over the bed. The big central pool is a definite plus; tour groups sometimes descend on the large restaurant.

Approximately 2.2 km southwest of town on the road to Agua Azul is the **Hotel Nututun,** Apto. Postal 74, tel. (934) 5-0100, fax 5-0161. in a lush, green setting on the Río Usumacinta. Most of the rooms are modern, with bathroom, TV, fan, and a/c, and a few have kitchen facilities; several of the rooms are of the older variety used when the newer ones are filled—ask for a newer room. You can swim in a pool and in the river, and an outdoor dining room overlooks the water and jungle. A small gift shop sells cards, T-shirts, suntan lotion, and a few sundries. Nighttime entertainment is presented during the high season. Bargain for cheaper rates without reservations, especially in the off-season. A car is a big help. Write or call to make reservations.

Hotel Maya Tucan, tel. (934) 5-0290, fax 5-0337, is across the road from the Hotel Plaza Palenque on the road to Catazaja. Another newish hotel, the Maya Tucan is a pleasant place to stay, though far from the ruins. The rooms are clean and cheery, with two double beds in each. It has a swimming pool and is very close to the highway. The restaurant is upstairs from the lobby.

Expensive

If you're a birdwatcher (or not), you'll enjoy **Chan Kah Resort Village,** for reservations Apto. Postal 26, tel. (934) 5-0318, fax 5-048, on Km 3 on the road to the ruins. Note: A car is really helpful here. However, taxis are available. One of the nicest things about Chan Kah is how it's maintained. Year after year it looks clean and fresh, and even nicer cabanas have been built. The rooms are spacious, with large open porches; many of them are perched on the edge of an arm of a river in the midst of thick jungle (ask not to be put in one on the entry road). The rooms are clean and fan-cooled, with decorative bathrooms and lots of privacy. Shallow, stone-lined pools in a large garden offer cooling relaxation and reading areas. An attractive *palapa*-roofed building houses the reception desk, lounge area, and dining room, with jungle vines dangling carefree down the open sides. The food is good and a wide selection of bar drinks is served. From your front porch, you can see many exotic jungle creatures. Owner Roberto Romano and his son Rocco both speak English, are fonts of information about Palenque, and can sometimes be found at mealtimes in the dining room.

In answer to the oft-asked question about drinking the water (which comes from a spring behind the Temple of the Inscriptions at the ruins), Señor Romano passes out a little card that explains it this way: "This water endowed the men who lived thousands of years ago on this site with the capability of a superior mind and who by drinking it brought to light the zero and discovered the infinite." However, if you still have doubts, ask for bottled water.

Bring a good book; at the hotel there's really no entertainment at night, only the chorus of insects and a black sky dotted profusely with dazzling stars. The hotel is about three km east of the ruins; transportation in a *colectivo* is available from the road that passes to and from town to the site about every 15 minutes. A taxi will cost about US$2 into town.

A Chan Kah guest related an experience that makes all travelers feel good. The young traveler decided to go out on the town and have a few drinks. To protect himself (from himself), he decided to take only the money he could afford to spend that evening. The rest of the pesos he slipped under his mattress. The evening was fun; he spent his allotment, came back to Chan Kah, and after a good night's sleep drove away bright and early the next morning. Fifty miles down the road he remembered he hadn't retrieved his money from under the mattress. When he and the manager returned to the room an hour later, he found that the maid had already cleaned and changed the sheets. Expecting the worst, he slipped his hand under the mattress to find the roll of pesos, all of them, neatly returned after the bed had been made.

The **Hotel Misión Palenque,** Rancho San Martín, tel. (934) 5-0241, fax 5-0300, is one of the most modern hotels in the area, complete with 160 rooms and suites, terraces, a/c, telephones, large swimming pool, green garden areas, bar, live music, travel agency, parking, and indoor/outdoor restaurant. One of the nice attractions at the Misión is the circular **Palapa Museo-Gráfica,** where changing exhibits are presented for guests. The much-talked-about Moises Morales, Chiapas guide extraordinaire and fine photographer (according to *National Geographic*), frequently shows his "stuff"—photographically and philosophically. Other times there is a showing of the costumes of the various villages of Chiapas. The hotel also provides transportation to and from Villahermosa airport and the Palenque archaeological zone.

Hotel Plaza Palenque, Carretera Playas de Catazaja Km 27, Apto. Postal 58, Palenque, tel. (934) 5-0555, fax 5-0395, about five km from the Maya statue at the entrance to town, is a modern hotel that has put down roots and 96 rooms. The three-story buildings frame a large swimming pool, and the grounds are backed by jungle where monkeys and parrots hide out. The rooms have been remodeled with rattan furnishings, cool tile floors, and satellite TV. The disco is one of Palenque's most popular night spots, but it is wisely set far from the rooms. Though large groups make up much of the clientele, the hotel is popular with those seeking peace away from the congestion of town. The restaurant and meeting rooms are decorated with photographs and drawings of the ruins.

RVs, Camping, and Cabins

Out of town, **María del Sol** campground, tel. (934) 5-0258, fax 5-0544, offers hookups for 86 trailers with good facilities including hot and cold showers, a clean pool, and a good restaurant called **María del Mar.** It's on the road to the Palenque archaeological site, just before you come to the Chan Kah Resort Village. Frequent (about every 15 minutes) minibuses travel back and forth from downtown to the ruins right past this RV park (about US50 cents).

Another local campground, the **Mayabel Trailer Park/Cabins,** lies about 2.2 km east of the ruins. This large grassy area has been known for its tents, camping vehicles, and hammock *palapas* (with room for four hammocks in each) for some time; now there are a few wooden cabins for rent as well. Rooms are large with two double beds, private bathroom, hot water, electricity, and very dim lights. Hammocks are available, but it's suggested you travel with your own hammock and mosquito netting (found easily at any marketplace); bring bug repellent and spray your netting as well as yourself. Toilet and shower facilities are fairly clean. A lively restaurant on the premises is open 7:30 a.m.-10 p.m. The *señora* in the office will keep valuables while you're out sightseeing. Rates: with tent, US$3 pp;

motorhomes depending on size are US$8-20; hammocks US$3 pp; and cabins US$20 d. Mailing address: Señora Nora del Karmen Morales, Apto. Postal 54, Palenque, Chiapas 29960.

Villas Kin Ha, Carretera Palenque Ruinas Km 2.7, tel. (934) 5-0533, fax 5-0544, has a campground with 60 RV spaces and hookups as well as tent spaces; RVs with hookups pay US$14 per night, and tent campers pay US$3 pp.

FOOD

Palenque has many small cafes with reasonable prices, and over the last years a few new, almost trendy cafes have sprung up. The marketplace is an inexpensive place to pick up picnic fixings or to eat a reasonably priced *comida corrida.* The **Restaurante Maya** on the plaza serves good regional food, and its prices are reasonable. The **Chan Kah Centro** on Av. Independencia serves tasty food and a good value *comida corrida,* tel. (934) 5-0318. Near the ADO bus station, **Girasoles** is a popular place for visitors, and sells kilos

If you venture out to Agua Azul, you'll likely encounter fruit vendors such as these. Some of these young women speak no Spanish, only Tzeltzal. Photographers take note—they have strong religious beliefs; please don't take photos without permission.

OZ MALLAN

of coffee beans grown nearby. Across from Chan Kah Centro, **Mara's** serves good hamburgers.

Las Tinajas, on Calle 20 de Noviembre not far from the bus station, offers great food at excellent prices in a simple setting, with three tables on a wooden porch and a few more inside. For about US$3 at breakfast you can have a full plate of *chilaquiles,* or eggs, beans, and toast, or an enormous *sope* with a corn base like a thick tortilla covered with beans, lettuce, and cheese. Full dinners cost about US$5-7.

Virgo, at Calle Hidalgo #5, is a second-story spot with an angled view of the plaza, a good cross breeze that's most welcome in humid Palenque, and live marimba music in the evening. The food is not exceptional (which can be said about most restaurants here), but the setting is nice. Another pleasant setting is the second floor of **Restaurant El Patio,** Av. Juarez #120, offering open air seating, good peoplewatching on the busy street below, breakfast, lunch, dinner, moderate prices, and good chicken tostadas.

In the same building as the Xibalba travel agency near Hotel La Cañada is a restaurant called **Mero Lec,** with outside dining under shade trees and an inside dining room decorated with Frida Kahlo posters. A lot of loving attention has gone into the decor, and it's the prettiest dinner spot in La Cañada, with live music on Friday and Saturday nights. The menu includes a fairly good tortilla soup, tacos, and salads.

For a little splurge, try **La Selva,** on the road to the ruins, about a 10-minute walk from the Maya statue. The traditional food is good, drinks are great, and the tropical *palapa* atmosphere is pleasing. You'll find indigenous artisans here, along with *típico* music. The dining rooms at the **Nututun** and the **Chan Kah Resort Village,** both out of town, serve meals in a lovely atmosphere. Bakeries and produce stands line Av. Juárez near the bus station, good for picking up a snack for the road. Keep looking; the town is growing small eateries like weeds.

SHOPPING AND SERVICES

Shopping is fun in Palenque, with more interesting indigenous crafts coming on the market all the time. Of course you will see the ubiquitous Guatemalan cloth and goods, but local art is ap-

pearing on the scene. Go to the **Casa de Artesanías Chiapeneca,** about a block from the *zócalo* on Av. Juárez. All it takes is a stroll along the downtown streets and you'll bump into shops for good perusing. Meandering through the *mercado* is always enlightening.

The **bank** cashes traveler's checks 9 a.m.-noon. The **post office** is a half block off the *zócalo* on Av. Independencia (about US50 cents to mail postcards internationally). The **long-distance telephone office,** at Caseta Cynthia, 20 de Noviembre, is open daily 7 a.m.-10 p.m. When calling collect (always cheaper), have your name, city, state, and number you want written down and be prepared for a long wait: there's only one operator and one line out of the village. The rumor is that this might change soon—believe it when you see it.

On Av. Juárez near El Chajul Restaurant is a doctor who speaks English. **Ela Laundry** service is in front of the Kashlan Hotel; **USA Laundry** on Av. Juárez has pickup and delivery service to the hotels, or you can drop off the laundry yourself.

Travel Agencies

In the past few years the number of travel agencies at Palenque has grown incredibly. Most offer tours to Bonampak and Yaxchilán, Misol Ha and Agua Azul, and other attractions, though the quality of the tours differs greatly. One of the oldest and most reliable agencies is **Viajes Shivalva** in the La Cañada area, tel. (934) 5-0411, in Mexico tel. (800) 2-3224, fax 5-0392. Owner Marco A. Morales Fimbres is extremely knowledgeable about the region and can help you decide the best way to tour out-of-the-way sights in Chiapas and Guatemala. **Viajes Yax-Ha,** Av. Juárez #119, tel./fax (934) 5-0767, offers all the typical tours and has a convenient money-exchange service open Mon.-Sat. 9 a.m.-2 p.m. and 5-9 p.m. **Anfitriones Turísticos Chiapas** (ATC) is the largest agency in the area, with offices in San Cristóbal de las Casas and Guatemala City and at the Hotel Kashlan, tel./fax (934) 5-0210.

TRANSPORTATION

By Air

Finally, the long awaited airport renovation and building has happened. Where once was a small unkempt landing field, there is now a lovely modern airport, including an indoor waiting area, ticket counters, and an open air waiting room. At press time, Aerocaribe Airlines was making flights to Palenque from Villahermosa and Merida. For flight information, contact Mexicana Airlines.

By Train
Until the much-promised improvements actually happen, traveling by train is not recommended. Many thefts have been reported.

By Bus
The bus situation has improved greatly in Palenque, and there are several choices of lines to San Cristóbal de las Casas (six hours); Mexico City (14 hours); Mérida (eight hours); and Villahermosa (two hours). Each bus line has its own terminal, most congregated on Av. Juárez and Calle 20 de Noviembre.

Autotransportes Rudolfo Figueroa on Juárez has the most deluxe buses to San Cristóbal and Tuxtla Gutiérrez, costing about US$12. The modern buses have curtained windows, a/c and heat, reclining seats, and movies shown en route. The only drawback is that the windows don't open, which can be frustrating if you grow nauseous along the winding road. **Mundo Maya** across Juárez by the Hotel Avenida has similar deluxe buses for about the same price. **Autotransportes Tuxtla** also on Juárez has less fancy service to Tuxtla and San Cristóbal for half the price.

ADO offers first-class service to Mexico City, Mérida, Chetumal, and Escárcega, and seven buses daily to Villahermosa. In Palenque the ADO first-class station is on Av. Hidalgo, three blocks north of the central plaza. The second-class bus station is on Calle 20 de Noviembre. It's always a good idea to check the schedule ahead of time, and if possible to buy your ticket a day in advance.

By Car
Car rentals are available both at the airport and at the large hotels in Villahermosa, from which it's a pleasant drive. The road from Villahermosa is in good condition most of the year, and it takes about two hours to cover the 150 km. From Villahermosa, drive 114 km on Hwy. 186 to the Catazaja junction, and then take the road to the right another 27 km to the village of Palenque. From there it's nine km to the ruins site.

Until the Zapatista situation has been resolved, traveling from San Cristóbal to Palenque

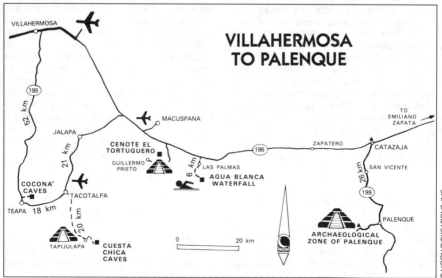

VILLAHERMOSA TO PALENQUE

is not recommended. Several robberies have been reported on this road (Hwy. 199). But if you take it, the highway is a fair road and the scenery is beautiful!

Upkeep is an ongoing problem and you may encounter rough spots and occasional potholes due to the excessive rain. Figure about five to six hours because of the twists and curves and steep switchbacks through the mountains. **Note:** It's strongly suggested that this drive be made during daylight hours, and never pass a gas station without topping off your tank; the next station down the road may be out of gas. *Magna sin* is available at Pemex.

BEYOND PALENQUE

SIGHTS NEARBY

Misol Ha

The lush rainforest around Palenque has an unbeatable combination of tall trees, thick tropical plantlife, beautiful waterfalls, and rushing streams. Don't leave Palenque without first exploring the surrounding areas! Take the Ocosingo road for 20 km; a side road goes off to the left to Misol Ha, a breathtaking waterfall (Misol Ha means "Waterfall" in Maya). The falls plunge from a height of 30 meters into a large shimmering pool, perfect for a cool swim. The fine spray in the air keeps everything cool and pleasant. You'll see a large, abandoned wooden platform where the view of the falls is stunning; if you decide to climb up there, be aware that the wood is rotting and even if you avoid the holes already there, a step on a weak board goes right through. It's a bit of a climb down the hill, but the swim is worth it.

Children from the area sometimes run a rope across the road at the entrance to Misol Ha and demand a fee for entrance. They are very insistent, and it's best just to give them a few pesos and consider it a donation to the community. The local *ejido* has formed the **Sociedad Cooperativa Turística Ejidal Palenque Misol Ha** to encourage tourism in the area, and it rents a group of cottages (originally built for researchers) for about US$20 d. The travel agencies in town have some information on the cottages.

Agua Azul

When returning to the main Ocosingo road, continue 50 km to a side road that turns off to the right for four km to Agua Azul—in Maya Yax-Ha ("Blue Water"). Most visitors to the National Park of Agua Azul are mesmerized by the beautiful aqua color and white falls surrounding the parking lot. Some hike upstream for a couple of hours and see even more. As you climb into the mountains you'll see the locals (including youngsters) making their way to small villages with large loads of wood, sweet potatoes, and full stems of bananas, all carried on their backs with tumplines around their heads. Milpas are cut from the thick forest; small huts, mostly with tin roofs, are grouped here and there. As you climb higher, the view below is dazzling, with brooks and rivers cutting across the green valley floor.

Agua Azul has more than 500 cascades crashing onto a limestone bed. The water boils and whirls, flows and ebbs, all a luxuriant blue. Calm pools provide good swimming, and the large grassy area (which fills with people when tour buses arrive) is great for flaking out and picnicking. Camping is permitted for a small fee at the site; in fact, campers will meet many fellow backpackers from all over the world, especially Europeans. You might see kayakers taking a turbulent ride down the cascades after toting their kayaks up into rampant wild jungle. The hardy might enjoy a hike upstream, following the cascades over rickety bridges (or just a log flopped across a rushing waterway) and into the small village above the falls. It takes plenty of time; start out early.

Back at Agua Azul are a small cafe and bathrooms (for a fee). The Lacandón Indians sell handmade arrows that not too many years ago were dipped in poison. Many of these Indians present a very intimidating attitude, totally unlike those found in the northern Yucatán Peninsula. Most speak no Spanish, only their own dialect, which can be Tzeltal, Tzotzil, or one of many others. Ask before you take their pictures.

The rivers of Chiapas run full and wild. Agua Azul is on the Yax Ha River, which begins as an

BOB RACE

just a few of dozens of cascades at Agua Azul

unceremonious stream in the jungle in the high peaks above. However, 200 inches of annual rainfall on the eastern slope expand the stream into a rushing, boiling entity with myriad channels cascading over and around scores of small steps to travertine falls from 10 feet to drops of 100 feet. Underground waterways emptying into the river add to the rampage of its rush to lower ground. The unique formations are similar to those found at Havasu Creek in the Grand Canyon. One of the few ways to really see these magnificent falls is by kayak. Obviously, only really experienced kayakers will attempt some of these circuits. However, a multitude of channels and rivers are exciting to explore without being dangerous.

Kayak trips in the area can take in the Río Jatate, Río Usumacinta, Río Chancala, and others. The rivers have been natural highways for centuries, and now provide white-water adventures as well as placid river trips past the thick, jungle-lined shores of Chiapas. For information about kayaking trips, contact **Slickrock Adventures, Inc.,** Box 1400, Moab, Utah 84532, tel. (801) 259-6996, fax (801) 259-8698.

TONINA

As you continue south of Agua Azul on the highway (less than a hundred km.), watch for the turnoff sign for Tonina, which is about 20 km farther on a dirt road. This nearly unheard-of site is believed to have been the last capital of the Maya empire. A 1,500-year-old frieze recently was discovered near the Acropolis in the 15-acre temple complex.

Archaeologist Juan Yadeun discovered the frieze in September of 1997. He describes it as one square yard in size, representing four nobles, called "grandfathers" and "the beginnings of the people." The stone figures are topped with headdresses and are dancing. The heads are believed to represent War, Agriculture, Trade, Tribute. Not only is the frieze an amazing archaeological find in itself, but some archaeologists say the stone carving of four important leaders or "governors" was described in the book called the *Popol Vuh.*

This codex tells the history of the Maya, by the Maya. It is believed to have been written sometime in the 1500s by Quiche Maya in their native tongue, and probably like their other codexes, in their own hieroglyphics on folded bark paper. The book was recovered by Friar Francisco Ximenez about 1701 in Chichicastenango, Guatemala. He was described as a "fine linguist with the trust of the Maya." With the help of his Maya friends, he translated the precious book into Spanish. The find was not made public until 1853. Because this codex was found only in its Spanish version, some have doubted its authenticity. Perhaps this new find will lend credence to the book that has long been the subject of skepticism. The Spanish copy of the *Popol Vuh* is the only book of the Maya not in hieroglyphs. The others were burned by early Spanish priests (who suspected they were works of the devil). Only three other codexes exist, all in museums in other parts of the world. The *Popol Vuh* is part of the Ayer Collection at the Newberry Library in Chicago, Illinois.

BONAMPAK AND YAXCHILAN

Calling all adventurers! A "don't miss" in the Palenque region is a trip to Bonampak or Yaxchilán. Leave the vendors and tour buses behind and get ready for a trip back in time. Both ruins lie in the lush Lacandón jungle and it takes some serious effort to get to the sites, especially Bonampak.

Since this is the home of the Lacandón people, you will undoubtedly encounter them along the trail. The Lacandón Maya have occupied the area for hundreds of years and refer to themselves as Hach Wink (the true people). Small in stature, they usually go barefoot. The men wear simple white sacklike gowns, and the women wear similar dresses but the fabric is flowered; both men and women have thick long black hair. Most of the men speak Spanish and their Maya dialect, while few women speak anything but Maya. Until early this century their jungle environment protected them from most outsiders. This Maya group's numbers have dwindled over the years from isolation, intermarriage, and the loss of their jungle. But traditions have remained the same; old rituals continue, the elders still direct and inspire with mythology and the ancient practices of agriculture.

Bonampak

The Maya translation of Bonampak means painted walls and it is certainly painted walls one sees at these exotic ruins. It's not an easy trek through the jungle: the site is 160 km by road southeast of Palenque and then another 10 km on foot along a sometimes muddy jungle path. The site is very near the Guatemalan border. Bonampak was constructed during the Maya Classic period and is still used by the Lacandón Indians for rituals and ceremonies. Three of the buildings' interiors are covered with murals and each chamber depicts insights into ancient Maya daily life.

One story goes that in 1946 a young American conscientious objector, Charles ("Carlos") Frey, took refuge in the jungles of east Chiapas in a small village called El Cedro. He soon became a familiar figure wandering the paths around the village and eventually met Kayon, one of 250 remaining Indians from the Lacandón *caribal* (village) between the Lacanha and Usumacinta Rivers. A warm friendship grew between the two men, and Frey began to learn the Indian language. The American was accepted so completely by the tribe that Kayon offered him one of his five wives (no record tells if he accepted or not). This small group of Indians lived isolated in the rainforest, still practicing polygamy and worshipping the ancient gods. Eventually, Kayon led Frey deep into the thick forest and shared the knowledge of a secret ceremonial center of his ancestors. Frey found nine structures and stelae scattered around the overgrown site. But the greatest discovery was the brilliantly colored frescoes in Building 1.

Apparently this discovery was too much for Frey to keep to himself, and he told Mexican federal authorities of the magnificent find. At first his news met with little enthusiasm, probably because getting there was a treacherous trip through some of nature's worst hazards, including trespassing on the land of aggressive, xenophobic Lacandón Indians. But, with the help of another American, John Bourne, Frey managed to pique the interest of several Mexican archaeologists; over the next few years several scientific expeditions were made to Bonampak. In 1949, Frey personally organized an expedition of Mexican artists, archaeologists, architects, photographers, and chemists, sponsored by the Mexi-

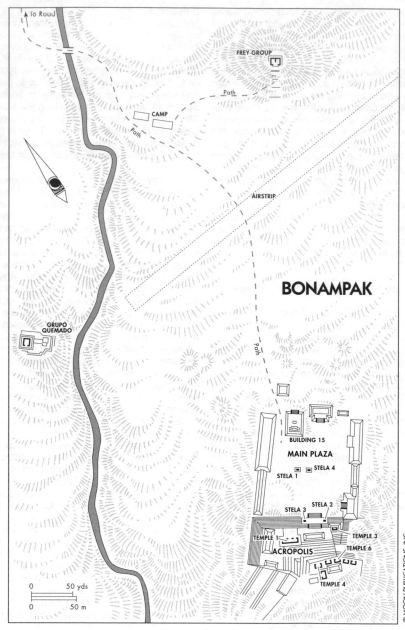

FREY GROUP

Path

CAMP

Path

AIRSTRIP

BONAMPAK

GRUPO
QUEMADO

Path

BUILDING 15

MAIN PLAZA

STELA 1   STELA 4

STELA 3   STELA 2

TEMPLE 1   TEMPLE 3

ACROPOLIS   TEMPLE 6

TEMPLE 4

To Road

0   50 yds
0   50 m

© MOON PUBLICATIONS, INC.

can National Institute of Fine Arts. This trip would pave the way for future scientific research, but it ended the life of Carlos Frey, who died trying to rescue an engraver, Franco Lázaro Gómez, when their canoe overturned in the rampaging water of the Lacanha River. None of this stopped other scientists from studying the site. Though Bonampak was once a trip for adventurers *only*, roads are being built and improved each year.

Bonampak was a small Late Classic (A.D. 600-800) center in the orbit of the nearby city of Yaxchilán. It achieved its present fame through the miraculous preservation of its brilliantly colored murals. They are now slowly flaking from the walls because of heat and light entering the rooms. Bonampak's murals are housed in Temple I, which stands on a low level of the Acropolis, a large stepped structure that backs onto a jungle-covered hill. In front of the Acropolis is a plaza with low buildings around the other three sides. Researchers believe that the story told through the murals should be read from left to right, from Room 1 to Room 3. The setting of Room 1's mural is the palace, where the child-heir is presented to the court and 336 days later is the focal point of a celebration with actors and musicians. Room 2 is set in the jungle and on a flight of stairs. These murals tell the story of a jungle battle, probably in honor of the heir, led by Chaan-Muan. This is considered the greatest battle scene in Maya art.

Next the scene moves to a staircase, where the captives are ritually tortured while Chaan-Muan watches from above. In Room 3 the setting is a pyramid, where costumed lords dance and a captive awaits his death. To the side, noble-women ritually let their blood, while a pot-bellied dwarf is presented to the court. Anthropologists believe that the child-heir never ruled Bonampak, because there is evidence that the site was abandoned before the murals were even completed. Visitors wanting to see the murals in something like their original glory should visit the reconstruction in Mexico City's Museo Nacional de Antropología.

When the first archaeologists arrived to see the paintings, it was necessary to scrape off the accumulation of centuries of limestone. The walls were then washed with kerosene, which temporarily brought out the brilliant colors; sadly, however, this was a mistake. The kerosene weakened the adhesion and contributed to the murals' deterioration. Today, there is very little color left on the walls. Fortunately, these fine paintings were duplicated in precise color and content by the early artists. You can see replicas at several other places. At Tuxtla Gutiérrez's Hotel Bonampak there's a large-scale reproduction from the central chamber; others are found in Villahermosa at the state museum; and farther away, Mexico City's Museo Nacional de Antropología has a full set of reproductions (the best quality) from each chamber. The murals are considered the finest example of fresco art thus found in the Maya world.

Yaxchilán

The Yaxchilán ruins lie on the Usumacinta River, which separates Mexico and Guatemala, so plan on taking a 20 km cruise up the river. Once you have climbed up to the small ledge overlooking the river, you'll find the Acropolis; to get to the Grand Plaza you must pass through structure 19, also called the "Labryinth" with connecting tunnels passing through its rooms—the bats hanging upside down taking their daytime sleep won't even notice you if you're quiet. In building 33, you'll see the beheaded sculpture of Jaguar Bird IV, who reigned after construction was complete. Lacandón legend has it that when the head of Jaguar Bird returns to its place, the world will be destroyed by celestial jaguars.

Yaxchilán was an extremely important and powerful central Maya city-state during the Classic era. Visitors who are lucky enough to visit the site can enjoy a wealth of elaborate stone sculptures. Archaeologists have found at least 35 stelae, 60 carved lintels, 21 altars, and five stairways covered with hieroglyphs—a treasure trove for translators. Yaxchilán's rulers were obsessed with venerating their dynasty and legitimizing their rule and endowed a major monument-carving operation to achieve these goals. The site's hieroglyphs provided

much of the raw material that led to the translation of the Mayan writing system.

Yaxchilán was ruled by the Jaguar dynasty, which traced its roots to A.D. 320 and a lord named Yat Balam ("Jaguar Penis"). The earliest date at the site is 10 December 435, and the first major monuments appeared early in the 6th century. The city flourished for the next 300 years (the last date glyph is 9 April 808). Yaxchilán's greatest ruler was Shield Jaguar, who was born in 647 and ruled from 681 to 742, or more than six decades. His primary wife was his first cousin, Lady Xoc, and Yaxchilán's Temple 23 is covered with reliefs in her honor—a unique homage for a Maya noblewoman. Anthropologists believe that he built Lady Xoc's temple to appease local lineages, because his actual heir-apparent was born to a wife of foreign birth. Shield Jaguar was succeeded by Bird Jaguar, who marked the stages of his 10-year-long accession to the throne (there were other pretenders) in a series of stelae and reliefs. According to this résumé, his achievements included participating in the ball game, blood letting, sacrificing captives, and fathering an heir with a wife from a politically powerful lineage. The Jaguar dynasty lasted until about A.D. 800, when the last ruler, Ta-Skull, constructed a small, badly built temple that celebrated his accession with one shoddy lintel relief. Thereafter Yaxchilán gradually returned to the jungle. The Lacandón Indians burned incense in Yaxchilán's temples as late as the 1970s.

BONAMPAK AND YAXCHILÁN PRACTICALITIES

A trip to Bonampak or Yaxchilán is still an adventure; it may be only for the dedicated naturalist or archaeology buff. A new paved road will be complete by the time you have this book. When you arrive expect no facilities. So far there's only one way to spend the night at Bonampak, and that's to rough it. The trailhead is marked by a house and no guides are available in the immediate area. Camping is permitted at the base of the ruins but expect primitive conditions. In other words, nothing is there, so bring everything with you. Sodas are sold by the man who collects admission (16 pesos).

Although most of the Indians in the area are aloof and keep their distance, there have been reports of robberies, even from locked cars. Women should *not* travel alone; there have been serious instances of assault. Everyone should be wary of offers of hospitality, which have been used as ruses for theft. Obviously, not all offers of kindness are would-be threats. Just use common sense. Once the road is completed it seems only natural that some sort of accommodations will be built.

Safety Tips
When traveling through the rainforest (especially if you're on your own), it's wise to dress for the occasion and carry a few extra necessities: a flashlight, a sharp knife (preferably a machete that will handle sturdy vines), extra batteries, and a strong bug repellent. Wearing long, lightweight cotton pants (jeans get hot) helps ward off insects and scratches from jungle growth. Make sure you have good water-repellent shoes (boots are best), and a waterproof cover-up wouldn't hurt. If you're sleeping in a hammock, bring good mosquito netting (some dangerous flying critters out there thrive on fresh blood and can cause severe problems). Before you leave home ask your doctor about malaria pills (some malaria medication must be taken in advance of exposure), and check with the State Department for a list of any other tropical diseases that might be ravaging the locals (hepatitis, etc.). Remember the other usuals if you're on your own; bring water and your own victuals. If this seems a little drastic, remember the Boy Scout motto: Be prepared.

Getting There
By Plane: It's possible to fly into Bonampak. It's quicker, but it's expensive. With the new road and the good bus service planned, fewer people will probably fly. However, if you're a dedicated Mayaphile, flying is another means of getting to the ruins in a much shorter time and it's possible to combine the trip with a stop at Yaxchilán, the larger, more architecturally important site. Trips can be arranged in small air-taxis from Villahermosa, Tenosique, Palenque, and San Cristóbal de las Casas. When making arrangements, make sure you have at least an hour at Bonampak and two hours at Yaxchilán, which seems to be the norm. The flight averages US$700-1,000

for a four-passenger plane, so traveling in a group saves a few pesos. Make all financial arrangements in advance, especially for the taxi ride. For information, check at the tourist office in Palenque, at travel agencies, or at the Na Balom Museum in San Cristóbal.

By Car: If driving your own car, continue on the road from the Palenque ruins. The drive on the new road should be quite pleasant, but do bring an extra tank of gas, as you'll see no gas stations once you're in the Lacandón. Four-wheel-drive vehicles are available to rent in San Cristóbal de las Casas. The only other way to get there is the way of the Indians: walking and boating down the river. From Palenque it's 160 km through thick rainforest.

Escorted Adventure Trips

Several tour operators offer a variety of trips to Bonampak and Yaxchilán. Day-trips from Palenque typically include one or the other and last about 14 hours. If you're really interested, it's best to spend the night. More involved trips start with a long drive in a 4WD vehicle, followed by a boat ride on the Río Usumacinta to Yaxchilán and possibly the ruins of Piedras Negras as well. The night is spent in rustic lodgings or camping on the river bed. The next day you boat back up the river, drive to Bonampak, and hike to the ruins. Most include a stop in the Lacandón town of Bethel.

Many operators now have tours that go on from the Chiapas ruins into Guatemala to Tikal. Some have more extensive river rafting and kayaking expeditions. For information contact: **Viajes Shivalva,** La Cañada Sector, Apto. Postal 237, tel. (934) 5-0411, fax 5-0392; **Transportadora Turística de Palenque** at Hotel Misión Palenque, tel. (934) 5-0066, fax 5-0499; or **Anfitriones Turísticos de Chiapas,** also called **ATC,** at Allende and Juárez, tel./fax (934) 5-0210, in San Cristóbal de las Casas, tel. (967) 8-2550, fax 8-3145.

BOOKLIST

The following titles provide insight into the Yucatán Peninsula and the Maya people. A few of these books are more easily obtained in Mexico, but all of them will cost less in the United States. Most are nonfiction, though several are fiction and great to pop into your carry-on for a good read on the plane, or for any time you want to get into the Yucatecan mood. Happy reading.

Coe, Andrew. *Archaeological Mexico: A Traveler's Guide to Ancient Cities and Sacred Sites.* Chico: Moon Publications, 1998.

Coe, Michael D. *The Maya.* New York: Thames and Hudson, 1980. A well-illustrated, easy-to-read volume on the Maya people.

Cortés, Hernán. *Five Letters.* Gordon Press, 1977. Cortés wrote long letters to the king of Spain telling of his accomplishments and trying to justify his actions in the New World.

Davies, Nigel. *The Ancient Kingdoms of Mexico.* New York: Penguin Books. Excellent study of pre-conquest (1519) indigenous peoples of Mexico.

De Landa, Bishop Diego. *Yucatán Before and After the Conquest.* New York: Dover Publications, 1978. This book, translated by William Gates from the original 1566 volume, has served as the base for all research that has taken place since. De Landa (though the man destroyed countless books of the Maya people) has given the world insight into their culture before the conquest.

Díaz del Castillo, Bernal. *The Conquest of New Spain.* New York: Penguin Books, 1963. History straight from the adventurer's reminiscences, translated by J.M. Cohen.

Fehrenbach, T.R. *Fire and Blood: A History of Mexico.* New York: Collier Books, 1973. Mexico's history over 3,500 years, told in a way to keep you reading.

Ferguson, William M. *Maya Ruins of Mexico in Color.* Norman: University of Oklahoma Press, 1977. Good reading before you go, but too bulky to carry along. Oversized with excellent drawings and illustrations of the archaeological structures of the Maya Indians.

Franz, Carl. *The People's Guide to Mexico.* New Mexico: John Muir Publications, 1972. A humorous guide filled with witty anecdotes and helpful general information for visitors to Mexico. Don't expect any specific city information, just nuts-and-bolts hints for traveling south of the border.

Greene, Graham. *The Power and the Glory.* New York: Penguin Books, 1977. A novel that takes place in the '20s about a priest and the anti-church movement that gripped the country.

Heffern, Richard. *Secrets of the Mind-Altering Plants of Mexico.* New York: Pyramid Books. A fascinating study of many subtances, from ancient ritual hallucinogens to today's medicines.

Laughlin, Robert M. *The People of the Bat.* Smithsonian Institution Press, 1988. Maya tales and dreams as told by the Zinacantán Indians in Chiapas.

Lewbel, George S. *Diving and Snorkeling Guide to Cozumel.* New York: Pisces Books, 1984. A well-illustrated volume for divers and snorkelers going to Cozumel. The small, easily carried volume is packed with hints about different dive sites, reefs, and marinelife of Cozumel.

Mallan, Chicki and Oz Mallan. *Colonial Mexico: A Traveler's Guide to Distinctive Lodging, Dining, and Shopping in Historic Districts and Artisans' Communities Throughout Mexico.* Chico: Moon Publications, 1998.

Meyer, Michael, and William Sherman. The Course of Mexican History. Oxford University Press. A good, concise one-volume history of Mexico.

Nelson, Ralph. *Popul Vuh: The Great Mythological Book of the Ancient Maya.* Boston: Houghton Mifflin, 1974. An easy-to-read translation of myths handed down orally by the Quiche Maya, family to family, until written down after the Spanish conquest.

Riding, Alan. *Distant Neighbors.* Vintage Books. A modern look at today's Mexico.

Sodi, Demetrio M. (in collaboration with Adela Fernandez). *The Mayas.* Mexico: Panama Editorial S.A. This small pocketbook presents a fictionalized account of life among the Maya before the conquest. Easy reading for anyone who enjoys fantasizing about what life *might* have been like before recorded history in the Yucatán. This book is available in the Yucatecan states of Mexico.

Stephens, John L. *Incidents of Travel in Central America, Chiapas, and Yucatán.* 2 vols. New York: Dover Publications, 1969. Good companions to refer to when traveling in the area. Stephens and illustrator Catherwood

rediscovered many of the Maya ruins on their treks that took place in the mid-1800s. Easy reading.

Thompson, J. Eric. *Maya Archaeologist.* Norman: University of Oklahoma, 1963. Thompson, a noted Maya scholar, traveled and worked at most of the Maya ruins in the 1930s.

___. *The Rise and Fall of the Maya Civilization.* Norman: University of Oklahoma Press, 1954. One man's story of the Maya Indian. Excellent reading.

Werner, David. *Where There is No Doctor.* California: The Hesperian Foundation. This is an invaluable medical aid to anyone traveling not only to isolated parts of Mexico, but to any place in the world where there's not a doctor.

Wolf, Eric. *Sons of the Shaking Earth.* University of Chicago Press. An anthropological study of Indian and mestizo people of Mexico and Guatemala.

Wright, Ronald. *Time Among the Maya.* New York: Weidenfeld & Nicolson, 1989. A narrative that takes the reader through Maya country of today with historical comments that help put the puzzle together.

MAYAN GLOSSARY

MAYA GODS AND CEREMONIES

Acanum—protective deity of hunters

Ahau Can—serpent lord and highest priest

Ahau Chamehes—deity of medicine

Ah Cantzicnal—aquatic deity

Ah Chhuy Kak—god of violent death and sacrifice

Ahcit Dzamalcum—protective god of fishermen

Ah Cup Cacap—god of the underworld who denies air

Ah Itzám—the water witch

Ah kines—priests, lords who consult the oracles, celebrate ceremonies, and preside over sacrifices

Ahpua—god of fishing

Ah Puch—god of death

Ak'Al—sacred marsh where water abounds

Bacaboob—the poureres, supporters of the sky and guardians of the cardinal points, who form a single god, Ah Cantzicnal Becabs

Bolontiku—the nine lords of the night

Chac—god of rain and agriculture

Chac Bolay Can—the butcher serpent living in the underworld

Chaces—priest's assistants in agricultural and other ceremonies

Cihuateteo—women who become goddesses through death in childbirth (Nahuatl word)

Cit Chac Coh—god of war

Hetxmek—ceremony when the child is first carried astride the hip

Hobnil Bacab—the bee god, protector of beekeepers

Holcanes—the brave warriors charged with obtaining slaves for sacrifice. (This word was unknown until the Postclassic era.)

Hunab Ku—giver of life, builder of the universe, and father of Itzámna

Ik—god of the wind

Itzámna—lord of the skies, creator of the beginning, god of time

Ix Chel—goddess of birth, fertility, medicine; credited with inventing spinning

Ixtab—goddess of the cord and of suicide by hanging

Kinich—face of the sun

Kukulcán—quetzal-serpent, plumed serpent

Metnal—the underworld, place of the dead

Nacom—warrior chief

Noh Ek—Venus

Pakat—god of violent death

Zec—spirit lords of beehives

FOOD AND DRINK

alche—inebriating drink, sweetened with honey and used for ceremonies and offerings

ic—chile

itz—sweet potato

kabaxbuul—the heaviest meal of the day, eaten at dusk and containing cooked black beans

kah—pinole flour

kayem—ground maize

macal—a type of root

muxubbak—tamale

on—avocado

op—plum

p'ac—tomatoes

put—papaya

tzamna—black bean

uah—tortillas

za—maize drink

ANIMALS

acehpek—dog used for deer hunting

ah maax cal—the prattling monkey

ah maycuy—the chestnut deer

ah sac dziu—the white thrush

ah xixteel ul—the rugged land conch

bil—hairless dog reared for food

cutz—wild turkey

cutzha—duck

hoh—crow

icim—owl

jaleb—hairless dog

keh—deer

kitam—wild boar

muan—evil bird related to death
que—parrot
thul—rabbit
tzo—domestic turkey
utiu—coyote
yac—mountain cat
yaxum—mythical green bird

MUSIC AND FESTIVALS

ah paxboob—musicians
bexelac—turtle shell used as percussion instrument
chohom—dance performed in ceremonies during the month of Zip, related to fishing
chul—flute
hom—trumpet
kayab—percussion instrument fashioned from turtle shell
Oc na—festival of the month of Yax; old idols of the temple are broken and replaced with new
okot uil—dance performed during the Pocan ceremony
Pacum chac—festival in honor of the war gods
tunkul—drum
zacatan—a drum made from a hollowed tree trunk, with one opening covered with hide

ELEMENTS OF TIME

chunkin—midday
chumuc akab—midnight
chumuc kin—midday
haab—solar calendar of 360 days made up with five extra days of misfortune, which complete the final month
emelkin—sunset
kaz akab—dusk
kin—the sun, the day, the unity of time
potakab—time before dawn
yalhalcab—dawn

PLANTS AND TREES

ha—cacao seed
kan ak—plant that produces a yellow dye
ki—sisal
kiixpaxhkum—chayote
kikche—tree the trunk of which is used to make canoes
kuche—red cedar tree

k'uxub—annatto tree
piim—fiber of the cotton tree
taman—cotton plant
tauch—black zapote tree
tazon te—moss

MISCELLANEOUS WORDS

ah kay kin bak—meat seller
chaltun—water cistern
cha te—black vegetable dye
chi te—eugenia, plant for dyeing
ch'oh—indigo
ek—dye
hadzab—wooden swords
halach uinic—leader
mayacimil—smallpox epidemic, "easy death"
pic—underskirt
ploms—rich people
suyen—square blanket
xanab—sandals
xicul—sleeveless jacket decorated with feathers
xul—stake with a pointed, fire-hardened tip
yuntun—slings

NUMBERS

hun—one
ca—two
ox—three
can—four
ho—five
uac—six
uuc—seven
uacax—eight
bolon—nine
iahun—ten
buluc—eleven
iahca—twelve
oxlahum—thirteen
canlahum—fourteen
holahun—fifteen
uaclahun—sixteen
uuclahun—seventeen
uacaclahun—eighteen
bolontahun—nineteen
hunkal—twenty

SPANISH PHRASEBOOK

PRONUNCIATION GUIDE

Consonants

c   as c in cat, before a, o, or u; like s before e or i
d   as d in dog, except between vowels, then like th in that
g   before e or i, like the ch in Scottish loch; elsewhere like g in get
h   always silent
j   like the English h in hotel, but stronger
ll   like the y in yellow
ñ   like the ni in onion
r   always pronounced as strong r
rr   trilled r
v   similar to the b in boy (not as English v)
y   similar to English, but with a slight j sound. When y stands alone it is
     pronounced like the e in me.
z   like s in same
b, f, k, l, m, n, p, q, s, t, w, x as in English

Vowels

a   as in father, but shorter
e   as in hen
i   as in machine
o   as in phone
u   usually as in rule; when it follows a q the u is silent; when it follows an h or g
     its pronounced like w, except when it comes between g and e or i, when it's also
     silent

NUMBERS

0	cero	11	once	40	cuarenta
1	uno (masculine)	12	doce	50	cincuenta
1	una (feminine)	13	trece	60	sesenta
2	dos	14	catorce	70	setenta
3	tres	15	quince	80	ochenta
4	cuatro	16	diez y seis	90	noventa
5	cinco	17	diez y siete	100	cien
6	seis	18	diez y ocho	101	ciento y uno
7	siete	19	diez y nueve	200	doscientos
8	ocho	20	veinte	1,000	mil
9	nueve	21	viente y uno	10,000	diez mil
10	diez	30	treinta		

DAYS OF THE WEEK

Sunday — *domingo*
Monday — *lunes*
Tuesday — *martes*
Wednesday — *miércoles*
Thursday — *jueves*
Friday — *viernes*
Saturday — *sábado*

TIME

What time is it? — *¿Qué hora es?*
one o'clock — *la una*
two o'clock — *las dos*
at two o'clock — *a las dos*
ten past three — *las tres y diez*
six a.m. — *las seis de mañana*
six p.m. — *las seis de tarde*
today — *hoy*
tomorrow, morning
   — *mañana, la mañana*
yesterday — *ayer*
day — *día*
week — *semana*
month — *mes*
year — *año*
last night — *anoche*

USEFUL WORDS AND PHRASES

Hello. — *Hola.*
Good morning. — *Buenos días.*
Good afternoon. — *Buenas tardes.*
Good evening. — *Buenas noches.*
How are you? — *¿Cómo está?*
Fine. — *Muy bien.*
And you? — *¿Y usted?*
So-so. — *Más ó menos.*
Thank you. — *Gracias.*
Thank you very much. — *Muchas gracias.*
You're very kind. — *Muy amable.*
You're welcome; literally, "It's nothing."
   — *De nada.*
yes — *sí*
no — *no*
I don't know. — *Yo no sé.*
it's fine; okay — *está bien*
good; okay — *bueno*
please — *por favor*
Pleased to meet you. — *Mucho gusto.*
excuse me (physical) — *perdóneme*
excuse me (speech) — *discúlpeme*
I'm sorry. — *Lo siento.*
goodbye — *adiós*

see you later; literally, "until later"
   — *hasta luego*
more — *más*
less — *menos*
better — *mejor*
much — *mucho*
a little — *un poco*
large — *grande*
small — *pequeño*
quick — *rápido*
slowly — *despacio*
bad — *malo*
difficult — *difícil*
easy — *fácil*
He/She/It is gone; as in "She left," "He's
   gone" — *Ya se fue.*
I don't speak Spanish well.
   — *No hablo bien español.*
I don't understand. — *No entiendo.*
How do you say . . . in Spanish?
   — *¿Cómo se dice . . . en español?*
Do you understand English?
   — *¿Entiende el inglés?*
Is English spoken here? (Does anyone
   here speak English?)
   — *¿Se habla inglés aquí?*

TERMS OF ADDRESS

I — *yo*
you (formal) — *usted*
you (familiar) — *tú*
he/him — *él*
she/her — *ella*
we/us — *nosotros*
you (plural) — *vos*
they/them (all males or mixed gender)
    — *ellos*
they/them (all females) — *ellas*

Mr., sir — *señor*
Mrs., madam — *señora*
Miss, young lady — *señorita*
wife — *esposa*
husband — *marido* or *esposo*
friend — *amigo* (male), *amiga* (female)
sweetheart — *novio* (male), *novia* (female)
son, daughter — *hijo, hija*
brother, sister — *hermano, hermana*
father, mother — *padre, madre*

GETTING AROUND

Where is . . . ? — *¿Dónde está . . . ?*
How far is it to . . .?
    — *¿A cuánto queda . . . ?*
from . . . to . . . — *de . . . a . . .*
highway — *la carretera*
road — *el camino*
street — *la calle*
block — *la cuadra*
kilometer — *kilómetro*

mile (commonly used near the
    U.S. border) — *milla*
north — *el norte*
south — *el sur*
west — *el oeste*
east — *el este*
straight ahead — *al derecho* or *adelante*
to the right — *a la derecha*
to the left — *a la izquierda*

ACCOMMODATIONS

Can I (we) see a room?
    — *¿Puedo (podemos) ver un cuarto?*
What is the rate? — *¿Cuál es el precio?*
a single room — *un cuarto sencillo*
a double room — *un cuarto doble*
key — *llave*
bathroom — *lavabo* or *baño*
hot water — *agua caliente*

cold water — *agua fría*
towel — *toalla*
soap — *jabón*
toilet paper — *papel higiénico*
air conditioning — *aire acondicionado*
fan — *ventilador*
blanket — *frazada* or *manta*

PUBLIC TRANSPORT

bus stop — *la parada del autobús*
main bus terminal
    — *terminal de buses*
railway station
    — *la estación de ferrocarril*
airport — *el aeropuerto*
ferry terminal
    — *la terminal del transbordador*

I want a ticket to . . .
    — *Quiero un boleto a . . .*
I want to get off at . . .
    — *Quiero bajar en . . .*
Here, please. — *Aquí, por favor.*
Where is this bus going?
    — *¿Adónde va este autobús?*
roundtrip — *ida y vuelta*
What do I owe? — *¿Cuánto le debo?*

DRIVING

Full, please (at gasoline station).
— *Lleno, por favor.*
My car is broken down.
— *Se me ha descompuesto el carro.*
I need a tow. — *Necesito un remolque.*
Is there a garage nearby?
— *¿Hay un garage cerca?*
Is the road passable with this car (truck)?
— *¿Puedo pasar con este carro*
(esta troca)?

With four-wheel drive?
— *¿Con doble tracción?*
It's not passable — *No hay paso.*
traffic light — *el semáfora*
traffic sign — *el señal*
gasoline (petrol) — *gasolina*
gasoline station — *gasolinera*
oil — *aceite*
water — *agua*
flat tire — *llanta desinflada*
tire repair shop — *llantera*

AUTO PARTS

fan belt — *banda de ventilador*
battery — *batería*
fuel (water) pump —
   bomba de gasolina (agua)
spark plug — *bujía*
carburetor — *carburador*
distributor — *distribuidor*
axle — *eje*
clutch — *embrague*

gasket — *empaque, junta*
filter — *filtro*
brakes — *frenos*
tire — *llanta*
hose — *manguera*
starter — *marcha, arranque*
radiator — *radiador*
voltage regulator — *regulado de voltaje*

MAKING PURCHASES

I need . . . — *Necesito . . .*
I want . . . — *Deseo . . .* or *Quiero . . .*
I would like . . . (more polite)
   — *Quisiera . . .*
How much does it cost? — *¿Cuánto cuesta?*
What's the exchange rate?
   — *¿Cuál es el tipo de cambio?*

Can I see . . . ? — *¿Puedo ver . . . ?*
this one — *ésta/ésto*
expensive — *caro*
cheap — *barato*
cheaper — *más barato*
too much — *demasiado*

HEALTH

Help me please. — *Ayúdeme por favor.*
I am ill. — *Estoy enfermo.*
pain — *dolor*
fever — *fiebre*
stomache ache — *dolor de estómago*
vomiting — *vomitar*
diarrhea — *diarrea*

drugstore — *farmacia*
medicine — *medicina, remedio*
pill, tablet — *pastilla*
birth control pills — *pastillas*
   anticonceptivas
condoms — *preservativos*

FOOD

menu — *lista, menú*
glass — *vaso*
fork — *tenedor*
knife — *cuchillo*
spoon — *cuchara, cucharita*
napkin — *servilleta*
soft drink — *refresco*
coffee, cream — *café, crema*
tea — *té*
sugar — *azúcar*
purified water — *agua purificado*
bottled carbonated water — *agua mineral*
bottled uncarbonated water — *agua sin gas*
beer — *cerveza*
wine — *vino*
milk — *leche*
juice — *jugo*
eggs — *huevos*
bread — *pan*

watermelon — *sandía*
banana — *plátano*
apple — *manzana*
orange — *naranja*
meat (without) — *carne (sin)*
beef — *carne de res*
chicken — *pollo*
fish — *pescado*
shellfish — *mariscos*
fried — *a la plancha*
roasted — *asado*
barbecue, barbecued — *al carbón*
breakfast — *desayuno*
lunch — *almuerzo*
dinner (often eaten in late afternoon)
— *comida*
dinner, or a late night snack — *cena*
the check — *la cuenta*

ACCOMMODATIONS INDEX

RESTAURANT INDEX

INDEX

ABOUT THE AUTHOR

Chicki Mallan discovered the joy of traveling with her parents at an early age. The family would leave their Catalina Island home yearly, hit the road and explore the small towns and big cities of the United States. Traveling was still an important part of Chicki's life after having a bunch of her own kids to introduce to the world. At various times Chicki and kids have lived in the Orient and Europe. When not traveling, lecturing, or giving slide presentations, Chicki and photographer husband Oz live in Paradise, California, a small community in the foothills of the Sierra Nevada. She does what she enjoys most when between books, writing newspaper and magazine articles. She has been associated with Moon Publications since 1983, as author of *Cancún Handbook, Belize Handbook,* and *Colonial Mexico Handbook,* and as co-author of *Mexico Handbook.* She also wrote *Guide To Catalina Island* (Pine Press).

In 1987, Chicki was presented the Pluma de Plata writing award from the Mexican Government Ministry of Tourism for an article she wrote on the Mexican Caribbean which was published in the *Los Angeles Times.* Chicki is a member of the Society of American Travel Writers.

ABOUT THE PHOTOGRAPHER

Oz Mallan has been a professional photographer his entire working career. Much of that time was spent as chief cameraman for the Chico *Enterprise Record.* Oz graduated from the Brooks Institute of Photography, Santa Barbara. His work has often appeared in newspapers and magazines across the country via UPI and AP. He travels the world with his wife, Chicki, handling the photo end of their literary efforts, which include travel books, newspaper and magazine articles, as well as lectures and slide presentations. Oz's photos are also featured in Moon's *Cancún Handbook, Mexico Handbook, Colonial Mexico Handbook,* and *Belize Handbook,* as well as in Pine Press's *Guide to Catalina Island.*

ABOUT THE ILLUSTRATOR

The banner art at the start of each chapter was done by Kathy Escovedo Sanders. She is an expert both in watercolor and this stipple style that lends itself to excellent black-and-white reproduction. Kathy is a 1982 California State University Long Beach graduate with a B.A. in Art History. She exhibits drawings, etched intaglio prints, and woodcut prints, as well as her outstanding watercolor paintings. Her stipple art can be seen in all of Chicki Mallan's Moon Handbooks.

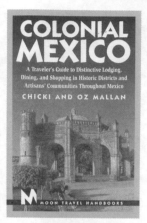
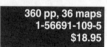

MOON TRAVEL HANDBOOKS

LOSE YOURSELF IN THE EXPERIENCE, NOT THE CROWD

For 25 years, Moon Travel Handbooks have been the guidebooks of choice for adventurous travelers. Our award-winning Handbook series provides focused, comprehensive coverage of distinct destinations all over the world. Each Handbook is like an entire bookcase of cultural insight and introductory information in one portable volume. Our goal at Moon is to give travelers all the background and practical information they'll need for an extraordinary travel experience.

The following pages include a complete list of Handbooks, covering North America and Hawaii, Mexico, Latin America and the Caribbean, and Asia and the Pacific.To purchase Moon Travel Handbooks, check your local bookstore or order by phone: (800) 345-5473 M-F 8 am.-5 p.m. PST or outside the U.S. phone: (530) 345-5473.

"An in-depth dunk into the land, the people and their history, arts, and politics."
—*Student Travels*

"I consider these books to be superior to Lonely Planet. When Moon produces a book it is more humorous, incisive, and off-beat."
—*Toronto Sun*

"Outdoor enthusiasts gravitate to the well-written Moon Travel Handbooks. In addition to politically correct historic and cultural features, the series focuses on flora, fauna and outdoor recreation. Maps and meticulous directions also are a trademark of Moon guides."
—*Houston Chronicle*

"Moon [Travel Handbooks] . . . bring a healthy respect to the places they investigate. Best of all, they provide a host of odd nuggets that give a place texture and prod the wary traveler from the beaten path. The finest are written with such care and insight they deserve listing as literature."
—*American Geographical Society*

"Moon Travel Handbooks offer in-depth historical essays and useful maps, enhanced by a sense of humor and a neat, compact format."
—*Swing*

"Perfect for the more adventurous, these are long on history, sightseeing and nitty-gritty information and very price-specific."
—*Columbus Dispatch*

"Moon guides manage to be comprehensive and countercultural at the same time . . . Handbooks are packed with maps, photographs, drawings, and sidebars that constitute a college-level introduction to each country's history, culture, people, and crafts."
—*National Geographic Traveler*

"Few travel guides do a better job helping travelers create their own itineraries than the Moon Travel Handbook series. The authors have a knack for homing in on the essentials."
—**Colorado Springs** *Gazette Telegraph*

MEXICO

"These books will delight the armchair traveler, aid the undecided person in selecting a destination, and guide the seasoned road warrior looking for lesser-known hideaways."

—*Mexican Meanderings* Newsletter

"From tourist traps to off-the-beaten track hideaways, these guides offer consistent, accurate details without pretension."

—*Foreign Service Journal*

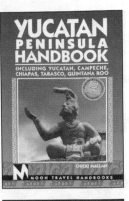

Archaeological Mexico	**$19.95**
Andrew Coe	410 pages, 27 maps
Baja Handbook	**$16.95**
Joe Cummings	544 pages, 46 maps
Cabo Handbook	**$14.95**
Joe Cummings	272 pages, 17 maps
Cancún Handbook	**$14.95**
Chicki Mallan	270 pages, 25 maps
Colonial Mexico	**$18.95**
Chicki Mallan	360 pages, 38 maps
Mexico Handbook	**$21.95**
Joe Cummings and Chicki Mallan	1,200 pages, 201 maps
Northern Mexico Handbook	**$17.95**
Joe Cummings	590 pages, 69 maps
Pacific Mexico Handbook	**$17.95**
Bruce Whipperman	580 pages, 68 maps
Puerto Vallarta Handbook	**$14.95**
Bruce Whipperman	330 pages, 36 maps
Yucatán Handbook	**$16.95**
Chicki Mallan	470 pages, 52 maps

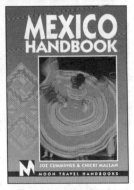

LATIN AMERICA
AND THE CARIBBEAN

"Solidly packed with practical information and full of significant cultural asides that will enlighten you on the whys and wherefores of things you might easily see but not easily grasp."

—Boston Globe

Belize Handbook	**$15.95**
Chicki Mallan and Patti Lange	390 pages, 45 maps
Caribbean Handbook	**$16.95**
Karl Luntta	400 pages, 56 maps
Costa Rica Handbook	**$19.95**
Christopher P. Baker	780 pages, 73 maps
Cuba Handbook	**$19.95**
Christopher P. Baker	740 pages, 70 maps
Dominican Republic Handbook	**$15.95**
Gaylord Dold	420 pages, 24 maps
Ecuador Handbook	**$16.95**
Julian Smith	450 pages, 43 maps
Honduras Handbook	**$15.95**
Chris Humphrey	330 pages, 40 maps
Jamaica Handbook	**$15.95**
Karl Luntta	330 pages, 17 maps
Virgin Islands Handbook	**$13.95**
Karl Luntta	220 pages, 19 maps

NORTH AMERICA AND HAWAII

"These domestic guides convey the same sense of exoticism that their foreign counterparts do, making home-country travel seem like far-flung adventure."

—Sierra Magazine

Alaska-Yukon Handbook	**$17.95**
Deke Castleman and Don Pitcher	530 pages, 92 maps
Alberta and the Northwest Territories Handbook	**$17.95**
Andrew Hempstead and Nadina Purdon	530 pages, 72 maps,
Arizona Traveler's Handbook	**$17.95**
Bill Weir and Robert Blake	512 pages,54 maps
Atlantic Canada Handbook	**$17.95**
Nan Drosdick and Mark Morris	460 pages, 61 maps
Big Island of Hawaii Handbook	**$15.95**
J.D. Bisignani	390 pages, 23 maps
British Columbia Handbook	**$16.95**
Jane King and Andrew Hempstead	430 pages, 69 maps

Colorado Handbook	**$18.95**
Stephen Metzger	480 pages, 59 maps
Georgia Handbook	**$17.95**
Kap Stann	370 pages, 50 maps
Hawaii Handbook	**$19.95**
J.D. Bisignani	1,030 pages, 90 maps
Honolulu-Waikiki Handbook	**$14.95**
J.D. Bisignani	380 pages, 20 maps
Idaho Handbook	**$18.95**
Don Root	610 pages, 42 maps
Kauai Handbook	**$15.95**
J.D. Bisignani	320 pages, 23 maps
Maine Handbook	**$18.95**
Kathleen M. Brandes	660 pages, 27 maps
Massachusetts Handbook	**$18.95**
Jeff Perk	600 pages, 23 maps
Maui Handbook	**$14.95**
J.D. Bisignani	410 pages, 35 maps
Montana Handbook	**$17.95**
Judy Jewell and W.C. McRae	480 pages, 52 maps
Nevada Handbook	**$18.95**
Deke Castleman	530 pages, 40 maps
New Hampshire Handbook	**$18.95**
Steve Lantos	500 pages, 18 maps
New Mexico Handbook	**$15.95**
Stephen Metzger	360 pages, 47 maps
New York City Handbook	**$13.95**
Christiane Bird	300 pages, 20 maps
New York Handbook	**$19.95**
Christiane Bird	780 pages, 95 maps
Northern California Handbook	**$19.95**
Kim Weir	800 pages, 50 maps
Oregon Handbook	**$17.95**
Stuart Warren and Ted Long Ishikawa	588 pages, 34 maps
Pennsylvania Handbook	**$18.95**
Joanne Miller	448 pages, 40 maps
Road Trip USA	**$22.50**
Jamie Jensen	800 pages, 165 maps
Southern California Handbook	**$19.95**
Kim Weir	720 pages, 26 maps
Tennessee Handbook	**$17.95**
Jeff Bradley	530 pages, 44 maps
Texas Handbook	**$18.95**
Joe Cummings	690 pages, 70 maps
Utah Handbook	**$17.95**
Bill Weir and W.C. McRae	490 pages, 40 maps

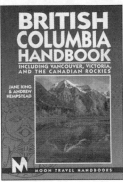

Washington Handbook	$19.95
Don Pitcher	870 pages, 113 maps
Wisconsin Handbook	**$18.95**
Thomas Huhti	590 pages, 69 maps
Wyoming Handbook	**$17.95**
Don Pitcher	610 pages, 80 maps

ASIA AND THE PACIFIC

"Scores of maps, detailed practical info down to business hours of small-town libraries. You can't beat the Asian titles for sheer heft. (The) series is sort of an American Lonely Planet, with better writing but fewer titles. (The) individual voice of researchers comes through."

—Travel & Leisure

Australia Handbook	**$21.95**
Marael Johnson, Andrew Hempstead,	
and Nadina Purdon	940 pages, 141 maps
Bali Handbook	**$19.95**
Bill Dalton	750 pages, 54 maps
Bangkok Handbook	**$13.95**
Michael Buckley	244 pages, 30 maps
Fiji Islands Handbook	**$13.95**
David Stanley	280 pages, 38 maps
Hong Kong Handbook	**$16.95**
Kerry Moran	378 pages, 49 maps
Indonesia Handbook	**$25.00**
Bill Dalton	1,380 pages, 249 maps
Japan Handbook	**$22.50**
J.D. Bisignani	970 pages, 213 maps
Micronesia Handbook	**$14.95**
Neil M. Levy	340 pages, 70 maps
Nepal Handbook	**$18.95**
Kerry Moran	490 pages, 51 maps
New Zealand Handbook	**$19.95**
Jane King	620 pages, 81 maps
Outback Australia Handbook	**$18.95**
Marael Johnson	450 pages, 57 maps
Philippines Handbook	**$17.95**
Peter Harper and Laurie Fullerton	670 pages, 116 maps
Singapore Handbook	**$15.95**
Carl Parkes	350 pages, 29 maps
Southeast Asia Handbook	**$21.95**
Carl Parkes	1,000 pages, 203 maps

South Korea Handbook Robert Nilsen	**$19.95** 820 pages, 141 maps
South Pacific Handbook David Stanley	**$22.95** 920 pages, 147 maps
Tahiti-Polynesia Handbook David Stanley	**$13.95** 270 pages, 35 maps
Thailand Handbook Carl Parkes	**$19.95** 860 pages, 142 maps
Vietnam, Cambodia & Laos Handbook Michael Buckley	**$18.95** 730 pages, 116 maps

OTHER GREAT TITLES FROM MOON

"For hardy wanderers, few guides come more highly
recommended than the Handbooks. They include
good maps, steer clear of fluff and flackery, and offer
plenty of money-saving tips. They also give you the
kind of information that visitors to strange lands—on
any budget—need to survive."

—*US News & World Report*

Moon Handbook Carl Koppeschaar	**$10.00** 141 pages, 8 maps
Moscow-St. Petersburg Handbook Masha Nordbye	**$13.95** 259 pages, 16 maps
The Practical Nomad: How to Travel Around the World Edward Hasbrouck	**$17.95** 575 pages
Staying Healthy in Asia, Africa, and Latin America Dirk Schroeder	**$11.95** 197 pages, 4 maps

MOONBELT

A new concept in moneybelts.
Made of heavy-duty Cordura
nylon, the Moonbelt offers
maximum protection for your money
and important papers. This pouch,

designed for all-weather comfort, slips under your shirt or waistband, rendering it virtually
undetectable and inaccessible to pickpockets. It features a one-inch high-test quick-release
buckle so there's no more fumbling around for the strap or repeated adjustments. This
handy plastic buckle opens and closes with a touch but won't come undone until you want
it to. Moonbelts accommodate traveler's checks, passports, cash, photos, etc.
Size 5 x 9 inches. Available in black only. **$8.95**

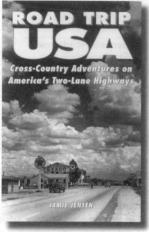

WHERE TO BUY MOON TRAVEL HANDBOOKS

BOOKSTORES AND LIBRARIES: Moon Travel Handbooks are distributed worldwide. Please contact our sales manager for a list of wholesalers and distributors in your area.

TRAVELERS: We would like to have Moon Travel Handbooks available throughout the world. Please ask your bookstore to write or call us for ordering information. If your bookstore will not order our guides for you, please contact us for a free catalog.

Moon Travel Handbooks
P.O. Box 3040
Chico, CA 95927-3040 U.S.A.
tel.: (800) 345-5473, outside the U.S. (530) 345-5473
fax: (530) 345-6751
e-mail: travel@moon.com

IMPORTANT ORDERING INFORMATION

PRICES: All prices are subject to change. We always ship the most current edition. We will let you know if there is a price increase on the book you order.

SHIPPING AND HANDLING OPTIONS: Domestic UPS or USPS first class (allow 10 working days for delivery): $4.50 for the first item, $1.00 for each additional item.

Moonbelt shipping is $1.50 for one, 50 cents for each additional belt.

UPS 2nd Day Air or Printed Airmail requires a special quote.

International Surface Bookrate 8-12 weeks delivery: $4.00 for the first item, $1.00 for each additional item. Note: We cannot guarantee international surface bookrate shipping. We recommends sending international orders via air mail, which requires a special quote.

FOREIGN ORDERS: Orders that originate outside the U.S.A. must be paid for with an international money order, a check in U.S. currency drawn on a major U.S. bank based in the U.S.A., or Visa, MasterCard, or Discover.

TELEPHONE ORDERS: We accept Visa, MasterCard, or Discover payments. Call in your order: (800) 345-5473, 8 a.m.-5 p.m. Pacific standard time. Outside the U.S. the number is (530) 345-5473.

INTERNET ORDERS: Visit our site at: www.moon.com

ORDER FORM

Prices are subject to change without notice. Be sure to call (800) 345-5473,
or (530) 345-5473 from outside the U.S. 8 a.m.–5 p.m. PST for current prices and editions.
(See important ordering information on preceding page.)

Name: _____ Date: _____

Street: _____

City: _____ Daytime Phone: _____

State or Country: _____ Zip Code: _____

QUANTITY	TITLE	PRICE

Taxable Total_____

Sales Tax (7.25%) for California Residents_____

Shipping & Handling_____

TOTAL_____

Ship: ☐ UPS (no P.O. Boxes)   ☐ 1st class   ☐ International surface mail

Ship to: ☐ address above   ☐ other _____

Make checks payable to: **MOON TRAVEL HANDBOOKS**, P.O. Box 3040, Chico, CA 95927-3040
U.S.A. We accept Visa, MasterCard, or Discover. **To Order**: Call in your Visa, MasterCard, or Discover number,
or send a written order with your Visa, MasterCard, or Discover number and expiration date clearly written.

Card Number: ☐ **Visa**   ☐ **MasterCard**   ☐ **Discover**

☐ ☐ ☐ ☐   ☐ ☐ ☐ ☐   ☐ ☐ ☐ ☐   ☐ ☐ ☐ ☐

Exact Name on Card: _____

Expiration date:_____

Signature: _____

U.S.~METRIC CONVERSION

1 inch = 2.54 centimeters (cm)
1 foot = .304 meters (m)
1 mile = 1.6093 kilometers (km)
1 km = .6214 miles
1 fathom = 1.8288 m
1 chain = 20.1168 m
1 furlong = 201.168 m
1 acre = .4047 hectares
1 sq km = 100 hectares
1 sq mile = 2.59 square km
1 ounce = 28.35 grams
1 pound = .4536 kilograms
1 short ton = .90718 metric ton
1 short ton = 2000 pounds
1 long ton = 1.016 metric tons
1 long ton = 2240 pounds
1 metric ton = 1000 kilograms
1 quart = .94635 liters
1 US gallon = 3.7854 liters
1 Imperial gallon = 4.5459 liters
1 nautical mile = 1.852 km

To compute celsius temperatures, subtract 32 from Fahrenheit and divide by 1.8. To go the other way, multiply celsius by 1.8 and add 32.

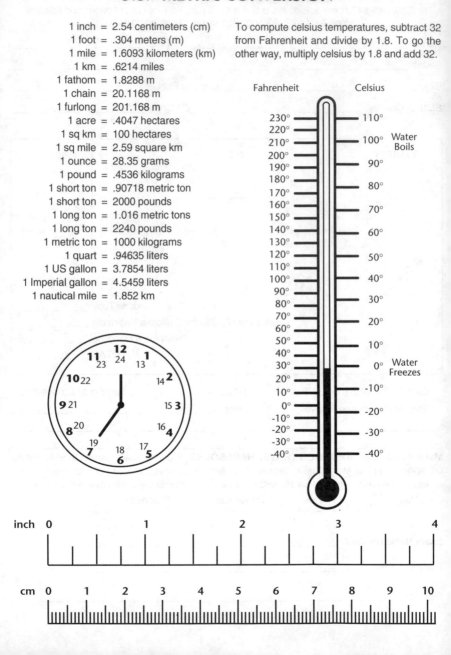